THE ROUTLEDGE COMPANION TO
IN THE TWENTIETH CENTU

The Routledge Companion to Britain in the Twentieth Century is a jargon-free guide to the social, economic and political history of Britain since 1900. Opening with a general introduction and overview of twentieth-century Britain, the book contains a wealth of chronologies, facts and figures, introductions to major themes, the historiography of twentieth-century Britain, a guide to sources and resources, biographies of the most important figures and a dictionary of key terms, providing a comprehensive and up-to-date introduction to this key period of change and development in this most urban of nations.

From the outbreak of the First World War, to the introduction of the NHS, to the first television set, this book covers in detail some of the most important events that shaped twentieth-century Britain. Topics discussed include:

- class: the working and middle classes
- gender: women's history
- ethnicity: immigration and the idea of multicultural Britain
- social policy: poverty and welfare
- economic paradox: decline and affluence
- economic change: manufacturing and services
- popular culture: music, fashion, sports, screen
- liberalisation: Victorian values and permissiveness
- political parties: the major and minor parties
- governments: achievements and problems
- the wider world: Ireland; decolonisation; European integration.

Packed with useful information, this guide will be an indispensable reference tool for all those seeking an introduction to twentieth-century British history.

Mark Clapson is Reader in History at the University of Westminster.

ROUTLEDGE COMPANIONS TO HISTORY
Series Advisors: Chris Cook and John Stevenson

Routledge Companions to History offer perfect reference guides to key historical events and eras, providing everything that the student or general reader needs to know. These comprehensive guides contain essential apparatus for navigating through specific topics in a clear and straightforward manner – including introductory articles, biographies and chronologies – to provide accessible and indispensable surveys crammed with vital information valuable for beginner and expert alike.

The Routledge Companion to Nazi Germany
Roderick Stackelberg

The Routledge Companion to Early Modern Europe, 1453–1763
Chris Cook and Philip Broadhead

The Routledge Companion to Britain in the Nineteenth Century, 1815–1914
Chris Cook

The Routledge Companion to European History since 1763
Chris Cook and John Stevenson

The Routledge Companion to World History since 1914
Chris Cook and John Stevenson

The Routledge Companion to Fascism and the Far Right
Peter Davies and Derek Lynch

The Routledge Companion to the Crusades
Peter Lock

The Routledge Companion to Historical Studies
Alun Munslow

The Routledge Companion to Decolonization
Dietmar Rothermund

The Routledge Companion to Britain in the Eighteenth Century, 1688–1820
John Stevenson and Jeremy Gregory

The Routledge Companion to the American Civil War Era
Hugh Tulloch

The Routledge Companion to the Stuart Age, 1603–1714
John Wroughton

The Routledge Companion to Central and Eastern Europe since 1919
Adrian Webb

The Routledge Companion to Britain in the Twentieth Century
Mark Clapson

THE ROUTLEDGE COMPANION TO BRITAIN IN THE TWENTIETH CENTURY

Mark Clapson

Routledge
Taylor & Francis Group

LONDON AND NEW YORK

First published 2009
by Routledge
2 Park Square, Milton Park, Abingdon, Oxon OX14 4RN

Simultaneously published in the USA and Canada
by Routledge
270 Madison Ave, New York, NY 10016

Routledge is an imprint of the Taylor & Francis Group, an informa business

Typeset in Times New Roman by
Book Now Ltd, London
Printed and bound in Great Britain by
TJ International Ltd, Padstow, Cornwall

British Library Cataloguing in Publication Data
A catalogue record for this book is available from the British Library

Library of Congress Cataloging in Publication Data
Clapson, Mark.
The Routledge companion to Britain in the twentieth century / Mark Clapson.
p. cm.—(Routledge companions to history)
Includes bibliographical references.
1. Great Britain—History—20th century—Handbooks, manuals, etc. I. Title.
DA566.C53 2009
941.082—dc22   2008054740

ISBN10: 0–415–27535–0 (hbk)
ISBN10: 0–415–27536–9 (pbk)
ISBN10: 0–203–87528–1 (ebk)

ISBN13: 978–0–415–27535–4 (hbk)
ISBN13: 978–0–415–27536–1 (pbk)
ISBN13: 978–0–203–87528–5 (ebk)

CONTENTS

CONTENTS

ACKNOWLEDGEMENTS

I am grateful to Philippa Grand, Emily Kindleysides, Eve Setch and Vicky Peters, at Taylor and Francis, for their advice and patience during the compilation of the *Companion*. Harriet Jones was also a great help in the early stages of preparation of the book. In addition I would like to thank the history students at the University of Westminster whom I really enjoy teaching. My warmest gratitude is to my colleagues at the university, both administrative staff and historians, in particular Tony Gorst and Martin Doherty. They are helpful and supportive in many ways, and assisted me with a couple of items in the text. As ever, any errors or lapses of judgement are my fault.

I

INTRODUCTION AND OVERVIEW OF TWENTIETH-CENTURY BRITAIN

1.1
INTRODUCTION

The *Companion to Britain in the Twentieth Century* is designed for anyone with an interest in modern and contemporary British history, whether students and teachers looking for a convenient reference book or the general reader wanting to learn more about Britain. Unlike many other fact-based textbooks on twentieth-century Britain, social and cultural history are given particular attention, in addition to political, economic and overseas developments. Furthermore, Britain was one of the most urbanised countries in the world by 1900, and it continued to be so throughout the twentieth century. Key aspects of British urban history and development are also included.

For those with little or no knowledge about Britain since 1900, the organisation of the *Companion* will both facilitate a broad understanding of modern and contemporary British history and allow for a more detailed exploration of key events, institutions, people and themes. And it will become clear that most of the major issues and problems faced by Britain in the early twenty-first century were shaped by the history of the previous hundred years.

The *Companion* is also a guide to the study of twentieth-century Britain. It introduces the historiography of the country since 1900, that is, the major approaches adopted by historians, and some of the key debates among them. It describes the wide range of sources – documents – that historians use, and indicates some of the strengths and problems of those documents. Guides to accessing and interpreting documents are included.

Organisation of the *Companion*

Four broad but overlapping categories form the substance of the *Companion*, namely:

- social and cultural history
- economic history
- political history
- Britain and the wider world, or overseas history.

Section 1.2 highlights the key periods in the twentieth century.

Section 1.3 gives an accessible overview of the major events, developments and key themes in twentieth-century British history. The aim of both of these sections is to establish a general understanding that can be built upon in subsequent sections of the *Companion*.

Part II is entitled **Landmarks**. It provides chronologies or timelines of the major Acts of Parliament and events in Britain.

Part III is a guide to the **Historiography** of modern and contemporary Britain, and also an A–Z checklist of some of the best-known historians working within this broad field.

Part IV, entitled **Sources and resources**, introduces the reader to the wide and growing range of contemporary documents, the very artefacts of history itself. It shows where these sources can be accessed and provides an approach to their interpretation.

Part V is an alphabetically arranged biography of many of the most famous or significant people of twentieth-century Britain. In common with other textbooks it lists the leading politicians, economists and reformers, but it also includes leading personalities from the worlds of popular culture and sport.

Part VI, the **Dictionary**, is about the major institutions, themes and isms in twentieth-century Britain, many of which are still very much a presence in our own lives. This includes the significant political, economic and civic institutions, but also social and cultural institutions, from television genres to the pub. The most significant thematic elements in the *Companion* are addressed in more detail here.

Throughout this *Companion* key events, names and themes are highlighted in **bold** at their first mention to assist in cross-referencing elsewhere in the book. As a kind of rule of thumb, think of the organisation of the book as follows:

- Major pieces of *legislation* and *events* are highlighted in **Landmarks**.
- Important *people* are discussed in the **Biographies**.
- Significant *themes* and *institutions* are elaborated upon in the **Dictionary**.
- **Historiography** is about what historians do.
- **Sources and resources** is about the archives, libraries, websites and documents that historians use.
- Page references to all entries in the *Companion* are listed in the Index to help with cross-referencing.

1.2
TIME FRAMES

Notes

- Time frames or significant periods in twentieth-century British history are outlined in this section. It is essential to have a basic understanding of the key time frames that historians use and why they use them. It is also essential to understand that no period of history remains in isolation from earlier or later time frames.
- Neither 'time frame' or 'periodisation' are particularly elegant words, but they are critically important when we seek to understand the history of twentieth-century Britain. While many historians seek to provide an interpretative overview of the entire century, others divide the century into smaller time frames or periods, in order to emphasise what was especially profound within those years. Wars and crises effectively mark both beginnings and ends of the major periods in twentieth-century British history.

The twentieth century in its entirety, 1900–99

A number of major works have covered the history of twentieth-century Britain from its beginnings to its conclusion. These are mostly survey histories, concerned with the most significant social, cultural, economic and political developments and with changes and continuities over the course of the century. Along with an emphasis upon key themes, the best books are attentive to detail, dates and chronology.

The Edwardian era, 1900–14

This period takes it name from the reign of King **Edward VII**, from 1901 to 1910. Although Queen Victoria died in January 1901, and King Edward in 1910, it would be over-precise to date the Edwardian years exactly from the date of her death to the demise of Edward. Thus there is room for overlap with both the last years of the Victorian period and the beginning of the reign of King **George V**. The Edwardian era is a convenient term for the years from the end of the nineteenth century to the outbreak of the First World War in 1914.

The First World War, 1914–18

The years from August 1914 to November 1918 saw the First World War, or the 'Great War' as it was then known. For some historians the war was the tragic climax to the 'long nineteenth century' that began with the French Revolution in 1789 and ended with the catastrophe of 1914 to 1918. There are many military histories of the First World War. However, its history is also studied for its consequences upon British society, culture, the economy and politics, both during the conflict and in its aftermath.

Because the First World War also witnessed the tragic culmination of Victorian and Edwardian militarism, and had a profound effect on Britain, it can usefully be included within other longer-term periodisations, from 1900 to 1918 and from 1914 to 1945, to give just two examples. For a country at war sees ends and beginnings, as well as drastic changes and accelerations in historical phenomena with both immediate and longer-term consequences.

The interwar period, 1918–39

The years from the end of the First World War to the outbreak of the Second form the interwar period. They were characterised by major social and economic changes and by the realignment of party politics. Again, there is room for overlap between the wars and the periods that preceded or followed them. For example, during the earliest weeks of the Second World War, plans for civil defence drawn up over previous years were put into place, and the legacy of **appeasement** between 1936 and 1939 became tragically evident into the war itself.

The Second World War, 1939–45

From the outbreak of the conflict in September 1939 to what is known as Victory over Europe Day (VE Day) in May 1945, the time span of the Second World War is relatively straightforward. However, historians sometimes date the ending of the conflict proper to August 1945, with the victory over Japan (VJ Day). Beyond military histories, the home front has been increasingly studied by social, cultural and political historians.

Many historians of Britain *since* the Second World War begin their analysis during the war itself, in order to grasp its longer-term effects from 1939. Addressing the nature of society and politics during the war encourages a focus upon forward linkages from wartime experiences and policy formation into peacetime.

Postwar Britain, 1945 to varying dates

The time frame of postwar Britain usually begins in 1945, with the defeat of Nazi Germany, and the near simultaneous general election of that year, which resulted in a momentous victory for the **Labour Party**. But when does the postwar period end? One possible year is 1973, with the impact of the **oil crisis**. Or did it cease with the year 1999, when the twentieth century ended? Or are we still living through it, until Britain endures another major war on its soil? Most historians of Britain since the Second World War wisely avoid the issue, treating the years from 1945 as a moveable feast in terms of when the period terminates.

Other time frames

Historians also divide the twentieth century into other periods. For example, a social history of Britain that ranges from the 1880s until 1914, or incorporates both Victorian Britain and the Edwardian era, can justify this time frame in relation to some key themes: the growing levels of **poverty** during the 1880s and since; the intellectual and political responses to it that led to **New Liberalism**, the beginnings of **tariff reform**, the growing popularity of **socialism**, and the rise of the **Labour movement**.

In recent years there has been a study of shorter time periods, notably within the postwar years. The study of **austerity** from 1945 to 1951 is a key example, because this period was distinguished by the recovery of war-damaged Britain and by a historically significant Labour government that, against great difficulties, instigated the **welfare state** and introduced a **mixed economy**.

Decades

Historians also focus upon decades not only because they form a convenient ten-year time frame, but also because decades were often characterised and even defined by significant social, cultural, economic and political phenomena. Any historian of a decade also understands that no ten-year time span is hermetically sealed, but rather is connected with earlier causes and later consequences.

The first two decades of the twentieth century tend not to be treated separately and distinctly because the short time span from 1900 to 1914 is a distinct period in itself – Edwardian Britain – which was abruptly terminated by the First World War.

In the aftermath of the **First World War**, the 1920s comprised a decade of contrasts. The economy endured major problems in **industrial relations** and high levels of **unemployment** on account of problems in the **staple industries**. Yet **new industries** sprang up across Britain, particularly in South-East England, London and the Midlands. Both socially and politically, the decade witnessed the incorporation of **women** into the franchise on equal terms with men. It saw the rise of **communism** and the beginnings of **fascism**, and the demise of the **Liberal Party** as Labour consolidated its growth and formed two minority governments.

The 1930s – sometimes called 'the devil's decade' – are still strongly associated with images of high unemployment and social problems during the **Great Depression**. The geography of economic **decline** and growth became painfully evident, as the industrialised distressed areas or **special areas** saw high levels of unemployment in the staple industries or the older manufacturing sectors, while other areas of Britain enjoyed investment from new industries and **service sector** expansion. Nominally beginning with the slump at the end of the 1920s, and ending with the onset of the Second World War, this was a fascinating decade of extremes: fascism threatened; **hunger marches** reminded millions of the plight of the poor, but politics and public opinion remained mostly moderate in temper. For most people, living standards and opportunities to enjoy **leisure** actually improved during the 1930s.

The 1940s witnessed the lows and highs that came with war, victory and readjustment to peace. Some studies of the decade, for example, assess popular politics and the Labour Party both in wartime and in the five or so years after the war was over because they seek to examine the relationship between political attitudes during war and early peacetime values. The 1950s are also increasingly studied by historians. Key reasons for this include the transition from the austerity of the years between 1945 and 1951 to full employment and **affluence**. This corresponded with three successive victories of the **Conservative Party** following the Labour governments of 1945–51.

As any fan of **popular music** or follower of **fashion** will be aware, the 1960s have been the subject of many histories because the decade witnessed new heights of cultural innovation and experimentation in popular culture. This was accompanied by a growing **permissiveness** and liberalisation in the social and cultural policies of government and in the values of millions of British people. The relationship between sexuality and society, from **censorship** to **contraception**, began to change rapidly. A conservative backlash against these trends also occurred.

The 1970s both intersected with the 1960s and generated a distinctive image. It is argued by some historians that the *zeitgeist* of the 1960s carried over into the early 1970s until the decade became beset with economic problems. The oil crisis, the return of mass unemployment and worsening industrial relations are typical fare on the menu of the 1970s. Politically, the rise of **Thatcherism** within this socio-economic background is commonly viewed as a break with the **consensus** politics that had endured since the later 1940s. British popular music, however, was hugely inventive and exciting during this decade.

The 1980s have been increasingly examined as the decade dominated by the right-wing conservative politics of Thatcherism. The weakness of political opposition was clearly evident: the Labour Party during the 1980s was in no position to be elected to government. Many conservative historians thus see the 1980s as the decade that remade Britain: the restructuring of the economy and the wave of patriotism generated by the **Falklands War** of 1982 restored self-confidence in Britain following the problems of the previous decade. During the 1990s, the long period of Conservative government came to an end, and in 1997 a new political agenda was evident in the rise of **New Labour**.

This last point is an important reminder that most historians never focus completely on one decade in isolation: they look for *continuities* between decades, and try to identify the consequences of a decade of change in its imme-diate or medium-term aftermath. The social and cultural innovations now asso-ciated with the 1960s, and the economic problems of the 1970s, for example, did not simply begin on the first day of each decade and end on 31 December 1969 or 1979.

On *modern* and *contemporary* history

The twentieth century witnessed the overlap between modern and contemporary history. By the modern period in Britain, historians often refer to the beginnings of mass **urbanisation** and industrialisation during the mid-eighteenth century, through to a cut-off date during the twentieth century. That cut-off date has been the First World War, the Second World War, and even later, including the present day. 'Modern' is a flexible adjective, and the time span associated with it is also moveable.

Historians also debate the legitimate temporal beginning of the 'contempo-rary' period. According to John **Barnes**, this is usefully viewed as the period within living memory for the majority of people. Hence the interwar period by this temporal definition may be viewed within the broad era of 'contemporary' history today. For the **Centre for Contemporary British History**, however, the years since 1945 define the contemporary period, and this appears to be the starting point that most historians are happy with – although some may begin with 1939, the start rather than the end of the Second World War. One thing is certain, however: contemporary history is equally as valid as the history of earlier times. And contemporary history is as ancient as history itself. In ancient Greece and ancient Rome, for example, many scribes were recording and commenting upon very recent history. It may raise interesting methodological issues, but it is essential to any humane and informed understanding of the past as prologue.

1.3
BRITAIN IN THE TWENTIETH CENTURY: A NARRATIVE OVERVIEW

Notes

• The most profound and dynamic developments and themes that shaped Britain are covered in this section, setting the scene for the remainder of the book. Its approach encourages you to make links between the social, cultural, economic and political history of twentieth-century Britain. Key terms in bold can be followed up elsewhere in the book.

Britain, 1900–14

Society and culture in Britain, 1900–14

At the beginning of the twentieth century, Britain was an urban nation: over four-fifths, or 80 per cent, of the **population** lived in a town or city. The population of the British Isles, including Ireland, numbered 38 million. Almost three-quarters of the British people were working class, engaged in industrial or manual labour. Britain was among the world's most prosperous nations in 1900, but poverty and inequality blighted the lives of millions of people the length and breadth of the land. **Social investigation** had found that up to a third of the working-class population of Britain's cities lived in poverty. Some poverty was extreme. Poor diet, pathetic clothing, dilapidated and overcrowded slum housing and many unpleasant illnesses blighted the lives of the worst-off families. In the heart of the world's leading imperial nation, the question of national efficiency posed itself to many leading politicians and professional experts. Why was there so much poverty in the midst of plenty? What were the implications for British power and prestige when so many young British citizens were unfit and incapable of undertaking industrial labour or military service? These questions appeared more urgent in the intellectual atmosphere generated by **social Darwinism** and its creed of natural selection.

In 1900, the vast majority of the British people were white. Close to the **docks** and ports of the largest cities, however, lived small communities of **black Britons**. Mostly poor and marginal, their presence in the country was consequent upon the trading system of the **British Empire**. In addition, by then the **East End of London**, Manchester and other large cities contained sizeable Jewish populations, and they also tended to live near docks or to inhabit the most affordable housing. The largest cities were the most multicultural areas of Britain, although the term **multiculturalism** would not be invented until the final quarter of the twentieth century.

In the towns and cities of Britain, an urban working-class culture had developed by the end of the Victorian period (Queen Victoria reigned from 1837 to 1901). There were regional variations across the country, but this was a culture of people living in a landscape of terraced streets, corner shops and pubs, churches or chapels, working-men's clubs and **sports** grounds. Going to the **pub** was a popular leisure pursuit, along with **football** and attendance and participation in other sports. But the prohibitive legacy of **Victorian values** cast a shadow over the leisure of millions of people. **Betting** with cash on **horse racing**, for example, had been illegal since 1853 unless the better (or 'punter') was actually at the course. Sex was also a lot less public than it is now. **Homosexuality** was still illegal, and pornography was accessible mostly for the wealthy. Getting hold of a condom was not impossible, but it was not until the 1920s that contraception and birth control became increasingly accessible. **Abortion** remained the preserve of the wealthy, while many poor and desperate women visited the back-street abortionist with often terrible consequences.

And the back streets were almost completely working class in social composition. In all large towns and cities **segregation** in housing was evident during the Victorian and Edwardian years in the growth of middle-class **suburbs**. Although some mixed-class suburbs existed, the **middle classes** had been moving to the outskirts in order to escape from the pollution, poverty and vice that existed in or near the town and city centres. From 1899 the **garden city** movement began as a concerted attempt to provide alternative experiments to unplanned and chaotic urban environments.

Despite the numerical dominance of the **working classes**, the middle classes were growing rapidly in numbers and continued to do so through the twentieth century as a consequence both of upward social mobility and of structural changes in the economy generating more employment suitable for the middle classes. Men still dominated this world. Some women ran small businesses, and some were involved in local political organisations, but no woman was head of a large business or a leading politician. In the middle-class professions, however, women were beginning to make major advances, notably in **education** and law. This was partly consequential upon the expansion of compulsory mass education initiated by the **Education Act** of 1870. Subsequent education acts extended schooling and its provision, creating opportunities for both women and men to become teachers and officials. The growing numbers of women in education also reflected the emphasis that middle-class families had placed upon learning and qualifications. The campaign for **women's suffrage** also brought middle-class women to the fore in Edwardian society.

Victorian values meant that sex was rarely discussed in public, but the art of the *double-entendre*, and the use of euphemisms to refer to the act of sexual intercourse, was evident in the popular culture of Edwardian Britain. Most large towns and cities had at least one **music hall** by 1900, and where there was more than one they were of varying size and quality. Many music hall acts were known for their scurrilous humour or suggestive songs. The **cinema**, however, a French invention that had made its first appearance in Britain in 1896, was set to become a hugely popular form of mass entertainment.

The British were also a more literate nation than ever before, spending their non-essential income on a variety of reading matter. **Newspapers** dominated the reading habits of the British public, however. This was a consequence of the coming together of a number of important developments: the **Education Acts** from 1902 that extended compulsory education to almost all **children**, growing levels of disposable income, and the commercialisation and expansion of the press. The Edwardian years witnessed the growth of the 'new journalism' and of cheap daily and weekly newspapers aimed increasingly at women and, more generally, at lower-middle-class and working-class readers. The *Daily Mail* began in 1896, and other now familiar newspapers such as the *Daily Express* and the *Daily Mirror* began during the early twentieth century.

Religion in Britain was dominated by Anglicanism or the Church of England, which stemmed from the Protestant reformation that divorced Britain from Roman Catholicism during the sixteenth century. Most people were practising Anglicans to a greater or lesser degree, mostly lesser. But Britain was no religious monolith. The large Roman Catholic minority continued to expand throughout the century, partly as a consequence of immigration from Catholic countries, notably Ireland. In London and other metropolitan areas lived Jewish populations which had grown since the 1880s. In Northern Ireland, Scotland and Wales, the nonconformist Protestant chapels provided alternatives to the Anglican Church. Religion was at the heart of different national identities within Britain, and also at the forefront of campaigns against alcohol and pubs, **betting and gambling**, and other vices.

Environmental issues and heritage conservation had emerged by the early twentieth century. During the nineteenth century, industrialisation and urbanisation had laid waste to much of the natural landscape and damaged or destroyed many fine buildings and rural environments. In the field of **architecture**, for example, the Arts and Crafts movement was inherently anti-urban, harking back to a pre-industrial past, while the **National Trust** was increasingly active in the Edwardian era. Both movements were harbingers of **environmentalism** and heritage consciousness in twentieth-century Britain.

The economy from 1900: powerful but vulnerable

Britain was the world's first industrial nation by the beginning of the nineteenth century. The great staple industries of textile manufacturing, iron and steel production, shipbuilding and coal mining were the predominant sectors of the British economy during the years before 1900, but they left a huge and complex regional legacy for the twentieth century. Working-class employment was dominated by a great variety of manufacturing and manual occupations, skilled, semi-skilled and unskilled. In the North-West of England, for example, the legacy of the industrial revolution was evident in the cotton manufacturing mills in Lancashire and Cheshire, and in woollens and some cotton textile making in west Yorkshire. Coal mining was another hugely important provider of jobs in the North-West, as it was across many other areas of England, and in Scotland and Wales. Shipbuilding was the great industry of a mercantile nation, and of a nation with a huge navy. And growing urbanisation was both caused by and consequential upon the growth of public transport. Workers in these industries were organised into **trade unions**. Problems in the sphere of industrial relations grew significantly during the Edwardian era. Indeed, industrial strife in Britain was evident in most decades of the twentieth century.

Britain faced increasingly successful competition from overseas countries during the later nineteenth and early twentieth centuries. In the wake of the unification of Germany in 1871 and industrialisation in the United States of America, the problems of Britain as a pioneer industrialising nation were exposed. These two countries and others had learned from British mistakes, and in Europe a number of nations benefited from greater levels of government assistance in industrial investment, as well as from tariffs (taxes) on imports which made domestically produced goods cheaper. Britain, however, had been wedded to **laissez-faire** economics since the abolition of the Corn Laws in 1846. Consequently, the textile, coal and metal industries faced a more difficult international scenario than during the earlier nineteenth century when British industry and the empire were dominant. From 1903, the movement for tariff reform sought to protect British markets from international competition.

But the British economy also continued to enjoy growth and success. Those staple industries of the nineteenth century remained at the heart of the manufacturing economy: many mills, mines and factories prospered. In addition a wide range of other industries contributed to the British economy. Many were traditional, such as foodstuffs, while others were new, for example **motor car manufacturing**. And throughout the twentieth century the service sector, in retail, banking and finance, and leisure and entertainment, continued to expand.

Politics, 1900–14: the mould begins to break

> Then let's rejoice with loud fal la, fa lal la!
> That nature wisely does contrive, fal la la la!
> That ev'ry boy and ev'ry gal,
> That's born into the world alive,
> Is either a little Liberal,
> Or else a little Conservative!
> (W. S. Gilbert, Iolanthe, 1882)

When *Iolanthe* was written, the challenge to the Conservative and Liberal parties was in its infancy. But by 1900 every child was no longer an automatic little

Liberal or a little Conservative. To carry the analogy further, there was a new kid on the block, an infant socialist party.

In 1900, British politics was, however, still dominated by Conservatives and Liberals, and a Tory government was in power. One hundred years later, British politics was still dominated by two major parties, but the nature of party politics had changed tremendously as a consequence of the birth in 1900 of the **Labour Representation Committee** (LRC). Formed from a number of socialist groups, notably the **Fabian Society** and the **Independent Labour Party**, it evolved into the most powerful vehicle for socialism in Britain. As its name suggests, it was staffed by leading members of the trade unions. The LRC was renamed the Labour Party in 1906, and in less than twenty years it had formed a government, replacing the Liberals as the second major political party at the ballot box, and of course in the House of Commons. The 'strange death of Liberal England' is a key theme of British politics before the Second World War, and the failure of the Liberals to re-emerge as a major force after 1918 was in part attributable to the rise of the Labour Party. But it was also a consequence of the electoral success of the Conservative Party. Throughout the twentieth century, the British electorate, never a homogeneous and always a changing entity, remained wedded to two-party politics. Alternatives on the extreme right and extreme left of the political spectrum were rejected – something for which the twenty-first century can be grateful.

The leading political positions in the Edwardian world were held by men. To be sure, Queen Victoria still sat on the throne in 1900, as she had since 1837. But she was an unelected and symbolic figurehead, and her wealth, and that of all the **monarchy**, was inherited and largely unearned. Victoria was at the apex of the aristocracy and the large landowning class termed the gentry, and the large landowners, as an elite class, remained hugely powerful in British parliamentary politics. But the nature of the ruling elites was changing. While retaining distinctive lifestyles, wealth and power, the aristocracy was increasingly merging with the wealthiest sections of the middle classes through intermarriage and commercial interests. These changes were reflected in the leading political parties of the late Victorian and Edwardian years, the Conservatives and Liberals.

By 1900 the Conservative Party was increasingly associated with the business elite, and the majority of aristocrats and other major landowners were more inclined towards Tory than Liberal politics. The growth of religious nonconformity among the membership of the Liberals partly explained this desertion of business interests to the Tories. Nonconformity was associated with teetotalism, hardly something on which the breweries and ancillary leisure industries were keen.

The nonconformist conscience was one of a number of contributory strands to New Liberalism, a set of interventionist policies including **national insurance** and **old-age pensions**. Since they were to be funded by increased taxation, such policies alienated many landowners, who did not relish the notion of high duties on their lands in order to pay for **social policy**.

Governments before the First World War were forced to confront the rise of organised labour politics, a political movement that intended to abolish poverty and to promote the interests of working-class people in parliament. As Labour grew in strength the electoral prospects of the Liberal Party were threatened, as millions of working-class voters who had previously been inclined to vote Liberal turned to Labour MPs. Working-class politics was also mostly dominated by men. The Labour Party was largely comprised of male trade unionists seeking to promote the interests of working people. Yet that is not to say that women were absent or inactive in working-class politics and trade unions. Many were involved in the new unions for unskilled and semi-skilled workers that were growing in influence during the early twentieth century.

Wealthy women property owners were able to vote for local councillors and were involved in **Poor Law** elections. But women could not vote at national **general elections**. No woman sat in the House of Commons – indeed a woman could not stand for parliament as an MP – and that fact led to the movement for women's suffrage. Within twenty years, as a consequence of the **Representation of the People Act** of 1918, many women had the vote in national elections. By 1928 all women over the age of twenty-one could vote in general elections. Women had also been able to sit in the **House of Commons** since 1919.

Britain and the wider world: imperialism before 1914

The British Empire in 1900 was at its most extensive, the culmination of centuries of overseas expansion, and Britain was the world's leading imperial nation. But just as the economy was facing increasing competition, so too was the empire under threat from a number of different countries. The so-called scramble for Africa during the 1880s manifested a more aggressive imperialism based upon not only economic exploitation but the subjugation of foreign peoples for the causes of material growth and national pride in Europe.

British expansion in Africa was being challenged primarily by France and Germany, the other great powers of Western Europe. Partly because of this international rivalry, Britain was at war in 1900. In the **Boer War** from 1899 to 1902 the mighty British army struggled to defeat the German-backed Afrikaans population in South Africa. A system of alliances or *ententes* between the great powers of Europe existed to create power blocs. Britain signed *ententes* with France and Russia between 1900 and 1914. Concomitantly, the armed services were strengthened by major reforms and increasing expenditure by the New Liberal governments.

The simmering question of home rule for **Ireland** also posed a powerful threat to Britain's imperial authority. The Victorian Liberal prime minister William Gladstone had advocated home rule in the face of huge opposition from the Conservatives, who viewed the ceding of any form of independent or even semi-autonomous government as the beginning of the break-up of the empire. Home rule bills were defeated in 1886 and 1893, and the question had moved down the parliamentary agenda during the Conservative governments of 1895–1905. With the election of the New Liberal government, however, the issue came to the fore once again. Irish Nationalist expectations were raised and dashed in the years up until the First World War, when home rule bills in 1912 and 1914 went unfulfilled. Irish anger overflowed in the **Easter Rising** of 1916.

Britain during the First World War

The social impact of the First World War

The First World War was by no means the first war to involve the civilian population. Because of mass civilian participation, it was a 'total war' (although there is no agreement among historians on exactly what a 'total war' is). Perhaps the American Civil War deserves the dubious accolade as the first modern total war. However, on British and European soil, the conflict from 1914 to 1918 was indeed the first total war. It involved the mass mobilisation of servicemen, first voluntarily and later via **conscription**. Gender relationships were greatly changed, as women went out to work in the munitions industries, in public transport, at the docks, in agricultural production and in a wide variety of uniformed and white-collar occupations usually reserved for or dominated by men. To be sure, women had worked in factories and on farms before, but the compelling need for their labour provided millions of women with new experiences and skills, and many enjoyed incomes independent of their boyfriends or husbands. Social historians have debated how far these experiences increased the self-confidence and broadened the expectations of many younger women. It was a common complaint among wealthier middle-class homes by 1920, for example, that women were less keen on domestic service than they had been before the war. Nonetheless, and unsurprisingly, inequalities continued and gender roles were affected only temporarily by the war. By 1918, for instance, it was still common for women to earn less than half or about half of what men earned for the same kind of employment.

Representations of war were also different from those of any previous conflict, with the minor exception of the Boer War. Newspapers had reported on wars for over a century, but for the first time, *en masse* in a modern conflict, the cinema brought newsreels of the battle front to the home front. From August 1914, the **Defence of the Realm Act** (DORA) had placed the government in control of key sectors of production and had led to greater regulation of civil life. And towards the end of the war in 1918 rationing was introduced, further directly affecting the consumption habits of the majority of British people. The war was also the first during which British towns and cities were attacked from both the sea and the air, as the civilian population was targeted directly by Germany. And, as soldiers and sailors returned from Belgium and France and other theatres of war from late 1918, **demobilisation** greatly increased the potential problems of unemployment.

The relationship of the First World War to social policy has been the subject of considerable historical debate. Planning for **reconstruction** began in 1917 and, with the advent of peace, education, national insurance, health, the Poor Law and **housing** were subject to further legislation.

Culture and the First World War

From its beginnings, the war was associated with a strong anti-German senti-ment and enthusiastic outpourings of **jingoism**, given expression both in a will-ingness to volunteer for military combat in the final third of 1914 and in newspaper and magazine articles and leader columns. The war poems of Rupert Brooke lyrically evoked the sense of elation and of youth sprung into action by the conflict. Ironic, then, that Brooke died while sailing to the Dardanelles in 1915. The cultural policy of government was clear, too. Following the Defence of the Realm Act the War Office Press Bureau introduced a tightly policed policy of censorship, attempting to block and modify anything that was written that might either lower morale in Britain and the empire or give heart to the Central Powers, the Germans and their allies. Letters written by those in military service to their families were also censored. The profound shock of the war, how-ever, muted such triumphalism and engendered cynicism towards government propaganda. The unprecedentedly high level of casualties in cruelly industrialised and merciless theatres of combat – over 720,000 mortalities and over 1.2 million injuries – led to a culture of disillusionment which could be seen in the paintings of official war artists, for example Wyndham Lewis and C. W. R. Nevinson, and in literature. A generation of artists and writers reacted with revulsion and vehe-mence to the idea of another conflict, perhaps most elegantly but powerfully expressed in the war poetry of Wilfred **Owen** and others. The writings of Robert **Graves** also manifested anger not only at the war but at the ruling elites that had engendered the conflict, and his *Good-bye to All That* (1929) reflected a powerful sentiment that the war had altered Britain for ever. Vera **Brittain**'s *Testament of Youth* was the autobiographical account of a nurse volunteer, and expressed her anger and despair at the impact of the conflict on the death and lives of so many young men and women. Contemporaries spoke of the 'lost generation', and several of Britain's weaknesses in the economic and political spheres since 1918 were blamed on the absence of many of the finest minds and physically able young men. It is important to note, however, that the culture of disillusion in Britain was less potent than that in Germany and Italy. Nonetheless, the conflict fostered strong anti-war feelings in Britain that were given expression in **pacifism** between the wars and in appeasement policies from 1936.

The wartime economy and the aftermath of war

Following the **Munitions of War Act** in 1915 the government assumed almost complete control of industrial production, the coal mines and public transport, and provided a hospital service that was designed to deal rapidly and effectively with the health problems of war workers. Leading staple industries changed production to generate munitions and materiel for the military, and a new atmosphere in industrial relations was created by the government crackdown on strikes and stoppages. Nonetheless, the war witnessed almost full employment as a consequence of labour shortages of manpower and increased production targets. At its conference in 1918, the Labour Party called for continued government intervention in the form of **nationalisation** of leading sectors of industry, partly to prevent the return to the unemployment and structural problems of the prewar years, but manufacturing and the coal mines were returned to private ownership soon after the war. Superficially, by 1919 the problems of the British economy appeared to be of no great dimension, as the majority of demobilised soldiers and sailors gained employment by the end of that year. The decommissioning of female labour was a major aspect of this readjustment. From early 1919 until 1921 the economy enjoyed a postwar restocking boom, although this was accompanied by inflationary pressures. Nonetheless, the difficulties of the staples were increasingly exposed as Britain's leading continental competitors, and in particular the United States of America, continued to eat away at British industrial power. The downturn in the economy from 1921 also negatively affected expenditure on social policy, notably housing. And during the war in 1918, and in 1919, industrial relations were less than harmonious.

Politics and the First World War

The war brought about a near terminal division within the Liberal Party from which it never fully recovered. In 1916, David **Lloyd George** took over as prime minister from Herbert **Asquith**, and served as leader of the **National Government** until 1922. Lloyd George's war cabinet included Liberals, Conservatives and also the Labour leader Arthur **Henderson**, who resigned before the war ended, not least because he was offended by Lloyd George's arrogance. This split between Asquith and Lloyd George, moreover, informed the latter's decision to remain as coalition prime minister in 1918, and to seek in the general election of that year a further mandate as 'the man who won the war'. The Conservatives, still divided over tariff reform, saw the political expediency in this, leaving the 'Squiffites' to nurse their wounds as a minority Liberal Party in parliament. The general election also witnessed the ascendancy of the Labour Party, which forewent any further reliance on Lib–Lab arrangements and began to construct a newer and more effective constituency machinery.

The general election, which came at the end of the war, was significant also because women voted for the first time, as did those in receipt of Poor Law dispensation who had previously suffered the pauper disqualification. As with social policy, however, any historical view that the Representation of the People Act having been passed prior to the general election was a kind of 'thank you' to women for their hard work and sacrifices during the war must account for the facts that, firstly, the right to vote for women had been accepted before the outbreak of war and, secondly, in 1918 only middle-class women over the age of thirty were given the right to vote. Millions of young middle-class and working-class women who had travailed for king and country during the war were forced to wait for full enfranchisement.

Britain, the Great War and the wider world

At the beginning of the war the Triple *Entente* of Britain, France and Russia faced the Central Powers of Germany, Austria-Hungary, Italy and the Ottoman Empire. The invasion of Belgium and northern France by Germany brought about some of the worst battlefield conditions of the twentieth century. The horrendous engagements in France and Belgium are now infamous for their terrible casualties and the apparent inhumanity of the military commanders who were prepared to sacrifice so many lives for such apparently limited strategic gains. The Gallipoli campaign in Turkey from April 1915 to January 1916, for example, led to the loss of 100,000 lives. The contribution there of soldiers from Australia and New Zealand demonstrated the significance of the British Empire to the war. And appalling loss of life ensued at the battles of the Somme in 1916 and Ypres in 1916–17. At sea, major encounters included the Falklands blockade in 1914–15, the battle of Jutland in 1916, and the submarine warfare of 1917.

The switching of allegiances by Italy following the **Treaty of London** in 1915 played only a minor role in the eventual victory of the Allies. The entry of the United States of America in 1917 was a much more decisive development, made more so by the decision of the emergent Russian communist state to withdraw from the conflict late that year, following the Russian Revolution. At the end of the war, a defeated and resentful Germany and a broken Ottoman Empire were somewhat at the mercy of the victorious British, American and French governments. The negotiations and settlements held at the **Paris Peace Conference** of 1919 were essentially about punishing and containing Germany and redrawing the maps of Eastern Europe and the former Ottoman Empire.

Britain, 1918 to 1939

A divided society? Britain between the wars

Historians continue to argue and debate about the nature and consequences of war and historical change during the twentieth century; among the key themes are the impact of war on social policy and on class and gender. From 1918 a further phase of social policy, affecting education, health, housing, national insurance, retirement and unemployment, was initiated. Many of the New Liberal reforms discussed above, however, had already laid the basis for subsequent legislation. Perhaps the most notable policy breakthrough came with housing, and the birth of a nationwide programme of **council estates** following the Housing and Town Planning Act of 1919.

Council housing did not begin from scratch in 1919, however, and herein lay some important considerations about war and historical change. Before 1914 many local authorities had already begun council housing schemes and slum-clearance programmes, but war accelerated and expanded an existing dynamic. Moreover, a major reform such as the abolition of the Poor Law in 1929 owed little to the so-called Great War. In short, the connections between war and expanded social policies are complex, and other longer-term factors must be accounted for. The effect of the war on women's enfranchisement was also nuanced. As noted, women were not finally enfranchised on equal terms with men until 1928, ten years after the war had ended.

The 1920s and 1930s saw the growth of mass entertainment. The most evocative was the cinema, which displaced music hall, and along with the pub became the main 'night out' for many millions of people every year. The cinema screen was heavily dominated by American films, however, so the government's cultural policy responded with the **Cinematographic Acts** to protect and promote the British film industry. In the more private context of home, the **radio** grew phenomenally following the establishment in 1922 of the British Broadcasting Company, which led during the mid-1920s to the formation of the **British Broadcasting Corporation**. Radio introduced a new era in domestic leisure, becoming a source of home-based entertainment and news in addition to the newspapers. So eventually would the **television**, introduced in 1936, although this was limited sociologically and regionally to a small number of wealthy Londoners and South-Easterners. Most households could afford papers and the radio, however, and a trip to the pictures, but the motor car, which became both a necessity and a luxury, was mostly reserved for the middle classes. Cars caused the spread of **motorisation** and greatly expanded suburbanisation between the wars. Because it ate up the countryside, suburbanisation became an environmental issue during the 1930s.

A new sport was introduced in its modern form into Britain in 1926, namely **greyhound racing**. A medium for gambling, dog racing took place in purpose-built stadiums. Other new forms of gambling included the football pools and the Irish Hospitals' Sweepstake. The cultural policy of the state, however, continued to restrict access to betting and gambling between the wars.

In short, the interwar years witnessed the makings of a twentieth-century **consumerism** that would be greatly augmented following the Second World War. Leisure and spending power, however, continued to reflect class and regional inequalities in British society, and these were exacerbated by the onset of mass unemployment during the Great Depression from 1929. Social investigation and **social observation** during the 1930s found that unemployment greatly aggravated poverty among the workers in the sectors where it was highest, namely coal mining (in which over 12 per cent of workers were unemployed in 1936), shipbuilding, cotton textiles, iron and steel manufacturing, the docks and the pottery-making industry. The writings of George **Orwell** and others have left us with some vivid and moving accounts of unemployment and poverty in the distressed areas.

The interwar economy: economic policy and the geography of growth and decline

Following the war, the British economy enjoyed a restocking boom as it returned to peacetime levels of demand and supply. During 1921, however, this boom collapsed, and the ongoing problems in the staple industries became more clearly exposed as persistent unemployment and problems in industrial relations, notably in the coal-mining industry, grew to a crescendo. Following the **General Strike** of 1926, the trade unions found their capacity for extensive strike action curtailed. With the calamitous Great Depression from 1929, many things changed. Unemployment rose from 1 million to over 3 million by 1932. Although most regions and urban areas were blighted by unemployment and short-time working, the North-West of England, Central Scotland and South Wales fared worst. These were the 'distressed areas', targeted for assistance by the **Special Areas Act** of 1934. Furthermore, migration from them to the wealthier regions of London, the South-East and the Midlands reflected the social geography of economic change. The new industries, notably motor car manufacturing and electrical and light engineering, were disproportionately located in London, the South and the Midlands. The service-sector industries – for example, retail, banking and finance, and tourism and leisure – continued to expand between the wars, but London and the South enjoyed more growth than other regions. However, even in the areas most hit by unemployment, levels of joblessness varied considerably. Areas based around a single industry and its ancillaries, for example Stockton-upon-Tees, were hardest hit. But nearby Newcastle possessed a wider employment portfolio and consequently suffered less unemployment as a percentage of the employable population.

Other sectors were hit by joblessness too, for example engineering, catering and food, building workers and labourers, even motor car manufacturing (in which 1 per cent of workers were unemployed in 1936). It is important not to see whole regions as uniformly devastated by unemployment or the prosperous cities and counties as enjoying unadulterated economic growth. With the coming of **rearmament** from 1936, and the **Second World War** from 1939, the problems of the staples were temporarily alleviated.

The economic crisis of the 1930s accelerated revisions to the economic policies of the government. Laissez-faire was effectively ended in 1932 with the introduction of **protectionism** by the **National Government**, while the ideas of John Maynard **Keynes** became increasingly germane as potential solutions to the problems of British capitalism.

Party politics after 1918: realignment and containment

The war ended with a coalition government led by the Liberal David Lloyd George, a coalition dominated by the Conservative Party. Wartime politics had produced that schism within the Liberal Party, and consequently Liberalism was unable to take advantage of the newly expanded electorate following the Representation of the People Act in 1918. Between 1918 and 1922 the coalition government fractured, and the Liberal Party lost its way. The Conservatives were elected to power in 1922 and, in that general election and all subsequent national elections, their major opponent became the Labour Party. Following its historic party conference in 1918, Labour vacuumed up the votes of millions of urban working-class men and women who had once voted Liberal, and it was able to form two minority governments, one in 1924, and again in 1929. Both were forced to cope with very difficult circumstances, however, and both were headed by Ramsay **MacDonald**. During the Great Depression, in 1931, a new coalition government in the form of the National Government replaced the second minority Labour government. It was headed for nearly five years by MacDonald. He was succeeded in 1935 by Stanley **Baldwin**, a former Conservative prime minister, who was leader until it dissolved into a Tory administration in 1937. The National Government was established to cope with the problems of the Great Depression, something it just about succeeded in doing, and by 1939 the worst of the economic and political threats had subsided.

Those political threats came from communism and fascism. The **Communist Party of Great Britain** (CPGB), established in 1920, operated to a considerable degree under diktat from Moscow, and worked hard to infiltrate leading trade unions and to exploit problems in industrial relations. Partly in opposition to and fear of communism, minor fascist groups emerged during the 1920s, but the **British Union of Fascists** (BUF), formed in 1932, became the largest of them – the largest, certainly, but the BUF never became a major force in British politics. The country remained in general immune to extremism from both left and right. Hence Britain continued to be a three-party system dominated by two major political parties, and the Conservatives emerged clearly as dominant between the wars. Other developments in interwar politics included the rise of pacifism in the face of fascist aggression in Europe, and the vexed policy of appeasement towards Nazism by the British governments between 1936 and 1939.

Britain and the wider world: war, peace and war again

Appeasement was in a sense both the culmination and the failure of the peace settlement established in 1919 by the **Treaty of Versailles**. In Europe, it did very little if anything to prevent the rise of totalitarian political regimes in Italy, Germany and other countries and the march towards war. Moreover, the dismemberment of the Ottoman Empire in the Middle East, in tandem with the consequences of the **Balfour Declaration** in 1917, led to destabilisation in

Palestine, a British protectorate, as a consequence of Jewish migration back to the heartlands of the Jewish heritage and religion. Further eastwards still, the beginnings of **decolonisation** became evident in **India**, as Gandhi lobbied the British government and people for the independence of his country. He was unsuccessful in the prewar years, but the dynamic of Indian independence re-emerged following the 1939–45 war. India, however, was not the first country in the twentieth century to liberate itself from British rule. That tribute went to Ireland, with the **Anglo-Irish Treaty** of 1921. The treaty did not completely free the whole island of Ireland: six counties in the north, with Protestant majorities, remained part of the United Kingdom. This was partition: Northern Ireland had become the focus of sectarian animosities that persisted until the end of the twentieth century.

The United States of America stayed mostly aloof from the League of Nations that had been created in Paris in 1919, and American isolationism continued throughout the rise of fascism in interwar Europe. British defence policy during the 1930s was an amalgam of facing up to the triple threat of fascist Italy, Nazi Germany and Japan. With the collapse of appeasement in March 1939, and the onset of war in September 1939, American isolationism worried many in Britain. Cultivated by Winston **Churchill**, who found a mostly sympathetic ear in President Roosevelt, the USA provided **Lend Lease**, philanthropy and some moral support. After the Japanese attack on Pearl Harbor in December 1941, American assistance in the defeat of the Axis Powers (Italy, Germany, Japan) became indispensable to the British during the Second World War.

Britain at war, 1939–45

Social change and cultural developments on the home front

'As I write, highly civilised human beings are flying overhead, trying to kill me.' Thus wrote George **Orwell** during the **Blitz** in *The Lion and the Unicorn*, one of his most significant polemics on **national identity** and on the social and political consequences of the war. He argued that the war would probably have little effect on national identity, which would remain essentially similar to its complex prewar character, anchored around class, regionalism and a host of stereotypes. And, as for society, he felt it would strengthen a demand for a 'better life' during the forthcoming peace. In this, Orwell was by no means alone, as many writers, film makers and others in positions of influence, and on the left of politics, entertained similar aspirations. However, Orwell and other broadcasters and writers were careful in what they said. Censorship during the Second World War, controlled through the **Ministry of Information**, was mostly effective, if not completely watertight. In wartime radio broadcasting and in **documentary film**, for example, many leading intellectuals came together not only to provide morale-building documents of the war effort, but also to make carefully cloaked calls for social change. Winston Churchill, the wartime prime minister from May 1940, often became vexed at what he derided as 'airy fairy visions of utopia', but since 1941 many leading writers and reformers had been building up the pressure for a radical reconstruction based upon a refreshed and egalitarian Britain.

The Blitz and the apparatus of air raid precautions (ARP), along with **evacuation**, rationing, munitions work for women, conscription and compulsory billeting, had also generated a desire for social change among the population of Britain, although its extent is impossible to calibrate. The strength of this collective aspiration was exaggerated by an earlier generation of experts on social policy, including Richard **Titmuss**, who argued that military participation by civilians led to an increased ratio of welfare spending. Social historians during the 1960s took their cue from this. From the later 1970s, however, historians became increasingly wary of the 'myth of the Blitz' and attempted to provide a more circumspect and nuanced account of the effect of total war on social change. The victory of the Labour Party at the general election of 1945 remains the most tangible demonstration of the mood for change that the war had created, and of the ability of Labour to seize the day. The great popularity of the **Beveridge Report** of 1942, albeit a document written by a Liberal, is further proof.

Certainly, the Second World War saw deeper and more prolonged interruptions to everyday life than had occurred between 1914 and 1918. Rationing and conscription were introduced earlier; the air raids were vastly more extensive and disruptive and involved dangerous voluntary service; evacuation brought the middle and working classes together as never before – or since; and women were more extensively involved in war work than during the First World War. In addition, special nurseries were provided to allow mothers to work while the state looked after their children. The promises of greater equality and a more modern Britain appeared bright for many on the left as the war drew to a close. Yet, by the mid-1950s, many were disappointed that a historic opportunity for socialism had apparently been betrayed: since 1945 the welfare state, in tandem with affluence and consumerism, had precipitated a new era of individualism, apathy, even conservatism. These are currently key themes in the social history of mid-century Britain.

The economy during the Second World War

The outbreak of war brought to an end the high levels of unemployment of the 1930s. Many workers now became soldiers, sailors and airmen, creating demands for labour, and, in common with the First World War, the British economy was placed under the strict command of the government from 1939. All sectors were subordinated to munitions production targets, and strict limitations were placed upon industrial action. Many strategically important manufacturing operations were dispersed away from the industrial city centres to remoter sites in the hinterland where they were less prone to destruction by aerial bombardment. Thus did economic dispersal accompany, to some degree, the dispersal of people and manpower via evacuation and billeting. Key ministries were established in 1939 and 1940 to coordinate munitions production, manpower needs, and billeting and emergency housing. Public transport was also strictly controlled by government: state intervention and government operation was labelled as 'war socialism', contributing to calls from the trade unions and from many Labour MPs for a permanent nationalisation of key sectors of industry once the war came to an end.

Party politics and the Second World War

As had happened in the Great War, the early phase of the Second World War brought about the downfall of the incumbent prime minister, in this case Neville **Chamberlain**, and his replacement by an altogether more dynamic figure, Winston Churchill. An emergency coalition government or National Government had been formed in 1939 to reflect mainstream party politics, but Labour politicians had refused to participate, a decision they reversed after Churchill took up the reins of power in May 1940.

Broadly speaking, Labour politicians proved effective and trustworthy, despite some significant ideological differences between Conservative and Labour leaders, and even within the Labour Party. But, against Churchill's instincts and wishes, the Labour Party quit the national government in 1945 to prepare to fight an earlier general election alone: Churchill had wanted the coalition to continue until victory over Japan. The performance of key Labour politicians during the war is another reason that helps to explain the general election result of that year. So too did the unimpressive electoral campaign by the Conservatives. Hence it was a Labour government that was tasked with handling a major programme of reconstruction at home, and of negotiating both the position of Britain vis-à-vis the rest of the world during the early stages of the **Cold War** and the onset of decolonisation.

The Liberal Party, however, despite the contribution of **Beveridge**, was unable to benefit from the war. Smaller parties remained marginal. The Communist Party of Great Britain mustered two MPs, but fascism by 1945 had a foul stench about it. Associated with the fallen and disgraced dictatorships of Germany and Italy, ultra-right-wing politics was confined to the remnants and personnel of various interwar fascist parties, notably Oswald **Mosley** and his British Union of Fascists. Unfortunately, fascism remained a toxic minor force in the street politics of Britain, as evidenced in the formation of Mosley's **Union Movement** in 1948 and in the anti-Semitic disturbances in London and other major cities during the latter 1940s.

Britain and the world at war

Britain's relationship with the wider world was shattered with the outbreak of war in September 1939, as it found itself fighting against the Axis Powers of Germany, Italy and Japan. In 1940 Britain faced arguably the most difficult year in its modern history. Following the fall of Norway (April) and France (May) and the heroic defeat at Dunkirk, the **Battle of Britain** and later the Blitz demonstrated the dangers Britain faced from Nazi Germany. From 1940–41, botched Italian invasions of Greece and Egypt led the Nazis to wage more effective incursions and occupations in the Eastern Mediterranean and North Africa, while Japan invaded the imperial possessions of Hong Kong and Malaya: the British were defeated in Singapore in February 1941.

In North Africa throughout 1941–2 the Allied forces faced near defeat until the decisive victory at Alamein, under Field Marshall **Montgomery**, in November 1942. This became a turning point of the war, eventually leading to the surrender of German and Italian forces in May 1943, and allowing the Allies a springboard to invade Italy and to conduct operations in the Eastern Mediterranean, particularly the attempted liberation of Greece. At sea, the Battle of the Atlantic from 1942 to 1943 was also won, thanks in no small part to the role of Bletchley Park, which cracked the German enigma codes, and to the role of the Royal Navy in facilitating cross-Atlantic traffic. The navy blockade of Germany was a further major contributing factor to Allied victory.

The **Royal Air Force** (RAF) assisted in the victories in North Africa, bombing Italian and German supplies and troops. The controversial Allied bombing of German and Japanese cities and industrial centres was also essential in the defeat of the Axis Powers. The atomic bombs dropped by the USA on Japan in the late summer of 1945 finally brought the bloody war in the Pacific and in Asia to its end.

Britain had drawn once more, as in the First World War, on the personnel and resources of the British Empire. In tandem with the United States from December 1941, and the USSR following the collapse of the Nazi–Soviet Pact in the summer of 1941, Allied strength began to outweigh that of the Axis Powers. The USSR became an essential ally in Eastern Europe, while the USA played a major role in both the Asian-Pacific and European theatres of war. Ironically, as the war drew to a close, the changed global position of Britain was exposed by the power of both the USA and Soviet Russia. And the countries of the Commonwealth, to whom so much was owed, were now seeking independence from Britain.

Britain from 1945

Social and cultural life, 1945–73: from austerity to affluence

At mid-century, Britain was enduring, with an amalgam of humour, annoyance, apathy and resignation, the so-called years of austerity. The classic time frame for austerity Britain is 1945–51, although the country was not fully restored to normality until 1954. During the Second World War and into the first half of the 1950s, rationing was a common and depressing feature of life: some of the controls on food and other resources imposed during the war were continued. New ones were introduced as scarce goods both raised costs and also led to a shortage of foodstuffs and clothing. The fuel crisis in the bitter winter of 1947 lent the early postwar years a totem of hardship that millions of people remembered for years afterwards. In the aftermath of victory over Nazi Germany, early happiness and relief following Allied victory had given way to some grim realities.

Yet the picture was not uniformly bleak. Going to the pub remained a popular weekly activity for millions. The second half of the 1940s also witnessed a boom in cinema-going and attendances at sports stadiums. Thousands of 'picture palaces' had been built between the wars and, despite restrictions and censorship, 'going to the pictures' remained popular during the Second World War. Leisure also intersected with environmental issues. During the Second World War, the National Parks Committee had been appointed, and its report of 1947 led to the creation in 1949 of the **National Parks**. They proved to be hugely popular for holiday-makers, tourists and walkers, and preserved huge areas of Britain from urbanisation.

At home, listening to the wireless, or radio, was still much more popular than watching television, and the three main channels were broadcast by the **BBC**, which retained its monopoly over the airwaves into the postwar years. After 1953, with the broadcasting of the **coronation of Queen Elizabeth II**, television swept the land, entering the great majority of homes and introducing a new level of exposure to light entertainment programmes and current affairs. From tiny beginnings in the 1930s, television became central to leisure and recreation in Britain. The **sitcom** was born in the 1950s, and **Americanisation** became increasingly visible as more and more programmes were imported from the USA, mirroring American success in the cinema. From 1955 commercial television was introduced in the form of **Independent Television** (ITV). It was ITV that introduced Britain's longest-running and most successful **soap opera**, *Coronation Street*, in 1960.

The onset of mass television also occurred during an era of liberalisation and greater permissiveness in British social and cultural life. For example, censorship in literature and in the theatre and cinema was relaxed during the late 1950s, and increasingly so during the course of the 1960s. The 'f' word, for example, was first used on television during this decade, and, although such language and the increasing depiction of sex and violence offended many, the relaxation of censorship encouraged greater levels of experimentation, whether in theatre, cinema or television.

All this was accompanied by great humanitarian strides in social policy. Within a few years during the 1960s, homosexuality was decriminalised, abortion became legally available, access to contraception was made easier, and **divorce** became more accessible and affordable. Victorian values were waning.

The majority of Britons had more money and time to spend on leisure than ever before. After 1950, the black and white television became the major feature of the growing affluence and consumerism among the population. Motor cars, record players, popular music, fashion clothing, and more and more exotic **holidays** were increasingly enjoyed and became ever more visible in British life. Luxury and leisure items that were once enjoyed mostly by the middle classes became accessible to working-class people to a far greater extent after the war. And electrically powered labour-saving devices in the home, such as washing machines, refrigerators and irons, became cheaper and so available to working-class households, particularly though hire purchase or credit payments.

Increasingly, the majority of homes were in the suburbs. Throughout the later nineteenth century and during the years until 1939, Britain, and especially England, had seen massive **suburbanisation** in the form of roads and houses spreading out from the towns and cities into the countryside. Those classic terraced streets with their corner pubs and shops now became inner suburbs, superseded by the familiar rings and sprawls of semi-detached and detached middle-class **suburbia**. The 1920s and 1930s especially had seen a huge boom in such building. By 1950, both **town and country planning** legislation and the Second World War had slowed down suburban growth, but it never completely stopped. Council estates continued to be built on the outskirts of towns, and cheaper land on those outskirts also tempted speculative private builders to construct houses for **home ownership**. The working classes increasingly moved not only to council estates but to the cheaper semi-detached homes available to them via credit in the form of mortgage loans.

And the British working classes underwent great changes during the 1950s as **immigration** from the Caribbean, India and **Pakistan** introduced larger communities of blacks and Asians in the major cities, and in smaller towns and cities too. They often moved into poorer housing areas from whence white people were migrating to the suburbs, creating an ethnic dimension to housing segregation. As noted above, small communities of blacks, Asians and people of European origin had existed in British cities for many decades, but historians now focus upon the docking of the SS *Empire Windrush* in 1948 as symbolising the beginnings of mass immigration into postwar Britain, following the **British Nationality Act** of the same year. African-Caribbean and Asian immigrants came to Britain in their hundreds of thousands, changing the character of many urban areas, notably the **inner cities**, and making a considerable contribution to the social, cultural and economic life of the country. The arrival of people of colour in any significant numbers into parliament would take longer, however – until the 1990s, in fact. Unfortunately, in many of the inner cities, and in other older urban areas, poverty afflicted people of all colours. By the later 1960s, sociology was 'rediscovering' the poor, just as social investigation had done during the 1880s.

The economy: growth and relative decline

Britain was victorious but financially exhausted at the end of the war. It was no longer the world's leading creditor nation. Despite the difficult financial context, the Labour government pursued the policy of nationalisation of the leading staple industries, of public transport and of the Bank of England. Based upon a mixed economy of nationalised key industries and a burgeoning private sector, Britain achieved almost full employment during the 1950s and 1960s. The return to peacetime prosperity in Europe, the United States and elsewhere also assisted British economic expansion during the later 1940s and 1950s. For these broad reasons, the years between the end of austerity during the early 1950s and the oil crisis of 1973 have been called the 'golden years', or the 'golden age'. This is unsurprising, given the difficulties encountered by the British economy from 1973, but there are dangers in simplifying the contrast between the golden years and the later problems of the British economy. For example, boom and bust, or the stop–go cycle of growth and its sudden halt, were endemic before the 1970s. The policies of Conservative chancellors of the exchequer during the mid- and late 1950s and early 1960s were partly responsible. The so-called golden years also saw many problems with inflation and the value of the pound, and the subsequent need for **devaluation** during the second government of Harold **Wilson**. Attempts during the 1960s to promote **economic planning** were largely unsuccessful.

This was because the problems of the British economy were longer term. By 1950 Britain was no longer the world's pre-eminent industrial nation, although its economy remained dominated by manufacturing. From 1957, moreover, the member states of the **European Economic Community** (EEC) enjoyed higher annual growth rates than Britain; however, the country joined the EEC only in 1973, when the Conservative prime minister Edward **Heath** completed the entry process. During the postwar years the growth of competition from the United States and the Asian-Pacific countries, notably Japan, posed further problems for British industry, both nationalised and privately owned.

Politics in an era of 'consensus'

The popularity of Churchill as war leader was extremely high by 1945, when the general election of that year was called. That Churchill lost the election, and Labour won with one of its largest majorities, is a source of much historical debate. Memories of the Tory-dominated 1930s had a great deal to do with this defeat. Moreover, the Tories had hardly been enthusiastic about the Beveridge Report in 1942. Under the new prime minister, Clement **Attlee**, Labour established the welfare state, with national insurance and the **National Health Service** as its cornerstones. Education was also restructured by the **Education Act** of 1944. As noted, a mixed economy was introduced. As William Beveridge was influential on social policy, so the ideas of John Maynard Keynes were institutionalised in the nationalisation of key industries and in the adoption of progressive taxation to fund the welfare state. The Conservative Party, in power from 1951, made a number of modifications to social and economic policies, but only a few Conservatives during the 1950s and 1960s, and even in the early 1970s, fundamentally challenged the rationale of the welfare state and the mixed economy. This became known as consensus politics.

In addition to the three major parties, a host of minor parties emerged during the 1940s and 1950s. Some were weaker versions of their interwar predecessors, notably the fascist groups such as the Union Movement, the **League of Empire Loyalists** and the **British National Party**. The Communist Party of Great Britain had seen no more than four candidates elected in the 1935 and 1945 general elections, and none in 1950 and since. In common with its fascist antagonists it remained a fringe movement in Britain, although more intellectually respectable, despite the atrocities and totalitarianism of Soviet Russia. Other parties included **Plaid Cymru**, the Welsh Nationalist grouping, and the **Scottish Nationalist Party** (SNP). Formed between the wars, they were relatively low-key at mid-century but grew in significance from the 1960s onwards.

Britain in the wider world: the Cold War, decline and decolonisation

In addition to losing its industrial pre-eminence, Britain ceased to be the dominant global power. Following the victory of the Allies in the Second World War, the United States of America emerged triumphantly onto the world stage as the so-called leader of the Free World. Its opponent, another federated country, namely the Union of the Soviet Socialist Republics, had occupied its neighbours, creating a bloc of communist countries. Hence, as the Cold War heated up, London was eclipsed by Washington and Moscow. The **Korean War** of 1950–53 was a further catalyst for polarisation between East and West.

Nonetheless, the Labour government of 1945–51 did play a major role in the establishment of the United Nations in 1945 and of the **North Atlantic Treaty Organization** (NATO) in 1949. This was at the heart of British attempts to maintain the **special relationship** with the United States within the sphere of defence and foreign policy. Yet, by contrast, neither the majority of British politicians nor public opinion manifested any great enthusiasm for perhaps *the* major international initiative of the 1950s, namely the beginning of the European Economic Community from 1957. Britain and **Europe** now became a problematic theme in postwar British history.

International decline was most sharply evident in the process of decolonisation. The so-called first colony, Ireland, had been an independent state since 1922, although the six counties of Northern Ireland remained a part of the United Kingdom – something bitterly resented by many Irish people and the longer-term cause of **The Troubles** from 1968. Ireland had been the closest colony to home, as it were, but the process of decolonisation further afield had also begun in earnest. India and Pakistan were born in troubled conditions during the latter 1940s. Later, when he made his **wind of change** speech in 1960, prime minister Harold **Macmillan** was referring to Britain's declining influence in Africa and to the wider decolonisation of countries that once made up the empire. Some gained full independence; others became members of the **Commonwealth**. Immigration to Britain from Commonwealth countries, as noted, began on a significant scale at mid-century following the British Nationality Act of 1948.

The Middle East continued to cause major problems for British foreign policy. The crisis in Palestine caused by the establishment of the state of **Israel** in 1948 and the hostility towards Israel from neighbouring countries, notably Egypt and Syria, were in part responsible for growing Arab nationalism in the region. This had major negative consequences for Britain, both between 1945 and the founding of the Jewish state and during the **Suez crisis** of 1956. A humiliation for the British and a clear demonstration of the power of the United States, Suez temporarily threatened the special relationship between Britain and America. Defence policy was also readjusted to the diminishing overseas role of Britain, as evidenced in the **East of Suez** strategy in 1967–8 and other retrenchments.

Britain, 1973–99

Choice and diversity: social and cultural life in the late twentieth century

By 1999 over 58 million people lived in Britain. Their society and culture had been influenced by a century and more of historical changes and short-, medium- and longer-term influences. It is now commonplace in social and cultural histories of Britain to emphasise its multiculturalism by the end of the twentieth century. As a consequence of mass immigration from Asia and the Caribbean during the 1950s and 1960s, Britain was certainly a more ethnically diverse country than ever before in its history. More than three hundred different languages are currently spoken in London. The much maligned British cuisine was enlivened by Indian, Pakistani and Bangladeshi restaurants. Pizzas and Italian meals, American fast-food outlets, and Greek and Spanish restaurants became increasingly common. Mosques and temples accommodated the religious practices of Muslims, Sikhs and Hindus. Among the Christian population, however, church attendances had declined over the course of the postwar years. **Secularisation** had eroded much of the influence of the Church of England and other Christian churches.

Multiculturalism, however, brought with it difficulties and tensions. The **Parekh Report** in the year 2000, entitled *The Future of Multi-Cultural Britain*, was welcomed as an enthusiastic statement of multiculturalism, but also criticised for its failure to emphasise some religious and cultural practices among immigrant groups that the majority found it difficult to accept, for example arranged marriages.

As a consumer society, Britain was wealthier but not necessarily healthier. In addition to pubs, continental-style wine bars and American-influenced sports bars became fashionable during the 1990s, and supermarkets sold ever increasing volumes of beers and wines from a growing range of global sources. Australian, Californian and South African wines now competed with French, Italian and Spanish wines, and passé German whites. The supermarkets, notably the giants Tesco, Sainsbury's, Asda and Safeway (later Morrisons), dominated shopping and consumerism. First introduced on a small scale between the wars, supermarkets grew massively during the postwar period, and were important in raising living standards. The abolition of resale price maintenance in 1964 removed the obligation for shops to sell goods at prices set by suppliers. It subsequently became possible for retailers to undercut others through offers, and the supermarket boom began. Convenience was also a major appeal and, if anything – although this is a controversial point in terms of environmental history – shopping at supermarkets became easier for most from the 1970s as rising car ownership led to the creation of out-of-town shopping centres, many of which were anchored around large supermarkets. In addition to those in the town centres, big new superstores rose up in big-box structures in edge-city style urbanisation. Increased shopping was also encouraged by the introduction of Sunday opening hours in 1994.

The weekly household shopping was no longer the preserve of women as it had been before the 1960s, and the growing numbers of women going out to work influenced some changes in household roles. The rise of the so-called symmetrical family meant more task-sharing at home and among family members, male and female. While this by no means brought about purely equal relationships within households, the everyday life of most women was less restricted than it had been in 1900. Inequalities also continued within the workplace, although the twentieth century witnessed huge improvements in women's pay and employment. A wider range of occupations, from manual unskilled jobs to the higher echelons of the professions, were increasingly filled by women. The **equal pay** legislation from 1971 made a significant if uneven impact, as did the effects of second-wave **feminism**.

Leisure was more abundant and more money was spent on it than before. Cinema-going had declined during the 1970s but made something of a comeback from the mid-1980s, with the opening of the first multiplex cinema in 1985. Cinemas with ten or more screens, and a greater variety of foods and confectionery than in older establishments, grew up in both the centres and around the outskirts of towns and cities. In common with shopping, going to the out-of-town cinema was one of many activities that encouraged the edge-city urbanisation.

The screen remained a dominant feature of most people's lives. Almost every house possessed at least one television set by 1990, and hundreds of thousands of homes had two or more. In addition, the personal computer (PC) was becoming a 'must-have' item for most people, both at work and at home, for business and for pleasure. In common with the **telephone**, the **internet** from the early 1990s enabled people to keep in touch by email. As for the telephone, the desire for sociable contact with family and friends was evident in the rise and rise of the mobile phone. From the 1990s onwards, both the PC and the mobile phone made it easier to contact people, and enabled kinship, friendship and more formal business and official communications to become increasingly flexible and less localised.

If life was more mobile and fluid for the majority, it was also freer. The permissiveness that had irrupted during the later 1950s and the 1960s continued to develop and grow during the 1970s, 1980s and 1990s. In matters of sex and relationships, it was no longer stigmatic to have children outside of marriage, or to live as an unmarried couple. The **Divorce Act** of 1969 had also contributed to the growth in the number of smaller households.

Cultural policy in the final two decades of the twentieth century demon-strated significant differences in emphasis to the consensus era. In cinema, for example, the legislation of the 1980s removed the framework of loans and quotas that had protected the British film industry since the 1920s. Any final lingering traces of Victorian censoriousness were wiped away by the introduc-tion of liberalised opening hours of pubs and bars, and by the introduction in 1994 of the **National Lottery**. Whereas once the state had tried to prohibit certain leisure habits, it now sought to promote and to profit from them.

The economy resurgent

By the end of the 1990s, the contribution of manufacturing to the British economy was shrinking while the service sector was growing. This represented a huge structural change, and one that was exacerbated by the oil crisis of 1973. But it is important to note that the growth of the tertiary sector was under way long before the 1970s, as were the endemic problems of some of the staple manu-facturing industries. By the year 2000 the service sector employed over 70 per cent of the total workforce and industry less than 30 per cent. **Agriculture** accounted for about 2 per cent of employed people. As a consequence of **privat-isation**, that is, **denationalisation**, staple industries were radically rationalised, trimmed down or terminated during the 1980s and 1990s: coal mining and ship-building became tiny shadows of their former selves, although steel remained a viable and sizeable industry. The infrastructure was also sold off by the state: public transport and the utilities companies became privately owned.

Compared with the 1970s, when a million unemployed emerged for the first time since the 1930s, and inflation and industrial relations gave an image of a country in either economic stasis or decline, the economic scenario was rosier twenty years later. Yet care must be taken not to overstate either the negatives of the 1970s or the positives since. Unemployment was higher under the Tory governments of the 1980s than it had been under Labour during the 1970s, and inflation grew much worse during the first Thatcher government before it got better. There were still over a million unemployed in the year 2000. Hundreds of thousands of the new jobs being created during the 1980s and 1990s were part-time, low-skilled and poorly paid. Following the **Big Bang** or the deregulation of the **City of London** in 1986, however, many financial positions became very highly paid.

The application of anti-**Keynesian** measures characterised economic policy during the 1980s and 1990s. **Monetarism** had become the new economic ortho-doxy on the right of politics, signalling the end of the so-called consensus era of economic and social policy. Committed to 'rolling back the frontiers of the state', however, the Conservative governments of the 1980s and 1990s were forced continually to adjust and expand social policy initiatives. Spending on most major aspects of social policy increased after 1980. And the Conservative record on privatisation was marked by error as well as success. Finally, the debacle of **Black Wednesday** in 1992, when the pound **sterling** crashed out of the European Exchange Rate Mechanism (ERM), lent the Conservatives an image of financial incompetence, something that had been previously been associated with the Labour governments of the 1960s and 1970s.

Politics: Conservative and Labour realignments and the rise of green and nationalist politics

The 1997 general election witnessed the return of a Labour government for the first time since 1974, a triumph for Tony **Blair** and New Labour. The Conservatives had won the general election of 1979 and went on to three further victories, in 1983, 1987 and 1992. And the centre-left of politics in Britain had been interrupted by the formation of the **Social Democratic Party** (SDP) in 1981, when leading Labour politicians quit their party to establish a new political movement. The Labour Party was to some extent rebuilt under Neil **Kinnock** following the general election defeat of 1983, and under John **Smith** from 1992 to 1994, and Blair's victory owed much to the work of his predecessors. But the popularity of New Labour also stemmed from the electorate's fatigue with the government of John **Major** between 1992 and 1997.

The 1997 general election confirmed that Labour remained the only real threat to the Conservatives. The **Liberal Democrats**, formed from an alliance of the Liberals with the SDP in 1988, remained a poor third, while a host of smaller parties were active in both general and local elections. The nationalist parties of the SNP and Plaid Cymru were buoyant as the promised national assemblies for their respective countries came into being at the end of the twentieth century. The issue of British membership of the European Union continued to burn, with the formation of a number of smaller anti-European Union parties and the continuing hostility of many Tories to the notion that Britain was ceding rights and freedoms to Brussels.

Green politics expanded in Britain following the formation of the **People's Party** during the early 1970s. Environmentalism remained a smaller cause here than in other Northern and Western European countries, but grew in significance, as was evidenced in the election of **Green Party** members of the European Parliament (MEPs) during the 1990s and since. The causes included nuclear power, the growth of motorisation and of road-building, and the impact of urbanisation on the environment.

For the first time since 1922, the dangerous situation in Northern Ireland appeared to have been visited with a possibly permanent solution, one that had at least brought about dialogue between Sinn Féin, the Social Democratic and Labour Party, and the Ulster Unionist parties. The Good Friday Agreement in April 1998, brought about within a year of Blair's election triumph, appears to have endured into the present century.

Britain and the wider world: America, the Commonwealth and Europe

The special relationship between Britain and the United States of America had been strengthened during the 1980s and 1990s. From 1979 to 1990 the prime minister Margaret **Thatcher** had enjoyed mostly amiable relations with the United States, particularly from 1980 to 1988 when Ronald Reagan was president. A close relationship was also forged between the New Labour and New Democrat parties (that is, between Tony Blair and Bill Clinton) during the 1990s, not least because the Labour Party learned much about how to win national elections from the American Democrats. Britain remained a leading member of NATO and of the United Nations, keeping itself at the heart of transatlantic negotiations.

Britain's growing participation in the **European Union**, however, was viewed by many contemporary historians and political scientists as placing the country in a triangular conundrum vis-à-vis Europe and America. Furthermore, the expansion of the economic and political apparatus of the EU led to continued soul searching within Britain, from fears about the loss of political sovereignty in legislative and legal matters to anger at key EU strategies over agriculture and fishing.

Although Britain had mostly remained free from involvement in major conflicts since the Korean War, the obvious and emotive exception was the Falklands War of 1982. In taking on the right-wing Argentine junta, the British government did much to restore national pride, while liberating a temporarily captive people and destabilising an unpleasant right-wing dictatorship.

In Africa, Asia and the Caribbean, British decolonisation proceeded throughout the postwar years. The final act came with the handing over of **Hong Kong** to communist China in 1997. It was poignant for its symbolism both as the decline of British rule and as the demise of democracy. By then, the British Empire was a long-distant memory for the majority of British people, but Britain could still continue to view itself as one of the leading world powers.

II
LANDMARKS

2.1
NOTES

- Landmarks provides a chronology or time line of the major developments in Britain since 1900 within the following four broad categories:

  1 Social and cultural history
  2 Economic history
  3 Political history
  4 Britain and the wider world.

- All Acts of parliament are given in bold.
- Names in bold are to be found in the **Biographies**.
- Key *themes* in bold are developed in the **Dictionary**.
- Some acts and events in bold may be found more than once under **Landmarks**. There is considerable overlap between many of these categories, so a number of Acts of parliament and key events will occur in a number of sets of Landmarks.

2.2
SOCIAL AND CULTURAL HISTORY

- Housing and town and country planning
- Environmental issues
- The monarchy
- Immigration and multiculturalism
- Religion
- Women
- Sexuality and permissiveness
- Social policy: health and welfare
- Social policy: education
- Media: the press – newspapers and magazines
- Media: cinema and television
- Media: radio broadcasting
- Sport
- Other leisure landmarks

Housing and town and country planning

1899   **Garden City** Association formed to promote the ideas of Ebenezer
        Howard for planned new garden cities in Britain to reintroduce people
        to the land in new settlements, and to relieve the overcrowding of
        London and other large cities. The association included members of
        the Land Nationalisation Society, committed to the more equitable
        distribution of land, Fabian socialists and New Liberal progressives.

1903   Ebenezer Howard's First Garden City Company began the con-
        struction of **Letchworth Garden City**, located in Hertfordshire in the
        South-East of England. Letchworth was the first of the British garden
        cities. The architect-planners were Barry **Parker** and Raymond
        Unwin.

1908   **Hampstead Garden Suburb** (HGS) opened in North London. The
        driving force in the creation of HGS was Henrietta **Barnett** and the
        architects were Barry Parker and, especially, Raymond Unwin. HGS
        became one of the most important practical exemplars of the garden
        suburb movement in Britain. Its avowed intention of a happy mix of
        social classes, however, did not come to pass.

1909   **Housing and Town Planning Act**: authorized local authorities to begin the clearance of some nineteenth-century slums, to build new houses, and to develop town planning schemes.

1915   **Increase of Rent and Mortgage Interest (War Restrictions) Act**: provided statutory control of rent rises during the First World War.

1916   **Ministry of Reconstruction** established; it was responsible for demobilisation, health, housing, national insurance and education.

1918   **Tudor Walters Report** (October): the report of the committee chaired by Sir John Tudor Walters on housing and reconstruction was enormously influential on subsequent council housing. The report argued that 500,000 new dwellings were required, and that suburban land around towns and cities should be purchased by councils for the purposes of a new national housing programme. Aiming for housing densities of twelve per acre in urban areas and eight per acre in the countryside, the Act recommended cottage designs and high standards of accommodation. Its recommendations were loudly endorsed by David Lloyd George and framed in the Housing and Town Planning Act the following year.

1919   **Housing and Town Planning Act (Addison Act)** (July): initiated the large-scale construction of council estates by local authorities through the provision of a central government subsidy to local councils. Hence government now took on the responsibility of providing housing for the working classes, a significant break with laissez-faire. The **public expenditure cuts** of the early 1920s curtailed council house building, to the anger of Addison and others in the emerging profession of town and country planning.

1919   **Rent Act**: carried on the principle of rent control established in 1915, a significant move that was continued by subsequent rent control legislation between the wars.

1919   **Housing (Additional Powers) Bill** (December): expedited the process whereby councils were directly subsidised to build homes.

1919   Ebenezer Howard initiated **Welwyn Garden City** (May): WGC was later, following the 1946 **New Towns Act**, redesignated as one of the **new towns**, a symbolic reminder that town planners working in the garden cities movement drove the government reconstruction agenda for new towns.

1923   **Housing Act (Chamberlain Act)**: a measure that provided a subsidy for private builders.

1924   **Housing (Financial Provisions Act) (Wheatley Act)**: provided subsidies to local councils for the building of council housing, a clear difference in emphasis to the Chamberlain Act. Half a million council dwellings had been built by 1934.

1930   **Housing Act (Greenwood Act)**: obliged local authorities, subsidised by central government, to begin or expedite slum clearance schemes.

Many new council estates were begun, often in tandem with the removal of the worst unfit housing in 'clearance areas'.

1933 **Housing Act**: terminated the previous subsidies and established a new public works programme of slum clearance.

1935 **Housing Act (Hilton Young Act)**: reaffirmed the commitment of local authorities to clear slums and introduced minimum standards for housing. Private sector rents were protected from competition with council house rents, continuing the problem that most council housing remained unattainable for the very poor. In addition, the Act obliged local authorities to measure overcrowding.

1935 **Ribbon Development Act** (also known as the Restriction of Ribbon Development Act): attempted to reduce road building which did not accord with the principles of good town planning. This was in turn intended to limit the suburbs sprawling into the countryside alongside the new main roads and many minor roads being built to accommodate the rapid rise of motorisation.

1940 **Barlow Report**: the report of the Royal Commission on the Distribution of the Industrial Population, first established in 1937, headed by Sir Montague Barlow, firmly endorsed the principle of the decentralisation or dispersal of both population and industry from the congested urban centres.

1940–41 The **Blitz** on British towns and cities from September 1940 to May 1941 damaged or destroyed many buildings, mostly in the larger industrial cities and towns, and made the housing shortage much worse. Preparation for the Blitz involved the evacuation of millions of poorer families from the industrial cities. All towns and cities that were bombed were required by government to produce plans for their blitzed and also blighted (slum) areas.

1941 **1941 Committee** established, comprised of leading professionals, politicians and social reformers, including Violet Bonham **Carter**, Michael **Foot**, Edward **Hulton**, J. B. **Priestley** and Richard Titmuss. It advocated a strong planning culture both for the waging of the war and for successful reconstruction, calling for a more civilised and rebuilt urban environment, full employment and better education and improved welfare for all.

1941 **Uthwatt Report**: the committee headed by Mr Justice Uthwatt to investigate land use and reconstruction provided an interim report (July) that made recommendations on the value of compensation for land taken by the state and a final report (September) that endorsed major extensions to central planning powers. It recommended the compulsory purchase of land in war-damaged towns and cities and of land required for reconstruction, and heightened power for the state in land development outside of built-up areas.

1943 **Ministry of Town and Country Planning** established (February): the culmination of the growth of the town planning profession in Britain since the later nineteenth century, it incorporated many of the leading town planners involved in the garden city movement as civil servants. They were essential in the preparation of wartime plans for reconstruction, liaising between local authorities and government. The ministry coordinated the enactment of the town and country planning legislation during the early postwar years.

1944   **Town and Country Planning ('Blitz and Blight') Act**: provided small sums for emergency rebuilding and replanning of bombed areas. Overall, the Act had little immediate effect on the rebuilding of the blitzed towns and cities.

1944   **Dudley Report**: also called *The Design of Dwellings*, the report laid down the types, standards and sizes of postwar accommodation. The product of the Dudley commission, chaired by Lord Dudley, among other issues addressed were densities of dwellings per acre and the contribution of flats to solving postwar housing problems.

1946   **New Towns Act**: initiated the programme of over twenty planned new towns in Britain, an essential element of reconstruction, and the realisation of intentions held by many leading town planners in Britain throughout the preceding years of the twentieth century.

1947   **Town and Country Planning Act**: introduced strict new planning laws in urban and rural areas and aimed to construct 300,000 dwellings per year. A particularly powerful tool was the green belt that local authorities could designate around towns and cities to prevent unwarranted sprawl. The Act created the system for postwar town and country planning intended to cope with pressure for development.

1949   **Housing Act**: augmented the principle of central government subsidy for housing by subsidising local authorities which acquired houses for upgrading and conversions.

1949   **National Parks and Access to the Countryside Act**: following the work of national parks survey committees in England and Wales, chaired by Sir Arthur Hobhouse, the Attlee government passed the National Parks Act. Ten national parks were designated in England and Wales during the 1950s. Among the 'Hobhouse criteria' for a national park were a high quality of natural beauty; clearly defined physical boundaries; minimisation of unsightly development; the absence of mining or quarrying unless absolutely necessary, followed by a rapid rehabilitation of the land; and the preservation of architectural, rural and scientific heritage.

1951   Dr Monica **Felton** removed from her post as chairman of Stevenage Development Corporation by Hugh **Dalton**, in a move seen by some as almost McCarthyite in its contempt for her career and reputation. Felton spoke out against atrocities by the United Nations forces – including British soldiers – while on a visit to Korea during the

Korean War with the Women's International Democratic Federation, a front organisation for Soviet communism. Despite claims of treason from some MPs, the attorney general found that she had not made any treasonous statements.

1951 During the general election campaign the Conservative home secretary Harold Macmillan promised the completion of 300,000 houses a year by a future Conservative government. This target was exceeded by the mid-1950s, hastening the redevelopment of many bombed-out urban areas, introducing a new generation of inner-city blocks of council flats, and allowing within the limits of the town and country planning legislation many new suburban housing estates.

1952 **Town Development Act**: introduced the planned expansion of existing towns, which hence became known as 'expanded towns'. Swindon in Wiltshire and Thetford in Norfolk were examples of expanded towns for the dispersal of Londoners.

1954 **Housing Repairs and Rent Act**: renewed the slum clearance programme mostly halted by the Second World War.

1957 **Rent Act**: liberalised rent controls, an unpopular move with many tenants. It facilitated the rise of unscrupulous landlords, typified at their worst by Peter Rachman.

1961 **Housing Act**: laid down maintenance regulations for landlords.

1961 **Parker Morris Report**, *Homes for Today and Tomorrow* issued by the Ministry of Housing to engender higher and more flexible standards in housing design in Britain.

1965 **New Towns Act**: this second New Towns Act introduced a fresh phase of planned new communities in Britain, of which Milton Keynes has become the most famous.

1965 **Rent Act**: provided security of tenure for unfurnished lets.

1968 **Town and Country Planning Act**: introduced a two-tier process for decision making, whereby an initial structure plan of a local authority was a statement of intent about policy and development, and a second-level process of refinement, including a public enquiry, modified and fine-tuned the plan.

1968 The collapse of the **Ronan Point** tower block in East London (May): two people were killed as a consequence of shoddy construction methods and materials.

1969 **Skeffington Report**: emphasised the need for more public participation in town planning.

1972 The reorganisation of **local government** created large new metropolitan councils in lieu of the older city councils, together with some county councils. Considerable anger was vented by many Conservatives at the demise of older 'shire' county councils.

1974 **Rent Act**: extended the provisions of the 1965 **Rent Act** to furnished rented accommodation.

1974   **Department of the Environment** established: it replaced the Ministry of Town and Country Planning with a much larger organisation.

1975   **Housing Rents and Subsidies Act**: introduced new subsidies for local authorities to maintain council houses and standardised them across the country. It was one of the last major government acts in the support of collective housing provision by local councils.

1980   **Housing Act**: an early and profound statement of Thatcherism, it brought to an end the era of collective housing provision by councils, mostly terminating the building of new housing and encouraging the 'right to buy' council houses among existing tenants. Council housing became increasingly known as social housing and was provided by housing associations.

1980s– 1990s   The relaxation of town planning controls assisted the creation of industrial and retail parks based upon 'big box' warehousing and out-of-town supermarkets. This facilitated the rise of **edge city**-style development in Britain. Out-of-town shopping centres became popular, but concern was raised about their environmental impact.

Environmental issues

1899   **Coal Smoke Abatement Society** established to lobby for legislation to deal with the unhealthy and polluting effects of coal fires.

1903   **Motor Car Act**: gave legal recognition to privately owned motor cars and indirectly facilitated road building. It also set the speed limit at 20 miles per hour.

1907   **National Trust Act**: conferred 'powers on the National Trust for places of historic interest or natural beauty'. This was the first of a number of twentieth-century acts designed to allow the National Trust to preserve areas, landscapes and buildings of beauty or historic interest.

1919   **Forestry Act**: established the Forestry Commission. During the First World War a dangerous shortage of timber occurred as imports of wood fell away, leading to the establishment in 1916 of the Acland committee to investigate the development of woodland resources following the conflict. Between the wars a national tree-planting programme was established. It was expedited during the late 1930s as war loomed with Nazi Germany.

1919   **National Trust Charity Scheme Confirmation Act** (August): empowered charity commissioners to manage the National Trust in its aim to preserve the nation's heritage.

1919   First Forestry Commission trees planted, at Egglesford Forest, Devon (December).

1925   **Council for the Preservation of Rural England**, a major pressure group comprised of environmental and rural interests, established following the efforts of Sir Patrick **Abercrombie** and others.

1926   **Public Health (Smoke Abatement) Act**: tightened regulations on use of coal in built-up areas.

1928   Publication of *England and the Octopus*, written by the architect and planner Clough **Williams-Ellis**, who decried the 'octopus' of ribbon road development and suburbanisation.

1929   **National Smoke Abatement Society** established.

1933   Greater London regional planning committee of the London County Council formally considered the establishment of a **green belt**, or 'green girdle', around London following the report by Sir Raymond Unwin.

1935   **Ribbon Development Act**: intended to prevent excessive road building and suburbanisation, it was only partly successful.

1936   **Public Health Act**: extended and improved local authority sewerage provision and increased responsibility of business in relation to discharge and pollution.

1937   **National Trust Act**: extended the financial powers of the National Trust. These powers were augmented in a further Act in 1939.

1938   **Green Belt Act**: preserved 25,000 acres surrounding London from urban development.

1942   **Scott Report**: called for the creation of a system of national parks to preserve Britain's most beautiful rural areas.

1945   **Wildlife conservation special committee** (the Huxley committee) set up to assess the protection of wildlife in nature reserves. It recommended the establishment of a body to manage sites of natural interest, which in 1949 became the **Nature Conservancy**.

1946   **New Towns Act**: created the first generation of postwar new towns. A major tool in reconstruction, the new towns were intended to relieve population and commercial pressures from the existing cities.

1947   **Town and Country Planning Act**: provided a statutory framework, including powers for local authorities, to protect rural areas and the nearby countryside around towns from unwarranted development.

1949   **National Parks Act**: established ten national parks in Britain (see under Housing and town and country planning). It also gave statutory powers to the Nature Conservancy, as recommended by the Huxley committee.

1951   Coventry established the first smokeless zone.

1952   London **smog** outbreak (December), the worst since the nineteenth century, killed over 4,000 people.

1953   **National Trust Act**: amended the previous National Trust legislation and bestowed further powers on the trust to conserve buildings and places of beauty or historical significance.

1955   London became a smokeless zone.

1956   **Clean Air Act**: passed as a response to the London **smog** of 1952 that killed about 4,000 people. A significant piece of environmental legislation, it introduced the restricted use of coal burning in smokeless zones nationally, an attempt to control domestic pollution caused by coal fires.

1957   Serious radioactive leak following a fire at Windscale nuclear power station in Cumberland (October). It created fears for the environmental health of the nearby Lake District, the Irish Sea and Morecambe Bay.

1958   **National Society for Clean Air** established, primarily to campaign against pollution from coal smoke.

1958   First stretch of motorway-standard road opened (December) – the Preston bypass in Lancashire. The subsequent British motorway system was modelled in part on American interstate highways, a further facet of Americanisation.

1960   **Radioactive Substances Act**: provided for more controls over nuclear facilities in the wake of the Windscale nuclear leak.

1963   Publication of the **Buchanan Report**, entitled *Traffic in Towns*. Researched and written by Colin Buchanan, with assistance from Ann McEwen and others, the report was a major contribution to the principles of British town planning at a time when the environmental implications of increased motorisation were not as well understood as they are now. Buchanan endorsed further road provision for motorisation in existing towns and cities.

1963   **Beeching Report**: called for major cuts to local and branch line services on the railways and for the development of the inter-city network. It led to the Beeching axe, signalling a shift in government thinking away from investment in railways and towards more motorisation and roads. The national rail route was cut by almost a third by 1970.

1965   The **Nature Conservancy** was incorporated into the new National Environment Research Council (NERC).

1966   **Aberfan disaster** in Wales (October): killed 144 people, mostly children. The tragedy was caused by the collapse of a slag heap of coal refuse onto a nearby school.

1967   *Torrey Canyon* shipping disaster (March): threatened oil pollution on a potentially devastating scale on the south-west coast of England. A great deal of oil leaked into the sea, causing a slick over 30 miles long and 20 miles wide.

1967   Outbreak of **foot and mouth disease** on British farms (October): over 2,200 cases, mostly in the English Midlands counties of Cheshire and Derbyshire and in North Wales, were confirmed in 1967–8.

1968   **Clean Air Act**: ordered the use of tall chimneys for the dispersal of smoke, leading to less sulphur dioxide poisoning on the ground.

1970   **Department of the Environment** created, with increased powers over urban and rural planning.

1971	**National Trust Act**: partly restructured the fund-raising apparatus of the **charity** and gave it further general powers to enhance and protect its properties.
1973	**Nature Conservancy Council Act**: abolished Nature Conservancy and replaced it with the National Conservancy Council (NCC), a grant-aided organisation operating under the aegis of the **Department of the Environment**.
1973	**People's Party** initiated: it was soon renamed the Ecology Party. This was the birth of green party politics in Britain.
1974	**Control of Pollution Act**: introduced regulations to improve air and water quality.
1974	**Flixborough chemical plant disaster** (June): killed twenty-eight people and injured more than thirty, causing major concern over the impact of such catastrophes in built-up areas.
1976	**Royal Commission on Environmental Pollution**: called for an inspectorate to monitor pollution in Britain
1980	**EEC** directives on environmental pollution and air quality introduced in Britain.
1981	**Wildlife and Countryside Act**: introduced protection for plants and animals, particularly threatened species, under the auspices of the Nature Conservancy Council.
1983	Government accepted the recommendation of the report of the Royal Commission on Environmental Pollution to introduce lead-free petrol.
1986	Radioactive leaks from **Sellafield** (Windscale) nuclear power station and the Chernobyl nuclear accident in the USSR greatly increased public concern over the threat to the environment and to people of radioactivity. Radioactive fallout from Chernobyl was detected on British uplands.
1986	**M25** motorway opened (October): it was intended to facilitate traffic flow both into and out of as well as around the capital city.
1987	Sizewell B power station in Suffolk approved by government following a prolonged public inquiry.
1987	**Ecology Party** changed its name to the **Green Party** for the 1987 general election, and stood over 130 candidates, none of whom was elected.
1988	**Piper Alpha oil rig disaster** (July): an explosion on the rig in the North Sea killed 167 of the 220 men on board. Many died trying to escape toxic fumes. It was the worst offshore drilling accident of the twentieth century.
1989	Green Party candidates received 15 per cent of the vote in European Union elections. The Liberal Democrats were relegated to fourth place.
1990	**Global warming** first raised as a major official issue in Britain by the

government white paper entitled *The Common Inheritance*: it committed Britain to making a contribution, along with other countries, to the reduction of the mean temperature of the world.

1990 **Environmental Protection Act**: aimed to improve the control of pollution and its causes, and to devolve nature conservancy to national authorities in England, Scotland and Wales.

1991 A devolution of natural conservation occurred when the **Nature Conservancy Council** was made responsible for England, becoming English Nature, while a new Countryside Council for Wales was begun. Scottish Natural Heritage was set up in 1992. The Joint Nature Conservation Committee became a forum for the three conservation agencies.

1993 *Braer* oil tanker disaster (January): the tanker ran aground on rocks near the Shetland Islands, Scotland, carrying over 85,000 tons of crude oil.

1994 Report of the **Royal Commission on Environmental Pollution** recommended a transition from private transport in cars to increased public transport on trains.

1995 **Brightlingsea protests** in the seaside town of Essex by animal rights activists concerned at the transit of live animals led to improvements in live animal transportation. The protests lasted for nearly ten months.

1996 **BSE scare**: this cattle disease was discovered to have spread to humans in the form of Creuzfelt–Jakob Disease (CJD) through the eating of beef products. CJD led to massive mental and physical deterioration, and most of Britain's herds were slaughtered. A ban on British beef followed in most countries.

1999 **Genetically modified (GM) crops** introduced into Britain, leading to protests from environmentalists. The spectre of monstrous hybridising consequences for humanity was often raised, but the government remained level-headed and allowed GM experiments to continue.

The monarchy

1901 Death of Queen Victoria (January): brought an end to her reign of some sixty-three years and initiated that of Edward VII. Identified inextricably with the nineteenth century, Victoria was the first monarch of twentieth-century Britain.

1901 Succession of King Edward VII, the eldest son of Queen Victoria and Prince Albert. Although his reign lasted less than nine years, Edward VII gave his name to the Edwardian era that lasted from 1900 to 1914, thus overlapping with the final Victorian years.

1910 Death of Edward VII (May): he was succeeded by his son George V.

1911 Coronation of George V (June): he became the first monarch of the

House of Windsor, which he himself created from the British derivatives of the German House Saxe-Coburg-Gotha.

1917   George V renamed the dynasty Windsor (July) in an attempt to distance himself and the royal family from anti-German sentiment during the First World War. The new name reflected the long-standing association of the monarchy with Windsor Castle in Berkshire.

1931   George V invited the prime minister, Ramsay MacDonald, to form a national government during the height of the slump in Britain. Inadvertently, the king was assisting in the death of MacDonald's reputation within the British Labour movement.

1936   Death of George V: following a reign of over twenty-five years, the death of this popular monarch led to considerable national sorrow, but also optimism following the coronation of **Edward VIII**, a relatively young and much admired member of the royal family.

1936   **Abdication crisis** (December): along with the death of **Diana, Princess of Wales** in 1997, the abdication crisis was one of the two worst misfortunes to affect the British monarchy during the twentieth century, and yet it did nothing to threaten its existence. The initiator of the crisis, Edward VIII, was a tortured man. Having been crowned early in the year, he was carrying on an affair with Mrs Wallis Simpson, an American and a divorcee. Until December, the newspapers had kept quiet about the affair, demonstrating a measure of restraint that would be rare in today's tabloid press. But once the news of the king's predicament was announced, the love interest captured the nation, temporarily taking their minds off such depressing matters as Nazi Germany and unemployment. When the king informed Stanley Baldwin of his intention to marry a commoner, and a divorced foreign commoner to boot, the prime minister worked hard to avoid bringing the monarchy and the Church of England into disrepute. The monarch was head of the Anglican Church, which blessed the sanctity of marriage. Sensing that the majority of British citizens would be disgusted with such a marriage, Baldwin ruled out a morganatic compromise that would have allowed it to go ahead but would have denied the status of queen to Edward's beloved. So Baldwin presented the king with a clear-cut choice: the crown or Mrs Simpson. Edward chose Mrs Simpson. Most leading politicians with the exception of Winston Churchill and a few others were in agreement with Baldwin's strategy. British public opinion, however, was quite supportive of the king, but to no avail. Edward gave his abdication broadcast on 10 December, making way for **George VI** to become monarch.

1947   **Royal wedding** of Princess Elizabeth and Lieutenant Philip Mountbatten, RN (November): coming as it did during a particularly bleak month during the years of austerity, politicians and royal officials were concerned at the possibility of a public backlash against the expense and opulence of the wedding and celebrations. Despite some criticisms, most British people appear to have welcomed the event as a colourful and glamorous respite in a gloomy winter.

1951 **Festival of Britain** opened by George VI (May): inaugurating the Festival of Britain, and opening Festival Hall, the king perhaps unwittingly signified that modernity as well as tradition is associated with royal deeds and functions. The festival was held on the one-hundredth anniversary of the Great Exhibition of 1851. Its main site was the South Bank of the River Thames in London, heavily bombed during the Blitz, and redesigned to be a showpiece for British modern architecture and an arena for the nation to celebrate British victory in the Second World War. Coming during the age of austerity, the festival was also intended to relieve the gloom of everyday life. Exhibits on the South Bank included the 'skylon', a cleverly designed optical illusion, and sundry fairground activities. The most enduring legacy of the event is the Royal Festival Hall, a concert venue.

1952 Death of George VI (February): following the funeral, the king's body lay in state for three days at Westminster Hall. His body was buried in St George's Chapel within the Windsor Castle estate.

1953 **Coronation of Queen Elizabeth II** (June): heralding a 'new Elizabethan Age', the coronation of Queen Elizabeth at Westminster Abbey was watched by millions of people on television, and the event did much to popularise that medium. The coronation began one of the longest reigns of a monarch in modern Britain and provided a certain flamboyant yet thoroughly British spectacle as the era of austerity drew to a close. Street parties were held across the country, signifying that popular support for the monarchy was widespread. In a study of the coronation, the American sociologist Edward Shils and his British colleague Michael **Young** observed that deference and respect for authority were major characteristics of the popular celebrations.

1960 **Royal wedding** of Princess Margaret to Antony Armstrong Jones (May): over 20 million British viewers watched the wedding, the first British royal wedding to be televised.

1969 **Investiture of Prince Charles** (July): Prince Charles had been created Prince of Wales aged nine. His investiture as the twenty-first Prince of Wales took place at Caernarfon Castle and was televised around the world. Aged twenty-one, in his speech the prince emphasised the need for Wales to look forward while never forsaking its traditions and heritage.

1973 **Royal wedding** of Princess Anne, the queen's daughter, to Mark Phillips (November).

1977 **Queen Elizabeth II** and most but not all of the British people celebrated the queen's silver jubilee (June): the event reignited debates about the role of the monarchy in Britain.

1981   **Royal wedding of Prince Charles and Lady Diana** (July): over 600,000 people thronged the streets of London to witness the marriage of Charles and Diana, already an iconic couple, and mostly adored by millions of British subjects as well as millions abroad. More than 750 million people around the world watched the televised wedding in St Paul's Cathedral. Aged just twenty, and wearing a bridal dress with a 25 feet train (7.6 metres) Diana stole the show, but the wedding initiated a new phase of a royal relationship that would lead to the birth of two male heirs to throne and unquantifiable media attention on the couple.

1996   Official divorce of **Prince Charles** and **Princess Diana** issued (August): the final termination of the marriage followed three years of separation and unseemly personal antipathies, aired in public, between the princess and the royal family.

1997   **Death of Diana, Princess of Wales** (August): a little over a year following the official divorce of Charles and Diana, the Princess of Wales was killed in a car crash in a road tunnel in Paris with her then partner, Dodi Al Fayed. Diana's funeral on 6 September followed a week of quite extraordinary displays of public grief, layered through with anger towards the royal family. The funeral was watched on television by millions of people in Britain and abroad. Across the country, for example on railings, in supermarket car parks, even on motorway verges, floral shrines were hastily set up for the deceased princess. Diana was buried in the grounds of her ancestral home in Althorp, Northamptonshire.

The causes of the crash that killed Diana were extensively revisited by the media in efforts to prove some sort of conspiracy, to blame the driver Henri Paul, or to cast blame on the chasing pack of paparazzi. A leading contender in the package of conspiracy theories was that Diana and Dodi were snuffed out by Prince Philip, her erstwhile father-in-law, who, working in tandem with MI6, a wing of the security forces, was determined to keep a Muslim out of the royal family. This theory was stated repeatedly in avuncular fashion by Mohamed Al Fayed, the owner of the hotel in Paris where Diana and his son Dodi had been staying. Mohamed Al Fayed was also the employer of Henri Paul. It was not until 2008 that the matter was ended, legally at least. An expensive and prolonged inquest into Diana's death found that she was not a victim of a conspiracy to kill her, but of Henri Paul's driving.

Immigration and multiculturalism

1905   **Aliens Act**: widespread popular and official concern at the social and moral degradation of the East End of London and at growing numbers of Eastern and Central European **Jews** led to its passage. It used the terminology of 'undesirable aliens' towards Jewish immigrants, and was the first Act designed to curb immigration into modern Britain.

1911   **Sidney Street siege** in North-East London (January): exacerbated **anti-Semitism** in the capital city and Britain more generally as a consequence of the murderous activities of a group of Latvian burglars and revolutionaries called the Gardstein gang. They had killed three policemen.

1914   **Aliens Restrictions Act**: in the context of the beginnings of the First World War, this Act required foreign nationals to register with the police lest they become the enemy within. The passage of the Act reflected an intensification in patriotism and perhaps xenophobia at a time of heightened tensions across Europe.

1919   **Race riots** in London and Cardiff. At a time of high unemployment and mass demobilisation of troops following the First World War, a number of ugly attacks were meted out to blacks living in the dockside areas of these mercantile cities, as well as to foreign seamen, including the Chinese. This unrest occurred in tandem with the 1919 Aliens Restriction Act.

1919   **Aliens Restriction (Amendment) Act**: placed limitations on the employment opportunities and rights of aliens already living in Britain, some of whom possessed British nationality.

1930s   Emigration to Britain of Jews fleeing Nazi persecution added considerably to the pool of professional expertise in Britain. Around 50,000 Jews came to Britain during the 1930s. Many stayed permanently, and included some leading artists and professionals. Others remained in Britain temporarily before moving to other countries, notably the United States of America.

1940–45   **Commonwealth war workers** and refugees created a temporary but critically important vortex of ethnic diversity in wartime London and other cities. Over 5 million Commonwealth citizens volunteered for the war effort. Some 3 million American servicemen and women passed through Britain between 1942 and 1945.

1948   **British Nationality Act**: granted British **citizenship** to 'subjects' of the British Commonwealth. This became known as an 'open door' policy that led to concerns over immigration during the 1950s and early 1960s.

1948   **SS *Empire Windrush*** docked at Tilbury carrying 492 West Indian men looking for work and housing (June): the arrival of the *Windrush* is commonly viewed as the historic beginning of postwar immigration into Britain.

1958   **Nottingham and Notting Hill race riots** (August): the first ugly disturbances between blacks and whites, many of them Teddy boys, in postwar Britain. Nottingham is in the English Midlands, and Notting Hill in North-West London.

1960   Publication of *Newcomers: The West Indians in London*. Written by Ruth **Glass**, it described the settlement patterns and culture of African-Caribbean migrants to the capital, and the context of the Notting Hill race riots.

1962   **Commonwealth Immigration Act** (April): terminated the 'open door' policy towards Commonwealth immigrants of the previous fourteen years. The Act was the first in postwar Britain aimed at restricting immigration, although it came four years after the race riots of 1958, suggesting that politicians were fearful at continued public concern over the 'race' problem.

1964   General election campaign tainted by racist language (October): at Smethwick in Birmingham, the Labour MP and shadow foreign secretary Patrick Gordon **Walker** lost his seat to the Conservative candidate Peter Griffiths, who is alleged to have stated, 'if you want a nigger for a neighbour, vote Labour'.

1965   The American Black Power leader Malcolm X visited Britain, including Birmingham (February), to express his concerns at the racism he felt was directed at blacks in Smethwick and elsewhere. His rhetoric was often fiery, and even racist against whites.

1965   **Race Relations Act** (December): established the Race Relations Board and outlawed racial discrimination in public places on 'the grounds of colour, race, or ethnic or national origins'. The act of racial discrimination, however, was not made a criminal offence, and shops and other purveyors of goods, for example estate agents, were exempt from the terms of this pioneering Act.

1968   **Kenyan Asians** expelled from Kenya: many headed to Britain, adding to concerns among many British people at the extent of immigration of people of colour into the United Kingdom.

1968   **Commonwealth Immigration Act** (November): enabled those with 'close ties' to Britain via family to enter while making it more difficult for those who did not have such ties, such as Kenyan Asians.

1968   Enoch **Powell** attacked British immigration policy in his infamous 'rivers of blood' speech (April): the speech also predicted a future of cultural decline and of blacks having the 'whip hand' over whites, a cynical reference to slavery.

1968   **Race Relations Act** (November): criminalised racial discrimination in the sale of properties, in employment, and in access to public services.

1971   **Immigration Act** (February): increased controls on immigration by restricting 'right of abode' and citizenship rights to those born in the UK or whose parents and grandparents were of British origin. The Act, which was in no small part directed at Kenyan Asians, came into force in 1972.

1972   **Asians** expelled from Uganda, the first arriving in Britain (September): the treatment of Ugandan Asians by Idi Amin bordered on genocide.

1976   **Race Relations Act** (November): extended previous legislation by making racial discrimination unlawful in almost all circumstances. The act defined two forms of discrimination, namely 'direct discrimination', which was treating a person less favourably on grounds of colour, ethnicity or nationality, and 'indirect discrimination', described as 'equal in a formal sense, as between different racial groups, but discriminatory in its effects on one particular racial group'. The independent Commission for Racial Equality (CRE) was established by the Act to ensure the principles of the legislation were met and to maintain good **race relations** in Britain.

1979   The **National Front** stood over 300 candidates at the general election, and all lost their deposits. It was a significant non-event in the history of the failure of fascism in twentieth-century Britain.

1979   Disturbances in **Southall**, West London, between National Front demonstrators and Asian youths. These race riots foreshadowed those in Britain's inner cities in 1980 and 1981.

1980   Inner-city **riots** in the impoverished district of St Pauls in Bristol, a city in the West of England. Most youths involved in the riots were black and Asian.

1981   **British Nationality Act**: largely replaced the British citizenship terms of the Act of 1948 by introducing three new categories: British citizen, citizen of territories dependent on Britain, and British overseas citizenship. Immigration based on parentage was restricted; the concern of the Act was mostly non-white entry into the UK.

1981   Inner-city riots in Liverpool, Manchester and London (April): a committee under Lord Justice Scarman was appointed to investigate the causes of the disturbances in Brixton, London. Scarman's report (November) blamed serious social and economic problems for exacerbating racial tensions in South London and, by implication and extension, elsewhere.

1985   **Broadwater Farm riot** in Tottenham, London (October): a police raid on the flat of a black woman caused her to die of a heart attack. In the subsequent disturbances, a policeman was hacked to death.

1987   Four ethnic minority MPs were elected to parliament at the general election.

1988   **Immigration Act**: targeted polygamy by removing special consideration given to men who had settled in the UK before 1973, whose wives and children had previously been able to enter the UK without accommodation, financial and marriage tests. Claims to British citizenship had to be established before right of abode was granted.

1989   Britain refused right of abode to over 3 million Hong Kong Chinese who held British passports. Official and popular fears were that the transfer of Hong Kong from Britain to China might lead to mass emigration to the UK.

1990   **British Nationality Act** (July): extended British citizenship to elite Hong Kong Chinese, for example professionals, business people and others who might create wealth or meet skills shortages in Britain. The Act discriminated against working-class Hong Kong Chinese.

1992   Inauguration of the Muslim parliament of Britain to raise the profile of **Islam** (January): one of its intentions was the creation of a 'non-territorial Islamic state' in Britain. Its members were all male. The parliament had declined in significance by 2000.

1993   A black teenager, Stephen Lawrence, was attacked and murdered by five white racists at a bus stop in Eltham, South London (April): police indecision and perhaps wilful inaction led Stephen's parents to launch a private prosecution against three of his suspected murderers.

1997   Trial of those accused of murdering black teenager Stephen Lawrence (February): the jury was unable to convict those primarily suspected of being his killers due to inadmissible evidence. The murder and the trial damaged **race relations** in London, where many felt the police had failed to prioritise the death of a young black man.

1997   The general election led to five black MPs and the first Muslim MP in Britain. Mohammed Sarwar represented Glasgow, Govan.

1997   Inauguration of Muslim Council of Great Britain (November): the council was established to promote understanding of **Islam in Britain** and to protect the rights of Muslims.

2000   Publication of the **Parekh Report**, *The Future of Multicultural Britain*, written by Lord Parekh on behalf of the Runnymede Trust.

Religion

1900   Unification of the Free Church of Scotland and the United Presbyterian Church of Scotland, both leading Scots **nonconformist churches**.

1903   Publication of seventeen-volume *Life and Labour of the People of London*, a survey by Charles **Booth** that included a 'Religious Series' detailing the spiritual life of the capital city at the turn of the century.

1905   Welsh revival of nonconformity as thousands of Welsh believers joined the chapels.

1906   Royal Commission on **Welsh Disestablishment** from the **Church of England** established: opposition to Welsh disestablishment formed the 'anti-disestablishment' movement in subsequent years.

1907   United Methodist Church formed from various Methodist sects.

1910   Beginning of the **ecumenical movement**, a project to promote greater union between the Christian churches.

1920	**Welsh Disestablishment Act**: the Welsh Church was disestablished from the Church of England, an important moment in both national and religious identity.
1921	**Church of Scotland Act**: the Church of Scotland, a Presbyterian church, became independent, another important moment reflecting both national and religious identity.
1926	World Union of Progressive Judaism established in London. It sought to promote Jewish integration within modern societies without vaporising the religious and cultural values and practices of **Jews in Britain**.
1932	Methodist Church established from the three main Methodist sects – the Primitive, United and Wesleyan Methodists.
1942	William Temple became the Archbishop of Canterbury. In the same year his book *Christianity and the Social Order* was published, calling for a more benign and fairer society.
1944	**Islamic Cultural Centre** opened in London (November).
1948	Publication of *Negroes in Britain: Race Relations in English Society* (about Cardiff in Wales) by Kenneth Little, containing observations on Muslims in Cardiff during wartime.
1960	The Archbishop of Canterbury visited the pope at the Vatican in Rome, the first head of the Anglican Church to do so since the Reformation of the sixteenth century.
1962	**Coventry Cathedral** consecrated: designed by Sir Basil Spence, it became a symbol of reconciliation between Britain and Germany, as Coventry had suffered heavily during the Blitz, and also of modernity, as it is a modern cathedral built adjacent to the ruins of the medieval cathedral.
1962	**First Hindu temple in Britain** (London): Hindu immigrants from India required their own places of worship.
1963	The theological tract *Honest to God* written by the Bishop of Woolwich, J. A. T. Robinson, created controversy in his personal exploration of faith, spirituality, the nature of God, and the future of the Christian Church.
1964	The Archbishop of York, Dr Donald Coggan, called for closer ties between the Church of England and the Methodist Church.
1969	**Sharing of Church Buildings Act**: aimed to encourage church buildings to be shared between different churches.
1972	United Reformed Church created from the Congregationalist Church of England and Wales and the Presbyterian Church in England.
1972	The Synod of the Church of England refused to approve the long-discussed plan to bring about Anglican and Methodist unity, illustrating continuing ideological differences between the Anglican and Protestant nonconformist churches.
1978	**London central mosque** opened: incorporating the Islamic Cultural

Centre, and designed by the architect Frederick Gibberd, its proximity to Regent's Park means it is also commonly called the Regent's Park mosque.

1982   Visit of Pope John Paul II, the first and only pope to travel to Britain during the twentieth century. Welcomed by most of Christian faith, particularly of course Roman Catholics, the visit was less enthusiastically greeted by nonconformists in Northern Ireland.

1985   Church of England *Faith in the City* report (November): a statement of 'urban theology' concerned with the synthesis between religious faith in the city and the moral and physical health of the urban context, the report called for the regeneration in the inner cities in the wake of riots in 1981 and 1985. The Conservative government was scathing about 'communist clerics' and defensive about the criticisms by the Church of its policy neglect of the inner cities. Some Tories were also angry at the failure of the report to emphasise the need for self-help among poorer communities. Nevertheless, at the general election of 1987 Margaret Thatcher called for more to be done for the inner cities.

1987   Anglican Synod first voted, by a considerable majority, to allow the ordination of women to become vicars (see women).

1988   First **Jain temple** in Britain inaugurated in Leicester.

1989   *Fatwa* issued by Iran's Ayatollah Khomeini against the British writer Salman Rushdie for his novel *The Satanic Verses* (February): the novel apparently carried 'blasphemous' depictions of the Prophet Mohammed. Some leading British Muslims did not demur. The Rushdie incident has since been viewed as a catalyst for the making of a more militant Islamic consciousness in Britain.

1994   First women priests ordained into the Anglican Church in a special ceremony in Bristol (March): the ordination was controversial, and traditionalists have argued to this day that only men, in accordance with the teachings of the Bible, should minister to Christians.

1995   Largest **Hindu temple** outside of India opened in Neasden, a suburb of North London. Both the size of the Hindu population and the diversity of London suburbia were expressed by its inauguration.

1997   **Muslim Council of Great Britain** formed to represent and promote Islam in Britain (November): it received strong support from the New Labour government.

2001   Terrorist attacks on the World Trade Center in New York (September) heightened tensions between Muslims and others in Britain and elsewhere in the West.

Women

1897   **National Union of Women's Suffrage Societies** (NUWSS): founded by Millicent **Fawcett** in 1897, the NUWSS coordinated societies dedicated to gaining the vote for women at national general elections and promoted the rights of women in other spheres of public life.

1903   **Women's Social and Political Union** (WSPU) formed (October): more militant than the NUWSS, the WSPU was headed by Emmeline **Pankhurst**, whose daughters Christabel and Sylvia were also leading suffragettes. Its slogan was 'deeds not words'.

1907   NUWSS organised first national demonstration for women's suffrage (February): it signalled an intensification of moderate as well as militant opinion among women's suffrage campaigners.

1907   **Qualification of Women (County and Borough Councils) Act**: women were enabled to become elected councillors in local government for the first time in modern Britain.

1908   WSPU organised demonstration for women's suffrage, resulting in violence and attempts to storm the Houses of Parliament (October): Emmeline Pankhurst was sentenced to a prison term for her role in the disturbances.

1910   Growing number of hunger strikes of suffragettes in British prisons as frustration grew at the slowness of Asquith and the government to promote women's suffrage.

1913   Death of the suffragette Emily Davison under the hooves of the king's horse at the Epsom Derby, a sacred home of horse racing.

1913   Intensification of violent campaign by the WSPU.

1913   **'Cat and Mouse Act'**, or Prisoner's (Temporary Discharge for Ill Health) Act: passed to assuage public opinion that militant suffragettes were not being abused through force-feeding in prisons. Women who refused food could be released early, under supervision, thus obviating the need for invasive treatments by the prison authorities.

1914–18   **First World War**: in this first 'total war' of the twentieth century the number of women in employment increased from 3,224,600 in July 1914 to 4,814,600 by January 1918. The experience of war work was not at first welcomed by many women, and yet hundreds of thousands of them gained new levels of experience and confidence – and money – from this expanded participation in the world of paid work. Women were employed in essential munitions industries, in the mines, in public transport, and on the land. Many others worked in ancillary and nursing duties for the armed services. Significantly, about 700,000 women became engineers, leading to fears among skilled men about the dilution of status and wages.

Moreover, the WSPU called a halt to its agitation for the vote very soon after the outbreak of war, and some of its members turned their campaigning skills to the recruitment of men for service in the trenches. Following the war, suffragism was mostly extinguished by the granting to some women of the right to vote in general elections.

1918   **Representation of the People Act** (February): extended the vote to all men aged twenty-one and to all women over thirty, but only if they were ratepayers or the wives of ratepayers.

1919 **Sex Disqualification Removal Act** (December): abolished limitations of female access to the major professions, although the Church was exempt. Lady Nancy **Astor** became the first female MP actually to sit in the **House of Commons**, although she was not the first woman to be elected.

1920 *Time and Tide* magazine launched by Lady Margaret Rhondda, perhaps the first periodical devoted to the literary and political discussion of women's issues in Britain. The title is ironic, being drawn from the old adage that 'time and tide wait for no man'. Originally socialistic in nature, its content moved increasingly rightwards over the coming decades.

1923 **Matrimonial Causes Act**: adjusted the causes or 'grounds' for divorce so that the rights of women became the same as those of men.

1928 **Representation of the People Act** (July): equalised votes for women with those of men: all adults aged twenty-one and over were now eligible to vote in national general elections. This was widely regarded as the 'flapper vote', following a fashionable style of dress among young women during the 1920s.

1929 Margaret **Bondfield** became first female cabinet minister, as minister of labour, in the second minority Labour government.

1935 London County Council lifted the ban on married women becoming or remaining as teachers (August). Among others, Evelyn **Denington** was able to continue her first career as a school teacher.

1937 **Matrimonial Causes Act**: extended the grounds on which people could petition for divorce to include adultery, desertion without cause after three or more years, cruelty, and insanity. The Act was steered through parliament by A. P. **Herbert**.

1939–45 **Second World War**: from March 1941 all women aged nineteen to forty, unless pregnant or otherwise incapable of doing so, were compelled to register at the labour exchanges for work. The age was later raised to fifty. By December 1943 over 7.5 million women were in paid wartime employment, an increase of over 2 million from the prewar figure. Women made an enormous contribution to the demands and exigencies of the home front: over 1.5 million worked in industry, particularly engineering and munitions. Many were billeted to areas of urgent demand for labour that were often miles away from home. More than 80,000 women also worked in the Land Army, assisting in the essential food supply. Almost half a million were in uniform in the women's armed services, principally the Women's Royal Naval Service (WRENS), the Women's Auxiliary Air Force (WAAF) and the Auxiliary Territorial Service (ATS). Although most did the 'traditional' work of women – cooking, cleaning, secretarial and of course nursing duties, etc. – some saw active service as code-breakers, as agents in the Special Operations Executive, flying in airplanes, and facing great danger as nurses at the front.

1940   **Old Age and Widows' Pensions Act**: reduced the pensionable age for women to sixty.

1945   **Family Allowances Act** (June): provided financial allowances to women to assist in the raising of their children. It came into operation in 1946 (August).

1967   **Abortion Act** (April): extended the grounds upon which the termination of a pregnancy could take place. The Bill was steered through parliament by Liberal MP David **Steel**, against fierce opposition from religious groups.

1967   **Matrimonial Causes Act**: liberalised access to divorce by allowing proceedings to begin in county courts, only transferring to the high court if one partner contested. The financial burden was partially eased by this Act.

1969   **Divorce Reform Act** (October): a major revision to the divorce laws, it established that divorce could be made on the basis of 'irretrievable breakdown'. A two-year period of waiting until the divorce became absolute was originally intended to enable couples to work out their differences and perhaps stay together, but from 1971, when the Act came into force, the statistics for divorce rose sharply. So-called quickie divorces were granted from that year, raising questions about the value of the two-year wait. Divorce also became much more affordable by this legislation, continuing a trend from 1967.

1970   **Equal Pay Act** (May): the Equal Pay Bill was concerned with equal conditions of employment for men and women, and was steered through parliament by the Labour MP Barbara **Castle**, for whom the noun 'feisty' could have been invented. It was passed under the Conservative government. The Act, intended to procure the same pay for women and men undertaking the same work, signalled the beginning of the end for the second-class status of women in employment. It came into force in 1975.

1972   Launch of *Spare Rib*, a publication strongly identified with the second-wave feminism that emerged in Britain during the early 1970s, and a self-proclaimed antidote to the mainstream women's magazines that populated the newsagent's shelves.

1975   **International Women's Year** celebrated in Britain and elsewhere.

1975   Dame Evelyn Denington became first woman chairperson of the Greater London Council (GLC).

1975   **Sex Discrimination Act** (December): discrimination on the grounds of unfair treatment because of an individual's gender became unlawful in employment, education, training, and the provision of goods and services. The Equal Opportunities Commission was established to enforce the legislation.

1979   Margaret Thatcher became Britain's first female prime minister at the general election (May).

1986   **Sex Discrimination Act**: enabled women to retire at the same age as men. Until this Bill, women had enjoyed an earlier age of retirement (sixty) than men, but now women could elect to work until sixty-five years of age.

1987   First woman editors of major British newspapers: Wendy Henry of the *News of the World* (a Sunday tabloid) and Eve Pollard of the *Daily Mirror*.

1992   Anglican Synod voted again for the ordination of women (November): in the face of considerable opposition, the reformers had achieved a second significant victory.

1992   The general election (April) led to the election of fifty-eight women MPs, represented in all three parties.

1994   The first women priests were ordained in Bristol Cathedral (March): the BBC sitcom the *Vicar of Dibley*, starring Dawn French as a woman of the cloth, was first shown in November 1994.

1997   General election (May) resulted in 120 women MPs, over a hundred of whom were in the Labour Party, partly as a consequence of its initiative to use women-only short-lists. Many were derided, both by the opposition and by the Left of the Labour Party, as 'Blair's Babes', a crabbed accusation given the historic achievement. Five women were appointed to cabinet posts.

1999   **Minimum wage** of £3.60 an hour introduced, assisting many low-paid female and male workers.

1999   **Child Support Agency** (CSA) reformed: the CSA had been seen to be failing adequately to serve the poorest women and children. A child maintenance premium was introduced whereby mothers were entitled to hold on to £10 a week per child without a corresponding reduction in benefit entitlements.

Sexuality and permissiveness

1908   Publication of Edward **Carpenter**'s *The Intermediate Sex*, exploring the emotional condition of 'transitional men and women' – namely homosexuals and lesbians.

1928   Radclyffe **Hall**'s novel *The Well of Loneliness* banned. It explored 'sexual inversion', a term coined by the medical sexologist Havelock Ellis, through its leading lesbian characters. The book was, however, published in the United States of America.

1953   The actor John Gielgud was arrested by an under-cover policeman for cottaging in a public lavatory.

1957   **Wolfenden Report** – the report of the departmental committee on homosexual offences and prostitution (September): named after the chairman of the committee, Lord Wolfenden, the report recommended that homosexual acts in private between consenting adults should no longer be a criminal offence.

1958   Formation of **Homosexual Law Reform Society**: its aim was to campaign for legislation defined by the recommendations of the Wolfenden Report the previous year.

1959   **Obscene Publications Act** (August): relaxed the definition of 'obscenity' as laid down in Victorian legislation. Any explicit and even the most mild descriptions of sex had been prohibited, as had the use of taboo swearwords. This Act of 1959 drew a distinction between works of literature and pornography.

1960   Parliament rejected the recommendations of the Wolfenden Report on homosexuality (June).

1960   *Lady Chatterley* trial (October): following the Obscene Publications Act the previous year, Penguin Books published *Lady Chatterley's Lover*, a novel originally written during the 1920s by the English author D. H. **Lawrence**. The novel became a test of the new laws, and the trial saw a number of leading writers, including Richard **Hoggart** and Raymond Williams, defending the artistic merits and humane message of the work. The book contained the 'f' word and even the 'c' word, more than enough to see it brought to trial. The case against Penguin was dismissed, a signal of the growing liberalisation and permissiveness associated with the sixties. In an unwitting statement of the Victorian values that, argue social historians, the 1960s are often seen to have challenged, the chief prosecutor inquired whether this was the type of material 'you would wish your wife or servants to read'.

1962   Leo Abse MP introduced a parliamentary Bill (March) to reform some of the more punitive aspects of the law pertaining to homosexuality; it was defeated.

1966   Lord Arran's Bill in the House of Lords to decriminalise adult homosexuality passed (June).

1966   Humphrey Berkeley's Bill to decriminalise homosexual acts passed in the House of Commons but fell as a consequence of the general election (March). In its wake, the Labour MP Leo Abse introduced a second Bill that was finally passed in the Commons in December.

1967   **Sexual Offences Act** (July): decriminalised homosexuality, while not endorsing homosexual relations as in any way normal.

1967   **Committee for Homosexual Law Reform** established to promote further revisions in the law within the new dispensation of decriminalisation.

1967   **Abortion Act** (October): extended the grounds for abortion; this helped to break down class discrimination in access to abortions.

1967   **The National Health Service (Family Planning) Bill** (February): greatly increased access to contraception and to advice in both family limitation and sexual health. Free contraception (on prescription) and advice was soon supplied to both married and unmarried women.

1969   The First International Symposium on Gender Identity held in London: it reflected medical, psychological and sociological interest in the growing numbers of sex-change operations performed around the world, including Britain. **Transsexuality** was established as an issue in sexual politics.

1970   Committee for Homosexual Law Reform changed its name to the **Campaign for Homosexual Equality**, not least to argue against the injustice of a differential age of consent for heterosexuals (sixteen) and gays (twenty-one).

1971   *Oz* **Trial** (June): originating in Australia during the 1960s, *Oz* caused a minor sensation in Britain with its psychedelic covers and uncensored language. However, the 'school kids issue' of May 1970, where the editors had invited pubescent boys to put together their own issue, had resulted in a graphic cartoon of Rupert Bear as he had never been seen before. Among other items was a 'jailbait of the month' photograph. The editors, Richard Neville, Jim Anderson and Felix Dennis, were found guilty and given prison sentences, but the case was turned over by the Court of Appeal because a magistrate had misdirected the jury. The trial became a cause célèbre of the libertarian left and the self-consciously 'young generation' who wished to shock their elders. However, the attitude towards women in some articles in *Oz* can hardly be said to have mirrored the aspirations of many feminists.

1972   *Gay News* founded by leading gay rights activists. It became a leading organ in the campaign for equality for gays and lesbians.

1972   First Gay Pride ('UK Pride') march held in London (July): it initiated gay homosexual events in Britain.

1976 · **Gay Christian Movement** set up to persuade the Church to become increasingly open about and tolerant of homosexuality.

1977   *Gay News* prosecuted on blasphemy charges. Given depictions of Christ in other media during the 1970s, the prosecution was a punitive affair.

1983   **Terence Higgins Trust** founded as a **charity** to work and care for the victims of AIDS and their relatives. The same year also witnessed the beginning of the government campaign with the slogan 'AIDS: don't die of ignorance'.

1987   Gay Christian Movement renamed **Gay and Lesbian Christian Movement**.

1988   Section 28 of the Local Government Act (March): prohibited local authorities from intentionally promoting teaching or materials that encouraged homosexuality or the acceptability of homosexuality as a 'pretended family relationship'. The clause was finally overturned in 2003, causing celebration by both gays and anyone concerned with sexual equality.

1990   OutRage formed, headed by Peter **Tatchell**, signalling a newer, more militant phase in the promotion of gay rights and the campaign against discrimination.

1992   Homosexuality decriminalised on the Isle of Man.

1994   Age of consent for gay men lowered from twenty-one to eighteen. Although an improvement, this was not equality, so OutRage, Stonewall and other gay rights groups continued their campaign.

1997   Chris Smith, the culture secretary, became the first openly gay cabinet minister.

1999   The House of Commons voted to equalise the age of consent for hetero- and homosexuals (March) but the decision was rejected by the House of Lords the following month, forcing the government to expedite the overturning of '**Clause 28**'. (The age of consent for males became sixteen in 2001.)

Social policy: health and welfare

1902   **Midwives Act**: designed to improve training and to raise standards of midwifery to increase the survival rates of babies, particularly among the very poorest in society.

1905   Majority report of the Royal Commission on the Poor Law into the working of the system of poor relief in England and Wales. A prominent member of the commission, Beatrice **Webb**, wrote a minority report calling for the end of the Poor Law and a new bureau to coordinate labour resources. It was rejected by the government.

1906   **Education (Provision of Meals Act)**: allowed local authorities (councils) to give free school meals, although most children did not receive them. It was an early Act concerned with **child welfare** and led to the establishment of the school meals service, universalised during the Second World War.

1907   **Education (Administrative Provisions) Act**: introduced the school medical service in order to provide inspection of the health of school children

1908   **Old Age Pensions Act**: a keystone of the New Liberal welfare reforms, the Act created means-tested non-contributory **old-age pensions**, payable at the age of seventy. Individuals received 5 shillings per week, and married coupled 7 shillings and sixpence. Their financing through taxation led in large part to the debacle of the **People's Budget** in 1909.

1908   **Children's Act**: an early definition of children's rights and child welfare, defining the responsibilities of parents, particularly the mother. It increased the role of paid local authority health visitors in the raising of working-class children.

1909   **People's Budget** (April): introduced by Lloyd George, the 1909 **budget** seriously affected relations between the House of Commons and the Lords over the costs of social policy and defence expenditure.

1911   **National Insurance Act** (December): established insurance for some workers against ill health and unemployment, on a basis of compulsory national insurance contributions made by worker, employee and state. It was an important foundation stone in the emergence of the twentieth-century welfare system.

1918   **Representation of the People Act** (February): removed the pauper disqualification from the franchise, enabling those claiming poor relief to vote.

1921   **Free milk** introduced for poor school children.

1921   **Local Authorities (Financial Provisions) Act**: allowed for greater transfer of funds between wealthier and poorer boroughs, and gave the Ministry of Health increased power to set scales and terms of poor relief.

1921   **Poplar revolt** in the East End of London came to a head, causing tensions between the Labour-led borough and central government. The Labour Party in Poplar, led by George **Lansbury**, sought to provide higher and more costly levels of relief to the poor of the borough.

1922   First **hunger march** held to protest against unemployment in the poorest industrial areas of Britain.

1924   **Old Age Pensions Act**: removed the earnings limit qualification for entitlement to pensions, an important step on the path towards universal pension provision.

1925   **Widows', Orphans' and Old Age Contributory Pensions Act**: created a contributory scheme, payable at the age of seventy (reduced in 1928 to sixty-five), which assisted thousands of women forced into poverty through bereavement.

1926   **Boards of Guardians (Default) Act**: gave powers to the government to reconstitute boards of guardians that were viewed as overgenerous with representatives from the Ministry of Health.

1929   **Local Government Act** (March), introduced by Neville Chamberlain: removed the administration of the Poor Law from boards of guardians to local authorities.

1930   **Poor Law Act**: renamed poor relief 'public assistance'. Benefits were henceforth paid via the public assistance committees.

1933   **Children and Young Person's Act**: removed the final vestiges and responsibilities of the Poor Law for those children who were in official care.

1934   **Unemployment assistance boards** established following the report of the parliamentary inquiry into unemployment. They were accompanied by the introduction of the means test. Loathed by the working classes, the test evaluated the assets and the income of a household in order to decide upon the levels of unemployment assistance to be allocated. Many saw their benefits reduced because they had inherited some heirlooms of meagre value or had saved for furniture and other domestic appliances when they were in work. The misery of the test was recorded in Walter Brierley's *Means Test Man* (1935).

1940   **Old Age and Widows' Pensions Act** (August): reduced the pensionable age for insured women to sixty.

1942   **Beveridge Report** (December): written by the Liberal William Beveridge and entitled *A Report on Social Insurance and Allied Services*, it emphasised the need to slay the five giants blocking the road to reconstruction – ignorance, disease, idleness, want and squalor. The report provided for a 'cradle to the grave' welfare system based upon universal national insurance. Full employment was also to become a major principle of social and economic policy. These recommendations were adopted by Labour and introduced between 1945 and 1950. The report was published during a phase of the war when many British people felt that the tide of conflict had turned in their favour, and that higher hopes for the future could be entertained. The indifference and even hostility towards it of the Conservative Party was one factor in their defeat at the general election of 1945, although historians disagree on the extent of the impact of the report on the British public.

1945   **Family Allowances Act** (June): provided non-contributory allowance of 5 shillings for the second and any subsequent child. The money was paid to the mother, partly because she was expected to know what was best for her children, and partly to avoid the father and husband from drinking, smoking or gambling the allowance away. The leading campaigner for family allowances was Eleanor **Rathbone**.

1946   **National Insurance Act** (August): extended compulsory insurance for all over sixteen. It provided benefits for everyone in unemployment, sickness or old age in return for regular contributions from wages. It was the realisation of a fundamental recommendation of the Beveridge Report.

1946   **National Health Service Act** (November): transferred control of voluntary and local authority hospitals, via regional hospital boards, to the Ministry of Health. Health care was intended to be free at the point of delivery. The remaining vestiges of the Poor Law were abolished.

1948   The National Health Service (NHS) came into operation on the 'appointed day' (5 July), establishing a major cornerstone of the welfare state. The minister for health, Aneurin **Bevan**, had fought the entrenched interests of the British Medical Association, the professional organisation of the doctors, and also considerable opposition from the Conservative Party. A standardised health system, based upon local doctor's surgeries and hospitals, came into being, replacing the *ad hoc* and unequal prewar apparatus of health care.

1948   **National Assistance Act** (January): this can be seen as the final defence against poverty, as it required local authorities to assess the needs of the poorest, or those with mental or physical problems, in order to provide adequate accommodation and care.

1954   **Institute of Community Studies** (ICS) formed by Michael **Young**. It attempted to relate social research to social policy. Among its most famous works was *Family and Kinship in East London* (1957), by Young and Peter **Willmott**, which became a best-seller and was republished many times in subsequent decades. Its compassion for poorer people in a welfare state that appeared to be treating the workers as pawns to be moved around in order to satisfy the diktats of housing policies appealed to many. Just three years later, however, Willmott and Young's *Family and Class in a London Suburb* (1960) revealed a more optimistic interpretation of suburban living in Essex, and yet this book received little of the attention garnered by its predecessor, suggesting that bad news captures the social imagination more than favourable tidings about the impact of affluence, consumption and improved housing on working-class life. Other important works by the ICS included Peter Townsend's *The Family Life of Old People* (1957). The ICS continues to the present day, and is now based at University College, London.

1959   **National Insurance Act**: brought in graduated pensions related to earnings, and came into effect in April 1961. The Act was a forerunner of the State Earnings Related Pensions Scheme (SERPS) introduced in 1978.

1970   **Family Income Supplements Act** (November): introduced a new type of benefit for low-income families. FIS was widely advertised in the newspapers and on television in order to raise awareness of it. One set of adverts was delivered by Marge Proops, the agony aunt of the *Daily Mirror*.

1971   **Free milk** for school children withdrawn by Margaret Thatcher, education secretary (June): she aimed to save £9 million. The move was resisted by many Labour-run councils.

1974   **Health and Safety at Work Act**: provided a comprehensive system of regulations.

1975   **Child Benefits Act**: child benefit replaced family allowances after thirty years of the latter system. The Act came into operation in 1977 (April).

1975   **Social Security Pensions Act**: introduced a variable element to pension contributions and payments in the form of the State Earnings Related Pensions Scheme. It began in 1978.

1986   **Social Security Act**: altered means-tested benefits with the stated intention of targeting them at lower-income households. Supplementary benefit became income support and family income supplement was replaced by family credit. The Joseph Rowntree Foundation and other charities working with poor households observed a deleterious impact upon the incomes of the poorest fifth of households. Many lost their benefit completely.

1990   **National Health Service and Community Care Act**: allowed hospitals to opt out of local authority control and to become self-governing trusts.

1991   **Child Support Act**: created the Child Support Agency, responsible for ensuring that, if possible, absent parents provided financial contributions for their children. Today, the reputation of the CSA is far from a positive one, as many parents have claimed unfair treatment or inadequate benefits, or both.

1997   New Labour general election victory: the incoming government promised to improve and democratise the National Health Service while maintaining a prudent fiscal regime. Increasing levels of public expenditure on the NHS were allied to a policy of modernisation and rationalisation. Hospital modernisation programmes were accompanied by new-build hospitals and the closure of older small sites, but any hospital closure was usually greeted with anger or fear by local communities. The culture of the 'traditional' family doctor or general practitioner was also revised, as Labour increasingly promoted medical centres during the early twenty-first century. This was by no means a new policy, but the mass murders of patients by Dr Harold Shipman gave impetus to the rationalisation: one GP working alone is less easily policed than a team at a medical centre. The British Medical Association voiced strong opposition to these changes during 2008. Furthermore, it appeared that no matter how much a government spent on the NHS it would never be free of problems, as proved by the 'superbugs' C Difficile and MRSA.

Social policy: education

1902   **Education Act**: school boards were abolished and local authorities (councils) were given powers to establish secondary education and provide aid to voluntary schools.

1904   Establishment of the Association to Promote the Higher Education of Working Men. The first branch was opened in Reading, Berkshire. This first twentieth-century landmark in adult education was renamed the **Workers' Education Association** in 1905.

1907 **Education (Administrative Provisions) Act**: introduced medical inspections at schools.

1918 **Education Act**: instigated compulsory attendance at school until the age of fourteen. The Act also abolished fees for elementary education in those schools where fees were still demanded. Herbert Fisher, as president of the board of education, also intended to introduce compulsory part-time teaching for those aged fourteen to eighteen, but public expenditure cuts put paid to his plans.

1926 The first of the three reports of the **Hadow Committee** called for the bipartite division of primary and secondary education, with the year of transfer from primary to secondary coming at the age of eleven. Elementary schools were incorporated into the primary school system. Particular teaching strategies were aimed at children aged five to seven and those aged seven to eleven. Local education authorities did not respond uniformly. By 1939 half of school children were in primary schools, the rest in elementary schools.

1936 **Education Act**: raised the school leaving age to fifteen, but this did not occur until 1944.

1944 **Education Act**: primary and secondary education was divided by the '11-plus' exam. Secondary education was divided into modern, technical and grammar schools. Grammar schools were the apex of this tripartite system.

1963 **Crowther Report**: recommended the raising of the school leaving age to sixteen, with the provision of part-time education thereafter for those who required it.

1963 **Robbins Report**: led to the opening of the first of the new universities from 1963. The report called for the expansion of the universities and the conversion of colleges of higher education into polytechnics. The growing number of teenagers who had qualified for university drove the expansion of higher education, which was anticipated to cater for double the number of students – 218,000 – by 1973. The 'new' universities of the 1960s, sometimes pejoratively referred to as 'plate-glass' as compared with the 'red-brick' Victorian institutions, included East Anglia, Essex, Kent, Lancaster, Stirling, Sussex, Warwick and York.

1965 **Certificate of Secondary Education** (CSE): introduced to give qualifications to those pupils deemed unfit for the ordinary level or 'O' level exam at sixteen years.

1965 Anthony **Crosland**, the secretary of state for education, announced that technical colleges would become polytechnics, not universities (April).

1965 Department of Education and Science, intending to end selection by the 11-plus, issued circular 10/65, which asked local authorities to plan for amalgamation of secondary schools into **comprehensive** schools (July). Crosland stated that he wanted to destroy 'every fucking grammar school' in the country.

1969   **Open University** (OU) established in the new town of Milton Keynes. Originally termed 'the university of the air', its concept was that university education was open to all adults, who could be taught both through course materials sent through the post and via programmes on television (originally **BBC2**). The idea was adapted from American experiments with broadcast teaching and was enthusiastically pursued by the Wilson government. Thousands of mature students took courses every year, attended summer schools and graduated in a wide variety of arts, social sciences and science subjects. By the year 2000 the OU had over 180,000 registered students, proof positive of its major contribution to adult education in Britain.

1972   Provision of nursery education announced for 90 per cent of four-year-olds and 50 per cent of three-year-olds within ten years.

1973   School leaving age raised to sixteen.

1980   **Education Act**: provided financial support for some pupils in independent schools.

1988   **Education Reform Act**: established the National Curriculum for schools and schools were given greater autonomy over their budgets.

1992   **Further and Higher Education Act**: expanded the number of new or 'post-1992' universities from previous polytechnics and colleges of further and higher education. More than sixty new universities were created by the Act.

1998   **Teaching and Higher Education Act**: abolished maintenance grants for university students, to be replaced by loans. Nearly all students were also required to pay tuition fees.

Media: cinema and television

1896   First screening of moving pictures at the Regent Street Polytechnic (now the University of Westminster) by the Lumière Brothers. The films were silent shorts, and the event was of enormous significance as a harbinger of the cinema in Britain.

1910   Empire Music Hall in Manchester converted to a cinema.

1912   **British Board of Film Classification**, otherwise known as the British Board of Film Censors, established by representatives of the film industry. The BBFC was initially intended to codify and standardise film classification in cinemas across Britain. It was also a product of its Victorian-born initiators, a paternalistic attempt to protect the public from anything sexual or seditious.

1915–18 **Topical Budget newsreels** shown in British cinemas, bringing censored moving images of war into the lives of hundreds of thousands of people for the first time.

1927 The first 'talkie' was shown in the United States, namely *The Jazz Singer*, starring Al Jolson. Soon afterwards talking movies crossed the Atlantic to Britain.

1927 **Cinematographic Act** (otherwise known as the Film Act): introduced to protect and promote the British cinema industry through quotas.

1929 Release of *The Drifters* (dir. John **Grierson**), a seminal film in the British documentary film movement. Made for the Empire Marketing Board, it depicted the lives of herring fishermen in Northern England.

1932 First experimental television broadcasts begun by the **BBC**.

1936 The BBC began regular television broadcasts in the London region.

1938 **Cinematographic Act** (Film Act): established the Cinematographic Films Council and reaffirmed the quota system in order to protect British film making.

1938 Release of *Spare Time* (dir. Humphrey **Jennings**), a documentary film emphasising the importance of leisure and recreation to the working classes of Bolton ('Worktown') during the 1930s.

1939 Television broadcasts suspended on the outbreak of war. The programme being shown at the time it was taken off air was a Mickey Mouse cartoon.

1940 *Gone with the Wind* (dir. Victor Fleming) became a sensational hit with the British viewing public on the eve of the battle of Britain during the Second World War. Based on the novel by Margaret Mitchell, its subject matter of love and death during the American Civil War must have struck a chord with millions of people as they contemplated the horrors and insecurities of the total war to come. Its success was also explained by the glamorous British-born actress Vivienne Leigh and the exotic accents and landscapes of the American South. Both escapist and topical, the film has remained a classic of Hollywood cinema and a staple viewing favourite with the British public on video and DVD.

1940 The **GPO Film Unit** was incorporated into the **Crown Film Unit** under the auspices of the Ministry of Information.

1941 *Love on the Dole* (dir. John Baxter) finally shown: based on the novel by Walter **Greenwood** and the adaptation for stage by Ronald Gow, the film had been banned before the war but was deemed acceptable for wartime viewing.

1945 *A Diary for Timothy* (dir. Humphrey Jennings) was completed towards the end of Second World War. Its message was that all classes had pulled together during the war, and that Timothy, a baby born in 1944, deserved a future of democracy and stability in which all would have to work hard and not take democracy for granted. Using 'real people' as well as famous actors and musicians, *A Diary for Timothy* possesses some contemporary poignant and moving scenes from everyday life. Written by E. M. Forster and narrated by actor Michael Redgrave, the film also reflected the mobilisation of theatrical and cinematic talent for the war effort on the home front.

1945   **Censorship** of cinema films was relaxed following the ending of war, but Victorian paternalism and strict censorship persisted until the thawing of attitudes during the later 1950s and afterwards.

1946   The BBC began regular television broadcasts, initiating what would eventually become the most significant postwar pastime of the British people.

1946   Release of the first **Ealing comedy**, *Hue and Cry*.

1949   Broadcasting committee report rejected advertising and firmly endorsed the BBC's monopoly status in public broadcasting.

1949   **British Film Institute Act**: provided for government to fund the British Film Institute (BFI).

1949   **Cinematographic Film Production (Special Loans) Act**: allowed for temporary loans to finance the production and distribution of films. It established the National Film Finance Company Ltd.

1953   **Coronation of Queen Elizabeth II** televised live (June), greatly boosting the popularity of the new medium

1954   **Television Act** (July): introduced commercial television, funded by advertising, under the Independent Television Authority (ITA).

1955   **Independent Television** (ITV) began broadcasting (September), the first and therefore the oldest independent commercial television company in Britain. It was and remains constituted of a number of different broadcasting companies with regional coverage.

1957   **Cinematographic Films Act**: imposed a levy on cinema exhibitors to assist in the funding of British film making. Subsequent legislation during the 1960s also raised funds through levies or loans.

1962   **Pilkington Report** (June): castigated standards of broadcasting and particularly attacked the Americanisation of British television, notably on Independent Television.

1962   Release of the first **James Bond** film, *Dr No*. Based on the novel by Ian Fleming, it was followed by other huge James Bond hits for the British cinema industry, among them From *Russia with Love* (1963), with a theme tune sung by Matt **Monro**, and *Goldfinger* (1964), whose theme song was sung by Shirley **Bassey**.

1964   Mary **Whitehouse** established the '**Clean up TV**' campaign in order to protest at 'filth' on the BBC and on television and radio more widely.

1964   **BBC2** began (April): the second television channel to be broadcast by the British Broadcasting Corporation, BBC2 more effectively expressed the values of the BBC's early head, John **Reith**, than did BBC1, which became increasingly populist in order to compete with the more commercial ethos of Independent Television (ITV). BBC2 also became known for more experimental programming.

1966   *Cathy Come Home* screened by BBC television as part of its 'Wednesday Play' season (November): a 'docudrama' directed by Ken **Loach**, and starring Carol White as Cathy, it was one of the most influential films of its genre shown on television. In harrowing terms, the film depicted the transition from the early cheerfulness and optimism of Cathy to the decline of her young family after her partner Reg (played by Ray Brooks, who later found fame as the hapless husband of Pauline Fowler in BBC's soap opera *EastEnders*) loses his job and becomes unemployed. In the final scene, children were snatched from the weeping mother by the social services in a railway station while the narrator details the crisis in housing provision for poorer people. *Cathy Come Home* was partly about the continuing housing shortage but was mostly concerned with the failure of the social services to understand and provide for the needs of a poor mother with a far from effective partner.

1967   BBC2 became the first channel to show programmes in colour (July): the snooker programme *Pot Black* was one of the shows used to trial colour.

1978   **Annan committee** report: led the government to propose a fourth television channel under the auspices of public broadcasting, but to be commercially funded and sensitive to the needs and aspirations of minority interests, including the Welsh language.

1982   **Channel 4** began broadcasting (November): privately funded but publicly owned, the channel was brought into existence to widen choice in addition to the three channels then on offer (BBC1, BBC2 and ITV) and to reflect minority interests.

1983   **Breakfast television** began on the BBC (January): the first presenters were Frank Bough, a previous sports reporter, and Selina Scott, a newsreader.

1985   The first 'multiplex' cinema, known as 'The Point' because of its pyramid design, was opened in the new town of Milton Keynes, beginning a revival of cinema-going in a decade when viewing films at home was also becoming more popular. The growth of satellite television and the use of video cassette players posed threats to the cinema, but the multiplex set new standards in choice, in the quality of screenings and in comfort.

1985   **Cinemas Act**: consolidated the Cinematographic Acts between 1909 and the 1950s. It specified licensing provisions for the showing of films and for Sunday opening, and made recommendations on the viewing of films in private houses.

1985   **Films Act**: repealed the legislation of the 1960s and 1970s and abolished the National Film Finance Corporation, both of which had provided much needed capital for the British film industry. From the perspective of Thatcherism, it terminated a culture of subsidy in British film making.

1989 **Sky satellite television** launched, broadcast to Britain via the Astra 1A satellite. Owned by the Australian entrepreneur Rupert **Murdoch**, the four main channels to be launched were Sky Channel, Sky News, Sky Movies and Eurosport.

1990 **British Satellite Broadcasting** (BSB) launched (April): the major government-funded but ultimately unsuccessful competitor with Sky.

1990 BSB merged with Sky (November): this came at the beginning of a proliferation in the number of satellite TV channels.

1994 **Internet** launched in Britain.

1996 **Broadcasting Act**: established the framework for the proliferation of satellite channels in Britain.

1997 **Channel 5** launched (March): the third major commercial terrestrial station, and the first launched since **Channel 4** in 1982, Channel 5 was firmly established ten years later, in part because it purchased some of the slickest new American TV series.

1997 Appointment of Britain's first minister of film, Tom Clarke. He was responsible for film and tourism, and his role was incorporated within the Department of Media, Culture and Sport.

Media: radio broadcasting

1922 British Broadcasting Company established during the 'wireless' boom. It soon became the **British Broadcasting Corporation (BBC)**.

1933 **Radio Luxembourg** began transmission, in the English language, from the Grand Duchy of Luxembourg. It can be viewed as a prototype 'pirate radio' station (although not anchored offshore) because it advertised goods and services, something forbidden by British legislation. By the 1970s, Radio Luxembourg had become more wedded to **rock music** and broadcast risqué songs banned in Britain.

1939 **BBC Home Service** began (September): all medium-wave regional programming was subsumed into one channel. It was dedicated mostly to news and current affairs, some light entertainment and, between 1939 and 1945, propaganda. Some of the leading wartime entertainers, for example Tommy **Handley** and **Flanagan and Allen**, also became household names via the Light Programme.

1940 Lord Haw Haw (William **Joyce**) made his first traitorous broadcasts from Nazi Germany.

1945 BBC **Light Programme** introduced as an alternative to the Home Service (July). The popularity of music, particularly American music and more light-hearted programming, was evident by the later 1930s, and especially through the wartime forces stations of the American troops.

1946   BBC **Third Programme** introduced (September), becoming the main channel for classical music.

1964   **Radio Caroline** began broadcasting offshore: a 'pirate radio station' anchored in the Irish Sea, its first track, played by DJs Chris Moore and Simon Dee, was *Not Fade Away* by the **Rolling Stones**.

1967   **BBC Radio 1** went on air for the first time (September), with DJ Tony Blackburn's *Daily Disc Delivery*. Radio 1 was very much the pop and rock end of the music spectrum, the station for the younger age group. Its evening and late-night programming became a vehicle for new trends in music.

1967   **BBC Radio 2** went on air for the first time (September): many programmes were broadcast simultaneously on both Radios 1 and 2. However, Radio 2 was established as the home of 'easy listening' for those beyond their twenties and for homey chit-chat.

1967   **BBC Radio 3** went on air for the first time (September): its content was very much aimed at a minority audience for arts and highbrow culture, with classical music a mainstay, along with jazz, music documentaries and live concerts. In a sense it was the most Reithian of the four new BBC radio stations.

1967   **BBC Radio 4** went on air for the first time (September): its mostly non-music programming was dominated by news, current affairs, documentaries, arts, and in-house drama and comedy shows. Radio 4 can claim to be the first 'talk radio' station in Britain.

1972   **Sound Broadcasting Act** (July): created commercial radio broadcasting in Britain, called independent local radio, under the auspices of the ITA, becoming the Independent Broadcasting Authority (IBA). The following year new radio stations began to proliferate.

1973   The domestic radio broadcasting monopoly of the BBC came to an end with the establishment of commercial radio. Radio wavelengths were expanded and adapted to allow the new channels on air. Among the first was London's Capital Radio, which launched in July.

1976   Radio 210 Thames Valley began broadcasting (March), one of the growing number of regional commercial channels.

1990   BBC **Radio 5** began broadcasting (August) as mostly live 'talk radio'. It later became Radio 5 live.

1992   Classic FM began broadcasting (September): its success demonstrated the continued and growing popularity of classical music in Britain.

1995   BBC introduced Digital Audio Broadcasting (DAB) transmissions (September), and its portfolio of radio stations increased thereafter, including Radio 6 and Radio 7, both introduced during the early twenty-first century.

Media: the press – newspapers and magazines

1870   **Education Act**: provided higher levels of mass literacy than before, facilitating a reading public increasingly hungry not only for news and current affairs but also for information on sports, entertainments and fashions.

1896   The *Daily Mail* launched by Alfred **Harmsworth**. It was the first mass-circulation newspaper 'below' *The Times*, *The Telegraph* and other broadsheets, and sold at one halfpenny. Within a few years it had become a staple mid-market paper aimed mostly at an affluent middle-class reading public. By the end of the twentieth century it was a staunch supporter of the Conservative Party.

1900   The *Daily Express* launched by Arthur **Pearson**, another mass-circulation newspaper that became a mid-market success. It remained mostly Conservative in its politics.

1902   The *Times Literary Supplement* launched (January) as an auxiliary newspaper on the arts and literature.

1903   Launch of the *Daily Mirror* (November) also costing one halfpenny. Aimed mostly at women, it was also the first newspaper to introduce half-tone photographs. Until the late 1930s its politics were Conservative, but it supported the Labour Party during the general election of 1945, since when it has remained a 'Labour paper'.

1907   **National Union of Journalists** founded; it was and remains a white-collar organisation to represent journalists, although its membership broadened to include journalists in broadcasting.

1908   Alfred Harmsworth acquired *The Times* newspaper, a purchase assisted by sales of the *Daily Mail*.

1909   Launch of the *Daily Sketch* (March), a mid-market newspaper reflective of the new journalism, which was by then quite old journalism.

1911   The *Daily Herald* originally founded (January) from a strike newspaper called *The World*. It was relaunched with the support of George Lansbury and other Labour leaders in April 1912 and became an organ of the Labour movement in Britain.

1913   The *New Statesman* founded by the Fabian Society socialists Beatrice and Sidney **Webb** and George Bernard Shaw as a middle-class periodical for socialist supporters in Britain.

1914   **Defence of the Realm Act** (August): introduced press and film censorship in Britain, which was relaxed following complaints from American journalists during the war and then more fully at the end of the conflict.

1915   The *Sunday Pictorial* launched by Alfred Harmsworth, Lord **Northcliffe**. It became the *Sunday Mirror* in 1963.

1916   The *Daily Express* purchased by Max Aitken (later Lord **Beaverbrook**).

1922	Death of Alfred Harmsworth (Lord Northcliffe), the brother of Lord **Rothermere**.
1926	The *British Gazette* produced by the government as a propaganda sheet against the **General Strike** (May). The *British Worker* was the newspaper issued by the TUC.
1930	Launch of the *Daily Worker* (January): a communist-backed newspaper, it was probably funded by the USSR until the fall of the Soviet bloc by 1991. In 1966 it became the *Morning Star*, and is still sold.
1930	The *News Chronicle* formed from the merger of the *Daily News* and the *Daily Chronicle* (June). It was incorporated into the *Daily Mail* in 1960.
1930	The *New Statesman* merged with the Liberal magazine *The Nation* and became the *New Statesman and Nation*.
1932	**British Library Newspaper Library** opened at Colindale, a suburb of North London (see Sources and resources).
1932–3	Circulation war between the *Daily Express* and the *Daily Herald* led to sales of over 2 million per day for both titles.
1932–4	The *Daily Mail* offered support to Sir Oswald Mosley and the **British Union of Fascists**. However, the support was withdrawn following fascist violence at a number of BUF meetings and in the streets.
1936	The first colour advertisements appeared in British newspapers, in the Glasgow *Daily Record*.
1938	*Picture Post* magazine launched by Edward Hulton (October): adopting a reformist stance during the Second World War, it became an important source of support for reconstruction and Labour's plans for the welfare state.
1940	Newspapers limited in both size and circulation on account of wartime paper shortages. Censorship was introduced as all publications were vetted by the **Ministry of Information**. The *Daily Worker* was banned.
1953	The **Press Council** established as a regulatory body along the lines suggested by the Royal Commission on the Press.
1959	The *Manchester Guardian* became *The Guardian*, the only left-liberal national broadsheet in Britain at the time.
1961	*Private Eye* launched (November): a satirical magazine at the heart of the boom in satire in 1960s Britain, its leading founders included the comedians Peter Cook and Willie Rushton.
1964	*The Sun* newspaper replaced the *Daily Herald*.
1969	*The Sun* was taken over by News International, owned by the Australian magnate Rupert Murdoch. A newspaper with a strong Labour heritage became Conservative in its politics during the 1970s and a strong supporter of Margaret Thatcher during the 1980s.
1978	Launch of the *Daily Star* (November): a tabloid newspaper that failed

to achieve the same level of sustained high-volume sales of the *Daily Mirror* or *The Sun*, it has nevertheless continued to the present day.

1979   *The Times* and the *Sunday Times* were not produced for most of the year as a consequence of industrial action.

1980   The *London Evening News* ceased circulation: London was left with only one evening newspaper, the *Evening Standard*.

1984   Robert **Maxwell** bought the Mirror Group, whose titles included the *Daily Mirror* and *Sunday Mirror*.

1984   Launch in Birmingham of the *Daily News*, Britain's first free daily newspaper.

1985   The *Daily Telegraph* bought by the American magnate Conrad Black.

1986   *Today* launched by Eddie Shah (March): the first colour national newspaper, it was short-lived, ceasing publication in November 1995.

1986   *The Independent* newspaper launched (October): originally with a mandate to be a neutral paper uncommitted to any political party or wing of politics, it became associated with many left causes by 2008.

1986   News International, whose titles included *The Times*, the *Sunday Times*, *The Sun* and the *News of the World*, moved its operations to Wapping in the London **docklands**. A bitter strike by printers accompanied the move.

1987   First woman editors of major British newspapers (see Women).

1990   The *Independent on Sunday* launched four years after its 'sister' daily, *The Independent*.

1991   The **Press Complaints Commission** replaced the Press Council.

1991   Robert Maxwell died, apparently having committed suicide by throwing himself from his private yacht in the Atlantic Ocean.

1991   Calcutt Commission established to research into press regulation at a time when many members of the public felt that 'the third estate' was over-invasive and poorly policed by its own regulatory body.

1993   **Calcutt Report**: recommended the establishment of a statutory complaints tribunal. The Press Complaints Commission responded by calling for enhanced voluntary self-regulation.

1994   The *Daily Telegraph* launched online (November): it was the first to go online, during the year the internet was introduced.

1995   The government white paper *Privacy and Media Intrusion* recommended voluntary self-regulation of the press according to a code of conduct laid down by newspaper editors.

1997–8 The reputation of the paparazzi, the photographers who supply photographs to the press, was hugely damaged by the **death of Diana, Princess of Wales** (September).

1998   *Sport First* launched (March): it was the first weekly national sports newspaper, published on Sundays.

1999   The *Sunday Herald* launched in Glasgow (February).

1999   *Metro* launched (March): the first free newspaper in London, aimed at users of the London Underground, it later spread to the wider train network.

Sport

1902   **Ibrox disaster** at a Scotland versus England football match in Glasgow (April): twenty-five people lost their lives and hundreds were injured.

1907   **Amateur Football Association** formed. Amateur football remained the alternative to the professional game. Today it is called the Amateur Football Alliance (AFA).

1908   **Olympic Games** held at White City, West London: the national football team, Great Britain and Ireland, won the gold medal for football. The Olympics are mostly remembered, however, for the controversial events surrounding the disqualification of Dorando di Pietri, the Italian winner of the marathon.

1908   The **Football Association** Charity Shield competition began.

1914   The First World War ended the regular fixtures of football and mainstream sports.

1920   The creation of the Football League Third Division.

1923   **Wembley Stadium** opened in the North London suburb. The famous twin towers made an iconic entrance to the English national sporting stadium, which played host not only to football but to other sports, notably the **London Olympics** in 1948.

1923   First **FA Cup Final** at Wembley, between Bolton Wanderers and West Ham United (April): Bolton won 2–0.

1926   First urban **greyhound racing** track opened in Manchester (July): utilising the electric hare device imported from the United States of America, it was emulated by other urban greyhound tracks.

1932   **Bodyline** scandal for English **cricket**: during the Ashes tour of Australia, the English team developed a fast-leg bowling tactic aimed directly at the body of the batsman. This was by no means unsuccessful in terms of results, but was widely viewed, particularly by the Australians and other cricket-loving countries in the British Empire, as rather un-English and certainly 'not cricket'.

1935   **Central Council of Physical Recreation** established: originally termed the Central Council for Physical Recreative Training, the organisation came into existence to provide a forum for clubs and organisations representing a wide variety of participant and spectator sports, and to protect and promote their interests.

1936   Fred **Perry** won Wimbledon for the third consecutive time, the last victory in SW19 for a British men's singles player during the twentieth century.

1937   British and Empire heavyweight **boxing** champion Tommy **Farr** beat the highly respected American boxer Max Baer (April), a major victory for the Welsh boxer. He also 'went the distance' (i.e. fifteen rounds) with Joe Louis (August).

1937   The BBC experimented with *Sports Review*, the first sporting magazine on British television, when numbers watching the small screen were still tiny. The programme was monthly and showed small extracts of films from major sporting events of the past four weeks.

1938   Two important football matches were televised live by the BBC in 1938: an England versus Scotland international and the FA Cup Final two weeks later.

1948   The **televising** of the **London Olympics** (the XIV Olympiad), the first major sporting event to be shown on the small screen in postwar Britain (August). They were called the 'austerity Olympics' because of the financial and material conditions in which the event was held. The previous country to hold the Olympics was Nazi Germany, in 1936.

1953   Hungary defeated England at football by 6 goals to 3 at Wembley Stadium (November): a humiliating defeat, partly because the English were outplayed by a fluid and inventive Hungarian side, it was also an embarrassing episode during the Cold War. International sporting events were always charged with propaganda opportunities for both capitalist and communist blocs.

1954   BBC television began to broadcast *Sportsview*, a weekly sporting magazine programme that ran until 1968. From 1957 to 1962 a version for children, called *Junior Sportsview*, was also broadcast, reflecting official concerns that youth required more exposure to sports. The programme was an early vehicle for sportsmen such as Danny Blanchflower and Billy Wright to become television celebrities. Well-known BBC presenters such as Cliff Michelmore and David Coleman also enjoyed initial exposure in their careers in these and other sporting programmes, notably *Grandstand*.

1954   Roger Bannister broke the 4-minute mile (May), an achievement that gave vent to much national pride during a relatively inauspicious period of British sports performances on the international stage.

1958   BBC television launched *Grandstand*: the Saturday afternoon sporting magazine ran until the early twenty-first century. *Grandstand* was the longest-running live sports magazine, and included half-time football results, late afternoon football results, horse racing and live screenings of other sports, notably cricket and football. The horse-racing service and the reading of football results represented a significant change in the BBC's attitude to betting and gambling, because betting on horses was widespread. The original nonconformist values of John Reith for the BBC, while remaining influential upon the character of television broadcasting, were compromised by that auxiliary sporting activity, betting.

1958   **Munich air disaster** (February): a talented Manchester United football team on a plane that crashed while trying to take off from Munich airport suffered greatly from the trauma of the incident and the deaths of several of its players and staff. Many moving tributes to those who died were paid in the newspapers and on television on the fiftieth anniversary of the crash in 2008. One of the most famous survivors was Sir Bobby **Charlton**, who never fully came to terms with his loss.

1961   The maximum wage of £20 per week for footballers was scrapped by the Football Association following a prolonged campaign by the Player's Union, latterly mobilised by Jimmy Hill (then a footballer himself; he later went on to become a football expert on the BBC).

1963   British heavyweight boxer Henry **Cooper** knocked down American champion Cassius Clay (later Mohammed Ali) (June) in front of a large crowd of spectators at Wembley Stadium. Clay won the fight.

1964   BBC2 first broadcast *Match of the Day* (August). A weekly programme during the football season that went out on a Saturday evening, and later during midweek for certain important matches, *Match of the Day* moved to BBC1 in 1966.

1965   **Sports Council** established by the Labour government: its four aims were: 1) to increase participation in sport; 2) to increase and improve sports facilities; 3) to raise standards of performance; 4) to provide information about sport.

1966   England won football's **World Cup**, beating West Germany by 4 goals to 2 on the home turf of Wembley Stadium (July): the match was of course an arena not simply of football but also of national pride for both countries. Not all British people shared in England's national joy, however. And from West Germany's point of view, the decision by the referee to award the third and game-turning English goal was a little unfair. It is still impossible to prove that the ball crossed the line of the German goal, and any disputed goal is to this day in Germany known as an 'Englische Ziel'.

1969   Tony Jacklin won the British Golf Open at a time when golf was becoming an increasingly popular sport in Britain.

1970   Tony Jacklin won the US Open.

1971   Second **Ibrox disaster** at the Rangers football ground in Glasgow (January): following more than sixty fatalities and hundreds injured, Ibrox became one of the first all-seater stadiums in Scotland.

1973   **Boycott of Wimbledon**: the **tennis** tournament was caught in the middle of a Cold War professional *contretemps* over the banning of the Yugoslavian player Nikki Pilić by his national tennis federation because he had played for a cash prize in Canada. Leading tennis players stayed away from Wimbledon in support of him.

1984   Jayne Torvill and Christopher Dean won gold for their ice skating at the Winter Olympics in Sarajevo (February). As amateurs, from Nottingham, they became hugely respected in Britain, and were voted BBC Sports Personalities of the Year for 1984. Following the Olympics they turned professional.

1985   **Heysel Stadium disaster** (May) in Belgium during the European Cup Final between Liverpool FC and Juventus. The match brought English football supporters, and particularly Liverpool supporters, a reputation for foul behaviour. Thirty-nine people died, most of them supporters of Juventus, following sickening crowd trouble. The European Football Association (EUFA) subsequently placed an indefinite ban on English football clubs in Europe.

1989   **Hillsborough Stadium disaster** (April): ninety-three football supporters were crushed to death at the Sheffield stadium during the Nottingham Forest versus Liverpool FA Cup semi-final. The tragedy led to the Taylor Report (1990) by Lord Justice Taylor, which recommended ground improvements and all-seater stadiums.

1990   Mike Gatting led the last of the England cricket team's rebel tours to South Africa, which since 1970 had been banned from the International Cricket Council (ICC) as anger at apartheid grew. Protests were held against the tours, and on their return leading players faced bans from test cricket.

1990   The Sports Channel began broadcasting on satellite television, later becoming Sky Sports.

1994   The **Sports Council** was remodelled as the UK Sports Council and the English Sports Council. Increasingly these groups enjoyed funding from the National Lottery.

1995   British heavyweight boxer Frank **Bruno** became world heavyweight champion (September) after beating Oliver McCall at Wembley Stadium.

1999   Manchester United won the treble: the FA Carling Premiership, the UEFA Champions League and the FA Cup.

1990s   Widespread introduction of satellite television led to growing levels of commercialised sponsorship in many major British sports and their televising to wider audiences. Football, **rugby**, golf, darts and one-day cricket were the main beneficiaries. These had all been shown on BBC and ITV, but now they reached audiences in Britain and abroad to a greater degree than before. Following the success of Eurosport, more events from Europe have been shown in Britain via Sky Sports.

Other leisure landmarks

1906   **Street Betting Act**: reaffirmed the illegality of ready money or cash betting and gambling in public spaces in Britain. Off-the-course cash betting had been illegal since 1853, but millions of working-class punters had continued to bet with bookmakers within an illegal network of street betting. The Act was spectacularly unsuccessful.

1915   **Defence of the Realm (Amendment) Act** (October): among other things, it restricted alcohol consumption for the duration of the First World War. Both the strength of beer and the opening hours of pubs were affected. Lloyd George denounced alcohol as potentially being as great an enemy as Germany in the waging of a successful war. The closure of pubs during the afternoon continued until liberalisation measures began in 1988.

1926   Veeraswamy became the first Indian restaurant to be opened in London during the twentieth century. 'Going out for an Indian' has become a major leisure pursuit since the 1970s.

1930   **BBC Symphony Orchestra** began: the Proms were broadcast from Sir Henry Wood Hall in Langham Place, an annual event that demonstrated the love of classical music among millions of British people.

1932   **Kinder Scout** mass trespass by over 400 ramblers in the Peak District, Derbyshire (April): both a protest and a call for the rights of walkers to enjoy more land of outstanding natural beauty that was under private ownership, the trespass was also a demonstration of the importance of walking to workers in the Northern and Midland industrial towns and cities. Cheap and accessible, walking continued to grow as a major leisure activity, and the National Parks from 1949 provided uniquely beautiful contexts for it.

1936   **Butlin's Holiday Camp** opened at Skegness on the east coast of England: it began a trend in self-contained family holidays accessible by rail and increasingly by road.

1938   **Holidays with Pay Act**: increased the entitlement of millions of workers to a week's holiday without loss of income. Increasingly, employees of factories and mills and other industrial workers were entitled to paid leave.

1951   **Royal Commission on Betting, Lotteries and Gaming** chaired by Sir Henry Willink: recommended liberalisation of the betting laws on horse racing. It had been illegal to make cash bets off the racecourse since 1853, and the Willink Commission signalled that liberalisation was essential to the modernisation of the betting laws.

1952   The BBC and the *New Musical Express* began to provide charts or lists of the best-selling single or 'pop' records of the week.

1955   *Gardening Club* launched on BBC television: hosted by Percy Thrower, the series demonstrated gardening techniques and taught knowledge of flowers, plants and vegetables. During the postwar years, as a consequence of planned dispersal from older urban areas through suburbanisation, growing numbers of working-class as well as middle-class people were able to enjoy gardens. The programme became *Gardener's World* in 1968, and is still one of the most popular programmes on BBC2.

1960   **Betting and Gaming Act**: legalised cash betting off the racecourse. This Act was an early signifier of the permissiveness now commonly and often simplistically associated with the 1960s.

1960   Lady Albemarle's report on **youth clubs** called for an expansion of youth centres, particularly on or near council estates. Its aim was to encourage young people to come together on terms of their own choosing, and among their peers, but the clubs themselves were to be provided from above, by local authorities. Fears of delinquency and the cult of the rebellious teenager also underpinned the introduction of a planned phase of youth clubs: they were intended to combat boredom and misbehaviour. The report was a landmark in the development of the youth service, a wing of the welfare state.

1964–6   Disturbances by **Mods and Rockers** at seaside towns spoiled many people's bank holidays, while signifying that casual or loosely organised petty violence was part of the leisure activities of youth subcultures.

1965   First **Pizza Express** opened in London, signalling the increasing popularity of Italian food in Britain, and of eating out, although pizzas owed much to Italian-American influences on global cuisine.

1969   First flight of the Anglo-French supersonic aeroplane **Concorde** (March): its maiden flight lasted just 27 minutes, but it ushered in a new era of high-speed transatlantic travel. Flying time from London to New York was reduced from 7 hours to just 3 hours, 30 minutes, both for leisure and business users. Concorde went out of service in 2003 (October).

1960s   Flights to Southern European coastal resorts expanded greatly, as package holidays in Spain, and to a lesser extent Greece, Italy and Portugal, were increasingly enjoyed by Britons. Discount flights offered by Laker Airways and other companies fuelled the boom. Right-wing dictatorships and ex-fascist countries which enjoyed better weather than Britain between the months of May and October took advantage of the overseas holiday boom.

1960s   **Garden centres** began to take off in the UK as gardening became a mass leisure activity, in no small part a consequence of the preference for suburban living among the majority of British and particularly English people. The Garden Centres Association, a trade organisation, was established in 1966.

1975   Laskarina holiday company began operations to Greece following the fall of the right-wing regime of the Greek colonels. Greece had been 'discovered' before the 1960s by middle-class travel writers and novelists, notably by Lawrence Durrell, Patrick Leigh Fermor and others, as a more remote and less commercialised tourist destination than Spain, but during the 1960s and 1970s it was increasingly attracting package tour holidays to some of its islands, notably Corfu and Skiathos. Laskarina was typical of the new flock of self-catering holiday companies for the discerning middle-class traveller. The company ceased trading in 2006.

1985   **Live Aid concert** (July): driven by the Boomtown Rats lead singer Bob Geldof, the concert attracted many leading performers of the 1980s and was televised live to millions of people to raise money for the ill and starving in Africa. Geldof later received a knighthood for this and further fund-raising activities, although many critics of Live Aid saw it as a self-promoting spectacle for the artists involved, who were clearly wearing their hearts on their sleeves. Nonetheless, most who witnessed the event will never forget it.

1988   **Licensing Act**: liberalised pub opening hours, allowing pubs and wine bars to stay open all day.

1994   **Channel Tunnel** opened (May): linking the south coast of England to the north coast of France, the 'chunnel' provided new opportunities for tourism for British and French weekenders and holidaymakers. Paris, Brussels and Lille became favourite destinations. The Eurostar ran from Waterloo Station until 2007, when it moved to the beautifully refurbished St Pancras terminal.

1994   **National Lottery** introduced (November). A government initiative, the lottery was intended to encourage or at least exploit the gambling instinct to make money for 'good causes'. It was also long overdue: most countries in Europe had long-established regional or state lotteries. Britain had abolished its government-supported lottery as long ago as 1826 and had officially frowned upon lotteries until the liberalisation of gaming during the 1960s. In its first year, the national lottery raised over £260 million for arts, heritage, sports and philanthropic charities. Expenditure of lottery money was often politically controversial, however, depending on the cause or charity that was supported.

2.3
ECONOMIC HISTORY
The British economy since 1900

Notes

This section introduces the major landmarks in the development of the British economy and in the economic policies pursued by British governments during the twentieth century. It focuses upon causes and consequences of changes in the direction of government economic policies, the major events and problems affecting the pound sterling, and the ownership of the staple industries. Trade unions and industrial relations remained at the heart of government concerns, as strikes or other forms of industrial action impacted upon the productivity and the image of the British economy.

- Economic policy
- Sterling
- Nationalisation and privatisation
- Trade unions and industrial relations

Economic policy

1903   Joseph **Chamberlain** made a speech in Birmingham on **tariff reform** (May). Chamberlain was particularly worried about metal manufacturing in Birmingham, where his family was at the heart of a dynastic local elite. The Conservative Party was divided over the issue: some Tories were willing to embrace it, while others remained committed to **free trade**.

1909   **People's Budget**: (April): intended to pay for the **Dreadnought** programme and old-age pensions through a policy of high taxation on land and property.

1919   The pound sterling came off the **Gold Standard**, a system of valuing currencies according to the price of gold.

1925   The chancellor of the exchequer, Winston Churchill, returned the pound sterling to the Gold Standard. It was an act of orthodox economic policy, underpinned by a belief in laissez-faire policies.

1925   Publication of John Maynard Keynes's *Economic Consequences of Mr Churchill*: Keynes attacked Churchill for returning the pound sterling to the Gold Standard, thus overvaluing the currency and making British exports more expensive during a difficult period for manufacturing industry.

1929   **Wall Street crash** (October) brought about the Great Depression in Britain. Following the slump in the autumn of 1929, the British economy, along with most other advanced capitalist economies, faced serious problems: lack of investment; credit recalls by banks and building societies in Britain and abroad; losses to the value of savings for hundreds of thousands of people; and a decline in demand that affected manufacturing. The staple industries in the North of England, Scotland and South Wales were hardest hit, but few sectors and regions of the country were completely unaffected. By 1931 unemployment had soared to 3 million. This coincided with the recent coming to power of the second minority Labour government wedded to **laissez-faire economics**, an orthodoxy undermined by the economic emergency of the early 1930s.

1929   *We Can Conquer Unemployment* manifesto launched by Liberal Party for the general election of that year: a Keynesian document, the manifesto was rejected by the electorate, and a less radical minority Labour government took power whose chancellor of the exchequer, Philip **Snowden**, was wedded to the orthodox economics of balancing the budget, and was therefore less committed to expensive public works projects.

1930   **Mosley memorandum**: written by Sir Oswald Mosley, it called for much higher levels of public expenditure on public services and public works programmes to put people back to work. The rejection of his memorandum caused Mosley to establish the unsuccessful **New Party**.

1932   **Ottawa Conference**: hastened the end of laissez-faire economics and the onset of **imperial preference**, a powerful tool of protectionism and trade agreements.

1932   **Import Tariffs Act**: effectively ended the era of laissez-faire dominance in government economic policy. Joseph Chamberlain had argued for tariff reform before 1914, and in 1922 Stanley Baldwin had converted to the cause, for which he paid the price of a lost general election the following year. Protectionism was now official government policy.

1933   **Anglo-German Trade Agreement** (April): the British government and the government of Nazi Germany signed an agreement to encourage further trade between both countries.

1934   **Anglo-Russian Trade Agreement** (February): in the wake of a deterioration in Anglo-Russian trade relations, this agreement aimed to stimulate mutual trade.

1934   **Special Areas Acts** (December): the official euphemism for the depressed areas of interwar Britain, the 'special areas' were those regions whose economies were dominated by the staple industries. Small sums were made available for limited public works schemes in these areas. Many historians argue that the governments of the 1930s did little but just enough to prevent worse manifestations of economic and social crises afflicting Britain. The Acts were limited in scope and success.

1936   Keynes's *General Theory of Employment, Interest and Money* challenged the assumptions of classical economics and government policies. It was a statement of progressive economic policy that was still controversial during the 1930s, yet would become something approaching a new economic orthodoxy just ten years later.

1939   All forms of economic policy except the command economy approach were suspended on the outbreak of the Second World War. The government took control of all aspects of the British economy.

1945–51   The Labour government introduced a Keynesian mixed economy, nationalising key industries, including the troubled staple industries of coal mining, steel production and shipbuilding. The use of taxation to fund nationalised industries would become a vexed political issue in the postwar period.

1947   Emergency budget by the chancellor of the exchequer, Stafford **Cripps**: adopting a Keynesian approach to the problems of introducing the public expenditure cuts and higher taxes required during a parlous year in Britain's finances, the budget became synonymous with austerity but also sustained investment in key social and economic policies.

1947   The **General Agreement on Tariffs and Trade** (GATT) followed the failure of governments to create the International Trade Organisation, one of the lynchpins of international cooperation agreed upon at the **Bretton Woods** conference in 1944. GATT became a series of negotiations among the world's leading countries to moderate the operation of tariffs – taxes on imports – in order to facilitate world trade.

1947   **Marshall Plan** endorsed by the British foreign minister, Ernest **Bevin** (June), who attempted to persuade European countries to accept this funding for European recovery. All countries in Western Europe were beneficiaries, particularly France, which received $4,237 million in military aid and $3,190 in economic aid. Britain subsequently received $1,035 million in military aid and $3,835 million in economic aid. Italy was granted over $2,292 million in military aid but considerably less than Britain in economic aid.

1951   R. A. **Butler** endorsed the commitment to welfare spending and investment in nationalisation established by the Labour governments of 1945–51.

1956   Harold Macmillan introduced **Premium Bonds** (November), a form of indirect taxation but also of saving that ensured the 'investor' always saw their 'stake' returned. ERNIE (the Electronic Random Number Indicating Equipment) regularly produced series of numbers which, if they matched the numbers on individual bonds, would result in a sum of money tantamount to winnings. The first draw was in 1957. Meanwhile the government utilised the sums invested by the British public to raise interest. Today over 22 million people hold more than £33 billion in premium bonds, and many large and small prize-winners have been created. The bonds are interesting relative to the government's increasingly liberalised attitude towards betting and gambling.

1958   The chancellor of the exchequer Lord **Thorneycroft** resigned from the Treasury over what he saw as overgenerous **public expenditure** plans.

1959   Britain organised the **European Free Trade Association** (EFTA) with other Northern European partners to create an alternative customs union to the Common Market.

1961   The **Plowden Report** attacked the piecemeal nature of planning for public expenditure, recommending a newly modernised accounting structure and more systematic planning. The public expenditure survey committee was established in light of the report.

1962   **National Economic Development Council** established. The NEDC was a key instrument in the development of Tory corporatism and economic planning during the early 1960s. Nicknamed 'Neddy', its aim was to bring together trade unions, employers' organisations and representatives of the government to promote ideas and strategies to increase national output. Its existence was significant for a number of reasons. It was a statement of Keynesian economics – of the need for governments to intervene in the 'free market' and within the industrial sphere to facilitate growth. Its presence also led to a recognition that there was an industrial relations problem in Britain – although this country was by no means alone in that – and to a growing realisation that British economic output could be improved. So-called little Neddies were established in 1964 in key sectors of the economy. Ultimately, the NEDC was mostly unsuccessful, falling foul of the wider demise of economic planning during the 1960s.

1965   **Capital Gains Tax** and **Corporation Tax** introduced on businesses.

1965   **Emergency budget** (July): reduced public expenditure and introduced prescription charges.

1965   **National Plan** published (September): drawn up by George **Brown**, the plan committed the Labour government to the modernisation of industry and to higher levels of productivity. It amounted to little by the end of the 1960s as the Wilson governments faced serious financial and industrial relations problems.

1973   **Oil crisis**: the Arab–Israeli War was the catalyst for a significant problem for both the world economy in general and the British economy in particular. It was little less than the abrupt termination of a period of growth that, despite some ups and downs, had continued since the early 1950s. The Conservative government of Edward Heath was gravely damaged by the crisis. A fourfold increase in the price of oil led to considerable inflation in the prices of a wide variety of oil-based goods. Growth rates fell in the advanced industrial nations, and consequently unemployment accelerated. In response to rising prices in the shops, and despite growing unemployment, public sector workers demanded higher wages, leading to a worsening of industrial relations between the Heath government and the unions, particularly the coal miners. The oil crisis thus exacerbated the problems that afflicted the Heath government of 1970–74.

1973   **Purchase Tax and Selective Employment Tax** (SET) abolished to prepare the ground for Value Added Tax.

1973   **Value Added Tax** (VAT) introduced on all goods and services, as in the European Economic Community.

1975   **Capital Transfer Tax** introduced as estate duty was abolished.

1986   '**Big bang**' in the City of London: financial markets in Britain were deregulated and share transactions automated. This enabled the City to compete effectively with New York and Frankfurt, maintaining the lead of the London Stock Exchange in Europe.

1997   Power to set interest rates transferred from the Treasury to the Bank of England by the new chancellor of the exchequer, Gordon **Brown**.

Sterling

1916   Sterling pegged at $4.77 during the First World War in order to stabilise its value.

1919   The pound 'went off' the gold standard following the disruption to international currencies and markets engendered by the war of 1914–18 and by the extraordinary period of global economic readjustment that continued into the 1920s.

1925   The pound returned to the gold standard by Winston Churchill. Sterling was fixed at $4.86.

1931   The gold standard was abandoned and floating rates were introduced, as orthodox classical economics was increasingly challenged by the harsh realities of the British economy during the global downturn during the Great Depression.

1939   **Exchange rate** fixed at $4.03 as part of wartime emergency measures to assist sterling.

1944   **Bretton Woods** conference in the United States of America: accepted the principle of intervention to maintain growth rates across the global economy. Bretton Woods was a considerable triumph for John

Maynard Keynes. The conference created both the International Monetary Fund and the World Bank. The location of the conference also signalled the growing influence of the United States of America in the global economy. The American dollar became the world's leading currency, against which the value of other currencies was fixed.

1949   **Devaluation** of the pound sterling (September) to a new fixed rate of $2.80, a devaluation of 30.5 per cent.

1951   The **ROBOT** Plan for the convertability of sterling to major European currencies was mooted, illustrating that Churchill and other leading politicians and economists were prepared to entertain the notion of a single European currency.

1967   **Devaluation** of the pound from $2.80 to $2.40 (November). The devaluation was accompanied by the assurance of the prime minister, Harold Wilson, that 'the pound in your pocket' would not be reduced in value. The context was the cost of the Middle East operations, ongoing and costly industrial relations disputes, and the need to reduce the value of the pound abroad to encourage British exports.

1971   The United States ended the Bretton Woods agreement: floating exchange rates were introduced in order to allow currencies to fix upon their most competitive value rather than an artificially high one.

1971   **Decimalisation** replaced the older imperial system of 'pounds, shillings and pence' with a metric system. This was introduced in order to prepare for membership of the European Economic Community. The television played a vital role in informing the British public of how the new metric system worked.

1972   The pound was 'floated' against the value of other major currencies.

1976   **Sterling crisis** (September): the governnment was forced to adopt public expenditure cuts in order to receive a loan from International Monetary Fund (IMF). Denis **Healey** was chancellor of the exchequer.

1980   **Medium Term Financial Strategy** (MTFS) introduced to bring about a reduction in the growth of the money supply. This was a key statement of monetarism by Sir Geoffrey **Howe**, chancellor of the exchequer.

1990   Britain joined the **Exchange Rate Mechanism** (ERM), intended as a precursor to the European single currency, at the rate of 2.95 Deutschmarks (October). However, subsequent events would prove to be unhappy ones for both the pound sterling in the short to middle-term and the Conservative party in the longer term.

1992   **Black Wednesday** (September): less than six months after the general election victory of John Major, the events of Black Wednesday were personally humiliating for the chancellor of the exchequer, Norman **Lamont**, and hugely embarrassing for the Conservative government.

The pound sterling crashed out of the European Exchange Rate Mechanism as radical fluctuations in the value of the currency made membership of the ERM untenable. Sterling was supposed to track the Deutschmark in order for Britain to become ready for the Euro, something it failed to do. The legacy of this currency crisis was manifold. In the short term terrible damage was done to the reputation for fiscal management of the Conservative government. The Eurosceptic wing of the Conservative Party felt emboldened, challenging Major's leadership and exacerbating divisions within the party over Europe. In the longer term, however, Black Wednesday proved to be beneficial to the British economy, as an independent pound performed more impressively than the Euro.

1997   Power to set interest rates was transferred from the Treasury to the Bank of England by the chancellor of the exchequer, Gordon Brown.

2002   **Euro currency, coins and notes**, launched (January): twelve countries participated; Britain did not, and enjoyed higher growth rates subsequently than many EU countries. Staying out of the Euro had increased the attractiveness of the pound to overseas investors. More widely, the British economy grew more impressively than that of the Euro zone, hence the reluctance of Gordon Brown to ally the pound immediately with the Euro.

Nationalisation and privatisation

1914–18   Major industries, public transport and the hospital service came under government control until 1918 for the coordination of wartime production and the allocation of resources. The industries were returned to private hands following the war, much to the disappointment of many trade unionists. The coal mines were returned to their owners in 1921, a longer-term cause of the General Strike of 1926.

1918   The Labour Party conference (July) supported **Clause 4** of its socialist constitution, drafted by George Bernard Shaw and Sidney Webb, committing the party to nationalisation or state ownership of industry.

1926   **Electricity (Supply) Act**: established the Central Electricity Board in order to standardise and regulate the 600 electricity supply companies and the local authorities that relied upon them.

1933   **London Passenger Transport Board** set up following the London Passenger Transport Act (April). Involving the extensive transfer of private holdings into the public sector, and with a monopoly on the coordination of London transportation, the LTPB was in a sense proto-'nationalisation' at a local level. The architect of the LPTB was Herbert **Morrison**, who was instrumental in the nationalisation programme in the Attlee governments.

1940–45 To an even greater extent than the First World War, the staple industries, public transport and health services were nationalised during
the Second World War. The government controlled and coordinated
these key sectors for almost six years. George Orwell termed this 'war
socialism'.

1946 **Bank of England** nationalised (March): the state inserted itself into
the heart of the City of London. The Bank of England has remained a
government-owned and run central bank since.

1946 **Coal Industry Nationalisation Act** (July): the National Coal Board
took over responsibility for the operation of coal extraction. The
assets of 800 private colliery companies were transferred to the NCB
in January 1947 when the Act came into effect.

1947 **Electricity** taken into public ownership (August): the grid was nationalised, ending private interests in the operation of the Central
Electricity Board, established in 1926.

1948 **Inland Transport Act** came into operation (January): the private rail
companies were abolished as railways came under the penumbra of
the British Railways Board. The canals were also nationalized.

1948 **Gas industry** nationalised (May): the third energy industry to be taken
into state ownership and control.

1949 **Iron and Steel Nationalisation Bill** received royal assent (November):
the Act did not come into force until 1951.

1953 Iron and steel and road haulage denationalized by the Conservative
Government.

1967 **Iron and steel renationalized** as British Steel (July).

1971 **Rolls-Royce**, an ailing but prestigious British car brand, bought out
by government following bankruptcy.

1975 **British Leyland Motor Group** nationalised to become British Leyland:
the company made some of the most famous British marques –
Mini, Rover, Jaguar – but performance remained unimpressive.
Nationalisation was reversed by the Conservatives in 1988, by which
time British Leyland had become Rover Group.

1977 Creation of **British Aerospace**, a nationalised company comprising
the British Aircraft Corporation, Hawker Siddeley and small aircraft
manufacturers.

1977 Creation of **British Shipbuilders**, a nationalised company incorporating Cammell Laird, Swan Hunter and other shipbuilding and steel-
manufacturing companies.

1979–90s **Privatisation**: Numerous state-owned interests were targeted in the
privatisation programme of the Conservative governments and sold
wholly in one move, or partially at different times, to private investors, including British Petroleum (partially, 1979); British Aerospace
(1980); British Sugar (1981); Cable and Wireless (partially, 1981);
British Rail Hotels (1982); British Petroleum (partially, 1983); Britoil

(1983); Cable and Wireless (partially, 1983); British Telecom (1984–5); National Bus Company (1984–5); Jaguar (1984–5); Land Rover (1984–5); British Gas (1986); Royal Ordnance (1987); British Airways (1988); British Steel (1988); Rover Group (1988); Water authorities (1989–92); Electricity companies (1991–2); British Railways (1993–4); British Coal (1994).

Trade unions and industrial relations

1900   **Labour Representation Committee** (LRC) formed in London (February): it became the major vehicle for trade union representation in parliament. The LRC was made up of representatives of the **Independent Labour Party** (formed in 1893), the Fabian Society (established in 1884) and trade union leaders.

1901   **Taff Vale** case (July): the railway workers' strike against the Taff Vale Railway Company, supported by the Amalgamated Society of Railway Servants, led to the injunction against the ASRS, making it liable for damages for lost profits. Picketing was prohibited. It was an important moment in stimulating a labour consciousness in Britain.

1905   The '**Caxton Hall concordat**' endorsed stronger relations between the LRC and the parliamentary committee of the TUC.

1906   **Labour Representation Committee** renamed the Labour Party.

1906   **Trades Disputes Act** (December): reversed the Taff Vale decision by removing the liability of unions for damages during industrial action.

1909   **Osborne judgement** (December): passed against the Amalgamated Society of Railway Servants to prevent the raising of funds for political purposes. It was an attack on the funding link between trade unions and the emerging Labour Party.

1909   Miners' Federation affiliated to the Labour Party, strengthening the presence of Labour not only within the coal industry but also in the coal-mining regions.

1910–11   **Tonypandy** coal strikes in Wales (August 1910–October 1911): the Tonypandy riot occurred in November 1910, witnessing violence between miners and policemen and some retributive action on both sides.

1910–14   Significant growth in industrial conflict in Britain leading up to the First World War, particularly involving the coal miners, dockers, seamen, transport and railway workers, and engineers.

1912   **Miners' Federation** brought about a national strike for a minimum wage in the coal-mining industry (February–April).

1912   **London docks strike** (May–August): the strikers sought better working conditions and higher pay, and wanted to build upon gains made in the unionisation of dock labour since the 1880s. The strike was at its most intense in July, but was unsuccessful due to the use of 'blackleg' or 'scab' labour. The docks industry was riddled with low and irregular wages.

1913 **Trade Union Act**: reversed most of the terms in the Osborne judgement of 1909. Moreover, the payment of MPs since 1911 had facilitated the presence of Labour representatives in the House of Commons.

1914 **Triple Alliance** begun, comprised of miners, railway workers and transport workers. The alliance aspired to cross-union solidarities in industrial action.

1915–18 Campaigns by skilled trade unions on **Clydeside** and elsewhere against dilution of work and wages by conscript unskilled workers, including women. Resentment at dilution sometimes boiled over into violent disputes.

1917 **Whitley councils** established to adjudicate over wartime disputes between employers and employees. Despite the conciliatory role of the councils, they were unable to prevent many working days being lost through industrial action. The councils continued after 1918.

1919 **Red Clyde**: in the near aftermath of the Russian Revolution, Britain experienced heightened levels of industrial disputes and demonstrations against the government's economic policies.

1919 **Sankey Commission** recommended nationalisation of the coal mines as industrial relations in the coal industry remained brittle. The government returned the mines to their owners.

1921 **Black Friday** (April): following the collapse of the postwar restocking boom in 1921, the coal mining industry in Britain, which had been under government control and support during the First World War, returned to the crises that had beset the industry before 1914. Redundancies and wage cuts for thousands of miners were threatened by the employers, many of whom were landowners with coal in their estates. Consequently the **Triple Alliance**, first formed in 1914, was re-established and threatened strike action in support of the miners. The transport and railway workers, however, withdrew from negotiations. This led the Miners' Federation of Great Britain to make bitter accusations of betrayal, accusations echoed by some on the left of the Labour Party. It was a failure of solidarity, caused by the strike-breaking activities of the British government, the intransigence of coal owners and the militancy of some miners' leaders. The General Strike of 1926 witnessed a similar failure of nerve.

1926 **General Strike** (May): following prolonged industrial unrest in the coal industry, the General Strike erupted partly as a consequence of the report of the **Samuel Commission** (March), which rejected nationalisation and recommended a longer working day and wage cuts. Hence the call of the miners' leader A. J. **Cook**, 'not a penny off the pay, not a second on the day'. The coal mines were perhaps the most troubled of the staple industries during the 1920s, and were further damaged in 1925 by a reduction of subsidies to the industry and the return to the gold standard, which contributed to the uncompetitive nature of British coal exports. The Trade Union Congress (TUC) came out in support of the miners following a lock-out by owners on 1st May, thus initiating the General Strike two days later. Transport workers (including dockers), builders, printers and engineers all struck on behalf of the miners.

The government of Stanley Baldwin issued the *British Gazette*, a propaganda sheet edited by Winston Churchill, and recruited volunteers and special constables to break the strike. The army was used to maintain essential food supplies and coal. Facing a depletion of resources and fighting funds, the TUC called off the strike on 12 May, after nine days, leading to further calls of betrayal from the angry and frustrated miners. Most stayed out, but traipsed back to lower wages and longer hours in August.

1927	**Trades Disputes Act**: introduced the new condition of 'contracting in' to Labour support with the political levy. General strikes were banned.
1928–9	**Mond–Turner talks**: aimed to create a more harmonious era in industrial relations.
1931–2	The new **National Council of Labour** formalised and strengthened relations between the TUC and the Labour movement.
1932	**Cotton textiles strike** in Lancashire to oppose wage reductions.
1939–45	Trade unions incorporated into the war effort by the government. The government clamped down on the ability to strike via Defence Regulation 58aa (July, 1940), which allowed the minister of labour to prohibit industrial action. Order 1305 provided a framework in the form of the National Arbitration Tribunal for the arbitration of industrial disputes. Ernest Bevin was appointed minister of labour, providing an important figurehead for trade unionists during wartime and a sense of union representation at the highest levels of the National Government. There were strikes during wartime, however.
1942	A **miners' strike** in Betteshanger colliery, Kent, led the government to prosecute over 1,000 miners deemed to be in contravention of Order 1305. The majority of prosecutions were later withdrawn.
1944	Miners' Federation of Great Britain became the **National Union of Mineworkers**.
1946	**Trades Disputes Act** of 1927 repealed by the Attlee government.
1958	Abolition of **National Arbitration Tribunal** established by Order 1305.
1961	**National Economic Development Council** established (July): it included the TUC, employers' organisations and government in the coordinated promotion of higher levels of industrial efficiency. This

was a major innovation in the rise of national economic planning during the 1960s, influenced by French indicative planning.

1962   **National Incomes Commission** established to regulate incomes where possible. It was replaced by Labour with a Prices and Incomes Board in 1966.

1964   **Department of Economic Affairs** established: in part, it aimed for improved industrial relations in order to facilitate economic planning.

1965   The **Trades Disputes Act** gave trade unions increased legal immunities.

1966   **Seamen's strike** (May–July): a crisis in industrial relations, during which the government was forced to declare a state of emergency. The seamen returned to work without having much success. The reputation of the second Wilson government was damaged.

1968   **Donovan Report** (June): The Donovan Commission called for greater levels of voluntary agreement between unions and employers in industrial relations. This was during a period of increasing levels of wildcat strikes, spontaneous stoppages that occurred without the support of the TUC.

1969   The government White Paper *In Place of Strife* proposed more powers to prevent sporadic wildcat strikes and improve industrial relations. The initiative was dropped after TUC pressure.

1971   **Industrial Relations Act**: signalled the attempt by the Conservative government of Edward Heath to deal with industrial disputes. It introduced the National Industrial Relations Council (NIRC) and a new system of compulsory registration for unions. Labour-supporting trade unionists hated it. The views of Tory rank and filers, however, are barely recorded in the annals of industrial relations during the 1970s.

1972   **Miners' strike** (January): led to a state of emergency as power cuts and fuel shortages crippled the normal functioning of the country. Following the report of the Wilberforce Commission, meeting some of the demands of the miners, the strike was ended in February.

1974   Miners' strike (January): led to the defeat of the Conservative government at the general election (February) over the question 'who governs Britain?'

1974   **Trade Union and Labour Relations Act**: repealed the Industrial Relations Act of 1971 with the exception of the NIRC.

1974   '**Social contract**' between the Labour government and the trade unions to promote a voluntary framework for industrial relations and to encourage shop-floor restraint in pay demands.

1978–9   '**Winter of discontent**': the trade unions rejected the 5 per cent pay increase norm (October). Industrial action by unions in the public services led to a widespread perception that Britain was wracked by

Bolshevism and that Labour was unable to deal with the unions effectively.

1980 **Steelworkers' strike** led to a short-term victory for the TUC in a wage hike for the workers, but a thorough rationalisation of British Steel followed.

1980 **Employment Act**: attacked the phenomenon of 'flying pickets' by limiting picketing to the place of work only. From the point of view of the TUC it was an attack on cross-workplace solidarity.

1982 **Employment Act**: limited the scope of the 'closed shop' principle whereby workers were obliged to join a workplace union. Now a ballot indicating 85 per cent support for a closed shop was required for it to become effective.

1983 **National Union of Mineworkers** (NUM), led by Arthur **Scargill**, voted for an overtime ban as a gesture against the government's closure of pits (mines).

1984 **Government Communications Headquarters** (GCHQ), at Cheltenham, suffered a ban on trade unions by the government. Its argument was that industrial action might compromise national security, but the TUC viewed this as an infringement on the rights of workers to belong to a union.

1984–5 **Miners' strike**: following the decision of the National Coal Board (NCB) to close pits and make 20,000 miners redundant, the NUM called for a nationwide strike in the coal industry without a national ballot (March). The last of the miners' strikes was under way. The conflict became increasingly bitter, as demonstrated at the battle of Orgreave (May) during which police and miners clashed and blood was spilt. The government opposed the use of flying pickets and fined the unions for their use, while the National Coal Board adopted divide-and-rule tactics by encouraging some miners to return to work. The Independent Union of Democratic Mineworkers was established by miners in Nottinghamshire in March 1985 for those who wanted to go back to work, fatally splitting the miners' front. The miners returned to work (March) having reached no agreements with the NCB. The strike was the angry and prolonged swansong of a heroic group of workers doomed to mass redundancies through a programme of privatisation and rationalisation of production in the coal industry.

1986 **Wapping dispute**: a stand-off between the newspaper magnate Rupert Murdoch and the print unions following mass sackings of print workers and the transfer of newspaper production from Fleet Street to the docklands site. New technology was at the heart of much of the problem, as printers were increasingly facing computerised formatting and production techniques.

1986–7   **Teachers' strike**: led to disruption in schools as a white-collar sector of workers, known more for verbal militancy than a history of active confrontation, rejected a government wage settlement.

1988   **Employment Act**: allowed workers to ignore ballots for industrial action.

1990   **Employment Act**: placed further restrictions on the closed shop and on secondary supportive actions between workers.

1992   **Trade Union and Labour Relations (Consolidation) Act**: consolidated enactments relating to industrial relations, including the rights of workers in industrial disputes, and the financing and regulation of trade union funding.

1993   Government abolished twenty-six wages councils, mechanisms involved in the setting of incomes.

1994   **National Union of Rail, Maritime and Transport Workers** struck against Railtrack, the organisation responsible for maintaining the rail infrastructure in the privatised rail industry.

1996   Amalgamation of civil service unions to establish the Public and Commercial Services Union (PCSU). It was one of the last amalgamations that considerably reduced the number of trade unions over the course of the twentieth century through the creation of larger organisations.

1997   Labour government restored the rights of **GCHQ** workers to belong to a trade union.

1999   **Minimum wage** introduced at £3.60 per hour to protect and enhance the wages of the lower-paid workers in Britain. Criticism from many employers that the minimum wage would prove too costly was mostly unfounded.

1999   **Employment Protection Act**: introduced paternity leave and improved maternity leave, and allowed for union recognition in organisations of more than employees if a majority of workers were in favour.

2.4

POLITICAL HISTORY

Party politics and elections

Notes

- This section provides a general and clearly signposted overview of party politics and governments from the beginning of the twentieth century until the government of Tony Blair from 1997. It covers key events which had immediate and longer-term repercussions for the development of party politics in Britain. This first chronology, however, does not contain general elections and **by-elections**, which are given in separate time lines.
- The major political parties are discussed more fully in the **Dictionary**.
- Each politician in bold is outlined in more depth in the **Biographies**.
- Key events in party politics
- Minor parties and political groups
- General election results
- By-election results

Key events in party politics

1900   **Labour Representation Committee** (LRC) formed in London (February): this initiated the rapid rise to power of the Labour Party in twentieth-century Britain.

1901   Lord **Salisbury** resigned as leader of the Conservative Party (July), and was succeeded by his nephew Arthur **Balfour**.

1904   **Chinese slavery** issue (March): Liberal leader Henry **Campbell-Bannerman** attempted to censure Prime Minister Balfour over the exploitation of Chinese labour in South Africa. Balfour appeared heartless to many following this incident.

1905   **Sinn Féin** formed in Ireland (November): the name means 'Ourselves Alone' – a clear statement of nationalist intent.

1906   Labour Representation Committee renamed the Labour Party following its impressive showing in the general election of 1905.

1909   **People's Budget** (April): soured the already strained relations between the Liberals in the House of Commons and the Conservative majority in the Lords. Lloyd George sought to levy high taxes on landowners in order to pay for old-age pensions and the naval programme, greatly angering the landed Tory members of the **House of Lords**.

1909   People's Budget rejected by the House of Lords (November): Lloyd George had mocked the Lords in the intervening period ('a fully equipped Duke costs as much as two Dreadnoughts') and he relished the subsequent struggle with the House of Lords.

1910   Two general elections were held as a consequence of the constitutional crisis brought about by the Lords' opposition to David Lloyd George, the chancellor of the exchequer, whose People's Budget was viewed as punitive to the propertied classes.

1911   **Parliament Act** (August): emasculated the House of Lords, which lost its power of veto over legislation passed in the House of Commons.

1915   **Coalition government** formed by Asquith following the so-called shells crisis, when a shortage of shells in the trenches was blamed on the government.

1916–18 **National Government** re-formed following resignation of Asquith as prime minister (December 1916). Lloyd George became premier.

1922   **Carlton Club revolt** (October): led by Stanley Baldwin, and emboldened by the growing weakness of Lloyd George in foreign affairs, the Conservatives exited the Tory–Liberal coalition. It also led to the formation of the 1922 Committee in the Conservative Party.

1924   **Campbell case** (September): the Liberal Party withdrew its support for the minority Labour government after the prosecution of J. R. Campbell for mutiny was withdrawn.

1924   **Zinoviev letter** published (October): in order to discredit the minority Labour government in the forthcoming election, a letter was published which was purported to have been written by the head of the Communist International, Gregori Zinoviev. It incited British communists and sympathisers in the Labour movement to revolution. While it was almost definitely a forgery, the letter was avidly deployed by the Conservative press against Labour.

1925   **Plaid Cymru** formed in Pwllheli (August): a minor movement in the short term, the party gained a number of parliamentary successes in the postwar years, leading to the growth of the politics of **devolution** for Wales.

1931   Ramsay MacDonald dissolved the Labour government and formed a **National Government** (August), which won a resounding victory in the subsequent general election (October). Labour secured only 52 seats in parliament.

1934   **Scottish Nationalist Party** (SNP) formed: born out of the National Party of Scotland and the more conservative Scottish Party, it was a major landmark in the history of devolution. Although the SNP was a tiny force in British politics during the 1930s, not least because of the negative connotations associated with nationalism in that decade, its influence grew, if unevenly, from the 1960s.

1935   MacDonald left office in humiliating personal and political circumstances (June): his successor as prime minister of the National Government was Stanley Baldwin.

1940   Neville Chamberlain was forced to resign as prime minster following the Norwegian debate in Parliament (May).

1956–7 **Suez crisis** led to the eventual resignation of Anthony **Eden** as prime minister.

1962   **'Night of the Long Knives'** (July): a poorly handled and ruthless cabinet reshuffle. The newspapers viewed this as a collapse of Macmillan's image. Writing in the *Sunday Telegraph* on 22 July, for example, the satirist Peregrine Worsthorne labelled Macmillan 'his own executioner' for the brutal yet seemingly incompetent manner in which the prime minister handled the matter.

1963   **Profumo scandal** erupted (June): the 'scandal' was the sexual relationship between the minister of war, John Profumo, a man in his late forties, and a 21-year-old prostitute called Christine Keeler. She, unfortunately for someone in such a strategic position, was also involved with a Soviet naval attaché. The public wondered whether state secrets had been whispered and passed on during or just after sexual intercourse. This was the era of the Cold War, and concerns for national security merged with outrage at the extramarital affair to force Profumo's resignation on 4 June 1963. Victorian values were by no means dead. A later report by Lord Denning found that national security had not been compromised, but Profumo's name was forever to be associated with this scandal. In redemptive fashion, Profumo went on to work at Toynbee Hall in the East End of London. For the Conservative government, however, the affair was a body blow that assisted in their defeat in the general election the following year. Many people felt that the prime minister, Harold Macmillan, had appeared ineffectual in his handling of the problem.

1974   **Crowther Commission** report: entitled *Democracy and Devolution: Proposals for Scotland and Wales*, it laid the basis for subsequent legislation on devolution.

1978   **Scotland Act** and **Wales Act** both called for referendums on devolution.

1979   Referendums on devolution of political power to Scotland and Wales resulted in rejection of the principle (March). For devolution to occur, 40 per cent of the population needed to vote for it.

1981   **Limehouse Declaration** (January): made by Roy **Jenkins**, David **Owen**, Bill Rodgers and Shirley **Williams**, it effectively marked the beginning of the Social Democratic Party. Other 'defectors' from Labour to the SDP included Lord George-Brown.

1986   **Westland affair** (June): a difficult time for the Thatcher government, the affair was caused by the resignation of the secretary of state for defence, Michael **Heseltine**, over the prime minister's reluctance to countenance a European package for the Westland helicopter company.

1990   Resignation of the foreign secretary Geoffrey Howe (November) over Margaret Thatcher's attitudes towards Europe and her opposition to the **single European currency**.

1990   Resignation of Margaret Thatcher (November): following Tory rebellion in the wake of the poll tax riots, the catalyst for her resignation on 22 November was the challenge to her leadership from a 'stalking horse' candidate, in the first instance, followed by a formidable challenge from Michael Heseltine. She had already been damaged by the resignation of Geoffrey Howe on 1 November. John Major became prime minister.

1993   '**Back to basics**' speech by Major at the Conservative Party conference in Blackpool (October): advocating a return to family values, fidelity and altogether less permissiveness in private and public life, the speech was badly judged in both content and timing, coming on the eve of the revelations of **sleaze** that rocked the Tory government until 1997.

1997   Referendums on devolution of political and administrative powers to separate assemblies (September) resulted in affirmative majorities in both Scotland and Wales.

2000   Publication of **Wakeham** Report on reform of the House of Lords (January): the Blair government had already cut the number of hereditary members of the second chamber, and this commission, chaired by an ex-Conservative MP, recommended 'radical evolutionary change', with increased representation from the regions, and more elected members. The decision not to adopt a fully elected Upper House angered many MPs, however.

Minor parties and political groups

1893   **Independent Labour Party** (ILP) formed. Initially developed by Kier **Hardie**, Ramsay MacDonald and others, it became an important influence on both the reformist ideology and the personnel of the Labour Party during the first four decades of the twentieth century: it was present at the birth of the Labour Representation Committee in 1900 and became affiliated to the Labour Party in 1906. Generally to the left of the Parliamentary Labour Party, it was particularly critical of the minority Labour governments, particularly that of 1929–31, and of Ramsay MacDonald's leadership of and policies in the National Government.

1919   The **Britons** established by Henry Hamilton Beamish: an anti-Semitic group with a very small basis of support, some of it from disenchanted ex-servicemen, the Britons published the *Protocols of the*

Elders of Zion, a fictitious but marginally influential tract that believed in a global Jewish conspiracy.

1920 **Communist Party of Great Britain** (CPGB) established: the communist party was re-established the following year, becoming the major vehicle for communism in Britain. It was partly funded by the Soviet Union, and sought influence and power in trade unions, on working-class council estates, and among students and intellectuals.

1921 **National Unemployed Workers' Movement** (NUWM) established: a front organisation for the Communist Party of Great Britain, it was led by Wal **Hannington**. Its most significant phase of activity was the organisation of the hunger marches during the 1920s and 1930s. At its peak between 1931 and 1933, membership of the NUWM probably reached about 50,000 and over 380 branches, less than the claims made for it by Hannington. Hannington's *Unemployed Struggles: 1919–1936* (first published in 1936) was a first-hand account of the main marches and of the indifference of the mainstream Labour movement, as he and the CPGB saw it, to the plight of the poor. Women and men belonged to the NUWM and many women took independent action. Membership was, however, transient and comprised mostly of workers from trade unions in the depressed areas of Scotland, Wales, Northern Ireland and Northern England and other industrial centres in the Midlands and London. Historians of the NUWM are generally sympathetic to it, but not uncritically so. Condemned by the Conservative Party and the predominantly Conservative national newspapers as subversives and communists, the NUWM also received short shrift from a Labour leadership wary of association with Moscow diktats. The popularity of the movement with unemployed or vulnerable workers was at its height at the worst of the Great Depression and waned as the economy began to improve after 1933. Its revolutionary goals were certainly far removed from the consciousness and values of most working-class people.

1923 **British Fascists** (British Fascisti) established by Rotha **Lintorn-Orman** following the example of Benito Mussolini and his fascist party in Italy. Little more than a small fringe group of disillusioned ex-combatants from the First World War and a rag-tag of middle-class anti-Semitic and anti-Bolshevik activists, the British Fascists tried to play an active role in defeating the General Strike, which they saw as a conflict promulgated by a Jewish world conspiracy and communist Russia. Later in the decade the British Fascists merged with the Imperial Fascist League and during the 1930s they went on to participate in the British Union of Fascists.

1928 **Imperial Fascist League** (IFL) formed by Arnold **Leese**. It was virulently anti-Semitic and anti-communist. Some members went on to join the British Union of Fascists.

1930   **New Party** formed by Sir Oswald Mosley. Angered by the rejection of his ideas for radical intervention during the slump, Mosley formed the New Party to fight for an alternative to the laissez-faire orthodoxy and to challenge the political establishment. It had failed to make any headway by the end of 1931.

1931   **Liberal National Party** formed to support the National Government of Ramsay MacDonald. However, in 1932 the Liberal National MPs divided over those who continued to support the National Government, under Sir John **Simon**, and those who did not, led by Herbert **Samuel**. Simon served in the National Governments of the 1930s and during wartime. In 1948 the party was renamed the National Liberal Party.

1932   **British Union of Fascists** (BUF) established (October): the successor to Mosley's New Party, the BUF signalled the minor ascendancy of fascism in interwar Britain and became the largest British fascist party of the twentieth century. Members of the BUF wore black shirts, hence their nickname, and engaged in paramilitary and extra-legal violence. Initially impressed with Benito Mussolini in Italy, Mosley and the BUF adopted an increasingly anti-Semitic position as the movement turned towards Nazi Germany after 1933 for its ideological inspiration. At the heart of its programme was a fascist state, to be led by Mosley, which would subordinate industrial and working-class interests to the planned economy and suppress democratic opposition by authoritarian government. Supported for some time by Lord Rothermere's *Daily Mail* newspaper, the BUF began to lose credibility as a consequence of its intimidating and violent activities at the Olympia rally in 1934. Its reputation was also tarnished by the **battle of Cable Street** in the East End of London in 1936. The improving economy and the decline in unemployment further damaged the party's fortunes, as did growing antipathy towards Nazi Germany, Mosley's second alma mater of extremism.

1934   **Peace Pledge Union** (PPU) founded (October). Disappointment at the growing talk of war and rearmament during the 1930s led to the initial formation of the PPU. The victory of the pacifist Labour candidate over the Conservatives at the **East Fulham by-election** during the previous year had puffed wind into the sails of pacifism, although bitter political gales were blowing across Europe. The founder of the PPU was Canon Richard ('Dick') Shepherd, who had probably borrowed the practice of signing the 'pledge' against drink and gambling in churches and chapels and extended it to the pursuit of peace. Along with his supporters, for example Vera Brittain, the novelist Aldous Huxley, and George Lansbury, Shepherd also used speeches, writings and broadcasts to spread the message against rearmament and war, including the Spanish Civil War and the conflict waged by Italy in Africa. Membership of the PPU peaked at perhaps 100,000 members in 1937. Some members were arrested for selling *Peace News* during wartime and for attempting to dissuade people from engaging in military service. In the postwar period, the PPU demonstrated against the development of British atomic weapons and British involvement in wars, from the Korean War to the Falklands. It has also been at the forefront of activism against the arms trade and in organising relief for the victims of conflicts abroad. Its newspaper, *Peace News*, is still available from left-wing bookshops.

1942   **Common Wealth Party** established (July), formed by leading members of the **1941 Committee**, including J. B. Priestley, concerned at the fate of socialism and of a more radical and egalitarian vision for reconstruction during the wartime coalition. The party won three by-elections during the war but fared badly at the general election in 1945.

1948   **Union Movement** formed: a second fascist party set up by Sir Oswald Mosley from his exile in France, it proposed a united Europe and sought respectability with the British electorate, but old habits died hard. The language of racism increasingly influenced the party's rhetoric as Mosley sought to appeal to white working-class Londoners fearful at the impact on their communities of immigration. Exploiting the race riots of 1958 in North Kensington, London, Mosley stood for parliament there in 1959, but failed. Further by-election and general election gambits also ended in miserable defeat.

1954   **League of Empire Loyalists** (LEL) formed: a fascist party, it fought a number of by-elections, opposing British decolonisation. A leading member was A. K. Chesterton, whose anti-Semitism influenced both the LEL and members of other neo-fascist groups, notably the British National Party (BNP) and the National Front. Having remained largely independent of the BNP during the later 1950s and 1960s, in 1967 the LEL merged with the National Front, the successor to the BNP.

1967   **National Front** (NF) formed: a neo-fascist political party, and successor to the first British National Party (BNP). Relying upon both extra-parliamentary activities and the ballot box to maintain a very minor role on the fringe of right-wing politics, the National Front was against immigration. Its leading members included A. K. Chesterton, a long-standing anti-Semite and veteran of the League of Empire Loyalists, John **Tyndall** and Martin Webster. Both had been involved with the BNP. During the 1970s and 1980s the NF was sometimes involved in street-based demonstrations and conflicts with their Trotskyite opponents, the Socialist Workers' Party, the Workers' Revolutionary Party and other **Trotskyite communist** groupings. The NF stood over 300 candidates in the general election of 1979, but gained less than 1 per cent of the national vote.

1973   **People's Party** founded: the first major political expression of environmentalism in Britain, it was renamed the **Ecology Party** the following year. While performing poorly at general elections, the People's Party had some success at local elections from 1976 and helped to sow the seeds of green politics for the 1980s and since.

1982   **British National Party** formed by some members of the **National Front** and other fascist groupings.

1985   **Green Party**, for England and Wales, formed out of the Ecology Party. The other major but separate green parties were the Scottish Greens and Northern Irish Greens. The prevalence of green issues did not convert into significant parliamentary representation for Green parliamentary candidates.

1993   **United Kingdom Independence Party** (UKIP) established: as its name broadly hints, it called for British withdrawal from the European Union. Its leading founder was Alan **Sked**.

1993   **Referendum Party** established by Sir James Goldsmith: along with UKIP, it fought against British membership of the European Union. It was financially powerful, but failed to win any seats in the general election of 1997 and was wound up.

1996   **Socialist Labour Party** (SLP) formed by Arthur Scargill, president of the National Union of Mineworkers (NUM). Both he and the NUM were by then a much diminished force. The SLP stood more than sixty candidates in the 1997 general election on a platform that included renationalisation and withdrawal from the European Union, but none were successful.

General election results

1900 (25 September–24 October)

Party	Total votes	MPs elected	Share of total vote %
Conservatives & Unionists	1,794,444	402	51.1
Liberals	1,568,141	184	44.6
Labour	63,304	2	1.8
Irish Nationalists	90,076	82	2.5
Others	544	0	0
Total	3,519,509	670	100

Context

The Conservatives had been in power since 1895. With the Liberal Party divided over the Boer War, Lord Salisbury called a general election in order to exploit

public patriotism, hence this became known as the 'khaki election'. The first
government of the twentieth century was Tory.

Chancellors of the exchequer	Sir Michael **Hicks Beach**; Charles Thomas Ritchie; Joseph Austen **Chamberlain**
Secretary of state for foreign affairs	Marquess of Lansdowne
Secretary of state for home affairs	Charles Ritchie; Aretas Akers-Douglas

1906 (12 January–7 February)

Party	Total votes	MPs elected	Share of total vote %
Conservatives & Unionists	2,451,454	157	43.6
Liberals	2,757,883	400	49.0
Labour	329,748	20	5.9
Irish Nationalists	35,031	83	0.6
Others	52,387	0	0.9
Total	5,626,503	670	100

Context

With the Conservative Party bitterly divided over the tariff reform question,
Lord Balfour resigned (December 1905) in the hope that the general election
might unite his party. He also hoped to exploit Liberal problems over the issue
of Irish home rule. The public voted strongly against the divided Conservative
government, and Sir Henry Campbell-Bannerman became Liberal prime minister.
The growing Labour interest was clearly in evidence in this election.

Chancellors of the exchequer	Herbert Henry Asquith; David Lloyd George
Secretary of state for foreign affairs	Sir Edward Grey
Secretary of state for home affairs	Herbert Gladstone

1910 (15 January–10 February)

Party	Total votes	MPs elected	Share of total vote %
Conservatives & Unionists	3,127,887	273	46.9
Liberals	2,880,581	275	43.2
Labour	532,807	40	7.6
Irish Nationalists	126,647	82	1.9
Others	26,693	0	0.4
Total	6,667,404	670	100

Context

The Liberal government had been in power since 1906. Following the resignation of Sir Henry Campbell-Bannerman in April 1908 due to ill health, Herbert
H. Asquith became prime minister. The year also saw a transition in the character of the Liberal government, which became increasingly committed to interventionist social policies, particularly old-age pensions, national insurance and
education. Following the unprecedented rejection of the People's Budget by the
House of Lords, Asquith called a general election to seek a renewed mandate for
the New Liberal government and to push the budget through the House of
Lords. He was to be disappointed.

The Labour Party secured an impressive forty MPs to represent trade union
interests, with assistance from electoral alliances with the Liberals, while the
Irish Nationalists remained useful to the new government in maintaining a
favourable balance of power in the House of Commons.

Chancellor of the exchequer	David Lloyd George
Secretary of state for foreign affairs	Edward Grey
Secretary of state for home affairs	Winston Churchill

1910 (3–19 December)

Party	Total votes	MPs elected	Share of total vote %
Conservatives & Unionists	2,420,566	272	46.2
Liberals	2,295,888	272	43.6
Labour	371,772	42	7.1
Irish Nationalists	131,375	84	2.5
Others	8,768	0	0.2
Total	5,228,369	670	100

Context

Parliamentary politics had been in near stalemate as the Conservative-dominated House of Lords continued its stand-off with the now depleted Liberal
majority following the election of January 1910. As can be seen from the statistics, the position of the main parties in the House of Commons changed very
little, but Asquith was able to retain power with the support of the Irish
Nationalists, who remained committed to home rule. Following the election,
King George V met his pledge to Asquith to create more Liberal peers in the
Tory-dominated House of Lords. The power of the Lords to interfere with
money bills, moreover, was greatly reduced.

Chancellor of the exchequer	David Lloyd George; Reginald **McKenna**; Andrew **Bonar Law**

Secretary of state for foreign affairs   Edward Grey; Arthur Balfour
Secretaries of state for home affairs   Winston Churchill; Reginald McKenna

National Government, 1915–18

With the outbreak of the First World War in 1914, the forthcoming election was suspended. The Conservatives joined the Liberals in a coalition in May 1915. Lloyd George became minister of munitions and from December 1916, following the resignation of Asquith, served as prime minister. He was replaced by Reginald McKenna as chancellor of the exchequer. Andrew Bonar Law took over in 1916.

1918 (14 December)

Party	Total votes	MPs elected	Share of total vote %
Coalition Conservative	3,504,198	335	32.6
Coalition Liberal	1,455,640	133	13.5
Coalition Labour	161,521	10	1.5
Irish Nationalists	238,477	7	2.2
Irish Unionists	293,722	25	2.5
Sinn Féin	486,864	83	4.5
Conservatives	370,375	3	3.4
Liberals	1,298,808	28	12.1
Labour	2,385,472	63	22.2
Others	572,503	10	5.3
Total	10,766,583	707	100

Context

This was the first general election to have been held since 1910. The war had led to the elevation of Lloyd George to the premiership at the expense of an allegedly dithering Asquith, thus splitting the Liberal Party between his followers, who supported his coalition with the Conservative Party, and the 'Squiffites', who remained loyal to their former leader and unwilling to remain in coalition. The 1918 general election was thus fought between the Liberal–Tory coalition, the Liberals, and the Labour Party, which had broken from its Lib–Lab alliance to fight mostly alone. The election was termed the **coupon election** on account of the letters issued to voters by the coalition. Both Conservatives and Lloyd George Liberals in the coalition sought to profit from the popularity of the prime minister as 'the man who won the war'. The increasing divisions and violence in Ireland impacted upon Irish representation in the post-election parliament.

This was also the first general election to include women voters, albeit on a limited basis – those aged thirty or over who were property owners or wives of property owners. Previously excluded paupers were also allowed to vote.

Chancellors of the exchequer	Austen Chamberlain; Sir Robert Horne; Stanley Baldwin
Secretaries of state for foreign affairs	Sir Edward Grey; Arthur Balfour
Secretary of state for home affairs	Edward Shortt

1922 (15 November)

Party	Total votes	MPs elected	Share of total vote %
Conservatives	5,500,382	345	38.2
National Liberals (Lloyd George)	1,673,240	62	11.6
Liberals (Asquith)	2,516,287	54	17.5
Liberal total	*4,189,527*	*116*	*29.1*
Labour	4,241,383	142	29.5
Others	462,340	12	3.2
Total	14,393,632	615	100

Context

The Conservatives grew increasingly disenchanted with the coalition. As a consequence both of alleged favours for his cronies and of the **Chanak crisis**, the prime minister, Lloyd George, became viewed as a liability rather than an asset. The **Carlton Club revolt** in 1922 led to the break-up of the coalition as the Tories became convinced they could win as an independent party once more. They were right. The Liberals subsequently reconsolidated, but it was too late, and they became the third party in mainstream politics. Labour doubled its number of seats in the Commons since 1918. Andrew Bonar Law became Conservative prime minister.

Chancellor of the exchequer	Neville Chamberlain
Secretary of state for foreign affairs	Arthur Balfour; Earl **Curzon**
Secretary of state for home affairs	William Bridgeman

1923 (6 December)

Party	Total votes	MPs elected	Share of total vote %
Conservatives	5,538,824	258	38.1
Labour	4,438,508	191	30.5
Liberals	4,311,147	159	29.6
Others	260,042	7	1.8
Total	14,548,521	615	100

Context

The issue of tariff reform dominated the hastily called election of 1923 as Stanley Baldwin, who became prime minister, converted to protectionism. He was probably seeking a mandate from the British public in favour of protectionism, but he was unsuccessful. The result was inconclusive: the Tories' share of the vote remained much the same as in 1922, but they lost seats, many to the ascendant Labour Party, who agreed to form a minority government. Ramsay MacDonald became the first Labour prime minister, with early support from the Liberals. MacDonald was also foreign secretary.

Chancellor of the exchequer	Philip Snowden
Secretary of state for foreign affairs	Ramsay MacDonald
Secretary of state for home affairs	Arthur Henderson

1924 (29 October)

Party	Total votes	MPs elected	Share of total vote %
Conservatives	8,039,598	419	48.3
Labour	5,489,077	151	33.0
Liberals	2,928,747	40	17.6
Communists	55,346	1	0.3
Others	126,511	4	0.8
Total	16,639,279	615	100

Context

The election was called by MacDonald after the Liberals withdrew their support over the **Campbell case**. However, the government had been under considerable attack from the Conservative-dominated national press as well as from the Labour left, including many members of the Fabian Society and its organ the *New Statesman*. The Labour government was forced to endure a dirty-tricks campaign involving the **Zinoviev letter**, and lost the election. Baldwin became prime minister.

Chancellor of the exchequer	Winston Churchill
Secretary of state for foreign affairs	Austen Chamberlain
Secretary of state for home affairs	William **Joynson-Hicks**

1929 (30 May)

Party	Total votes	MPs elected	Share of total vote %
Conservatives	8,656,473	260	38.2
Labour	8,839,512	288	37.1
Liberals	5,308,510	59	23.4
Communists	50,614	0	0.3
Others	243,266	8	1.0
Total	22,648,375	615	100

Context

Stanley Baldwin called an election at the end of his five-year term. Memories of the General Strike lingered on in the minds of many trade unionists, and by-election results were by no means favourable for the Conservatives. The government adopted a 'safety first' approach to complement the image of the steady 'squire' Baldwin, supported by the optimistic language of 'lighthouse' and 'sunray' policies designed to appeal to aspirational suburban voters. The result was no overall majority, and for the second time during the 1920s Labour formed a minority government. Labour had by 1929 consolidated its vote in many urban industrial areas.

Chancellor of the exchequer	Philip Snowden
Secretary of state for foreign affairs	Arthur Henderson
Secretary of state for home affairs	John R. **Clynes**

1931 (27 October)

Party	Total votes	MPs elected	Share of total vote %
Conservatives	11,978,745	473	55.3
National Labour	341,370	13	1.6
National Liberals	809,302	35	3.7
Liberals	1,403,102	33	6.5
Total Nat. Govt	14,532,519	554	67.1

continued on next page

Continued from previous page

Party	Total votes	MPs elected	Share of total vote %
Opposition	486,864	83	4.5
Labour	6,649,630	52	30.6
Independent Liberals	106,106	4	0.5
Communists	74,824	0	0.3
New Party	36,377	0	0.2
Others	256,917	5	1.2
Total	21,656,373	615	100

Context

With many Labour MPs bitterly critical of the decision by Ramsay MacDonald and Philip Snowden to reduce unemployment payments, MacDonald accepted the invitation of George V (August) to form a National Government comprised mostly of Conservative MPs. The prime minister sought a mandate via a general election. Although he was successful in the short term, he did infinite damage to his long-term reputation within the Labour movement.

Chancellors of the exchequer	Philip Snowden; Neville Chamberlain
Secretaries of state for foreign affairs	Rufus **Isaacs**; John Simon
Secretaries of state for home affairs	Herbert Samuel; John **Gilmour**

1935 (14 November)

Party	Total votes	MPs elected	Share of total vote %
Conservatives	11,810,158	432	53.7
Labour	8,325,491	154	37.9
Liberals	1,422,116	20	6.4
Communists	27,117	1	0.1
Independent Labour	139,577	4	0.7
Others	272,595	4	1.2
Total	21,997,054	615	100

Context

Ramsay MacDonald left office in June 1935, and Baldwin became prime minister. Baldwin called a general election to continue the work of the Conservative-dominated National Government and also to gain a mandate for rearmament in the face of Italian fascist aggression in Europe and Africa and an increasingly warlike Nazi Germany.

Chancellors of the exchequer	Neville Chamberlain; John Simon
Secretaries of state for foreign affairs	Samuel Hoare; Anthony Eden; Lord Halifax
Secretaries of state for home affairs	John Simon; Samuel Hoare

National Government, 1939–45

General elections were suspended because of the outbreak of war. Prime ministers were Neville Chamberlain until May 1940 and Winston Churchill from 1940 to 1945. The chancellors of the exchequer were Sir Howard Kingsley **Wood** and Sir John **Anderson**. Anthony Eden was foreign secretary. Labour had refused to serve under Chamberlain but participated in the coalition under Churchill. Clement Attlee was deputy prime minister. Herbert Morrison was secretary of state for home affairs from 1942, briefly succeeded by Sir Donald Bradley Somervell following Labour's resignation from the National Government three months before the general election of 1945. Ernest Bevin was minister for labour.

1945 (26 July)

Party	Total votes	MPs elected	Share of total vote %
Conservatives	9,988,306	213	39.8
Labour	11,995,152	393	47.8
Liberals	2,948,747	12	9.0
Communists	102,780	2	0.4
Others	126,511	19	3.0
Total	16,639,279	615	100

Context

Following Labour's exit from the National Government with victory over Europe, Winston Churchill, prime minister since May 1940, called a general election for July, both in the hope of gaining a mandate for his caretaker government and in the expectation that his highly regarded service as war leader would coast him back into Number 10 Downing Street. He was wrong. The Conservative election campaign was poorly conceived, and the Labour Party achieved a momentous victory based largely on its war record and its manifesto. Clement Attlee became prime minister, and was driven to Buckingham Palace by his wife.

Chancellors of the exchequer	Hugh Dalton; Stafford Cripps; Hugh **Gaitskell**
Secretary of state for foreign affairs	Ernest Bevin
Secretary of state for home affairs	James Chuter **Ede**

1950 (23 February)

Party	Total votes	MPs elected	Share of total vote %
Conservatives	12,502,567	298	43.5
Labour	13,266,592	315	46.1
Liberals	2,621,548	9	9.1
Communists	91,746	0	0.3
Others	290,218	3	1.0
Total	28,772,671	625	100

Context

Between 1945 and the general election of 1950 Labour had introduced important welfare legislation, the National Health Service and a programme of nationalisation that created a Keynesian mixed economy. Labour defended its record and held most of its urban working-class seats, but lost many marginal constituencies.

Chancellor of the exchequer	Hugh Gaitskell
Secretaries of state for foreign affairs	Ernest Bevin; Herbert Morrison
Secretary of state for home affairs	James Chuter Ede

1951 (26 October)

Party	Total votes	MPs elected	Share of total vote %
Conservatives	13,717,538	321	48.0
Labour	13,948,605	295	48.8
Liberals	730,556	6	2.5
Communists	21,640	0	0.1
Others	177,329	3	1.0
Total	28,595,668	625	100

Context

The Labour Party was split over welfare expenditure and the financing of the Korean War. Hence Attlee went to the country to try to unite the party and gain a larger number of seats. Labour's majority was in single figures, despite an impressive share of the vote that was higher than in 1945. The Conservatives fought their campaign against Labour's apparent ineffectualness, targeting its slowness to deliver the requisite number of houses since 1945. Winston Churchill was elected as prime minister for the first time.

Chancellor of the exchequer	R. A. Butler
Secretary of state for foreign affairs	Anthony Eden
Secretaries of state for home affairs	David **Maxwell-Fyfe**; Gwilym **Lloyd George**

1955 (26 May)

Party	Total votes	MPs elected	Share of total vote %
Conservatives	13,286,569	344	49.7
Labour	12,404,970	277	46.4
Liberals	722,405	6	2.5
Communists	33,144	0	0.1
Others	313,410	3	1.1
Total	26,760,498	630	100

Context

Following the resignation of Winston Churchill, the new prime minister was Anthony Eden, who went to the country within the context of full employment, an income tax cut, the end of austerity, and the onset of enhanced affluence among the majority of the population. Eden gained the largest share of the vote of any prime minister at a general election.

Chancellors of the exchequer	Harold Macmillan; Peter Thorneycroft; Derick Heathcoat-Amory
Secretary of state for foreign affairs	Selwyn **Lloyd**
Secretaries of state for home affairs	Gwilym Lloyd George; R. A. Butler

1959 (8 October)

Party	Total votes	MPs elected	Share of total vote %
Conservatives	13,749,830	365	49.4
Labour	12,215,538	258	43.8
Liberals	1,638,571	6	5.0
Others	142,670	1	0.4
Total	27,859,241	630	100

Context

Following Anthony Eden's resignation after the Suez crisis, Harold Macmillan became prime minister. Known for his moderate views, and with economic conditions in his favour, aided by the budget of 1959, Macmillan was returned as prime minister with a comfortable majority. This third consecutive election defeat accelerated the modernisation of the Labour Party under Hugh Gaitskell, who had replaced Clement Attlee as Labour leader in 1955.

Chancellors of the exchequer	Derick Heathcoat-Amory; Selwyn Lloyd; R. A. Butler
Secretaries of state for foreign affairs	Selwyn Lloyd; Alec **Douglas-Home**
Secretaries of state for home affairs	R. A. Butler; Henry **Brooke**

1964 (15 October)

Party	Total votes	MPs elected	Share of total vote %
Conservatives	12,001,396	304	43.4
Labour	12,205,814	317	44.1
Liberals	3,092,878	9	11.2
Communists	45,932	0	0.2
Plaid Cymru	69,507	0	0.3
Scots Nationalists	64,044	0	0.2
Others	168,422	0	0.6
Total	27,655,374	630	100

Context

Harold Macmillan was succeeded by Sir Alec Douglas-Home in 1963 following the **Profumo scandal**. Parliament had almost come to the end of its maximum five-year period. Labour was now led by Harold Wilson after the death of Hugh Gaitskell in 1963; Wilson achieved a narrow but historic victory, ending thirteen years of Tory government. Race relations was an issue for the first time at this general election.

Chancellor of the exchequer	James **Callaghan**
Secretaries of state for foreign affairs	Patrick Gordon Walker; Michael **Stewart**
Secretaries of state for home affairs	Frank **Soskice**; Roy Jenkins

1966 (31 March)

Party	Total votes	MPs elected	Share of total vote %
Conservatives	11,418,433	253	41.9
Labour	13,064,951	363	47.9
Liberals	2,327,533	12	8.5
Communists	62,112	0	0.1
Plaid Cymru	61,071	0	0.2
Scots Nationalists	128,474	0	0.5
Others	201,301	2	0.6
Total	27,263,374	630	100

Context

With a majority of just four seats in the House of Commons, and as the economic news improved during the latter months of 1965 and early in 1966, Wilson went to the country to gain an increased mandate, and was successful. The new Conservative leader, Edward Heath, was relatively unknown.

Chancellors of the exchequer	James Callaghan; Roy Jenkins
Secretary of state for foreign affairs	George Brown
Secretary of state for foreign and Commonwealth affairs	Michael Stewart
Secretaries of state for home affairs	Roy Jenkins; James Callaghan

1970 (18 June)

Party	Total votes	MPs elected	Share of total vote %
Conservatives	13,145,123	330	46.4
Labour	12,179,341	287	43.0
Liberals	2,117,035	6	7.5
Communists	37,970	0	0.1
Plaid Cymru	175,016	0	0.6
Scots Nationalists	306,802	0	1.1
Others	383,511	0	1.4
Total	23,344,798	630	100

Context

Against the background of problems in industrial relations, but with economic trends apparently favourable, Harold Wilson dissolved parliament, to be surprisingly defeated by the Conservative leader Edward Heath in 1970.

Chancellors of the exchequer   Iain **MacLeod**; Anthony **Barber**
Secretary of state for foreign and
    Commonwealth affairs   Alec Douglas-Home
Secretaries of state for home affairs   Reginald **Maudling**; Robert Carr

1974 (28 February)

Party	Total votes	MPs elected	Share of total vote %
Conservatives	11,686,906	297	37.9
Labour	11,639,243	301	37.1
Liberals	6,036,470	14	19.3
Communists	32,741	0	0.1
Plaid Cymru	171,364	2	0.6
Scots Nationalists	632,032	7	2.0
National Front	76,865	0	0.3
Others GB	131,039	2	0.4
Others N. Ire.	717, 986	12	2.3
Total	31,333,226	635	100

Context

Following bitter disputes with the trade unions in the wake of Heath's attempted industrial relations reforms, the Conservatives fought the general election with the slogan 'who governs Britain?' Their defeat was unexpected given the public's weariness with strikes, although the prime minister was wounded by the three-day week and recent memories of power cuts. The trade unions gained more influence in the governance of Britain with the election of Harold Wilson as prime minister, albeit of a government with no overall majority.

Chancellor of the exchequer   Denis **Healey**
Secretary of state for foreign and
    Commonwealth affairs   James Callaghan
Secretary of state for home affairs   Roy Jenkins

1974 (10 October)

Party	Total votes	MPs elected	Share of total vote %
Conservatives	10,464,817	277	35.8
Labour	11,457,079	319	39.2
Liberals	5,346,754	13	18.3
Communists	17,426	0	0.1
Plaid Cymru	166,321	3	0.6
Scots Nationalists	839,617	11	2.9
National Front	113,843	0	0.4
Others (GB)	81,227	0	0.3
Others (N. Ire.)	702,094	12	2.4
Total	29,189,178	635	100

Context

Harold Wilson went to the country for the second time in 1974 in order to gain a majority – which was even slimmer than the one he had gained in 1964. Key issues at the election were industrial relations, and Britain and Europe. Labour offered a referendum on whether to stay in or withdraw from the European Economic Community. The Labour left (in common with the right wing of the Tory Party) was particularly keen to quit.

Chancellor of the exchequer	Denis Healey
Secretaries of state for foreign and Commonwealth affairs	James Callaghan; Anthony Crosland; David Owen
Secretary of state for home affairs	Merlyn **Rees**

1979 (3 May)

Party	Total votes	MPs elected	Share of total vote %
Conservatives	13,697,690	339	43.9
Labour	11,532,148	269	36.9
Liberals	4,313,811	11	13.8
Communists	15,938	0	0.1
Plaid Cymru	132,544	2	0.4
Scots Nationalists	504,259	2	1.6
National Front	190,742	0	0.6
Ecology	38,116	0	0.1
WRP	13,535	0	0.1
Others (GB)	85,338	0	0.3
Others (N. Ire.)	695,000	12	2.2
Total	31,220,010	635	100

Context

Recent memories of the 'Winter of Discontent' caused by industrial relations problems, unfavourable press coverage of the minority Labour government's leading politicians, notably James Callaghan and Denis Healey, and a clever campaign by the Conservatives targeting both unemployment and Labour's alleged incompetence – 'Labour isn't working' – brought the Conservatives to power. In Margaret Thatcher, Britain gained its first female prime minister.

Chancellor of the exchequer	Geoffrey Howe
Secretaries of state for foreign and Commonwealth affairs	Lord **Carrington**; Francis **Pym**
Secretary of state for home affairs	William **Whitelaw**

1983 (9 June)

Party	Total votes	MPs elected	Share of total vote %
Conservatives	13,012,315	397	42.4
Labour	8,456,934	209	27.6
Liberals	4,210,115	17	13.7
SDP	3,570,834	6	11.6
Communists	11,606	0	0.04
Plaid Cymru	125,309	2	0.4
Scots Nationalists	331,975	2	1.1
National Front	27,065	0	0.1
Others (GB)	193,383	0	0.6
Others (N. Ire.)	764,925	17	3.1
Total	30,671,1136	650	100

Context

Despite considerable economic difficulties from 1979, the Falklands War and the 'Falklands factor' it generated in 1982, in addition to a reduction in the rate of inflation, gave Mrs Thatcher a lead in the opinion polls that carried her to victory the following summer. The condition of the Labour Party, led by Michael Foot, whose manifesto was described as the 'longest suicide note in history', also assisted the Conservatives. Furthermore, the Labour vote was split by the Social Democratic Party, although combined Labour and SDP votes amounted to fewer than those polled by the Conservatives.

Chancellor of the exchequer	Nigel **Lawson**
Secretary of state for foreign and Commonwealth affairs	Geoffrey Howe
Secretaries of state for home affairs	Leon **Brittan**; Douglas **Hurd**

1987 (11 June)

Party	Total votes	MPs elected	Share of total vote %
Conservatives	13,763,066	376	42.3
Labour	10,029,778	229	30.8
Liberals	4,173,450	17	12.8
SDP	3,168,183	5	9.7
Plaid Cymru	123,599	3	0.3
Scots Nationalists	416,473	3	0.3
Others (GB)	151,519	0	0.5
Others (N. Ire.)	730,152	17	2.2
Total	32,529,568	650	100

Context

Margaret Thatcher won her third consecutive election, a feat equalled in recent times only by Tony Blair. Reasons for the Conservative victory included tax reductions in the budget and a Labour Party undergoing a slow reconstruction of its values and policies under Neil Kinnock. The centre-left vote remained sundered by the SDP. The combined results for the Liberal Party with the SDP were their best since the 1920s.

Chancellors of the exchequer	Nigel Lawson; John Major
Secretaries of state for foreign and Commonwealth affairs	John Major; Douglas Hurd
Secretaries of state for home affairs	David **Waddington**; Kenneth **Baker**

1992 (9 April)

Party	Total votes	MPs elected	Share of total vote %
Conservatives	14,082,283	336	41.9
Labour	11,559,735	271	34.4
Liberal Democrats	5,999,384	20	17.8
Plaid Cymru	154,439	4	0.5
Scots Nationalists	629,552	3	1.9
Others (GB)	436,207	0	1.0
Others (N. Ire.)	740,485	17	2.2
Total	33,612,693	651	100

Context

John Major had replaced Margaret Thatcher as Conservative leader and prime minister in 1990, following her enforced resignation. He called an election at the end of the five years of parliament as opinion polls pointed to Conservative defeat. In fact, Major gained more votes than Margaret Thatcher had managed in a single general election, although many urban marginal constituencies returned to the Labour Party. The SDP had merged with Liberals in 1988 to become the Liberal Democrats.

Chancellors of the exchequer	Norman Lamont; Kenneth **Clarke**
Secretary of state for foreign and Commonwealth affairs	Douglas Hurd; Malcolm **Rifkind**
Secretary of state for home affairs	Kenneth Clarke; Michael **Howard**

1997 (1 May)

Party	Total votes	MPs elected	Share of total vote %
Conservatives	9,600,940	165	30.7
Labour	13,517,911	419	43.2
Liberal Democrats	5,243,440	46	16.8
Plaid Cymru	161,030	4	0.5
Scots Nationalists	622,260	6	2.0
Referendum	811,827	0	2.6
Others (GB)	549,874	1	1.7
Others (N. Ire.)	790,778	18	2.5
Total	31,287,702	635	100

Context

After almost eighteen years as an opposition party, Labour achieved its third largest share of the vote in its history to gain power with a huge majority. The avowedly centrist New Labour model developed by Tony Blair, now prime minister, Gordon Brown and others swept aside a Conservative government widely perceived as arrogant, incompetent and mired in sleaze.

Chancellor of the exchequer	Gordon Brown
Secretary of state for foreign and Commonwealth affairs	Robin **Cook**
Secretary of state for home affairs	Jack **Straw**

By-election results

1922 Newport	The Conservatives defeated the Liberals, encouraging the Tories to leave the coalition (October).
1931 Westminster	The Conservatives defeated the Empire Crusade Party, encouraging the party to countenance protectionism (March).
1933 East Fulham	A pacifist Labour candidate defeated the Conservatives during the year the Nazis came to power. Housing and unemployment, however, were also key issues at this by-election (October).
1938 Oxford	An Independent Progressive challenge to the Conservatives failed as appeasement became the major issue at the by-election (October).
1938 Bridgewater	An Independent Progressive defeated the Conservatives as appeasement continued to divide the country (November).
1942 Grantham	An independent candidate defeated the Conservatives, indicating the unpopularity of the party with many among the electorate (March).
1942 Maldon	Labour defeated the Conservatives despite the dominance of the Tories in a wartime coalition with Winston Churchill as prime minister (June).
1943 Eddisbury	The Common Wealth Party won its first election victory; the party was mostly a wartime phenomenon, however (April).
1945 Motherwell	The Scottish Nationalist Party (SNP) won its first by-election victory and gained a seat from Labour three months before the Labour landslide at the general election (April).
1957 Lewisham	Labour narrowly defeated the Conservatives in this inner suburb; the **Rent Act** rather than the Suez crisis was the reason (February).
1958 Torrington	The first Liberal victory at a by-election since the 1920s (March).
1962 Orpington	A Liberal victory in a safe Tory seat in the London–Kent suburban commuter belt (March).
1965 Leyton	Labour's foreign secretary, Patrick Gordon Walker, lost this by-election in the year following his defeat in Smethwick at the general election (January).
1965 Roxburgh etc.	The Liberal candidate David Steel took a safe Conservative seat, becoming the youngest member of the House of Commons (March).

1966	Carmarthen	The first victory by Plaid Cymru at a by-election (July).
1967	Hamilton	The first postwar victory of the SNP (November).
1968	Dudley	A large swing to the Conservatives against Labour in an urban constituency in the West Midlands two years before the Tories' general election victory (March).
1972	Rochdale	A Liberal victory in a northern industrial town where Labour had been in power (October).
1973	Sutton and Cheam	A Liberal victory in a suburban Conservative seat (March).
1973	Lincoln	The Labour maverick Dick Taverne won the seat as a 'Democratic Labour' candidate in the city where he had been a Labour MP (March).
1973	Glasgow Govan	An SNP victory, increasing the nationalist pressure for devolution (November).
1976	Walsall North	A safe Labour seat was won by the Conservatives on a swing of almost 23 per cent. The reputation of Labour's John Stonehouse influenced the result (November).
1979	Liverpool Edge Hill	A Liberal victory with a swing of over 32 per cent in a safe Labour seat in the Lancashire port city (March).
1981	Crosby	The Social Democratic Party (SDP), with Shirley Williams as candidate, won its first by-election victory in the Liverpool suburb, a safe Conservative seat (November).
1983	Glasgow Hillhead	The SDP candidate Roy Jenkins gained the seat from the Conservatives, the second by-election victory for the Social Democrats (March).
1987	Ryedale	The SDP gained a seat from the Conservatives for the third time in a 1980s by-election (May).
1987	Greenwich	The SDP gained a seat from the Labour incumbent in a relatively safe Labour seat (February).
1987	Glasgow Govan	The SNP gained the seat from Labour with swing of over 33 per cent (November).
1989	Vale of Glamorgan	Labour gained the seat from the Conservatives (May).
1990	Mid Staffordshire	Labour gained the seat from the Conservatives in its best postwar by-election result (March).
1990	Eastbourne	The Liberal Democrats gained a seat from the Conservatives in their first by-election victory (October).

1991 Ribble Valley		The Liberal Democrats gained the seat from the Conservatives in the aftermath of the poll tax debacle (March).
1993 Newbury		The Liberal Democrats gained the seat from Conservatives with a swing of 29 per cent in a southern country town, normally safe Tory territory. It was the first by-election since the general election the previous year (May).
1993 Christchurch		The Liberal Democrats gained the seat from Conservatives in a southern country town; the swing was a huge 36 per cent (July).
1994 Eastleigh		The Liberal Democrats gained the seat from Conservatives in another southern country town with a sizeable swing of 21 per cent (June).
1995 Dudley West		Labour gained a seat from Conservatives with a swing of 29 per cent (December).
1995 Perth and Kinross		The SNP gained the seat from the Conservatives as nationalism grew while the Tory vote plummeted in Scotland during the 1990s (May).
1997 Winchester		The Liberal Democrats won the seat soundly following a disputed general election victory (May).

2.5

BRITAIN AND THE WIDER WORLD

Notes

Despite a century of diminishing influence overseas as a consequence of decolonisation, Britain retained its position as a leading European power. It played a fundamental role in the extinguishing of fascism and militarism in two world wars, and a key part in establishing the United Nations. Eclipsed by the USSR and the USA following 1945, Britain nevertheless remained an important player in world affairs. The special relationship with the United States was essential to this, while sometimes coming under strain. Britain's relationship with Europe, however, was more nuanced still, as will become apparent from the following chronologies:

- Decolonisation and the Commonwealth
- Wars and conflicts
- Defence policy
- Britain and European integration.

Decolonisation and the Commonwealth

1910   **South Africa** gained dominion status within the British Empire, eight years after the end of the Boer War.

1916   **Easter rising** (April): evidenced growing nationalist Irish anger at being part of Britain. Irish nationalists were divided between those who wanted outright independence, and those who might have settled for dominion status.

1916   Formation of Indian Independence Society, a leading mover in which was Annie **Besant**, who campaigned fervently in Britain for India's right to separate from the British Empire.

1916–21   **Anglo-Irish War** (or War of Independence in Ireland): led to the partition of Ireland in 1921 (December).

1917   **Balfour Declaration** (November): a year before the ending of the First World War, the British foreign secretary, Arthur Balfour, issued a communication to Lord Rothschild, a leading Anglo-Jewish businessman and landowner, supporting the establishment of a Jewish homeland in Palestine. Palestine had been Turkish-administered for many centuries until the British defeated the Ottomans there during the war. Balfour had insisted upon a number of conditions to ensure the rights of Palestinians as Jews began to move there in large numbers. During the 1930s, many politicians and commentators in Britain articulated their fear at the consequences of the Jewish migration to a predominantly Muslim region. With the Ottoman Empire in ruins, Palestine became British mandated territory following the League of Nations conference at San Remo in 1920.

1919   **Montagu-Chelmsford reforms** (March): drawn up by Edwin Montagu, the secretary of state for India, the reforms created autonomous provinces in India which were given a limited measure of self-government.

1919   **Rowlatt Acts** (March): passed to clamp down on independent Indian political activities viewed as subversive to British rule and to law and order.

1921   **Anglo-Irish Treaty** (December): brought about the partition of Ireland into the Southern Irish Free State and the six-counties compromise in Northern Ireland, which eventually led to the Troubles.

1922–3   **Irish Civil War** (*Cogadh Cathartha na hÉireann*): in the wake of the Anglo-Irish Treaty civil war broke out in June 1922 and continued for ten months.

1927   **Balfour Report**: recommended the use of the term 'British Commonwealth of Nations' as an alternative to 'British Empire'.

1933   **Arab boycott** of British goods in Palestine (February): indicated strengthening of Arab hostility to the British support for a Jewish homeland.

1937   The **Peel Commission** recommended the partition of Palestine (July): the British government continued to investigate further the possibility of partition of the Arab and Jewish populations in Palestine, but the outbreak of the Second World War ended this momentum.

1930s   Mahatma Gandhi campaigned in Britain for Indian independence, adopting a dignified strategy of non-violence. Winston Churchill was critical of Gandhi to the point of racism.

1942   The Mission of Sir Stafford Cripps to India during the Second World War offered the Indians dominion status once the war was ended. This was rejected by both Indian nationalists and communists.

1947   **India** granted independence, the largest of the countries in the British Empire to do so in the postwar period.

1947   **Pakistan** granted independence. Unlike India, Pakistan was a predominantly Muslim state, and the rationale for the partition of India owed much to religious questions. Jinnah became prime minister of Pakistan.

1948   Ceylon (Asia) granted independence.

1948   Burma (Asia) granted independence.

1948   **Israel** declared as a Jewish nation-state, ending the status of Palestine as a British protectorate.

1949	**Ireland** (Éire) withdrew from the Commonwealth and became the independent Republic of Ireland.
1949	The term 'British Commonwealth' was replaced by the less Anglo-centric 'Commonwealth'.
1950	India became the first ex-colony to join the Commonwealth.
1952	Mau Mau insurrection in Kenya (Africa) began the state of emergency and a conflict that lasted for eight years.
1956	Suez crisis proved to be a major blow to British interests in the Middle East.
1956	Mau Mau insurrection in Kenya contained.
1957	Ghana became the first British colony in Africa to gain independence.
1957	Malaya (Asia) gained independence.
1958	West Indies Federation (Caribbean) formed.
1960	Harold Macmillan made '**wind of change**' speech (February). Reflecting on African nationalism to the South African parliament, Macmillan accepted the inevitability and acceleration of African decolonisation.
1960	Cyprus (Europe) gained independence.
1960	Nigeria (Africa) gained independence.
1960	Tanganyika (Africa) gained independence.
1961	South Africa withdrew from the Commonwealth.
1961	Tanganyika (Africa) gained independence.
1961	British Cameroon (Africa) gained independence.
1961	Sierra Leone (Africa) gained independence.
1962	Trinidad and Tobago and Jamaica (Caribbean) left the West Indian Federation.
1962	Western Samoa (Asia) gained independence.
1962	Uganda (Africa) gained independence.
1963	Zanzibar (Africa) gained independence.
1963	Kenya (Africa) gained independence.
1964	Commonwealth Secretariat established (December) to improve administration and promote new initiatives to enhance cooperation between member states.
1964	Malta (Europe) gained independence.
1965	Rhodesia (Africa) made Unilateral Declaration of Independence.
1966	Basutoland (Africa) gained independence.
1966	Bechuanaland (Africa) gained independence.
1966	British Guyana (Caribbean) gained independence.
1966	Barbados (Caribbean) gained independence.
1967	Aden (Africa) gained independence.
1968	Mauritius (Asia) gained independence.
1968	Swaziland (Africa) gained independence.
1970	Fiji (Asia) gained independence.

1970	Tonga (Asia) gained independence.
1972	Bangladesh (formerly East Pakistan) gained independence from Pakistan.
1973	Bahamas (Caribbean) gained independence.
1974	Grenada (Caribbean) gained independence.
1975	Papua New Guinea (Asia) gained independence.
1976	Seychelles (Asia) gained independence.
1978	Dominican Republic (Americas) gained independence.
1979	Rhodesia (now Zimbabwe) settlement reached, following guerrilla warfare between fighters for Zimbabwean independence.
1980	Zimbabwe gained independence
1981	Belize (South America) gained independence.
1982	Maldives Islands (Asia) gained independence.
1984	Brunei (Middle East) gained independence.
1984	Sino-British agreement on the future of Hong Kong (Asia): the agreement was opaque about democracy, while ensuring a capitalist economic base for Hong Kong.
1987	Fiji left the Commonwealth following a military coup.
1988	Namibia (Africa) gained independence, becoming the fiftieth member of the Commonwealth.
1990	**British Nationality Act (Hong Kong)**: extended British citizenship to elite Hong Kong Chinese, for example professionals, business people and others who might create wealth or meet skills shortages in Britain.
1994	South Africa rejoined the Commonwealth. Over three years after the release of Nelson Mandela in 1990, South Africa held free elections in 1994.
1997	**Hong Kong** handed back to China (July) as Hong Kong mandate ended.

Wars and Conflicts

1899–
1902   **Boer War**: also called the South African War. The conflict was fought between the superior forces of the British Army and the Boers, the Afrikaans-speaking descendents of Dutch settlers, most of whom were still farmers and small traders. The Boers gained considerable support from the Germans and other nations seeking to undermine British imperial authority in Africa. Fearful of British attempts to annex their territories of the Orange Free State and the Transvaal, the Boers fought a sometimes devastating guerrilla campaign. Led by Lord **Kitchener**, British forces gained a number of significant and much celebrated victories, notably the relief of Ladysmith and Mafeking and the fall of Pretoria in 1900. The war finally came to an

end following the Treaty of Vereeniging in 1902. From the British point of view, these were welcome triumphs amid a conflict that worried politicians in the world's leading imperial nation. One source of concern was the appalling deaths and diseases suffered by Boers in the British concentration camps: these were both a humanitarian and a global public relations disaster.

1914–18 **First World War**: sparked by the assassination of Archduke Ferdinand of Austria, the First World War began in August 1914 and ended on the eleventh hour of the eleventh day of the eleventh month in 1918. Among the most significant land battles involving British military forces against the Germans were the Somme (1915), Ypres (1916) and Paschendaele (1917), while the battle of Jutland (1916) was the most significant battle at sea. Appalling slaughter and loss of limb occurred in the trenches of the Western Front, and the use of mustard gas and tanks for the first time greatly increased the suffering and mortality. 'Shell-shock' was a war-induced mental illness from which thousands of servicemen suffered. The so-called Great War was also the first in the twentieth century in which the British mainland was attacked from both air and sea. German ships attacked east coast ports from the North Sea, for example, while London was subjected to Zeppelin bombing and raids by Gotha airplanes. Over 670 people were killed in London by aerial attack between 1915 and 1918. In total, British and British Empire mortalities totalled more than 900,000. Over 2 million were wounded.

1916–21 **Anglo-Irish War**: begun with the Easter rising in April 1916 and concluded by the Anglo-Irish Treaty in December 1921, the conflict in Ireland led to the increased conscription of British troops, as the British Army was also engaged in the trenches of the First World War. Atrocities were committed by both the Republican Sinn Féin forces and the Black and Tans unit of the Royal Irish Constabulary. The treaty established the Irish Free State. (Given the close relationships between Britain and Ireland, and the fact that the war was fought on British soil until 1921, **Ireland and Britain** warrants an extended narrative history: see Dictionary.)

1918–19 **Russian Civil War**: an ultimately futile British intervention in the conflict between the 'Reds' and the 'Whites'. Hoping to undermine the Bolsheviks by supporting the counter-revolutionary Whites, Winston Churchill ordered the dispatch of British troops to accompany American and French forces. Many British lives were lost, Bolshevik rule was strengthened, and the British withdrew during the summer of 1919.

1919 **Third Afghan War** (May): the British presence in northern India was deeply resented by the Islamic leader Amir Amanullah, who declared *jihad* or holy war on Britain and invaded the neighbouring country. The superior forces of the British Army and the RAF suppressed the Afghan revolt, which was formally ended by the Treaty of Rawalpindi in August.

1919   **Amritsar massacre** (April): a key moment in the worsening of relations between the Indian population and the British Raj. The passage of the **Montagu-Chelmsford reforms** and the **Rowlatt Acts** in 1919 caused great anger among millions of Indians, who felt that the assistance that India gave to Britain during the First World War had been betrayed by only timid moves towards greater self-determination. Tensions in the Punjab grew, and as violence increased the British Army garrison opened fire on a crowd of protesters. About 380 Indians were killed and over 1,200 injured. Brigadier-General Dyer, who gave the order to fire, was subsequently relieved of his command.

1939–45   **Second World War**: over 388,000 British people were killed during the war; 62,000 of these were civilian deaths. The declaration of war on Germany was made by Neville Chamberlain on 3 September 1939, cruelly exposing the failure of appeasement against the cynical and irrational use of diplomacy and force by Nazi Germany. In Western Europe, the German Blitzkrieg subjugated Belgium, France, Holland and other democracies to occupation by May 1940, while Italy, a fascist power, was allied with the Nazis. Britain stood alone until the Soviet Union took up arms against Germany in June 1941. The entry of the USA into the war following the attack by the Japanese in December 1941 was also hugely significant. The effect of other countries in Western Europe proved negligible, however. Spain and Portugal were both fascist dictatorships, professing neutrality. Other neutral countries were democracies, but they made at best a peripheral contribution to British morale and war activities, and many people in those countries – for example, Ireland, Sweden and Switzerland – were sympathetic to the Nazis. It was thus a great and justifiable source of national pride that Britain withstood Nazi invasion during the difficult years of 1940 to 1941 in the battle of Britain and the Blitz.

1939   **Evacuation**: among the major disruptions to people's lives during wartime, evacuation remains the most poignant. It began on the eve of war, and was maintained, despite the unwarranted return of some evacuees to their homes, or what was left of their homes, during the conflict. Over 3.5 million people were evacuated, the majority of whom were mothers and children. Some children went alone or with other siblings, but all were uprooted from their homes or institutions in the industrial cities and moved away to relative safety. Metropolitan suburbs, provincial towns and villages were the most likely destinations, but many children were shipped overseas to the

United States and Canada via the US committee for the evacuation of European children. Thousands were also evacuated to South Africa and other dominions. Within Britain, a class divide existed among evacuees. Middle-class parents were much more able to arrange for their children to stay with family or friends living in the suburbs or in locations away from the big cities, while working-class children and their mothers were much more likely to be evacuated to the official reception areas. Many working-class evacuees were billeted with wealthier households. Several Labour politicians and social reformers felt that this narrowing of the class divide helped to bring about a new 'rediscovery' of poverty that helped to explain Labour's victory at the general election of 1945.

1939–40 **Phoney war**: during the early months following the declaration of war the term 'phoney war' was coined by a visiting American journalist who was somewhat puzzled and perhaps even disappointed at the lack of action to report back to the USA. From September 1939 to May 1940 the home front was not attacked in any significant way. However, the battle of Britain from May 1940 brought the phoney war to the beginning of its end, an end confirmed by the defeat at Dunkirk, also in May 1940. With the Blitz on London from September 1940, British civilians were now direct targets of the Nazi war machine. The phoney war was decidedly over.

1940 **Battle of Britain**: 'Never in the field of human conflict has so much been owed by so many to so few' was Churchill's much-quoted judgement on the aerial conflict that was fought out in the skies over Britain from early summer to October 1940. As the Luftwaffe's planes swarmed into British airspace, Royal Air Force Hurricanes and Spitfires defended the country against a numerically superior enemy. Over 1,200 German aircraft were lost compared with 800 British planes. More than 500 allied pilots lost their lives, but all became heroes. Both during the war and afterwards many pilots involved in the battle of Britain carefully crafted an image of casual bravery along the lines of 'It was nothing, old chap'. Victory against the odds was of course an enormous and a morale-boosting relief, but it also led to a further alteration in German tactics. As the number of dogfights petered out in the autumn of 1940, the Nazi air campaign shifted to the mass bombardment that became known as the Blitz.

1940–41 The **Blitz**: The aerial bombardment of Britain during the Second World War, notably the phase of sustained attacks from September 1940 to May 1941. Derived from the German word 'Blitzkrieg', meaning 'lightning war', the Blitz encompasses and describes the German aerial bombardments from 1940 to 1945. It was the most visible and terrifying visitation of the war on the home front. The most sustained periods of bombing were from September 1940 to

November 1940 in London, and from November 1940 to May 1941 in London and other British cities and towns. There were small-scale blitzes in 1942, and the so-called Baedeker raids occurred when the Luftwaffe bombed some of England's most attractive historic provincial towns and cities. And in 1944 and 1945 the pilot-less **V1** rockets and **V2** missiles unleashed new technologies of death and destruction upon the stoic but war-weary British.

Aerial bombardment had first occurred during the First World War, when Zeppelins attacked London and other areas of Eastern England and Gotha fighter planes had also terrified the capital. Civil defence planning for possible aerial attack initially began during the 1920s, as tensions continued in Europe. Its intentions were revealed by the infamous prediction of the Conservative leader Stanley Baldwin in 1931 that 'the bomber will always get through'. Certainly military strategists and politicians feared that mass bombings might paralyse cities, kill or maim thousands of people, and shatter the morale of the citizens, who would be reduced to anarchy, chaos and submission until the ground forces rolled in to conquer and take control. They were wrong. The blitzing of East London on 7 September 1940 finally ended the so-called **phoney war**, but the subsequent raids failed to stop the capital from functioning or its people from defying their hated antagonist.

The East End of London was worst hit. The City of London, close to the East End, was heavily blitzed: a third of its buildings was damaged or destroyed. The Houses of Parliament were severely damaged in places, as were many other iconic buildings in Central London. The suburbs did not escape either. The London County Council's bomb damage maps at the London Metropolitan Archive, for example, detail the devastation. Elsewhere in Britain, the larger industrial centres were heavily bombed as the Nazis attempted to disrupt war production and to demoralise the British people. The city of Coventry in the English Midlands, notably, saw its centre almost completely obliterated in the raids in November 1940, and many of the larger port cities were also attacked in order to break up supply lines. In total about 60,000 people were killed in Britain by bombing raids between 1940 and 1945 and nearly 2 million were made homeless. The V1 rockets took a particular toll in 1944: they were responsible for the deaths of over 5,400 Londoners. The V2s that followed were less successful but deadly when they hit their targets. London's built environment suffered greatly: over 100,000 buildings were destroyed or damaged beyond repair, and more than 1 million were damaged to lesser degrees. Other cities suffered too from heavy damage: Liverpool and Birkenhead, for example, had over 7,300 dwellings damaged or destroyed.

But some good did come of the Blitz. Many slums and poor housing areas were too badly damaged for *ad hoc* repairs, and during the process of reconstruction new housing was built in the inner cities. However, much of the new housing was unpopular. Furthermore, the war witnessed the planned dispersal of over 3 million people through evacuation schemes. The principle of dispersal from the overcrowded urban industrial city centres echoed the planned programme of new towns from 1946. The Blitz also assisted the adoption of modern architecture in Britain.

1944–5 **V1** and **V2** pilot-less missile and rocket attacks on Britain: discharged from mobile rocket launchers in the Netherlands, the attacks came in the final phases of the war, when the Allies were approaching victory, lending an added poignancy to the deaths from Nazi technology.

1945–6 **Vietnam**: it was impossible for France to police its entire empire after the war, so Britain played a major role in Vietnam between September 1945 and March 1946. Nearly forty service personnel were killed, mostly from the Commonwealth, and the defeated Japanese were used to instil order among the Vietnamese population.

1945–8 **Palestine conflict**: a British protectorate under the League of Nations, Palestine had witnessed the in-migration between the wars of thousands of Jewish refugees from Nazi Germany and elsewhere. Israel increasingly became a site of Zionist struggle for an independent Jewish state, and in the immediate aftermath of the Second World War Jewish 'terrorists' (from the British point of view) waged a guerrilla war to that end. The bombing of the King David Hotel, in July 1946, was the most extreme of the attacks on British interests: more than ninety people were killed, but others lost their lives in other atrocities committed by the Israelis. The state of Israel was declared in May 1948, leading to British withdrawal. Between 1945 and 1948 Britain spent over £200 million on the conflict, sending in 100,000 troops. Casualties were high: more than 170 British troops died in 1947–8.

1948–60 **Malayan emergency**: Malaya left the British Empire in February 1948, one of a number of early acts of postwar decolonisation. British military involvement in Malaya began with the state of emergency in June and aimed to prevent the spread of communism in the Burmese Federation. The emergency ended in July 1960, the communist-backed forces having been largely removed.

1950–53 **Korean War**: conflict erupted in June 1950 between Soviet-supported North Korea and the American-backed Republic of Korea in the South, when the former invaded the latter. British troops were sent to assist the USA in late August and formed part of the United Nations forces that entered North Korea in October 1950, although the American military presence was the largest. Fighting between UN and communist forces led to over 1,700 British killed or missing and 2,500 wounded. The Korean War was the first defining major conflict of the Cold War.

1952   The **Mau Mau** insurrection in Kenya (Africa) began a state of emergency and a conflict that lasted for eight years.

1956   **Suez crisis**: in July 1956 President Nasser of Egypt had nationalised the Suez Canal Company, to the chagrin of the French and British interests in this hugely important waterway between Europe and the Middle East. His pretext was the need for dues to pay for the Aswan Dam. Increasing tensions between the Egyptian president, who was viewed as something of a neo-fascist dictator by the prime minister, Anthony Eden, and Britain and France were exacerbated by the hostility between Egypt and Israel. Britain sought to exploit an Israeli contretemps with the Egyptians, which led to British and French forces attacking military bases in Egypt. The United States of America was highly critical of the Anglo-French actions, and the reputation of the British government plummeted. Soviet Russia supported Egypt, thus strengthening its presence in the Middle East. The crisis led to the resignation of Eden. It also temporarily damaged the special relationship between Britain and the USA, which Harold Macmillan, who took over as prime minister from Eden, assiduously rebuilt with President Eisenhower in the aftermath. Historians of the Suez crisis also explore its repercussions for Britain's reputation overseas and how it exposed London's weakness in international relations when compared with Moscow or Washington, DC. The debacle became synonymous with British imperial decline.

1961   **Kuwait intervention** (July): British forces prevented an Iraqi invasion of Kuwait.

1961   **Kenyan state of emergency** lifted by the British after eight years of violence. The Kikuyu tribe led the Mau Mau rebellion against white British and European rule. More than thirty whites were killed, but over 11,000 black Africans died. The Mau Mau themselves killed more blacks that whites, but the British also put suspected terrorists to death. In 2006 a delegation to Britain of Mau Mau veterans claimed they had been the victims of a systematic campaign of rape and torture by the British Army, a claim contested by the government.

1968   The Troubles began in Northern Ireland, spreading during the 1970s to England following the intervention of British troops in 1969. Given that the Troubles occurred on UK soil and were a prolonged and painful conflict in recent British history, a fuller narrative account is provided in the Dictionary.

1982   **Falklands War** (April–June): The Falklands had been a British colony since the 1830s. For many years Argentina had claimed that the islands, sovereign British territory in the South Atlantic Ocean, were Argentinian. Tensions had long been in evidence between Britain and the Latin American power, and in 1977 the Labour government warned off a possible Argentinian raid on the islands by sending a nuclear submarine. But the invasion of the islands on 2 April 1982 by the conscript forces of a right-wing dictatorship was mostly unexpected, and was certainly resented by the 2,000 Falkland Islanders themselves. In response, Margaret Thatcher's government hastily assembled a 'task force' to remove the Argentinian military. Following a courageous and skilful British military campaign, involving land, sea and air, the islands were recaptured. The Union Jack was flying again in Port Stanley, the capital of the Falklands, by mid-June. Almost a thousand men lost their lives from both sides, and hundreds were injured.

The Argentinian annexation of 'the Malvinas' provoked outrage among millions of British people, and victory became a source of patriotic pride. Such pride was expressed in ebullient tabloid headlines, increased sales of alcohol and huge gatherings at the ports to welcome home the returning heroes. The left saw the Falklands War and its accompanying behaviour as unpleasant jingoism. Hence when the Argentinian cruiser the *General Belgrano* was sunk on 2 May by HMS *Conqueror* as it operated away from the theatre of conflict, killing over 360, some were quick to condemn the British military and the government that exonerated it, despite the *Belgrano*'s exocet missile capabilities. One woman member of the public famously embarrassed Margaret Thatcher when talking about the *Belgrano* incident on a live television interview during the general election campaign. Critics of the war, however, were mostly silent about the British servicemen who were injured or killed. Hence Conservatives contrasted what they saw as the glorious victory of 1982 with the pessimism and unpatriotic positioning associated with the left of the Labour Party. Yet throughout the crisis the Labour leader Michael Foot offered mostly uncritical support to the government.

1991   **Gulf War**: although Britain was uninvolved in the liberation of Kuwait from the Iraqi dictatorship, it gave strong support via the United Nations to the United States of America. The conflict may be viewed as the first of two Gulf Wars: the second was the war in Iraq from 2003.

Defence policy

1904   ***Entente cordiale*** (April): the Anglo-French *entente* of 1904 was agreed during a period of rising international tensions within Europe. As the continent moved towards a series of alliances between the Great

Powers, Britain and France sought to solve significant mutual disagreements between the two countries over territories in Africa and Asia. For much of the nineteenth century, official and public opinion in Britain was often anti-French and pro-German. However, the rise of German military might following the unification of the country in 1871, and growing German influence in Africa, presented Britain and France with an interest to develop more cordial international relations, and the two nations agreed to be allies to each other in the event of a major conflict with their Teutonic rival.

1905   **Morocco crisis** (March): Germany's challenge to French rule in Morocco was also intended test the *entente cordiale*, but both Britain and France held firm in mutual support.

1906–8   **Haldane reforms**: As secretary of state for war, **Haldane** established the British Expeditionary Force (BEF) and the Officer Training Corps. He also reorganised the military reserve of the British Army, creating the Territorial Army and increasing the number of men available for military conflict.

1906   HMS *Dreadnought* launched by the Royal Navy (February): it was a key moment in the Anglo-German naval race.

1907   **Anglo-Russian** *entente* over spheres of influence in Asia (August): Britain had been fearful of a Russian invasion of India.

1909   **Navy Act** introduced dreadnoughts, a superior generation of battleships. There was considerable argument in government and in the Royal Navy about the number of required. Four were commissioned in March, and four later in the year as concern mounted over the rise of German naval power.

1912   **Royal Flying Corps** established, signifying the growing awareness of air power and its military significance.

1914   **Defence of the Realm Act** (August): empowered government to take control of key industries, and to control the media and other areas of social and economic life.

1915   **Munitions of War Act**: the government took control of the munitions industry, suspending normal industrial relations. Labour resources were critical: hundreds of thousands of women worked in munitions by 1918, making an essential contribution to munitions production yet provoking fears of dilution of wages and working conditions among many male trade unionists.

1915   **Treaty of London** (April): signed in secret by Britain, France, Russia and Italy, the treaty guaranteed Italy significant territorial gains on the condition it switched allegiance from the Central Powers to the Allies. This occurred, but following the war, as a consequence of various renunciations of the conditions of the treaty from Soviet Russia and the USA, Italy gained much less of the Adriatic lands than it wanted. Anger and disappointment in the country contributed to the rise of Italian nationalism and fascism.

1916   The **Military Service Bill** (January) introduced conscription to twentieth-century Britain. The unwitting testimony of the Bill, introduced by the prime minister, H. H. Asquith, was that earlier expectations of a short-lived war were shattered. It applied to single men aged from eighteen to forty-one but was extended in May 1916 in the light of new pressures in Ireland. Conscription was lifted in 1920.

1918   **Royal Air Force** (RAF) formed from the merger of the Royal Flying Corps and the Royal Naval Air Service: overseen by the Air Ministry, it became independent of both the army and the navy. During the 1920s, and for most of the 1930s until the latter stages of rearmament in the lead-up to the Second World War, as military and political understanding of the potential of aerial attacks on Britain grew, the RAF remained small. Its much vaunted 'finest hour' during the battle of Britain was dependent upon the rapid supply of Spitfire and Hurricane fighter planes.

1919   **Paris Peace Conference, Versailles**: in the aftermath of the 'war to end all wars', the Paris Peace Conference in 1919 produced the **Treaty of Versailles**, a considerable contributory cause of the Second World War. Providing for reparations against Germany, and dismantling the final vestiges of the Ottoman Empire that had held order, albeit with a considerable degree of barbarism, the treaty established a shaky peace in both Europe and the Middle East.

1922   **Chanak crisis** (September–October): a crisis in Anglo-Turkish relations. Wounded from defeat in the First World War and the dismantling of the Ottoman Empire, Turkey responded aggressively to the Greek military presence following the Treaty of Sèvres in 1920, which ceded Smyrna to Greece. Britain and some other countries feared that the Turkish military under Kemal Ataturk might deploy into Greek territory from Chanak in the Dardanelles and pose a threat to the British Army. The Conservatives and Labour argued that the decision by the prime minister, David Lloyd George, to send British reinforcements to the Dardanelles threatened to bring about war with Turkey. Along with the Newport by-election and the Carlton Club revolt, both in the same month, the Chanak crisis greatly damaged the reputation of Lloyd George.

1922   **Washington Nine Power Treaty** (February): signed by Britain, the USA and Japan to establish a battleship ratio of 5-5-3, with no new battleships and cruisers to be built for ten years. The tonnage of battleships was also restricted.

1923   **Treaty of Lausanne** (August): obliged Turkey to cede large swathes of Ottoman territory to Greece. Turkey also conceded the annexation of

Cyprus by Britain and accepted demilitarisation of the Bosporus and the Dardanelles.

1925 **Treaties of Locarno** (December): A conference in October the purpose of which was to ease international tensions led to the signing of the treaties in December. Britain and Italy were to guarantee the Franco-German and Franco-Belgian borders and the demilitarised Rhineland.

1928 **Kellogg–Briand Pact** (August): also known as the **Kellogg Pact**, by which Britain, France, Germany, Italy, Japan and other powers agreed to renounce aggressive warfare.

1930 **London Naval Treaty** (April): Britain, France, Italy, Japan and the USA agreed to the restriction of naval armaments for six years.

1935 **Anglo-German Naval Agreement** (June): ostensibly aimed to curb Nazi German naval and submarine capacity. It had little effect.

1936–9 **Appeasement**: originating with Baldwin and culminating with Neville Chamberlain, appeasement was predicated on the assumption that British defence against aggression by Germany, Italy and Japan was most effectively served by negotiation with and even placation of dictators. The policy was thrown into sharp relief by the position adopted towards Hitler and German expansionist plans for Czecho-slovakia. Appeasement was not the only defence policy towards fascism: rearmament was also begun in 1936, although by no means wholeheartedly.

1936–9 Rearmament ran parallel with appeasement, but was generally under-funded, reflecting the belief among many politicians and of prime ministers Baldwin and Chamberlain that war was and should be avoidable. However, increasing investment in military materiel and weaponry failed to provide Britain with adequate resources by 1940, when the threat of imminent invasion forced the mobilisation of industry for war production, notably fighter planes.

1938 Anthony Eden, the foreign secretary, resigned (February) following the British government's recognition of the Italian king as emperor of Ethiopia. Eden was disgusted at the appeasement of Italian fascism by Chamberlain.

1938 **Munich Agreement** (September): events in September revealed the weaknesses of appeasement politics, and may be viewed as a desperate example of shuttle diplomacy by Chamberlain. He was determined to avoid war at all costs, pressing the Czechs to make territorial conces-sions to Nazi Germany and to allow a German military presence. Hitler's demands increased between two meetings with Chamberlain at Berchtesgaden on 15 September and Godesberg on 22 September, and at the Munich Conference on the 29th – involving Britain, Germany, France and Italy, but not the Czechs – Hitler called for the Sudetenland to be handed over to Germany. Britain, France and Italy would guarantee the independence of the remainder of Czechoslovakia, which was expected to accept the Munich Agreement. This was viewed in the short term as a victory for Chamberlain, but Churchill and other leading politicians were angered at this capitulation to dictatorship. They viewed it as a step towards war, not back from it.

1939   Territorial integrity of Poland guaranteed by Britain (March): appeasement was practically and symbolically terminated by this act, and British preparations for war were accelerated and expanded over the coming months.

1939   **National Service Act** (April): reinstated conscription for the first time since the First World War against the background of the demise of appeasement. Conscription applied to all men aged twenty and twenty-one years. Following the outbreak of war all men aged from eighteen to forty-one were to be enlisted, with exemptions for skilled men for essential war work on the home front.

1939   **Lend Lease**: in the USA, an earlier Neutrality Act was repealed (November) and the Lend Lease Act was passed. It allowed for £32,385 million in aid for the Allies, with a facility for further assistance as the war continued. Churchill declared it 'the most unsordid act in the history of any nation'.

1939   **Emergency Powers Act** (August): enabled government to coordinate and control the British economy during wartime. This was essential for both the home front and munitions production.

1939   Declaration of war on Germany by Neville Chamberlain (September).

1945   **Yalta Conference** (February): a late wartime summit between Churchill, Stalin of the USSR and Roosevelt of the USA, which agreed to carve postwar Germany into zones of occupation and to establish the United Nations. Significant decisions were also reached over the prosecution of German war criminals.

1945   **Potsdam Summit** (July–August): the final wartime summit, held in Germany. Clement Attlee and Ernest Bevin attended for Britain (in the wake of Labour's general election victory in July), while President Truman of the USA and Stalin represented the other leading victorious nations. Key issues included reparations and the endgame against Japan.

1946   **'Iron curtain' speech** by Winston Churchill at Westminster College in Fulton, Missouri. One of the earliest significant moments signalling the beginning of a Cold War in Europe and elsewhere, Churchill's apocalyptic vision of the iron curtain stretching from the Baltic to the Balkans, separating the free West from the communist Eastern European countries, became a powerful metaphor for the Cold War.

1946   **USS *Sequoia* Summit** (September): strengthened the special relationship between Britain and the USA at the dawn of the Cold War. Both Montgomery and American joint chiefs of staff agreed upon the necessity for Anglo-American military cooperation.

1947   British ministers agreed that the United Kingdom required its own atomic bomb (January) as the USA and USSR began the arms race. The USA had dropped atomic bombs on Japan in 1945, and the USSR had begun to develop its own atomic capability; hence Britain felt committed to its own bomb as a defence deterrent but also as a symbol of world influence.

1947   British troops completed their withdrawal from Egypt to the Suez Canal zone (March): North Africa and the Middle East were major theatres of war from 1941 to 1945. The Suez Canal had been built by Anglo-French interests during the nineteenth century.

1947   **Palestine Mandate** referred to the United Nations (April) against the background of continuing conflict in the area of Palestine that would soon become the state of Israel.

1947   British withdrawal from Palestine began (November) following the United Nations vote for the partition of Arab Palestine and Jewish Palestine. They completed their withdrawal in 1948 (May).

1947   **Marshall Aid**: a twofold American strategy to promote economic growth in Europe and other parts of the world and to contain the communist threat. In Europe, Britain was a major beneficiary, receiving $1,035 million in military aid between 1947 and 1965, and $3,835 in economic assistance.

1948   Communist insurgents in **Malaya** (June) brought about a state emergency requiring British intervention until 1960. The conflict can be viewed within the contexts of both decolonisation and the Cold War.

1949   **North Atlantic Treaty Organization** (NATO) established in Washington by the United States of America and eleven Western European governments (April). Formed primarily to cement defence relationships between Britain, Western Europe and the United States, NATO must be understood within the context of the early Cold War and the desire for peace in Europe. It was a major achievement for the British foreign minister, Ernest Bevin.

1950   Rearmament programme intensified within the context of austerity at home and growing tensions abroad caused by communist expansionism, notably in Korea.

1950   **Korean War** (July): British servicemen sent to Korea under the aegis of the American-led United Nations forces.

1950   **National Service** (conscription) extended to two years (July) for every soldier, sailor or airman in response to the situation in Korea.

1951   Middle East problems intensified (May): the Iranian government

	nationalised the Anglo-Iranian Oil Company, prompting the British government to debate military action.
1951	Egypt made the first moves towards the nationalisation of the Suez Canal (October) by attacking previous Anglo-Egyptian agreements.
1952	**NATO** formally came into existence (April).
1952	The **Mau Mau insurrection** in Kenya (October) led to a state of emergency, one of the bloodier chapters in the British process of decolonisation.
1952	First atomic bomb tested by Britain at Monte Bello in the Pacific Ocean (October).
1954	**Anglo-Egyptian Treaty** commenced the British withdrawal from its base in Suez.
1955	**Cyprus** witnessed the beginnings of terrorism (April) in its campaign for independence from Britain with the formation of the EOKA, led by Archbishop Makarios.
1955	**Baghdad Pact** signed by Britain with Turkey and Iraq (April): Pakistan and Iran joined later the same year.
1956	**Defence review** begun by the Conservative government (June) to adjust British foreign policy and defence needs to the country's economic capability.
1956	**Suez crisis** engulfed Britain (June–November), a catastrophe in British military and diplomatic history.
1957	Harold Macmillan met with President Eisenhower to rebuild the battered special relationship with the USA in the diplomatic aftermath of Suez (March). The need for reconciliation had been brought about by Eisenhower's previous words and deeds about Britain's reduced status as a world power together with American criticism of Anglo-French military action in the Suez crisis.
1957	**The defence review** by Duncan **Sandys** (April) recommended the abolition of national service in the new age of nuclear weapons.
1957	Britain tested its first hydrogen bomb in the Pacific Ocean (May). The **Campaign for Nuclear Disarmament** was formed the following year to campaign for unilateral nuclear disarmament.
1960	**Conscription** finally terminated in Britain, while other European countries without a nuclear deterrent or for expedient domestic reasons continued to maintain a conscripted force.
1960	The British government agreed to purchase the American **Skybolt** missile in return for the use of Holy Loch in Scotland as an American submarine base (March).
1960	The Labour leader Hugh Gaitskell rejected unilateral disarmament for his party. His rationale was that the majority of British people probably saw the common sense in possessing a nuclear deterrent, while the unilateralist left of his party did not.
1961	Britain used military force to prevent the invasion of **Kuwait** by **Iraq**

(July): Iraq had left the Central Treaty Organisation (CENTO), and until that point named the Baghdad Pact, which was designed to keep peace in the Middle East.

1962   British troops sent to the British protectorates in **Aden** in the Middle East (September) to put down nationalist uprisings.

1962   **Polaris** submarine replaced Skybolt in an agreement reached by Harold Macmillan and President John F. Kennedy (December).

1963   A **Ministry of Defence** called for by a defence White Paper (July): the following year the War Office, the Admiralty and the Air Ministry amalgamated with the Ministry of Defence.

1963   **Aden**: state of emergency declared (December).

1963   **Cyprus** situation deteriorated (December): Archbishop Makarios called for British military intervention as tensions grew between Greek-Cypriot nationalists and the Turkish population.

1964   Denis Healey appointed as secretary of state for defence by the prime minister, Harold Wilson (October). Healey quickly announced a **defence review**.

1965   Cancellation by Healey of the contract for the American fighter aircraft the **TSR2** (April).

1967   **East of Suez** decision (July): made by Denis Healey, it recognised Britain's increasing difficulty operating east of the Egyptian Suez zone in the Middle East. Britain began the process of withdrawal that was to continue into the mid-1970s.

1967   British forces evacuated Aden (November). The People's Republic of Southern Yemen was subsequently declared.

1968   East of Suez withdrawal was expedited (January) with completion brought forward to 1971, and endorsed by NATO.

1969   British troops intervened in Northern Ireland as the Troubles grew worse (August).

1971   The Ministry of Defence was extended with the addition of the Ministry of Aviation Supply: the MOD now had responsibility for supplying guided weapons and military aircraft.

1972   **Strategic Arms Limitation Talks** (SALT I) (January): agreed by leading nuclear powers, including Britain, in order to prevent nuclear proliferation.

1973   Enhancement of the **Polaris** nuclear-powered submarines programme between Britain and the USA.

1974   **Defence review** instigated to enable Britain to reduce overseas military commitments beyond the alliance with NATO (March), thus affirming the need to avoid overstretching British forces – a need implicit in the East of Suez decision some six years previously.

1978   Special relationship damaged by the decision of President Carter (April) to cancel the Anglo-American neutron bomb project.

1979	NATO decision to deploy American-made **cruise missiles** in Britain and across Western Europe (January), reigniting the **Campaign for Nuclear Disarmament**.
1980	**SALT II Treaty** signed (June), but it remained unratified.
1981	**Defence review** by Sir John Nott (June): facilitated reductions in the size of the Royal Navy.
1982	British government announced its decision (March) to purchase **Trident nuclear missiles** from the USA.
1982	**Falklands War** (April–June): became the largest conflict in which the British were involved during the final quarter of the twentieth century. It took place in the year following the defence review that had called for reductions in the size of the navy.
1983	**Cruise missiles** deployed in Britain (November): the move strengthened the Campaign for Nuclear Disarmament in Britain, leading some local councils to declare themselves 'nuclear free zones'.
1987	**Nimrod** early warning system cancelled: a British product, it was cancelled in preference for the American-made Boeing aircraft warning and control system (AWACS).
1988	Neil **Kinnock** began to move the Labour Party away from the position of unilateral disarmament favoured by the left of his party (June). There were considerable historical echoes of the similar move by Gaitskell some twenty-eight years earlier.
1989	The **fall of the Berlin Wall** accelerated the end of the Cold War (December): this engendered considerable revisions to the military rationale and role of NATO as communist Eastern Europe faded into contemporary history.
1990	The defence secretary, Tom King, announced cutbacks to the British Army of the Rhine (July) and other reductions in the British armed forces.
1991	The USA announced its withdrawal from the submarine base at Holy Loch in Scotland and of F-111 bomber planes from bases in Britain.
1991	**Gulf War** (January–March): The war was the second attempt by Iraq to attack Kuwait during the postwar period. The Iraqi invasion was a considerable threat to the oil supplies of the West and to the sovereignty of its Islamic neighbour. Britain gave support to US forces' removal of Saddam Hussein's forces.
1992	**Defence review** announced by the defence secretary, Malcolm Rifkind (July): it accepted Britain's status as a mid-ranking power in Europe with global obligations.
1997	**Defence review** *Options for Change* initiated by the New Labour government.
1997–	New Labour governments constantly strived to sustain the special relationship with the USA in military and diplomatic affairs. Tony

Blair came under severe domestic criticism for his decision to support the American invasion in Iraq from 2003, and was even accused of deference to the American president.

Britain and European integration

1940   Anglo-French Union declared (June) following German invasion of France.

1946   Winston Churchill called in Zurich for a 'United States of Europe' (September).

1947   **Marshall Plan** to finance European-wide reconstruction in order to rebuild Europe to make it safer for democracy, and to increase American influence.

1947   Belgium, Netherlands and Luxembourg forged economic union in **Benelux** trading bloc (October).

1948   Formation of **Convention for European Economic Cooperation** (April).

1949   Statute of the **Council of Europe** signed (May) by Belgium, Denmark, France, Ireland, Italy, Luxembourg, the Netherlands, Norway, Sweden, and the United Kingdom.

1950   **Pleven Plan**, proposed by the French premier for a European Defence Community (October). Ernest Bevin opposed the plan.

1951   **European Coal and Steel Community** (ECSC) established to the framework proposed by Robert Schuman (April). Belgium, France, Germany (West), Luxembourg, Italy and the Netherlands were the signatories. Britain was involved neither in this nor with further steps towards European integration during the 1950s.

1953   The ECSC in coal, iron and scrap begun (February): the common market in steel was initiated (May).

1955   **Messina Conference** (June): proposed further moves towards European integration.

1957   **Treaties of Rome** (March): established the European Economic Community (EEC) and the European Atomic Energy Community (EURATOM). The signatories were Belgium, France, Germany, Luxembourg, Italy and the Netherlands, the original 'six'.

1958   Treaties of Rome enacted as the EEC and EURATOM (January).

1959   **European Free Trade Association** (EFTA) established (November): the so-called seven, namely Austria, Denmark, Norway, Portugal, Sweden, Switzerland and the United Kingdom, intended EFTA as an alternative trading bloc to the EEC.

1961   The United Kingdom and the Republic of Ireland requested negotiations for membership of the EEC (July to August).

1963   President de Gaulle of France rejected British moves for membership (January). Despite, or perhaps because of, a widespread scepticism about Europe, but also angered by a French 'betrayal' following Britain's assistance to de Gaulle and the Free French during the Second World War, British public opinion became hostile towards France.

1966   Harold Wilson announced new plans to drive forward British membership of the EEC (November).

1967   The United Kingdom applied for membership of the EEC (May).

1967   De Gaulle vetoed the British application (November), leading to his vilification in sections of the British press.

1969   Following de Gaulle's resignation as president of France, the United Kingdom, Denmark, Ireland and Norway began negotiations for membership of the EEC (December).

1970   **Luxembourg negotiations** on UK membership (June). Edward Heath became prime minister in the same month.

1971   'D Day': the introduction of **decimal currency** or decimalisation in the United Kingdom (February). Sterling was prepared to come in line with European currencies. The new currency was greeted with enthusiasm among those who favoured EEC membership and bemusement or hostility by many who did not.

1971   The **Council of the European Union** reached a historic agreement for UK membership of the EEC (June) following a transitional period of preparation for membership. The House of Commons voted in favour of British entry (October).

1972   **Treaty of Accession** signed in Brussels (January), accepting Denmark, Ireland, Norway and the UK into the EEC.

1973   The United Kingdom became a formal member of the EEC (January).

1974   At the British general elections the anti-EEC Conservative MP Enoch Powell recommended the electorate vote Labour because its left wing wanted Britain to quit the EEC following a referendum. Many on the left felt strongly that EEC membership would divert the Labour movement from the 'British road to socialism'.

1975   **Referendum on EEC membership** (June): Britain voted to remain in the EEC by a majority of over two-thirds, a significant defeat for the anti-EEC lobby.

1976   The EEC reached an agreement on direct elections to the European Parliament in Brussels (July).

1979   **European Monetary System** began (May), creating a common currency unit, the ECU, whereby exchange rates between different currencies were to be linked together, laying the basis for an EEC-wide currency in the near future.

1979   First direct elections to the **European Parliament** held (June): there were 410 members (MEPs) to represent the member nations of the EEC.

1982 British veto on agricultural prices in the EEC defeated (May): France saw this as a particular victory for its farmers.

1983 **Common Agricultural Policy** reform agreed and Common Fisheries Policy initiated (June).

1984 The EEC adopted a draft treaty of European Union (EU) (February), paving the way for it to be phased into the EU.

1984 Second direct elections to the European Parliament (June).

1984 **Fontainebleau Summit** agreed to UK budget rebate (June), a considerable achievement for Margaret Thatcher.

1987 **Single European Act** came into force (July): the first significant modification of the Treaties of Rome, it aimed to break down all trade barriers within the EEC area and to generate common social policies in the form of a social charter.

1988 **Bruges speech** by Margaret Thatcher (September): her attack on further European integration and the spectre of a 'European superstate' led to the formation of the 'Bruges Group' of Eurosceptics within the Conservative Party.

1990 Third direct elections to the European Parliament (June).

1990 Britain joined the **Exchange Rate Mechanism** (October) while remaining out of step with most other EEC countries on monetary union.

1991 The **Maastricht Summit** (December) made concessions to Britain for opt-outs over monetary union and the social charter.

1992 **Black Wednesday** (September): the pound sterling and a number of other European currencies crashed out of the ERM.

1993 The **Maastricht Bill** was passed in the House of Commons (July) after considerable debate and open rebellion in the Conservative Party.

1993 **United Kingdom Independence Party** (UKIP) and **Referendum Party** both established to campaign to get Britain out of Europe.

1994 The European Union came into force (January), replacing the EEC.

1994 Fourth direct elections to the European Parliament (June).

1994 Continuing rebellion by Eurosceptics in the Conservative Party (November) led to the removal of the whip from eight of them.

1996 **Referendum Party**, led by Sir James Goldsmith, launched a campaign against what it saw as the imminent federal European superstate and loss of British sovereignty (November).

1996 Tony Blair promised a referendum on British membership of the single European currency (August). No referendum was subsequently forthcoming.

1998 Britain took the presidency of the European Union (January): among the early key issues with which it was faced were the ratification of the 1997 Amsterdam Treaty's revision of the Maastricht settlement and the problem of unemployment in Europe, as discussed in Luxembourg the previous year.

1999 Launch of the **Euro** (January) the common currency of Europe. Britain remained outside European Monetary Union (EMU) into the early twenty-first century.

1999 The fifth direct elections to the European Parliament (June) saw the small but increasing presence of anti-European and Green MEPs.

III

HISTORIOGRAPHY AND A–Z OF KEY HISTORIANS OF TWENTIETH-CENTURY BRITAIN

3.1

NOTES

- The term 'historiography' refers to the theories and practices of historians, and to the researching and writing of history. Some very useful textbooks and guides have been written on the nature of history as a discipline, so there is no need to reproduce a generalised approach here. Instead, this section develops themes within historiography specific to twentieth-century Britain. It also highlights some of the most important theoretical approaches and practices.
- This section also provides a kind of 'history of history', a historical account of the evolution of twentieth-century history – social, cultural, economic and political – and the major theoretical and practical positions adopted by historians working within these broad and diverse areas of enquiry. It will become clear that these approaches were continually evolving during the twentieth century, but that in a number of critically important decades the assumptions of historians of earlier periods were challenged, with consequences for the subsequent study of history in general and of twentieth-century Britain in particular.
- The section is divided into three broad but intersecting areas as follows:

  - First, the major theoretical approaches to the study of modern British history are introduced and their strengths and limitations evaluated.
  - Second, the emergence of the historical study of twentieth-century Britain is outlined, influenced as it was by the study of earlier periods and the reactions to the studies of leading historians. Twentieth-century history evolved from a number of differing broad fields of historical enquiry: social and cultural history, economic history, and political history and its connected disciplines.
  - The third section is an A to Z of key historians in the fields of social and cultural, economic and political history; some military and defence historians with research and publications in twentieth-century Britain have been included, as have urban historians in keeping with the themes of the book.

3.2
APPROACHES TO HISTORY

Traditional empirical history

Most historians of Britain in general, and of twentieth-century Britain more specifically, would describe themselves as 'traditional' and 'empirical' in their approach to the study of the past. This point was made by L. J. **Butler** in 1997, but it remains true today despite attacks on traditional historians from post-modernism, discussed below. So what is traditional history? And, specifically, what does a traditional historian do when studying Britain during the twentieth century? More or less all writers of historiographical textbooks point to the influence of the eighteenth-century German historian Leopold von Ranke on the so-called common-sense approach to historical enquiry and the writing up of results. Ranke was a Protestant and a conservative-minded scholar who placed enormous faith both in the meticulous reading of contemporary sources and in the harvesting of as many facts as possible to sustain the validity of the historians' judgement. This was akin to positivism, wherein objective judgements were made from a careful process of scientific observation. Ranke's famous dictum was that interpretations of the past should 'tell it as it actually was'. This maxim has been open to misunderstanding and mockery, but on closer examination and careful adaptation it can be viewed as a valuable, even indispensable, guiding principle.

'Telling it as it actually was' has often been misunderstood by critics of Ranke, who argued that there was never one achievable objective account of a particular historical episode or period. But those working within the Rankean tradition argue that he never really said that. Looking back on twentieth-century Britain, no serious historian would argue that a particular event (for example, the General Strike of 1926, the Blitz of 1940–41, or the Profumo scandal of 1963) could be subjected to a singular telling of the truth which cancelled all other accounts. Rather, the historian, no matter what their politics or perspective, should harness as many objective 'facts' as possible to validate their account. Although some 'facts' are open to debate, many are not. For example, let us take the General Strike of May 1926, and the following sentence: 'The chancellor of the exchequer and chief antagonist of the Triple Alliance during the General Strike was Winston Churchill. The government's newspaper the *British Gazette* was a tool of the government during the strike.' These points are facts. They cannot really be disputed. But take this sentence: 'The government won the

General Strike because the Triple Alliance backed down after less than ten days, and a few months later the defeated miners returned to work.' That sentence, which might have been written by a Conservative historian, has a ring of truth about it. It is, however, much more debateable than the facts of the previous sentence. For many Labour historians, the General Strike can be viewed as something of a victory for working-class solidarities within a very difficult context. And when the numbers of workers involved, across many important sectors of industry, and the amount of working days lost are calculated, then the seemingly implausible view of a working-class victory takes on a certain rationality: it uses validated facts and attempts to challenge orthodoxy. In this act of original thinking and application of argument, new insights into the past are continually produced.

Traditional empirical history is intrinsically flexible and applicable to all fields of historical enquiry. Social, cultural, economic and political history, and the disciplines of defence, diplomatic and military history, all require close readings of contemporary sources and a knowledge of both the short-term and the wider historical context that informed the authorship and timing of those sources. This is also true for urban history and planning history, both of which emerged as increasingly self-confident and distinct fields of enquiry during the final third of the last century. Let us take the example of urban history. While I do not wish to sound like a marketing executive on behalf of the discipline, it offers exciting opportunities for both original and engaging local histories and also for the 'bigger picture' urban histories of such grand subjects as urbanisation, suburbanisation, demographic change and the city, and the social life and cultures of cities. It is both micro and macro. And there are both hard facts – demographic data, for example – and fluid areas for well-informed judgement: the complex reasons for the emergence of suburbia, for instance, have formed a highly contested field of study. Therefore an ability to make links between a wide range of sources, to create synthesis, is also essential within the act of interpretation. The range of sources is outlined in **Sources and resources**.

Marxist history

Many British historians have been influenced by the work of Karl Marx (1818–88), a nineteenth-century economist, philosopher and writer who argued that capitalist society was essentially bound to self-destruct because of its internal contradictions. Marxism has made a hugely important contribution to the historical study of economic history, social and cultural history, and imperialism.

The most fundamental and destabilising contradiction was that between the owners of the means of production, the bourgeoisie, or, to give their English label, the capitalist middle classes, and the much larger class of the proletariat, known colloquially in Britain as the working class. Hence class was at the very heart of Marxist analysis. According to the Marxist pattern of historical development, the social, economic and political epoch that preceded capitalism, feudalism, had declined because it generated the seeds of its own destruction, namely capitalism. Aristocratic landowners and petty property owners became more profit-orientated, and the peasantry, the massive social bedrock of the feudal system, was decommissioned by the aristocracy. In turn the peasantry was forced to commute or sell its labour to a burgeoning bourgeoisie.

This was a developmental and a deterministic view of history. It anticipated the decline of capitalism through a gathering process of class conflict, leading eventually to its revolutionary overthrow by leading sections of the politically conscious working classes. Marx earnestly argued that a socialist system would eventually lay the historical platform for a communist society in which money and profit were irrelevant. It must be emphasised that, from the vantage point of the early twenty-first century, anticipations of the collapse of capitalism were greatly exaggerated. But we have the benefit of hindsight. During the 1950s, and particularly the 1960s and 1970s, left-wing ideologies were increasingly influential among historians in the established universities. In the history departments of the new universities and new polytechnics brought into being by the expansion of higher education, many Marxist historians were convinced that capitalism would eventually be defeated by Marxism. There were, of course, working models – if flawed – of communist societies in Eastern and Central Europe, and the Russian Revolution of 1917 was inspired by Marx. However, quite the opposite occurred: the 'state socialist' or communist regimes collapsed in the late 1980s and the 1990s. They were overthrown by popular pressure from within, assisted to a degree by the West. A major problem for Marxist historiography was its assumption that history was progressing towards a more socialistic future.

This account of the Marxist interpretation of history is necessary because it enables us to understand the basis of Marxist understandings of twentieth-century British history. The values of the working class, their 'trade-union' consciousness, for example, stemmed from a Marxist–Leninist concern with the pivotal role of workers' organisations in securing revolution. The failure of a trade-union consciousness to develop a revolutionary potential is at the heart of many left histories of the organised working class. And a disproportionate amount of research and analysis, conversely, was spent on looking for the signs of a revolutionary potential among the masses. Significantly, however, the tendency of the majority of the workers to avoid communism was also a major question for analysis. In this, Marxist historians developed an increasingly flexible set of tools for analysis, even though their abiding assumption was that capitalism was inherently unstable and perhaps inevitably doomed to terminal decline. This can be understood in social and cultural Marxist history, notably in the work of historians who, from the 1970s, adopted the categories of analysis of the Italian Euro-communist Antonio Gramsci. In place of an earlier crude emphasis upon repressive state organisations, 'false consciousness' and the inevitability of revolution, Gramsci underlined the significance of 'hegemony', the moral, intellectual and practical leadership of the bourgeoisie, to which the working classes or 'subordinate' layers of society appeared to give their consent. Consent was maintained within the 'superstructure' of civil society and governed with varying degrees of persuasion by the state and the media.

To summarise, the Marxist emphasis upon class in social and economic histories of modern Britain helped to place that variable at the heart of historical study in the postwar years. Today, many historians, not always Marxist but usually socialist or social democratic in their politics, continue to privilege class in their approaches to the past. However, the rise of feminism and of feminist history since the early 1970s increasingly emphasised gender as a driving force in historical change and as a framework for understanding.

Feminist history

Historical approaches are informed by recent and current social, cultural, economic and political movements and trends, and this is one major reason why the 'truth' in historical writing is never absolute, that is, fixed in the same meaning for eternity. Historians continually adapt, reinterpret and discover evidence according to the ideological influences on their own lives, and feminism led to a major reinterpretation of British history, both in general and for the years since 1900. The emergence of 'second wave feminism' during the 1970s became highly influential in British and European universities. Its origins were manifold. Longer-term influences included the 'first wave' feminists of the early twentieth century who fought for women's suffrage and fairer employment opportunities for female workers. Their actions were also increasingly studied by feminist historians after 1970. During the 1960s Marxist student politics, and a belief in permissiveness that gave women – in theory – the same sexual licence and satisfactions as men came together with political struggles for equal pay and working conditions for women to produce a powerful feminist moment. It was never a monolithic or one-dimensional movement, something which its male critics often misunderstood. Nonetheless, a unifying theme of the feminist approach to history was an initial and obvious emphasis upon women's history, and soon afterwards on gender as a driving force in historical change.

A further central component of feminist history was that women's experiences and achievements had been obscured from historical analysis by the dominance of men writing history mostly or wholly concerned with men. Hence the need for *herstory*, and the title of the powerful historical polemic by Sheila **Rowbotham** entitled *Hidden from History: Three Hundred Years of Women's Oppression and the Fight Against It* (1973). It made the close connection between women's second-class citizenship and patriarchy: women were subordinate in history, a reflection of their subordination in a patriarchal society – that is, a society where men are socially, economically and politically dominant. Coterminous with Rowbotham's analysis, feminist historians increasingly explored the myriad aspects of the female experience. Feminism lent itself particularly to **oral history**, which could and did tease out ways in which women were often active and passionate participants in the past rather than passive recipients of the patriarchal path of historical development. In this relationship to oral history, feminism made an original, significant and ongoing contribution to the study of twentieth-century Britain. For, as noted in **Sources and resources**, oral history is now mostly a history of the twentieth century. The great majority of witnesses to historical change were born after 1900. Some of the most original social history of twentieth-century Britain has been undertaken by feminist oral historians, or by those inspired by this fusion. Moreover, many feminist historians by no means rejected class as a useful category of analysis – far from it. The lives of poorer women and middle-class and wealthy women were explored in the context of their income, status and class position. Some very moving feminist oral histories, for example, have been written about the lives of poor women in twentieth-century England, notably in the work of Elizabeth **Roberts**.

Developing from the concern with gender, the social history of sexualities emerged during the 1970s. The taboos of homosexuality and lesbianism had meant that gays had also been 'hidden from history'. Again, oral history has been a useful tool in opening up the histories of and giving voice to the testimonies of those beyond the mainstream before the more liberalised attitudes of the later twentieth century.

Feminism posed a serious challenge to traditional historiography because it challenged patriarchy and the practice of history within patriarchal society. Male assumptions and values underpinned both academic and social practices, something reflected powerfully in the language used by historians. In this interrogation of language and its reinforcement of received patriarchy, feminism greatly influenced an emerging new agenda in historiography: postmodernism (L. J. Butler, 'History: theory and practice', in L. J. Butler and A. Gorst (eds), *Modern British History*, 1997, p. 25). However, we should also remember that many feminist historians could accurately be termed feminist empiricists.

Postmodern perspectives

When Butler argued that most historians would describe themselves as 'traditional', he was writing at a time when passionate debates were emerging between traditional historians and postmodernists. The origins of postmodernism lie in the reaction of some leading French and American philosophers during the 1970s and 1980s to what they perceived as the failure of modernism. Challenging the 'meta-narrative', the all-embracing or totalising philosophies associated with major belief systems, postmodern historical approaches argued that the certainties of the earlier twentieth century were dissipating as a growing range of beliefs and values made for a more fractured ideological landscape. The ideas of the founding fathers of postmodernism, notably Roland Barthes, Jean Baudrillard, Jacques Derrida and Michael Foucault, were taken to heart by those academics who wished to destroy traditional empirical historiography. In particular,

Jean-François Lyotard, in *The Postmodern Condition* (1979), ridiculed the notion of scientific positivism and a belief in progress that underpinned the certainties implicit within the work of academics in the later twentieth century.

Marxism, with its emphasis upon historical materialism and the class-based evolution of historical progress, was a meta-narrative. Another was feminism, which explained women's history almost entirely as one of the feminist struggle against oppression by patriarchy. However, the relative recentness of feminism, and its influence upon postmodernism, ensured that the relationship of feminist thought to postmodern theory remained close. Religion is also a kind of meta-narrative: Christians explained the universe in terms of creationism, and historical development thereafter may be viewed as God's will. For postmodernists it follows that, if such massive, influential grand theories were merely flawed stories, then other stories have equal or even greater validity. Postmodernism did not completely reject Marxist, religious or feminist approaches and other meta-narratives, but argued that they needed to embrace the postmodern condition.

Furthermore, American postmodernist academics, notably Frank Ankersmit and Hayden White, argued that historians could never produce accurate narrative accounts of historical events or developments because they could not really know the past: it was now inaccessible on account of the shifting nature of language, developments in knowledge or epistemology, and of changing interpretations over time. In this sense, another assumed meta-narrative – that of 'common sense' based upon an understanding of 'human nature' – was also deeply flawed and useless because it rested upon contemporaneous and culture-bound viewpoints that praised objectivity and realism when there was no longer anything 'real' or any earlier intended 'meaning' that could not be contested.

Armed with these approaches, British postmodernists attacked traditional history as essentially a limited and biased modus operandi: it was naïve, bourgeois, white, gendered on behalf of the male, unchallenging of the capitalist status quo, Western rather than Eastern, and more northern hemisphere than southern hemisphere. Furthermore, and here we can see the influence of Ankersmit and White, postmodernism was sceptical of any empiricist notion that there was some 'objective' truth or original meaning that could be gleaned from the documents – the contemporary sources – that historians use. *Language* – not context – was the key to understanding, and language was multidimensional and problematic, never reducible to one or even a few meanings, but open to an almost infinite number of interpretations. Ergo, any particular interpretation of any document through the prism of language has as much viability or validity as any other reading of that text.

Key protagonists of postmodernism in Britain include Keith **Jenkins**, Alan **Munslow** and Beverley Southgate. Munslow, for example, is editor of the journal *Rethinking History: The Journal of Theory and Practice*, which began life in 1997 and is an important vehicle for postmodern debates. Jenkins wrote an accessible guide to postmodernism with the same title, *Rethinking History*. Postmodernists argue that the old certainties of the modern era have dissipated, and express their frustration at the failure of most historians in Britain to adopt postmodern perspectives.

It is fascinating to consider some as yet under-explored parallels between the postmodern attack on 'certaintist' histories, as Jenkins terms them, and the critique of Whig history outlined below in section 3.3. Most historians continue to question the assumptions of previous generations of historians according to fresh perspectives gained in the light of historical developments in their own times. To that extent they can be what the historian Herbert Butterfield once termed 'present-minded' – updating historical enquiry to accommodate and deploy new directions and insights into the past. But they are, perhaps, less 'present-minded' than the postmodernists who assume that we are living in a new era of history – the postmodern era – that makes traditional modes of historical enquiry as potentially as redundant as the coal miners of the late twentieth century. Certainly postmodernist academics can offer new insights into the past, but the discipline of history continually refreshes itself beyond the parameters of postmodernism.

You may also wish to consider the notion that there is no inherent meaning or intention in the original document. Certainly, interpretations of original texts vary from one generation to another and from differing ideological standpoints. But does this mean that the original author's intentions are now not really worthy of serious consideration *on their own terms*? Is this akin to what E. P. **Thompson** once castigated as 'the enormous condescension of posterity'? By that he meant that, from our own historical vantage point, we patronise or dismiss as irrelevant the deeds and words of those in earlier periods of history.

Postmodernism has also been criticised by traditional historians, left and right, for the problem of self-cancellation. If documents have no inherent meaning save for that pronounced by their interpreter, then the outputs of post-modernists themselves are by self-definition meaningless except for the inter-pretation placed on them by other historians. Yet of course postmodernists feel their own arguments have meanings and wish to have them discussed seriously. Are they therefore exempt from their own laws of analysis?

Finally, how fashionable now is postmodernism in the Anglophone world of historical studies? For one contributor to the *American Historical Review* (vol. 6, no. 4, 2001), postmodernism was already 'old hat' in Britain and America and increasingly off-trend even in France. This was perhaps in part a consequence of the weight of traditional approaches and in part a consequence of Richard J. **Evans**'s *In Defence of History* (1999). Evans highlighted the moral dangers of 'hyper-relativism', dangers that stem from the notion that any story about the past is as valid as any other. Hyper-relativism is a key issue of which all students of modern and contemporary history should be aware. The Holocaust, notably, has been passionately discussed in relation to it, as the work of Dan **Stone** and Sir Ian Kershaw elucidates.

Debates about postmodernism in relation to other historical approaches are still ongoing among historians. Some leading historians are postmodernists, hence claims about its *passé* status may yet be exaggerated. You can get a sense of how passionate the arguments between traditional historians and post-modernists are by looking at the **Institute of Historical Research** web pages on historiography (see www.history.ac.uk). A number of historians contributing to the debate concede that it is very difficult to be a neutral participant.

What do historians do now?

L. J. Butler was basically right in 1997, and he would be right today. Because of what they see as problems inherent in postmodern approaches, and because they prefer to work creatively, sensitively and with a sense of operational objectivity while being aware of their own biases, a majority of historians would probably still describe themselves as 'traditional' in their approach to documents and in their interpretations of the past. In short, a careful evaluation of contemporary documents and an attempt to provide a fair-minded and original assessment as is possible should remain an important modus operandi. And that does not imply either simple-minded neutrality or homogeneity of assumption. A Marxist, socialist, Liberal or Conservative historian with a particular axe to grind about a historical event should always look for as much evidence as possible to support their viewpoint, and then accept modifications and nuance when they discover sources that conflict with their understanding.

No matter what period of history we are interested in, and no matter what our politics may be, good practice acknowledges certain biases and tendencies in interpretation and should always be guided by the following: a knowledge of the arguments of other historians and of previous generations of historians in order to be able to develop original criticisms and insights; a humane ability to empathise with people in previous periods of history, even quite recent times, and to understand their emotions and values; a continuing imperative to connect a document as closely and comprehensively as possible to the immediate and wider historical context (this necessitates historical knowledge of the period); a scepticism about projecting our own assumption and values uncritically into the past (this is present-mindedness, discussed in section 3.3); and the detection of both witting and unwitting testimony in source materials. Please refer to **Sources and resources** for further guidance.

3.3

THE CHANGING LANDSCAPE OF TWENTIETH-CENTURY BRITISH HISTORIOGRAPHY

Whig history and the end of optimism

In 1931 a highly influential little book was published entitled *The Whig Interpretation of History*. Its author, Herbert Butterfield, argued that historians during the nineteenth and into the early twentieth century had tended to adopt a teleological view of history, that is, they worked with an assumption that the conclusion was an automatic given in the process. This meant that the parliamentary democracy that Britain had become during the nineteenth and early twentieth centuries was viewed in terms of continued improvement and progress from medieval through early modern politics to the Victorian era. Furthermore, the rise to power of Britain as the leading imperial and industrial nation of the nineteenth century could be traced via a Whiggish interpretation of the collapse of feudalism and the heroic endeavours of entrepreneurs and inventors during the industrial revolution.

The nineteenth-century belief in a forward path of inevitable improvement was much less pertinent to twentieth-century British history. The very history of Britain itself since 1900, with its uncertainties and considerable reversals of fortune – economic and imperial – rendered a Whiggish interpretation of earlier periods increasingly inappropriate while appearing almost irrelevant to the historical study of Britain post-1900.

A further danger of which Butterfield warned was 'present-mindedness'. As John **Tosh** summarises Butterfield:

> present-minded history exhibits a tendency to underestimate the differences between past and present: to project modern ways of thought backwards in time and to discount those aspects of past experience which are alien to modern ideas. In this way it reduces history's social value, which derives largely from its being a storehouse of past experiences contrasted to our own. Nowadays the charge of 'present-mindedness' or 'presentism' is often levelled at left-wing exponents of people's history or women's history. Butterfield's book is a useful reminder that goal-oriented or teleological history has been prevalent among establishment historians of every persuasion.
>
> (J. Tosh, *The Pursuit of History*, 1998, p. 145)

Historians of all political persuasions, therefore, could be culpable of present-mindedness. This raises some fascinating questions for the historian of twentieth-century Britain. We are, of course, relatively closer in time to events and developments in contemporary history than earlier periods. Looking back on the 1970s, 1980s and 1990s may by definition be a 'present-minded' thing to do, partly because many of us remember some or all of those decades, and partly because we think we can trace developments to our own time much more easily as a consequence. Contemporary historians should still adopt a position of rational detachment, however, acknowledging that personal memory is no substitute for wide-ranging research and hard analysis and expecting to process countervailing evidence to their own assumptions. And without a doubt the study of the history of, say, economic or foreign policy in all decades during the last century, whether we lived through those decades or not, requires the same disciplines and standards that would be required for the study of other periods.

British historiography was not only simplistic in its naïve optimism, it was also 'top down', focusing upon the 'great men' in history, those hallowed few, often dressed in uniform or wearing an Eton collar and a suit, who were considered to have shaped the paths of historical development or to have personified its most significant moments. This elitism was challenged by the emergence of relatively new fields of historical enquiry during the twentieth century, notably social history, cultural history, political history, urban history and economic history. The related disciplines of diplomatic, defence and military history also enjoyed new directions in travel throughout the course of the twentieth century.

Social history

The well-known book *English Social History* by G. M. Trevelyan, first published in 1944, is often held up as the standard text in the social history of modern Britain. Trevelyan famously defined social history as 'history with the politics left out' in order to privilege the study of social change for its own sake, although by no means in isolation from economic history. However, the origins of a more democratic concern with the development and experiences of 'ordinary people', albeit written by leading intellectuals, stems from the work of historians of the later nineteenth and early twentieth centuries who argued strongly that industrialisation and urbanisation had by no means benefited all people in Britain, and that Britain in many respects remained an unequal and inhumane country deserving of new political strategies. This point reminds us that historians often developed their views and their writings in relation to current concerns and policies, and that many wish to use history to shape public opinion and policy agendas.

Two married couples were significant in this respect, namely Beatrice and Sydney Webb and Barbara and J. L. **Hammond**. They were at the forefront of a new pessimistic school of history that pointed not to the quantitative story of improvement and progress but to the subjective and experiential dimensions of history. The Webbs, both founders of the Fabian Society, had strong connections with social science and with leading social reformers of the late nineteenth and early twentieth centuries, with whom they shared a concern to improve the lives of ordinary people. One such method was to promote the historical study of the lower classes. The Webbs's study *English Poor Law History* (1927) was an extended historical and moral critique of the system of poor relief as it continued to exist into the twentieth century.

Coterminous with much of the Webbs's work was that of the Hammonds. In *The Village Labourer* (1911), the *Town Labourer* (1917), *The Skilled Labourer* (1919) and *The Bleak Age* (1934) they highlighted the destructive effects of industrial 'progress' on the lives of the working poor. Focusing upon the poor during the industrial revolution from 1750 to 1830, they argued in *The Bleak Age* that the experiences of millions of workers were those of loss: the loss of the known and familiar village as a consequence of urbanisation and urban migration; the decline of common land as a site for social activities and for foraging and grazing as the enclosure movement and agricultural 'improvement' changed the English landscape; the demise of an informal pattern of work and leisure for the new rigidities of the factory system; and the rise of overcrowded and polluted proletarian zones in the largest industrial cities.

Similar arguments were proposed by G. D. H. **Cole** and Raymond Postgate, whose seminal book *The Common People* was first published during the 1930s and republished during the postwar years partly as a reminder of continuing inequality and poverty within the welfare state. Tosh draws attention to Cole's argument, in *A Short History of the British Working-Class Movement, 1789– 1947* (1948), that, 'as the working-class grows towards the full exercise of power, it should look back as well as forward, and shape its policy in the light of its own historic experience' (Tosh, *The Pursuit of History*, 1998, p. 98).

Labour history has its origins in such sentiments. The formation of the Society for the Study of Labour History (SSLH) in 1960 both reflected and promoted the growing interest in the organised working classes that Cole had helped to pioneer: the trade unions, whose rationale was the collective interest of workers in the workplace and who had sought parliamentary influence since 1900. Furthermore, histories of trade unions also dovetailed with the study of industrial relations in Britain during the 1960s and 1970s. There was no coincidence in such overlap, or in the expansion of the study of labour history. For the 1960s and 1970s were decades during which industrial relations were often problematic, and academics sought to explain strikes and other forms of industrial protest as symptomatic of the position of the workers within industrial capitalist Britain.

Labour history thus had linkages with economic history, but was ideologically closer to social history. Leading Labour historians, notably Cole and Eric Hobsbawm, were also social historians. And just three years after the foundation of the SSLH the Centre for Social History was established at the University of Warwick by the Marxist social historian E. P. Thompson. Thompson's interests lay primarily in the social and political history of lower-class organisations in eighteenth- and nineteenth-century England, but the twentieth century was increasingly studied in the work of many of his contemporaries and those who followed him. Thirteen years later, as social history continued to expand, the **Social History Society** was founded by Harold **Perkin** at the University of Lancaster in 1976. A great deal of the work of social historians was concerned with the eighteenth and nineteenth centuries; however, interest in the twentieth century began to expand as the century drew to its close. Increasingly sports, leisure and popular culture in all their diversity were subjects of serious academic study. Historians sought to discover the meanings and values in the lives of people beyond the workplace. Other fields of enquiry included children's history, the history of ethnic minorities, dietary history, sexuality, ageing . . . the list was almost endless.

By the 1970s new areas of social history were forming, notably the study of gender within women's history and the cultural history of modern and contemporary Britain. As John **Stevenson** argued, these broad fields of historical endeavour now took on lives of their own (Stevenson, 'Social history', in L. J. Butler and A. Gorst (eds), *Modern British History*, 1997, p. 207).

Cultural history

Social history contributed to the growing interest in cultural history. Cultural history is harder to define than social history, however. When asking ourselves what cultural history is, we may usefully draw upon the following definition by Arthur **Marwick**, in his book *Culture in Britain since 1945* (1991). The word 'culture' signified the arts, intellectual attainments, entertainments and leisure pursuits reflecting the values and ways of life – cultures – of a people or a nation. A more limited working definition of culture emphasises cultural *products*: 'books', 'the arts', 'entertainments' and 'the media'. These two definitions overlap closely.

During the postwar period, cultural history also came to mean the study of cultures of groups, their norms, values and lifestyles: working-class culture, the culture of armies, **youth culture**, and so on. Social history has tended to overlap with the study of culture in this broad definition. Hence Marwick usefully draws the distinction between *cultural* products and their *social* construction: books, paintings, television programmes, cinema movies, newspapers and magazines were the cultural products of – in our case – twentieth-century British society.

Two broad but intersecting schools have dominated cultural history. One, influenced by the French Annales school, focuses upon *mentalities* and upon collective manifestations of consciousness, values and lifestyles: working-class culture, middle-class culture, the cultures of ethnic minorities or other marginal groups, and even national cultures. A second school, an important practitioner of which was Arthur Marwick, focuses upon cultural products, as noted above, and places these in their historical context.

Both broad categories of cultural history were also influenced in postwar Britain by the emergence of cultural studies. The character of cultural studies initially owed much to the work of the social scientist Richard Hoggart, whose study of the mass **media**, literacy and working-class culture and community during the 1950s proved hugely influential in sociology and social history. Hoggart himself established the Centre for Contemporary Cultural Studies (CCCS) at the University of Birmingham during the 1960s.

This was an important moment in the growth of interdisciplinary approaches to cultural history. Historians have borrowed from approaches and insights in literary studies and media studies. A leading figure in this respect was Raymond Williams. A Marxist, he may also accurately be described as part literary critic, part novelist, part journalist and part cultural historian. During the 1970s and 1980s, Williams interrogated a diverse range of what he thought were fundamental questions about class and culture. Both the CCCS and Williams were linked by their belief, pioneered by E. P. Thompson in British historiography, that culture was not only meaningful but could be agency, that is, a mover of history, and not simply the dumping ground of ideas and representations within a dormant superstructure. Hence Williams explored the cultural significance of literature as influencing values and both reflecting and causing emergent social and cultural trends.

Unfortunately for Marxist cultural studies, an emergent socio-political trend was the growing support for Thatcherism among the British electorate during the 1970s and 1980s. The election of Margaret Thatcher in 1979 was brought about in part by the voting behaviour not only of the middle classes but of millions of affluent workers who were sick of militant trade unions, and also by some of the poorer sections of the working classes, whom Marx had once dismissed as the *lumpen proletariat* – those beyond the organised working classes who were instinctively patriotic and fearful of socialism. Hence, at the peak of their intellectual powers and influence, Hobsbawm and Williams were writing against the tide of cultural and political history. Although they were certainly far from being 'present-minded', it could be argued that they were also falling short of a comprehensive understanding of the very classes and marginal groups in society they sought to liberate. In that sense, a more present-minded approach could be advantageous, and would prove to be so for the new generation of historians who owed little or nothing to Marxist cultural studies. Younger or newer historians adopted an increasingly nuanced approach to social and cultural change. As John **Tosh** has written, the general election of 1979 'marked a political and cultural watershed, with the collapse of the postwar social democratic consensus, and its replacement by a new and strident version of Conservatism' (Tosh, *The Pursuit of History*, 1998, p. 178). This watershed brought about a new revisionism in historians' understandings of society and culture. A similar broad pattern from Marxism to revisionism, with continuing currents of conservative and liberal historiography, can be seen in the origins and character of political historiography in twentieth-century Britain.

Political history

The status of political history declined during the twentieth century yet remained an increasingly vibrant field of study. Unlike social and economic history, political history was firmly established before the beginnings of the twentieth century. Indeed, most historical endeavour occurred within the fields of political history or diplomatic history. As Arthur Marwick has argued in *The Nature of History* (1989), while the disciplines of social and economic history emerged and took root before the Second World War, most professional historians 'continued to be preoccupied with constitutional and political history' (p. 89). Hence much political history was undoubtedly and by its very nature elite history. As Robert Pearce has noted, political history could be written 'as if politics were part of a closed world', devoid of inter-connections with social and economic developments (Pearce, 'Political history', in L. J. Butler and A. Gorst, *Modern British History*, 1997, p. 155). That closed world may be summarised as 'the corridors of power': the sphere of the prime minister, the cabinet and cabinet committees, the ministries, and the civil service.

Before the First World War, the classic two-party system of Tories and Liberals was the framework within which most political historical analysis of the nineteenth and early twentieth centuries was undertaken. However, the rise of Labour and of mass movements that impacted upon party-political fortunes caused many political historians of twentieth-century Britain to address the connections between politics and social change. This led to a growing number of studies of 'grass-roots' political organisations and their origins. One of the major historiographical contexts for this was the emergence of labour history. This refers to the history of trade unions, their role in the formation of the Labour Party, and their ongoing relationship with that party. The Webbs (again) were at the early stages of this with their *History of Trade Unionism* (1894), which viewed trade unions as rational collective responses to industrial capitalism. Increasingly however, labour historians focused on the achievements and performances of Labour governments and politicians, reflecting once more the truism that historians respond to their own contemporary historical context, for example in the work of Henry **Pelling**, Kenneth O. **Morgan** and a more recent generation of labour historians.

Political history also evolved in relationship with political science and the discipline of politics as taught in universities. The work of opinion pollsters, and of psephology – the study of voting behaviour and election results – contributed towards greater understanding of the relationship of political performance to social and economic developments. Furthermore, the growth of affluence and consumerism during the postwar period stimulated historians to investigate more closely the relationship between, on the one hand, rising incomes, material comforts and home ownership and, on the other, voting behaviour and party-political allegiances. The failure of the Labour Party to win successive general elections during the booming 1950s and the 'Thatcherite' 1980s was particularly significant, as was the enduring relationship between the Conservative Party and the majority of middle-class voters. Here, as with social and cultural history, the changing political landscape of late twentieth-century Britain engendered more nuanced interpretations of politics. Many historians on the left, as noted above for G. D. H. Cole for example, had endorsed a kind of socialist–Whig view of the Labour Party as an ascending force. By the early 1980s many labour historians were re-examining the so-called British road to socialism and the forward march of Labour halted, a re-examination that was, ironically, coterminous with the apogee of the left of the Labour Party.

What was the character of political history by the end of the twentieth century? Although the eighteenth and nineteenth centuries remained important periods of study, the twentieth century and particularly the years since 1945 were increasingly fashionable. While in no way given to hermetically sealed interpretations of postwar politics, leading contemporary historians of politics remained focused on decision-making and decision-makers, on political policies and policy-makers, on the significance of by-election and general election results, and on the performance and reputations of leading politicians. To be sure, political historians can also be social historians – Peter **Hennessey** is a case in point – but the bulk of his work, and probably the majority of work connected with the Institute of Contemporary British History from 1986, treated politics as *primus inter pares* within the study of Britain since 1945.

The political history of the twentieth century remains a diverse and vibrant field of historical endeavour, although it is no longer as dominant within the canon of British historiography as it was a hundred years ago. This was a very different story from the fields of urban and economic history. We will look at each in turn.

Urban history

The study of urbanisation and of the history of towns and cities has become increasingly popular in recent years. The work of the Urban History Group (UHG) at the University of Leicester is one reflection of this, as is the number of urban history courses in British universities, particularly at postgraduate level. Urban history is a broad and diverse field of study, embracing local histories as well as much grander investigations into urbanisation and urban change in regions, countries and continents – even global urban development. It enables us to connect up local or micro-level developments, for example slum clearance or the rise of suburbs in a particular town or city, with much broader processes. These can include population growth and urbanisation, legislation and its effects, the impact of wars and conflicts upon the urban environment, growing affluence and rising expectations, and the changing economy. It follows from this that urban history is also strongly interdisciplinary: for example, considerable work has been undertaken on the social history of towns, on the politics of slum clearance, on suburbanisation, consumption and class, on urban economies, and on architecture and urban change. There are also considerable creative synergies between urban history and town planning history, although historians of town planning focus more often upon the impact of the garden city and garden suburb movements, on key town planners, and of course on town and city plans themselves.

Among leading lights in the establishment of urban history are Asa **Briggs**, H. J. **Dyos** and Anthony Sutcliffe. Much of their work was about the nineteenth and early twentieth centuries, although they and many other historians have studied towns and cities in Britain since 1918.

Economic history

Economic history first emerged during the late nineteenth century and had become a small but established discipline by the 1920s. The **Economic History Society** was founded in 1926, and its journal the *Economic History Review* began publication the following year. The discipline of economic history developed partly in harness with social history, but also in reaction to the perceived failure of social history to get to grips adequately with hard economic data. Both T. S. Ashton and J. H. Clapham were significant in this respect. Clapham notably, in his three-volume *Economic History of Modern Britain*, published during the 1920s and 1930s, challenged the work of the Hammonds and other social historians who reflected upon the qualitative experience of industrialisation and urbanisation for the poor, and instead put his faith in statistics, in a quantitative account of the development of modern Britain. As Jeremy **Black** and D. M. MacRaild have argued, Clapham was in many ways a nineteenth-century positivist, believing in the forward march of economic growth. 'Under Clapham's aegis', they have written,

> the emphasis shifted from the social impact of industrialisation to looking at the emergence of the great staple industries – cotton, coal, iron and steel, and shipbuilding. Clapham was concerned with the origins of the industrial revolution, not its impact.
>
> (Black and MacRaild, *Studying History*, 2000, p. 60)

Clapham's emphasis on the staples provides a convenient and significant point of synthesis for the economic history of twentieth-century Britain. He was concerned to describe the growth of these staple industries and their contribution to the modern British economy. As he wrote his magnum opuses, however, British staple industries were increasingly battered by effective competition from overseas and the global economy was undergoing turbulence and transition. Subsequently, traditional manufacturing industries would come to be at the heart of many economic analyses of British decline. As Jim **Tomlinson** has argued, Clapham's work remained influential into the postwar period, in part because of the disinclination of Marxist labour and social historians. Eric

Hobsbawm and E. P. Thompson, for example 'showed little concern with or knowledge of economics in their work' (Tomlinson, 'Economic history', in L. J. Butler and A. Gorst (eds), *Modern British History*, 1997, pp. 235–6). One exception to this may be Hobsbawm's *Industry and Empire*, a work of synthesis that traced Britain's industrial rise and decline partly to its marshalling of resources in the colonies from the eighteenth to the twentieth centuries.

Hobsbawm, in common with Clapham, focused on the history of the staple industries, and as he was completing his influential textbook economic historians were increasingly getting to grips with the problem of Britain's relative **decline** since the later nineteenth century. As Tomlinson argues:

> Pioneered by such writers as Burn in the 1940s, by the 1960s it was emerging as a commonplace among British economic historians that for nearly a century the British economy had been on a path of relative decline. This perception drew upon the general political debate on economic decline which emerged in Britain at the end of the 1950s, but pushed back the beginnings of the problem to well before the First World War.
>
> (Tomlinson, 'Economic history', in L. J. Butler and A. Gorst (eds), *Modern British History*, 1997, p. 239)

A central theme of this perspective was that of entrepreneurial failure in investment and innovation. British economic decline could be explained by the rise of an anti-industrial culture among the elites and the middle classes and a growing flirtation with learning and letters. Martin Wiener is an American advocate of this view. More caustically, the British historian Corelli **Barnett** accused the welfare state and nationalisation – in short, Labourite socialism – for Britain's postwar economic problems. Consensus politics, it follows, both consolidated and extended the errors of socialism. Both Barnett and Wiener have been trenchantly criticised for narrowness of interpretation. Tomlinson has mounted the critique of '**declinism**' against such pessimistic interpretations, noting that 'the dominance of declinism in writing about recent British economic history produced simplistic accounts of a much more complex pattern of economic development' (Tomlinson, 'Economic history', in L. J. Butler and A. Gorst (eds), *Modern British History*, 1997, p. 241). Barnett and Wiener are good examples of this: they were writing in the 1980s, and yet during the 1990s the British economy began to expand more rapidly than those of many of its leading competitors, by no means solely as a happy consequence of Tory government.

More widely, economic historians of Britain have focused upon a variety of central themes that, in synthesis, explain relative decline, for example the growing strength of foreign competition; the debilitating economic impact of the Second World War; and the failure of state-led initiatives to introduce economic planning during the 1960s. Many contemporary difficulties and downward trends were exaggerated by a failure to understand the postwar restructuring of the British economy as the services expanded while staple industries contracted.

The British economy continued to grow throughout the twentieth century, but the same cannot be said for Britain's influence overseas.

Britain and the wider world: diplomatic history, defence history and military history

In tandem with political history, diplomatic history had dominated British historiography both before and during the nineteenth and early twentieth centuries. As Anne Lane has argued, the Rankean method of documentary scrutiny and analysis governed the methodology of diplomatic history. A Rankean assumption that international history and the fate of nations were driven purely by foreign policy was also a central defining characteristic of diplomatic history. Marxist historians, however, mounted a 'sustained attack' on diplomatic history, 'arguing that markets and raw materials, not foreign policy, are the driving forces in history, and that ergo the reading of diplomatic history was of questionable value' (Lane, 'Diplomatic history', in L. J. Butler and A. Gorst (eds), *Modern British History*, 1997, p. 168).

Diplomatic history is also open to the charge of being 'elite' history. Yet there is little value in this charge, for in some respects the elitism of diplomatic historians is inevitable. As with a concern for high politics, by its very nature diplomatic history focused upon the leading politicians who were involved in the highest and most critical echelons of diplomacy, and upon the ambassadors and diplomats from Britain who liaised and negotiated with their foreign counterparts in order to improve international relations, prevent conflicts, or engage in conflict resolution.

Diplomatic history following the First World War became heavily focused upon the causes of that terrible conflict. The failure of diplomacy and negotiations among the European Great Powers during the later nineteenth century and the Edwardian years were viewed as both cauldron and catalyst for the so-called Great War. From 1945, diplomatic historians continued to debate the causes of the First World War but increasingly, of course, those desperate historical circumstances that had led to Second World War. Tracing the international linkages between these two conflicts was a key theme. The weaknesses of the settlement at the Paris Peace Conference in 1919 and the failure of appeasement have been endlessly picked over and re-examined. The realm of postwar diplomatic history, moreover, was further stimulated by the break-up of the British Empire through the process of decolonisation and the negotiations between the British and foreign governments for the independence of former subject nations. The continuing success, as well as some failures, in the special relationship between the United States of America and Britain has remained at the heart of the work of many diplomatic historians, while the partly risible story of Britain and Europe, and the relationships with the EEC since the early 1970s (and the EU since 1994), has been a growing area of study.

The history of defence policy is located, in common with diplomatic history, within the sphere of international relations. Key themes in defence history are the conflicts of decolonisation; the causes of war; appeasement and rearmament; the civil and military defence apparatus during wartime; the maintenance of peace through diplomacy and military preparation, for example major defence contracts; and the changing relationship of Britain to other world powers, notably the special relationship with the United States of America, the Soviet bloc and Western Europe. As in other historical disciplines, the most effective historians of defence do not work in splendid isolation from the methodologies and even the subject matter of other fields of historical enquiry. The relationship of the British economy, and of government public expenditure cuts, to the army, navy and air force has been a key theme of the history of postwar British defence, while Donald Cameron Watt and other leading defence historians have success-fully endeavoured to locate foreign and military policy within a wider frame-work of the political culture of postwar Britain and of elite networks.

Military history in a sense begins where defence and diplomatic history come to an end. War, as Clausewitz famously stated, was the extension of diplomacy by other means. Military conflict often reflected the failure or the impossibility of diplomatic solutions. Twentieth-century Britain had a close relationship with a number of wars: the Boer War, the totality of the First and Second World Wars, the Korean War, the Falklands War and later the **Gulf Wars**. British forces were also involved in counter-insurgency in overseas colonies. Increasingly, military historians have adopted not just the 'toy soldiers' approach of how battles were won and lost, but also the cultures of countries or groups that generated military conflicts. In the work of recent military historians, a more total picture of the military arena has emerged which has focused increasingly upon the nature and potency of nationalism, from the First World War to the Falklands War. Social histories of the British Army at war also throw new light onto the class relations of the battlefield, the pitilessness of modern warfare, and the vulnerability of men under fire. Increasingly, the comparative history of coun- tries at war illuminated the shared and differential characteristics of the British experience from 1914 to 1918 and between 1939 and 1945.

We saw above how the emergence and consolidation of social history led to responses in diplomatic, economic and political history. So too did the work of social historians meld with military history, notably, unsurprisingly, within the context of total war and the home front. As Ian F. W. **Beckett** has argued, the work of the social historians Angus **Calder** and Arthur Marwick, to take but two examples, opened up a more synthetic approach to the impact of total war on historical change. They disagreed on key aspects of war and change, for instance on the nature of the wartime solidarities on the accelerating or postponing effect of war on social policies, but made hugely important connections between war and historical development. Economic historians also debate the complex and often positive impact of war on British economic development, for example on technological innovation, the lessons learned from state coordination of industry on the home front, and the restocking booms that followed in the wake of total wars (Beckett, 'Military history', in L. J. Butler and A. Gorst (eds), *Modern British History*, 1997, pp. 183–90). Hence, unfashionable though it is to say so, military, political and social historians have all drawn attention to the beneficial consequences of conflict. Within the context of the military-political arena, wars have prevented dictators from flourishing and liberated peoples from tyranny. And, as is evident from **Landmarks**, total war produced benevolent social policies.

The contemporary historical study of small wars and counter-insurgencies also gathered pace as the Cold War drew to its close, and expanded thereafter. This was a reflection of the causes and nature of the conflicts that scarred the partial decolonisation of Ireland, the Troubles from 1968, and the end of empire in African and Asian countries. It was also consequential upon the growth of radical political nationalism and religious fanaticism during the final fifth of the twentieth century, a growth that had such tragic consequences for both 'East' and 'West' during the early twenty-first century.

3.4
A–Z OF KEY HISTORIANS

Notes

- What follows is by no means a comprehensive list of the major historians of twentieth-century Britain, rather an index of those who are best known and quite frequently cited. To search for other historians use www.history.ac.uk/ihr/Resources/Teachers/index.html. In addition you can purchase the latest hard-copy issue of *Teachers of History in the Universities of the United Kingdom* at www.history.ac.uk/bookshop. It contains the addresses and telephone and fax numbers of all departments of history, email addresses of most historians, and their teaching area and research interests. It is not focused solely on twentieth-century Britain, of course, but many key historians are listed there.
- Please note that most historians now have web pages, and some have their own websites. You can also use online search engines to find their major publications and reviews of their work.
- The main research interests of each historian given below reflect the British twentieth century: some of them have wider interests than might be suggested here.

ADDISON, PAUL *Social history; political history*: made a significant contribution to the understanding of the Second World War and its relationship to social and political change in Britain. He has also written on military conflicts, namely the battle of Britain and the bombing of Dresden.

ALEXANDER, SALLY *Social history; cultural history*: a pioneering feminist historian with interests in historiography, the women's movement in Britain, and psychoanalysis and history. She became known beyond the profession of history for using autobiography to explore women's subjective experiences.

BALL, STUART *Political history*: a foremost historian of the Conservative Party in modern and contemporary Britain and a biographer of leading Tory politicians. Ball's work has been used by the Conservative Party on its website.

BANKS, OLIVE *Social history; cultural history*: primarily a sociologist of education, towards the end of her life Banks also made a considerable contribution to the history of feminism in Britain. Her books on the subject were influential, and she has been credited with pioneering the terms 'first-' and 'second-wave feminism'(see also entry in Biographies).

BARNES, JOHN *Political history; historiography*: a prolific historian of modern and contemporary Britain who has made an important contribution to the history of twentieth-century politics and to the practice of contemporary history.

BARNETT, CORELLI *Economic history; political history; military history*: a Conservative historian, Barnett was closely in sympathy with the Thatcherite critique of the effects of socialism and consensus on British society and the economy during the 1980s. He has also written on major conflicts involving Britain during the twentieth century and on Britain's declining overseas influence post-1945.

BEACH, ABIGAIL *Political history*: has written on political history, on citizenship and national identity in twentieth-century Britain, and also on the nursing profession.

BECKETT, IAN F. W. *Military history*: Beckett's major interests include the British Army; the changing nature of warfare; the growth of small wars; and counter-insurgency responses of the state and of the military. He has also written on total war.

BÉDARIDA, FRANÇOIS *Social history*: a French historian of England whose work incorporates both the nineteenth and the twentieth century, Bédarida cannot really be viewed as an Anglophile, but nor was he an Anglophobe. His work was essentially dialectical, emphasising the dynamism of the ostensible contradictions in English social and cultural history.

BLACK, JEREMY *Political history; military history; social history*: a prolific and wide-ranging historian of Britain since 1700, Black has also written on the country's recent history, on newspapers and on international relations.

BLAKE, LORD ROBERT *Political history*: a leading historian of the Conservative Party in modern Britain from Robert Peel to John Major and also a biographer of key Conservatives. Blake was knighted in 1971 by Edward Heath. He also wrote on overseas affairs, for example a history of Rhodesia (now Zimbabwe).

BOOTH, ALAN *Economic history*: Booth has made a significant contribution to the study of the British economy in the twentieth century, particularly after 1945, and to understanding industrial and technological change.

BOURKE, JOANNA *Social and cultural history*: a wide-ranging historian who has made important contributions to the history of warfare, notably the First World War and concepts of masculinity, within a wider body of work that examines gender and cultural change in twentieth-century Britain. She has also written a history of the working classes during the twentieth century.

BRENDON, PIERS *Social and political history; historical biography*: Brendon's wide-ranging research and publications include work on the British newspaper press barons, the holiday company Thomas Cook, Winston Churchill, and the decline of the British Empire.

BRIGGS, ASA *Social history*; *labour history*; *historical biography*; *urban history*: a leading historian of modern Britain whose work is wide-ranging, embracing the history of class, politics, cities, the British Broadcasting Corporation, and a biography of the leading reformer Michael Young.

BRIVATI, BRIAN *Political history*; *historical biography*: a leading member of the Institute of Contemporary British History (ICBH) during the 1990s, Brivati is perhaps best known for his biography of Hugh Gaitskell, but he has made many other contributions to the study of Labour's history.

BULLOCK, ALAN *Political history*; *historical biography*: the author of a respected biography of the Labour politician and trade unionist Ernest Bevin. However, he is best known for his work on Hitler.

BURK, KATHLEEN *Political history*; *historical biography*: within the broad penumbra of Britain and the wider world post-1945, Burk's area of expertise includes the Marshall Plan, the special relationship, and a biography of A. J. P. **Taylor**.

BUTLER DAVID *Political history*: Butler is primarily a political scientist, and his collations with other academics of *British Political Facts* is a goldmine for students of twentieth-century British politics.

BUTLER, L(AWRENCE) J. *Political history*; *historiography*: the co-editor of some very useful textbooks on modern British history whose work on history and theory has been useful to this volume. Butler has research interests in Britain and decolonisation.

C

CAIRNCROSS, ALEC *Economic history*: with a background in economic policy-making, Cairncross made an important contribution to the study of the British economy and of economic policy since 1945, notably on the economic legacy of the Second World War and on postwar British economic policy.

CALDER, ANGUS *Social history*: a pioneering historian of war and historical change who questioned earlier historians' interpretations of the wartime experiences and the Blitz as having created a cosy social consensus during the 1940s.

CANNADINE, DAVID *Social history*; *political history*; *imperial history*; *urban history*: a wide-ranging historian of modern British history from 1800 to 2000 whose interests include class relations, symbolism and the monarchy, and the British Empire.

CATTERALL, PETER *Political history*; *media history*; *historiography*; *historical biography*: the director of the Institute of Contemporary British History (ICBH) from 1989 to 2000. Catterall's work includes the practice of contemporary history, the launch of Channel 4, the editing of the diaries of Harold Macmillan, and some useful textbooks on postwar Britain.

CESARANI, DAVID *Social history*; *political history*: a prolific writer who has published on the history of Jews in Britain and more widely on Jewish history and on anti-Semitism.

CHARMLEY, JOHN *Political history*; *historical biographer*: a conservative-minded historian who has written on Britain and international relations, the Conservative Party and also Winston Churchill.

CHERRY, GORDON *Planning history*: a pioneering historian of town and country planning in Britain and of the garden cities. With Anthony Sutcliffe, he founded the **International Planning History Society**.

CHILDS, DAVID *Political history*: a wide-ranging historian with interests in British and overseas history. His textbook on British politics since 1945 is very useful to undergraduate students. He has also written on immigration history.

CLARKE, PETER F. *Political history*; *economic and social history*; *political biography*: originally a historian of Liberalism in Lancashire. Clarke's thesis on working-class politics in the county raised some important questions about divisions within the working classes and the rise and fall of Liberalism. He also made studies of a number of prime ministers and other politicians and wrote two significant studies of the interventionist economist John Maynard Keynes, who in some ways was an heir to New Liberal politics. Clarke is best known for his readable and impressive synthesis of twentieth-century Britain, *Hope and Glory*.

COLE, G(EORGE) D(OUGLAS) H(OWARD) *Social history*; *political history*: a pioneering social and labour historian of Britain from the eighteenth to the twentieth century. Cole was originally a journalist and was a keen member of the Fabian Society.

COOK, CHRIS *Political history*; *social history*: an author of useful textbooks on twentieth-century British history and also of source books on modern and contemporary Britain. With John Stevenson, he made an original contribution to under-standing interwar experience, but has also written on a wide range of subjects.

D

DAUNTON, MARTIN *Economic history*; *urban history*: an expert on globalisation and Britain since the mid-nineteenth century, he has also written on housing in modern Britain. Daunton has interests in the taxation of the British Empire in the nineteenth and twentieth centuries and the changing relationship between domestic and international economic policies in the postwar years.

DOCKRILL, MICHAEL *Political history*; *diplomatic and defence history*: a historian of British **defence policy** since 1945, of the special relationship or Anglo-American overseas alliances, and of Anglo-European international relations during the Cold War. Dockrill has been concerned to relate the disciplines of defence and diplomatic history to wider historiographical developments in social and political history.

DOCKRILL, SAKI *Political history*; *diplomatic and defence history*: an expert on international relations, including diplomacy and the special relationship during the Cold War, and the related field of British defence policy since the Second World War.

DYOS, H. J. *Urban history*: with particular interests in Victorian and Edwardian slums and suburbs and the influence of public transport on town expansion, Dyos made a pioneering contribution to the rise of urban history in Britain. Along with David Reeder, he was a leading proponent by the 1970s of urban history at the University of Leicester

EVANS, ERIC *Social history*; *political history*: a wide-ranging historian of modern and contemporary Britain whose work includes the development of the modern state, the politics of Margaret Thatcher, and national identities.

EVANS, RICHARD J. *Historiography*: although primarily a historian of modern Germany, Evans has contributed, in his *In Defence of History*, to debates over the nature and practice of modern and contemporary history.

FIELDING, STEVEN *Political history*: a Labour historian whose analysis is very much within the revisionist tradition from High Gaitskell through to Tony Blair. Fielding has half-dismissed the history of the Communist Party of Great Britain as 'interesting but irrelevant'. His work is particularly concerned with how the Labour Party adapted to cultural change in Britain.

FREEDMAN, LAWRENCE *Defence history*; *military history*: a leading historian of contemporary conflicts, Freedman is author of the most significant histories of the Korean War and the Falklands War.

GAMBLE, ANDREW *Economic history*; *political history*: primarily a political scientist, Gamble brings a historical perspective to his work on the decline of twentieth-century Britain and on Britain's relationship to the wider world. His range includes the British economy and its problems during the twentieth century; the British Empire and decolonisation; British attitudes to and interactions with Europe; and, more recently, Britain's special relationship with the United States of America.

GARDINER, JULIET *Social history*: a former editor of *History Today* with a wide-ranging portfolio, she has made an important contribution to the history of the Second World War and also to both Edwardian and postwar Britain.

GILBERT, MARTIN *Military history*; *political biography*: a leading historian of the First and Second World Wars, of the Holocaust and of British relations with Germany between the wars, and perhaps the most eminent scholar of Winston Churchill. He is also an international historian, the author of a three-volume history of the twentieth century.

HAGGITH, TOBY *Social history*: specialising in film history, Haggith has written or edited many key works on the history of film during war as well as on film and the Holocaust.

HALL, SIR PETER *Urban history*; *town-planning history*: Hall's work is international in focus and oriented towards urban and town planning policies. Within his prodigious outputs, he has made some important studies of the British garden cities movement and of new towns.

HALSEY,   A(LBERT)   H(ENRY) *Social history*: primarily a sociologist, Halsey nonetheless deserves pride of place in any pantheon of twentieth-century historians on account of his work on social trends and social change in British society. Many of the facts and figures in this book are drawn from works written or edited by Halsey. His edited volumes *Trends in British Society since 1900* (1974) and *Twentieth-Century British Social Trends* (2000) are among a number of key text-books that historians and journalists rely upon for basic facts and figures about social, economic and political develop-ments since 1900. He has also written *A History of Sociology in Britain* (2004).

HARRIS, JOSÉ *Social history*; *historical biography*: an expert in the history of social policy from the late Victorian years to William Beveridge and on social change in late Victorian and Edwardian Britain.

HARRISON, BRIAN *Social history*; *political history*; *biography*: Harrison was editor of the *Oxford Dictionary of National Biography* (2004). He has written on alcohol and the pub and on modern British political history, and is currently working on a history of postwar Britain.

HARRISSON, TOM *Social history*: although primarily an anthropologist rather than a historian, Harrisson is noteworthy as the co-founder in 1937 of the **Mass Observation** movement, which provides invaluable information on British society during the 1930s and 1940s. *Living Through the Blitz* (1976) is a revealing social history of wartime Britain drawing upon the work of Mass Observers from 1939 to 1945 (see also entry in Biographies).

HATTERSLEY,   ROY *Political   history*; *Labour history*; *historical biography*: an ex-Labour politician, now a journalist, polit-ical historian and biographer, Hattersley is lacking in original insights but strong on readability.

HENNESSEY,   PETER *Political   history*; *social history*: a co-founder of the Institute of Contemporary British History (ICBH) in 1986, Hennessey has made a major contribution to understanding the opera-tion and shortcomings of government and also the civil service in twentieth-century Britain, particularly in the postwar years. He has written two books on the social and political history of Britain from 1945 to 1960 – *Never Again: Britain, 1945–1951* and *Having it So Good: Britain in the Fifties*. He is, broadly speaking, a social democrat in politics.

HEWISON, ROBERT *Cultural history*: the author of highly original studies of elite and popular culture in Britain during the era of the Cold War and on art and society in Britain during the 1960s.

J

JAMES, LAWRENCE *Social history*; *political history*: a wide-ranging author of some notable histories, particularly on the rise and fall of the British Empire and on the middle classes in modern Britain.

JEFFERYS, KEVIN *Political history*: his work is concerned with the leadership of major political parties and governments and with key events and turning points in British political history during and since the Second World War.

JENKINS, KEITH *Historian of philosophy*: a postmodernist who is keen to deconstruct the nature and practice of 'traditional' empirical history.

JENKINS, ROY *Political history*; *biography*: a Labour and Social Democratic Party politician (see Biographies), Jenkins was also a historian and wrote biographies of Clement Attlee, Stanley Baldwin and Winston Churchill.

JOHNSON, PAUL *Political history*: an editor of *New Statesman* magazine during the 1960s, Johnson became a convert to Conservative politics and a supporter of Margaret Thatcher during the 1980s. He has written on modern British history and also United States history.

JOHNSON, PAUL A. *Economic history*; *social history*: Johnson has written on old-age pensions, standards of living, and spending and saving habits and has also edited a useful textbook on British history in the twentieth century:

JONES, HARRIET *Contemporary political history*; *the Cold War*: a member of the Institute of Contemporary British History during the 1990s. As a historian of postwar conservatism, Jones has challenged notions of a shared 'consensus' between the Conservative and Labour parties during the 1940s, 1950s and 1960. She is also co-editor of some useful textbooks for students of twentieth-century Britain.

for students of electoral history. With Anthony **Seldon** of the Institute of Contemporary British History, Kavanagh made a number of very recent contemporary historical studies of prime ministers. He has also contributed to the debate on the postwar political consensus.

KILLINGRAY, DAVID *Political history, overseas history*: within a wide portfolio of articles and books he has made a strong contribution to the history of people of African descent in Britain, and of decolonisation.

KUSHNER, TONY [Antony Robin Jeremy] *Social history*: with interests in race and ethnicity in modern and contemporary Britain, Kushner has written on the history of Jews in Britain, anti-Semitism, the heritage of the Holocaust, and immigration.

KYNASTON, DAVID *Political history*; *business history*; *postwar British history*: Kynaston made his authorial debut with a history of the Labour Party. He has written a major history of the City of London and the financial institutions of the Square Mile within London, and is currently working on three in-depth revisionist histories of postwar Britain, the first of which, on austerity, was published in 2007.

KAVANAGH, DENNIS A. *Political science*; *political history*; *political biography*; *psephology*: a political scientist whose work is careful to provide a historical context for the elections, political developments and politicians about whom he is writing. Analyses of each general election, made with David **Butler**, are essential readings

LAYBOURN, KEITH *Political history*; *social history*: a wide-ranging survey historian, with particular interests in Labour Party history, social policy, and social conditions in Britain between the wars.

LEESE, PETER *Social history*: the author of some accessible and important histories of immigration and the migrant experience to Britain during the nineteenth and twentieth centuries, and more specifically the postwar period, he has also written on shell-shock during the First World War.

LEWIS, JANE *Social history; social policy; women's history*: a feminist historian of women in nineteenth- and twentieth-century Britain and of social policy from the later nineteenth century. Lewis has also written a survey history of women in England since 1945.

LOWE, RODNEY *Social history*: a historian of social policy with particular interests in welfare policies in twentieth-century Britain and in the evolution of the welfare state since 1945. He has also written on British welfare policy since 1942 within a comparative perspective.

McKIBBIN, ROSS *Social history; cultural history*: a major historian of British society and cultures in the nineteenth and twentieth centuries. McKibbin's work encompasses class relations, working-class cultures, leisure and the Labour Party.

MANDLER, PETER *Social history; cultural history*: a highly respected historian of nineteenth- and twentieth-century Britain whose interests include architectural history, voluntary association, and the notions of national identity and national character.

MARWICK, ARTHUR *Social history; cultural history*: Marwick made a major contribution to the understanding of war and historical change, notably the First World War. He was the author of a number of useful general textbooks on postwar Britain and also wrote a large comparative study of Britain and other countries during the so-called cultural revolution of the 1960s. His analysis of 'witting' and 'unwitting' testimony in historical sources is very helpful to students looking to understand the multi-layered meanings of texts.

MASON, TONY *Social history; sports history*: working at the Centre for Social History at the University of Warwick during the 1970s and 1980s, Mason moved the analysis of the working classes significantly beyond the study of trade unions and the workplace into the spheres of sports and leisure. He addresses the issues of solidarities and social action in sport and leisure activities, mostly football – both informal and commercially organised. He has also written on the Blitz in Coventry.

MIDDLETON, ROGER *Economic history*: his work on industrial problems, on the policies of 1950s and 1960s governments, and on relative decline clearly explains many difficult concepts and developments in economic history.

MORGAN, KENNETH O. *Political history; political biography*: a prolific historian of politics in nineteenth- and twentieth-century Britain, best known for his history of the Labour Party, his biographies of Labour leaders, and his history of modern Wales.

MORGAN, KEVIN *Political history; historical biography*: a historian of the left in twentieth-century Britain, Morgan has focused on the social, cultural and political history of communism in Britain. Other key works include a biography of Harry **Pollitt**.

MOWAT, CHARLES LOCH *Social history*; *political biography*: an American historian of late Victorian, Edwardian, interwar and early postwar Britain. Eminently readable, and covering almost all significant aspects of social, cultural, political and economic history, Mowat's work continues to offer students concise but comprehensive summaries and interpretations of the major themes and events in interwar Britain, notably class conflict and class quiescence, conservatism, Liberal decline and the rise of Labour, political movements of the far left and right, affluence, consumerism and poverty, the new and declining sectors of the interwar economy, and the onset of war.

MUNSLOW, ALAN *Historian of philosophy*: a postmodernist and an editor of the journal *Rethinking History: The Journal of Theory and Practice.*

NEVILLE, PETER *Diplomatic history*; *political history*: a prolific and wide-ranging historian who has written on Sir Nevile Henderson, the British ambassador to Nazi Germany during the phase of appeasement, and on Britain and **Vietnam** in the years immediately after the Second World War.

OVENDALE, RITCHIE *Defence history*; *political history*: the author of a useful survey of defence policy since 1945, he has also worked on the special relationship and the Cold War.

PELLING, HENRY *Political history*; *social history*: a socialist historian of the Labour Party and trade unions, his work included a biography of Winston Churchill and a study of the Marshall Plan. He was also interested in the British left and the special relationship between Britain and the USA.

PERKIN, HAROLD *Social history*: spanning the eighteenth to the twentieth centuries, Perkin challenged Marxist historiography through an emphasis, derived from the sociology of Max Weber, upon status in addition to class. His work on Britain since 1880 emphasised the rise of professional status and values, reflecting the increased bureaucratisation of society and the inexorable expansion of the professional middle classes. He founded the Social History Society at the University of Lancaster in 1976. Perkin was also a historian of public transport, notably the railways and motorisation.

PIMLOTT, BEN *Political history*; *historical biography*: a member of the Fabian Society, Pimlott wrote an important history of the Labour Party during the 1930s and biographies of Hugh Dalton, Harold Wilson and Queen Elizabeth II. He was a trenchant critic of Thatcherism during the 1980s and 1990s.

PORTER, BERNARD *Imperial history*: he has written on British imperialism, the rise and fall of the British Empire, and the difficulties and problems facing the British during decolonisation.

PUGH, MARTIN *Social history; political history*: a prolific historian of twentieth-century Britain. In addition to some highly recommended key textbooks on general British history, he has written accessible books on the women's suffrage movement, British fascism, electoral politics during the First World War, and interwar Britain.

PURVIS, JUNE *Social history; political biography*: a feminist historian who has made a considerable contribution to the understanding of women's suffrage in Edwardian Britain and its consequences. She has also made a number of biographical studies of key women in twentieth-century Britain.

R

RAMSDEN, JOHN *Political history*: a historian of the Conservative Party in the twentieth century and also a specialist on Winston Churchill.

REID, ALASTAIR J. *Political history; social history*: a socialist, he has updated Henry Pelling's long-standing and much respected history of the Labour Party. Reid is also a founder and co-editor of the website 'History and policy' (www.historyand-policy.org); its aim is to connect up more closely with policy formulation the historical work on social change and social policies undertaken by historians.

RICHARDS, JEFFREY *Cultural history*: Richards has made a considerable contribution to the cultural history of Britain during the twentieth century, including studies of cinema-going during the late 1930s and 1940s, national identity, the monarchy, and imperialism.

ROBERTS, ANDREW *Political history*: a conservative political journalist whose historical works include studies of Winston Churchill, of the monarchy, and of Britain and the English-speaking peoples in the international arena.

ROBERTS, ELIZABETH *Oral history; social history*: Roberts's most significant contribution to social history has been her oral history of working-class women in the North-West of England, mostly in Barrow and Lancaster.

ROSE, SONYA *Social history*: within a feminist perspective Rose has made a significant contribution to the history of women at war in twentieth century Britain, to an historical understanding of masculinities, and to national identities.

ROWBOTHAM, SHEILA *Women's history; social history*: a leading proponent of 'second-wave' feminism from the early 1970s, Rowbotham has remained a radical feminist whose core argument was that men write history primarily from their own gendered perspective. Hence women were 'hidden from history' both as subjects in the past and in the practice of history by (mostly) white middle-class men.

ROYLE, EDWARD *Social history*: a readable historian of modern and contemporary Britain, Royle emphasises twentieth-century historical developments in a wider historical context.

RUBINSTEIN, W(ILLIAM) D. *Social and economic history*: with interests in both the nineteenth and the twentieth century, Rubinstein has made a major contribution to the study of modern and contemporary British history and to debates over economic decline. He has also written on Jews in Britain and produced a comprehensive textbook on British party politics and elections since 1900. (His work has been useful to the politics sections of this book.)

S

SAMUEL, RAPHAEL *Social and cultural history*: Samuel was a Marxist academic and historian and a critic of postmodernism. Among his earliest work was the sociology of the East End of London, written with Michael Young and Peter Willmott. His interests in working-class and labour history continued throughout his life, and were particularly but by no means exclusively focused on the East End. He was one of the founders of the social history journal *Past and Present*. His archives and private papers are held at the Guildhall Library.

SANDBROOK, DOMINIC *Social history; cultural history*: Sandbrook is also a journalist and broadcaster, and his books on Britain during the 1950s and 1960s provide lively and readable introductions to the major social, cultural and political developments of those decades.

SELDON, ANTHONY *Political history; practice of contemporary history; contemporary biography*: a co-founder of the Institute of Contemporary British History (ICBH), Seldon has written mostly on the contemporary Conservative Party, its leaders, achievements, shortcomings and political culture. However, he has also acknowledged and lauded the political acumen and achievements of Tony Blair. In addition, he has made a number of useful contributions to the methodology of contemporary British history and written a history of Brighton and Hove.

SHAPELY, PETER *Political history; social history*: with research interests in housing and urban politics in both nineteenth- and twentieth-century Britain, specifically Manchester in the North-West of England, Shapely has explored council housing and consumerism. He has also written on charity and poverty.

SHERIDAN, DOROTHY *Social history*: an archivist and foremost scholar of the Mass Observation Archive at the University of Sussex, Sheridan focuses particularly upon wartime experiences, women's social history, the social experience of cinema-going, and the history of Mass Observation itself.

SKED, ALAN *Political history*: Sked is a conservative historian of both Britain and Europe (and also a politician opposed to British membership of the European Union). His work on postwar Britain provides useful introductions to the key themes of economic and imperial decline and to political history.

SKIDELSKY, ROBERT *Political history; historical biography*: primarily a political scientist, Skidelsky has written on Labour Party history; he is also the author of a somewhat controversial biography of Oswald Mosley.

STEVENSON, JOHN *Social history; political history*: Stevenson's textbooks provide very useful, wide-ranging and insightful introductions to modern and contemporary British history. With Chris **Cook**, Stevenson has complied some useful compendiums of British history (this volume has benefited from them) and made a highly original contribution to the history of the slump and the Great Depression in Britain. In addition (also with Cook), he has compiled a number of books on modern and contemporary British history based on facts and figures.

STONE, DAN *Cultural history; history of ideas*: covering both Britain and Europe, Stone has made some key contributions to the history of fascism and eugenics in twentieth-century Britain.

SUMMERFIELD, PENNY *Social history; oral history*: a feminist historian who has made an original contribution to understanding the many roles of women during wartime through the use of oral history.

TAYLOR, A(LAN) J(OHN) P(ERCIVALE) *Social history; political history; historical biography*: originally a Marxist who became a liberal social democrat in politics, Taylor was a well-known historian concerned with nineteenth- and twentieth-century political and social change in Britain (and Europe), with leading political figures, and with war. He came to prominence as much for his newspaper journalism and television lectures as his published work. His study of the origins of the Second World War was particularly provocative, emphasising the role of accident and contingency in historical development rather than Hitler's cunning and ruthlessness. Always controversial, Taylor is now regarded by many historians as inconsistent and opportunistic. Nonetheless, he did much to popularise interest in British history during the 1950s, 1960s and 1970s, and his range of interests and writings was uniquely wide.

THANE, PAT *Social history; political history*: a leading member of the Centre for Contemporary British History, Thane has written on the history of the Labour Party and on social policy, and is at the heart of

the history into policy initiative (see www.historyandpolicy.org).

THOMPSON, E(DWARD) P(ALMER) Social history: a leading Marxist historian and founder of the Centre for Social History, Thompson was concerned mostly with eighteenth- and nineteenth-century British history. He was also involved in the Campaign for Nuclear Disarmament during the 1970s and 1980s.

THOMPSON, F(RANCIS) M(ICHAEL) L(ONGSTRETH) *Social history; urban history*: Thompson's work on the twentieth century is embedded within a wider historical perspective that also includes the eighteenth and nineteenth centuries. He has made a particularly important contribution to the rise of the urban middle classes.

THOMPSON, PAUL *Social history; oral history; political history*: Thompson was a founder member of the **Oral History Society** during the latter 1960s. In addition to studies of Edwardian England, much of his work is historiographical, examining the rationale and practice of oral history:

THURLOW, RICHARD *Political history*: a leading and of course highly critical historian of British fascism, of leading fascists, and of anti-Semitism.

TIRATSOO, NICK *Economic history; political history*: a revisionist historian keen to debunk myths and accepted orthodoxies about Labour politics and the British economy, particularly during the postwar years. His work is useful to students for its analysis of such subjects as the 'thirteen wasted years' of Tory government from 1951 to 1964. He has also confronted the lazy view that Britain during the 1970s was in economic ruin before Margaret Thatcher came along to save it.

TOMLINSON, JIM *Economic history*: Tomlinson is particularly well known for his work on British economic decline during the twentieth century, and in particular the postwar period. One of his central arguments is that notions of decline became institutionalised during the 1950s and 1960s, leading to a belief among political elites in 'declinism' that took on its own dynamics in political and economic debates about postwar Britain.

TOSH, JOHN *Historiography*; *overseas history*; *gender history*: Tosh has a wide range of interests, including the study of masculinities, and has made a strong contribution to the teaching of history in *The Pursuit of History* (4th edn, 2006) and *Why History Matters* (2008).

WEBSTER, WENDY *Social and cultural history*: Webster's work is focused particularly on gender, race, ethnicity and national identity, for example on the impact of immigration into postwar England and the relationship of Englishness to the British Empire.

WEIGALL, DAVID *Political history*: a general historian of modern Britain and an expert in contemporary international relations. He has written on Britain and the European Union, and is recognised for his accessible work on international relations during the Cold War. He has also co-written textbooks for 'A' level and undergraduate students in British history.

WEIGHT, RICHARD *Cultural history*: Weight is the co-author of a useful A–Z of modern Britain. He has particular interests in national identity during and since the Second World War.

WHITE, JERRY *Social history*; *political history*: a historian of London working very much within the neo-Marxist *History Workshop* tradition of social, cultural and political history.

WIENER, MARTIN *Cultural history*: he is mostly known as the author of a widely discussed but unconvincing book on English culture and the alleged demise of the entrepreneurial spirit.

WRIGLEY, CHRIS *Economic history*; *political history*; *historical biography*: a historian of trade unions and industrial relations and of the leading figures in twentieth-century politics, particularly in the Labour movement.

ZEIGLER, PHILIP *Social history*: Zeigler's work encompasses both elite and popular social history, to wit the monarchy and the home front in London during the Second World War.

IV
SOURCES AND RESOURCES

4.1

NOTES

- This section introduces the major sources that historians use to research twentieth-century British history. These are traditionally placed into two broad categories, namely *secondary* sources and *primary* sources. Secondary sources are history books and journals and teaching websites. Primary sources are original documents, generated at the time that the event, events or developments occurred. In relation to the twentieth century, however, the term 'primary sources' is less appropriate than 'contemporary sources', and in some ways it is also unhelpful. In the purest sense of the term a 'primary source' is an artefact such as a weapon, or a manuscript – for example, a handwritten or typewritten document produced by the historical figure under analysis. A 'secondary' source, however, refers to work that has been subject to interpretation. Ergo, a letter written by a soldier from the trenches at the battle of the Somme is a primary source, while a newspaper report on the battle may be viewed as a secondary source because there has been some mediation between the battle and the historian. This definition is only partly useful, because both communicate the experience of the war in an acute way. 'Contemporary sources' is a much more revealing term. Furthermore, a history of the First World War written during the 1930s would in the previous definition be a secondary source, but surely it is a contemporary source that uncovers a great deal about the view of the First World War from the perspective of the 1930s. And, finally, because we are also looking at the latter period of the twentieth century, the distinction between primary and secondary sources can become blurred. For example, an article in a political science journal in 1998 on the general election result in 1997 is neither primary nor secondary given the recentness in time, but contemporary.
- The twentieth century was richer in contemporary source materials than any previous century, so the historian of Britain since 1900 has a huge variety of documents to choose from. Their uses are many. Interpretation of documents develops intellectual skills. It forms the basis of understanding historical issues and periods in history both from our own time and from that of the people involved in the making of the document. And 'documents' is a huge category, including books, journals, the press, cinema, television and broadcasting, parliamentary materials, official reports from myriad public and private professional organisations, autobiographies, memoirs and oral history. Many sources, or guides to those sources, are also available online.

- Secondary sources (history books) on the broad categories in this section are to be found in the **Bibliography**.

This section is divided as follows:

Secondary sources: history books, journals and websites
- History books
- History journals
- Online resources: teaching websites

Contemporary sources
- The press: newspapers and magazines
- Illustrations: cartoons
- Illustrations: photographs
- The screen: cinema
- Television
- Radio broadcasting
- Social investigation
- Social observation
- Parliamentary materials
- Private papers
- Diaries
- Oral history
- Memoirs and autobiographies
- Fiction
- The built environment

Resources: archives and libraries
- National archives and libraries
- University-based archives

History organisations

Approaches to documents
- Witting and unwitting testimony

4.2

SECONDARY SOURCES

History books, journals and websites

History books

It is impossible to give a detailed guide to all the history books on twentieth-century Britain. Below are a sample of some of the most reliable and comprehensive texts, some of which have been useful in the compilation of this *Companion*.

The twentieth century in its entirety

A growing number of series issued by publishers are dedicated to the twentieth century. Within the catalogue of the Longman Seminar Studies series, for example, initiated in 1966, one of the later themes introduced was twentieth-century Britain, which included studies of the Labour Party and Labour governments; the Conservative Party and Conservative governments; the decline of the Liberal Party; unemployment between the wars; war and society; women's suffrage campaigns; the British economy; and Britain and Europe. In 2007, every British prime minister of the twentieth century was the subject of a short historical biography in a series issued by Haus Publishing. The books are full of facts and are accessible introductions to their subjects.

Individual histories of Britain over the course of a century usually adopt a survey approach, aiming for comprehensiveness and up-to-date reviews of the historiography. Those written by a single author aim for synthetic or over-arching and inclusive interpretation of historical change, while edited collections may be more of a compendium of key themes and subjects. Please note that, in addition to the history of twentieth-century Britain in its entirety, the books in this section are valuable for the study of the more specific time frames here.

Black, Jeremy, *Modern British History since 1900* (2000), provides a comprehensive and thematic overview of the major themes and issues in modern and contemporary British history.

Butler, Lawrence, and Gorst, Anthony (eds), *Modern British History* (1997), provides a useful introduction to historiography, to using archives and libraries, and to the broad areas of social, economic, gender, political, diplomatic, military, imperial and commonwealth and business history. It was one of the first books to get to grips with the uses of the internet for historians, although the world wide web has developed and expanded since the book was published.

Carnevale, Francesca, Strange, Julie Marie, and Johnson, Paul (eds), *Britain in the Twentieth Century: Economic, Cultural and Social Change* (2007), discusses what is indicated in the title, focusing mainly upon major themes shaping the course of the century.

Clarke, Peter, *Hope and Glory: Britain, 1900–1990* (1996), covers social, cultural, economic and political history. The book is the final instalment of the Penguin History of Britain series.

Cook, Chris, and Stevenson, John, *The Longman Handbook of Modern British History: 1714–2001* (2001), includes many key facts, figures and people for twentieth-century Britain within a much wider time frame, and is all the more useful for that.

Garnett, Mark, and Weight, Richard, *Modern British History: the Essential A–Z Guide* (2004) is a quirky, not really comprehensive, but mostly informative collection of short essays on over 200 key issues, events and people in modern Britain. The social and cultural history of the twentieth century is particularly well covered.

Halsey, A. H., with Webb, Josephine (eds), *Twentieth-Century British Social Trends* (2000), is more than just a catalogue of statistics on social trends. It is a mine of information on social, economic and political developments since 1900.

Lowe, Norman, *Mastering Modern British History* (1998), allows students to gain immediate information and provides effective summaries of political, economic and military developments.

Palmer, Alan, *The Penguin Dictionary of Twentieth-Century History* (1999), covers world history but has some very useful fact-based entries on key aspects of British history from the Boer War to the fall of Margaret Thatcher.

Pugh, Martin, *Britain: A Concise History 1789–1998* (1999), is a readable introduction to modern Britain from the age of the French and industrial revolutions to the era of New Labour. Pugh's *State and Society: British Political and Social History: 1870–1997* (1999) is another widely used textbook on undergraduate courses.

Rubinstein, W. D., *Twentieth-Century Britain: A Political History* (2003), is a clearly written and well-informed history of the major governments of the twentieth century and of their leading personalities. It provides many key facts, figures and dates.

Early twentieth-century Britain

The early twentieth century can involve a number of different time frames, but usually tends to mean 1900–14, or the Edwardian period, as indicated in section 1.2, **Time frames**, above.

Harris, José, *Private Lives, Public Spirit: Britain 1870–1914* (1994), covers social, cultural and political changes during an era that represented a distinctive break with the previous Victorian years. Edwardian Britain is viewed largely in terms of continuities from the late nineteenth century, the rise of socialism, and growing social and reform movements.

Thompson, Paul, *The Edwardians: The Remaking of British Society* (1984), is an oral history of a country celebrating but wary of its imperialism, and witnessing the rise of women's suffrage, the decline of agriculture, and major disputes in industrial relations.

Wrigley, Chris (ed.), *A Companion to Early Twentieth-Century Britain* (2002), includes contributions from leading historians on social and cultural changes, the irruptions in domestic politics, and essays in both economic history and urban and planning history.

Britain between the wars

Unsurprisingly, the study of the interwar years usually begins with the ending of one war and the start of the other, but most histories of this period are dovetailed with the experience and significance of both world wars.

Constantine, Stephen, *Social Conditions in Britain, 1918–1939* (1983), is a clearly organised and readable summary of the major social problems and conditions in Britain between the wars. It is particularly useful for 'A' level, high school and undergraduate students.

Graves, Robert, and Hodge, Alan, *The Long Weekend: A Social History of Britain, 1918–1939* (1941). As its title suggests, this contemporary history by Graves, the well-known classics scholar and screenwriter, and Hodge emphasises positive developments in interwar Britain in addition to social and economic problems. Leisure and culture are discussed in a lively manner, anticipating some of the later historical approaches to the social landscape of interwar Britain.

Mowat, Charles Loch, *Britain Between the Wars, 1918–1940* (1978), by an Anglophile American historian, was originally written during the 1950s. It is still a very comprehensive and readable account of the major social, cultural, political and economic developments in Britain from 1918 to 1940.

Pugh, Martin, *We Danced All Night: A Social History of Britain between the Wars* (2008), takes some cues from Stevenson and Cook's *Britain in the Depression*, providing a readable account of 'the long weekend'.

Stevenson, John, *British Society, 1914–45* (1984), is a wide-ranging survey of society and culture from the beginnings of the First World War to the end of the Second.

Stevenson, John, and Cook, Chris, *Britain in the Depression: Society and Politics, 1929–39* (1994) (first published as *The Slump*), is an influential revisionist textbook that draws attention to an increasingly affluent and leisured British population beyond the poverty and unemployment of the poorest areas.

Britain since the Second World War

The historical study of postwar Britain has exploded in recent decades. A significant expression of this was the formation in 1986 of the Institute of Contemporary British History (ICBH) by Peter Hennessey and Anthony Seldon. As its title suggests, the ICBH was focused almost completely on the twentieth century, and mostly on the years including and since the Second World War. Many studies incorporated the years before 1939. However, the great majority of political histories have concentrated on the years since 1945, as is evidenced in the subject matter of series Making Modern Britain, edited by Seldon and Hennessey: the prime ministers since 1945; British general elections since 1945; consensus politics from Attlee to Blair; Britain and the Korean War; the Suez crisis; the end of the British Empire; British defence policy since 1945; Britain and Europe; Britain and the Falklands War; British public opinion; the British media (press and broadcasting) since 1945; town planning in Britain since 1945; women in Britain since 1945; and culture in Britain, unsurprisingly, since 1945.

There are many useful general textbooks for the years since 1945, but these are particularly useful both for those seeking a well-informed introduction to key themes and for students looking for varied perspectives. As noted in section 1.2, **Time frames**, above, some periodisations vary in terms of both starting and finishing dates.

Addison, Paul, and Jones, Harriet (eds), *A Companion to Contemporary Britain: 1939–2000* (2007), is an up-to-date and thematic approach to Britain which explicitly incorporates wartime developments and covers society, culture, the economy, urban history, defence, and Britain and the wider world.

Cook, Chris, *Routledge Guide to British Political Archives: Sources since 1945* (2006), is a user-friendly guide to the archives of organisations and societies since 1945 and to personal archive collections. It also contains indexes to colonial and military records since the Second World War.

Cook, Chris, and Stevenson, John, *The Longman Companion to Britain since 1945* (1996), provides a wealth of facts and figures as well as key events, names and terms.

Hollowell, Jonathan (ed.), *Britain since 1945* (2003), is divided into sections on government and politics, society and economy, and is notable for its clearly focused and well-explained chapters written by leading or up-and-coming historians.

Marwick, Arthur, *British Society since 1945* (2001), is a solid narrative view focusing upon social and cultural changes and continuities, and the arts, but also touching on politics. Many historians, it must be said, particularly of the postmodern schools, find Marwick to be narrow in his approach.

History journals

There are some useful and powerful guides and research engines to history journals on the world wide web. Some are more extensive than others, and many are compiled for use by individual libraries, so it is possible to browse the web and find many more titles than are listed below. This section, however, indicates the journals most relevant to twentieth-century British history. Most of them have online archives and indexes that can be browsed free of charge through the various online research gateways used by schools and universities, or for a small price if accessed privately. JSTOR and Blackwell Synergy are among the major gateways to accessing historical journals.

Contemporary British History (formerly *Contemporary Record*) is the journal of the Centre for Contemporary British History. Available online at www.tandf. co.uk/journals/titles, it is certainly orientated more towards political history than other fields, but is generally quite inclusive.

History Today and *BBC History Magazine* are published monthly, and are therefore on the shelves of the major newsagents. Back copies are available in libraries but are more accessible online: www.historytoday.org and www. bbchistorymagazine.com both provide a wealth of articles on most periods and countries, but twentieth-century Britain figures regularly. The articles are well written, frequently topical, and provide fascinating and often original insights into aspects of modern and contemporary British history.

20th Century British History (http://tcbh.oxfordjournals.org) is a relatively recent addition to the canon of academic history journals. Its subject matter includes politics, overseas history (defence, diplomatic and military history), and economic, social and cultural history.

Twentieth Century British History and *Contemporary British History* are dedicated to Britain in the twentieth century. Most journals are not, nor are they even primarily focused, on the British Isles, but they contain many articles, book reviews and other items of interest and relevance about Britain since 1900, for example lists of conferences, museum and archive exhibitions, and seminar programmes.

Other general titles containing articles and book reviews on twentieth-century Britain that range across social, cultural, economic and political history and Britain and the wider world are listed below. Again, they are available both in local and educational libraries and online. Private users are required to pay a small fee. The online research gateways or engines used by schools and universities should enable articles in the other journals to be accessed.

American History Review
Contemporary European History
Contemporary History
English Historical Review
European History Quarterly
Historian
Historical Journal
History
Journal of British Studies
Journal of Contemporary History
Journal of Modern History
Modern History Review

Some other journals falling within the broad fields that structure this book, namely social and cultural history, economic history, political history and Britain and the wider world are given below. Again (with the exception of the two titles that include parliamentary history) it is important to recognise that they are not only about Britain.

Social and cultural history journals

Film and History: An Interdisciplinary Journal of Film and Television Studies
Historical Journal of Film, Radio and Television
History Workshop
International Review of Social History
Journal of Gender Studies
Past and Present
Race and Class
Cultural and Social History (formerly *Social History*)
Women's History Review

Economic history journals

Business History
Economic History Review
European Review of Economic History
Journal of Economic History

Political history

Local Government Studies
Parliamentary Affairs
Parliamentary History

Britain and the wider world

Diplomacy and Statecraft
Diplomatic History
Journal of Imperial and Commonwealth History
Journal of International Affairs
Journal of Military History
Journal of Public Policy

Urban and town planning history journals

Journal of Urban History
Planning History
Planning Perspectives: An International Journal of Planning, History and the Environment
Urban History

Online resources: teaching websites

Browsing with intent to commit to the study of history is an enormously rewarding experience. The number and variety of websites is quite astounding, and what follows here is but a tiny sample of those available. However, you need to be aware that they vary considerably in terms of quality. Those selected below provide useful and in some cases excellent introductions and useful guides to the study of history in general, and to twentieth-century British history in particular. Many are direct teaching websites, containing inputs from historians and a variety of contemporary sources.

For history taught at schools, and those wishing to find out about the levels required, the following sites are useful if a little uneven. None are concerned solely with twentieth-century Britain. Some subjects are treated with more depth than others.

www.spartacus.schoolnet.co.uk is a comprehensive website for people of school age, particularly teenagers. It contains a wealth of information on key events, themes and people in modern British history. Its sections on twentieth-century Britain include:

> black people in Britain and immigration
> the world wars
> the Cold War
> trade union history
> cartoons, 1700–1980
> towns and cities (very useful for urban history)
> Scotland

Wales
religion and society
newspapers
and more general British history from the eighteenth century to 1960.

www.bbc.co.uk/history has a great deal of lively information on twentieth-century Britain, much of it drawn from BBC television or radio news items and reports. The website also contains many useful categories for searching, for example British history, Recent history, World Wars, Historic figures and Timelines.

More widely, www.bbc.co.uk has a didactic ethos (we can mostly thank John Reith for that), and contains many other items of great value to students of the twentieth century, notably 'on this day' (www.bbc.co.uk/onthisday), which provides little features and some moving film segments from BBC news reports for many events. Most of these reports date from the Second World War into the present.

www.thehistorynet.com is an American site, owned and operated by Weider History Group, a major publisher of history magazines. Its focus is predominantly American, and it is by no means confined to the twentieth century, but it does have some useful items on major people and events in Britain since 1900. It is also uneven: you will find more than a few references to Winston Churchill, for example, but very little on Clement Attlee.

www.britannia.com/history contains some useful introductions to many key themes in modern British history and provides a well-informed narrative history of twentieth-century Britain. However, some of its sections are hyper-links to other sites.

www.besthistorysites.net is an American website run by university academics, very easy to use and with links to many history websites, both academic and commercial. Its content ranges across many periods and countries, not only modern Britain. It also advertises books.

www.historylearningsite.co.uk is maintained by a history teacher. It ranges from ancient to contemporary history and includes many countries. For twentieth-century Britain it contains pages on the two world wars, women, and politics. Users are invited to make additions or corrections.

www.schoolhistory.co.uk provides a basic introduction to history, and will be useful for anyone seeking an introduction to modern British history. It begins in Roman times but contains some useful pages for students aged eleven years and above on the First and Second World Wars.

For students preparing for or panicking about exams, www.revisionlink.co.uk has links to the major sites to assist school students with revision and exam prep-aration, among them www.revisioncentre.co.uk, www.revisiontime.com and www.revision-notes.co.uk. This last, for example, covers history subjects on British school curricula from ages fifteen to eighteen.

What should we do about Wikipedia?

Wikipedia, an online encyclopaedia, is often the first site to pop up on a major search engine when a subject in history is keyed in. Teachers of history have been engaged in debate about Wikipedia, because some of its facts and figures have been found to be erroneous or misleading, and occasionally very erroneous and very misleading. Yet students at school, college and university continue to use it, and millions of people worldwide consult it for introductions to key events or people in history. It must also be emphasised that academics themselves write entries or sections of entries for Wikipedia, and that some of its content is verifiable, fascinating and useful.

If your teacher or lecturer specifically prohibits you from using Wikipedia, or recommends that you do not use it, then it is wise to follow that advice. However, if you are prepared to use Wikipedia as one resource among others, and to check off facts and arguments against other websites and published hands-on materials, then it does have its uses as a quick way into a particular topic. Anyway, relying solely upon one source for information to support arguments in essays or even work for publication is not acceptable. But if used with care, Wikipedia is by no means devoid of value to students of British history.

4.3

CONTEMPORARY SOURCES

Notes

- This section provides some essential guidelines to using the key types of documents in twentieth-century Britain, indicating the strengths and potential of sources, but also some of their inherent dangers or weaknesses.
- It also provides you with the major locations where you can access some documents, either in person or online.

The press: newspapers and magazines

It is common for historians to refer to newspapers and weekly or monthly journals as providing the 'first rough drafts of history'. For this reason, and also as a record of the huge diversity of newspapers published, the British Library's Newspaper Library at Colindale in North London holds almost all of the titles published in modern Britain. However, Colindale Newspaper library will be closed down by 2011, and thereafter newspapers will be available at the British Library or at its Boston Spa site. This collection embraces the national press, local newspapers, and literally thousands of special-interest papers, from sports to almost all leisure activities. Some are available online.

Most newspapers have adopted a political standpoint – left, centre but usually right-wing – and many different journalists and writers have analysed and opined in newspapers from a variety of political interests. In addition, most titles have long held a leader column, the statement of the views of a newspaper on a particularly important news item. This is not cause for concern: the biases and partisanship of newspapers and their writers, once understood, are advantageous to the historian, not a handicap. When exploring a particular incident in history, various newspapers can be drawn upon to gain insights into differing party-political views.

Newspapers have many other uses for the historian beyond political history, however. Both national and local papers contain articles on important events in national and local life as well as letters, leader columns, opinion columns, photographs, cartoons, sports coverage, and reviews of arts and culture. In addition there are many hundreds of titles based around specific interests in sports and leisure. Magazines, too, are usually centred within specific fields, from sociological, economic, cultural and political to myriad titles again within the broad categories of sports and leisure.

Where can I access twentieth-century newspapers and periodicals?

The best place to look for almost all newspapers and magazines is the British Library Newspaper Library's online search facility: www.bl.uk/collections/ newspapers.html (see also Archives and libraries below).

Both *The Times* and *The Guardian* have websites which can be searched for articles on modern British history. The site www.timesonline.co.uk/archive has a searchable database by keyword covering 200 years of world history, with Britain, of course, prominent among its contents. It runs from the late eighteenth century to 1985 (later years are available on the main *Times* website). This link will take you to the search box for key words, with which you can also set time parameters. For many keywords, you will be impressed at the amount of hits you receive on this website.

The Guardian has also been busy making its past issues machine-readable. Its website http://century.guardian.co.uk/ is arranged by decade from 1899, and also by theme. It is clearly presented and easy to use. At the time of writing a digital archive of all back issues of *The Guardian* and *The Observer* since 1821 was being created. These will be available from 2009, with various pricing options.

Illustrations: cartoons

Cartoons (in the sense of drawings as opposed to moving animations for entertainment) are to be found in a wide variety of newspapers and magazines. Illustrations depicting people or events have been in existence for centuries, and all of the major events and key people in twentieth-century British history – and many minor events and relatively unimportant people – were the subject of caricature. Such caricatures could be born of mockery and outrage or of sensitivity and humanity towards their subjects. Many cartoons, however, capture the gravity, irony, humour, joy or tragedy of a major moment in history.

A leading cartoonist was Eric Partridge of the magazine *Punch*: he was a Conservative satirist whose cartoons on politicians and political events during the Edwardian and the interwar years were almost always beautifully drawn, sometimes sentimental, and often scathing. Sidney Strube of the *Daily Express* and David **Low** are among the most highly regarded political cartoonists of the twentieth century.

Where can I access cartoons?

Cartoons are readily available in the newspapers and magazines in which they were published. These are available at the British Library Newspaper Library at Colindale (www.bl.uk/collections/newspapers.html) and of course on *The Times* and *The Guardian* websites mentioned in the section above.

The British Cartoon Archive at the University of Kent, Canterbury, is a rewarding place to begin researches into cartoons (http://library.kent.ac.uk/

cartoons). It contains over 100,000 cartoons and its database has a quick and accessible keyword search facility. The archive at the university also holds about 2,000 books on cartoons and cartoonists.

Some of the teaching websites listed above, notably Spartacus, have cartoons within their selections of contemporary sources.

Illustrations: photographs

Many of the most iconic photos of the last century are available from major photographic archives. When using photographs as historical documents, it is necessary to know, where possible, the newspaper or journal from whence it came, as this may assist in the interpretation of its content. Most photographs used by historians are derived from newspapers or magazines, and so are available on the websites of those newspapers. Again, online newspaper archives contain accompanying photographs to their articles.

Where can I access photographs?

It is usually more difficult to trace who took a photograph than it is to know who wrote the accompanying text. But you still need to know about the newspaper or periodical the photograph is from. Unflattering photos of politicians often accompany a critique of them in a newspaper of a different political persuasion, for example. However, many photographs, especially of major events, were often taken by professional freelance photographers and syndicated to more than one newspaper. The websites www.hultongetty.com and www. photoarchivenews.com contain thousands of photos from twentieth-century Britain. These have to be purchased for private use. Most photographs from newspapers and magazines will also raise copyright issues, so personal reproduction without permission or payment or both is often impossible.

A good photograph will convey the gravity or sheer joyfulness of a momentous event. Many others are concerned with the details, be they minor or significant, of everyday life. A particularly fine website in this respect is that of the 'Worktown' collection of photographs taken by Humphrey Spender for the **Mass Observation** project of the same name and held at Bolton Museum (see http://spender.boltonmuseum.org). It contains many black and white images of Bolton during the late 1930s on a variety of topics, among them **Blackpool**, children, religion, leisure, including pubs and sports, politics and street-life. Local history libraries generally contain collections of photographs of the locality, often deposited by keen local amateur photographers. Many of these often find their way into histories of cities, towns and villages written by local amateur historians.

The screen: cinema

From its late nineteenth-century origins in the most basic but revolutionary single reels of moving film to the sophisticated fiction feature films of today, the cinema provides historians of twentieth-century Britain with a rich and fascinating range of different types of film. The beginning of television broadcasting during the 1930s, and the huge expansion of television from the 1950s, has left a massive legacy of recorded programmes for historians to explore and to enjoy.

Cinema newsreels

Newsreels ranged from silent shorts to voiced-over news items on important and not so important items of current affairs. The era of silent newsreel in Britain stretched from the Edwardian years until the end of the 1920s. The main company providing silent newsreels was Topical Budget, which during the First World War was taken over by the War Office and hence became the major wing of British government propaganda during the conflict. The narrative took the form of sentences posted up between sequences of film. Newsreels with voice-overs began during the later 1920s. Among the largest companies of the talking newsreel were Pathé and Movietone.

Even simple newsreels were edited and presented according to strict criteria. During the Second World War, as in the previous global conflict, nothing was broadcast that might be of any value to the enemy or that was felt to demoralise those on the home front. And the choice of words used in voice-overs was sometimes calculated to present a certain point of view. Most key events in the political, social and cultural history of the country were the subject of newsreels, as were more 'human interest' stories or humorous items.

Documentary film in Britain

As noted in the **Dictionary** in this *Companion*, documentary film was one of the finest genres in British screen history. The 1930s and 1940s, before the television became the most important screen-based context for documentaries, were its most productive decades. From the 1950s documentary film-making in Britain was mostly absorbed by the BBC. Documentary films provide often politicised commentaries on key issues of the day or representations of people and places. They were never completely neutral, nor were they intended to be. More than that, many 'real-life' events or locations were often staged: many wartime documentaries, for example, included re-enactments or staged sets. Hence 'docudrama', as it is now called, was in existence from the early decades. Some documentary films aimed for hard-hitting realism, while others adopted a more poetic or aesthetic approach. Most were didactic to a greater or lesser degree – that is, intended to be informative. Documentaries remain a useful source material for social historians.

Fiction feature films

Great care must be exercised when making use of fiction film. First, its year of production is of critical importance, because the content of a film is often shaped by its historical context. The year a film was made may also influence the intentions of the film makers. For example, *In Which We Serve* (1942) was made during the Second World War, and its aim was to boost morale by presenting a picture of heroism and bravery and of unity across class divisions. However, a film such as *The Dam Busters* (1955) was made ten years after the war, so its subject matter, the ingenious bombing of dams in wartime Germany, was more about self-congratulation than propaganda, but it was also a paean to the bravery and dedication of British airmen in the conflict.

Second, genre is all important. Some films were made in a 'kitchen-sink' or realistic style, while others were much more glamorous or orientated towards visual effects for the 'wow' factor. To take one example of the genre of kitchen-sink films which emerged out of British new-wave cinema during the later 1950s and 1960s, the film *Saturday Night and Sunday Morning* (1961) was set in the terraced streets of working-class Nottingham. It is a contemporary film because it was based upon the novel of the same title by Alan **Sillitoe**, a native of the city, who was well acquainted with Nottingham and its people during the 1950s. Sillitoe took a particular angle, the **angry young man** called Arthur Seaton who is far from satisfied with his life and his future, yet trapped in a culture of instant gratification based around women, drink and gambling.

The film is useful in many ways. It contains the witting testimony of Sillitoe about working-class life and culture in an industrial city. Perhaps its unwitting testimony, however, reveals that he was less sympathetic or sensitive towards the women of the working poor: in one scene an unsympathetically acted middle-aged woman gets shot in the backside by Seaton. The film also provides a sense of the atmosphere of Nottingham during the late 1950s and gives tantalising glimpses of the streets, pubs, shops and houses of so-called traditional working-class culture, those who had not moved to the newer housing estates in the suburbs but remained in the old by-law terraced housing. At the very end of the film, in fact, Seaton is forced to realise that his bachelor days are going to end in marriage and a semi-detached home on a council estate. The content of the film can also be compared with the novel of the same name to see how far its attitudes and values were accurately portrayed in the cinema. Many of those attitudes and values would appear foreign to many younger people today, yet perhaps are still easily remembered by those over the age of sixty.

Television

Television is a twentieth-century technology that recorded twentieth-century news and current affairs. In addition, many different genres of programme have left a valuable and hugely diverse archive that reveals much about the history of the medium itself as well as of society. Americanisation is a major theme too. The news bulletins, soap operas, sitcoms, quiz shows, documentaries, contemporary and historical dramas, sports programmes, and leisure and hobby-based series are all windows into the viewing habits and preferences of the British people. Many series were long-running, such as the soap opera *Coronation Street*, while some sitcoms became firm favourites in the collective memory of the nation, for example almost anything from the 1970s starring Ronnie Barker. It is possible that the great proliferation of programmes from the 1980s and 1990s as a consequence of satellite and cable TV will be archived, but information on many series and programmes will be available from *Radio Times*, *TV Times* and newspaper television pages.

Where can I access films and television programmes, and information about them?

An excellent free website for newsreels is www.movietone.com, whose online collection begins mostly in 1929 – although there are some earlier silent reels – and terminates in 1979. The content is not only about Britain, of course, but if you have a powerful PC, or one that can show small segments of film, this site can be browsed by year, decade and subject-based searches.

Another newsreel website is www.britishpathe.com, which covers the years from 1896 to 1970. This is a pay-to-view site, operated by ITN, but it does provide some free high-quality segments from thumbnails. It is interesting to note that the most popular downloads from this site were about the *Titanic* disaster (1912), the accession to power of Adolf Hitler (1933), the London Blitz (1941), the 'events of the year' for 1940 when Britain held out against fascism in Europe, and the winning of a music prize in 1965 by the **Beatles**.

A useful website for accessing details on British cinema film is www.imdb. com. Its summaries of films are often gnomic but provide valuable pointers for further research. Another useful site, with clearly laid out summaries of content and the personnel involved in the making of the film, is www.filmreference.com.

For an excellent introduction to British film and television, with online research guidance, see www.bfi.org.uk. The BFI database has over 810,000 film and television titles and information on more than 1.2 million people. It also contains a major research collection of documents on the history of film and television.

The British Film Institute (BFI) operates a free viewing for schools of some twentieth-century films: see www.screenonline.org.uk.

On television specifically, www.bbc.co.uk is a mine of information on itself and its broadcasting history. For programmes on Independent Television (ITV), see TVTIP: TV Times Project, 1955–1985, based at Bournemouth University. It appears to be accessible to members only or via registered academic search engines (email asktvtip@bufvc.ac.uk).

Selected news items from the Independent Television (ITN) news archive and from Reuters are available to subscribing colleges, schools and universities via News Film Online (www.nfo.ac.uk). Its content spans most of the twentieth century and is both national and international in scope. Non-subscribers may search and browse for free.

An encyclopaedia on British television programmes is Tise Vahimagi's *British Television* (1996), compiled with the BFI.

Radio broadcasting

The radio, in common with television, was a twentieth-century medium. From the 1920s it made a major contribution to the social and family lives of the British people, providing not only entertainment but also news and current affairs.

Many important radio broadcasts, such as the abdication speech of Edward VIII, the declaration of war on Germany by Chamberlain, and some of Churchill's wartime speeches, are available on vinyl and cassette tape (both increasingly outmoded forms of reproduction), on CD, or to download from some of the various media websites mentioned in this section.

For those too young to remember these events, understanding the context is as important as the recording itself. Listening to the broadcasts with some knowledge of their causes and consequences is a highly rewarding experience. However, we must bear in mind that politicians and others were not only reacting to a difficult situation. Many were also attempting to use the medium for maximum effect and were changing their tone of voice for persuasive purposes. As for the listeners, there were millions of individualised responses, some influenced by personal politics or by particular views of the politician. For example, a miner's wife in Scotland, perhaps with communist sympathies and who could remember Churchill during the General Strike, may have had a different response to a Conservative-voting civil servant in a South London suburb when listening to some of Churchill's earliest wartime speeches. Nonetheless, all listeners shared in the power of the moment, and almost all were aware of the threat of Nazi Germany.

Where can I access information on radio programmes?

Many of the BBC's radio broadcasts are available on its website (www.bbc.co. uk) and at the National Sound Archive (www.bl.uk/collections/sound-archive).

As with so many larger websites, however, you should take the time to browse and to use internal search engines.

Social investigation

A key theme of this book is the uses of social investigation and sociology for the social historian of twentieth-century Britain. We should distinguish between two broad types of social investigation – social surveys and community studies.

Social surveys

Social surveys were pioneered in late Victorian Britain by Charles Booth and Benjamin Seebohm **Rowntree**. Booth went on to work in social policy during the Edwardian era while Rowntree continued as a social investigator until the 1950s. The scientific social survey is characterised by a large dataset and a concern to represent social class and social conditions statistically as facts. Many surveys were intended to compile information for the purposes of social policy. Following Booth's studies of London and Rowntree's of York, the twentieth century produced many important social surveys, a number of them concerned with the social life and class structure of cities, home and paid work for women, poverty, and – consequent upon immigration – race and ethnicity in the city.

Community studies

Using a smaller sample group, focused on local areas, and often concerned with particular issues in relation to community life, community studies were often rather narrow and even impressionistic. Ruth Glass was no great admirer of community studies, viewing the sociologist who ventured among the working classes as something of a nosy amateur, although her study of the North London suburb of Edgware during the 1930s was as much a community study as a social survey. During the 1950s, the foundation of the **Institute of Community Studies** gave rise to a new phase in community sociology and has left us with some fascinating publications on the working classes of the 1950s and 1960s. Subjects for study by community sociologists also included elderly people in the welfare state, education, the family, race and ethnicity, and the social life of suburbia. Others have investigated the worlds of employment, health and medicine, **crime** and children.

Where can I access social investigations?

The British Library of Political and Economic Science (or BLPES) at the London School of Economics (www.lse.ac.uk/library/archive) has been a major repository of social studies since the beginning of the twentieth century, and has an unequalled collection of the published social investigations, the documents and the papers of leading social scientists as well as myriad smaller social studies.

Also consult www.lse.ac.uk/library/pamphlets for more than 90,000 titles on the nineteenth and early twentieth centuries.

The British Library, of course, contains all published social studies made in Britain (see www.bl.ac.uk), and many of the older universities hold a great deal of social survey materials. Most university libraries with significant archives of sociological materials now have a comprehensive index or finding aid that is available online.

Academic journals, notably the *British Journal of Sociology* and the *Sociological Review* (new series), and more thematic titles, for example *Race and Class*, are also essential for shorter reports on aspects of British society since the 1940s. Many sociological journals can be accessed online. Hard copies are held at the BL and the LSE and in many university libraries.

Social observation

Often sharing similar concerns with social investigations – for example, social problems, inequalities in society, and the lived experience of marginal or oppressed groups – social observation is usually less empirically rigorous and researched than the more academic discipline of sociology. Yet social observation provides the historian with often profound insights into the problems being described. In his *People of the Abyss* (1902) the American writer Jack London visited the slums of the very poor in Edwardian England, those who had next to nothing, and provided some powerful descriptions of hopelessness and degradation that are moving in their own right but may also be usefully set alongside the social investigations of Booth or Rowntree.

Between the wars, the novelist and journalist George Orwell also wrote about poverty, his methodology being his willingness to live among the poor, whether it was the homeless of Paris and London or the unemployed or low-paid workers of Lancashire. Both *Down and Out in Paris and London* (1933) and *The Road to Wigan Pier* (1937) provide atmospheric and sensitively written, if occasionally rather pompous, descriptions of the impoverished people and places in urban Britain during the 1930s. In his *English Journey* (first published in 1934) the playwright J. B. Priestley observed and evoked social conditions in the countryside, the smokestack cities of industrial Britain, and the newer suburban areas of prosperous outer London and of the South-East in general.

Since the Second World War, social observation has produced no household names like Orwell or Priestley, but the activity has proliferated. For example, Jeremy Seabrook wrote extensively on the losers in social change: neglected old people, poor working-class children, and those living in poorer urban communities that were about to be ripped down to make way for redevelopment. During the 1980s, Beatrix Campbell, also lived among poor working-class women, recording their experiences and hardships during the decade of Thatcherism.

Where can I access social observations?

Social observation resulted in many contemporary books of great moment, held in the British Library, university libraries and many local libraries. However, many shorter or less well-known articles can be found in the broadsheet newspapers and in weekly or monthly magazines, such as *New Statesman* and *New Society*.

Parliamentary materials

Records of parliament are the archive of the heart of British democracy: they are the words and deeds of elected representatives to the House of Commons. Parliament also records the workings of the House of Lords, most of whose members were not directly elected by the people during the twentieth century. Parliamentary functions can be broadly divided into legislative, financial, representational and judicial. Materials include the debates of the both the Commons and the Lords; the work of MPs; the inquiries and findings of special committees and commissions into key issues and problems; Bills proposing legislation; the legislation itself; and a wide range of other data.

Where can I access parliamentary materials?

A useful introduction to and overview of these functions is available on the website of the United Kingdom Parliament (www.parliament.uk). This is an essential introduction to the contemporary workings of parliament and to the resources available to historians. Parliamentary records date from the thirteenth century to the present.

One of the important sources accessed by historians is *Hansard*, the daily debates of the Commons and the Lords, given as HC (Deb) and HL (Deb). *Hansard* is the record of British democracy in action in Westminster. It is almost verbatim, about as verbatim as record-keeping can get, with the exception of the exclusion of pregnant pauses in debate, coughs and the occasional 'ah' and 'err'.

Hansard is also kept in the Parliamentary Archives at the Palace of Westminster. Other records held in the Parliamentary Archives include private papers of leading politicians or those who took on affairs of state, for example Andrew Bonar Law, Lord Beaverbrook and David Lloyd George.

The British Library's Social Sciences room and most university libraries have an off-the-shelf facility. The House of Commons debates are available online from the 1988–9 session of parliament, and the House of Lords debates from the 1995–6 session (www.parliament.uk/publications/index.cfm). These can be searched via the names of individual MPs or Lords and by category and subject in addition to the dates and the index provided.

Most usefully of all, the website http://hansard.millbanksystems.com contains all *Hansard* debates from 1803 until 2005. It is searchable by this entire time period – by century, by decade, by year, or even by reigns of monarch – via a keyword search engine. It is a superb resource, although it does not contain the detailed minutes and proceedings of select committees and parliamentary inquiries. The British Library and National Archives remain the best resources here, or major university libraries.

Other parliamentary materials are bracketed under 'parliamentary papers' and include the following:

Bills: the drafts of legislation that precede Acts of Parliament, and the *Acts* themselves

command papers: the papers of information, or about decisions and problems, that the government or MPs wish to bring to the attention of parliament

select committee papers: the debates, investigations and reports of parliamentary committees into key issues and problems

reports of parliamentary and *royal commissions*: these are reports of parliamentary committees of inquiry into major contemporary issues and problems.

Among further materials are *house papers*, namely documents resulting from the work of parliament and its committees; and *accounts and papers*, namely correspondence between MPs and others; statistics; census data; treaties; and other materials.

Students of twentieth-century British history can search these online via http://parlipapers.chadwyck.co.uk. The website contains some very useful contextual information and an accessible guide to its use. These records are also available as bound volumes in the British Library, other national libraries, and some university libraries.

Major government publications have traditionally been published by His/Her Majesty's Stationery Office (HMSO). Its work is now subsumed under the Office of Public Sector Information (OPSI) (see www.opsi.gov.uk), which since 2006 has worked with the **National Archives** to encourage access to official publications.

Finally, a point about the infamous thirty-year rule, which prevents the release of official parliamentary documents into the public domain if these may be deemed to be damaging either to the public interest or to certain key individuals in the events or problems that were under investigation. This rule has been subject to review, and the report can be accessed at www.30yearrulereview. org.uk.

Private papers

The highly respected archivist Angela Raspin described private papers, which may contain private and public correspondence, drafts of policy papers, and official papers, as 'the physical survivals of a life' (Raspin, 'Private papers', in Anthony Seldon (ed.), *Contemporary History: Practice and Method*, 1988, p. 89). They may also contain newspaper and magazine cuttings, book reviews and even little souvenirs of places visited or people met. Many leading politicians, statesmen, stateswomen, public servants, writers, sports personalities and entertainers have kept private papers. They are hugely revealing of a person's life and work, but some may be more complete than others.

Where can I access private papers?

Many private papers have been archived and are available in university special collections and archives or, in the case of some leading politicians, in the Parliamentary Archives. Others may have been left with other types of repository, for example local libraries. Others still may not have been given to the public record at all, and will be held by the individual's close family or friends. In the latter case, they may viewed privately for academic use if the credentials of the historian and the purposes to which the work is being put are approved by those holding the papers.

As for tracing the location of private papers, this is not difficult: an internet search engine will usually turn up the information required. In the case of major figures, such as Winston Churchill or John Maynard Keynes, the repositories will be many rather than singular, while the papers of the town planner Frederic **Osborn**, for example, a less prominent historical figure, are held at Welwyn Garden City Local Library. In the case of more minor characters, one archive is usually the convenient result of an online search.

Diaries

The written thoughts, feelings and recent memories of events provide us with fascinating records of people's lives in earlier times. These may be the diaries of 'the great and the good' and sometimes of the lowly and the bad. They are vital for providing us with the individual or the subjective dimension of history, and they are records of earlier value systems and perhaps prejudices and beliefs that might appear outmoded or reactionary – or progressive – when seen from the perspectives of the early twenty-first century. However, we need to take care with diaries by asking some simple questions: How can we be sure this was written at the time, and not remembered some while later but presented as current? How 'me-directed' is this account? Does it pay due care and attention to the views of others, or is it dismissive? And how does the historical record in a particular diary square with the accounts of others? Does it add to knowledge or confirm what we already know?

Where can I access diaries?

Many diaries have been published, almost always edited by a historian, a confidante or a professional with a well-informed interest in his or her subject. Other diaries are archived, and may be available on similar terms to private papers.

Oral history

Oral history is the application of the tape recorder, or more contemporaneously the digital voice recorder, to record the memories of a person or persons who were witnesses to history.

When you think about it, almost all oral history undertaken today is twentieth-century history. In studies, for example, of agricultural and rural history during the first half of the twentieth century, almost all interviewees were born in the late Victorian or Edwardian years, and most of their significant memories were of the twentieth century. Oral history was concerned mostly with the experiences of the lower classes. The British oral history movement emerged during the later 1960s when a growing interest in folk culture, and even a romantic view of the countryside and of urban working-class life before the Second World War, stimulated historians to venture among the people and to record them. The work of such oral historians of rural Britain is evocative but does sometimes fall victim to a sense of nostalgia for a lost world.

By contrast, elite oral history provides us with a 'top-down' perspective, and it was given a major fillip by the Institute of Contemporary British History from 1986: the 'witness seminar' programmes of the ICBH (now the Centre for Contemporary British History) host mostly leading politicians and professionals. As noted above, however, most oral history is 'bottom-up' history – a silly term really, but one widely used by oral historians. The affinity of oral history with social history is a multifaceted one. However, it must be said that the plethora of titles in oral history along the lines of 'speaking for ourselves', 'we can speak for ourselves', 'speaking out', 'speaking up' or 'speaking up, speaking out' does irritate many non-oral historians. Similarly, the image of a serious professional middle-class historian clutching a tape recorder and venturing into the lives of the poor in order subsequently to 'empower' them in a publication is one that lends itself to ridicule.

But some of the best publications in turn justify the premise and practice of oral history. Few subjects are now taboo, and most can and have been, or will be, explored by oral historians. Hence oral history has been used to record the experiences of gays and lesbians in the years before decriminalisation or the worlds of illicit love affairs: Steve Humphries's *A Secret World of Sex: Forbidden Fruit: the British Experience 1900–1950* (1988) imaginatively and sensitively explored the personal dimensions of sex and sexualities during the twentieth century. It was also televised, another example of the affinity between oral history and the screen.

In *Oral History and the Local Historian* (1994) Stephen Caunce illustrates just how compatible oral history is with the study of local history, as it may explore local employment, housing, significant events, or the details of everyday life in a town or village. Individuals outside of academia, school and university students have also undertaken small oral history projects to research aspects of social history. Some museums and archives undertake or collect oral history for projects of varying scope and scale. The Imperial War Museum's *Voices of the Blitz and the Battle of Britain* is a good example of a larger oral history project that concentrated mostly on London but drew its interviewees from further afield.

Oral history is not without its problems, however. Memories become less sharp over time. Furthermore, people are often selective, choosing to highlight those aspects of an event which reflect well upon themselves or to suppress things for a variety of personal reasons. This is retrospective contamination. It is always necessary, where possible, to check testimonies for accuracy. But if handled with care oral history is a very useful tool for discovering something new and for recording the recollections of less well-known and even hidden areas of personal experience in the past. Discretion is required when exploring delicate or controversial subject matter.

Where can I access further information and guidance on oral history?

For online guidance on how to go about setting up an oral history project, see www.ohs.org.uk.

For hard copy guides, see Paul **Thompson**'s *The Voice of the Past* (1978). Robert Perks, *Oral History: Talking about the Past* (1992), and Alastair Thomson and Robert Perks (eds), *The Oral History Reader* (2006), both contain sections on the practice and problems of oral history. Many other minor guides have been published.

It is essential to note, however, that some of these books were out of date or about to go out of date in terms of the technology of oral history. During the 1960s and early 1970s the reel-to-reel tape recorder was the main instrument for recording the voices of the past, though sometimes historians would even take direct notes. During the later 1970s and 1980s the cassette tape recorder became the most common device, but digital voice recording has increasingly been used since its introduction, and many existing collections of testimonies, recorded on tapes, have been or are being digitised in order to improve data storage and accessibility. And accessibility does not just mean the availability of the source: digitisation enables historians to search back over recordings using key words as well as indices.

The website of the Oral History Society (see www.ohs.org.uk) is a fascinating introduction to the diversity of oral history; to the problems associated with recorded testimonies; to practising oral historians; to publications, including the *Oral History* journal; and to undertaking projects in oral history.

Furthermore, www.bl.uk/collections/sound-archive/nlsc.html has an indexed guide to interviews and recordings held at the **National Sound Archive** of the British Library in London.

Many oral history collections and projects have been undertaken, ranging from the large-scale to those by small local groups based in families, in communities, at local history libraries and museums, and at schools and universities. The following list gives some prime examples of how oral and local history fuse together.

Aberdeen and Region Oral History Association (AROHA): www.arohascot-land.org

Age Exchange, The Reminiscence Centre, London: www.age-exchange.org.uk/

Ambleside Oral History Group: www.aohghistory.f9.co.uk

BBC Education – History – 20th Century Vox: www.bbc.co.uk/education/20cvox

Birmingham People's History Archive (Carl Chinn Archive): http://lives.bgfl.org/carlchinn

Bracknell Forest Heritage: www.bfheritage.org.uk

Centre for North-West Regional Studies (including the Elizabeth Roberts Archive, Penny Summerfield Archives, etc.): www.lancs.ac.uk/depts/cnwrs

Dartmoor National Park Authority's Moor Memories Oral History Project: www.dartmoor-npa.gov.uk/dnp/oralhist/ohhomepage.html

East Midlands Oral History Archive: www.le.ac.uk/emoha

Exmoor Oral History Archive: www.somerset.gov.uk/archives/exmoor

King's Cross Voices Oral History Project: www.kingscrossvoices.org.uk

Museum of Welsh Life, St Fagans, Cardiff: www.nmgw.ac.uk/www.php/195

North-East Oral History Network: www.oralhistorynortheast.info

Refugee Communities History Project: www.refugeestories.org

School of Scottish Studies, University of Edinburgh: www.sss.ed.ac.uk

Society of Archivists Film and Sound Group (UK): www.pettarchiv.org.uk/fsgmain.htm

South Wales Coalfield Collection/Miners Library, University of Wales, Swansea: www.swan.ac.uk/swcc

Ulster Folk and Transport Museum, Belfast, Northern Ireland www.uftm.org.uk

Waltham Forest Oral History Workshop: www.wforalhistory.org.uk

Memoirs and autobiographies

Published autobiographies and memoirs by great and not-so-great people are of immense use to historians. They are produced by a wide variety of people: politicians, civil servants, writers, economists, film, television and radio personalities – even newsreaders – sportsmen and women, trade union leaders, freedom fighters, people from the armed forces, and well-known academics. There is also a growing number of autobiographies of 'ordinary' men and women. Neil Richardson, for example, ensured that many working-class autobiographies and memoirs from Manchester and Salford were published and thus preserved for posterity. Yet his website www.mlfhs.org.uk/Bookshop/richard.htm is by no means the only repository for the life stories of the un-famous. These reveal much about everyday life for working or unemployed people, of 'housewives' and amateur footballers, and give but a tiny sample of the autobiographies available.

It will be evident that many of the people included in the **Biographies** section of this *Companion* wrote their own version of their lives or accounts of events or episodes of significance with which they were intimately involved. Such accounts can give an insider's view of the processes and personalities involved, and this can provide vivid or even detailed insights into past events and people. They also reveal, often through that unwitting testimony mentioned above, flaws in the personality of the writer. And therein become evident some of the disadvantages of autobiographies and memoirs. They are mostly partisan, more or less fair-minded in their recollections, but always based upon conscious or unconscious selection in the way in which a 'true' story is told. In this sense, autobiographies and memoirs share some of the problems of oral testimony, although the historian is not present at the creation of the written testimony in the way that she or he is during an oral history recording. So at least historians who use the recollections in autobiographical writings can emphasise that the subject matter and the manner of argument reflects the choices of the writer. This in turn reveals a great deal about the writer.

The character or flavour of autobiographical work is thus as varied as the people who have written themselves into history. It is interesting to compare the rather modest output and tone of Clement Attlee in *As it Happened* (1954) with that of Margaret Thatcher's *The Downing Street Years* (1993). Many autobiographies rely on diaries written by their authors.

Fiction

Novels also throw light onto the lives of people and events in the twentieth century, and have been written about almost every area of human experience. Some examples will suffice to illustrate the uses and abuses of fiction for the historian. In Walter Greenwood's *Love on the Dole* (1933), for example, which was also made into a play and a film, the grinding effects of poverty and unemployment upon a slum in interwar Salford were closely observed and sympathetically treated. The novel evokes the atmosphere of urban Lancashire during the Great Depression, and is written in local dialect as well as 'proper' English to portray many aspects of slum life: the cheap appeal but also the perils of alcohol and gambling; the dangers of unwanted pregnancy; the lack of a politicised class consciousness despite the presence of left-wing Larry Meath and communist agitators; the decent hard-working woman driven to semi-prostitution by her family's poverty; and of course the fact that the textile mills, an important staple industry of the North-West, are in recession. These concerns reveal much about the values of the author himself: Greenwood had a strong grasp on reality but he was also a thinking man of his time, a writer who understood the appeal of gambling and drinking but felt the need to highlight their corrosive potential.

Greenwood was on the left of British politics. He was writing at a time, between the wars, when unemployment and its associated problems were deeply worrying to anyone with a social conscience. And, on this note, we must acknowledge an important distinction in fiction. Many novels are not contemporary or of their time. They are written after the event and, although they may be beautiful evocations or re-creations of atmosphere and of character and tell stories that reveal the hopes and fears, aspirations and problems of a previous generation, they must be treated with caution. For example, few would disagree that Pat Barker's *Regeneration* (1991) and Sebastian Faulks's *Bird Song* (1993) are powerful and moving depictions of the trenches and the tragic destruction of life and limb during the First World War. Yet, as accounts of that war, many novels will be coloured by the sensibilities and values of writers at three or four generations removed from that terrible conflict. The trenches are now a convenient historical landscape upon which current literary and philosophical debates about warfare itself are sent into battle. An objective and comprehensive grasp of the causes and nature of the Great War is often the first casualty of many literary approaches.

More widely, then, anyone using fiction to appreciate and understand the twentieth century, whether contemporary literature or a historical novel, must be cautious. As John Barnes has written, 'novels, films, plays and other works of fiction [can] give an insight into the manners, mores and ways of thinking of a particular period':

> They can be dangerous allies, however, and need to be used with great care. No author is typical and most have a message of sorts. In this sense the more commonplace novels may be of more use than great works of literature. By all means read Isobel Colegate on Suez, or John Mortimer's account of his slowly developing postwar disillusion, but do not swallow them whole. They are not a substitute for the kind of detailed research a sociologist or anthropologist carries out, or at least should do, but they may nevertheless stimulate imaginative insight into a period and so be of help to the contemporary historian.
>
> (John Barnes, 'Books and journals', in Anthony Seldon (ed.), *Contemporary History: Practice and Method*, 1988, p. 50)

Note that when Barnes refers to films and plays he means fiction feature films and dramatisation. The cinema and, to some extent, the stage have other uses for the historian because films and drama are often highly contemporary or written as key events and changes were taking place.

The built environment

The heritage industry, now so essential to our service sector economy, advertises and conserves historic buildings and sites from pre-Roman times. Prehistoric sites, churches and cathedrals, royal palaces, the homes of famous people, government buildings, and a wide variety of public buildings and famous streets and spaces are essential not only to our historical experience but also to the tourist experience (see www.englishheritage.org.uk and www.historic-scotland. gov.uk).

Increasingly, the most important or attractive environmental artefacts built during the twentieth century are being preserved for posterity. This takes the form of listing – that is, of using conservation and planning legislation to ensure that private individuals, commercial developers or councils cannot just knock down buildings of great architectural merit or historic significance. Such structures are listed because they are worth conserving to the highest degree of integrity that is possible.

The BBC's Broadcasting House for example, on Portland Place in London, is listed. It is an interwar building reflecting modern architectural styles, but it is also a building where a great deal of history occurred, from the earliest radio programmes, through wartime news broadcasts, to the expansion of radio programming during and since the 1960s.

Beyond the most famous buildings, however, the cities, towns and villages of Britain are full of artefacts and sites of great significance. Almost every settlement in Britain has a memorial to the dead of the First and Second World Wars, for example. But we need to know where to look to find out why these and other artefacts and buildings are significant. Many examples may be drawn upon when using the built environment, but a case study of the effects of the Blitz and its consequences for British cities is both a fascinating and revealing exercise for our understanding of wartime and postwar Britain.

In Coventry in the English Midlands, the old cathedral in the centre of its once medieval quarter is preserved as a symbolic reminder of the inhumanity of aerial bombings during the Second World War. It is also a reminder that Coventry's architectural heritage suffered terribly in 1940. A new modern cathedral stands close by, a site of reconciliation between Britain and Germany in the postwar years. Each was constructed at a different time, but both tell of the impact of war on the built environment and its people. In London, the Houses of Parliament and Broadcasting House were also bombed, as were vast tracts of residential neighbourhoods.

Two useful books are Sayre Van Young's *London's War* (2004) and Clive Harris's *Walking the London Blitz* (2003). When you take a walk around the streets and squares and compare what you see against the official bomb damage maps held at the National Archives in Kew, or the London Metropolitan Archives near Farringdon in London, it is fascinating to see what is now built upon the blitzed areas of the capital city. In addition, blue plaques in heavily bombed areas give basic information as to what existed before the war. Students can also consult Nikolaus **Pevsner**'s *The Buildings of England* series, which is arranged by county – except for London, for which there are a number of volumes (see www.pevsner.co.uk). Pevsner was an émigré to Britain with a great enthusiasm for British architecture. He and his associates itemised and recorded the merits and the address of almost every building of note, including those designed and constructed since 1945.

Buildings also housed important people, from the twentieth century and of course before. Blue plaques are useful and fascinating signposts to further enquiry, indicating key people associated with those buildings. The plaques mention many leading figures of the twentieth century, making an important pedagogical contribution to the city as well as a tourist attraction. For example, on Brook Street in London W1, there are blue plaques commemorating both the classical composer Handel and the rock guitarist Jimi Hendrix (see www.blue-plaques.com).

In addition, local history libraries contain a wide range of resources on the built environment, including maps, illustrations and paintings, and collections of old photographs.

4.4

RESOURCES

Archives and libraries

Online, the first website to visit for British archives is www.nationalarchives.
gov.uk/a2a (previously www.a2a/org.uk; a2a stands for 'access to archives').
The website does not give the contents of archives, but rather indices to those
contents. Its keyword search facility can yield some truly fabulous results. The
website also contains a search facility on the location of archives in Britain,
although, as it readily admits, its information on smaller local archives may be
less comprehensive than that on larger collections.

Many who want to undertake historical research for the first time are often
put off by the images associated with the terms 'archives' and 'libraries', terms
that often bring to mind old-fashioned and even intimidating places. All those
rows of shelves leave many people cold. Yet archives and libraries in Britain are
of course essential for historical research, and they have been changing greatly
in recent years. Many new library buildings have been constructed for schools,
universities and local authorities, and many others have been modernised. And
all archives and libraries have been made more accessible via the growth of
remote online searching and in-house online catalogues. For the convinced hater
of computers, many archives still contain card or paper indexes; an archivist or
a librarian is also on hand to help out. Alternatively, someone else can be
employed to do the research for you if you are willing to pay. A number of
archives have links to researchers.

National archives and libraries

The National Archives

The most important repository for the United Kingdom is the National Archives
(NA), based in Kew in the western suburbs of London (the nearest tube station
is Kew Gardens on the District Line). The archive was formerly known as the
Public Records Office (PRO), and some older textbooks or history books use
that term. While many Scots records are held at Kew, Scotland also has its own
National Archives, although it is much smaller than its southern counterpart.

The NA is the government archive – the repository for central government
records that date back to the eleventh century. With the growth of government
during the twentieth century, the expansion in the number of departments
and ministries led to data proliferation. Although not every single government

document or record is preserved at the NA, almost all of the most significant official materials are kept there. The NA is thus essential to the historian of social and economic policies in the UK and of almost all aspects of Britain's changing role in the wider world, notably defence and foreign policy. Family history or genealogical sources are also held.

The NA website (www.nationalarchives.gov.org) is well designed, easy to use and quickly conveys the huge variety of documents available in Kew. The following categories are of particular use to the historian of modern and contemporary Britain, and are partly drawn from the online A to Z *research guide* of the NA website. They are listed here both to provide a sense of the materials available by theme and to highlight the fact that some areas overlap. One of the first lessons to learn about the NA is that the system is very accessible, but many subjects can be found in more than one category of records or in more than one of the so-called *record groups*.

Admiralty
Armed forces
British Army
British Commonwealth
British Empire
Cabinet committees
Census
Citizenship
Civil service
Colonial Office
Crime
Death records
Education
Emigrants
Family records
Film and television
First World War
Foreign Office
Garden history
Gay and lesbian history
Health, 1919–39
Home Office correspondence
Housing and local government
Immigrants
Imperial and Commonwealth history
Ireland – the Easter rising
Ireland – Roger Casement
Jewish history
Labour history

League of Nations
Maps
Medals
Ministry of Housing and Local Government
Ministry of Labour
National Farm Survey, 1940–43
Naturalisation and citizenship; grants of British nationality
Newspapers and the press, sources for
Old Bailey and Central Criminal Court records of trials
Palestine
Parliamentary papers, printed
Passport records
Photographic collections
Police: Metropolitan Police (London)
Police: transport police
Poor Law
Prime Minister's Office
Prisoners of war in British hands
Propaganda, British in twentieth century
Railways
Refugees and minorities
Rights of way
Royal Air Force
Royal Marines
Royal Navy
Second World War: home front
Second World War: war cabinet
Second World War: war crimes
Ships wrecked or sunk
Titanic
Treasury board
Unidentified flying objects
War dead: First and Second World Wars
Wills and probate

These categories are starting points from which you can delve deeper through online searches. You will find, for example, that the experience of the home front in the Second World War will also be included under Maps, as the bomb-damage census maps are held here (those for London are also held at the London Metropolitan Archives), while homosexuality may also be included in Crime before the 1960s.

In common with all archives, the search engine of the NA can of course be used to search for much narrower terms. You might wish to search, for example, for a particular person, event or place. It is useful to practice on the NA website to see what is available. Some documents can be copied and sent on to you; others may be available only at the archive itself.

National Archives of Scotland

At the time of writing (2008) this user found the website of the National Archives of Scotland (www.nas.gov.uk) contained more crowded pages and was therefore less user-friendly than the mother of all national archives in London. However its summary of contents is clear:

> The National Archives of Scotland (NAS) keeps records created by Scottish government, as well as private records created by businesses, landed estates, families, courts, churches and other corporate bodies.

Some governmental records relating to Scotland are not held at NAS, but the emphasis is clearly upon recent records.

The British Library

The British Library is housed in an 'interesting' red-brick building on Euston Road in Central London (the nearest tube station is Kings Cross–St Pancras, and it is a short distance from those two major rail stations, and also from Euston Station). It contains almost every book or article printed in Britain and abroad in the English language. It is also the host for a wide variety of other archives and collections, for example the National Sound Archive, which contains a growing collection of oral history testimonies.

The British Library website (www.bl.uk) is easy to navigate and conveys the sheer breadth of books and journals and other materials available. Herein, of course, there is also a danger that minor specific topics will not be immediately apparent, so there is a search window for specific terms. Users can search on keywords, surnames and titles. For the historian of twentieth-century Britain, an obvious starting point is the *Modern Britain* collection, searchable online as well as in-house.

National Library of Scotland

Many of the books and materials held at the National Library of Scotland (see www.nls.uk) are also held in the NA in London. However, Edinburgh does have some significant specific collections for Scotland, namely the *Scottish Theatre Programme Database* and a series entitled *Scottish Political Press Releases*. The latter series coincided with the opening of the Scottish Parliament in 1999, so it is very contemporary history as well as being a collection of records of a fascinating and in some ways experimental period in British governmental history. The number of press releases issued by the Scottish National Party has been particularly influential on the collection.

National Library of Wales/Llyfrgell Genedlaethol Cymru

Although many of the books and other printed materials held in the National Library of Wales are also to be found in London, the National Library of Wales in Cardiff contains some collections specific to Wales and Welsh cultural identity. It holds, for example, records of Welsh archives and museums deposited before 1999. In addition, the crime and punishment database are of particular interest for social historians, and there are extensive collections of photographs and pictures. The National Screen and Sound Archives of Wales collection is held at the National Library of Wales (see www.llgc.org.uk)

British Library Newspaper Library

This is the major national repository for (in theory) all newspapers published in modern Britain and a number of major newspapers and periodicals published overseas. The collection is certainly phenomenal, containing all national newspapers existing or extant, local newspapers, and special-interest papers too. From 2011 Colindale's contents will be housed at the British Library's sites in London and Boston Spa.

Please bear in mind that in some cases visits to the Newspaper Library may not be necessary. Many newspapers have online search engines. Both *The Times* and *The Guardian* certainly do, and *The Times* is perhaps the best example of a paper whose articles are also available online as downloadable files. Other national and local newspapers also have online search facilities, but these are often confined to limited and recent time frames. In this respect, if, for example, someone wished to research on a particular event, such as a murder or riot that was known to have happened in a particular town during the 1920s, and the newspaper's online facility does not stretch back that far, there is no substitute for using the archives at Colindale.

University-based archives

The school or university library is often the first place to go to pick up history books or read history journals. Most will also contain online facilities to assist research. But many of the university libraries contain specific and important archival collections. As noted above, several are local and oral history collections, partly because universities have increasingly wished to enhance their local presence and importance.

Other collections are more extensive, embracing one or some of the following categories: social and cultural history, economic history, political history, and some military and defence history. Others may include all of these broad fields. It is impossible to include here the full range of university-based and specialist archives within these four categories, but those below are included because they are particularly useful for historians of twentieth-century Britain. Browsing them will give you a strong idea both of how to use the archives and of their contents and relevance to your own interests:

Social and cultural history

The Mass Observation Archive at the University of Sussex has a guide to the keyword search facility for its large collection of file reports, diaries, surveys, and the 'Worktown' collection. It has two website addresses. The stuff of everyday life is the basis of the collection, but the categories and thousands of entries under both general and more specific topics make this a first-class resource for social and cultural historians of contemporary Britain: see www.massobs.org.uk or www.sussex.ac.uk/library/speccoll/collection_introductions/massobs.html.

You should also look at the LSE library (BLPES) website (www.lse.ac.uk/library) for its unrivalled collection of sociological materials and private papers.

Economic history and political history

The Modern Records Centre at the University of Warwick (www2.warwick.ac.uk/services/library/mrc) has particular strengths in trade union history, employers' organisations, radical political groups and pressure groups (unilateral nuclear disarmament, human rights), the motor car manufacturing industry, and collections of private papers.

Military and defence history

The Liddell Hart Archive at King's College, London (www.kcl.ac.uk/iss/archives/about/lhcma.html), was begun in 1964 and has become the leading research repository on British defence history, with particular strengths in conflict and decolonisation and the world wars. It also contains private papers.

General university archives

Indexes to many university collections may be searched online at www.archive-shub.ac.uk. This website has powerful 'quick search', 'subject finder' and 'advanced search' engines, which will alert you to where key collections on specific subjects may be located.

The UK Data Archive based at the University of Essex (www.data-archive.ac.uk) is also useful. Established in 1967, it holds many thousands of datasets and contains links to major collections of official surveys, for example large-scale government surveys such as the Social Attitudes and British Households surveys, and major economic data studies, both national and international. This website also hosts the Arts and Humanities Data Service for historians (http://ahds.ac.uk/history/index.htm), which includes some twentieth-century British history datasets.

4.5
HISTORY ORGANISATIONS

Notes

- The organisations given here are wide-ranging and cover the broad themes in this *Companion*. Please be aware that several much smaller history organisations and research groups exist in social, cultural, political and military and defence history. Many are professional organisations based at universities, while others are more 'antiquarian' or run by enthusiasts who are not necessarily qualified historians.

Centre for Contemporary British History (CCBH)

The CCBH, based at the Institute of Historical Research at the University of London, is a leading research centre for twentieth-century British history (www. ccbh.ac.uk; see also www.historyandpolicy.org). It developed from the Institute of Contemporary British History, established in 1986, whose major journal was *Contemporary Record* (now *Contemporary British History*). The CCBH holds regular conferences, seminars and talks, including a 'witness seminar' programme based on the oral testimonies of leading figures in postwar British history. It has also been active in promoting the history of the struggle for equal rights in postwar Britain: this is one aspect of its wider commitment to emphasise the uses of history for policy formulation.

Centre for Urban History

Based at the University of Leicester, the Centre for Urban History (www.le.ac. uk/urbanhist/uhg) is the base of the Urban History Group, comprised of leading urban historians of modern Britain and of other countries. It is also a base for local and urban history, and hosts an annual conference in association with the Social History Society.

Economic History Society

The aim of the Economic History Society, established in 1926, was the promotion of the study of economic history alongside the established disciplines of political and diplomatic history and the emergent subject area of social history.

It began to publish the *Economic History Review* soon after it was founded, and both the society and the journal became important forums for the economic history of modern Britain, although interests went much wider than Britain. Over the course of the postwar years, both economic history and social history were brought together in an increasing number of 'socio-economic' histories of modern Britain, so that today the constitution of the EHS states that it promotes 'the study of economic and social history', a synergy that had positive consequences not just for historical research and writing but also for the organisation of conferences and research bids by historians. Today, the EHS has active links with other leading professional history societies, including the Social History Society, the Urban History Group, the Association of Business historians and the Institute of historical Research. Its web address is www.ehs.org.uk.

British Society of Sports History (BSSH)

Founded in 1982, the BSSH promotes the study of sports history, particularly the relationship of sport to British culture both at home and overseas. Its website provides a good idea of the key areas of sports history, and is useful for looking up some of the leading historians in the field and their publications. The journal *Sport in History* is closely associated with the BSSH; its web address is www.bssh.org.uk.

History of Warfare Research Group

Based at King's College, London, the History of Warfare Research Group (www.umds.ac.uk/schools/sspp/ws/groupresearch/military/hwrg) is international in scope but obviously includes Britain. Its research encompasses the nature and consequences of modern warfare; intelligence and espionage and the **secret state**; international relations; and the relationship of the military to the state.

International Association for Media and History (IAMHIST)

As its title suggests it is not only about modern British media, but it covers all aspects of media history, local, national and international, and from production and personnel to representation and reception. It contains leading British media historians, and the website includes resources, a forum for discussion, and links to other media history groups: www.iamhist.org.

Institute of Historical Research (IHR)

Based in the University of London's Senate House in Malet Street, the Institute of Historical Research is akin to the headquarters of professional historians and of teachers of history in British universities. The website (www.history.ac.uk)

contains a list of most of those teachers and has subsections on publications and book reviews. The IHR hosts regular seminar programmes and conferences. **British History Online** at www.british-history.ac.uk is a valuable IHR learning resource for more undergraduate and postgraduate history students.

International Planning History Society (IPHS)

First founded in 1974 by Gordon **Cherry** and Anthony Sutcliffe as the Planning History Society, the IPHS (www.planninghistory.org) became the successor to its parent body in 1993. It is genuinely interdisciplinary, and has important synergies with urban history, economic history, social history, geography and urban studies. Most of the work of planning historians is focused on modern and contemporary town planning history, and is thus concerned largely (but, it must be emphasised, not exclusively) with the nineteenth and especially the twentieth century as a consequence of the development of large-scale town planning and the town planning profession in advanced urban societies. Britain, as the original home of the IPHS, and, in addition to pioneering town and country planning legislation, as the home of the garden city and garden suburb movements, is commonly studied in *Planning History*, until recently the tri-annual publication of the IPHS, and in *Planning Perspectives: An International Journal of Planning History and the Environment*.

Oral History Society

The Oral History Society (www.ohs.org.uk) was formed in 1973 and is based at the University of Essex. It is now a global as much as a British organisation, and closely connected with the National Sound Archive at the British Library in London. Its journal is entitled *Oral History*.

Social History Society

Formed in 1976 by Harold Perkin, professor of social history at the University of Lancaster, the Social History Society (www.socialhistory.org.uk) was established to promote the study of the history of society through university teaching, research and publications, and conferences. It is now an international organisation. In 2004 its bulletin *Social History* became the journal *Cultural and Social History*. The instigation of the SHS reflected the growing popularity of social history more generally during the 1960s and 1970s, and an increasing number of social historians have working interests in the twentieth century as well as earlier periods. The society also has links with the Urban History Group.

4.6

APPROACHES TO DOCUMENTS

Published documents in textbooks

A number of very useful documentary source books have been produced on twentieth-century Britain. A good starting point is Lawrence Butler and Harriet **Jones**'s two-volume *Britain in the Twentieth Century: A Documentary Reader, 1900–1939* (1994) and *1939–1970* (1995). Both volumes provide a wide range of sources on political, economic, social and cultural history.

A highly respected work containing gobbets or sections from contemporary sources is Norman Lowe's *Mastering British History* (1998). Chapters 17 to 33 cover twentieth-century Britain, and the documents he includes are clearly explained and placed within their historical context. Many other works by historians, too numerous to mention in total here, involve contemporary sources. For example, Stephen Constantine's *Unemployment in Britain between the Wars* (1980) contains many useful short selections from contemporary documents from the 1920s and 1930s.

In addition, many history websites provide documents or extracts from primary sources: www.spartacus.schoolnet.co.uk is by no means the only one.

What sort of questions do historians ask of documents?

A careful, thoughtful and well-informed approach must always be adopted when using contemporary sources. Key questions must include:

- Who wrote or produced this?
- Why was it written?
- What can it tell about the values and beliefs of the author/s?
- What was the historical context of this document? (This refers not only to the month and year of its publication but also to the cause or causes that brought the document into existence. These may be immediate, but medium- and longer-term causes should also be emphasised in your interpretation.)
- What are the key words, allusions and most meaningful sentences in the text?
- Can I identify any consequences of this document in history?
- How reliable is this document? Is it an accurate or a heavily biased account?

Witting and unwitting testimony

The importance of identifying witting or unwitting testimony in primary sources is usually associated with Professor Arthur Marwick, of the Open University in Britain. His definition of witting and unwitting testimony can be found in a number of his writings. The following is drawn from the Institute of Historical Research website (www.history.ac.uk/ihr/Focus/Whatishistory/marwick1.html):

> In their work, historians have always recognised that primary sources, as well as containing many kinds of imperfection, also contain many types and many layers of evidence, even if they have tended not to make explicit statements about this. The crucial, though never absolutely rigid, distinction is between the 'witting' testimony and the 'unwitting'. 'Witting' means 'deliberate' or 'intentional'; 'unwitting' means 'unaware' or 'unintentional'. 'Testimony' means 'evidence'. Thus, 'witting testimony' is the deliberate or intentional message of a document or other source; the 'unwitting testimony' is the unintentional evidence (about, for example, the attitudes and values of the author, or about the 'culture' to which he/she belongs) that it also contains. Actually, it is the writer, creator, or creators of the document or source who is, or are, intentional or unintentional, not the testimony itself, so these phrases are examples of a figure of speech, the transferred epithet, where the adjective, which strictly speaking should be applied to a person, is transferred to what the person produced – the phrase is all the more effective for that.

A student of history should scrutinise a document not only for its most obvious points and allusions, but also for what is not said, or for aspects of the source which may reveal the values of the author in ways the author did not intend. Here, of course, knowledge both of the historical context and of the author or authors is essential to the fullest understanding of a document.

V
BIOGRAPHIES

5.1

NOTES

- The following secondary sources were very useful in the compilation of this biographical section, and readers are encouraged to consult them to build upon the details on the people mentioned, particularly the *New Oxford DNB*:

  - Accessible online at www.oxforddnb.com, the *New Oxford Dictionary of National Biography* (2004) contains biographies of almost anyone of significance who died during the twentieth century. It can also be searched by keywords.
  - *The Hutchinson Encyclopaedia of Modern Political Biography* (1999)
  - Cook, Chris, and Stevenson, John, *The Longman Companion to Britain Since 1945* (1996); *The Longman Handbook of Modern British History, 1714–2001* (2001).
  - www.spartacus.schoolnet.co.uk

- Biographies have been written on many of the most important figures below. In many instances more than one biographical study has been made.
- Many of the individuals have websites, established either by themselves or by admirers, and sometimes by critics. Take care to look for biases when using them, as with any other text-based interpretation.
- The biographies in this section are concise accounts and cannot really explore the personality and personal lives of the subjects in any depth; biography as a form of writing history has become increasingly popular, although it is not without its problems – not least a tendency to over-praise or alternatively to demonise the subject. The best biographies, however, are sensitive to their subjects, and nuanced, avoiding one-dimensional portrayals.
- Most key terms in bold may be cross-referenced to other points in this *Companion*, notably under **Landmarks**, in the **Dictionary**, and via the index.

5.2

BIOGRAPHIES

A

ABERCROMBIE, SIR PATRICK (1879–1957) Architect and town planner. A leading campaigner for the green belt around London and the most famous architect at the London County Council (LCC), he was joint author of the *County of London Plan* (1943) for the reconstruction of the LCC area following the war. The plan was succeeded, however, by the *Greater London Plan*, which emphasised the planned decentralisation of population into new towns and council estates and the rebuilding of the blitzed areas of the capital. Abercrombie also drew up postwar plans for other cities, for example the *Clyde Valley Regional Plan*.

ACLAND, SIR RICHARD (THOMAS DYKE) (1906–90) Liberal politician; MP for Barnstaple, Devon, from 1935 until the Second World War. Acland was one of the founders of the **Common Wealth Party** in 1942. During the postwar period he joined the Labour Party, and from 1947 to 1955 he was MP for Gravesend in Kent. He resigned from the party over Gaitskell and his support for the British atom bomb.

ADAMS, GERRY [Gerard] (1949–) Northern Irish Republican politician; MP for West Belfast from 1983 to 1992 and from 1997; president of Sinn Féin, the political wing of

the Irish Republican Army, since 1983. Adams is considered a folk hero among many Catholics and Republicans in Northern Ireland, and his reputation was enhanced following his internment in 1971 for alleged involvement in terrorism. Having been released in order to participate in secret peace talks between the IRA and the British government in 1972, he was rearrested the following year and held in the Maze Prison. He refused to sit in the Westminster parliament after he won the seat of Belfast West in the general elections of 1983 and 1997 because he would not take an oath of allegiance to the queen. Adams met with the Unionist leader David **Trimble** at the Stormont Conference in 1998, a meeting that has been viewed as the beginning of the cessation of The Troubles that had afflicted Northern Ireland, and occasionally England, since 1968. Against great difficulties, he was able to persuade Sinn Féin to sign up to the Good Friday Agreement in 1998. The violence did not completely disappear, but Adams's reputation as a statesman and politician was mostly improved except in the eyes of the hard-line Real IRA. His autobiography is entitled *Before the Dawn* (1996).

ADDISON, CHRISTOPHER, 1ST VISCOUNT ADDISON (1869–1951) Liberal, later Labour, politician; MP for Hoxton in East London (1910–18), Shoreditch (1918–22) and Swindon (1925–31, 1934–5). He went on to play an important role in the promotion of national insurance legislation before the First World War. During the war Addison was an ally of David Lloyd George. At the Ministry of Munitions from 1916 he was responsible for expanding munitions production, and in 1917 he was appointed minister of reconstruction. Addison is perhaps most commonly remembered for the **Housing and Town Planning Act** of 1919. He became a Labour politician during the 1920s.

ALEXANDER, A(LBERT) V(ICTOR), 1ST EARL ALEXANDER OF HILLSBOROUGH (1885–1965) Labour politician; minister of defence (1947–50) and chancellor of the Duchy of Lancaster (1950–51); Labour leader in the House of Lords (1955–64).

AMERY, LEO(POLD CHARLES MAURICE STENNETT) (1873–1955) Conservative politician, journalist, military historian of the Boer War, and intelligence officer during the First World War. Conservative and Unionist MP for South Birmingham from 1911 to 1945, Amery was also a prominent protagonist for imperial preference, or protectionist policies, during the 1930s.

ANDERSON, JOHN, 1ST VISCOUNT WAVERLEY (1882–1958) Civil servant and Conservative politician. Following a distinguished career in the civil service during which he worked in Ireland, India and Bengal, he became a National MP in 1938, under Neville Chamberlain. During the war he served as home secretary: one type of air raid shelter was named after him. Anderson became chancellor of the exchequer in 1943 following the death of Sir Howard Kingsley Wood.

ANDERSON, LINDSAY (GORDON) (1923–94) Film maker. He was a proponent of the Free Cinema phase of documentary films released during the later 1950s. Among his most respected if controversial films was *If* (1968), a study of the leader of a rebellion

in a public (i.e. expensive private) school. The film satirised hypocrisy, the church, schooling and class relations in contemporary England. *O Lucky Man!* (1973) was another satire, while *Britannia Hospital* (1982) viewed Britain under Margaret Thatcher as a poorly run hospital. The film was also a clumsy comment on the National Health Service. Anderson also wrote on film making and on other film makers, including Humphrey Jennings.

ARCHER, JEFFREY (HOWARD), BARON ARCHER OF WESTON-SUPER-MARE (1940) Conservative politician and novelist; MP for Louth (1969–74). His short tenure as deputy chair of the Conservative Party from 1985 to 1986 is explained by Archer's involvement in a libel case about a prostitute. He won the case against the tabloid *Daily Star* in the short term but was later found guilty of perjury, and jailed. This was a massive fall from the political stratosphere, and it discredited both him and his party, reminding the British public of the sleaze associated with the Conservative Party during the 1990s.

ASHDOWN, PADDY [Jeremy John Durham], **Baron Ashdown of Norton-sub-Hamdon** (1941–) Liberal politician; MP for Yeovil in Somerset (1983–2001); leader of the Liberal Democrat Party formed in 1988, which included Liberal politicians and members of the former Social Democratic Party. Under Ashdown, the Liberal Democrats enjoyed considerable success at the general election of 1997, although he was subsequently disappointed at a lack of progress on constitutional reform under the New Labour government of Tony Blair. He resigned as leader of the Liberals in 1999.

ASQUITH, H(ERBERT) H(ENRY), 1ST EARL OF OXFORD AND ASQUITH (1852–1928) Liberal politician; MP for East Fife

(1886–1918) and Paisley (1920–24); home secretary (1892–5); prime minister (1908–16). He spoke out for free trade when Joseph Chamberlain of the Tories was endorsing tariff reform. As chancellor of the exchequer in Campbell-Bannerman's Liberal government he introduced means-tested old-age pensions for people aged seventy and over. Asquith became prime minister on the resignation of Campbell-Bannerman, and in the short term he became an ally of the new chancellor of the exchequer David Lloyd George, as both supported the People's Budget of 1909, about which the landed Conservative interest was so bitterly critical. In common with Gladstone, Asquith supported home rule for Ireland, and his government became increasingly dependent upon Irish Nationalist MPs from 1911 as the resurgent Conservative and Unionist Party campaigned against it. Asquith was attacked by the suffragettes for his tardiness on votes for women, and faced growing industrial militancy from 1911 to 1914.

As prime minister at the outbreak of the First World War, Asquith came under considerable criticism for his alleged lack of dynamism, characterised by the phrase 'wait and see'. His formation of a **coalition government** in 1915 did little to stem the criticism, and a Liberal–Tory alliance between Lloyd George, Bonar Law and Balfour forced his resignation in late 1916. Asquith lost his East Fife seat in 1918, but was subsequently elected as MP for Paisley in 1920. He returned as leader of the Liberal Party in 1923, but the Liberals were by then in steep decline, having been replaced by the Labour Party as the natural alternative to the Conservatives.

ASTOR, NANCY (WITCHER), VISCOUNTESS ASTOR (1879–1964) Conservative politician; Britain's first woman MP (Plymouth Sutton, 1919–45). Born as Nancy Witcher Langhorne in the United States, she married Viscount Astor in 1906 and entered parliament as a Conservative MP not in the general election in 1918 but the following year. A temperance campaigner and advocate of women's rights, Astor was also a prominent hostess and member of London society between the wars.

ATTLEE, CLEMENT (RICHARD), 1ST EARL ATTLEE (1883–1967) Labour politician; MP for Limehouse (1922–50) and West Walthamstow (1950–55) in East London; prime minister of the reforming postwar Labour government from 1945 to 1950 and its short-lived successor of 1950–51. Attlee began his working life as a barrister, while also being employed as a tutor at the London School of Economics. He joined the Fabian Society in 1907 and the Independent Labour Party in 1908. Following service during the First World War he was mayor of Stepney and MP for Limehouse. When that constituency was abolished in 1950 he became MP for West Walthamstow. In the first short-lived Labour government of 1924 Attlee was under secretary for war, and during that of 1929–31 he was chancellor of the Duchy of Lancaster and postmaster general. He refused to serve in the National Government of Ramsay MacDonald and succeeded George **Lansbury** as leader of the Labour Party in 1935, remaining in the post until 1955. During the wartime coalition government he served as lord privy seal (1942–3), lord president of the council (1943–5) and deputy prime minister 1942–5.

Attlee's Labour Party defeated Churchill's Conservatives in the general election of May 1945, and he became the prime minister of the government of 1945–50, the first Labour government with a proper working majority. It oversaw the introduction of the welfare state, the establishment of a mixed economy based upon the nationalisation or public ownership of key industries, and the independence of India. When Labour was returned to office with a greatly reduced majority following the general election of 1950, in 1951 Attlee decided to go to the country once more, when he lost to the Conservatives. His memoirs were given the modest title *As it Happened* (1954)

AUDEN, W(YSTAN) H(UGH) (1907–73) Writer and poet. Auden was also involved in documentary films during the 1930s, notably *Night Mail* (1936). Perhaps his most famous poem, *Funeral*, was read out at the funeral in the 1994 film *Four Weddings and a Funeral*.

B

BAKER, KENNETH (WILFRED), BARON BAKER OF DORKING (1934) Conservative politician; MP for Acton (1968–70), St Marylebone (1974–83) and Mole Valley (1983–97. He was education secretary from 1986 to 1989, during which he introduced 'gerbil', the Great Education Reform Bill, which brought in the National Curriculum. Home secretary in John Major's government from 1990 to 1992, he later become a back-bench critic of the **Maastricht Treaty**.

BALDWIN, STANLEY, 1ST EARL BALDWIN OF BEWDLEY (1867–1947) Conservative politician; MP for Bewdley, Worcestershire (1908–37); prime minister of Britain in 1923–4, from 1924 to 1929, and during the National Government between 1935 and 1937. Previously he had held minor office in the National Government of 1916–22. He played an important role in the Carlton Club meeting on 19 October 1922, during which leading Conservatives ended their commitment to that government. Baldwin served as chancellor of the exchequer (1922–3) in Andrew Bonar Law's Conservative government, and he succeeded Law as prime minister in May 1923. His small majority following the general election of that year led to his resignation and the short-lived Labour government of 1924. However, he returned as prime minister late in 1924 and led the country through some turbulent industrial disputes, notably the General Strike in 1926 and high levels of unemployment.

Baldwin ceased to be prime minister in 1929 after the instigation of the minority Labour government of 1929–31 and served as lord president of the council in Ramsay MacDonald's National Government from 1931 to 1935. Following MacDonald's fall he was again prime minister until his resignation in 1937, a period in which the Great Depression continued to ease, but which saw the beginnings of appeasement. He was created Earl Baldwin of Bewdley in 1937.

BALFOUR, ARTHUR (JAMES), 1ST EARL OF BALFOUR AND VISCOUNT TRAPRAIN (1848–1930) Conservative politician; MP for Hertford (1874–85), Manchester East (1885–1906) and the City of London (1906–22). Balfour had a long and mostly well-regarded career. He succeeded his uncle, Lord Salisbury, as prime minister, serving from 1902 to 1905. In the general election of 1906 the Conservatives were defeated by the Liberals, the party having been fractured by the issue of tariff reform, something which Balfour himself opposed. In 1915–16 he was first lord of the Admiralty, and from 1916 to 1919 during the National Government he was foreign secretary. Leader of the Conservative Party from 1902 to 1911, he remained active in politics until the late 1920s. He was created Earl of Balfour in 1922.

BANKS, OLIVE (1923–2006) Sociologist of education and historian of feminism. Her major works in the latter category were *Faces of Feminism: A Study of Feminism as a Social Movement* (1986), *Becoming a Feminist: The Social Origins of 'First Wave' Feminism* (1987), *The Biographical Dictionary of British Feminists* (1985) and *The Politics of British Feminism* (1993). Banks appears to have been the first academic to have coined the term 'second wave' feminism.

BARBER, ANTHONY (PERRINOTT LYSBERG), BARON BARBER OF WENTBRIDGE (1920–2005) Conservative politician; MP for Doncaster (1951–64) and Altrincham and Sale (1964–74); minister of health (1963–4). Following the premature death of Iain Macleod in 1970, Barber was appointed by Heath as chancellor of the exchequer. He retired from parliament in 1974 and became a life peer.

BARNETT, DAME HENRIETTA (1851–1936) Social reformer and Christian socialist. Barnett lived with her husband, Canon Samuel Barnett, in the East End of London and worked among the poor, for a time with Octavia **Hill**. In 1908, with the architects Barry Parker and Raymond Unwin, she founded **Hampstead Garden Suburb** in North London, perhaps the most significant exemplar of the garden suburb movement in Britain.

BASSEY, DAME SHIRLEY (VERONICA) (1937–) Singer. One of very few black female singers from Britain to become a global name, she was born into a working-class home in Cardiff, South Wales, and enjoyed her first hit with *Banana Boat Song* in 1957, which reached the BBC's Top Ten. She went on to have a huge variety of singles and albums on various record labels and recorded three of the **James Bond** themes, namely *Goldfinger* (1964), *Diamonds Are Forever* (1971) and *Moonraker* (1979). Bassey was created a DBE in

1999. It was testament to her talent, beauty and staying-power that she was a leading act at the Glastonbury Music Festival in 2007.

BEATLES, THE Pop band. In alphabetical order by surname, the Beatles were George Harrison (lead guitar, occasional vocals, and other instruments), John Lennon (guitar, vocals, keyboard), Paul McCartney (bass guitar, vocals) and Ringo Starr (drums, occasional vocals). The 'Fab Four' emerged as the leading lights of the Liverpool rock scene during the early 1960s and were the most famous and successful British band of that decade. They had numerous number one hits on both sides of the Atlantic, enjoying considerable fame in the USA, and also starred in a number of semi-autobiographical whimsical films. After splitting in acrimonious circumstances in 1970, each band member went on to enjoy a solo career. Lennon, with his wife Yoko Ono, enjoyed critical acclaim with early albums by the Plastic Ono Band, but his song-writing abilities waned during the later 1970s; he was assassinated outside his home in New York in 1980. McCartney enjoyed a second and prolonged lease of life with the band *Wings* during the 1970s before deciding to become a solo performer. His individual career has made him one of the best-selling British musicians of all time. Ringo Starr enjoyed a few singles hits, and also narrated the *Thomas and Friends* (*Thomas the Tank Engine*) television series, while George Harrison had some significant hits during the 1970s and promoted movie-making in Britain via Hand Made Films during the 1980s. The Beatles are significant not only for the imaginative partnership of Lennon and McCartney as songwriters but also for a number of highly original albums, namely *Rubber Soul* (1966) and the experimental and highly influential *Sergeant Pepper's Lonely Hearts Club Band* (1967).

BEAVERBROOK, MAX [Aitken, William Maxwell], **1st Baron Beaverbrook** (1879–1964) British newspaper magnate; Conservative politician. Born in Canada, he migrated to Britain in 1910 and soon became MP for Ashton under Lyne (1910–16). He served during the wartime National Government under David Lloyd George as chancellor of the Duchy of Lancaster and as minister of information (1918). Beaverbrook took over the *Daily Express* in 1919 and established the *Sunday Express* two years later, and between the wars was a prominent advocate of free trade, against the prevailing nostrums of Stanley Baldwin. He was a member of Winston Churchill's wartime cabinet, successively as minister of aircraft production (1940–41), minister of supply (1941–2), minister of war production (1942) and lord privy seal (1943–5). Beaverbrook became a prominent opponent of the independence of **India and Pakistan** during the 1940s and of British membership of the European Economic Community during the 1950s and 1960s.

BECKETT, MARGARET (MARY) (1943–) Labour politician; MP for Lincoln (1974–9) and Derby South (1983–). By the early twenty-first century she had proved to be one of the most enduring and multi-tasked of Labour's leading women politicians. She was deputy leader of the Labour Party from 1992 and briefly became leader following the death of John Smith in 1994, the only woman to have led the party. After the 1997 general election she was appointed secretary of state for trade and industry, and in 2006–7 she served as foreign secretary, the first woman to do so.

BENN, TONY [Wedgewood Benn, Anthony Neil] (1925–) Labour politician; diarist; MP for Bristol South-East (1950–83). Benn disliked his inherited peerage and refused to accept it under the Peerages Act

of 1963, for which he had been a leading campaigner. He lost his seat in 1983, but was elected MP for Chesterfield in Derbyshire in a by-election the following year. His most important positions were as minister of technology (1966–70) in Harold Wilson's government, opposition spokesman on trade and industry (1970–74), chair of the Labour Party (1971–2), and secretary of state for industry, also under Wilson (1975–6). He is one of the few members of his party who has met with both the shah of Iran and the deposed quasi-fascist Iraqi leader Saddam Hussein.

Benn was a prominent critic of Britain's entry into the EEC in 1973 and was strongly anti-American in his politics. He was defeated by Denis Healey in his challenge to become deputy leader of the party in 1981. He also called for automatic reselection of MPs and for tighter control of the national executive committee of the Labour Party over the writing of the election manifesto. He denounced many of the party reforms of John Smith and Tony Blair that made Labour electable again by 1997.

BESANT, ANNIE (1847–1933) Feminist; campaigner for improvements to wages and working conditions for the poor. Although most immediately associated with the match girls' strike of 1888, which she led, she was active into the twentieth century, supporting the cause of the independence of India, where she established the Indian Home Rule League in 1916.

BETJEMAN, SIR JOHN (1906–84) Poet. Among his best-known poems is *Slough* (1938), a witty statement of anti-suburban values, although in later life he manifested more of a love–hate relationship with suburbia, as was evident in his *Metroland* travelogue for BBC television (1973).

BEVAN, ANEURIN ('NYE') (1897–1960) Labour politician; MP for Ebbw Vale

(1929–60). Bevan was one of the most significant ministers in the Labour governments of 1945–51. Born into a poor miner's family in Wales, he knew about the problems and depredations of poverty and unemployment and was a committed trade unionist. A passionate and skilled orator, he was a leading spokesman for the miners of South Wales during the General Strike of 4–12 May 1926.

As minister for health from 1945, Bevan was pivotal in establishing the National Health Service, which he steered into place, despite considerable opposition from the medical profession, on the 'appointed day' of 5 July 1948. From that day the government ran all medical services, which were, for the time being, free to people at the point of need. However in 1951, as minister of labour, Bevan resigned from the second Attlee government in protest at the introduction of dental charges. During the 1950s he was the leading light of the eponymous 'Bevanite Left', which opposed high defence expenditure to the detriment of more spending on health and welfare. He was defeated by Hugh Gaitskell for leadership of the Labour Party after the resignation of Clement Attlee in 1955 and the following year became spokesman for foreign affairs.

BEVERIDGE, WILLIAM (HENRY), 1ST BARON BEVERIDGE (1879–1963) Liberal politician; reformer; MP for Berwick on Tweed (1944–5). The most important architect of the welfare state, he was both an economist and a social reformer. From 1903 he worked at Toynbee Hall, the settlement house in London's East End, and from 1906 for the *Morning Post* newspaper. In 1908 he joined the civil service, where he was a central figure in the instigation of national insurance from 1911. In the tradition of Charles Booth and other leading Victorian-born intellectuals, Beveridge believed in the dynamic relationship with – that is, the hook-up between – social investigation, social research and social policy. This influenced him to join the London School of Economics, of which he was director for most of the interwar period. Also a master of Balliol College, Oxford, he is best known for the Beveridge Report or, to give it its more prosaic title, the *Report on Social Insurance and Allied Services*, published at the end of 1942. Beveridge was made a Liberal peer in 1946. He also headed the new town development corporations at Peterlee and Newton Aycliffe in County Durham.

BEVIN, ERNEST (1881–1951) Labour politician; MP for Central Wandsworth (1940–52). A trade union activist, he became assistant secretary of the Dockers' Union in 1911. The previous two decades had seen a considerable growth in the organisation of previously non-unionised unskilled and semi-skilled manual workers, and Bevin was one of many Labour leaders produced by this rank-and-file groundswell in the docks. He was an active campaigner for general unions, and in 1921 oversaw the creation of the Transport and General Workers' Union during a time of growing unemployment and industrial militancy.

Bevin and Churchill were on opposite sides during the General Strike of 4–12 May 1926. During the Second World War, however, Churchill invited Bevin to become minister of labour, a shrewd political gesture that incorporated organised labour more fully into the war effort, although its loyalty was rarely in doubt from Bevin's point of view. From May 1945 until his death in 1951 Bevin was an effective and respected foreign secretary. He played a key role in the instigation of the Marshall Plan, the Independence of India and Pakistan, and the formation of the North Atlantic Treaty Organization (NATO).

BIRKENHEAD, LORD [Smith, F(rederick) E(dwin)], **1st Earl of Birkenhead** (1872–1930) Conservative politician; MP for Liverpool Walton (1906–18) and Liverpool West Derby (1918–19). Widely known as F. E. Smith, he made a profound contribution towards the creation of the Irish Free State in 1922 and held a number of offices during the preceding coalition governments of 1916–22. He was secretary of state for India in Stanley Baldwin's Conservative administration from 1924 to 1928. During the General Strike Birkenhead played an active role as 'peacemaker' on behalf of the government, and was certainly more moderate than Winston Churchill, Neville Chamberlain and others who wanted mercilessly to break the trade unions.

BLAIR, TONY [Anthony Charles Lynton] (1951–) Labour politician; MP for Sedgefield (1983–2007); a major architect of New Labour, and prime minister from 1997 to 2007. In purely electoral terms, Blair was the most successful leader in the history of the British Labour Party, and he remains a charismatic if controversial politician into the present century. He won the leadership in 1994 following the death of John Smith and began a considered and successful attempt to moderate and modernise the party, a path already being followed by Smith following the failure of the 'dream ticket' of Neil Kinnock and Roy **Hattersley** at the 1987 and 1992 general elections. The abolition of Clause 4, which committed Labour to nationalisation, was a major triumph for Blair. He explicitly adapted the language and policies of his party to appeal to those sections of the population that had increasingly swung to the Conservatives since 1979, namely the affluent working classes and sections of the middle classes. If the older Labour Party had drawn its votes disproportionately from the poorer inner-city areas, New Labour drew more widely from the suburban majority. Prudence in public expenditure and a continuation of privatisation and moderate taxes meant that Blair was frequently accused by the left and sections of the media of following a 'Thatcherite' policy agenda. Nonetheless, the New Labour governments from 1997 introduced the **minimum wage** for all, lifted hundreds of thousands of children out of poverty, and spent large sums of money on the National Health Service, education and public transport, albeit with mixed results. Blair's first administration also assisted in bringing about in 1998 a cessation of The Troubles in Northern Ireland, where previous governments had failed. The long-standing issue of devolution was addressed with the establishment of the Scots parliament and the Welsh Assembly.

BLUNKETT, DAVID (1947–) Labour politician, MP for Sheffield, Brightside (1987–); leader of Sheffield City Council (1980–87). He was a leading member of the shadow cabinet before 1997, and his major ministerial positions thereafter were as secretary of state for education and employment (1997–2001) and home secretary (2001–4).

BOATENG, PAUL (YAW) (1951–) Labour politician; MP for Brent South (1987–2005); barrister and broadcaster. The first black MP to hold a front-bench post as a member of Labour's shadow Treasury team, in 1997 he became parliamentary under secretary for health, and hence the first black government minister. He held the same post in the Home office in 1998, and in 2001 became financial secretary to the Treasury. On his promotion to chief secretary to the Treasury in 2002 he became the first black cabinet member.

BONDFIELD, MARGARET (GRACE) (1872–1953) Trade unionist and Labour politician. She was a leading founder of the

National Federation of Women Workers in 1906 and the first woman chair of the Trade Union Congress (TUC) from 1923. An MP in the first two Labour governments (Northampton, 1923–4; Wallsend, 1926–31), in 1929 she became the first woman member of the cabinet, as minister of labour and a privy councillor. Bondfield proved unpopular with many rank and file trade unionists for her belief in reductions to unemployment payments during the slump of 1929–31.

BONHAM CARTER, (HELEN) VIOLET, BARONESS ASQUITH OF YARNBURY (1887–1969) Advocate of a National Government in the spring of 1940; president of the Liberal Party (1945–7). The daughter of the former Liberal prime minister H. H. Asquith, she was created a baroness in 1964.

BOOTH, CHARLES (1840–1916) Social investigator, social reformer and businessman. He was a founder of modern empirical sociology in Britain, and his enormous survey *Life and Labour of the People in London*, which ran to seventeen volumes, was begun in 1886 and completed during the early twentieth century. Among his assistants was his relative Beatrice Webb. An advocate of old-age pensions, Booth was integrated into a wider network of social reformers and was a significant figure in the development of social investigation and social policy in late Victorian and Edwardian Britain.

BOOTHBY, ROBERT (JOHN GRAHAM), BARON BOOTHBY (1900–86) Conservative politician; MP for East Aberdeenshire (1950–58). During the 1930s, with Churchill, he was a leading advocate of rearmament, and in 1938 called for the introduction of conscription. During the Second World War he worked in food supply and undertook military service.

Following the war he became an avowed consensus politician. From 1947 to 1954 he served on the Council of Europe and from 1957 became a leading advocate of British membership of the European Economic Community. A bisexual, Boothby had affairs with Dorothy Macmillan, the wife of Harold Macmillan, and was involved with Ronald Kray, a notorious gangster in the East End of London. He also found time to become a broadcaster and writer.

BOOTHROYD, BETTY, BARONESS BOOTHROYD (1929–) Labour politician; MP for West Bromwich (1973–2000); speaker of the House of Commons (1992–2000). She was a member of the European Parliament from 1975 to 1977 and served on the select committee on foreign affairs, and in other parliamentary roles, until she became deputy speaker in 1987. This was the first time the post was contested by voting. She became Baroness Boothroyd in 2001.

BOTTOMLEY, VIRGINIA (HILDA BRUNETTE MAXWELL), BARONESS BOTTOMLEY OF NETTLESTONE (1948–) Conservative politician; MP for Surrey South-West (1984–); health secretary (1992–5); and national heritage secretary (1995–7).

BOWIE, DAVID [Jones, David] (1946–) Singer. He was a mime artist during the 1960s before becoming a singer. Few of his 1960s works are memorable, but a 1969 song *Space Oddity*, became his first significant hit. A number of distinctive albums followed, notably *Hunky Dory* (1971), *The Rise and Fall of Ziggy Stardust and the Spiders from Mars* (1972), *Aladdin Sane* (1973) and *Diamond Dogs* (1974), which produced some highly original chart hits to challenge the American dominance over cutting-edge rock 'n' roll. At its peak from 1973 to the early 1980s, Bowie's work was characterised by a camp singing style, some outrageous personas, changes in genre from rock to soul, and a continuing inventiveness. Both *Low* (1977) and *Heroes* (1977) were among his most experimental albums of the decade. Bowie was also successful overseas, notably in Germany, Japan and the United States of America, a country from which his music had borrowed extensively, and where he lived for many years.

BRAINE, JOHN (GERARD) (1922–86) Novelist. In his mid-thirties he became known as one of the **Angry Young Men** of the latter 1950s. He is best known for *Room at the Top* (1957), a novel made into a film starring Lawrence Harvey and released in 1959.

BRITTAIN, VERA (MARY) (1893–1970) Pacifist, feminist, socialist and writer. Brittain gave up her education at Somerville College, Oxford, to serve as a nurse during the First World War. Her autobiographical *Testament of Youth* (1933) was a best-seller, detailing her life and service during the war and its effects on her generation. She was the mother of Shirley Williams.

BRITTAN, LEON, BARON BRITTAN OF SPENNITHORNE (1939–) Conservative politician; MP for Cleveland and Whitby (1974–83) and Richmond, Yorkshire (1983–8); chief secretary to the Treasury during Margaret Thatcher's first government; home secretary (1983–5). Brittan was forced to resign his position as secretary of state for trade and industry in 1986 over the **Westland affair**. In the late 1980s his career became increasingly concerned with external trade relations with the EEC. From 1989 to 1993 he was a European commissioner, and from 1995 to 1999 he served as vice president of the European Commission.

BROCKWAY, (ARCHIBALD) FENNER, BARON BROCKWAY (1888–1988) Labour politician; MP for Leyton East (1929–31) and Eton and Slough (1950–64). Brockway was imprisoned for being a conscientious objector during the First World War, and became one of the leading proponents of pacifism between the wars and afterwards. He was also an anti-poverty campaigner.

BROOKE, HENRY, BARON BROOKE OF CUMNOR (1903–84) Conservative politician; MP for Lewisham West (1938–45) and Hampstead (1950–66); financial secretary to the Treasury (1954–7); minister of housing and local government (1957–61); home secretary (1962–4). A politician in the consensus mould, he continued Conservative policies on the promotion of housing inherited from Harold Macmillan and was a liberal-minded home secretary.

BROOKE, PETER (LEONARD), BARON BROOKE OF SUTTON MANDEVILLE (1934–) Conservative politician; MP for the City of London and Westminster South (1977–97) and the Cities of London and Westminster (1997–2001); Northern Ireland secretary (1989–92); national heritage secretary (1992–4). In the face of Conservative and Unionist anger, Brooke suggested dialogue with the Irish Republican Army some years before the New Labour government acceded to such a process.

BROWN, GEORGE (ALFRED), LORD GEORGE-BROWN (1914–85) Labour politician; MP for Belper (1945–70); secretary of state for economic affairs (1964–6); foreign secretary (1966–8). He was supposed to have been a personal powerhouse behind the enactment of Labour's **National Plan** from 1965, a plan which was mostly abandoned. Sometimes lachrymose after a few drinks – and he drank a lot – the phrase 'tired and emotional' was coined for him by *Private Eye*. His autobiography was entitled *In my Way* (1970). He later joined the Social Democratic Party.

BROWN, (JAMES) GORDON (1951–) Labour politician; MP for Dunfermline East (1983–). Brown became shadow chancellor of the exchequer after John **Smith** was elected leader of the Labour Party in 1992, and remained in this position until Tony Blair was elected prime minister in 1997, when he became chancellor. He granted independence to the Bank of England over the setting of interest rates in order to prevent the 'stop–go' cycle of boom and bust that had undermined much British economic performance in previous decades, imposed a one-off corporate tax to fund welfare policies, and cleverly used indirect taxation to promote social reform. A moderniser, he played an essential role in the creation of New Labour during the mid-1990s. Brown became prime minister in the summer of 2007.

BRUNO, FRANK (1961–) Boxer. Along with Lennox Lewis (a fellow boxer) and Linford Christie, he was one of the most famous black sportsmen in late twentieth-century Britain. Following his successful bid as world heavyweight champion in 1995, he retired from boxing and became a television personality.

BUTLER, R(ICHARD) A(USTEN), BARON BUTLER OF SAFFRON WALDEN (1902–82) Conservative politician; MP for Saffron Walden (1929–65). Known as 'Rab', Butler held minor posts in governments of the 1930s, and was under secretary of state for foreign affairs in 1938 and a supporter of appeasement. As chairman of the Board for Education during the wartime coalition government of Winston Churchill, he was responsible for the Education Act of 1944. He was chancellor of the exchequer from 1951 to 1955, lord privy seal from 1955 to 1959, and foreign minister from 1963 to

1964. Butler was defeated by Macmillan for the party leadership, and therefore the prize of prime minister, following the fall of Eden, and was overlooked for Douglas-Home in 1963.

BUTLIN, BILLY [William Heygate Edmund Colborne] (1899–1980) South African-born entrepreneur. He established a number of holiday camps around the British coast, beginning in 1936 with **Butlins at Skegness**, Lincolnshire. He understood that increasingly affluent working-class families wanted convenient all-in American-style vacations by the seaside. Other holiday camps were opened in the later 1930s and 1940s, and Butlin also developed a chain of holiday hotels. As a British holiday institution, Butlins is still going strong.

C

CAINE, MICHAEL (1933–) Actor. His first major films included *Alfie* (1966) and *The Charge of the Light Brigade* (1968). Born in London, Caine personified the cool upwardly mobile cockney during the 1960s, and has become one of Britain's leading film stars.

CALLAGHAN, (LEONARD) JAMES, BARON CALLAGHAN OF CARDIFF (1912–2004) Labour politician; MP for South Cardiff (1945–50) and South-East Cardiff (1950–87); prime minister (1976–9). He served in the Royal Navy during the Second World War and was elected MP for Cardiff South in Labour's historic victory of 1945. Defeated by Harold Wilson for the party leadership following the death of Hugh Gaitskell, he subsequently served in Wilson's government as chancellor of the exchequer (1964–7), home secretary (1967–70) and foreign secretary (1974–6) before becoming prime minister after Wilson's resignation in 1976. Callaghan was vilified by the conservative press for his alleged weakness and mishandling of the '**Winter of Discontent**' in 1978–9, and he lost the general election the following summer to Margaret Thatcher. Known as 'Sunny Jim' to his friends and supporters, Callaghan was on the centre-right of the Labour Party. He was father of the House of Commons for some years. His writings include *A House Divided* (1973) and *Time and Chance* (1997).

CAMPBELL, ALASTAIR (JOHN) (1957–) Journalist. He was invited in 1993 to become Tony Blair's press secretary, a position that led to Campbell serving as director of communications and strategy for the Labour Party from 1994 to 2003. His exploits, providing many insights into the workings of the Blair governments and key political issues of the 1990s and since, are recorded in *The Blair Years* (2007).

CAMPBELL-BANNERMAN, SIR HENRY (1836–1908) Liberal politician; MP for Stirling (1868–1908); prime minister (1905–8). He held a number of key positions during the Victorian years and became a supporter of the moral Liberalism of William Gladstone, whose belief in home rule for Ireland he shared. Campbell-Bannerman became Liberal leader following a fractious and damaging debate over the Boer War and Ireland. At the general election in 1906 the Liberals heavily defeated the Conservative and Unionist Party, which was bitterly divided over the issue of tariff reform. This initiated a significant period of reforming legislation now associated with the New Liberals, although Campbell-Bannerman has only a limited claim to be a New Liberal. Apart from the Education Act of 1906, most of the important pieces of legislation were passed after his death, during the government of his successor, H. H. Asquith. Unlike Asquith, however, he was a supporter of women's suffrage.

CARPENTER, EDWARD (1844–1922) Poet, philosopher, mystic, vegetarian and socialist. Carpenter was a founding member of the Fabian Society in 1884 and was involved in the early Labour Party during the twentieth century. His homosexuality was well known, and the communitarian Edward Carpenter Community of Gay Men still exists to promote his teachings and example.

CARRINGTON, PETER (ALEXANDER RUPERT), 6TH BARON CARRINGTON (1919–) Conservative politician; defence secretary in Edward Heath's government of 1970–74 and opposition leader in the House of Lords during the Labour governments of 1964–70 and 1974–9. As foreign secretary in Margaret Thatcher's first government (1979–82) he negotiated the independence of Zimbabwe (formerly Rhodesia), but he resigned following the invasion of the Falklands by Argentina. He also served as Secretary General of NATO from 1984 to 1988.

CASEMENT, ROGER (DAVID) (1864–1916) Irish nationalist. His pro-German and pro-Irish activities during the First World War earned him a trial for high treason in London, following which he was hanged. His homosexuality was used by the British state to discredit him.

CASTLE, BARBARA (ANNE), BARONESS CASTLE OF BLACKBURN (1911–2002) Labour politician, MP for Blackburn (1945–79); minister for overseas development (1964–5), minister of transport (1965–8) and minister of employment (1968–70). This last office of state coincided with a continuing rash of wildcat strikes – strikes unsanctioned by the official trade union leaders – which led her to attempt to solve the industrial relations problems with *In Place of Strife*. Castle also served as minister for social services in Wilson's government of 1964–6. Opposed to British entry into the European Economic Community (EEC), she nonetheless led the Labour Party in the European Parliament from 1979 to 1989, and was made a life peer in 1990. Her autobiography *Fighting All the Way* (1993) played very much to her image as the red-haired, red-hearted Bevanite loyalist.

CHAMBERLAIN, SIR (JOSEPH) AUSTEN (1863–1937) Conservative and Unionist politician; MP for Worcestershire East (1892–1914) and Birmingham West (1914–37). The elder son of Joseph Chamberlain, he was a leading member of the great Birmingham dynasty of the Chamberlains. He was secretary of state for India in 1915–17 and foreign secretary during Stanley Baldwin's Conservative government from 1924 to 1929, during which time he won the Nobel Peace Prize for his emollient and constructive role in the forging of the **Treaties of Locarno** (1925). In 1931 he was appointed first lord of the Admiralty.

CHAMBERLAIN, (ARTHUR) NEVILLE (1869–1940) Conservative politician; MP for Birmingham, Ladywood (1918–29) and Edgbaston (1929–40); prime minister (1937–40). The son of Joseph Chamberlain and half-brother to Austen Chamberlain, Neville was a businessman and local politician in Birmingham. He worked briefly as director general of national service during the coalition government of the First World War.

Chamberlain was minister of health in Stanley Baldwin's second government during the 1920s, and from 1931 to 1937 he served as chancellor of the exchequer, first

under Ramsay MacDonald and then from 1935 under Baldwin, whom he succeeded as prime minister in 1937. Lacking in charisma, he was roundly criticised by Winston Churchill and other leading Conservatives for his appeasement of Adolf Hitler during 1937–8, although Chamberlain was by no means alone in wanting to adopt a non-combative policy towards Nazi Germany. His reputation suffered greatly as a consequence. Furthermore, in a not dissimilar manner to Asquith during the First World War, Chamberlain was widely accused of lacking dynamism as leader of the coalition government, and in the wake of the disastrous Norwegian campaign he resigned in May 1940, to be replaced by Winston Churchill as wartime prime minister.

CHAMBERLAIN, JOSEPH (1836–1914) Liberal, later Unionist politician; Birmingham businessman and mayor; colonial secretary during the Boer War; anti-slum campaigner. 'Joe' was a staunch advocate of tariff reform from 1903.

CHAPLIN, SIR CHARLIE [Charles Spencer] (1889–1977) Actor. During a career in music hall as a leading pantomime or slapstick comedian he toured in the United States, where he was spotted by the American film maker Mack Sennett, who gave him work in comedy films. In this American stroke of fortune, Chaplin did not follow an exactly typical trajectory from music hall to cinema, but he was perhaps the most famous of many stars who transferred from stage to screen after the First World War. As a silent movie actor he became a British-born box-office success on both sides of the Atlantic. Among his finest films was *The Great Dictator* (1940), in which he played a dual role as a parody of Adolf Hitler and of a Jewish barber in Nazi Germany. Part of the significance of Chaplin's American fame was that, along with Stan Laurel (of Laurel and Hardy fame), he was one of a growing number of British talents who 'made it' in the United States within a sphere of popular culture – the cinema – that was predominantly Anglo-American in Britain.

CHARLTON, SIR BOBBY [Robert] (1937–) Footballer. Charlton was a leading member of the England football team during the 1950s and 1960s, winning over 100 caps. His club football was with Manchester United, with which he won three league titles and the FA Cup. He played for England during the **World Cup Final** of 1966, and has been a leading board member of Manchester United FC into the present century. His autobiography is entitled *My England Years* (2008).

CHURCHILL, SIR WINSTON (LEONARD SPENCER) (1874–1965) Conservative and Liberal politician; prime minister of the wartime government (1940–45) and Conservative prime minister (1951–5). Churchill was born in Blenheim Palace, Woodstock, Oxfordshire, to Jennie Jerome, the American-born wife of Lord Randolph Churchill. Following a varied military career in the later nineteenth century, in 1900 he was elected MP for Oldham, a textile manufacturing town in Lancashire, although he soon went off to 'fight' in the Boer War, where his exploits became the subject as much of glorification as of reality. Committed to free trade principles and possessing a modicum of social conscience, Churchill quit the Conservative Party, divided as it was over tariff reform, to join the Liberals, for whom he was MP for Manchester North West from 1906 to 1908 and for Dundee from 1908 to 1922. He gained his first cabinet post in Asquith's government, where he was a progressive in social policy, promoting the employment

exchanges or 'labour exchanges' legislation in 1910. This was the same year when, as home secretary, he deployed the military against striking miners in **Tonypandy** in South Wales. He used the army to break the **Sidney Street siege** in London in January 1911.

From 1911 to 1915 Churchill was first lord of the Admiralty, but he resigned as a consequence of the British military tragedy at the Dardanelles in Turkey. From 1917, following service in the trenches in France, he was minister of munitions under the wartime coalition government of David Lloyd George and secretary of state for war and air in the coalition government from 1919 to 1921.

After a brief stint as 'Constitutional Anti-Socialist' MP for Epping, Churchill rejoined the Conservative Party in 1924, representing the Essex constituency of Woodford. As chancellor of the exchequer from 1924 to 1929 in Stanley Baldwin's government, he returned Britain to the gold standard, provoking the critical wrath of John Maynard Keynes. Churchill's intense dislike of industrial action, manifested in Tonypandy, again came to the fore in his attempts to break the General Strike in 1926, during which he edited the government propaganda newspaper the *British Gazette* and encouraged strike-breaking.

The 1930s were a relatively marginal period for Churchill, although his denunciations of Indian independence and his hostility regarding Neville Chamberlain's policy of appeasement towards Nazi Germany were by no means the sum of his busy political and literary life. At the beginning of the Second World War he returned to the Admiralty. Following the downfall of Chamberlain in the wake of the Norwegian disaster, Churchill became prime minister on 10 May 1940, although he was not the first choice of the Conservative leadership. He had found his greatest moment and, with his speeches, leadership and untiring commitment, led the British people and their Allies to victory. He adeptly used his special relationship with Franklin D Roosevelt, the American president, and welcomed Russian intervention to defeat the Nazis in Eastern and Central Europe, while retaining his suspicion of the expansionist intentions of the USSR.

Churchill's defeat in the general election of July 1945 can be blamed partly on an ill-judged speech and his failure to grasp the aspirations of large sections of the British electorate. Nonetheless, defeat gave him the opportunity to warn the world of the threat of the USSR. In Fulton, Missouri, in 1946, during the emergent period of the Cold War, he used the term '**iron curtain**' to describe the division of Europe between the 'free' capitalist West and the communist-controlled Eastern and Central European countries. He became an advocate of European unity with Germany at its heart, while emphasising the need for Britain and her Commonwealth to retain a strong measure of independence. Following the Conservative victory at the general election of 1951, which at long last gave him the popular mandate he had long sought, Churchill served as prime minister until 1955. He was suffering health problems by the time he offered his resignation in that year.

Churchill was voted the greatest Briton of all time by BBC television viewers in 2002. This is largely explained by his wartime leadership, but also by his literary and oratory skills and a number of political achievements. He was certainly an inspirational figure at a time of national crisis. Nonetheless, his paternalism towards the poor could give way to a desire to crush the organised resistance of economically vulnerable working-class people, and his biographers also list some significant political and military failures. Perhaps

Churchill is admired by so many people for his contradictions and weaknesses as much as for his palpable strengths.

CITRINE, WALTER (MCLENNAN), BARON CITRINE OF WEMBLEY (1887–1983) Trade union leader. He was secretary of the Trade Union Congress (TUC) from 1926 to 1946 – that is, from the year of the General Strike to the first full year of peace following the Second World War. From a working-class Liverpudlian background, Citrine reflected rank-and-file pragmatism in the Labour Party rather than the more ideological socialism of many trade union leaders and middle-class Fabians. He fought against the Trades Disputes Act that resulted from the General Strike. Citrine also served on the National Coal Board and the Central Electricity Authority. He was knighted in 1935 and became a peer in 1946.

CLARK, COLIN (GRANT) (1905–89) Economist. He was author of *The Conditions of Economic Progress* (1940) and other works that emphasised the **de-industrialisation** of mature or advanced capitalist societies and pointed to post-industrial conditions.

CLARKE, KENNETH (HARRY) (1940–) Conservative politician; MP for Rushcliffe (1970–). He served as minister of health during Margaret Thatcher's third administration and as education secretary from 1990 to 1992 during John Major's first period of tenure. Clarke became chancellor of the exchequer following Norman Lamont's resignation in the aftermath of Black Wednesday.

CLYNES, JOHN R(OBERT) (1869–1949) Labour politician; MP for North-East Manchester (1906–18) and Manchester Platting (1918–31, 1935–45); home secretary from 1929 to 1931.

COLLINS, MICHAEL (1890–1922) Irish Republican politician, revolutionary and leading founder of the Irish Free State. Collins was chair of the Provisional Government during 1922, and was shot and killed while on active duty for the Irish Republican Army (IRA).

CONNOLLY, JAMES (1870–1931) Irish Republican, socialist, revolutionary and trade unionist. He was executed by the British for his role in the Easter Rising.

COOK, ARTHUR (JAMES) (1883–1931) Trade unionist; leader of the South Wales branch of the Union of Mineworkers. He was a key activist in the General Strike of 1926 and a socialist committed to the Labour movement.

COOK, ROBIN (FINLAYSON) (1946–2005) Labour politician; MP for Livingstone (1974–2004); foreign secretary (1997–2001). An advocate of an 'ethical foreign policy', he resigned from his post as leader of the House of Commons in 2003 in opposition to the British involvement in the War on Terror in Iraq.

COOPER, (ALFRED) DUFF, 1ST VISCOUNT NORWICH (1890–1954) Conservative politician; MP for Oldham (1924–9) and Westminster St Georges (1931–45). He was minister for war in the National Government of 1935–7 and a leading critic of appeasement. From 1940 to 1942 he was minister of supply in the wartime coalition government led by Winston Churchill, and from 1944 to 1947 served as ambassador to France.

COOPER, SIR HENRY (1934–) Boxer. Cooper won the British, European and Commonwealth heavyweight titles. He was the BBC Sports Personality of the Year in 1967 and was later awarded an OBE.

COTTON, SIR BILL [William Frederick] (1928–) Television executive. As head of light entertainment at the BBC from 1970, Cotton was involved in the production of some leading British series, including *Monty Python's Flying Circus*. He was controller of BBC1 from 1977 to 1981, and one of the more successful BBC chiefs who addressed the competitive threat of Independent Television (ITV).

COWARD, SIR NOËL (PEIRCE) (1889–1973) Playwright, screenwriter and songwriter. Coward's talents were conscripted by the government during the war to write morale-boosting songs and scripts for cinema films, of which *In Which We Serve* (1842) and *This Happy Breed* (1944) were among the most famous. A particularly poignant film, now regarded as a classic example of understated British film making, was *Brief Encounter* (1945), directed by David **Lean** and starring Stanley Holloway.

CRIPPS, SIR (RICHARD) STAFFORD (1887–1952) Labour politician; MP for Bristol East (1931–52). Cripps was a nephew of Beatrice Webb. A barrister with a reputation for his formidable intellect and whose politics were on the left of the Labour Party, he was expelled in 1939 for supporting a popular front to challenge Neville Chamberlain's policy of appeasement, following which he remained as an independent Labour MP. He was readmitted to the Labour Party in 1945.

Cripps was ambassador to Moscow from 1940 to 1942, and from 1943 to 1945 served as minister for aircraft production. He was appointed president of the board of trade in Clement Attlee's government in 1945, and was chancellor of the exchequer from 1947 to 1950. During that time he became the personification of austerity, insisting on a wage freeze and high taxation in order to suppress inflationary pressures in the economy. In 1949 he unwillingly agreed to the devaluation of the pound sterling, something that he feared damaged the reputation of the currency. Although he was seen as a possible successor to Attlee, Cripps's political future was cut short by illness.

CROSLAND (CHARLES) ANTHONY (RAVEN) (1918–77) Labour politician; MP for South Gloucestershire (1950–55) and Grimsby (1959–77); cabinet minister, notably as Labour minister for education (1965–7), president of the board of trade (1967–9), secretary of state for local government and regional planning (1974–6) and foreign secretary (1976–7). As a moderate to right-wing member of his party, he opposed unilateral nuclear disarmament and Clause 4. His publication *The Future of Socialism* (1956), following two consecutive general election victories of the Conservative Party, adroitly understood that the increasing affluence and consumerism of the working classes posed problems for Labour's vote. In this, he anticipated some of the revisions to left-wing positioning that Gordon Brown and Tony Blair would address during the 1990s.

CROSSMAN, RICHARD (HOWARD STAFFORD) (1907–74) Labour politician; MP for Coventry East (1945–74); minister for housing and local government (1964–6) and of health and social security (1968–70). *The Backbench Diaries of Richard Crossman* (1981; edited by Janet Morgan) provide many accounts and insights into the Labour Party in opposition from 1951 to 1964.

CURZON, GEORGE (NATHANIEL), 1ST MARQUESS CURZON OF KEDLESTON (1859–1925) Conservative politician; viceroy of India (1899–1905). A staunch advocate of the British Empire, Curzon was one of a number of failed contenders for the leadership of the Conservative Party after the demise of Arthur Bonar Law in 1923. He was the chief British negotiator with Turkey following the Chanak crisis of 1922, signing the **Treaty of Lausanne** in 1924.

DALTON, (EDWARD) HUGH (NEALE), BARON DALTON (1887–1962) Labour politician; MP for Peckham (1924–9) and Bishop Auckland (1929–31, 1935–59). He occupied a number of important wartime posts, notably minister of economic warfare. His experiences of wartime economic coordination by government endorsed his commitment to nationalisation, and when he was chancellor of the exchequer (1945–7) he managed the introduction of the nationalisation of the **Bank of England**. As chancellor during the financial crisis and the fuel crisis of 1947 he introduced austerity measures for which he was subsequently remembered by many. Following his resignation he held other cabinet posts, including minister of town and country planning (1950–51). Among his publications were *High Tide and After* (1962) and *Call Back Yesterday* (1973).

DENINGTON, EVELYN (JOYCE), BARONESS DENINGTON OF STEVENAGE (1907–98) Labour politician; school teacher and housing reformer; leader of the National Association of Labour Teachers (1938–47). Denington became the chairwoman of Stevenage New Town Development Corporation in 1966. She was made a dame of the British Empire in 1974, and achieved another high point by becoming the first chairwoman of the GLC in 1975. From

1978 she was a life peer, speaking in the House of Lords on housing, local government and transport.

DIANA, PRINCESS OF WALES (1961–97) Diana became one of Britain's and indeed the world's most famous media icons during the late twentieth century. She was born in July 1961 on the royal family's Sandringham estate in Norfolk into the aristocratic Spencer family, and her childhood at Althrop House in Northamptonshire is widely reported to have been unhappy, not least because of the break-up of her parents' marriage. During her early career as a nursery assistant to the very wealthy, she became engaged to Prince Charles, the Prince of Wales, and in a now infamous interview with him before their wedding spoke of her love for him, while her fiancé responded opaquely with a comment about 'whatever "love" is'. From her televised marriage to Prince Charles in July 1981, when she wore one of the longest bridal trains in the history of marriage, to her death in August 1997, 'Lady Diana' was a major presence in British life. Her passing caused a massive wave of mourning to sweep the country, and that is no overstatement. As the alleged victim of an unfaithful husband, and because of her attractive looks and media-savvy activities, including work with landmine victims and posing, lonely and vulnerable, in front of the Taj Mahal, Diana elicited great support and sympathy from the British public. Conspiracy theories, much debated by some, tiresome to many others, abounded about her untimely death.

DOUGLAS-HOME, ALEC [Alexander Frederick], **Baron Home of the Hirsel** (1903–95) Conservative politician; MP for South Lanark (1931–45), Lanark (1950–51) and Kinross and West Perthshire (1963–74); foreign secretary (1960–63,

1970–74); prime minister (1963–4). Home renounced his earldom in 1951 in order to remain in the House of Commons, and he succeeded Macmillan as prime minister in the wake of the Profumo affair. A patrician Tory, he was over sixty years old by the time he fought and lost to Harold Wilson in the general election of 1964. He was given a life peerage as foreign secretary in Edward Heath's government.

EDE, JAMES CHUTER, BARON CHUTER-EDE (1882–1965) Labour politician; MP for South Shields in North-East England (1929–31, 1935–64); home secretary in the 1945–51 Labour government; leader of the House of Commons (1951).

EDEN, ANTHONY, 1ST EARL OF AVON (1897–1977) Conservative politician; MP for Warwick and Leamington (1925–57); prime minister (1955–7); under secretary at the Foreign Office (1931–3); lord privy seal and minister for League of Nations affairs (1935). In the wake of the resignation of Samuel Hoare following the Italian invasion of Abyssinia in 1935, Eden became foreign secretary, famously resigning in 1938 in protest at Neville Chamberlain's policy of appeasement. Other key positions included secretary for the dominions (1939–40), secretary for war (1940) and a second term as foreign secretary (1940–45).

Following Winston Churchill's resignation, Eden, a handsome and charismatic politician, won a considerable victory in the 1955 general election and became prime minister. However, his term of office will forever be associated with the disastrous Suez crisis in 1956, which was a cruel blow. Eden resigned partly through ill health and partly through loss of reputation post Suez. He became Earl of Avon in 1961.

EDWARD VII [Albert Edward] (1841–1910) Edward VII became king of Britain and the empire on the death of his mother, Queen Victoria, in January 1901. A one-nation conservative, he was opposed to the New Liberal governments and their reforms and to women's suffrage. He played a significant role in the constitutional crisis following the People's Budget of 1909, insisting that reform of the House of Lords, a cause of David Lloyd George and Asquith, should be the subject of a general election.

EDWARD VIII [Edward Albert Christian George Andrew Patrick David] (1984–1972) Edward VIII reigned only from January to December 1936, following the death of George V, and prior to his abdication; he was never crowned. The **abdication crisis** was brought about solely because he wanted to marry Mrs Wallis Simpson, an American and a divorcee, and that was unacceptable to the government, the Church and the monarchy. He and his wife lived in France following the war until his death in 1972.

ELIZABETH II [Elizabeth Alexandra Mary] (1926–) The daughter of George VI, Elizabeth became queen of Great Britain and Northern Ireland in 1952. Her coronation took place the following year. Married to her third cousin, Prince Philip, the Duke of Edinburgh, she gave birth to four children – Prince Charles (the Prince of Wales), Princess Anne, Prince Andrew and Prince Edward. The queen faced a difficult time from 1997 to 1998 in the wake of the death of Diana, Princess of Wales, who millions of people felt had been badly treated by the royal family and whose death had not met with the requisite show of sympathy from the head of state. During the first term of Tony Blair as prime minister, Elizabeth made the monarchy a more approachable institution. The fiction feature film *The Queen* (2005), starring Helen Mirren, provides a well-acted and atmospheric narrative of the events of 1997.

EVANS, GWYFOR (1912–2005) Plaid Cymru politician. A leading Welsh nationalist and prominent campaigner for the Welsh language, Evans was elected as the first MP for Plaid Cymru, at the Carmarthen by-election in 1966, holding the seat until 1970, and again from 1974 to 1979. He campaigned successfully for a Welsh Channel Four, even threatening a hunger strike, and SC4 began broadcasting in 1982.

FARR, TOMMY [Thomas George] (1914–86) Boxer. One of the most famous Welsh sportsmen in the twentieth century, Farr fought his way out of poverty and the coal mines to become British and empire heavyweight champion during the 1930s. Although he never won the world title, he fought and sometimes defeated some of the greatest boxers of the interwar years.

FAWCETT, DAME MILLICENT GARRETT (1847–1929) Women's suffrage campaigner. She was a key figure in the **National Union of Women's Suffrage Societies** (NUWSS), of which she was elected president in 1890. Broadly a Liberal in her own politics, she was a moderate but committed advocate of votes and rights for women, although disenchanted with Asquith, the Liberal prime minister who opposed women's suffrage. She eschewed

the violent tactics of the militant suffrag-
ettes. The NUWSS changed its name to the
London and National Society for Women's
Service and then in 1953 to the Fawcett
Society, invoking the spirit and example
Dame Fawcett in the ongoing campaign to
reduce inequalities between women and
men.

FELTON, MONICA (1907–70) Planner,
communist activist and writer. A member
of the Labour Party, Felton was a prominent figure in the early postwar new towns.
She was chairman of the Peterlee
Development Corporation from 1948 to
1949, when she left to become chairman of
the Stevenage Development Corporation.
During 1951 she went on an unsanctioned
visit to communist North Korea. There she
claimed to have witnessed atrocities by the
United Nations forces, including British
soldiers, and was sacked from her job in
Stevenage. She subsequently moved to
India, where she lived as a writer until her
death.

FIELDS, DAME GRACIE (1898–1979)
Actress and singer. Fields became famous
during the 1930s as a chippy but likeable
working-class lassie from Lancashire. Her
identification with the culture of mill girls
in the textile factories of the North was at
its strongest in the British cinema classic
Sing as We Go (1935). Gracie married an
Italian, and lived much of her life on the
island of Ischia in the Bay of Naples, something of a contrast with the gritty back
streets of industrial mill towns with which
she is more usually associated.

FLANAGAN AND ALLEN Comedy and
singing double act consisting of Bud
Flanagan [Weintrop, Chaim Reuben]
(1896–1968) and Chesney [William] Allen
(1893–1982). They made the successful
transition from music hall to radio between
the wars. Also members of the Crazy

Gang, another comedy act, Flanagan and
Allen became best known for their singing
routines during the Second World War.
Their songs were homely, reassuring, patriotic, and characterised by gentle and
catchy tunes. They include *Run Rabbit Run*
and *Underneath the Arches*.

FOOT, MICHAEL (MACKINTOSH) (1913–)
Labour politician; MP for Plymouth
Devonport (1945–55) and Ebbw Vale
(1960–92); leader of the Labour Party
(1980–83; secretary of state for employment (1974–6); leader of the House (1976–
9). A member of the left-leaning Tribune
Group, Foot led the Labour Party at its
lowest postwar ebb, when the left was more
powerful than at any time since 1945. Also
a journalist and writer, he attacked the late
1930s Tory leadership in *Guilty Men* (co-
authored with Frank Owen and Peter
Howard and published in 1940 under the
pseudonym Cato) and wrote a number of
biographies.

FRIEDMAN, MILTON (1912–2006) American
economist. An advocate of monetarism,
Friedman was influential upon the
emerging New Right economic agenda of
the 1970s, manifest during the 1980s in
Thatcherite economic policies. He was at
the heart of an Anglo-American culture of
neo-liberal economics that challenged
what it saw to be the discredited and failed
interventionist policies of **Keynesianism**.

G

GAITSKELL, HUGH (TODD NAYLOR) (1906–
63) Labour politician; MP for Leeds
South (1945–63); chancellor of the
exchequer (1950–51). In 1955 Gaitskell

defeated Aneurin Bevan, whom he had greatly criticised for his opposition to National Health Service charges, for the leadership of the Labour Party. He did, however, find common ground with Bevan in attacking the British operation in Suez. Opposed to unilateral disarmament, and to Clause 4, Gaitskell promoted the modernisation of the Labour Party by the end of the 1950s. He died unexpectedly, and was succeeded as leader by Harold Wilson.

GALLACHER, WILLIE [William] (1881–1965) Communist politician; MP for West Fife (1935–50); trade unionist. An activist in the **Clydeside** demonstrations of 1919 and a founding member of the Communist Party of Great Britain (CPGB), Gallacher was one of only a few communist parliamentary candidates to be elected an MP. In the CPGB he was in favour of an out-and-out challenge to reformism, taking, along with Sylvia **Pankhurst** and others, an avowedly revolutionary direction. His autobiography was entitled *The Chosen Few* (1940).

GEORGE V [George Frederick Ernest Albert] (1865–1936) His reign stretched from 1910 until 1936, encompassing the First World War, the Irish Civil War and the creation of the Irish Free State, the General Strike, and the first Labour governments. During the First World War, mindful of the unpopularity of Germany, he changed the surname of the royals from Saxe-Coburg-Gotha to Windsor.

GEORGE VI [Albert Frederick Arthur George] (1896–1952) Following the abdication crisis at the end of 1936, George succeeded his brother Edward VIII as king. During the Second World War he and his family famously resided in Buckingham Palace, ostensibly in order to express solidarity with those in the East End of

London and others who were in danger from the Blitz. He awarded the George Cross and George Medal to brave citizens. His daughters were Elizabeth II and Princess Margaret. He died prematurely of a lung condition in 1952.

GILMOUR, SIR JOHN (1876–1940) Conservative and Unionist politician; MP for East Renfrewshire (1910–18) and Glasgow Pollok (1918–40). Among other senior positions, he was secretary of state for Scotland (1926–9) and home secretary (1932–5), during a period which included the fascist disturbances. His son John Gilmour was also a Conservative politician.

GLASS, RUTH (ADELE) (1912–90) Sociologist. A German-born Jewish émigré to London during the 1930s, she made an important contribution to British sociology from the 1930s to the 1960s. Her interests included urban sociology, for example the issues and problems of community and association on new housing estates, and the sociology of ethnicity and race relations. London was the context for most of her work. A selection of her articles and chapters was published in her edited collection *Clichés of Urban Doom* (1988).

GOONS, THE *The Goon Show* was a radio comedy on the BBC that ran for most of the 1950s. Comprising Spike Milligan, Harry Secombe and Peter Sellers, the Goons were known for some outrageous jokes and a pioneering use of sound effects. An avant-garde act, the Goons blazed a trail for later experimental humour, such as *Monty Python's Flying Circus*. Secombe went on to a singing career on television; Sellers became a cinema actor, starring most famously in the *Pink Panther* movies, and Spike Milligan became a television comedian with his own series.

GRAVES, ROBERT (1895–1985) Writer, playwright and classical scholar. Graves wrote bitterly of the First World War in *Goodbye to All That* (1929) and also a contemporary history of the interwar period, *The Long Weekend* (first published 1941). He is perhaps best known through the BBC television adaptation of *I, Claudius*.

GREENE, (HENRY) GRAHAM (1904–91) Novelist, playwright, screenwriter and travel writer. Greene was most famous for his novels, a number of which he adapted for the cinema, notably *Brighton Rock* (1938) and *The Quiet American*. The first is a somewhat pitiless portrait of the working classes, both innocent and criminal, while *The Quiet American* (1955) dealt with the United States of America's espionage during the Cold War.

GREENE, SIR HUGH (CARLETON) (1910–87) Director general of the BBC (1960–69). Greene's reign at the 'Beeb' is generally viewed as one of increased permissiveness with which the 1960s are so commonly associated. He is also credited by historians of television with strengthening public sector broadcasting in the face of increasing commercial pressures from ITV.

GREENWOOD, WALTER (1903–74) Writer. His most famous work was *Love on the Dole* (1933), set in Salford during the Great Depression. The novel was made into a stage play and a film, and sensitively portrayed the corrosive effects of poverty and unemployment upon individuals and communities.

GREER, GERMAINE (1940–) Australian-born feminist and writer. She first came to prominence with *The Female Eunuch* (1971). Greer has written widely on women's issues, art and literature, and regularly contributes to newspapers and television. For a while she was editor of the semi-pornographic magazine *Suck*, which among other messages depicted cartoons and photographs and carried written items and stories on all aspects of sexual love and lust, including child pornography, incest and rape.

GRIERSON, JOHN (1898–1972) Leader of the British documentary film movement. He is known for *Drifters* (1929), but was mostly proactive in establishing the principles of documentary film making in Britain. He supported other film makers at the General Post Office Film Unit during the 1930s.

GRIMOND, JO(SEPH), BARON GRIMOND OF FIRTH (1913–93) Liberal politician; MP for Orkney and Shetland (1950–83); leader of the Liberal Party from 1956 to 1967 and again briefly in 1976. He is credited by historians with helping to revive the Liberal Party by the mid-1960s, and indeed under Grimond the Liberals enjoyed their first by-election success since the 1920s at Orpington, Kent, in 1962. General election results began to improve thereafter.

H

HAGUE, WILLIAM (JEFFERSON) (1961–) Conservative politician; MP for Richmond, Yorkshire, from 1989. Hague first became famous as a teenager during the 1970s when giving an amusing speech at a Conservative Party conference, which certainly revealed confidence and ambition. Among other leading offices, he was minister for social security and the disabled (1994–5) and secretary of state for Wales (1995–7). He replaced John Major as Tory leader in 1997, following the Conservatives' general election defeat of that year, but was resoundingly defeated himself at the general election in 2001.

HALDANE, RICHARD (BURDON SANDERSON), 1ST VISCOUNT HALDANE (1856–1928) Liberal (later Labour) politician. He was a leading light in the establishment of the London School of Economics in 1895. An expert in military affairs, in 1905 he was appointed as minister for war by Sir Henry Campbell-Bannerman and initiated and oversaw significant military reforms until 1912.

HALL, (MARGUERITE) RADCLYFFE (1880–1943) Novelist and mystic. Her novel *The Well of Loneliness* (1928), with its lesbian themes, is the work most usually associated with her. It was temporarily banned in Britain for obscenity. Hall wrote a number of other books.

HAMM, (EDWARD) JEFFREY (1915–94) Fascist. A school teacher originally from Wales who settled in England, Hamm stood as a candidate in local elections in the postwar years for Oswald Mosley's Union Movement. In 1947 he participated in the anti-Semitic disturbances in London, disturbances that were also associated with the crypto-fascist British League of Ex-Servicemen and Women.

HAMMOND, BARBARA (1873–1961) and **Hammond, J(ohn) L(awrence)** (1872–1949) Historians. Following their marriage in 1901, they played a leading role in establishing the discipline of social history in Britain during the Edwardian period and between the wars. Drawing upon the work of Arnold Toynbee and the Webbs, the Hammonds advocated the pessimistic view of the industrial revolution that considered industrialisation and urbanisation as mostly harmful to the social fabric of the poor. Their writings influenced the schol-

arly study of the working classes both in Britain and abroad, particularly *The Bleak Age*, published during the mid-1930s, a time of great hardship for millions of urban workers.

HANCOCK, TONY [Anthony John] (1924–68) Comedian and actor. He came to fame on the radio during the 1950s with *Happy Go Lucky* and *Hancock's Half Hour*. The latter series was transferred to television and became a hugely popular sitcom. Hancock went on to work on television comedy and radio. He committed suicide in Australia.

HANDLEY, TOMMY [Thomas Reginald] (1892–1949) Liverpudlian comedian. He became a national figure during the 1940s through *ITMA* (It's That Man Again). A hugely popular radio comedy show, making fun of the war and Germans but also of the English class system, *ITMA* was know for its catchphrases, some of which entered everyday conversation in Britain – for example, 'I don't mind if I do.' Handley died of a brain haemorrhage in 1949, and the BBC ended *ITMA* in tribute to him.

HANNINGTON, WAL(TER) (1886–1966) Communist. As leader of the National Unemployed Workers' Movement between the wars, Hannington inspired and led a number of the hunger marches. His experiences, communist views, anger at unemployment, and contempt for the reformist politics and politicians are evident in his two books, *Unemployed Struggles: 1919–1936* (1936) and *The Problem of the Distressed Areas* (1937).

HARDIE, (JAMES) KEIR (1856–1915) Socialist, trade unionist, peace campaigner and founder of the Labour movement. From 1886 he was secretary of the Scottish Miners' Federation. He stood as Labour candidate in London and became MP for

West Ham (1892–5) and later for Merthyr Tydfil in Wales (1900–15). Hardie founded the Independent Labour Party (ILP) in 1893 and was, until his death in 1915, a prominent spokesperson both for the poor and for pacifism.

HARMSWORTH, ALFRED (CHARLES WILLIAM), 1ST VISCOUNT NORTHCLIFFE (1865–1922) Newspaper proprietor. At the heart of the late Victorian and Edwardian expansion in newspaper reading, Harmsworth founded the *Daily Mail* in 1896, and the re-launched *Daily Mirror* in 1903. He took over *The Times* later in his career. In 1918 he was appointed minister of propaganda by Lloyd George, who understood the importance of an on-message and powerful newspaper owner not only during wartime but also in peacetime. He became a viscount in 1919.

HARMSWORTH, HAROLD (SIDNEY ROTHERMERE), VISCOUNT ROTHERMERE (1868–1940) Newspaper proprietor. He founded the *Sunday Pictorial* in 1915 and following the death of his brother, Viscount Northcliffe, in 1922 he became the owner of the latter's newspaper empire, to which he added other titles between the wars. During the 1930s a number of his newspapers, notably the *Daily Mail* and the *Daily Mirror*, were sympathetic to the British Union of Fascists. He supported appeasement before the Second World War.

HARRISSON, TOM (1911–76) Social anthropologist. With Charles Madge and Humphrey Jennings he founded Mass Observation (MO) in 1937. He wrote or edited a number of books based upon MO materials, including *Mass Observation Day Survey: May 12 1937* (1937); *Britain by Mass Observation* (1939) and *Living through the Blitz* (1976).

HEALEY, DENIS (WINSTON), BARON HEALEY (1917–) Labour politician; MP for Leeds South-East (1952–5) and Leeds East (1955–92); deputy leader of the Labour Party during the 1970s and early 1980s. Healey was defence secretary in Harold Wilson's second government from 1964 to 1970, and oversaw a reduction in British forces east of Suez. As chancellor of the exchequer from 1974 to 1979, he was associated with public expenditure cuts and the apparent humiliation of the loan from the International Monetary Fund (IMF). He retained an important position as a right-wing gradualist influence over what by 1980 was an increasingly divided and fratricidal Labour Party. Healey was made a life peer in 1992. His autobiography was entitled *The Time of my Life* (1989).

HEATH, SIR EDWARD (RICHARD GEORGE) ('TED') (1916–2005) Conservative politician; MP for Bexley (1950–74) and Old Bexley and Sidcup (1974–2001); prime minister (1970–74). Heath has been widely viewed as having been eclipsed by Margaret Thatcher. Yet he enjoyed a long and distinguished career, characterised by humanity, progressiveness and a number of significant triumphs. He came from a relatively modest skilled working-class background. The son of a parlour maid and a carpenter, he was educated at Oxford University and took a keen interest in European affairs, witnessing the horrors of fascism and communism. He became the personification of a consensus politician during the postwar years, committed to full employment at home and good working relationships with the trade unions, at least until his time as prime minister.

Heath was chief whip of the Conservative Party (1955–9), minister for labour (1959–60) and secretary of state for trade and industry (1963–4). He was the first Tory leader to be elected by Conservative

MPs, in 1965. In 1970, against most predictions, he won the general election. During his term as PM Heath attempted unsuccessfully to curb the power of the trade unions in industrial relations, and was forced to confront growing militancy, notably among the coal miners, power workers, transport workers and dockers. His policy to establish a wage freeze to control inflation was a failure. The impact of the oil crisis in 1973 did great damage to the British industrial economy, and forced unemployment to rise sharply for the first time since the 1930s. Heath called a general election in 1974, asking 'who governs Britain?', and lost by a small majority to his adversary, Harold Wilson. Heath, however, successfully negotiated British entry into the Common Market, namely the European Economic Community (later the European Union), in the face of much opposition from his own party and the left of the Labour Party. Defeated by Thatcher for the Tory leadership in 1975, he became much less prominent in politics thereafter, but continued to be regarded as a more consensus-minded politician than his successor. His autobiography was entitled *The Course of my Life* (1988).

HENDERSON, ARTHUR (1863–1935) Labour politician. He was born in Scotland but was strongly associated with the North of England, where he represented a variety of constituencies. He was first elected as MP for Barnard Castle in 1903. Having taken over the Labour leadership from Ramsay MacDonald in 1914, when the party was split over the war, Henderson became the first Labour MP to reach a cabinet position, namely in the coalition government during the First World War, but he resigned before the war ended. He was home secretary in the first Labour government of 1924 and served as foreign secretary from 1929 to 1931. He was awarded the Nobel Peace Prize in 1934 for his efforts to promote peace in the years after 1918.

HERBERT, SIR ALAN (PATRICK) (1890–1971) Politician and lawyer; independent Member of Parliament for Oxford University (1935–50) before the university constituencies were abolished. Herbert was a reformer, having fought for an amendment to the divorce laws in 1937. He was also a novelist.

HESELTINE, MICHAEL (RAY DIBDIN), BARON HESELTINE (1933–) Conservative politician; MP for Tavistock (1966–74) and Henley-on-Thames (1974–2001); minister for aerospace and shipping (1972–4); minister for the environment (1979–83; minister for defence (1983–6); secretary of state for the environment (1990–92); secretary of state for trade and industry (1992–5). Heseltine was often a colourful parliamentarian, defending tradition against what he saw as the irresponsibility of many socialists. His resignation over the Westland affair in 1986 ended his term as minister of defence. He was also a critic of Margaret Thatcher's views on Europe, and was frustrated by some of the militant Eurosceptic members of his party. His challenge to Thatcher's leadership in 1980 effectively induced the end of her term as prime minister. Heseltine's important contribution to **urban regeneration** is often overlooked by contemporary historians. He is, however, certainly remembered by many working-class people in the industrial areas for his announcement in 1992 that the Conservative government intended radically to reduce the coal industry in Britain. Many mines were closed and communities damaged. Heseltine was also deputy leader of the Conservative Party from 1995 to 1997. Nicknamed 'Tarzan', his political autobiography was entitled *Life in the Jungle* (2000).

HICKS BEACH, MICHAEL (EDWARD), 1ST EARL ST ALDWYN (1837–1916) Conservative politician; MP for Gloucestershire East (1864–85) and Bristol West (1885–1906). During the Victorian period he had been president of the board of trade and occupied other senior positions. As chancellor of the exchequer during the Boer War, he used taxation to assist in paying for the conflict.

HILL, OCTAVIA (1838–1912) Social reformer in the East End of London. An early advocate of social housing in the form of model dwellings, Hill was a leading member of the Charity Organisation Society, which advocated home visiting, the birth of social work. She served on the royal commission on the Poor Laws in 1905, and remained a staunch advocate of **self-help** as the key to a stable life.

HOBHOUSE, L(EONARD) T(RELAWNY) (1864–1929) Academic and philosopher. Hobhouse was the first professor of sociology in Britain, a position he held at the London School of Economics from 1907. His views on the need to regulate capitalism and improve urban society were influences upon the development of New Liberalism during the later nineteenth and early twentieth centuries.

HOGGART, (HERBERT) RICHARD (1918–) Literary critic, sociologist and cultural commentator. In 1964 he founded the Centre for Contemporary Cultural Studies at the University of Birmingham. He was the author of *The Uses of Literacy* (1958), a key text in understanding the impact of the media and Americanisation on working-class culture.

HOWARD, SIR EBENEZER (1850–1928) Social reformer and town planner. Inspired by American pastoralism, and by his own experiences on the American frontier, Howard endeavoured to provide planned alternatives to the ugly, sprawling and polluted industrial cities of Britain. As outlined in his *Tomorrow: A Peaceful Path to Reform* (1898), which was later retitled *Garden Cities of Tomorrow* (1902), he advocated garden cities, where the best of both town and country living could be fused in sociable cities provisioned with good, attractive housing, parklands, social facilities, and zoned places of employment – zoned meaning separated from residential areas. The first experiment to this end was Letchworth, in the county of Hertfordshire. Promoted by Howard via private investment in the Garden Cities Pioneer Company from 1903, it schooled a generation of twentieth-century architects and town planners in the design of new communities. So too did **Welwyn Garden City**, also begun by Howard, from 1920. These garden cities and the planners who worked in them went on to influence the new towns programme following the end of the Second World War. The war gave planners the opportunity to reconstruct urban Britain, and planned new communities formed one mechanism to this end.

HOWARD, MICHAEL (1941–) Conservative politician; MP for Folkestone and Hythe (1983–); home secretary (1993–7). An unsuccessful contender for the Tory Party leadership in 1997, he replaced Iain Duncan Smith as party leader in 2003, but was soundly defeated by Tony Blair at the 2005 general election.

HOWE, (RICHARD EDWARD) GEOFFREY, BARON HOWE OF ABERAVON (1926–) Conservative politician; MP for Bebington (1964–6); Reigate (1970–74) and Surrey East (1974–92); solicitor general (1970–72); minister of trade and consumer affairs (1972–4). Howe served in Margaret Thatcher's governments as, successively, chancellor of the exchequer, foreign secretary and deputy prime minister. His resignation speech in 1990, directly criticising Thatcher's leadership style and views on Europe greatly, damaged the prime minister and precipitated the challenge to Thatcher by Michael Heseltine. Howe's memoirs were entitled *A Conflict of Loyalty* (1994).

HULTON, EDWARD (GEORGE) (1906–88) Newspaper proprietor. A Conservative in politics, Hulton owned various titles, but in 1938 he founded the one for which he is most usually associated – *Picture Post*, a pioneering organ of photo-journalism in Britain.

HUME, JOHN (1937–) Northern Ireland politician; leader of the Social Democratic and Labour Party (SDLP) (1979–2001). Hume made an important contribution to the peace process in Northern Ireland, emphasising the civil rights of all of Northern Ireland's people, and meeting with Sinn Féin leader Gerry **Adams** during the 1990s. This led to the Anglo-Irish peace initiative, which resulted in a temporary ceasefire. Hume continued to work for peace following the end of the ceasefire, and helped to secure the Good Friday Agreement of 1998.

HURD, DOUGLAS (RICHARD), BARON HURD OF WESTWELL (1930–) Conservative politician; MP for Mid Oxfordshire (1974–83) and Witney (1983–97); home secretary (1985–9; foreign secretary (1989–95). He retired from parliament in 1997 and was made a baron.

ISAACS, GERALD (RUFUS), 2ND MARQUESS OF READING (1889–1960) Conservative

politician; under secretary of state for foreign affairs (1951–3) and minister of state for foreign affairs (1953–7).

ISAACS, RUFUS (DANIEL), 1ST MARQUESS OF READING (1860–1935) Liberal politician; MP for Reading (1904–13); foreign secretary in the National Government of Ramsay MacDonald. He was the first Jewish foreign secretary in modern Britain, during a decade of noticeable anti-Semitism.

JENKINS, ROY (HARRIS), BARON JENKINS OF HILLHEAD (1920–2003) Labour, Social Democrat and Liberal politician; MP for Southwark Central (1948–50), Birmingham Stechford (1950–77) and Glasgow Hillhead (1982–7); home secretary (1965–7); chancellor of the exchequer (1967–70); home secretary (1974–6); leading founder of the Social Democratic Party (SDP) (1981); president of the European Commission (1977–81). Jenkins was a right-of-centre member of the Labour Party, a moderate and a modernizer, and his period as home secretary during the 1960s coincided with a wider liberalisation of values in Britain, although his austere budget of 1970, while achieving an improved balance of trade, has been viewed by some political historians as contributing to Labour's electoral defeat of that year. Increasingly frustrated with the leftist direction of the Labour Party from the late 1970s, Jenkins was one of the Gang of Four who in 1981 established a new left-liberal Social Democratic Party.

JENNINGS, HUMPHREY (1907–50) Documentary film maker. Admired for his poetic techniques in film making, and for his commitment to social reform, Jennings was also a founder member of Mass Observation in 1937. He joined the General Post Office Film Unit, run by John Grierson, during the mid-1930s, and went on to make the elegiac *Spare Time* (1938) about the leisure of the working classes in Bolton, Lancashire, the textile town that Mass Observation labelled 'Worktown'. During the war he directed *London (Britain) Can Take It* (1941), *Listen to Britain* (1942) and *A Diary for Timothy* (1945).

JOHN, ELTON [Dwight, Reginald Kenneth] (1947–) Singer and pianist. He gained fame during the 1970s with a number of best-selling albums, including *Tumbleweed Connection* (1971), *Madman across the Water* (1972), *Don't Shoot Me, I'm Only the Piano Player* (1973) and *Goodbye Yellow Brick Road* (1973). Many hit singles were drawn from these albums, among them *Candle in the Wind*, from *Yellow Brick Road*. About Marilyn Monroe, this was reinterpreted as a paean to Diana, Princess of Wales, in 1997. John went on to have many hits singles and albums and, along with David **Bowie** and Rod **Stewart**, has been a leading solo act, and a gay icon, in an Anglo-American culture of popular music.

JOSEPH, KEITH (SINJOHN), BARON JOSEPH (1918–94) Conservative politician; MP for Leeds North-East (1956–87); minister of state at the board of trade (1961–2); minister of housing and local government (1962–4); secretary of state for social services (1970–74); secretary of state for industry (1979–81); secretary of state for education and science (1981–6). Associated from the 1970s with the New Right, Joseph served in the governments of Harold Macmillan, Alec Douglas-Home, Edward Heath and Margaret Thatcher. He was most influential upon Thatcher, who was in sympathy with his monetarist ideas, and with whom he founded the right-wing Centre for Policy Studies.

JOYCE, WILLIAM ('LORD HAW HAW') (1906–47) Irish-American sympathiser of Adolf Hitler and Nazi Germany. His risible radio broadcasts on behalf of Britain's enemy during the Second World War elicited more humour than fear. It is highly doubtful whether morale in Britain was ever lowered by this. Nonetheless, despite the possession of an American passport, Joyce was put to death for treason in 1947.

JOYNSON-HICKS, WILLIAM, 1ST VISCOUNT BRENTFORD (1865–1932) Conservative politician; MP for Manchester North-West (1908–10), Brentford (1911–18) and Twickenham (1911–29). Joynson-Hicks enjoyed a wide portfolio of senior parliamentary positions before serving as home secretary in the Conservative government of Stanley Baldwin from 1924 to 1929.

K

KEYNES, JOHN MAYNARD, 1ST BARON KEYNES (1883–1946) Economist. He was an advocate of greater government intervention during the era of laissez-faire Treasury policies. In his *The Economic Consequences of the Peace* (1919) he was highly critical of reparations levelled against Germany by the Treaty of Versailles, and in *The Economic Consequences of Mr Churchill* (1925) he attacked the decision to return the pound sterling to the gold standard because it damaged British exports. During the 1920s his ideas for deficit spending by government in order to reduce unemployment influenced the Liberal Party's 1929 manifesto *We Can Conquer Unemployment*. In 1936 Keynes's *General Theory of Employment, Interest and Money* advocated regulation of financial markets through greater government control, heightened government management of the economy, and a programme of public works in order to maximise productive capacity, put people back to work and attain full employment. He was the British delegate and the dominating influence at the Bretton Woods conference in the United States in 1944. Keynes served as chief economic advisor to the Treasury during the Second World War. His endorsement of a proactive and strategic role for government was adopted by both Labour and Conservative governments, but was increasingly challenged by the New Right in the 1970s.

KINNOCK, NEIL (GORDON), BARON KINNOCK (1942–) Labour politician; MP for Bedwellty (1970–83) and Islwyn (1983–95). Kinnock was leader of the Labour Party from the ending of the tenure of Michael Foot in 1983 to 1992, when his second general election defeat forced his resignation. Despite his failure to become prime minister at two general elections, he can be credited with rebuilding a Labour Party that was demoralised and unelectable following the general election of 1983.

KITCHENER, (HORATIO) HERBERT, 1ST EARL KITCHENER (1850–1916) Military leader. He served in a number of battles, including the Boer War, and attained the highest rank of field marshal in 1910. From 1914 to 1916 he was secretary of state for war, overseeing a hugely successful recruitment drive to staff the volunteer armies that fought in the trenches of Northern France and Belgium. He was drowned when his ship was sunk in 1916.

L

LAMONT, NORMAN (STEWART HUGHSON), BARON LAMONT OF LERWICK (1942–) Conservative politician; MP for Kingston-upon-Thames (1972–97). Lamont was chancellor of the exchequer at the time of Black Wednesday in 1992, when the pound sterling was suspended from the European Exchange Rate Mechanism.

LANSBURY, GEORGE (1859–1940) Labour leader; pacifist; MP for Bow, in East London (1910–12, 1922–40). Lansbury was a progressive left-winger, an advocate of votes for women, and the leader of the **Poplar revolt** against unfair Poor Law levies and dispensations during the 1920s. During the second Labour government he was the commissioner of works. He led the Labour Party from 1931 to 1935. His autobiography was entitled *Looking Backwards – and Forwards* (1935).

LAW, (ANDREW) BONAR (1858–1923) Canadian-born Conservative politician; MP for Glasgow Blackfriars (1900–06), Dulwich in South London (1906–10), Bootle (Liverpool) (1911–18) and Glasgow Central (1918–23); prime minister (1922–3). Against the background of much criticism of Arthur Balfour from both leading and rank-and-file Tories, Law became leader of the Conservative Party in 1911. He was colonial secretary in the wartime government in 1915–16, chancellor of the exchequer from 1916 to 1918, and leader of the Commons from 1915 to 1919. He became lord privy seal soon after the First World War ended. A critic of continued cooperation with the Liberals led by Lloyd George by 1922, Law became prime minister following the Carlton Club revolt of 1922.

LAWRENCE, D(AVID) H(ERBERT RICHARD) (1885–1930) Novelist. Among his best-known works is *Lady Chatterley's Lover*, banned from the 1930s until the 1960s, and the subject of a famous trial for obscenity in 1960.

LAWSON, NIGEL, BARON LAWSON OF BLABY (1932–) Conservative politician; MP for Blaby (1974–92); chancellor of the exchequer (1983–9). Lawson oversaw the deregulation of British financial markets during the 1980s, notably the Big Bang of 1986. He resigned following the over-heating of the British economy in 1988–9 as a consequence of tax cuts, and under criticism from Margaret Thatcher over his handling of British membership of the European Monetary System. He entered the House of Lords in 1992. His daughter, Nigella Lawson, is a celebrity chef.

LEAN, SIR DAVID (1908–91) Film producer and director. Among his most famous films was *This Happy Breed* (1944), written by Noël **Coward**, a gentle morale-boosting film about the basic decency and good humour of British families in good times and bad. The movie *Brief Encounter* (1945), also written by Coward, was no box-office hit but became highly regarded later as a quintessentially British film because of its coded references to an extra-marital affair that did not even include any sex. Following the war, Lean's adaptations of Dickens's novels were hugely popular, while his film *Bridge on the River Kwai* (1957) was devoid of any smug triumpha-lism about the Allied victory in the Second World War. Lean contributed to other major British films, including *Lawrence of Arabia* (1962), *Dr Zhivago* (1965) and *Ryan's Daughter* (1970).

LED ZEPPELIN Rock, blues and folk-rock band. Led Zeppelin surfaced during the late 1960s and became internationally famous during the 1970s. Singer Robert Plant and guitarist Jimmy Page were estab-lished as the most prominent of the four-piece act, but bassist John-Paul Jones and drummer John Bonham were a powerful rhythm section. 'Led Zep', as they became commonly known, along with the Beatles and the Rolling Stones, popularised British rock music in the USA. Coinciding with the fashion for reading J. R. Tolkien, whose *The Hobbit* and *Lord of the Rings* novels captured the imagination of millions, the band also performed folksy and mythical ballads with Tolkien in mind.

LEESE, ARNOLD (SPENCER) (1877–1956) Fascist; veterinary surgeon with a speciality in camels. Leese was associated with the **British Fascists** in the 1920s and early 1930s, and founded the **Imperial Fascist League** (IFL) in the late 1920s. Based in Stamford, Lincolnshire, the IFL was vehemently anti-Semitic. Leese was little more than a very marginal and risible figure in British politics between the wars. His autobiography was entitled *Out of Step: Events in the Two Lives of an Anti-Jewish Camel Doctor*.

LINTORN-ORMAN, ROTHA (BERYL) (1895–1935) Fascist. In common with so many fascists in Britain and Europe after 1918, Lintorn-Orman had been radicalised by the First World War. She was a committed anti-socialist and hater of communism, and saw the rise of both as a betrayal of the victory of 1918. In 1923, in the early wake of Mussolini's example in Italy, she estab-lished the British Fascisti, later renamed the British Fascists. As a leading woman fascist, she has some significance in history. Apart from that, she is a deservedly minor figure.

LIVINGSTONE, KEN(NETH ROBERT) (1945–) Labour politician; MP for Brent East (1987–2001); leader of the Labour-controlled Greater London Council from 1981 until its abolition in 1986. On the left of the Labour Party, Livingstone baited Margaret Thatcher during the 1980s: he was critical of her record on unemployment, and of her diminution of London government. He stood for mayor of London, without the support of the Labour Party leadership, and was elected in 2000. However, in 2008 he lost the mayoral elections to the Conservative Boris Johnson.

LLOYD, MARIE [Wood, Matilda Alice Victoria] (1870–1922) Music hall entertainer. Born into a working-class family in East London, she was the most successful of a number of siblings with ambitions to become stars of the London music hall. Her repertoire of songs included *A Little of What You Fancy Does You Good*, with allusions to sex and alcohol, and *One of the Ruins that Cromwell Knocked About a Bit*, an unwitting statement of the sad fact that Lloyd was the victim of an alcoholic and abusive husband. Her career exemplified the pressures on successful working-class young women in show-business, where the filial, financial and educational props available to aspirant middle-class entertainers were often lacking.

LLOYD, (JOHN) SELWYN (BROOKE) BARON SELWYN-LLOYD (1904–78) Conservative politician; MP for The Wirral (1945–76). He was foreign secretary during the Suez crisis and continued to serve in this position under Macmillan (1955–60). From 1960 to 1962 he served as chancellor of the exchequer, and in the latter year was instrumental in establishing the **National Economic Development Council**. A victim of Macmillan's **night of the long knives** in July 1962, Lloyd became a back-bencher, but was leader of the House of Commons under Douglas-Home and later a prominent member of the House of Lords.

LLOYD GEORGE, DAVID, 1ST EARL LLOYD-GEORGE OF DWYFOR (1863–1945) Liberal politician; MP for Caernarfon Boroughs (1890–1945); prime minister (1916–22). Lloyd George was born in Manchester but brought up in North Wales. A New Liberal, he was a fiery advocate of social policies that led to the creation of a proto-welfare state before 1914. His introduction of **old-age pensions** in 1908 was particularly controversial because it was financed by raised taxation, notably on land values. The People's Budget in 1909 led to a prolonged constitutional crisis that resulted in the passing of the **Parliament Act** 1911, which asserted the supremacy of the Commons over the House of Lords.

The First World War was a good time for Lloyd George personally. He was an effective minister of munitions under Asquith and, as the latter lost his reputation due to perceived slowness and mismanagement of the crisis, in 1916 moved to replace him as prime minister of the coalition government. This, while successful for Lloyd George in the short to medium term, opened a breach in the Liberal Party that never fully closed until the latter was incapable of winning power in a general election. Endorsing a programme of social reform for the reconstruction of postwar Britain, which famously included his 'homes fit for heroes' call for council housing, Lloyd George also won a huge majority for his coalition with the Tories in the **'coupon election'** of 1918.

But he lost face over the coming years. The Conservatives were very critical of his actions towards the Irish Free State in 1921. His handling of the Chanak crisis in 1922 was also attacked, and in the immediate aftermath of the Carlton Club revolt in the same year the Tories broke with the coalition and in the subsequent general election returned to power as a unified Conservative Party. Lloyd George was now forced to heal a divided Liberal Party that was pushed into third place during the 1920s by the ascendant Labour Party. He was converted to Keynesianism, endorsing interventionist politics in the Liberal manifesto of 1929, *We Can Conquer Unemployment*. He was created an earl in the year of his death.

LLOYD GEORGE, GWILYM, 1ST VISCOUNT TENBY (1894–1967) Liberal, later Conservative, politician; MP for Pembrokeshire (1922–4, 1929–50) and Newcastle upon Tyne North (1951–7). Lloyd-George held a number of leading positions during the 1950s, including home secretary and minister for Welsh affairs, a period that encompassed three prime ministers. In 1955 he decreed that Cardiff was to be the capital of Wales.

LOACH, KEN(NETH) (1936–) Film maker and television director. Among his most respected works are the television docudrama *Cathy Come Home* (1966) and his film *Kes* (1971). Both were depressing, sympathetic and moving portrayals of life among the poorest sections of British society.

LOW, SIR DAVID (ALEXANDER CECIL) (1891–1963) Cartoonist. Low worked for a variety of publications, including the *New Statesman*, *Punch* and the *Evening Standard*. His politics were pragmatic and sometimes radical: he was a staunch critic of fascism during the 1930s. Low invented the character of 'Colonel Blimp', a pompous, reactionary, militaristic and jingoistic Tory caricature.

LYNN, DAME VERA [Welch, Vera Margaret] (1917–) Singer. Linked in the minds of millions of British people with her wartime songs of hope such as *We'll Meet Again* and *White Cliffs of Dover*, she was also the 'forces' sweetheart'. Her singing career continued long into the postwar years. In 1975 he was made a DBE.

M

MACDONALD, (JAMES) RAMSAY (1866–1937) Labour politician; MP for Leicester (1906–18) and Aberavon (1922–9); and National Labour MP for Seaham (1929–35); Labour prime minister (1924, 1929–31); prime minister of the National Government (1931–5). Born in Scotland to a poor labouring family, MacDonald had a formidable and impressive rise: with Kier Hardie and others he established the Labour Representation Committee in 1900, and was its first secretary. He served as chairman of the Independent Labour Party from 1906 to 1909 and became leader of the Labour Party following his chairing of the parliamentary Labour Party in 1922, a position he held until 1931. As Labour's first prime minister in 1924, he was also foreign secretary. His second term as prime minister coincided with the slump and the onset of the Great Depression. His government's orthodox economic policies were attacked from most sides for failing to get to grips with the problems of high unemployment and industrial decline. Cuts to unemployment payments angered many in his party, and the decision to form a national government in 1931 split the Labour movement, leading to his expulsion from the party. Even today, Labour historians find it difficult to provide enthusiastic accounts of MacDonald.

MCKENNA, REGINALD (1863–1943) Liberal politician; MP for North Monmouthshire (1895–1918). McKenna served in a number of senior parliamentary positions, and became home secretary under Asquith from 1911 to 1915 and chancellor of the exchequer in 1915–16. No supporter of David Lloyd George, he resigned over the issue of conscription in 1916.

MACLEOD, IAIN (NORMAN) (1913–70) Conservative politician; MP for Enfield West (1950–70). He was colonial secretary from 1959 to 1961, overseeing a key period of decolonisation in Africa. In 1970 he became chancellor of the exchequer, but he died shortly afterwards and was succeeded by Anthony Barber.

MACMILLAN, (MAURICE) HAROLD, 1ST EARL OF STOCKTON (1894–1987) Conservative politician; MP for Stockton-on-Tees (1924–9, 1931–45) and Bromley (1945–64). During the 1930s, the social problems of the North-East of England, and of his constituency of Stockton-on-Tees in particular, led Macmillan to embrace the 'middle way' in politics. He was a conservative consensus politician, patrician and paternalistic. As minister for housing and local government (1951–4) he facilitated the delivery of over 300,000 houses per year, an achievement that fulfilled a key election promise made in 1951. Macmillan was minister for defence in 1954–5 and foreign secretary briefly in 1955. While chancellor of the exchequer (1955–7) he introduced **Premium Bonds**. He took over as prime minister following Eden's resignation in 1957, and won the general election of 1959 with a sizeable majority. His subsequent years as premier, however, were characterised by problems with Tory discipline and a resurgent Labour Party under Gaitskell and Wilson. Macmillan resigned in the wake of the Profumo scandal and became much less active in politics. He published six volumes of memoirs, and his diaries have been edited by Peter **Catterall**.

MCMILLAN, MARGARET (1860–1931) Social reformer, educationalist and supporter of the Fabian Society, the Independent Labour Party (ILP) and other socialist and progressive movements of the Victorian and Edwardian years. Witnessing the effects of child poverty in Bradford led her to campaign for both health and educational policies, including school meals – a policy enacted in the 1906 **Education (Provision of Meals) Act**. McMillan pioneered a number of school-based clinics and established a centre for the training of nurses. She was also a campaigner for women's suffrage.

MAJOR, SIR JOHN (1943–) Conservative politician; MP for Huntingdonshire (1979–83) and Huntingdon (1983–2001); prime minister (1990–97). Following a number of junior posts Major became a cabinet member in 1987. He was foreign secretary in 1989, and became chancellor of the exchequer that same year after the resignation of Nigel Lawson, under whom the economy had greatly overheated. Britain joined the European **Exchange Rate Mechanism** in 1990 under Major, but his portfolio was greatly enhanced when he became prime minister following the enforced resignation of Margaret Thatcher. His generally right-of-centre politics and apparently affable if uninspiring personality were favoured by a number of Tory MPs, and many voters, who returned Major to the prime minister's office in 1992. However, the government from 1992 to 1997 was scarred by the unseemly conduct of many Tory MPs, which gave the Conservative Party a reputation for sleaze despite its rhetorical commitment to '**back to basics**' in terms of values. The problems with the Exchange Rate Mechanism severely damaged any claim that the Conservatives were the natural party of sound governmental finances.

MARSHALL, T(HOMAS) H(UMPHREY) (1893–1981) Sociologist. Marshall played a leading role in establishing the *British Journal of Sociology* in 1949. His collection of essays *Citizenship and Social Class* (1950) connected citizenship with entitlement to welfare state policies and other rights. He remained a staunch advocate of progressive social policy throughout his professional career.

MAUDLING, REGINALD (1917–79) Conservative politician; MP for Barnet (1950–74) and Chipping Barnet (1974–9). Maudling held a number of important senior positions in the Conservative Party and in government, including chancellor of the exchequer (1962–4). He unsuccessfully challenged Edward Heath for the leadership of the Tory Party.

MAXWELL, (IAN) ROBERT [Hoch, Ján Ludvik] (1923–91) Labour politician; MP for Buckingham (1964–70); businessman and newspaper magnate. Czech-born, he emigrated to Britain on the eve of the Second World War. His parents were murdered by the Nazis, against whom Maxwell fought during the war. He became the owner of the publishing house Pergamon Press, and his business drive grew during the 1970s and 1980s. In 1984 he acquired Mirror Group newspapers, subsequently changing the appearance and style of the *Daily Mirror*, making it a more competitive newspaper against the *Sun* while retaining the newspaper's pro-Labour politics. Maxwell and his family were undone by the scandal of his companies' pension funds. As news broke that he had raided the pensions of his employees to sustain his ailing business empire, Maxwell probably threw himself off of his yacht as it sailed in the Atlantic Ocean.

MAXWELL-FYFE, DAVID (PATRICK), EARL OF KILMUIR (1900–67) Conservative politician; MP for Liverpool West Derby (1935–54). He was a key British member of the Council of Europe from 1949 to 1952 and home secretary in the government of Winston Churchill from 1951 to 1954, following which he moved to the House of Lords.

MONRO, MATT [Parsons, Terence Edward] (1930–85) Singer. Born in the East End of London, he had a number of minor jobs before his singing voice was recognised for its star potential. He signed with the Parlophone record label, enjoying five hits in the British charts during the 1960s, and recorded the theme to the second James Bond film, *From Russia with Love* (1963). His range from gentle crooning to strong vocal delivery came close in style to that of Frank Sinatra.

MONTGOMERY, BERNARD (LAW), 1ST VISCOUNT MONTGOMERY OF ALAMEIN ('MONTY') (1887–1976) Army officer. He served in India before the First World War, in Belgium and France from 1914, and in Palestine between the wars. During the Second World War his role as commander of the Third Army during the events at Dunkirk and of the Eighth Army at Alamein in November 1942 earned him enormous respect, the status of general, and a knighthood. His major defeat, however, came with the battle of Arnhem in November 1944. He was killed by an IRA bomb.

MONTY PYTHON'S FLYING CIRCUS Perhaps the most famous of all the BBC comedy series made during the postwar period, *Monty Python* was a blend of surreal animation, inventive dialogue, extreme caricature and satire. Running for just two series, in 1969–70 and from 1972 to 1974, it became a worldwide phenomenon and launched the careers of John Cleese, Terry Gilliam (an American animator), Eric Idle, Terry Jones and Michael Palin. A number of *Monty Python* feature films were made during the 1970s, notably the controversial *Life of Brian* (1979), assisting the launch of the team into global stardom. Cleese gained further success in the BBC2 sitcom *Fawlty Towers* and as a cinema actor, while Gilliam worked as a cinema animator.

Palin became a regular fixture of the British television screen.

MORRIS, WILLIAM (RICHARD), VISCOUNT NUFFIELD (1877–1963) Businessman, motor car manufacturer and philanthropist. Using mass-production techniques influenced by Ford, Morris's plant at Cowley, Oxford, became the largest car manufacturer in Britain, incorporating Austin into Austin-Morris in 1952.

MORRISON, HERBERT (STANLEY), BARON MORRISON OF LAMBETH (1888–1965) Labour politician; MP for South Hackney (1923–4, 1929–31, 1934–45), Lewisham East (1945–50) and Lewisham South (1950–59). During the First World War Morrison worked on the land in the garden city of Letchworth and was the leading member of the London Labour Party (LLP), formed in 1915. Although defeated in 1935 by Clement Attlee for the leadership of the Labour Party, he was leader of the London County Council from 1934 to 1939 following the successful rise to power of the LLP. The personification of a moderate Labour politics, eschewing the left of his party for a careful and corporate vision of municipal socialism and nationalisation, Morrison realised that the middle-class vote was necessary for Labour's electoral success, and should not be alienated by high taxation and angry class-based rhetoric. He was minister of transport from 1929 to 1931, and during the Second World War he was minister of supply in 1940 and home secretary and minister of home security from 1940 until 1945. After 1945 Morrison served as deputy prime minister and leader of the House of Commons. He became foreign secretary for nearly eight months in 1951, following the death of Bevin. He was made Lord Morrison of Lambeth in 1959. His autobiography was entitled *Herbert Morrison: An Autobiography* (1960).

MOSLEY, SIR OSWALD (ERNALD) (1896–1980) Conservative, Labour, Independent Labour, New Party and Fascist politician, but now known mostly as a fascist. Mosley began his political career as Conservative MP for Harrow from 1918 to 1924, following which he was an 'Independent' until he joined the Labour Party in 1924, for which he was MP for Smethwick, in Birmingham, from 1926 to 1931. During Ramsay MacDonald's 1929–31 government he was disappointed at the position of chancellor of the Duchy of Lancaster, because it is not a powerful cabinet role. Increasingly frustrated about the inability of orthodox economic policy and an elderly political elite to find a radical solution to the social and economic problems of the slump, in 1930 he proposed the **Mosley memorandum**, a document influenced by Keynesianism. Frustrated by its rejection, he formed the **New Party**, which met with disaster at the general election of 1931. Increasingly impressed with Italian fascism, Mosley ended the New Party and formed the British Union of Fascists (BUF), by no means the first fascist party in Britain but certainly the largest. The BUF was at its height in 1933–4 but was a marginal movement, partly because of Mosley himself. The image of a self-important product of the minor gentry stamping up and down in a paramilitary uniform lent itself to comedic caricature. In a number of his Jeeves and Wooster novels set in England during the 1930s, P. G. **Wodehouse** drew upon Mosley as the basis for the risible yet sinister character of Roderick Spode, leader of the Black Shorts. Yet Mosley's growing rapport with Hitler and Nazi Germany also alienated most British people. As Britain increasingly positioned itself for a war with Germany during the later 1930s, Mosley seemed increasingly like an outsider. During the Second World War he was interned under Regulation 18b as a possible traitor. He left for France after the war and attempted, unsuccessfully, to rekindle his political career in Britain in 1947 by founding the Union Movement, which fought unsuccessfully in a number of London constituencies. Mosley sought to exploit the **Notting Hill race riots** of 1958, even making a speech on the spot where a young black man was murdered some months after the riots were over. His autobiography was entitled *My Life* (1978).

MOWLAM, MARJORIE ('MO') (1950–2005) Labour politician; MP for Redcar (1987–2001). As Northern Ireland Secretary from 1997 to 1999 she played a leading part in the Good Friday Agreement. Mowlam also found a career post-1999 as a writer for the *Daily Mirror*. Known as 'Mo, the woman in the know', she achieved a genuine connection with the working-class public.

MURDOCH, (KEITH) RUPERT (1931–) Newspaper magnate. An Australian-born proponent of tabloid journalism, Murdoch has a vast empire, including News International, which owns *The Sun*, the *News of the World* and *The Times*, and the Sky satellite television network.

O

O'NEILL, TERENCE (MARNE), BARON O'NEILL OF THE MAINE (1914–90) Unionist MP; minister of finance in the Ulster government (1956–63); prime minister of Northern Ireland (1963–9). In adopting a generally conciliatory attitude towards Catholics, including local government reforms, O'Neill was opposed by more militant Unionists, and was unable to assuage the growing anger of Northern Ireland's Catholics during the beginning of The Troubles in 1968. He was created a life peer in 1970.

ORWELL, GEORGE [Blair, Eric Arthur] (1903–50) Novelist, journalist and broadcaster. Orwell was a socialist whose most famous books include *Homage to Catalonia* (1938), an account of the Spanish Civil War during which Orwell fought on behalf of communist Republicans. *Animal Farm* (1945) is a famous satire on the Russian Revolution, and *1984* (1949) is a grim vision of a totalitarian Britain dominated by the screen. Orwell himself was a broadcaster and journalist during the war. The experience of the austerity years from 1945, furthermore, shaped the writing and context of the world of *1984*.

Orwell has inspired a number of mostly favourable, even affectionate, but by no means uncritical biographical studies. His writings, for those who were able to access them in secret, were of considerable comfort in totalitarian countries before the Berlin Wall was pulled down in 1989, and the television series *Big Brother* (based upon the all-seeing screen in *1984*) is an unwitting insult to him.

OSBORN, SIR FREDERIC (JAMES) (1885–1978) Town planner. A leading advocate of garden cities, and committed to a programme of planned new towns, Osborn was influenced by Ebenezer Howard and worked in both Letchworth and Welwyn Garden City. He became influential in the Ministry of Town and Country Planning, formed in 1943 in order to plan for postwar reconstruction.

OSBORNE, JOHN (JAMES) (1929–94) Playwright. Osborne was in his late twenties when he became famous as one of the Angry Young Men. He remains best known for *Look Back in Anger* (1956), *The Entertainer* (1957) and his adaptation of the bawdy novel *Tom Jones* for cinema during the 1960s.

OWEN, DAVID (ANTHONY LLEWELLYN), BARON OWEN OF PLYMOUTH (1938–) Labour politician; MP for Plymouth Sutton (1966–74) and Plymouth Devonport (1974–92; foreign secretary (1977–9). Along with Roy Jenkins and Shirley Williams, Owen was a founding member of the Social Democratic Party (SDP) in 1981. Although a joint leader with David Steel of the Alliance, a Liberal–SDP electoral pact, Owen opposed the merger with the Liberals and the formation of the Liberal Democrats in 1988.

OWEN, WILFRED (EDWARD SALTER) (1893–1918) Poet. Born into a working-class background, he expressed his disgust and horror at the First World War in a number of poems, for example *Dulce et decorum est*. During the war he was a victim of shell shock, and was killed in November 1918, just a week before the Armistice was signed.

P

PAISLEY, REVEREND IAN (RICHARD KYLE) (1926–) Northern Ireland politician; MP for North Antrim (1970–); founder of the Free Presbyterian Church of Ulster. A fierce defender of the Protestant majority in Northern Ireland and denouncer of Catholicism, Paisley formed the Democratic Unionist Party (DUP) in 1971. Although he was intractably opposed to the Anglo-Irish Agreement of 1985, and originally refused to cooperate in the peace process, he accepted the outcome of the power-sharing agreements that brought an end to The Troubles.

PALME DUTT, RAJANI (1896–1974) Communist; general secretary of the Communist Party of Great Britain from 1939 to 1941, following the resignation of Harry Pollitt. These were quite difficult years for British communists. The Nazi–Soviet pact was viewed as a dangerous alliance between dictatorships, but its breakdown following the German invasion of Russia temporarily rehabilitated Russian communism in the eyes of many British people. Palme Dutt remained a loyal Stalinist throughout his life, unlike many other members of the CPGB, who were deeply critical of the foreign policy of the USSR.

PANKHURST, DAME CHRISTABEL (HARRIETTE) (1880–1958) Suffragette. The daughter of Emmeline and sister of Sylvia Pankhurst, Christabel favoured only limited women's suffrage, believing the vote should be given only to wealthy and educated middle-class women. During the First World War she argued for a woman's right to work for her country and for men's duty to fight in the charnel houses of Belgium and Northern France, although she was by no means alone in that. Defeated as a Women's Party candidate in the general election of 1918, she moved to the United States of America and became a prophetess of the Second Coming.

PANKHURST, EMMELINE (1858–1928) Suffragette. The mother of Christabel and Sylvia Pankhurst, Emmeline was the founder of the Women's Social and Political Union (WSPU) in 1903. Given that the issue of votes for women was already on the parliamentary agenda, but held up by Herbert Asquith and opponents of women's suffrage, it is questionable whether such tactics were any more successful than the moderate strategy of Millicent Fawcett. During the First World War Pankhurst campaigned for young men to be sent to the Western Front. She died in 1928, the year that women were finally given equal voting rights with men.

PANKHURST, (ESTELLE) SYLVIA (1882–1960) Suffragette, feminist and communist. The daughter of Emmeline and sister of Christabel **Pankhurst**, she was at first a militant suffragist who was arrested and imprisoned under the 1913 **Cat and Mouse Act**. A pacifist, Sylvia played a leading role in the establishment of communism in Britain in 1920, and during the 1930s her anti-fascism led her to help Jewish refugees from Nazi Germany. She was also critical of the Italian invasion of Ethiopia, the country in which she chose to live after the war.

PARKER, BARRY (1867–1947) and **Unwin, Raymond** (1863–1940) Architects and town planners. Involved in the garden city and garden suburb movements, they designed **Letchworth Garden City** and Hampstead Garden Suburb, both of which were very important experiments in planned new communities begun during the Edwardian years. The style of the housing designed by Parker and Unwin was influenced by the Arts and Crafts movement in architecture, being small-scale, traditional and cottage-like, with naturalistic decorations, although new construction techniques and building materials were trialled in some of the housing forms at Letchworth. Unwin was also responsible for the design of housing at New Earswick, the model village of the Rowntree company at York, while Parker designed and planned the council estate of Wythenshawe in Manchester, built during the 1930s. Unwin became a leading town planner and civil servant between the wars.

Both individually and together, Parker and Unwin may be credited with influencing the design of mass housing in England during the first third of the twentieth century. Bastardised versions of their domestic architecture found their way into the council estates of the interwar period.

PATTEN, CHRIS(TOPHER FRANCIS), BARON PATTEN OF BARNES (1944–) Conservative politician; MP for Bath (1979–92); environment secretary (1989–90). As governor of Hong Kong from 1992 to 1997 he was responsible for handing over the colony to the Chinese. Patten was greatly concerned at the possible democratic deficit that might exist once the British had left Hong Kong, and advocated British citizenship to those who might have wished to leave once the Chinese took over.

PEARSON, SIR (CYRIL) ARTHUR (1866–1921) Newspaper proprietor and philanthropist. In 1900 he began the *Daily Express*, which became an enduring centre-right mid-market newspaper. He was a supporter of tariff reform.

PERRY, FRED(ERICK JOHN) (1909–95) Tennis player. Unlike many leading tennis players, Perry was working class, the son of a Cheshire cotton spinner, lay preacher and Cooperative and Labour MP. He spent much of his young life in Brentham Garden Suburb in London, a fitting context to acquire his tennis skills. Perry was a Davis Cup champion, and won Wimbledon three times in a row during the 1930s. He then turned professional, alienating many in the All England circles, and following the Second World War put his name to a lucrative sportswear contract. Perry commentated on Wimbledon fortnight for BBC radio during the 1980s.

PEVSNER, SIR NIKOLAUS (BERNHARD LEON) (1902–83) Architectural historian.

A German-Jewish émigré from Nazi Germany, Pevsner followed an academic career in Britain at Birkbeck College, London, the University of Birmingham, and Oxford and Cambridge universities. Smitten with the rich diversity of English architecture, both housing and also public buildings, he researched his architectural guides to England. Every county was surveyed. These were subsequently published in *The Buildings of England* series, issued by Penguin. Pevsner worked with a number of assistants, and since his death the series has been updated by others.

PIRATIN, PHIL(IP) (1907–95) Communist politician. A Jewish East Ender and a leading member of the Communist Party of Great Britain (CPGB), Piratin was elected as MP for Mile End at the general election of 1945. Reasons for the support given to the CPGB in 1945 include the appalling housing shortage brought about in East London by the Blitz.

POLLITT, HARRY (1890–1960) Communist politician, leader of the London Boiler-maker's Union, and a founder of the CPGB in 1920. He was also instrumental in establishing the *Daily Worker*, the newspaper of the CPGB. A revolutionary socialist and a staunch defender of Russia, Pollitt led the 'Hands off Russia Campaign' during the British intervention of Bolshevik Russia from 1918 to 1921. He resigned as general secretary of the CPGB in 1939 because he supported the war, and was unhappy at the official CPGB line, which was to oppose entry.

POWELL, (JOHN) ENOCH (1912–98) Conservative politician; MP for Wolverhampton South-West (1950–74); minister of health (1960–63); Official Unionist MP for South Down, Northern Ireland (1974–87). His political career was long-standing

and varied. As minister for health he allowed thousands of West Indians and others to work for the National Health Service, but in 1968 he became infamous for his 'rivers of blood' speech. This polemical warning against mass immigration was certainly ill-judged in its language, but nonetheless Powell expressed the insecurities of the white working-class population during an era of immigration and the changing demographic profile of many urban communities. Given the race riots that have occurred in a number of areas, perhaps his views are now worthy of reconsideration beyond the knee-jerk accusation of 'racism'. His words also revealed, perhaps, both high Tory and populist misconceptions about an increasingly multicultural society.

Powell was committed to continued Protestant majority rule in Northern Ireland – hence his fulsome conversion to Unionism in 1974. He was also an outspoken critic of membership of the European Economic Community (EEC), warning of the erosion of British sovereignty.

PRIESTLEY, J(OHN) B(OYNTON) (1894–1984) Playwright, broadcaster, keen social observer and socialist. Priestley made a considerable contribution to the arts and media in Britain from the 1920s through to the postwar years. During the Great Depression of the early 1930s he toured England, recording his observations in *English Journey* (1934). Priestley worked as a broadcaster for the BBC during the Second World War, during which he was a co-founder of the Common Wealth Party. He was also instrumental in establishing the Campaign for Nuclear Disarmament in 1958.

PYKE, MARGARET (AMY) (1893–1966) Advocate of contraception in Britain. Although less well known than Marie

Stopes, during the 1930s Pyke was secretary of the National Birth Control Association, which later became the Family Planning Association, of which she was chair from 1954.

PYM, FRANCIS (LESLIE), BARON PYM (1922–2008) Conservative politician; MP for Cambridgeshire (1961–83) and Cambridgeshire South-East (1983–7). Pym served in a number of senior cabinet posts, including secretary of state for Northern Ireland (1973–4), secretary of state for defence (1979–81) and foreign secretary (1982–3).

QUEEN Rock band. Comprised of flamboyant and openly gay lead singer Freddie Mercury, guitarist Brian May, bass guitarist Deacon John, and vocalist and drummer Roger Taylor, Queen began their rise to global stardom in 1973 with their eponymous first album. Their rock classics *Bohemian Rhapsody* (1975) and *We Are the Champions* (1977) became two of the best-known pop songs of the later twentieth century. The name Queen was an ironic use of a slang term for an effeminate gay man.

RATHBONE, ELEANOR (FLORENCE) (1872–1946) Social reformer, campaigner for women's suffrage and politician. A leader of the National Union of Women's Suffrage Societies from 1919, Rathbone was also a member of the Women's Industrial Council and an ardent critic of low wages for women and of the treatment of women by the Poor Law. During the 1930s she was an outspoken critic of fascism and a critic of appeasement. She also successfully campaigned for **family allowances**, introduced during the Second World War.

REES, MERLYN, BARON MERLYN-REES (1920–2006) Labour politician; MP for Leeds South (1963–83) and Morley and Leeds South (1983–92). As secretary of state for Northern Ireland (1974–6) and home secretary (1976–9) he faced many difficulties. He was unable to bring peace to Northern Ireland, but he was not alone in that, and his period at the Home Office is perhaps now unfairly associated with an inability to deal with growing industrial relations problems.

REISZ, KAREL (1926–2002) Film maker. A Czech-born Jewish escapee from communism, he was a leading light among the Free Cinema directors of the 1950s. Among his best-known works are *We Are the Lambeth Boys* (1959), a documentary about working-class lads in South London. Of his fiction feature films, which reflected the social realism born of kitchen-sink dramas of the later 1950s, *Saturday Night and Sunday Morning* (1960) and *This Sporting Life* (1963) are the most familiar. He also directed the Harold Pinter screenplay *The French Lieutenant's Woman* (1981).

REITH, JOHN (CHARLES WALSHAM), 1ST BARON REITH (1889–1971) Broadcasting executive. Reith was a Scotsman from a nonconformist religious background who was instrumental in the formation of the British Broadcasting Company in 1922. Aiming at providing a monopoly of radio broadcasting in Britain, unlike the free-market system in the United States, the company became the British Broadcasting Corporation (BBC) in 1927, and was the world's first official broadcasting body. Reith was director general until 1938, and his influence over the BBC can be felt to this day. He believed that entertainment should be rational recreation – that is, life-enhancing and educational. The introduction of television broadcasting in 1936 bore this imprint of didacticism. As television expanded greatly during the 1950s and since, the 'Reithian' broadcasting of the BBC also sat alongside more populist offerings such as situation comedies and dramas. The fact that the BBC was funded by a licence fee gave the corporation the ability to experiment with more serious programming in current affairs and documentary film making than purely commercial operations.

In 1940 Reith was appointed as minister of information; later during the war he was minister of transport and minister of works and building, becoming involved in the debates over reconstruction. He chaired the New Towns Committee (1945–6) which produced the 1946 New Towns Act. After the war he held a number of key posts, including chairman of the Commonwealth communications board and chairman of Hemel Hempstead Development Corporation. Reith wrote two autobiographical works, *Into the Wind* (1949) and *Wearing Spurs* (1966).

RICHARD, SIR CLIFF [Webb, Harry Rodger] (1940–) Singer. He was born in India, but his family moved to London following Indian independence in 1948. Richard became famous in 1958 while still a teenager with his top ten hit *Move it*, and his first number one followed the next year. Both on his own and with his support band, *The Shadows*, he has enjoyed hits ever since. He came second in the Eurovision Song Contest in 1968, a risible

annual reminder that Britain and the United States are superior forces at making popular music, and third in that contest in 1973. During the 1960s he became an active Christian. Richard was knighted in 1995 for his continuing contribution to the British popular music industry: he had more than seventy hits at home and abroad, selling over 250 million records.

RICHARDSON, TONY [Cecil Antonio] (1928–91) Film maker and producer. Richardson was associated with the new wave of realist films during the later 1950s and early 1960s. Among his best-known films are *Look Back in Anger* (1958) and *The Entertainer* (1960), both of which were based upon plays by John **Osborne**. *A Taste of Honey* (1961) and *The Loneliness of the Long Distance Runner* (1962), written by Alan Sillitoe, also reflected his interest in and commitment to portraying working-class lives on screen.

RIFKIND, SIR MALCOLM (LESLIE) (1946–) Conservative politician; MP for Edinburgh Pentlands (1974–97) and Kensington and Chelsea (2005–). His ministerial posts include secretary of state for Scotland (1986–90), for transport (1990–92) and for defence (1992–5) and foreign secretary (1995–7).

ROLLING STONES, THE Rhythm and blues-based rock band formed in London during the early 1960s, comprising Mick Jagger (vocals), Keith Richards (guitar), Brian Jones (guitar), Bill Wyman (bass), Ian Stewart (piano) and Charlie Watts (drums). Perhaps their best-known chart-topper was *(I Can't Get No) Satisfaction* in 1965, but the band had three previous number ones and enjoyed many subsequent hits. Following the death of Brian Jones in 1969, a number of changes in personnel ensued, and the band took a more mellow musical direction. Along with the Beatles and **Led Zeppelin**, the Stones broke the dominance of American popular music in Britain, while owing a huge debt to the country that invented rock and roll in the first place.

ROWNTREE, (BENJAMIN) SEEBOHM (1871–1954) Social scientist. A Quaker, he was the son of the York chocolate maker Joseph Rowntree. He made studies of the extent of poverty in York and other urban areas, notably *Poverty: A Study of Town Life* (1899) and *Poverty and Progress* (1941). Along with Charles Booth, Rowntree pioneered more flexible and humane definitions of poverty than were allowed by the more austere interpreters of the Poor Law. His co-written *English Life and Leisure* (1951) is an important snapshot of leisure at mid-century, although by no means devoid of social criticism born of his nonconformity.

S

SALISBURY, LORD [Cecil, Robert Arthur Talbot Gascoyne-], **3rd Marquess of Salisbury** (1830–1903) Conservative politician; MP for Stamford, Lincolnshire (1853–68); prime minister (1886–92) and (1895–1902). Naturally a supporter of the British Empire, he was strongly in favour of the Boer War from 1899. He retired as prime minister in 1902.

SAMUEL, HERBERT (LOUIS), 1ST VISCOUNT SAMUEL (1870–1963) Liberal politician; MP for Cleveland (1902–18) and Darwen (1929–35). A supporter of Asquith, he was home secretary in 1916. In 1925–6 he chaired the eponymous **Samuel commission** whose recommendations on the coal industry contributed to the General Strike

of May 1926. He became Viscount Samuel in 1937, and was Liberal leader in the House of Lords from 1944 to 1955. It was Samuel who appears to have been the first British politician to have used the term 'Holocaust' to describe the organised anti-Semitic atrocities taking place in Germany and German-occupied countries, in 1943.

SANDYS, (EDWIN) DUNCAN, BARON DUNCAN-SANDYS (1908–87) Conservative politician; MP for Norwood-Lambeth (1935–45) and Streatham (1950–74). Sandys held a number of senior parliamentary positions during the Second World War, including chairman of the war cabinet committee for defence against German flying bombs and rockets (1944–5). Among later cabinet positions were minister of supply (1951–4), minister of housing and local government (1954–7), minister of defence (1957–9), minister of aviation (1959–60) and secretary of state for Commonwealth relations (1960–64). He initiated a major defence review during the late 1950s and oversaw an important phase of decolonisation.

SASSOON, SIEGFRIED (LORAINE) (1886–1967) Poet and writer. In common with Robert Graves and Wilfred Owen, he was disgusted at the massive loss of life and bloodshed during the First World War, as evidenced in his controversial poetry. He also wrote autobiographical works, for example *Memoirs of an Infantry Officer* (1930).

SCARGILL, ARTHUR (1938–) Trade union leader. An advocate of industrial action in the coal industry on behalf of the National Union of Mineworkers (NUM), Scargill played a pivotal role in the miners' strikes of the 1970s that damaged the Heath government. As NUM president, he was at the centre of the **miners' strike** of 1984–5.

He also founded the **Socialist Labour Party** in 1996.

SHONFIELD, SIR ANDREW (AKIBA) (1917–81) Economist. Shonfield was an expert on economic policy and more widely on public policy, markets and their relationship to the state. He wrote a number of important books, including *Modern Capitalism*.

SILLITOE, ALAN (1928–) Working-class writer. His most famous works associate him with the Angry Young Men of the later 1950s and early 1960s, namely *Saturday Night and Sunday Morning* (novel, 1958; film, 1960) and *The Loneliness of the Long Distance Runner* (novel, 1959; film, 1962). The provincial city of Nottingham – known for its bicycle manufacturing, lace textiles and coal mining – was the setting for both films. His autobiography was entitled *Life without Armour* (1995).

SIMON, ERNEST (EMIL DARWIN), 1ST BARON SIMON OF WYTHENSHAWE (1879–1960) and **Simon, Shena Dorothy** (1883–1972) Ernest was an industrialist, philanthropist and Liberal MP for Manchester Withington (1923–4, 1929–31). He joined the Labour Party in 1946. Shena was a social reformer and housing campaigner and also a member of the Labour Party. Together, the Simons made a localised but significant contribution to the evolution of council housing in England by purchasing the country estate of Wythenshawe during the 1920s and donating it to the city of Manchester for a large new council estate. Shena became a civic leader in the development of Wythenshawe.

SIMON, JOHN (ALLSEBROOK), 1ST VISCOUNT SIMON (1873–1954) Liberal politician; MP for Walthamstow in East London (1906–18) and Spen Valley (1922–40). Home secretary during the First World War under H. H. Asquith, he remained loyal to Asquith as an opponent of David Lloyd George. In 1931 he became leader of the National Liberals, the Liberals who supported the National Government of Ramsay MacDonald. He was chancellor of the exchequer from 1937 to 1940.

SMITH, JOHN (1938–94) Labour politician; MP for Lanarkshire North (1970–83) and Monklands East (1983–94); secretary of state for trade (1978–9), shadow chancellor (1989–92) and leader of the Labour Party (1992–4). As Labour leader before his untimely death Smith was responsible for accelerating the modernisation of the party begun by Neil Kinnock.

SNOWDEN, PHILIP, 1ST VISCOUNT SNOWDEN (1864–1937) Labour politician; MP for Blackburn (1906–18) and Colne Valley (1922–31). A conscientious objector, he opposed British involvement in the First World War, as did a number of other Labour leaders. Appointed by Ramsay MacDonald as chancellor of the exchequer in both the 1924 and 1929–31 Labour governments, he was given to cautious, orthodox economic measures. He was marginalised within the Labour Party, along with MacDonald, for his cutbacks to unemployment relief in the Depression of 1930–31 and did not stand for parliament in the general election of 1931. Snowden resigned as lord privy seal in 1932, taking up his seat in the House of Lords.

SOSKICE, FRANK, BARON STOW HILL (1902–79) Labour politician; MP for Birkenhead East (1945–50), Sheffield Neepsend (1950–55) and Newport in Wales (1956–66). The son of a Russian émigré, he was home secretary in the first government of Harold Wilson, the first under whom no **capital punishment** took place.

SPICE GIRLS, THE Pop group. Following some unsuccessful recordings after their formation in 1994, the Spice Girls charted impressively in 1996 with *Wannabe* and became a pop sensation. Comprised of Victoria Adams ('Posh Spice'), Mel Brown ('Scary Spice'), Emma Bunton ('Baby Spice'), Mel Chisholm ('Sporty Spice') and Geri Halliwell ('Ginger Spice'), the girls sold over 55 million records globally and made a musical film, *Spice World* (1997). Halliwell was the first to leave, in 1998, and the group finally broke up in 2001: spliced girls. They then enjoyed solo careers of varying renown, although the marriage of Victoria to the footballer David Beckham probably kept her in the news more than her solo career. The Spice Girls re-formed in 2007 for a major world tour. Some cultural commentators, particularly feminists, viewed them as prominent role models for fun-loving and self-confident teenage girls and young women.

STEEL, DAVID (MARTIN SCOTT), BARON STEEL OF AIKWOOD (1938–) Liberal politician; MP for Roxburgh, Selkirk and Peebles (1965–83) and Tweeddale, Ettrick and Lauderdale (1983–97). When he gained his seat at a by-election in 1965 Steel became the youngest member of the House of Commons. His first political measure was to steer through parliament the private member's bill on abortion, which became the **Abortion Act** in 1967. Following the fall of Jeremy **Thorpe** in 1976, Steel became leader of the Liberal Party, participating in the Lib–Lab pact that assisted the Labour government to remain in power. In 1981 he joined the Liberals in an alliance with the Social Democratic Party (SDP) and became a joint leader with David Owen. General election results in 1983 and 1987 were probably better than the Liberals could have hoped for as an independent party, but still emphasised that they were a long way away from taking power. In 1988 Steel stood down and Paddy **Ashdown** became Liberal leader. Steel went on to forge a role in European politics and in the devolved Scottish parliament. He entered the House of Lords in 1997.

STEWART, (ROBERT) MICHAEL (MAIT-LAND), BARON STEWART OF FULHAM (1906–90) Labour politician; MP for Fulham East (1945–55) and Fulham (1955–9). A Fabian, he served as minister of education (1964–5) and foreign secretary (1965–6). He supported both the American intervention in Vietnam and British entry into the EEC during the 1970s, becoming a leader of the Labour group in the European parliament.

STEWART, ROD(ERICK DAVID) (1945–) Singer. Of Scottish parentage, Stewart grew up in London. He began as a solo artist but worked with both the Jeff Beck Group and the Faces during his career. His first major hit with the Faces was *Maggie May* (1971), from the album *Every Picture Tells a Story*. His early rockier beginnings, however, led to a highly successful trajectory as a soloist, his distinctively gravely singing voice achieving him major international sales during the later 1970s and the 1980s, particularly in Britain and the USA.

STOPES, MARIE (CHARLOTTE CARMICHAEL) (1880–1958) Campaigner for birth control. She established the first British birth control clinic in London, in 1921, and her book *Married Love* (1918) was one of the first sex manuals of the twentieth century, urging women to enjoy safe protected sex within marriage. Many men, and women too, were shocked at the suggestion that women should actually enjoy sexual relations. There was an element of cultural pessimism in Stopes's attitude to the poorer sections of the working classes, some of whom she wanted to prevent from having children lest they procreate in too large a number.

STRAW, JACK [John Whitaker] (1946–) Labour politician; MP for Blackburn (1979–). Straw was a leading opposition front-bencher from 1987 to 1997. A prominent New Labour minister, he served as home secretary from 1997 to 2001.

TATCHELL, PETER (GARY) (1952–) Gay rights campaigner. Increasingly known for his militant gay rights stand in Britain through his organisation OutRage, Tatchell has been highly critical of foreign countries with a poor record on human rights and homosexuality. He also spoke out against nuclear weapons and British troops in Northern Ireland.

TEBBIT, NORMAN (BERESFORD), BARON TEBBIT (1931–) Conservative politician; MP for Epping (1970–74) and Chingford (1974–92). During the 1970s Tebbit was critical of trade unions for their propensity to strike and of Labour politicians for supporting the 'closed shop', the obligation to belong to a trade union or to suffer either unemployment or group estrangement. In the late 1980s he stated that a large proportion of ethnic minority people in Britain failed to pass the 'cricket test', meaning people who had settled in Britain should support England, not, for example, Pakistan or the West Indies. Tebbit was minister for employment from 1981 to 1983, minister for trade and industry from 1983 to 1985, and chancellor of the Duchy of Lancaster from 1985 to 1987. He became

a life peer in 1992, the year the Conservatives won their fourth consecutive general election.

THATCHER, MARGARET (HILDA), BARONESS THATCHER (1925–) Conservative politician; MP for Finchley in North London (1959–92); secretary of state for education (1970–74); joint shadow chancellor (1974–5); prime minister (1979–90); Conservative Party leader (1975–90). Thatcher was the first woman party leader and the first female prime minister in Britain. She came from the lower middle classes, the aspirational daughter of a grocer, and graduated from Oxford with a degree in chemistry. In 1975 she challenged Edward Heath, following his failure to be re-elected the previous year, for the Conservative Party leadership, and won. She defeated James Callaghan in the general election of 1979 and went on to win two more substantial election victories. Her government was committed to cuts in public expenditure and to a programme of privatisation – that is, of 'rolling back the frontiers of the state' and removing uncompetitive and costly nationalised industries. The legacy for the coal industry, notably, was a painful one. However, economic policy during the 1980s should also be viewed within the context of an accelerated de-industrialisation. The deregulation of financial markets and the Big Bang of 1986 were aspects of this.

Her conduct of the Falklands War in 1982 won Thatcher many friends and admirers, some grudging, both at home and abroad. She remained a staunch defender of the special relationship with the United States of America, finding an ideological ally in President Reagan. Following the poll tax debacle in 1989–90, she was turfed out of the party leadership by a coalition of disgruntled Tory MPs who were increasingly fearful of her apparent arrogance, and forced to resign as prime minister.

Thatcher's views were anchored in a distrust of socialism, a dislike of high taxation, a suspicion of Europe, a fear of too many immigrants, and a self-help philosophy whose strength was hard work and enterprise, but whose downside was often a selfish and crabbed utilitarian outlook upon life. Her autobiography was entitled *The Downing Street Years* (1993).

THORNEYCROFT, (GEORGE EDWARD) PETER, BARON THORNEYCROFT (1909–94) Conservative politician; MP for Stafford (1938–45) and Monmouth (1945–66). He famously resigned as chancellor of the exchequer in 1958 over the issue of public expenditure. He held other important ministerial posts, including minister of aviation (1960–62) and minister of defence (1962–4).

THORPE, (JOHN) JEREMY (1929–) Liberal politician; MP for North Devon (1959–79); leader of the Liberal Party (1967–76). Under his leadership the Liberals slowly improved their performance in general and local elections, but Thorpe's political career was ended following allegations of a homosexual affair and of an attempt to murder his gay lover. Although he was cleared of all charges, he lost his seat in the general election of 1979.

TILLETT, BEN(JAMIN) (1860–1943) Trade unionist; Labour MP for North Salford (1917–24, 1929–31). As a leader of the dockworkers' union from the 1880s, Tillett was one of many new trade union activists who linked Victorian trade unions with the twentieth century, and the interests of unskilled and semi-skilled working folk with the emergent Labour Party after 1900. He was a founder of the Independent Labour Party.

TITMUSS, RICHARD (1907–73) Social scientist and historian of social policy.

Titmuss began writing the history of the Second World War during the war itself. This led to his *Problems of Social Policy* (1950), which focused on the extended role of the state, on its successes and difficulties from the Blitz to the end of the war, and on the issues and problems involved in evacuation and the emergency services. Other key books included *Essays on the Welfare State* (1958).

TRIMBLE, (WILLIAM) DAVID, BARON TRIMBLE (1944–) Ulster Unionist politician; MP for Upper Bann (1990–2005). In the face of much opprobrium from Ian **Paisley** and others, Trimble became a leading proponent of the Good Friday Agreement signed in 1998, and with John **Hume** he was awarded the Nobel Peace Prize.

TYNDALL, JOHN (1934–2005) Fascist. He was a leading light, along with Martin Webster, of the National Front during the late 1960s and 1970s. A portly man, looking very unlike an Aryan hero, Tyndall was also associated with the Greater Britain movement, and he assisted in the foundation of the **British National Party** in 1982.

W

WADDINGTON, DAVID (CHARLES), BARON WADDINGTON (1929–) Conservative politician; MP for Nelson and Colne (1968–74), Clitheroe (1979–83) and Ribble Valley (1983–90); home secretary (1989–90).

WADE, (SARAH) VIRGINIA (1945–) Tennis player. She was the last British woman to win Wimbledon during the twentieth century, in 1977. She subsequently enjoyed a career as a television commentator on the

BBC and became the first woman to be elected to the Wimbledon Committee.

WALKER, PATRICK GORDON (CHRESTIAN), BARON GORDON-WALKER (1907–80) Labour politician; MP for Smethwick (1945–64) and Leyton (1966–74). He served in a number of senior parliamentary positions, for example as parliamentary private secretary to Herbert Morrison (1946) and leader of the House of Commons during the Attlee government. Gordon Walker was controversially defeated during the 1964 general election, the first in which racism was involved but returned to parliament as MP for Leyton in East London in 1966.

WATT, (RAYMOND EGERTON) HARRY (1906–87) Documentary film maker. Working under John Grierson in collaboration with other directors, he made a number of important wartime documentary films, including *Target for Tonight* (1941).

WEBB, (MARTHA) BEATRICE (1858–1943) and **Webb, Sidney (James), Baron Passfield** (1859–1947) Fabian socialists, writers and historians. The Webbs were instrumental in the formation of the London School of Economics. In 1912 they established the *New Statesman* magazine. Beatrice was the more skilled writer of the two; among her targets were Ramsay MacDonald and Sir Oswald Mosley. She was an admirer of Stalin's Russia during the 1920s. Her early professional life is narrated in *My Apprenticeship* (1926), which includes her work (as Beatrice Potter) with her relative Charles Booth on social investigation and her interest in socialism, and her life with Sidney is detailed in *Our Partnership*, published in 1948, five years after her death. Sidney was MP for Seaham from 1922 to 1929, president of the board of trade in 1924 and secretary of state for dominion affairs in 1929–30.

WHITEHOUSE, (CONSTANCE) MARY (1910–2001) Moral campaigner. She was the founder of the '**Clean up TV**' campaign in 1964 and the first president of the National Viewers' and Listeners' Association from 1965. Whitehouse saw herself as a Christian woman of common sense who challenged permissiveness in broadcasting, particularly on the BBC under Sir Hugh **Greene**.

WHITELAW, WILLIAM (STEPHEN IAN), VISCOUNT WHITELAW ('WILLIE') (1918–1999) Conservative politician; MP for Penrith and the Border (1955–83); secretary of state for Northern Ireland (1972–3) and for employment (1973–4). He was home secretary under Margaret Thatcher from 1979 to 1983, following which he took up his peerage in the House of Lords.

WILLIAMS, SHIRLEY (VIVIEN TERESA BRITTAIN CATLIN), BARONESS WILLIAMS OF CROSBY (1930–) Labour and Social Democrat politician; MP for Hitchin (1964–74), Hertford and Stevenage (1974–9) and Crosby (1981–3). Williams served in Harold Wilson's second Labour government from 1966 to 1970 at the Ministry of Labour, the Department of Education and Science and the Home Office. She was opposition spokesperson on social services and home affairs from 1970 to 1974, minister for prices and consumer protection from 1974 to 1976, and minister of education and science from 1976 to 1979.

A one-time member of the Fabian Society, along with Roy Jenkins, David Owen and William Rodgers, the so-called Gang of Four, Williams was a founder member in 1981 of the Social Democratic Party (SDP), of which she was president from 1982 to 1983. In 1981 she also scored a significant by-election victory at Crosby, Liverpool. However, she lost her parliamentary seat in the general election in 1983. From 1988 she became a prominent Liberal politician when the SDP merged with the Liberal Party to form the Liberal Democrats. Her writings include *God and Caesar: Reflections on Politics and Religion* (2003).

WILLIAMS-ELLIS, SIR (BERTRAM) CLOUGH (1883–1978) Architect. Williams-Ellis was best known for his romantic model village Portmeirion in North Wales. He was also a leading campaigner against 'the octopus' of suburban sprawl in England between the wars, and played a leading role in the establishment of the national parks.

WILLIS, NORMAN (DAVID) (1933–) Trade union leader. He was general secretary of the **Trades Union Congress** (TUC) from 1984 to 1993, a period of hostile media criticism of the trade unions, Conservative legislation that circumscribed the activities of the unions, and also the remodelling of Labour Party policies to reduce the negative relationship with more militant trade unionists. Willis was a voice of moderation but also a critic of Thatcherism.

WILLMOTT, PETER (1923–2000) Sociologist. He worked with Michael Young to establish the Institute of Community Studies in 1954. He also co-researched and co-wrote with Young the highly influential *Family and Kinship in East London* (1957) and the less well-known but equally important *Family and Class in a London Suburb* (1960). His study of the council estate of Dagenham in East London, *The Evolution of a Community* (1962), also developed the theme of working-class suburbanisation.

WILSON, (JAMES) HAROLD, BARON WILSON OF RIEVAULX (1916–95) Labour politician; MP for Ormskirk (1945–50) and Huyton (1950–83). Until Tony Blair completed his ninth year as prime minister in 2006, Harold Wilson, as a consequence of his two governments of 1964–6 and 1966–70 and his tenure during the 1970s, was the longest-serving Labour premier.

Born in Huddersfield in Yorkshire, Wilson was grammar-school educated. He was elected as MP for Ormskirk, Lancashire, in Labour's historic general election victory of 1945. During the first full-term Labour government from 1945–51 he held a number of key positions, including president of the board of trade. Along with Aneurin Bevan, he resigned over the introduction of health service charges during the decline of Attlee's postwar Labour government.

Following the death of Hugh Gaitskell, Wilson became the leader of the Labour Party, and narrowly defeated Alec Douglas-Home in the general election in 1964. With a slender majority, his first government was hampered in its policy initiatives, but the decision to go to the country again in 1966, made to coincide with an upturn in the British economy, gave Labour a larger majority. Now the picture became one of economic and industrial difficulties on the one hand and some important and forward-looking pieces of social legislation on the other. Industrial relations deteriorated from 1966, and other economic problems included inflationary pressures and the need to devalue the currency. Wilson's 'the pound in your pocket' speech following **devaluation** in 1967 was exploited by his political foes as a sign of flannel and weakness.

In the sphere of social policy, however, the Labour governments under Wilson passed important reforms, for example in the fields of abortion, divorce, contraception and race relations. Wilson was expected to win the general election of 1970, but the economic and industrial problems with which he and his government were associated, and the breezy personality of the Tory leader Edward Heath, contributed to a Conservative victory. This left Wilson as leader of the opposition until 1974, when industrial action contributed to the termination of the Heath government. Wilson was re-elected as prime minister for the third time, but resigned in 1976.

WINTRINGHAM, MARGARET (1879–1955) Liberal politician; MP for Louth (1921–4). A supporter of women's suffrage and one of the first female members of parliament, she was also an early campaigner for the right of women to sit in the House of Lords.

WODEHOUSE, SIR P(ELHAM) G(RENVILLE) (1881–1975) Comic novelist. Best known for his characters Psmith, Ukridge, Jeeves and Wooster, his books were quintessentially English in their mild satire and outright mirth-making at the expense of English class culture, notably the gentry. Of both Bertie Wooster, a wealthy propertied man, and his butler Jeeves, by far the most accomplished brain belonged to the latter. Although he is now widely admired, it is noteworthy that for some time during the Second World War and afterwards the name of P. G. Wodehouse had its own hapless associations. On the outbreak of war Wodehouse was in Germany and was subsequently interned there, and then allowed to live in, but not leave, the Third Reich. In an essay showing a fine sense of common sense and forgiveness, George Orwell argued that Wodehouse never colluded with the Nazis, and deserved no opprobrium.

WOOD, SIR (HOWARD) KINGSLEY (1881–1943) Conservative politician; MP for Woolwich West (1918–43). He held a number of senior cabinet positions, including minister of health (1935–8) and minister for air (1938–40). From 1940 to 1943 he served as chancellor of the exchequer.

WRIGHT, BASIL (1907–86) Documentary film maker. He worked for the Empire Marketing Board, for which he made *Song of Ceylon* in 1934, but is best known for *Night Mail* (1936), which he co-directed with Harry **Watt**. Along with other leading British documentary film makers, Wright also worked during the Second World War for the Crown Film Unit under the Ministry of Information, where he produced Humphrey Jennings's *A Diary for Timothy* (1945).

YOUNG, MICHAEL, BARON YOUNG OF DARTINGTON (1915–2002) Social reformer. An important figure in social policy, social investigation, and the history of the Labour Party, Young worked for Political and Economic Planning (PEP) before the Second World War and was instrumental in writing the Labour Party manifesto for the general election of 1945. During the mid-1950s, with the sociologist Peter Willmott, he researched and wrote a hugely important study of the working class in the East End of London entitled *Family and Kinship in East London* (1957). Republished many times since, it warned of the break-up of extended working-class families as a consequence of planned dispersal from the old East End to suburban council estates. Willmott and Young's *Family and Class in a London Suburb* (1960), however, provided a more upbeat appraisal of social change. During his long and distinguished career, Young was a founder member of the consumer association Which? and also a committed educationalist, notably in the field of adult education. He played an important role in the establishment of the **Open University** from 1969.

VI
DICTIONARY

6.1
NOTES

- This Dictionary provides further historical analysis of, and context for, the most significant *institutions* and major *themes* introduced earlier in the *Companion*. This includes social and cultural institutions, notably sports and popular culture. Major themes and 'isms' in social, cultural, economic and political history will also be found here. A particular emphasis upon urbanisation also brings together many of the key themes in the *Companion*.
- Smaller groups and minor political parties are not included in the dictionary. They can be found under **Landmarks** for the year of their formation.
- For information on the people referred to, see **Biographies**.

6.2

DICTIONARY

ABORTION As the film by Mike Leigh entitled *Vera Drake* (2005) sadly illustrates, before the Abortion Act of 1967 working-class women were often forced to turn to the so-called back-street abortionists to terminate an unwanted pregnancy. Although the film is a work of fiction, it powerfully conveys the tawdry atmosphere of illegal abortion, and the desperation felt by women who were pregnant yet wished they were not. Many women also attempted to terminate pregnancies themselves. In *Vera Drake* the subject is sympathetically treated; however, back-street abortion was sometimes a murky underworld of petty profiteering from other people's misery. It was also very dangerous. A variety of means could be used to terminate or to try to terminate a pregnancy, sometimes resulting in death to women through internal injuries. Some women died or were badly injured when attempting self-termination. These brutal facts made the hypocrisy of British law all the more appalling. For, despite its illegality, wealthier women could get an abortion using private doctors. In the fiction feature film *Alfie* (1966), based on the novel by Bill Naughton, a woman felt compelled to have an abortion to avoid the shame of being found out following a sexual liaison with Alfie. And Alfie himself,

played by Michael **Caine**, was able to walk away, saddened by the termination, but not forced to endure it. It was this state of affairs that the Abortion Bill of 1967 sought to correct. Steered through parliament by the young Liberal MP David Steel, the Abortion Bill faced many powerful moral objections over the rights of the foetus, and the still powerful condemnations of sex outside of marriage. The Society for the Protection of the Unborn Child (SPUC) and the Roman Catholic Church were particularly prominent opponents of liberalised abortion laws, and indifferent to the torment of pregnant women who did not want to have a child. Yet the Bill prevailed, and the Act came into force the following year.

Since then, per thousand live births, the ratio of abortions rose from 27 in 1968 to 256 by 1996, although the figures must be qualified by a lack of accurate data on the number of illegal terminations before the Act. Although the Abortion Act was a landmark in the growing permissiveness of the time, the issue of abortion did not disappear after 1967. Pro- and anti-abortionists continued to argue, and debates have raged over the acceptable and safest limits for a termination given advances in medical technology. However, any return to the pre-1967 situation was unpalatable for the majority of British people, and social historians primarily reflect such values. So too did a majority of the House of Commons which, in May 2008, following a passionate debate, rejected the cutting of the upper limit for abortions from 24 weeks.

AFFLUENCE Affluence in the context of twentieth-century Britain refers to the growing wealth and purchasing power of the population. In turn, that meant increasing consumerism. Affluence has been a hugely important socio-economic fact of modern Britain, and historians examine the implications of elevated levels of wealth and prosperity for personal choices and political behaviour. During the 1950s, in particular, a decade of full employment and rising wages, when more people than ever before were 'never having it so good', the Labour Party was forced to address the problem that millions of voters who moved to the new council estates, and even homes that they were buying for themselves, were unconvinced that Labour served their aspirations more effectively than the Conservative Party. The Tories were in power for most of the 1950s. Labour revisionists who followed Hugh Gaitskell were acutely aware of the need to look favourably upon working-class prosperity rather than present a grim image of Labour as the party only of the poor. The 1980s and 1990s also exposed Labour's weakness. Although unemployment remained high in the latter decades of the twentieth century, the Conservatives were in power from 1979 until 1997, and during the 1980s a left-leaning Labour Party was forced to revise its values in the light of continued popular preferences for a Tory Party that appeared more in touch with the aspirations of affluent **Middle England**. In that sense, affluence defined New Labour politics more than a redistributive socialism, and New Labour was spectacularly successful at the 1997 general election.

AGRICULTURE At the beginning of the twentieth century, British agriculture was enduring a prolonged depression that had begun in 1873 and which continued until the salvation of war in 1940. Growing imports of foodstuffs were the major cause of agriculture's problems, and the primary sector made a smaller and smaller contribution to the British economy and to the consumption of British-produced food in the United Kingdom. The exceptions were during the world wars, when food production was controlled and coordinated by the government. Following the Second World War, the **Agriculture Act** of 1947 provided significant subsidy and hence security for British farmers. From 1973, however, membership of the European Union had mixed consequences for British agriculture, and also for the fishing industry.

Throughout the twentieth century, farmers and larger landowners remained at the heart of the agricultural economy of rural Britain, and were represented in political and economic affairs by the National Farmers' Union. Many were tenant farmers, working for others, and many were landowners. Lowland farming tended to be dominated by crop growing and cattle, while most upland farming was the preserve of sheep farmers. While the size and scale of farming operations varied greatly, the average British farm was larger and more efficient than its counterparts in other European countries, notably France, where agri-business was conducted in smaller units. Membership of the European Economic Community from 1973 meant increased competition, while British taxpayers were forced to subsidise the less efficient agricultures of the member states through the Common Agricultural Policy. Overproduction was one consequence of the culture of subsidisation, and farmers were paid 'set-aside' grants simply to leave their fields uncultivated.

In 1970, 80 per cent of food consumed in Britain was produced at home. By 1999, this figure was less than 60 per cent. Imports from the EU were partly responsible, but so too was multiculturalism and a widespread desire for ethnic foods. A preference for fresh and exotic fruits and vegetables all year long in the supermarkets led to higher imports. British agriculture had exported very little since 1900, and certain trades, for example beef, were greatly damaged by outbreaks of **foot and mouth disease** during the 1960s and the BSE crisis during the 1990s. By 1999, agriculture accounted for less than 2 per cent of the British workforce, compared with 5 per cent of the French workforce, and 3 per cent in Germany.

Agriculture defined rural Britain and, as agricultural practices changed throughout the nineteenth and twentieth centuries and suburbanisation and road building eroded the countryside, a sense of nostalgia for a lost age of rural living and the idealised rural community was often to be found in romantic histories. More seriously, historians view rural Britain during the twentieth century as in decline. The number of agricultural workers fell from over half a million in 1950 to 110,000 in 1999, when it formed less than 2 per cent of the workforce.

Just as soap operas such as *East Enders* and *Coronation Street* pandered to an unrealistic notion of urban community, so did the ITV soap *Emmerdale Farm* (later *Emmerdale*) romanticise the country village. First broadcast by ITV in 1972, this long-running television series depicted the life and times of hard-working folk in the Yorkshire Dales, one of Britain's largest and much-loved national parks. The success of the parks in attracting tourism owed much to the work of the national park authorities with such voluntary bodies as the National Trust, with local councils, and with the farmers themselves. Income from tourism was one of an increasingly diverse number of sources of revenue enjoyed by many farmers at the end of the twentieth century.

Historians of agriculture and of rural Britain focus upon the changing economy of the countryside; its increasingly middle-class rural populations; the impact of socio-economic change and urbanisation upon both landscape and the much vaunted 'rural community' and country ways of life; the marginalisation of the rural poor; and the continuing identification of cherished landscape with national identities.

AMERICANISATION AND ANTI-AMERICANISM In 2003, as American and British forces removed the crypto-fascist and genocidal regime of Saddam Hussein in Iraq, a ferocious wave of anti-Americanism, most of it on the left of British politics, swept through Britain. One of the most outspoken critics of the USA, the novelist Margaret Drabble, was forthright:

> I now loathe the United States and what it has done to Iraq and the rest of the helpless world. [I] detest Disneyfication, I detest Coca Cola, I detest burgers, I detest sentimental and violent Hollywood movies that tell lies about history.
>
> (Quoted in Nick Cohen, *What's Left? How Liberals Lost their Way* (2007), p. 263)

Drabble's views reflected over a century of anti-Americanism among the *bien pensant*. Like so many novelists, she brought her own personalised sense of moral outrage to a common sensibility that the USA was the world's bully, and that made it convenient to despise many of those aspects of commercialised mass culture that self-consciously cultured people make a point of despising. But the history of America's relationship with Britain – the special relationship – is nuanced. Anti-Americanism had accompanied America's rise to power during the twentieth century. At its very beginning, the United States was challenging the industrial might of Britain, and American mass-produced goods were flooding the British market. As a laissez-faire country, Britain was prone to foreign competition, and the United States was at the forefront of much of it while using its own selective tariffs to protect American producers. Many British social commentators and economists railed against the Americanisation of Edwardian Britain – for example, the new shaving devices, Coca-Cola, tinned foods and Tin Pan Alley music. Fortunately, and against its instincts of isolationism from European conflicts, the USA joined the Allies in 1917, hastening the end of the immense waste of human lives and ensuring victory. Victory in 1918 also increased America's global standing and opened up markets in Europe. Many new consumer goods and labour-saving devices, the cinema and popular music reshaped a culture of leisure and consumption. They helped to bring about the comfortable suburban living described but by no means praised by J. B. Priestley in his *English Journey* (1934). The new suburbs of London and the South-East, with their bungalows and garages and 'factory girls looking like actresses', were a 'third England' that contrasted with the rustic simplicities of the 'first' England and the terraced houses and smokestacks of industrial or 'second' England. 'America', wrote Priestley, 'was its real birthplace.'

Feelings towards the Americans were mixed during the Second World War. Great relief was felt at American aid and intervention, but mild resentment was also evident at the American presence on the home front from 1942. The rapid withdrawal of Lend Lease by the USA and the terms of the American loan negotiated by John Maynard Keynes after the war were felt to be punitive by millions of British people. The war, however, elevated the United States to superpower status. It became the leading capitalist country, the enemy of Soviet Russia and the dominant power at the United Nations, whose headquarters were, symbolically, in New York. The USA also went from strength to strength in the context of commercialisation and cultural product. The Americanisation of everyday life in Britain, first observed during the Edwardian years and expedited between the wars, was particularly evident from the 1950s in the rise of a youth culture that was hugely influenced by American rock 'n' roll and popular music and casual clothing fashion. American television and film continued to provide exotic images and accents to the British public. The burger chain McDonald's first opened in Britain during the late 1960s, and Kentucky Fried Chicken was also widely on sale by the early 1970s. As one of the most visible facets of Americanisation, the modern interiors of these burger restaurants provided a convenient context for critics to rail against the grossness and superficiality of Americana compared with everything associated with older European countries. After the fall of the Berlin Wall and the ending of communism, anti-Americanism became if anything even more virulent. Capitalism and liberal democracy had won the Cold War, and the United States was ostensibly the most powerful victor.

What were the deeper reasons for this continuing feeling against the democratic republic of the USA? Again, the answers lay in both foreign policy and cultural elitism. Certainly disasters overseas, notably the Vietnam War, alienated millions of people worldwide against the United States. Many on the left secretly or explicitly wanted Soviet Russia to win the Cold War, and after 1989 were depressed at the failure of global leadership to break away from the United States. And, as

Hollywood and American products continued to capture the imagination of the masses, it was difficult to avoid the conclusion that cultural snobbery was rampant among Britain's opinion-forming elites. The alleged crassness of Americanisation was ridiculed by those from the aristocratic right of the Conservative Party to the left of the Labour Party. But, as a social historian has argued, millions of British working people were 'enthralled' by the geography, literature and culture of the 'promised land' of America: 'That country has always fascinated the European proletariat as much as it has repelled the European educated classes', argued Jonathan Rose, 'because it promised the former a measure of freedom and affluence that the latter was not prepared to grant' (Rose, *The Intellectual Life of the British Working Classes* (2002), p. 353). Furthermore, this was no one-way process: for centuries, American culture has been influenced by Britain and Europe. Today, however, the simple term 'Americanisation' appears a pejorative one that obscures the positive influences of the USA and the complex pattern of cultural, economic and political interchanges that have occurred since 1900.

ANGRY YOUNG MEN The Angry Young Men were novelists and playwrights in their twenties and thirties who emerged during the second half of the 1950s and whose subject matter was mostly the boredom and frustration of provincial and suburban life. Such realist content was also termed '**kitchen sink drama**' on film and the stage. Among the best-known angry texts was John Osborne's play *Look Back in Anger* (1956). Two of Alan Sillitoe's novels, *Saturday Night and Sunday Morning* (1958) and *The Loneliness of the Long-Distance Runner* (1959), were literally about angry young men in Nottingham, a town known for its lace making and genteel cricket.

Both Sillitoe's books were made in the early 1960s into critically acclaimed British cinema films of the same name. Living rooms and the pub rather than glitzy mansions and Hollywood, and the terraced streets of a northern city rather than the tourist locales of glamorous Manhattan, formed the essence of the new novels, plays and films of the later 1950s and early 1960s. Some historians give credence to some of the Angry Young Men, for example Osborne, as having something profound to say about the crabbed and boring life of provincial Britain just before the eve of the more permissive era of the 1960s. However, a textual and historical interrogation of these writers is long overdue. They were, for example, hardly progressive and egalitarian in their attitudes towards women. Furthermore, they rarely captured the sense of excitement and optimism generated among the young by affluence and an emergent youth culture. Banality was a state of mind as much as a social reality in late 1950s England.

ANTI-SEMITISM Anti-Semitism refers to the irrational fear and prejudice directed towards Jews. It has a long history in Britain that has been examined by both Jewish and non-Jewish historians. Overt and sometimes violent anti-Semitic activities were evident by the late nineteenth century in East London and in other larger cities where Jewish populations were expanding as a consequence of persecution in Eastern and Central Europe. The East End of London housed the largest immigrant Jewish community in Britain by the early twentieth century, but Jews were increasingly spreading out to the suburbs and more salubrious housing even before the First World War. An ugly manifestation of anti-Semitic hostility during the early twentieth century occurred in the Sidney Street siege in January 1911. Between the wars, a number of marginal political organisations were vehemently anti-Semitic. The **Britons**, the Imperial Fascist League and the British Union of Fascists (BUF) all adopted anti-Jewish rhetoric. The Britons and their patron Henry Hamilton Beamish were responsible for publishing *The Protocols of the Elders of Zion*, a scurrilous piece of conspiracy mongering that is still read in reactionary and some religious circles even today. A certain strain of anti-Semitism was also fashionable on the left of British politics between the wars, partly because of Stalin's attacks on Jews, partly because of sympathy for the Arabs, and partly because of a prejudice that Jews were overly incorporated into business and commerce. Fascist anti-Semitism was evident in the battle of Cable Street in East London in 1936. Over a decade later, ugly anti-Jewish disturbances occurred in London and other areas in 1947 and 1948. The bombing of the King David Hotel by Jewish-Israeli nationalists in 1947, with British casualties, was partly responsible. Hence, just a few years following a war against a barbaric racist regime, anti-Semitism was back on the streets, and an insightful social study by J. H. Robb, *Working-Class Anti-Semite* (1954), addressed its causes and the psychology that sustained it. Such sentiment, however, was by no means confined to poorer people. Between the wars an anti-Jewish tendency was almost fashionable among some within the intellectual elite. Anthony Eden was quietly anti-Semitic, and his condemnation of Nazi genocide was mild when compared with the genuine outrage vented by Winston Churchill. Many who supported the Palestinians blamed Jews for their plight, and that feeling intensified in the decades following the establishing of **Israel** in 1948 and the military successes of that country in the wars of 1967 and 1973. It is impossible to measure anti-Semitism, and also impossible to calibrate the various degrees

of feeling against Jews, from the humorous caricature to vehemence. As George Orwell observed during the Second World War, anti-Semitism in Britain was rarely as virulent as it was in Germany, but nonetheless it was manifest in cruel humour, caricature and indifference. A mannered indifference to the suffering of the Jews was later evidenced in the use of the swastika or the insensitive references to Jews, for example the Belsen concentration camp, by British punk rock bands during the 1970s. Anti-Semitism was less in evidence than colour prejudice during the later twentieth century, but it had not entirely dissipated.

APPEASEMENT The term given to the strategy of the British government towards Nazi Germany from 1936 to 1939. Neville Chamberlain is commonly viewed by historians as more naïve in his grasp of Nazi foreign policy than his arch-critics Churchill and Eden. The events of 1937–9 undoubtedly haunted the prime minister to his wartime grave and blighted his subsequent reputation. More recently, however, a revisionist school has tried to provide a more nuanced account of appeasement and of Chamberlain's role. So, was it fair to blame Chamberlain for the shortcomings of appeasement? Not entirely. He inherited both the ethos and the strategy from his predecessor, Stanley Baldwin. Although Baldwin had pushed for rearmament, his response to the German reoccupation of the Rhineland in 1936 had been muted. Moreover, the British carried out negotiations with the support of the French, who showed little inclination to challenge Germany. Chamberlain, furthermore, had witnessed the awful carnage and death toll of the First World War and was determined to avoid further European conflict at all costs. In so doing, how far did he fail to grasp the mendacity of Adolf Hitler and the Nazi government? Believing that tactical responses to German military and territorial aggression might satisfy and thus contain the Nazis, he certainly appeared to possess little empathy for the country stamped upon by the Third Reich during the period of appeasement. The **Munich Agreement** of 1938 illustrated in sharp relief the weaknesses, moral and practical, of the policy. Chamberlain accepted the German occupation of the Sudetenland in Czechoslovakia for assurances that the rest of the country would remain independent. The following year Hitler broke his assurances and in March invaded what was left of independent Czechoslovakia. On 1 September the invasion of Poland broke German promises to the British and French and caused the declaration of war on Germany on 3 September. The experience of appeasement in Western Europe between 1936 and 1939 had indicated with appalling clarity how difficult it is to negotiate with dictators.

ARCHITECTURE Architecture here is divided into domestic architecture, or housing, and commercial and public building design. Housing will be discussed first, then public and commercial buildings.

To the frustration of many modernists and those who prefer to live in apartments, traditionally styled suburban houses with gardens remained enormously attractive to a majority of British people throughout the twentieth century, particularly in England. The Victorian and Edwardian villa, the interwar semi-detached house, and the variety of terraced, semi-detached and detached homes built since the 1880s remained popular with the public. The 'Arts and Crafts' movement in domestic architecture, with its romantic rustic motifs, was perhaps at the apex of Edwardian housing design. Both English Heritage and the **National Trust**, along with many private individuals, are owners of some fine Arts and Crafts housing. Moreover, the garden cities and garden

suburbs which pioneered that movement, notably in the designs of Barry Parker and Raymond Unwin, laid the basis for cottage-style mass suburban housing designs between the wars, although the millions of suburban houses designed by volume builders were often cruder than their progenitors.

Despite this, wartime surveys such as *People's Homes* (1943) by Mass Observation and many postwar surveys on housing preferences affirmed that most people wanted a suburban home with a garden rather than a flat in a city centre or a dwelling in the countryside. Surveys of popular housing preferences found much the same fifty years later. The love of traditional vernacular architecture in Britain was complemented by a hatred or indifference towards modern architecture. During the era of reconstruction the international modern movement became more influential, as many local authorities sought to meet housing targets by building tower blocks and systems-built homes. Unfortunately, tower blocks became infamous as one symptom of 'what went wrong' with the rebuilding of postwar Britain: bold, modern, new and tall in the later 1950s and 1960s, they were associated by the 1970s with social breakdown and an uncomfortable, even alienating, urban environment. The partial collapse of **Ronan Point** in 1968 brought the era of new build in tower blocks to an end and symbolised the crashing to the floor of a modernist dream. A clear lesson emerged from such experiments in Britain: public buildings lent themselves to modern architecture much more effectively than private dwellings. Leading architectural historians, moreover, have deplored the design standards of many modern buildings during the reconstruction of postwar Britain.

Yet there were some significant examples of a successful and explicitly twentieth-century architecture in Britain, some designed by émigré architects. The 1930s saw the construction of some fine modern structures, notably the Penguin Pool and Gorilla House at London Zoo, the Finsbury Health Centre, and the De La Warr pavilion at Bexhill-on-Sea. The American Art Deco style on cinemas also introduced a distinctly twentieth-century flavour to the high streets of interwar Britain. And the Royal Festival Hall, designed for the **Festival of Britain** in 1951, remained a popular modern cultural centre on London's South Bank, and certainly appears less brutish than the nearby National Theatre, completed during the 1970s. A number of fine understated buildings influenced by Bauhaus in Germany were also constructed during the early 1950s. In later decades some striking modern architecture was evident in the office buildings of the City of London. However, the collapse into postmodern medley during the 1980s signified the partial rehabilitation of traditional styles with large new buildings. Its unwitting testimony spoke to the preferences of a majority of British people for naturalism and detail over an explicit emphasis upon form and function.

AUSTERITY Austerity describes a condition that is lacking in comforts and luxuries. In twentieth-century British history, the years of austerity really began during the Second World War. Rationing of foodstuffs, clothing, fuels and other goods was introduced at the beginning of 1940 and the final restrictions were lifted during the 1950s. Some new restrictions were even introduced once the war was over, as the British economy and British people struggled to cope with shortages engendered by interruptions to supply and demand in the immediate aftermath of war. Hence 'austerity Britain' more specifically refers to the period between the end of the war in the summer of 1945 and the final lifting of

rationing and restrictions by 1954. Another periodisation refers to the years 1945 to 1951, the years of the Attlee governments. Against a very difficult economic background, Labour was able to bolt into place the welfare state and the mixed economy. However, two chancellors of the exchequer, Hugh Dalton and Sir Stafford Cripps, came to be identified with harsh economic measures, particularly Cripps, whose tight-lipped and stiff-collared manner appeared to many people to personify austerity. Dalton was chancellor during the financial crisis and fuel crisis of 1947, while Cripps, as chancellor from 1947 to 1950, initiated a number of new rationing schemes and in September 1949 oversaw the **devaluation** of the pound sterling. During the 1951 general election the Conservative Party cleverly exploited continuing dissatisfaction and frustration with rationing and queues, yet the government of Winston Churchill was unable to lift rationing on sugar and sweets until 1953, and the coal supply remained under government control until 1958. Leading historians have successfully attempted to capture the moods that British people felt in early postwar Britain, from the elation of victory in 1945 through the wearying years that followed, notably the fuel crisis in the bitter winter of 1947, to the return to full employment. The era of austerity was over by 1954 at the very latest, although the final restrictions on coal were not removed until 1958.

B

BETTING AND GAMBLING The verbs 'to bet' and 'to gamble' mean the same thing: to risk a sum of money or an item on a sporting or other event with an unknown outcome. The notion that income could be gained from chance, with no effort or talent expended, offended nineteenth-century religious reformers because it mocked the tenets of the Protestant work ethic. Prohibition was the answer. The National Lottery was abolished in 1823, and from 1853 off-the-course cash betting on horse racing was made illegal. During the Edwardian period the National Anti-Gambling League campaigned hard for the **Street Betting Act** of 1906, which maintained the prohibition of cash betting. It was still legal to bet on horses with cash if one was at the race itself. The law was biased, moreover, in favour of the wealthy. Punters who could afford a cheque-based account with a bookmaker could bet off the race-course because no cash was transacted. The sums were settled via credit arrangements. Between the Victorian years and 1961 a colourful open secret was to be found on the streets of Britain, namely street betting, an illegal but irrepressible system of ready-money betting on horse races and other sports.

The forces for commercialised betting and gambling eventually defeated those of paternalism and prohibition. During the 1920s, for example, the football pools emerged, a weekly flutter enjoyed by millions who sought to predict the draws that might occur at forthcoming Saturday afternoon football matches. Greyhound racing from 1926 also offered new opportunities to bet, and both persisted into the postwar years, proving that betting was a popular pastime. Moreover, the betting shops which are now familiar on the high streets were finally introduced in 1961. The licensed betting office, to give it its official title, was originally intended to be a grim and unwelcoming place, unlike the shops that today have television screens, comfortable seating and coffee machines. A disagreeable environment was aimed to prevent loitering with intent to bet too

much. This was because the lifting of Victorian values in relation to this particular leisure activity was still somewhere between the older disapproval of the nineteenth century and the current liberalisation that characterises the betting and gambling culture of early twenty-first century Britain. Lotteries for gaming were also technically illegal until gaming legislation of the 1960s relaxed the laws on casinos. Bingo grew from this time as a form of gambling particularly enjoyed by working-class women and holiday-makers at the seaside, where gifts replaced cash prizes.

Historians have explored the organisation and significance of both informal and commercialised betting and gambling activities, and have focused upon the reasons for liberalisation after 1945. These included the fact that the laws on betting and gambling were unpopular and brought the police and judiciary into ill favour with millions of otherwise law-abiding punters. As British people enjoyed the fruits of affluence, consumerism and full employment during the 1950s and 1960s, a hypocritical Victorian paternalism that tried to protect the poor from 'wrong' spending while allowing the wealthy to gamble on regardless appeared outmoded and was resented. There was also the issue of the state and its need for income: governments could raise taxes from betting and gambling. During the 1950s, the chancellor of the exchequer Harold Macmillan had been attacked from the left and from the Anglican and Protestant churches for introducing the Premium Bonds, a savings scheme that assured the original sum invested but also offered winnings in the form of a regular draw. It was state-sponsored quasi-gambling, and Macmillan was ahead of his time. Following a number of instances of liberalisation between 1960 and the 1990s, the exchequer drew increasing revenues from taxes on betting and gambling. In 1994 the conservative government of John Major introduced the National Lottery. Once an arch-opponent of popular gambling, the government now profited handsomely from it.

BLACKPOOL, LANCASHIRE Along with Brighton on the south coast of England, Blackpool is the most famous seaside resort in Britain. Unlike Brighton, Blackpool has no royal connections enshrined in exotic buildings with a Georgian heritage. Nor does it enjoy the relative proximity to London that benefits Brighton's tourist economy, and it has no racy 'alternative' image. Brighton has been a gay capital in southern England for over thirty years, and a haunt of bohemian artistes. Graham **Greene**'s novel *Brighton Rock* (1938), about a petty psychotic gangster, further contributed to its seedy enigma. Blackpool, however, is unashamedly proletarian. It was established as a major holiday destination for industrial workers and their households before the end of the nineteenth century, and for much of the twentieth century it continued to draw the workers *en masse* for their annual vacations. Guest houses and hotels provided the accommodation for most holiday-makers. Before the Second World War, the railways were the most common form of public transport to Blackpool. In the film *Sing as We Go* (1935), starring Gracie **Fields**, the mill girls from Lancashire took time out from the troubles at the mill to have fun there. Millions of working-class visitors, mostly from the North-West of England, turned Blackpool into a hedonistic holiday destination, renowned for its famous ballroom in the Blackpool Tower, its seafront tram, the large funfair known as the Pleasure Beach, Blackpool Pier, and the sand and shingle beach squeezed between a cold Irish Sea and the English mainland.

During the postwar years the growth of motorisation encouraged holiday-makers to travel to Blackpool from other parts of Britain, a transition encouraged by the appearance of the Blackpool Tower Ballroom on national television shows such as *Come Dancing*. Over 10 million people still visited Blackpool for the day, for a weekend or for an annual holiday by the year 2000. The Pleasure Beach on its own attracts over 5 million people every season.

BOXING Boxing has long been a sport indulged in mostly by working-class men from what Karl Marx once dismissed as the lumpen proletariat: casual and itinerant workers beyond the organised working class. With its origins in bareknuckle prize fighting and fairground fisticuffs, boxing was codified and cleaned up during the later Victorian years. Although it failed to reach the pinnacles of respectability enjoyed by other professional sports, it became a mass spectator sport and multimillion pound leisure industry as a consequence of both the growing American and international presence and the television. The American dominance was signalled between the wars by Joe Louis and other practitioners of what some sporting historians, almost all of them male, view as the noblest of sports. All professional boxers originally learned to fight in amateur clubs, and amateur boxing continued to thrive during the twentieth century. Boxing survived an attack by feminism during the 1980s and 1990s which led to attempts to ban the activity in some council premises. The British Medical Association (BMA) was also highly critical of the sport, and called for it to be banned in 1998. However, any such ban would have forced boxing underground into a less well-regulated culture, so the introduction of protective headwear was the compromise.

Major British names in professional boxing during the twentieth century were Tom Causer and Tommy Farr, who were successful between the wars, and Henry Cooper, Lennox Lewis and Frank Bruno. Their success was positive proof of the route offered by boxing and other sports out of the working classes and into fame and fortune. Increasingly, as a consequence of immigration, boxers were black and Asian. The continuing popularity of amateur boxing was evident in the support given to boxers in the Olympics in 2008. Furthermore, women were increasingly participating in both amateur and professional boxing before the end of the last century; the sport of women's boxing has grown considerably since 2000.

BRITISH BROADCASTING CORPORATION (BBC) The most important cultural institution in Britain, the BBC was born in the age of the radio during the early 1920s. The long-lived successor to its short-lived predecessor the British Broadcasting Company, the BBC enjoyed a near monopoly over the airwaves which was only broken by the introduction of offshore radio broadcasting, namely **Radio Luxembourg** during the 1930s and **Radio Caroline** in the 1960s. During the 1970s commercial radio stations also challenged the BBC's dominance, but the corporation remained a powerful presence. From its outset, the BBC was defined by John Reith, whose emphasis upon rational recreation and the educational potential of broadcasting established an ethos of programming still strongly identified with the corporation, and which for millions of people provided an antidote to the crasser commercial outputs of its rivals, whether on the radio or on television.

The BBC enjoyed a complete monopoly of television broadcasting from its limited inception during the 1930s until the introduction of Independent Television (ITV) in 1955. A common misunderstanding is that the BBC began the first regular television broadcasts, but it was in fact Nazi

Germany that did so, in 1935. Early television in 1930s Britain was limited to London and the nearby home counties, but some key features of later BBC broadcasting were established, namely regular news bulletins, light entertainment and sports, including the first football matches shown live. In September 1939 the programme taken off the air when war was declared was a Mickey Mouse cartoon, testimony to the fact that the BBC would become a major vehicle for American cultural products in postwar Britain. TV broadcasting was resumed in 1946, and grew dramatically thereafter as the number of television sets proliferated. Almost every home had one by the mid-1960s. During that decade, under director general Hugh Greene, BBC television broadcasting was restructured into two channels, namely the more populist BBC1 and BBC2.

Radio, however, also remained at the heart of the BBC. The national home of radio was and remains Broadcasting House, opened in Langham Place, London, in 1932. During the war of 1939–45, Broadcasting House suffered external and internal damage from bomb raids, and some broadcasts were made from the Langham Hotel opposite. The **Home Service** was the BBC major channel for news and current affairs, beginning in 1939. After the war the **Light Programme** and the **Third Programme** were started, both Reithian in content. These three channels were superseded as the now familiar channels of radios 1, 2, 3 and 4 were introduced in 1967. However, the BBC World Service, begun in 1930 and based at Bush House in the Aldwych, continued to maintain as far as possible an impartial news service that was relied upon and trusted throughout the globe. Many people living in war zones or under dictatorships secretly tuned into the BBC World Service for news denied them by their rulers.

The BBC has a rich heritage and archive for historians of Britain since the 1930s, as discussed in **Sources and Resources**. More importantly, while publicly funded through the licence fee, the BBC clung tenaciously to its independence and commitment to free speech beyond the requirements of moral censorship. Its ethos and programmes were inextricable from the cultural and political life of twentieth- and early twenty-first-century Britain. Hence historians have written the history of the BBC itself and explored the relationship of its programmes to British society, culture and politics.

BRITISH EMPIRE Britain was the foremost imperial nation in modern Europe, and had created an empire of almost fifty subject states by the beginning of the twentieth century. The empire was a source of great national pride for millions of people, and it required a large army and navy to police *Pax Britannica*. Economic exploitation and development was accompanied by cultural and political influence. With the exception of Ireland, however, whose native Gaelic was marginalised by the British, the English-speaking countries were by 1914 dominions, self-governing entities that continued to owe allegiance to the British monarch. Parliamentary democracy was the major political export of the British, unsuccessful in some countries, but taking root in others. Culturally, the ramifications of empire were complex and immeasurable, but among the most visible cultural residues of British occupation were religion, notably the exporting of Christianity, and sports: both cricket and rugby football are often highlighted as the most visible remnants of British rule, although the Canadians preferred North American sports, while the Irish proudly promoted Gaelic sports and games after 1900 as counterweights to Anglicisation.

The seeds of decay in British imperialism had been sown for some time, but began to flourish during the later nineteenth and early twentieth centuries. Much of the history of the British Empire during the twentieth century is situated within the historical debates about the decline of Britain. The expansion of other European empires intensified during the 1870s, with the scramble for Africa, and afterwards, while the industrialisation of leading European powers, and also the United States of America, led to challenges to British overseas trade. Within the colonised countries themselves, moreover, the rise of nationalism and of anti-colonial movements led the more far-sighted politicians in Britain to grasp that the global stretch of the empire could never be permanently maintained. The campaign and conflicts for Irish independence before 1921 were closest to home. Furthermore, the struggles for Burmese and Indian independence gathered pace during the 1930s. By then, some leading British politicians had already conceded the principle of a looser Commonwealth of nations rather than the continuation of a global empire. Other politicians looked to the principle of imperial preference to attempt to shore up the economic underpinnings of the empire and to assert Britain's role as a colonial trading nation that was *primus inter pares* with its partners. The Second World War interrupted the demise of the British Empire and accelerated it. However, over 5 million people from the empire fought for Britain between 1939 and 1945. Following the war, the process of decolonisation led to the growth and consolidation of the Commonwealth.

Until the 1950s, most histories of empire tended to celebrate Britannia's ruling of the waves, but increasingly Marxist historians came to view it mostly as exploitative. Today, Britain's adjustment to the loss of empire and a more nuanced understanding of the pros and cons of British rule in former colonies are key approaches to imperial history.

BUDGET The once-yearly statement by the chancellor of the exchequer on the condition of the British economy and on government policies to promote its growth and stability and to finance other government legislation. A ritualised affair, the budget always takes place in midweek, and the chancellor carries the details in an old red briefcase before he reads them out to a packed House of Commons.

'BUTSKELLISM' The term coined by *The Economist* magazine during the early 1950s for the new consensus in British party politics. It draws together the 'But' of the Conservative chancellor of the exchequer R. A. Butler with the 'skell' of his Labour shadow, Hugh Gaitskell. Specifically, Butskellism was mostly a phenomenon during the 1950s of the front benches in parliament – that is, the cabinet – and a majority but never a unanimous number of Treasury officials.

BY-ELECTIONS Between general elections, if a member of parliament (MP) dies, retires, voluntarily resigns or is forced out of office on account of indiscretions in financial or personal life, a by-election is held to elect another MP for his or her constituency. Many by-elections are relatively minor affairs, simply replacing the MP with a candidate from the same party. Others are more historically significant. If a government MP is voted out, this may indicate a decline in its popularity. If a smaller party sees its candidate elected to parliament, this could augur well for its fortunes. Such new parties were the Labour Party during the first two decades of the twentieth century, Plaid Cymru and the Scottish Nationalist Party during the postwar years, the Common Wealth Party during the Second World War, and the

Social Democratic Party (SDP) during the 1980s. Ironically the SDP was an offshoot of the Labour Party. Occasionally, single-issue groups won by-elections, for example candidates supporting pacifism during the 1930s and nationalist candidates during the late twentieth century. At no point did a fascist candidate win a parliamentary by-election.

C

CAMPAIGN FOR NUCLEAR DISARMAMENT (CND) In the early postwar fallout from the American nuclear attacks on Japan in 1945, many on the left of the Labour Party in Britain advocated unilateral disarmament. They hoped that Britain might stay out of the Cold War arms race, but the testing of the first British atomic bomb in 1952 put paid to such unworldly optimism. On 15 May 1957, moreover, Britain dropped its first hydrogen bomb, or 'H' bomb, leading to a revitalisation of unilateral currents of opinion in the fallout of another nuclear device. The Campaign for Nuclear Disarmament was formed the following year. Many of its members had been involved in pacifism between the wars; some had not, nor were they pacifists, but rather anti-nuclear bomb. For the government, however, the 'bomb' was deemed essential to maintain Britain's status as a leading world power, while simultaneously providing a deterrent to the communist bloc. The seemingly insane ratio of mutually assured destruction (MAD) kept the nuclear peace during the Cold War.

In protest at the awful possibility of nuclear holocaust, however, and also at the financial costs of the bomb, the movement for unilateral disarmament engaged in both written and active protest. Leading members of **CND**, such as the Labour politician Michael Foot, the playwright J. B. Priestley and the philosopher Bertrand Russell, denounced atomic weaponry, and thousands took to the streets to march, usually from Aldermaston, the Berkshire town that housed the Atomic Weapons Research Establishment, to London. Yet the majority of British people remained grudgingly in favour of nuclear weapons for their protective cover. The Labour leader Hugh Gaitskell instinctively understood this, and steered the party away from a unilateral position in 1960, at the peak of the CND's influence. After 1964 the campaign declined, partly as a consequence of the relief at the benign outcome of the Cuban missile crisis in 1962, although 'Ban the Bomb' marches and stickers never completely disappeared, and were kept alive mostly by students in university campuses and colleges. The movement gained new momentum during the early 1980s as **cruise missiles** became part of Britain's nuclear arsenal. The unilateralism of the Labour left re-emerged within a new discourse entitled 'Protest and Survive', a play on words of the 'protect and survive' advice given by governments in the unlikely event of a nuclear attack. Under the leadership of Michael Foot, the Labour Party from 1980 once more moved towards unilateralism, a position that proved to be an electoral liability as the party almost reached meltdown in the general election of 1983. The ending of the Cold War after the fall of the Berlin Wall in 1989 defused the unilateralists once more. However, the threat of nuclear attack has never completely disappeared, and possession of the bomb continued into the twenty-first century. Historians of CND and nuclear disarmament highlight the role of protest in keeping alive the issue of atomic weaponry since the 1940s and the relationship of anti-nuclear sentiment to the left wing of politics.

CAPITAL PUNISHMENT ('DEATH PENALTY')

Capital punishment was colloquially known as the 'death penalty'. A couple of tragic cases had brought capital punishment under closer scrutiny. In 1953, Derek Bentley was hanged for the murder of a policeman, but many years later was posthumously pardoned. Ruth Ellis, the last woman to be hanged, in July 1955, had apparently been abused by the man she killed. The possibility of wrongful death sentencing was highlighted even in feature films, for example *Dial 'M' for Murder* (1954), one of many classics by Alfred Hitchcock.

During the 1950s and 1960s, therefore, Conservative home secretaries became increasingly worried and upset about the decisions they had to make over capital punishment. Its abolition was not a party-political issue. MPs on both sides of the House of Commons had views against and for it, but those against it won the day. However, this was not a question about which the majority of British people were particularly liberal or permissive. Opinion polls proved that over three-quarters of the country in 1965 wanted to keep the hangman's noose, and a considerable majority since have continued to support the death penalty. For most British people, the rape and murder of children, the killing of police officers, the blowing up of innocent civilians by IRA 'terrorists', and cold-blooded premeditated murders have consistently been at the top of a list of offences for which a sentence of death appears a proportionate response. The common belief is that the Old Testament moral equation of 'an eye for an eye' is a straightforward antidote to a relativistic liberalism which waxes clever about the technicalities of manslaughter as opposed to murder, and even lets offenders go free or enjoy lax sentencing if those technicalities remain contested. The notion that capital punishment is a deterrent was often trotted out by tabloid newspapers and those who wrote letters to them, who blamed the rising number of murders and violent offences on a lack of fear of the consequences of such actions. Evidence from the United States of America, however, where some states retain the death penalty, did not sustain such a position. Neither deterrence nor a harsh retributive justice held sway among the lawmakers in post-1950s Britain, and historians have tended to treat the abolition of capital punishment as one facet of liberalisation. And, during the 1980s and 1990s, the overturning of some high-profile convictions for murder and IRA terrorism seemed to validate such liberalism. Had the hangman still been in his post, some of those convicted would have been unable to witness their warranted redemption.

CENSORSHIP The history of censorship has been viewed largely as one of a qualified retreat from Victorian values towards permissiveness. Censorship is the monitoring and editing of the content of cultural products by the government or other authorities. Its intention is to prevent corruption or sedition. A landmark in censorship during the twentieth century was the establishment in 1912 of the **British Board of Film Classification** (BBFC) in order to regulate film content. The lingering persistence of Victorian values contributed to a culture of censoriousness in Britain, and local authorities could also engage in censorship of films, something which often varied from region to region because of religion. Wartime greatly increased the censorship of the cinema. During the First World War, **Topical Budget newsreels** were only allowed to show Allied victories, for example, while the Ministry of Information during the Second World War rigorously policed film content. Boosting morale was a major motive, but so too was the fear of Nazi propaganda. In addition, many poli-

ticians, notably Conservatives, were angry at the inclusion of social reformist messages in some documentary films and wartime radio broadcasts. However, the effect of censorship was nuanced. The British movie *Love on the Dole*, the reworking of the novel by Walter Greenwood, was banned during the 1930s for exaggerating 'the sordid side of poverty'. But the film was released during the war with a morale-inspiring coda attached.

In 1948 the 'X' certificate was introduced to prevent children under sixteen watching the growing number of horror films. The permissiveness of the 1960s is widely argued to have relaxed censorship rules, although the protection of children from harmful influences persisted. In 1970, censorship at the cinema was updated by the BBFC in the following categories: U – universal; A – children over five years admitted with parental knowledge; AA – no children under fourteen admitted; and X – no admission for young people aged below eighteen years. These were subsequently reworked, but the over-eighteen principle remained mostly intact. In 1984 the Video Recordings Act also brought video cassettes under the jurisdiction of the BBFC, although private home viewing remained much more difficult to monitor than the open cinema. It has been even more difficult to regulate since the rise of the internet during the 1990s.

Censorship was abolished in the theatre in 1969, but content was more closely scrutinised on television because policing the home was more complex than regulating the cinema or the theatre. The showing of unsuitable content to children and minors remained a major issue. When the film critic Kenneth Tynan used the 'f' word on television during the 1960s, opinion was polarised between those who were outraged and those who gave a libertarian shrug. Today, however, that word is used frequently on British television after the 9 p.m. watershed. Some of those films that were categorised as adult during the 1970s, to be broadcast on television only after 10 p.m., are now shown with impunity in the afternoons.

CHARITY Charity is the provision of assistance and relief to the poor, and to those who require help as a consequence of accident or circumstance. A charity is an organisation or fund established to these ends. Charities can also assist with causes that are less important, for example the arts and sports. Beyond the primary care and nurture provided by the family, and in addition to the state welfare services, charity has tackled social problems in modern Britain. Religion was closely harnessed to charity during the nineteenth century, and the later Victorian years witnessed an emergent culture of philanthropy that greatly influenced the last century. For example, the Charity Organisation Society under the auspices of Octavia Hill attempted to coordinate almsgiving to working-class families and elderly and poor individuals in need, while insisting that recourse to charity should be very much a last resort.

The major fields of charitable endeavour during the twentieth century included animal welfare (the Royal Society for the Prevention of Cruelty to Animals had been formed in the 1820s) and child welfare. The National Society for the Prevention of Cruelty to Children was established in 1889, and Dr Barnardo funded his first home for orphans and children in need during the 1870s. Care of the sick and the terminally ill remained at the heart of philanthropy, and was tragically augmented by the onset of the twentieth-century illness AIDS and the formation during the 1980s of the Terence Higgins Trust. Many elderly people also remained recipients of charity: Help the Aged was formed in 1961 partly as a consequence of the demise of the extended family leaving many old people on their own. The care of the elderly was also dovetailed with that of hundreds of thousands of injured ex-servicemen who were given help and treats by the British Legion, formed in 1921.

War was a catalyst for other charities. The crises caused by hunger and poverty abroad were recognised in the formation of OXFAM during the Second World War, while in Britain it became impossible to differentiate poverty from postwar housing conditions. Poverty and slum housing had not disappeared during the 1960s, despite reconstruction and the postwar housing programme, as testified to by the formation in 1966 of Shelter and the transmission in the same year of *Cathy Come Home* by the BBC. Homelessness remained a stubborn and miserable reminder of the limitations of both charity and official policy into the twenty-first century. During the later twentieth century, moreover, the tragedy of sexual violence against children and women came to the fore, the former becoming an aspect of child welfare while the latter was partly tackled by women who came together during the late 1970s to form the Rape Crisis Centre movement. Most sexual abuse occurred within the family: the ostensibly loving focus of primary care was a living hell for many.

Surveys of charitable activity by the government during the 1990s and into the present century indicated that over half the population gave regularly to charity. These were the years that followed Margaret Thatcher's infamous comment that 'there is no such thing as society'. And that figure was independent of the charity gain produced by the National Lottery from 1994, which purloined the giving impulse for the gambling impulse, but by the end of 2007 it had provided £12 billion for good causes. Historians of charity focus on the social problems addressed by philanthropic organisations, and also the voluntary impulse that accompanied it. From church and chapel fetes to the car-boot sales at schools, from fun runs to city marathons, and from the Poppy Appeal to the BBC's Children in Need, the desire to give and to organise was a reminder that the best in human nature could be relied upon to counteract the worst.

CHILD WELFARE Modern child welfare legislation began during the nineteenth century. The use and abuse of children in industrial workplaces led to the regulation of children's employment in Britain from 1833, although this continued often illegally in sweatshops into the last century. The treatment of child paupers led to a series of acts that reduced the role of the Poor Law in child welfare. The **Children's Act** of 1908, moreover, outlined the rights of young people to care and support. Increasingly during the twentieth century, child welfare policies were harnessed to education policies and family welfare policies. Payments to poorer mothers were systematically introduced by the Family Allowances from 1945, pioneered by Eleanor Rathbone. Policy evolved up to the **Family Income Supplement** during the 1970s and its replacements, all designed to reduce child poverty. But by the end of the century they had failed to eliminate it. Hence one of the loudest pledges of New Labour was to end child poverty, a goal that is still a long way from being realised.

Beyond the role of the state, child welfare was also in the hands of charity. Orphans and victims of abuse could find assistance and nurture in a number of children's charities, most of which carried out their duties and responsibilities to vulnerable children with a concern and commitment that seems to have been somewhat obscured by the revelations, during the 1990s and since, of child abuse in care homes. The **Child Support Agency** introduced in 1991 was the final main act

of the state in attempting, and failing, to provide the necessary level of protection and support for children – in this case, the children of divorced parents. It was reformed, with miserable failings, in 1999.

CHILDREN AND CHILDHOOD With the exception of ground-breaking work by the French social historian Philippe Ariès, the history of childhood was reduced mostly to a focus on the consequences of legislation affecting children, particularly in the fields of education and health and child welfare. It was not until the 1970s that a body of work began to emerge on the history of childhood in modern Britain. There was considerable overlap between the nineteenth and twentieth centuries in terms of the periodisation of this history. The changing definitions of childhood from the eighteenth to the twentieth century formed one reason, connected as they were to official education and Poor Law policies that affected the lives of young people. The discovery of considerable abuse towards children, including sexual violence and infanticide, and their exploitation in sweatshops and other unregulated workplaces had led to the rise of a child protection movement during the Victorian years. During the Edwardian period the **Children's Act** initiated the language of children's rights. The moors murders in 1963–4 were among the most gruesome of the appalling cases of abuse and murder of children in postwar Britain, and during the 1990s abuse in care homes reminded a shocked public that children remained among the most vulnerable people in society, as did the discovery of paedophilia on the internet. Crime against children remained a filthy underbelly in most countries.

More widely, however, the character of childhood was influenced by increasing material prosperity and the cult of toys, although class and income defined the level and costs of consumption between children. Television from the 1950s also introduced a new range of children's programmes that assisted in the definition of childhood, greatly adding to the range of cultural products available to children beyond the literature that millions of young people had enjoyed since the Victorian years: the Education Act of 1870 had proved to be an enduring boon to writers of children's novels. As Robert and Iona Opie found in their social anthropology of *Children's Games* (1969), childhood was also a context where certain socialising habits, practices and values were learned independently of adults: parks, playgrounds and street corners remained locales of hopscotch, tag and other free informal games that were never taught by grown-ups but learned by children through a culture of folk memory that remained uniquely and fascinatingly age-specific.

By the end of the twentieth century, the media expressed considerable concern at the shrinking window of childhood innocence, yet it was the media that had done so much to undermine any golden age of childhood innocence through the sexualisation of the young. Girls especially were exposed to a range of magazines that targeted older children and young teenagers. A chatty but insensitive emphasis upon the body beautiful, the need to 'pull' boys or girls or feel left out, and the importance of that latest item of fashion could lead to misery in the lonely bedroom of the teenager who was poor or who felt different from her or his peers. The poorly censored internet, moreover, made available to all thousands of websites whose content should have been strictly limited to those aged over eighteen.

CINEMA The history of moving pictures in Britain began in 1896, when the Lumière Brothers exhibited their experimental and influential moving slides at the Regent Street Polytechnic (now the University of Westminster) in London. Before cinema, on-stage entertainment for the masses was provided by the music hall, where a variety of acts, including singers, dancers, stand-up comedians, magicians, jugglers and other fly-by-night performers, would entertain the paying public.

By 1914, however, the music hall was in decline, as moving films captured the imagination of the people. The First World War added to the popularity of 'a night at the pictures' because newsreels about the war and other current events accompanied the showing of fiction feature films. Between the wars, cinema supplanted music hall as the local 'good night out'. Many old music halls were indeed converted to cinemas even before the First World War, and such conversions continued into the 1920s. But the 1920s and the 1930s were also the decades when American-style modern cinema buildings were built all over Britain. Many of those interwar cinemas are now 'listed buildings', protected by town planning legislation from demolition or unplanned alteration. Many others were smaller and less well-built and designed affairs. But no matter what the style, size or opulence of the individual cinema, the activity of cinema-going became firmly established as a major form of leisure activity between the wars. Moreover, the prewar Cinematographic Acts and the postwar Film Acts tried to protect the British film industry via loans and quotas. Their success is debateable, not least because people flocked to see American films, and the best of British too. After 1945, cinema admissions peaked and troughed. In 1950 they reached a high of 1,396 million admissions to the 4,600 cinemas in Britain. By 1987, however, admissions numbered just 67 million, and the number of outlets was fast declining. By 1990 the figure had risen again, to 79 million admissions to the 500 cinemas in Britain, thanks in part to the opening of the new multiplex movie theatres in the edge-city-style developments of late twentieth-century Britain. This dispersal of cinema locations coincided with the consequences of the cinema legislation of the mid-1980s, which cut indigenous state funding to British film.

Going to the cinema was mostly a sociable affair, undertaken in groups, in couples and in families. It was a visual and exotic introduction to the world of the United States of America, as Hollywood, a catch-all descriptor for the output of most American film studios, continued to produce films that entertained the public, from the interwar years into the present century. 'Westerns', films about the American frontier, remained hugely popular, but so too did historical fiction films, romances, musicals, comedies, and crime and police thrillers. Horror films were another favoured genre, leading to their censorship in early postwar Britain.

While American products dominated, Britain possessed an indigenous film industry, although it was tiny compared with the American cinema. The Cinematographic Acts of 1927 and 1938 provided for screen quotas for the exhibition of British-made films in British cinemas with a modicum of success. Some of the most popular films in British cinema were home-made, just as some of the best-known and much loved actors and actresses were British. During the 1930s such films as *Sing as We Go* (1934), written by J. B. Priestley and starring Gracie Fields, were windows into the lives of the urban working classes. Many other films are now widely recognised by critics as essentially 'British' cultural products. Among the most highly regarded genres in British cinema were the documentary films of the 1930s. After the war until the 1960s there was a predictable proliferation of war films, many of which

were congratulatory and heroic in tone, while others were more nuanced. Globally, the spy films of the *James Bond* series from the early 1960s, based upon the novels by Ian Fleming, were among the most famous Cold War products of British cinema, although financial backing came from the United States. Comedy was a staple feature, from the Ealing comedies of the 1940s and early 1950s to the *Carry On* films, over thirty of which were made from the 1960s. However, the social comment and subtle humour in the Ealing comedies was a long way away from the immature but undeniably inventive attitudes towards sex and partial nudity to be found in the *Carry On* films. Gritty realism may be viewed as another genre of postwar British film. *Room at the Top* (1958), based on the novel by John **Braine**, and *Saturday Night and Sunday Morning* (1960), by Alan Sillitoe, also dealt partly with the working-class social landscape and its discontents and brought illicit sex into mainstream cinema. And British cinema produced a number of famous international classics, from David Lean's *Lawrence of Arabia* (1962) to Richard Attenborough's *Gandhi* (1983).

During the latter twentieth century, television and cinema came closer together. Channel 4 introduced *Film on Four*, which produced some famous movies, among them *My Beautiful Laundrette* (1985), *Trainspotting* (1996) and *East is East* (1999). In 1998 Channel 4 launched its subscription channel *Film Four*, which became free to view in 2006. Further boosts to British film making came with funding from the National Lottery.

Historians of the cinema in Britain have explored the cultural content of films and the social significance of going to the cinema. Many histories also, and for obvious reasons, focus upon both the cinema and the television screen as texts reflective of historical contexts.

CITIZENSHIP 'Citizen' can mean a number of key things. It literally means a member of a city or town, but more widely it refers to the legally recognised subject or national of a nation-state. The latter notion of citizenship was connected with many aspects of postwar British social history. The social scientist T. H. **Marshall**, in *Citizenship and Social Class* (1950), defined the characteristics of citizenship as the possession of civil, political and social rights, underpinned by a democratic and accessible welfare system. Working-class entitlement to welfare benefits meant, in principle at least, duties to pay national insurance and obey the law.

Beyond Marshall, the notion of citizenship had implications for inclusion and exclusion by ethnicity or gender. A modern democracy was distinguished by the rights and duties contained with the concept of citizenship. Hence the differential access to the rights and benefits that, in theory, accompanied citizenship has been taken up by historians of different sections of society, for example Asians, blacks, women and the poor. During the 1960s the civil rights movement in the United States of America demonstrated that citizenship was at the heart of racial politics, and American civil rights strongly influenced the debates around race and citizenship that led to the race relations legislation passed by the governments of Harold Wilson. The notion that citizenship meant equal rights and duties for all was also useful for feminist analyses of the framing during the 1970s of equal-pay legislation and of discrimination on the basis of gender. In 1991 the *Citizen's Charter*, issued under the government of John Major, guaranteed the rights of *all* British citizens to redress in any failure in access to or dealings with public services. The early twenty-first century witnessed a newer direction in the language of citizenship. The New Labour government sought to assuage fears about immigration from Eastern Europe, and about Islam, by insisting that migrants who settled in Britain should be subject to a citizenship test in order to encourage knowledge of and loyalty to the host nation; in return they would receive the rights and protections offered by British citizenship.

CITY OF LONDON The heart of the financial services in Britain, the City of London is somewhat confusingly not a part of the administrative framework of London itself. It is a little over 1 square mile in size, and is governed by the Corporation of London and the lord mayor. It also has its own police force. During the industrial revolution and the expansion of the British Empire, the City's wealth was built upon its heritage of livery companies and expanding overseas trade. During the twentieth century it suffered aerial attack in both world wars and was extensively damaged in the Blitz: over a third of its buildings were hit, many of them beyond repair. Since 1945 the pre-eminence of the City of London as the home of the Stock Exchange appeared to be threatened by the rise of Wall Street in New York, and by European and Asian competitors. During the 1970s the City's workforce fell by over 14,000 to 360,000. Almost all of these were commuters, as most accommodation in the City is for business and trade. However, the Big Bang of deregulation during the 1980s powered the City to greater heights, bringing increasing levels of inward investment and employment, and creating not a little resentment at the spiralling fortunes to be earned by many of its company owners and key employees. That the City of London is adjacent to some of the most impoverished streets of the East End of London threw the contrasts between rich and poor into sharp relief.

The Guildhall, Mansion House and livery halls continue to remain at the heart of metropolitan and international business and elite networks, and to make a hugely important contribution to the capital's wealth and influence. Into the twenty-first century, the City of London remained the pre-eminent financial centre in Europe.

COLD WAR The diplomatic and political conflict between the Western powers and the communist Eastern bloc was termed the 'Cold War' as early as 1946. Supported by the United States of America, Western European nations resisted communist infiltration between 1946 and 1989. The **Marshall Plan** was an early and significant move by the Americans to prevent communism from gaining ground. Key moments in the embedding of the Cold War in the public consciousness included the spectre of the 'iron curtain' across Europe lamented by Winston Churchill in his speech of 1946; the Berlin blockade in 1948; the Russian invasions of Hungary and Czechoslovakia during the 1950s and 1960s; the Korean War; the launch of Sputnik in 1961; the Cuban missile crisis of 1962; America's heightened involvement in **Vietnam** between 1965 and 1974; the Apollo moon landings of the later 1960s and early 1970s; and the occasionally reported assassinations of secret agents, for example the murder of the Bulgarian dissident Georgi Markov in London in 1978, almost certainly by an agent of the USSR. (In May 2008 the Metropolitan Police re-opened the case.) Worse still, the Cold War carried the threat of nemesis, of nuclear apocalypse, as the world's leading powers developed nuclear weapons as a deterrent threat.

The **fall of the Berlin Wall** in 1989 signalled the final cessation of the Cold War, although a few communist regimes would soldier on until brought down by citizens who were seeking more democratic and wealthier societies. With the ending of communism, however, came the begin-nings of the historical study of the Cold War, a historiography that is likely to grow. The political history of the **secret state** is one such area of analysis. Another rich field of study has been the nature and role of culture during the Cold War. The arts, media and sports, for example, were battlegrounds for the ideological positions of East and West. Major international sporting events became struggles between the free world and the Eastern bloc, while the representations of communism in newspapers, cinema and television contin-ually served to remind people that there was a Cold War going on.

COMMONWEALTH, THE The system that replaced the British Empire as a conse-quence of decolonisation, and whose seeds were sown during the empire. Before 1950 the term 'British Commonwealth' was more commonly used for the British colo-nies. It first came into official usage following the **Balfour Report** during the mid-1920s, which recommended that all countries that were either dominions or colonies be labelled 'the British Com-monwealth of Nations'. Trading links with the British Commonwealth were strength-ened with the ascendancy of protectionist policies during the 1930s following the **Ottawa Conference** of 1932. The growing demands in Burma and India for indepen-dence, however, were symptomatic of the rising nationalism in the British Empire which would lead to its break-up in the postwar years. The Second World War brought about a kind of mega postponing effect, however, as Commonwealth coun-tries played a hugely important role in the defeat of the Axis powers. Yet the war also weakened Britain's longer-term ability and power to retain global leadership, and the Commonwealth came into being as former British colonies gained independence. As if to reflect the imminent demise of British influence, the 'British' had been dropped from 'British Commonwealth' by 1949, the year of the first Commonwealth Conference. By then, Burma, India and Pakistan had already gained independence. Most countries that subsequently sought independence chose to stay within the Commonwealth for its economic dispensations: their dates of independence are listed in **Landmarks**. By 1980 there were thirty-six members of the Commonwealth.

The growing number of Commonwealth members met periodically at the Commonwealth Conferences. From 1949 through 1951, 1953, 1955, 1956, 1957, 1960, 1961, 1962, 1965, 1969 and 1977 these were held in London; however, other major Commonwealth Conferences were hosted in Nigeria in 1966, Singapore in 1971, Canada in 1973, Jamaica in 1975, Zambia in 1979, Australia in 1981, India in 1983 (twice) and the Bahamas in 1985.

COMMUNISM: THE COMMUNIST PARTY OF GREAT BRITAIN (CPGB) In the continuing aftermath of the Russian Revolution, the Communist Party of Great Britain (CPGB) was first formed in June 1920, and then refounded in 1921 with the merger of other leading communist organisations under the umbrella of the CPGB. Small Marxist parties already existed in Britain, for example the British Socialist Party, the Communist Unity Group of the Socialist Labour Party, and a variety of workers' communist guilds and groups. A number of members of the Independent Labour Party also affiliated to the CPGB. It was the product of the Third International, or the Comintern (an abbreviation of international communism), founded in 1919. The Russian Bolsheviks, now firmly in power, were seeking to promote communist parties around the world, parties that would follow the diktats of Lenin, and later any party leader, from Moscow. Leading founders of communism in Britain included Willie **Gallacher**, Arthur Horner, Albert Inkpen, Sylvia Pankhurst, Harry Pollitt, T. J. Watkins and Edgar Whitehand.

Communist historians have written a number of fascinating histories exploring the nature of British communism, the problems facing revolutionary politics in a democracy between the wars and during the Cold War, and the relationship of British communism, as well as individual communists, with Moscow. The role of communism in trade unions and industrial relations, and in a variety of protest movements from rent strikes to 'ban the bomb' marches, has also been explored. As will be evident from the general election results, however, the CPGB had very little success in its dalliance with the reformist blind alley that was democracy, but at least it was a better record of achievement than fascism ever mustered in British parliamentary politics. With the exception of its appeal to some middle-class intellectuals and to a minority of blue-collar workers who had read Marx and Lenin, British communism remained a marginal force, and it came to an inauspicious ending. Following the people-led demise of communist regimes in Eastern Europe, the CPGB wound itself up in 1991.

COMMUNISM: TROTSKYITE GROUPS IN BRITAIN The arch-opponent of Stalin, Leon Trotsky, was murdered by an agent of the Soviet state in 1940. Since his death, revolutionaries who loathed the totalitarianism of Soviet Russia have viewed Trotsky as someone who was working towards an alternative vision of a more democratic workers' state. The leading Trotskyite groupings in Britain, some of whom emerged in the radical moment of the later 1960s and early 1970s, have been the International Socialists (who became the Socialist Workers Party (SWP) in 1978), the International Marxist Group (IMG) and the Workers' Revolutionary

Party (WRP). To say they were marginal to British politics is no overstatement. They were never as sizeable as the Communist Party of Great Britain, and that was little more than a fringe political movement itself. And when Trots worked their way into mainstream politics, notably the Labour Party during the 1980s, the party suffered as a consequence.

Incidentally, the Anti-Nazi League (ANL), begun in 1977, was a Trotskyite-backed campaign to kick racism out of rock music and off the streets. Gaining support from many university students, trade unionists and pop stars during the later 1970s and early 1980s, the success of the ANL demonstrated that the Trots could do something right, sometimes. As for the history of Trotskyite communism in Britain, such as it is, the student needs to be aware that much of it is written by members or supporters of the various marginal cells mentioned above.

CONSCRIPTION Known in the United States of America as 'the draft', and alternatively in Britain as 'national service', conscription describes the compulsory military service required of men and occasionally women during times of conflict or national crisis. During peacetime, with the exception of the 1950s, all recruitment to the military was voluntary. The First and Second World Wars were major catalysts for compulsory enlistment to the armed services, and in 1950 the outbreak of the Korean War also led to the extension of national service. Over 2.3 million conscripts had served in the British forces by 1918, for example, and were demobilised thereafter. Between 1945 and the end of conscription in 1963, more than 2.5 million men were drafted into national service.

Opposition to conscription came from conscientious objectors, who were stigmatised by most people. Over 10,000 men refused to don a uniform during the First World War. Much anti-conscription sentiment was increasingly channelled through the **Peace Pledge Union** in the 1930s and 1940s. More than 60,000 people refused military service during the Second World War. As the latter point suggests, pacifism was inherently opposed to national service. A key concern of historians is how far conscription 'militarised' individuals and society. Another is the experience of both military service and demobilisation. The National Sound Archive contains many testimonies of conscripted servicemen.

CONSENSUS

> Britain has undergone one of the greatest social revolutions in her history. [The] strength of the Tory Party [and] its continuance as a major force lie in its empirical approach to current problems and its readiness to accept facts. [We] accepted the revolution of 1832 and governed England for a considerable part of the nineteenth century in consequence. I am glad to tell you that we have accepted the revolution of 1945 and are looking forward to governing England for a good part of the rest of this century.
>
> (Robert Boothby, Conservative MP, 1949)

'Consensus' was the term given to the general agreement between the parliamentary front benches of the major political parties for an era of broad unanimity, despite differences, over the management and funding of social and economic policies. The role of the Second World War in the creation of the welfare state from 1945 is also viewed as an essential plank establishing a consensus politics, and, as the quotation from **Boothby** above indicates, whatever their misgivings, the Tories had realised before the 1951 general election that to abolish or question the welfare state and nationalisation might affect their popularity with the electorate. In that year *The Economist* magazine coined the term '**Butskellism**' to describe the ideological and practical harmonies between the Tory chancellor of the exchequer R. A. Butler and the Labour shadow chancellor Hugh Gaitskell. From the 1950s until the later 1970s there was little fundamental disagreement over social and economic policies. A number of historians, however, have tried to question the notion of a consensus in Britain, pointing to divisions between the two main parties over welfare expenditure, the denationalisation of certain industries in 1953, and the introduction of Independent Television (ITV) in 1955 to break the state monopoly in broadcasting. Furthermore, right-wing views that had questioned the high taxation of the welfare state were occasionally manifested before the 1970s, but were given political expression by Margaret Thatcher, whose promise to 'roll back the frontiers of the state' and attack the so-called dependency culture appeared to affirm those on the right who had been critical of the postwar consensus. However, it is difficult to avoid the conclusion that a broad front-bench commitment to nationalisation and the welfare state existed in the House of Commons from the early 1950s until the 1970s.

CONSERVATISM AND THE CONSERVATIVE PARTY The principles of modern British Conservatism were established by the Irish philosopher Edmund Burke in the immediate aftermath of the French Revolution of 1789 and by Sir Robert Peel in his Tamworth Manifesto in 1834. Both definitions of Conservatism emphasised tradition, antipathy towards radical revolution, a pragmatic response to social and economic changes, and a belief in the primacy of individualism as opposed to the dominance of the state. By extension, this also embraced a notion of organic and voluntary communities rather than the agency of state-sponsored schemes for social advancement and cohesion. The spectrum of Conservative opinion accepts these nostrums to varying degrees. 'One-nation Toryism', deriving a great deal from the Victorian Conservative prime minister Benjamin Disraeli, believed in an organic hierarchical social-class system that made concessions to the working classes while emphasising nation over sectional interests. Most Conservative prime ministers of the twentieth century, from Lord Salisbury to Edward Heath, may be viewed as one-nation Tories. Margaret Thatcher probably had the weakest claim to that title.

Statistically, the Conservatives were the most successful party of the twentieth century as measured by general election victories and years in power, forming named governments in eight decades – the exceptions being the 1920s and the 1940s. In all, the party achieved almost fifty years of government. The Tories led by Stanley Baldwin also dominated the National Government of 1931–5 and shared power with the other political parties during the wartime national governments, as well as in the coalition government of 1918–22. Between the wars the Conservatives were the largest party in the House of Commons, whether in coalition or as the party of government, and they governed postwar Britain for almost thirty-four of the fifty-five years after 1945. As the quotation from Boothby (under **consensus**, above) indicates, the Conservatives had adopted consensual politics in order to prosper at the ballot box, sometimes driving the political agenda, at other times responding to it. This led notably to an acceptance of Keynesianism by most but by no means all leading members of the Conservative Party during the 1950s and

1960s. This pattern, however, was broken during the 1970s when the more consensual one-nation Conservatism was attacked by the New Right. One of the earliest and most influential texts associated with the New Right was Frederick Hayek's *The Road to Serfdom*, published during the 1940s, which warned against the dangers of a powerful socialist state. Rejecting the economics of John Maynard Keynes in favour of monetarism, and extolling Victorian values as opposed to permissiveness, the New Right became personified by Thatcher. Her attempts to encourage a new phase of individualism in British society, and to limit the power and reach of the state, were very popular with large sections of the middle-class and affluent working-class electorate. In fact, she initiated a period of eighteen years of unbroken Conservative government, an achievement unequalled by any other twentieth-century politician. Not all Conservatives, let alone Conservative-minded historians, however, necessarily admired her. And by the end of the twentieth century the Tories were quite unpopular with the public, a consequence of the performance of the Major government and of the less successful aspects of privatisation during the 1980s and 1990s. A Conservative government had ushered in the twentieth century, but a Labour government, owing much to the 'business-friendly' political environment of Thatcher's influence, ended it.

Broadly, historians of the Conservative Party emphasise its split over tariff reform from 1903 and its inability to win power again until 1922, following its break with the coalition government headed by Lloyd George. By contrast, Conservative dominance in parliamentary politics between the wars, its pragmatic embrace of consensus politics from the latter 1940s, and the adoption of New Right policies during the 1980s are evidence of its power

both to adapt to as well as to lead political trends. This was one explanation for Tory general election victories during the 1950s. Leadership qualities are another major theme, with Baldwin, Churchill, Macmillan and Thatcher standing out as the great Tory prime ministers, despite some flaws in their record.

CONSUMERISM Consumerism has two meanings. One refers to consumption, to the growing range of consumer goods available to more and more people in an increasingly affluent society. The other refers to the organisation of consumers to promote their own interests. Taking the former definition first, we can see that throughout the course of the twentieth century (as in previous centuries) the majority of people became better-off in a material sense, but also that considerably higher levels of disposable income among working-class as well as middle-class households greatly democratised access to consumption.

Real wages hardly rose between 1900 and 1938, but from 1950 they grew considerably, if unevenly. Increasingly households enjoyed higher levels of disposable income to maximise their consumption of luxury goods and foodstuffs. The interwar years had witnessed the beginnings of a modern consumer and leisure culture among the majority of the population, but the 1950s and beyond saw the acceleration and consolidation of a consumerism oriented towards labour-saving devices, leisure goods, clothing and fashions, more and better foods, increasingly exotic holidays, and motor cars.

By the year 2000, many writers deplored the so-called McDonaldisation of British consumer culture, and the apparent banality and homogeneity of supermarket chains, notably Tesco, but also Sainsbury's and Safeway (later renamed Morrisons). Yet the supermarkets had managed to cut costs for their customers to a degree that smaller shops could not meet. Furthermore, the range of goods on the supermarket shelves increased dramatically from overseas during the last two decades of the twentieth century, both cause and effect of a growing diversity of tastes in multicultural Britain. This was sometimes bad news for British agriculture as imports displaced home-grown products, but good news for consumers, who enjoyed more exotic foods at increasingly affordable prices. Moreover, the provision of parking around most of the larger supermarkets and superstores during the final quarter of the twentieth century also made life more convenient for the majority of British people who had access to a motor car. With the rise of the symmetrical family and greater role-sharing between men and women in the household, the weekly shop at the supermarket became part of the mass rhythms of British life, although women continued to be more responsible for shopping than men. And, for those who had no car, most supermarkets were on a bus route. Asda even ran their own buses to their new superstores from the early 1980s. Supermarkets made a contribution to the quality of life in postwar Britain that, in different ways, was as significant as socialism.

The importance of shopping for both essentials and luxuries was evident in the growing consciousness of consumers in postwar Britain. The consumer's association Which? was formed in 1957, and its magazine *Which?* soon became a useful guide to the quality of products on sale. The organisation cooperated with Consumer Unions, whose membership totalled 150,000 by 1960. By then the magazine had become monthly.

Historians have focused on the importance of affluence and the purchase of goods in shaping consumer identities, on the formation of consumer's organisations, and on the relationship between British and American consumerism.

CONTRACEPTION Crude and ineffective forms of contraception had existed for hundreds of years, but the twentieth century saw huge improvements in contraceptive technology and in the propagandising of contraception. As a consequence, family planning became accessible to millions. Among the most important names in the promulgation of family planning were Margaret **Pyke** and Marie Stopes. Stopes's book *Married Love*, first published in 1918, was widely read. Contraception was, as the term makes clear, a barrier to conception. It is a commonplace in social history that the middle classes pioneered family-size limitation before 1900. However, working-class family limitation increased considerably between 1900 and 1939, a consequence of the realisation that fewer mouths to feed meant more income to go round. Factors such as the decline in staple industries also encouraged caution among industrial workers in calculations of the number of children. And of course a growing access to contraception, sanctioned by Stopes and the birth control movement, also worked to restrict family size among the less well-off. An ideology derived in part from eugenics informed the actions of Stopes and other propagandists for birth control among the poor. An increasingly literate and educated working class could see the benefits for itself, however.

The Second World War itself was an effective contraceptive, although the number of babies born – and secretly terminated – as a consequence of liaisons between British women and American servicemen was immeasurable testimony to the strength of illicit relationships between 1939 and 1945. During the war, nonetheless, 76.8 per cent of families whose head of household was manually employed used contraception, and this had risen to 90 per cent by the mid-1960s, only a little behind that of middle-class levels.

The potential of contraception for liberating young women from the burden of unwanted children, and for allowing sexual experimentation of both sexes outside of marriage without the probability of conception, became fully evident during the later 1960s and early 1970s. The **Family Planning Act** of 1969 was a significant example of the growing permissiveness discussed elsewhere in this book, facilitating as it did access to free contraception. The pill became the most commonly used form of contraception among both married and 'cohabiting' women. Another commonly used method was the condom, and a number of other devices were also used by women. Some couples still practised the withdrawal method. However, during the late twentieth and early twenty-first centuries, Britain continued to manifest one of the highest rates of teenage pregnancy in Western Europe, leading to the conclusion that sexual knowledge about contraception was either poorly promoted, wilfully ignored, or both.

COUNCIL ESTATES Council estates were comprised of public housing, the accommodation lived in by millions of Britons who could not afford home ownership. The clearance of slum housing and the relocation of the poor to new housing estates was begun by a number of local councils during the Victorian period. In London, for example, the London County Council cleared a number of terrible slums during the 1890s, not least 'the Nichol' in the East End of London, adjacent to the Whitechapel haunts of Jack the Ripper, who in his ghastly way had publicised the moral degradation of slum districts. And the Edwardian beginnings of town and country planning legislation also introduced further public housing schemes. The first Act that created council estates across Britain, however, was the **Housing Act** of 1919, championed by Christopher **Addison**, who by 1923 was disappointed with the impact of expenditure cuts on council housing and on reconstruction more generally. Further Acts followed between the wars. The 1920s and the 1930s witnessed the birth and expansion of mass council housing in Britain: 1.5 million council dwellings were built during this period. Some of them were blocks of flats in town and city centres, others were in villages, but the majority were built in the suburbs of existing towns and cities, where land was cheaper. Some were absolutely enormous. To take some examples, Dagenham in Essex, just east of London, became home to one of the largest council estates constructed between the wars. Built by the London County Council between 1921 and 1934, the estate housed 110,000 people in 25,000 dwellings by the end of the 1930s. In common with other council estates, Dagenham was designed to relieve overcrowding in the capital city, as were other peripheral council housing developments. And, like Wythenshawe in Manchester and Hall Green in Birmingham, Dagenham was a cottage estate, with small single-family dwellings in the form of houses with gardens. Dagenham was sustained economically between the wars by the introduction of a Ford motor manufacturing plant, and was thus representative of the new working-class suburbia and also the new industries that comprised a large part of that landscape which J. B. Priestley labelled 'the third England'. It was neither the old England of the countryside nor the industrial England of nineteenth-century staple industries and rigid streets of terraced housing. Nor was Dagenham a suburban graveyard. It gave rise to the Dagenham Girl Piper's Band, numerous amateur football teams, and the professional football club Dagenham and Redbridge FC. A number of famous people grew up there, including the comedian Dudley Moore and the pop singer Sandie Shaw. Its social and community life from the 1920s to the 1950s is discussed by Peter Willmott in *The Evolution of a Community* (1963). During the 1990s, the nearby **edge city** development of Thurrock provided a convenient major new shopping centre and leisure opportunities for the residents of Dagenham.

Wythenshawe in Manchester, a large interwar council estate associated with the reforming zeal and philanthropy of Ernest and Shena **Simon**, is also worthy of comment. Designed by Barry Parker, who had been a leading architect in Letchworth Garden City in Hertfordshire, the estate accommodated over 30,000 people by 1939 and illustrated both the close connections between Edwardian garden cities and garden suburbs and the design and planning of many council estates between the wars.

During the Second World War council house construction came to a halt as spending priorities by government were redirected. The impact of the Blitz exacerbated the housing shortage in the large cities. Once the war ended, one solution to the housing crisis was a renewal of the government subsidy for local councils, inherited from the interwar legislation for a new generation of council housing. The other major solution was a programme of planned new towns. It is now well known that the minister for health and housing, Aneurin Bevan, oversaw a slower rate of housing construction than the public would have preferred before 1951, and during the 1950s the Conservative governments achieved impressive levels of house building, albeit often at the cost of quality over quantity. The construction of high-rise tower blocks under both Conservative and Labour governments had been one method of meeting housing demand. They were among the most powerful symbols of modern architecture, and of its unpopularity. The towers on the Red Road estate in Glasgow, completed in the late 1960s, were scheduled for demolition during the early twenty-first century.

Council housing continued to be subsidised by both Labour and Conservative administrations throughout the 1960s and 1970s. At its peak, council housing was lived in by over 30 per cent of households. But by the end of the 1990s less than a quarter of the population rented from local authorities or housing associations. Hence social historians of housing have treated the years from the 1920s to the 1970s as a prolonged era of collective housing provision for the working classes. The Conservative **Housing Act** of 1980 terminated this era of 'collective' housing provision. The right to buy council accommodation was radically extended, and semi-independent charitable housing associations grew to meet the demand for what was increasingly renamed 'social housing'. Housing action trusts from 1988 were intended to provide tenants with greater levels of power within the context of social housing, although how far they did so is a moot point.

CRICKET Unlike the sports of football or rugby, cricket is associated with a county structure, but the big county grounds themselves are usually in large cities: Lords in London and Trent Bridge in Nottingham are examples. Cricket's governing body, the Middlesex Cricket Club (MCC), has been based at Lords since before 1900. Cricket was and continues to be played all over the world, mostly as a consequence of the British Empire: England, Australia, India, New Zealand, Pakistan, South Africa and the West Indies are all great cricketing nations, as demonstrated in the international test matches. Cricket is also played in other countries, sometimes where there are sizeable expatriate communities:

Kenya and Spain have cricket leagues, for example.

During the course of the last century, English international dominance in cricket declined as the colonies – later the countries of the Commonwealth – became increasingly adept at the game and keen to defeat their sporting alma mater. One of the first great controversies in English cricket came with the **bodyline** tour of South Africa during the early 1930s, when the English were accused of rough tactics in bowling. Later, the rebel cricket tours to South Africa during the 1980s associated leading English cricketers with a cynical self-interest in the face of the iniquitous apartheid regime. The rebel tours, in fact, signalled a new phase in the capitalisation and media amplification of the sport, which eventually led to the introduction of shorter games for the benefit of a television-viewing public. Yet although cricket still had the power to excite controversy, and while recent victories by the England side have received much media attention, its international prominence was not mirrored at the grassroots. County matches could draw over 10,000 spectators during the 1950s, but an attendance of 1,000 was more commonplace into the early twenty-first century.

CRIME In Britain in 1900 there were 312 murders. By the year 2000 the number had more than doubled, to 681. In 1900 the number of burglaries was 3,812, but one hundred years later the figure was 1.1 million. The number of thefts from the person had also risen considerably, from 63,600 in 1900 to over 2.3 million by the year 2000. On the surface this looks to be a very depressing increase in crime, but the picture is a complex one. First, the population had grown by over 20 million people – admittedly less rapidly than the crime rate – and more people meant more crime. Secondly, as the British people enjoyed increasing affluence there was more to steal: motor car theft, driving offences and other criminal activities involving motor cars grew considerably from the 1920s. More mobility and greater affluence contributed to the startling fact that since 1945 over half of all crimes have been car crimes. And during the postwar years the arrival of the television, the personal computer and particularly the mobile telephone added huge upward trends to the statistics of burglary and theft. There is a further problem with these ostensibly simple facts, however: much crime went unreported throughout the twentieth century, and that means that the real crime rate was much higher in both 1900 and 2000, but we cannot know exactly how much higher. Furthermore, many cases of domestic sexual assault in the home went unrecorded. Unfortunately, sadly, sexual crime appears to have increased considerably since the 1960s. The first refuge for women fleeing from abusive partners opened in West London in 1971, so the problem has been more openly discussed since. Pornographers and libertarians, conservatives and feminists, remain bitterly divided about the causes of reported sexual violence.

Which groups were more involved in criminal activity than others? This was and remains a difficult and controversial question to answer. Young people, particularly young men under the age of twenty-five, were disproportionately involved in petty theft, minor assault and some more violent crimes through the last century, and they still are. The related panics about juvenile delinquency following the Second World War and during the early 1970s were also mostly about the tendency of boys and young men to commit minor thefts and acts of violence. The working classes and immigrant minorities, furthermore, were often viewed by the tabloid newspapers as responsible for 'crime waves' of violence and varying degrees of burglary and theft. However, a great deal of middle-class white-collar crime, involving silent scams and fiddles, went unrecorded because the paper trail was non-existent or was covered up.

A further problem when comparing overall crime rates during the twentieth century is the changing definition of criminal activity. The aforementioned problem of domestic violence is a case in point, because this was not viewed as a criminal activity, unless it resulted in reported death or injury, until a Home Office circular of 1990. Abortion was a crime before 1967, but not following the act of that year. Betting and gambling is another good example. Before the **Betting and Gambling Act** of 1960 it was technically illegal to place a cash bet on a horse unless one was at the racecourse, and that criminalised thousands of punters who from 1961 were suddenly criminals no longer.

When seeking to explain rises in crime, social historians have certainly focused on economic decline in poorer areas and the culture of low expectations that contributed to crime as a perceived solution to poverty. Perhaps the demise of religious observance, furthermore, had created a more materialistic and godless society by 2000? The first proposition implies that the nature of the poorest was more criminogenic than that of the richest, but much wealthy crime went unreported. It also leads to a conclusion that perhaps atheists or secular humanists are less moral than those of a religious persuasion. But when, for example, one considers the appalling sexual abuses practised by some leading members of the Roman Catholic Church, which first came to light quite recently, and the terrible murders committed by professional doctors, it becomes clear that simple generalisations are usually unhelpful when attempting to explain the crime rates of twentieth-century Britain.

D

DECLINE Britain was the predominant global power in 1900, but could not claim to be so one hundred years later. The decline of the British Empire and the rise of foreign economic competition during the twentieth century were at the heart of British decline. So decline here means decolonisation and the relative demise in the global sphere of economic competition. In terms of economic troubles, we cannot say that the entire British economy declined, because it did not. In fact it continued to grow in macro-economic terms during the twentieth century, sometimes impressively, sometimes less so. However, in the years before the First World War international competition grew fiercer, and between the wars the problems in Britain's staple industries, that is, the leading sectors of nineteenth-century industrialisation, became painfully apparent. During the postwar years the staple industries continued to play an important role in the mixed economy, but the docks were in almost terminal decline by the 1950s and, during the 1970s and since, coal mining, shipbuilding and steel production were radically 'restructured'.

Britain was increasingly challenged by the growth of overseas competition. Before the First World War, the United States of America, Germany and other European countries had undermined Britain's pre-eminence in iron and steel production and in coal. Between the wars the rise of new industries – motor car production, light engineering, labour-saving devices and electrical goods – continued the pattern, while in the postwar years the growth of the European Economic Community (EEC) and of Japan and other Asian 'tiger economies' took their toll on British manufacturing. By the 1970s, rising unemployment, industrial disputes and the palpable difficulties of the nationalised industries compounded the image of Britain as 'the sick man of Europe'.

Historians have entertained various other explanation for economic decline: the fact that Britain was the first country to industrialise and the inevitable 'catch-up' of other countries; the failure of entrepreneurial culture among the middle classes; nationalisation and its subsidisation of inefficient labour-intensive industry; the problems of class and their effect on poor industrial relations and productivity; the early unwillingness to join the EEC; the ineptness of economic policy making by government, notably the stop–go economics of the 1950s and 1960s and the related failure of economic planning during the 1960s – all of which frustrated the modernisation of the British economy. A serious and balanced analysis of the nation's difficulties might incorporate all or some of these explanations. However, any analysis should also bear in mind that the British economy bounced back during the 1980s and 1990s. Both the tertiary, or service, sector and a smaller but nonetheless productive manufacturing sector were at the heart of this resurgence in Britain's fortunes.

'DECLINISM' British economic decline relative to other countries may be attributed to myriad causes, and the reality of the economic and imperial readjustment of Britain during the twentieth century has been harnessed to various ideological positions. Historians have demonstrated how economic decline in particular became a highly politicised concept during the postwar years. For example, Labour attacked the Conservatives for 'thirteen wasted years' in 1964, while Thatcherite conservatives during the 1980s were bitterly critical of the economic legacy of the welfare state

and of **nationalised** industries. Two unfortunate consequences of declinism were, firstly, to overemphasise and embed an unduly negative and pessimistic sense of national demise which, for some Conservative historians, reached its miserable apogee during the 1970s. A second danger was the simplistic present-mindedness during the 1980s of historians who explained decline as a failure of consensus politics until Mrs Thatcher came along to save Great Britain PLC.

DECOLONISATION Decolonisation refers to the break-up of the British Empire and the independence of the former subject nations, most of whom signed up to the Commonwealth, perhaps the world's most successful global geo-political village. Fifty countries, mostly in Africa and Asia, achieved independence, a fact that was at the heart of British global decline during the postwar years. In some cases the transition was violent, but for the most part it was orderly. The wider legacy of British and European imperialism, however, continues to be manifest across the former colonial territories. Other European countries, for example Belgium and France, underwent a painful dismantling of empire in the years after 1945.

Historians of Britain overseas view decolonisation as a major process of decline, a prolonged fall from global leadership as newer power blocs emerged during the Cold War, notably the USA and the USSR. Other important fields of enquiry concern the complex legacies for the former colonies themselves of decolonisation, both economic and political. From a Marxist perspective, decolonisation continued the exploitation and subjugation of previously colonised peoples within a new framework of British and European hegemony. More Conservative-minded historians, however, argue that the legacy of both the British Empire and decolonisation is nuanced, and that British investment and the heritage of democracy was no disaster for former colonies.

DEFENCE REVIEWS The defence reviews listed in the **Landmarks** section were responses to both Britain's changing position in the wider world and the constant requirement to assess and address the economic impacts of defence expenditure. In turn, defence expenditure had to address the real and potential threats to home security. A number of defence reviews were undertaken during the twentieth century, for example in the lead-up to the two world wars and during the era of the Cold War and of decolonisation. The last defence review of the twentieth century was *Options for Change*, a New Labour document, commissioned in 1997.

DE-INDUSTRIALISATION De-industrialisation describes the historical transition away from an economy based upon industrial manufacturing towards one evolving increasingly around the services, namely the tertiary sector. During the final third of the twentieth century the British economy rapidly de-industrialised as a consequence of both foreign competition and privatisation programmes that closed down 'uneconomic' manufacturing and mining in preference to growing service-sector employment. The environmental impact of de-industrialisation was nuanced: polluting coal mines and smokestack industries were greatly reduced in scale, yet the trend for cleaner and more mobile technologies also led to land-grab, as companies often sought to locate beyond the suburbs where land was cheaper. Hence de-industrialisation led to post-suburban growth or edge city-style expansion across Britain.

By 1999, 27 per cent of the British workforce was still engaged in industry, but the services accounted for over 70 per cent of all employment. When this is compared with the prominence of industrial labour at mid-century, this was indeed a process of de-industrialisation. However, more sophisticated economic historians also emphasise the continuing importance of manufacturing industries; the interdependence between the industrial and tertiary sectors; the complexity of the tertiary sector, both private and public; and the increased globalisation of a post-industrial economy.

DEMOBILISATION The two great demobilisations of military personnel into civilian life in twentieth-century Britain were those following the world wars. Both involved millions of servicemen and women, although demobilisation in the aftermath of the 1914–18 war has enjoyed more attention from historians than that of 1945. Key concerns for the demobilised airmen, sailors and soldiers were the availability of work, the reforging of relationships after long periods of separation, and a desire to return to normal as quickly as possible. Despite official concern that the numbers of returning demobilised ex-servicemen might outstrip the availability of employment and housing and thus cause social friction, no major discord resulted. Hence historians have focused on how the governments managed demobilisation, and on the economic and social impact of the return to civilian life of such large numbers of people of employable age. Feminist historians have looked at how far the demobilisation of millions of men was accompanied by a return to normal prewar expectations and experiences for women.

DENATIONALISATION Most of those industries nationalised between 1945 and 1951 remained under the auspices of the state until the Conservative governments of the 1980s and 1990s, although the government of Winston Churchill denationalised the road haulage industry and steel making in

1953. After 1980 the term privatisation was used to describe the denationalisation programme of the Thatcher and Major governments.

DEVOLUTION: SCOTTISH AND WELSH Devolution means the devolving of administrative and political power from the centre – Westminster in London – to quasi-independent authorities at local, regional and national level. The demands for home rule in Ireland during the later nineteenth and early twentieth centuries were initially demands for devolution, but became increasingly nationalistic. In Scotland and Wales, nationalist parties, the Scottish Nationalist Party (SNP) and Plaid Cymru respectively, were formed between the wars and established small and fragile platforms for devolved government. However, they remained marginal to British politics during the 1930s. During the postwar years Scotland and Wales created an increased momentum for devolved government, and long-held intra-national tensions and resentments in Britain became more visible, bound up as they were with Celtic national identity versus an Anglo-Saxon-dominated Britishness.

Beyond political accounts of devolution, social and cultural historians emphasise cultural influences that impacted on a sense of Scottishness and Welshness. Resentment at the Act of Union with England had long simmered in Scotland. Culturally a sense of both Scots and Welsh nationalism owed much to sports and religion. Some memorable performances by the Scots and Welsh rugby and football teams and some miserable defeats must have played their part in creating a glow of pride or in nursing resentment at the English, who after all had a larger sporting population. The independence of the **Church of Scotland** and the prominence of **Welsh disestablishment** from the Church of England by the 1920s were quite significant

moments in the promotion of separate national identities. Religious nonconformity in Wales, for example, led to higher levels of abstinence and dry Sundays in many parts of the country. Language, too, was at the heart of a sense of separateness from England. Wales remained a bilingual country, and the calls for Welsh-language programming on the BBC, and for a Welsh television channel equivalent of Channel 4 in the 1980s, were expressions of a related desire to protect and spread the language while expanding a sense of Welsh identity.

During the postwar period, both Plaid Cymru and the SNP scored a number of significant by-election victories. However, when the opportunity came in 1978 to vote for a devolved national assembly in Scotland, the country failed to reach the 40 per cent mark required. In Wales, the referendum of 1979 was a resounding rejection of the idea of devolved government: more than one in three of those who bothered to turn out voted against. Yet the Labour Party persisted in appeasing its more nationalistically motivated MPs from Scotland and Wales, and in 1997 both the Scots and the Welsh voted in referenda for separate assemblies. These were introduced in 1999 as a consequence of the Scotland Act and the **Government of Wales Act** the previous year.

DIVORCE The formal separation and termination of a married couple, divorce was by no means new to the twentieth century, but the divorce rate grew quite substantially after 1900, dipping only during the 1930s and 1950s. In 1900 there were fewer than a thousand petitions for divorce per year in England, Scotland and Wales combined. By the mid-1990s, however, this had risen to over 170,000 formal marriage separations every year.

Rising numbers of women petitioning for divorce was a key characteristic of the trend during the latter decades of the twentieth century. About half of the petitions issued for divorce were by husbands and half by wives during the Edwardian years, and the picture had not altered dramatically by the 1950s. From the 1970s onwards, however, over 70 per cent of petitions were initiated by women. This was a consequence of the Divorce Act of 1969, which made divorces less costly and easier to obtain.

Reasons for growing divorce rates were many, and often charged with emotional and moral arguments. Increasing affluence facilitated the making of a new life following the break-up. This is evident in the fact that, before the 1969 Act, the middle classes had higher rates of divorce than the working classes. The almost simultaneous introduction of equal-pay legislation also assisted women who were in paid work, and thus their ability to gain freedom from an unhappy marriage. More widely, the impact of feminism and of a discourse of women's rights gave many women the self-confidence to leave their erstwhile spouse. Feminist historians view the growing number of divorces initiated by women as evidence of both their increasing self-confidence and their liberation from unhappy relationships. Other factors contributing to rising rates of separation include the break-up of the working-class extended family. Often romanticized by middle-class social investigators as the bedrock of stability in poorer housing areas, the multi-generational localised family was undermined by the migration of younger households to council estates or into home ownership engendered by upward social mobility. Subsequently, less pressure was applied from the elders to 'make the marriage work for the sake of the children' than might have occurred had the young family stayed closer to the matriarchy and patriarchy of the traditional working-class housing areas. Moving

home itself, however, often threw young married couples closer together, sometimes strengthening but oftentimes exposing problems in their relationship. Such points were made by the sociologist Ronald Fletcher in *The Family and Marriage in Modern Britain* (1974) and in Michael Young and Peter Willmott's *The Symmetrical Family* (1973). Yet it should be remembered that every year hundreds of thousands of people continued to walk up the aisle or between the municipal chairs of a registry office, and not all were first-time married couples. Despite the rising numbers of cohabiting couples, marriage remained a popular institution.

DOCKS AND DOCKLANDS The docks in the major port cities of Britain – notably Belfast, Bristol, Cardiff, Liverpool, London and Glasgow, although there were many smaller docks around the British coast – were the major conduits for both imports and the exports upon which British manufacturing industry was so dependent. The existence of large docks or series of docks in a city provided unskilled employment for hundreds or even thousands of people. The types of jobs available, however, were casual – that is, dependent on trade cycles and the weather. The East End of London was adjacent to a massive series of docks, a fundamental explanatory factor in the high levels of petty crime and vice with which the area was associated by the beginning of the twentieth century.

Social historians have focused upon the legacy of lowly paid and often casual labour at the docks for the poorer sections of the working classes. Although poverty blighted such areas, the docks were also one of the major sectors from the 1880s of unskilled new unionism, a movement that contributed from 1900 to the rise of the Labour Party. They also remained at the heart of many industrial relations problems that beset British industry. During the

Edwardian years and between 1919 and 1926, the dockworkers cooperated with the Triple Alliance of miners, transport workers and railway workers. In the postwar years a number of docks strikes affected both Conservative and Labour governments, but the proverbial writing was on the wall for the docks industry. As a consequence of air freight, but more generally of de-industrialisation, the docks declined rapidly during the postwar years. London's docklands were already in decline in 1965 when their cranes were lowered as a mark of respect for the passing cortege of Winston Churchill. Today, only a few of the cranes remain. They are historical artefacts, a testament to the decline of the docklands and their resurrection as a consequence of urban regeneration policies pursued since the 1980s. A similar pattern of decline and regeneration was centred in the docklands of other port cities. In Liverpool, for example, the Albert Docks were regenerated from the 1990s, and now house professionals living in lofts and flats, as well as restaurants, shops and tourist attractions. These last include, as does Canary Wharf in London, a museum to the heritage of the once-busy docks, providing a historical perspective on their role in local social and economic life. The changing class structure of docklands during the 1980s and 1990s, however, often caused anger among existing residents, who felt squeezed out by rising prices and the *embourgeoisement* of their once proletarian, if deprived, neighbourhoods. Today, the urban watersides are no longer the hubs of an *entrepôt* nation but the site of recreational and residential amenities. Liverpool, the City of Culture in 2008, proudly displayed its dockland redevelopments to the visiting tourists. Economic historians are increasingly focusing upon the transition of the docks over the twentieth century, emphasising their fate within the decline of British sea power and the rise of invisible exports.

DOCUMENTARY FILM MOVEMENT From its origins at the beginning of the twentieth century, documentary film was concerned with the details, issues, practices and problems of real life. During the First World War, film makers in Britain and in other nations made propaganda films on behalf of the government and the military. Intended to raise morale, they were heavily censored by the government, along with newsreel footage of the war. Between the wars, however, the British documentary film movement established itself as generally left-leaning, progressive, and at the cutting edge of film making. During the 1930s John Grierson promoted and coordinated documentary film making at the Empire Marketing Board and the **GPO Film Unit**, giving rise to some of the finest documentaries of the twentieth century. Leading film makers included Humphrey Jennings and Harry Watt. Following the outbreak of the Second World War in 1939, the GPO Film Unit was placed under the control of the Ministry of Information and renamed the **Crown Film Unit**. Morale-boosting and moving documentaries were made about the Blitz and the fighting, but so too were coded films about the need for postwar reforms, particularly, in the films of Jennings and Paul Rotha.

During the 1950s, documentary film making diffused into the rapidly expanding medium of television. Many important documentary documentaries were made, including the docu-drama *Cathy Come Home* in 1966. *Panorama* became a major BBC series for in-depth documentary analysis of news items, while ITV promoted *World in Action*. A major moment in the evolution of human interest documentaries came with BBC television's *The Family*, in the so-called fly on the wall format, broadcast in 1974, which was a major influence on subsequent documentary film making for TV.

DREADNOUGHT PROGRAMME A new superior generation of warship introduced by the defence review during the government of H. H. Asquith, the Dreadnoughts were really brought into existence as a consequence of the build up in imperialism in Europe that originally began with the scramble for Africa during the 1870s. Internal tensions within Europe were heightened by the rise of German industrial might and its military presence abroad. The unification of Germany in 1871 had also led to the rise of the German Navy, a development that posed problems for Britain and France and other countries with an extensive overseas empire. At the heart of the Anglo-German naval race before the First World War, the new Dreadnoughts made the previous fleet appear almost obsolescent and played an important role in the war at sea from 1914 to 1918.

E

EALING COMEDIES The Ealing comedies generated much laughter for film-goers in austerity Britain, and starred aspiring British actors and actresses of the 1940s and 1950s. Some went on to become household names, notably Sir Alec Guinness, while Thora Hird and Jack Warner made their reputations on television. Today, Ealing comedies are a rich source for social historians. For example, the first film, *Hue and Cry* (1946), provides an evocative atmosphere of bombed-out London. The best-known Ealing comedies, such as *Passport to Pimlico* (1949), *The Lavender Hill Mob* (1951) and *The Ladykillers*

(1955), were also based in London. However, *The Titfield Thunderbolt* (1952) was a rural comedy, while *The Magnet* (1950) and *The Man in the White Suit* (1951) were set in the industrial North-West of England. Humorous representations of authority figures, notably the police force, and amusing interactions between the often snobbish middle-class characters and diffident or rude working-class figures were recurring themes in Ealing comedies. *The Magnet* also has some tantalising glimpses of the wealthy middle-class suburbs of Birkenhead and of the bomb sites in central Liverpool, a port city heavily blitzed in 1940–41. The film features a Chinese Liverpudlian boy and his mother living in a tenement block, a reminder of the presence of Chinese people in the poorest areas of British cities at mid-century. Most Ealing comedies, as with most British films of the 1940s and 1950s, were in black and white, but *The Ladykillers*, the last of the series, was in colour.

EAST END OF LONDON Situated to the east of the centre of the capital city, and adjacent to the City of London, the East End is probably the most famous local district in England. Many people will know of it from the fictional and somewhat ridiculous representation of Walford and its cockney inhabitants in the BBC television soap opera *EastEnders*, begun in 1985. 'East Enders' are portrayed as the relatives of the old 'pearly kings and queens' and of the market traders who worked the streets before the 1960s. They are depicted as community-minded, generous-hearted, given to drinking, gambling and, in some cases, crime, and fiercely proud of their family and their neighbourhood (when they are not running away from them, that is). The very fact of the soap opera and its success, however, was based upon the enduring power of a wide range of facts, images and myths. They were derived from gloomy gas-lit streets associated with the Jack the Ripper atrocities during the 1880s and the bawdy or mawkish music hall acts of the Victorian and Edwardian years that portrayed East End 'characters'. But different intelligence about the East End was available to a more academic audience. Social investigation during the 1880s and 1890s uncovered appalling poverty generated by structural underemployment because of the high incidence of casual labour at the docks. During the 1880s and 1890s, moreover, the immigration of Jews into the East End greatly increased, bringing about one of the first distinctively Jewish areas of Britain in Bethnal Green and Whitechapel, but also engendering anti-Semitism.

Between the wars the East End became associated with communist politics. It was one of the few areas in Southern England where the Communist Party of Great Britain gained power in both local and national politics. At the other end of the political spectrum, the British Unions of Fascists targeted the Jews living in the East End during the Great Depression in an attempt to impress the resentful poor, some of whom were suffering because of the problems in the docks. However, the economic problems of the East End were temporarily suspended by the Second World War. During the Blitz, the East End suffered acutely, more so than other areas that were subjected to aerial bombardment, but the collective experience of aerial bombardment of East Londoners was a source of local pride, and admired by many elsewhere. The reasons for the blitzing of East London were simple: the docks were at the heart of the wartime distribution of essential resources. The high population density and numerous industries also added to its value as a target for death and destruction. Most East Enders, however, saw either military service or essential war work. The Bethnal Green Tube Disaster of 1943, unfortunately, was a tragic and inauspicious episode.

The demise of the docks during the postwar period contributed to the continuing problems of East London. The face of the East End, as of many other areas of the capital city, was changing as a consequence of reconstruction policies. Large tower blocks were built there during the 1950s and 1960s, and many slums were cleared. During the later 1940s and in subsequent decades, many white Londoners moved out to suburban council estates and new towns. Socially, a growing influx of mostly Asian migrants, particularly from Pakistan during the 1960s and increasingly from the Sylhet region of Bangladesh, changed the ethnic composition of the area. Asian in-migration coincided with continuing Jewish out-migration to the affluent suburbs of North London. Consequently, the East End, particularly Bethnal Green and Whitechapel, remained poorer than other parts of the capital city, but it never lacked the ethnic vitality that had characterised the area for over a hundred years.

ECONOMIC PLANNING Like the Keynesians, economic planners believed in government intervention in the economy. In their view, however, demand management alone was insufficient, and the mixed economy was in need of more rational direction from above. One version of this approach, influenced by French policies, was known as indicative planning. This involved both the setting of growth targets agreed between unions, employers and government and the removal of 'restrictive practices' by both sides of industry. Planning attracted cross-party support and was particularly influential during the late 1950s and the 1960s. The Conservative governments during the early 1960s attempted a more effective management of the economy through the mechanism of the National

Economic Development Council (NEDC). The National Plan produced by George Brown in Harold Wilson's first government was not a success, and was abandoned partly as a consequence of its own limitations but also because of the financial exigencies faced by the second Wilson government. Economic historians mostly view economic planning as a failure. From the left it has been seen as a missed opportunity for a more modernized and coordinated economy, while neo-Liberal historians argue that planning thwarted enterprise and innovation and was a poor substitute for the free market.

EDGE CITIES During the 1980s and 1990s two major forms of urban development changed the face of large parts of Britain. One was urban regeneration in the depressed areas of established towns and cities. The other was the 'edge city', a term made popular by the American writer Joel Garreau during the early 1990s. When applied to Britain, the term describes the growth of new out-of-town retail outlets, industrial estates, leisure facilities and low-rise housing developments on the suburban edges of existing towns and cities. This was essentially 'post-suburban' urbanisation during the final twenty years of the last century. The large housing estate of Lower Earley, between Reading and Wokingham in Berkshire, with its Asda superstore, office parks and recreational facilities at Winnersh Triangle, was typical of English edge-city-style development. The fact that it grew up along the M4 corridor linking London with South Wales was also typical of the effect on urban expansion of new road building or the upgrading of arterial routes. Elsewhere in Britain, new out-of-town shopping centres such as Meadow Hall near Sheffield, Thurrock near East London, or Trafford Park near Manchester, completed during the 1990s, stimulated further suburban development

on the edges of towns. Each of those three centres was adjacent to a major motorway intersection in order to increase catchments from further afield. From the perspective of many environmental and urban historians, **edge cities** were a further extension of urbanisation into the countryside, with deleterious ecological consequences. Social historians, however, have argued that they were an additional expression of urban democracy, bringing employment, leisure and retail facilities closer to households living in the outer suburbs.

EDUCATION Compulsory mass education began with the Education Act of 1870, which introduced local board schools across the country. Further significant education acts followed during the Edwardian period, placing the board schools under local authority control, raising the school leaving age, and improving the nutritional and health standards of millions of working-class boys and girls. The latter directives stemmed from the fact that, following the Boer War and during the years of the Conservative and New Liberal governments, the education of the working classes was linked to the problems of national efficiency. In 1918 the **Education Act** of H. A. L. Fisher strengthened the auxiliary provision of medical services and introduced nursery schools. However, the most significant restructuring of education was brought about by R. A. Butler's Education Act of 1944. It raised the school leaving age to fifteen and introduced the system of primary, secondary and further educational stages. At secondary level, from ages eleven to fifteen, the tripartite principal was clear in the grammar, technical and secondary modern schools. Grammar schools were opened up to non-fee-paying students, while the provision of the latter two types of school led to a major schools-building programme and the adaptation of existing school buildings.

The notion enshrined in Butler's Act was that education should be appropriate to ability as indicated in aptitude tests, notably the Eleven Plus exam that sifted children into grammar school or relegated them into the secondary moderns. This rationale came under considerable attack and scrutiny during the 1950s and 1960s by educationalists who favoured a more egalitarian and less hierarchical system of educational provision known as the **comprehensive** school system. The first comprehensive was opened in South London in 1954, and, following the initiatives by Anthony Crosland during the mid-1960s, the comprehensive system was rolled out across Britain throughout the later 1960s and the 1970s. The Eleven Plus was mostly abolished, and streaming was subtly downplayed within the comprehensives. By 1980 about three-quarters of all secondary schools were comprehensives. However, many Conservative local authorities reacted strongly against what they saw as socialist social engineering, claiming that the brightest children were being held back by those of lesser intelligence. This was a major theme of the so-called black papers on education during the 1970s. Many middle-class parents who could afford it put their offspring into private schools. Two Conservative **Education Acts**, in 1979 and 1980, repealed the statutory obligation for schools to become comprehensives. Schools were enabled to opt out of local educational authority control and become funded as self-run entities by the head and the board of governors. The 1988 Education Act introduced the National Curriculum and changed the examination system at age sixteen.

Access to higher education was also democratised during the twentieth century. Small but growing numbers of working-class people entered Oxford, Cambridge and the Victorian and Edwardian universities as a consequence of grammar school education after 1945, leading to the need for more university places, and hence more universities. The report by Lord Robbins of 1963 called for investment in a programme of new universities, and six were initiated by the Conservative government. Britain's lagging performance in technical education was addressed by the creation of 'polytechnics' to provide for skilled qualifications. Many of these polytechnics, along with some colleges of higher education, were converted into the 'new universities' of the 1990s, following the **Further and Higher Education Act** in 1992 which created over sixty new universities in often outdated buildings with insufficient resources and inadequate managements. Nonetheless, after a painful period of birth and infancy, many had begun to perform well in the university league tables. In sum, education was extended, modernised and democratised during the twentieth century. Britain became a more intelligent and literate country as the century developed, but education did little to undermine the class system.

An important field of the history of education exists in Britain, focusing upon the expansion of schooling and its consequences; the role of leading or minor educationalists and social reformers; and the differential educations between middle-class and working-class, black and white, girls and boys. Social historians have also examined the complicated contribution of secondary and higher education to the upward social mobility of working-class students and the reasons for working-class underachievement. In this they often shared common interests with the sociology of education pioneered during the 1950s and 1960s by Olive **Banks** and other postwar social scientists.

ENVIRONMENTALISM Concern about the impact of industrialisation and urbanisation on the natural environment has a long history. Many leading intellectuals of the Victorian and Edwardian years warned of the destructive onward march of philistine capitalism over the architectural glories and natural beauties of Britain. It is often forgotten, furthermore, that an environmental consciousness informed the professions of architecture and town and country planning: worries over the sprawl of suburbs into the countryside and the extension of railways and roads across areas of outstanding natural beauty had produced some significant pieces of restrictive legislation before 1950. A further problem was that of coal-fired factories and power-stations and the use of coal in home fires. This had generated 'smog', a mixture of smoke and fog, which killed over 4,000 people in Britain, mostly in London, during the early 1950s. **The Clean Air Act** of 1956, the **Town and Country Planning Acts** of 1946 and 1947, and the Nature Conservancy apparatus were all significant evidence of an environmental consciousness before the rise of green politics during the 1960s and 1970s. However, during those two decades a number of movements coalesced to produce what is now known as the green movement. Significant momentum was given by the publication in the United States of America of Rachel Carson's *Silent Spring* (1962), which warned of the effects of pesticides and chemicals on the earth's ecology. Europeans took their cue from this and other texts in the American ecological movement. In 1971 Friends of the Earth was formed in Britain. And much of the momentum for a more proactive environmentalism was located in Northern Europe, notably in the person of Petra Kelly, a German ecologist and founder of green politics in that country. In Britain, the forerunner of the Green Party was the People's Party, formed in 1973. The 'Greens', as they became collectively known, had very little success at general elections in Britain: there were no Green MPs in the House of Commons before 2000. However, a number of Green members of the European parliament were elected from Britain from the 1990s onwards.

EUROPE: THE EUROPEAN ECONOMIC COMMUNITY AND THE EUROPEAN UNION
In the aftermath of the Second World War, attempts to build a stronger sense of unity in Western Europe culminated in March 1957 in the **Treaties of Rome**, which established the European Economic Community, or 'Common Market'. Both ambivalence and also downright hostility towards the EEC were common sentiments in Britain, and the **European Free Trade Association**, formed in November 1959, was anticipated to become an alternative vehicle for British influence and economic growth in Europe. As the EEC began to produce higher rates of economic growth among its member states, however, the position changed. An application by Harold Macmillan in August 1961 for Britain to join was vetoed by President de Gaulle, who also rejected an application made by Harold Wilson in May 1967. Against strong opposition in his party, and also within the Labour Party, Edward Heath successfully took Britain into the EEC in January 1973. Denmark and Ireland joined at the same time. Entry into the Common Market was preceded by a process of decimalisation of sterling. Public opinion did not seem at all favourable towards the new currency system, or to membership of the EEC, and Labour promised a referendum on the issue of membership if it won the forthcoming general election. But in June 1975 over two-thirds of those who voted in the referendum opted to stay within the EEC. Many on the left of the Labour Party, and many more in the Conservative Party, were disappointed at the result.

Opposition to the EEC and the issue of British sovereignty rumbled on throughout the later 1970s and 1980s, and came to a head during the debates over the **Treaty of Maastricht** in 1990–91. The aim of the Maastricht settlement was to extend the EEC into a social as well as an economic entity called the European Union, and to promote a common notion of citizenship and citizens' rights for all members. Despite strong misgivings about the loss of British sovereign powers, articulated in her **Bruges speech** in 1988, Margaret Thatcher acceded to the treaty. During those debates, and in their wake, anti-European sentiment bubbled up more strongly than before, causing a major rift in the Conservative Party between a vocal Eurosceptic wing and those who were in favour of further EU participation. Anti-European Union political parties were formed in 1993, namely the **United Kingdom Independence Party** (UKIP) and the **Referendum Party**; the latter party was terminated in 1997. UKIP polled 7 per cent of votes in the 1999 European elections and 16 per cent in 2004, beating the Liberal Party into fourth place, and gaining twelve MEPs. How far this could be viewed as an endorsement of a British exit strategy from the EU is a matter for debate. Furthermore, anti-European parties are basically single-issue organisations, and this may count against them in general elections to the British parliament, when the electorate's mind is concerned not only with EU membership but also with a host of other economic and political issues.

F

FABIANISM AND THE FABIAN SOCIETY The Fabian Society was a progressive, reformist and gradualist socialist organisation formed in Britain in 1884. Labour historians have extensively researched the ideological origins of Fabianism, its contribution to the reformist character of the Labour Party, and its role in the formulation of socialist policy. Leading members were mostly middle class, and included Beatrice and Sidney Webb, the writer H. G. Wells, the philosopher and poet Edward Carpenter, and the Irish playwright George Bernard Shaw. As with so many comfortably-off metropolitan middle-class socialists, many early individual members of the Fabian Society had little experiential knowledge of the working classes. Yet Fabians were hugely influential on the character of the early Labour Party, reminding us that Labour was never solely the party of the working classes. In 1918 Sidney Webb was instrumental in drafting Labour's constitution. His wife Beatrice soon became a caustic critic of the Labour leader Ramsay MacDonald, possibly because her expectations far exceeded what the Labour Party was able to deliver in government during the 1920s. She greatly admired Herbert Morrison, however, for his electoral successes in London and his commitment to municipal socialism. The Webbs, along with other Fabians, also expressed admiration for Stalin, wilfully underestimating his capacity for oppression, while balefully accepting his propaganda about Russian economic growth and modernisation. All Labour prime ministers have been members of the Fabian Society, proving that it was ultimately a broad church. The Fabian Society published a continuing series of pamphlets during the twentieth century – it still does – and remained a research unit committed to gaining information for public policy.

FASCISM Experts on fascism and its history emphasise the requirement to define fascism as closely as possible, or at least to provide a template by which an individual, group or party can be labelled 'fascist'. Fascism as a political creed is anti-capitalist, anti-democratic, anti-socialist, anti-communist, anti-trade union, anti-Semitic, racist, nationalistic and mostly anti-religious. An ideal-type fascist state is totalitarian because the state controls all aspects of social, cultural, economic and political life. It privileges the nation and country, and exhorts romantic myths of blood and soil over such sectional categories as class and gender. Religion is replaced by the iconography and apparatus of a dominant fascist party in which the people worship dictator and nation. Immigrants and ethnic minorities of colour are deemed inferior and are to be repatriated, enslaved or exterminated. The economy is operated on the basis of state-controlled cartels wherein business interests and workers' needs are subordinated to the demands of the nation-state. The media, unsurprisingly, is a state monopoly. The totalitarian aspects of fascist regimes such as Nazi Germany and fascist Italy met such a template to varying degrees, but also bore some strong semblance to communist regimes. In that sense, the communist ex-leaders of East Germany were more 'fascist' than General Franco of Spain. The largest fascist party in Britain was the British Union of Fascists (BUF), led by Sir Oswald Mosley from 1932 to 1940. Mosley's dream of a totalitarian Britain forged in the heat of reactionary revolt failed miserably, proof of the profound anti-extremism of the majority of British people and unwitting testimony of Mosley's misreading of his country's values. Emulating anti-Jewish rhetoric was not popular with most, but it did appeal to some, notably middle-class traders and businessmen resentful of what they saw as Jewish-run big businesses above them and socialist and communist trade unions below. Some working-class groups in the poorest areas of the big cities,

for example the East End of London, also succumbed to Mosley's message. But an increasing association with violence and street marches alienated such high-level support, and the Cable Street disturbances in East London led to the **Public Order Act 1936**, which prohibited the wearing of paramilitary uniforms in public demonstrations. Partly because of this, but also because of the improving economy, the BUF waned from 1936. It is also pertinent to note that the British people remained mostly wedded to constitutional politics during the difficult years of the slump and the Great Depression, and viewed extremists with suspicion.

During the postwar years, Oswald Mosley's Union Movement, the League of Empire Loyalists, the British National Party, the National Front and other fascist groups remained marginal to British mainstream politics. Nonetheless, historians of fascism point to the continuing underbelly of racism and fascism in Britain. They explore the contexts for the emergence of fascism during times of economic crisis or social change in poorer city areas, and explain the ideological attractions of fascism for small sections of the working and the middle classes.

FASHION (CLOTHING) Trends in fashion changed repeatedly during the twentieth century, and were influenced by both domestic and overseas designers. Historians of fashion focus upon the skills and ingenuity of key designers, the gendered nature of clothing, the *zeitgeist* of certain fashions, for example the mini-skirt of the 1960s, and the shared taste cultures that were reflected by fashion. Underpinning the individual clothing choices of people was mass production: the British laid the basis for mass modern fashion with the industrial revolution in textiles manufacturing during the nineteenth century, while the Americans invented the sewing machine and applied more sophisticated mass-production techniques to fashion in the early twentieth. The rise of the cinema between the wars also influenced fashion trends. In his *English Journey* (1934), J. B. Priestley made his famously patronising statement about 'factory girls looking like actresses.'

Some of the most famous fashion styles of the twentieth century in Britain unwittingly proved that hemlines rose and fell in quick succession; the fashion for long or short hair was similarly changeable. The late Victorian and Edwardian bustles were followed during the 1920s by the shorter flat-fronted skirts above the knee and the 'bob' hairstyle. The chic Parisian New Look of the 1950s followed the 'make-do-and-mend' era of austerity, while the mass adoption of jeans and the mini-skirt during the 1960s was a manifestation of the rise of youth culture and the teenager, as were the various styles of dress that accompanied rock music – the natty suits of the early Beatles and the Mods, for example, or long hair and jeans. During the 1970, fashion reacted to the trends of the previous decade: mini-skirts gave way to the longer mid- and maxi-skirts. And tight, straight, angular punk fashions offered an angrily mannered rebuff to the lingering hippie styles born of the late 1960s counter-culture.

A growing range of magazines and newspaper items on fashion alerted the reading public to what was *à la mode* that season or year. Affluence and consumerism between the wars, and particularly from the mid-1950s, expanded the market for fashions. From department stores to boutiques, and by the 1990s the superstore, outlets reflected the varying levels of income that people could spend on looking good. Fashion was also beneficial to the image of Britain, particularly its capital city. Although Britain no longer exported textiles in any volume, it could and did export style. London Fashion Week began in 1959, and by the 1990s London had risen to challenge, if not to displace, Paris and New York as a leading centre of innovation in clothing, make-up and hair styling. Mary Quant, Vivienne Westwood and other prominent designers all played their part in establishing London as a cool, cutting-edge city. Little wonder, then, that during the 1960s Twiggy became so iconic, as did Kate Moss during the 1990s. Twiggy was a working-class girl who looked great in the latest styles, as did many other fashionable women of the time, such as the singer Sandie Shaw. Both Twiggy and Shaw were identified with the swinging London of the 1960s. More recently, Moss is closely associated with 'the London look'. Famous models evidenced the *cachet* attached to British fashion, but they also personified something else that was compelling: the notion that fashion was democratic. For both Twiggy and Moss, style was less to do with looking good in ridiculously exclusive clothes and much more about looking good in the main fashions on the street. Although most of the influential styles began as *haute couture* experiments, they went fully on-trend when millions of people started to wear them.

FEMINISM Feminism is defined by the advocacy of women's rights and of sexual equality with men. Modern feminism in Britain took shape during the Victorian period and flourished during the campaigns for women's suffrage. Feminist historians are increasingly exploring how far, if at all, feminism declined in significance between the attainment of the vote and the rise of 'second wave' feminism during the 1960s. Between the 1920s and the 1960s, feminism was also connected with pacifism, communism, and continuing struggles for improved access to pay and conditions in spheres of employment.

Elements of a feminist consciousness can also be identified in diaries, memoirs, autobiographies, novels and other testimonies of sexual and personal lives.

Certainly feminism gained a new and powerful momentum during the 1960s and 1970s, contributing towards important legislation over equal pay, but perhaps more significantly creating a powerful discourse of social, sexual and legal rights for the latter twentieth century. Among some key texts by feminist academics was Ann Oakley's *Housewife: High Value, Low Cost* (1974), which emphasised the extent to which women's roles in society were traditionally characterised by financial dependency and an expectation that economically productive tasks were the primary preserve of men. The very role of 'housewife' itself overdefined a woman's place in society. Juliet Mitchell's *Women's Estate* (1971) was an early text in radical feminism, inspired by Marxism and revolutionary in nature. Mitchell was an editor of *New Left Review*. Revolutionary feminism was adopted by many black women and others from ethnic minorities who saw themselves as disadvantaged both by their skin colour and by class and gender. Perhaps the best-known feminist text of all was *The Female Eunuch*, by Germaine **Greer** (1971), deploring the ways in which women were subordinated and held back by patriarchy, or male-dominated society. Today, terms such as 'post-feminism' and 'new feminism' may unwittingly reveal that feminism is less dynamic and novel than it was, although women have by no means achieved full equality with men.

FREE TRADE The era of free trade was initiated by the abolition of the protectionist Corn Laws in 1846 and terminated by the introduction of imperial tariffs under the banner of **imperial preference** in 1932. Free trade was dominated by the notion of laissez-faire or minimum government intervention in the workings of the market. The issue of free trade versus tariff reform caused an ongoing rift in the Conservative Party from 1903 until the early 1930s.

G

GENERAL ELECTIONS General elections were held in twentieth-century Britain on twenty-six occasions to decide which of the three main parties was to be in government. Before the Representation of the People Act in 1918 general elections lasted more than one day. Following the decline of the Liberal Party after the First World War the Conservative and Labour parties were the two most significant forces in contention. Communist, fascist, nationalist and a host of other minor political parties and single-interest groups were formed to fight general elections. Individually and *en masse*, however, they failed to break the two-party dominance which persisted strongly throughout the twentieth century. In 1931 and 1935 the usual pattern of general elections was altered by the election of the National Governments, Conservative-dominated coalitions with which the majority of Labour MPs felt ill at ease. General elections were cancelled during the world wars.

Prime ministers call general elections. Unlike other countries, where there are fixed-term parliaments and thus regular elections for government, the PM can wait for the entire length of his party's government, five years, or call an election early if it is politically expedient to do so. Some governments lasted only a few months or a few years in order that majorities might be increased, and many general elections were called before the ending of the five-year term. See **Landmarks** for the election results and the governments that they produced.

GREYHOUND RACING Greyhound racing had its origins in whippet racing, which was derived in turn from hare coursing. By the early twentieth century, however, a form of dog racing held in 'flapping tracks' was a common pastime in the wastelands near working-class areas of industrial cities. Flapping races did use not live bait as did coursing with hares. Instead scented rags were waved and flapped about by somebody towards whom the canine athletes, once released by their owners, would race. This was a male pastime, used as a vehicle for informal betting. Dog keeping was a hobby that expressed a sense of competitiveness in working-class life, but also a shared interest. Whippets were kept in kennels in the back yards of houses in the industrial towns and cities and were raced on the nearest common lands or on wastelands. Local authorities forbade dog racing in public parks because it created a nuisance, and because it was a medium for informal betting and gambling.

The flapping track, however, was marginalised by the introduction in 1926 of the electric hare, which first sped along the rails at the Belle Vue stadium in Manchester. The electric hare was an American invention. Greyhound racing proved to be a hugely popular evening out for the urban working classes, and the large greyhound tracks, licensed by the National Greyhound Racing Society, were built in most cities and some large towns between the wars. Nearly 18 million punters visited the stadiums each year during the late 1920s, and their main aim was to have a bet on the dogs. At a time when off-course cash betting on horses was illegal, the conveniently placed greyhound track was a punter's dream. In addition to licensed bookmakers at the tracks, by 1930 the totalisator, or 'Tote', a mechanism for *pari mutuel* or pool betting, was available. It also provided betting revenue for the track owners.

It is hardly surprising, perhaps, that one of the leading sports personalities of the interwar period was not human, but a dog: the successful greyhound Mick the Miller starred with Flanagan and Allen in the British film *The Wild Boy* (1934) and, posthumously, became an exhibit in the Science Museum in Kensington. After the suspension of the major races between 1939 and 1945 the immediate postwar years saw a resurgence in the popularity of nightly greyhound racing once more. During 1949 there were over 50 million visits to the licensed dog tracks. Yet the sport failed to retain this peak of popularity in subsequent decades. A minor revival occurred during the 1980s, when many young men and women making good wages in financial employment, the so-called yuppies, visited the tracks. And during the 1990s the expansion of satellite television also assisted in maintaining a degree of popularity. But as an urban sport greyhound racing is going to the dogs: sixty years ago there were more than seventy major dog tracks; now there are fewer than thirty. Greater London itself used to have over twenty tracks; now it has four.

HOLIDAYS Holidays are an important barometer of social and economic trends. Throughout the twentieth century entitlement to time off for holidays for manual and industrial workers increased beyond the bank holidays and religious festivals shared by almost all. The **Holidays with Pay Act** of 1938 was a landmark in that respect. During the postwar years two weeks' paid leave was increasingly the norm. In 1950, 66 per cent of full-time manual workers had this entitlement, rising to over 95 per cent by the end of the decade. And by 1990 over 90 per cent of manual workers enjoyed four weeks or more of paid leave, partly because Britain came into line with European Union legislation and partly through negotiated agreements between trade unions and employers.

There was a great upsurge in taking holidays in Britain. Days out to stately homes, amusement parks, national parks and theme parks became increasingly popular, and a week or two by the cold sea remained the aspiration of millions who flocked to the guest houses and hotels of the resorts. Blackpool continued to be to the northern industrial cities what Brighton and Southend were to London: accessible coastal towns with cheap accommodation in guest houses or the more affordable hotels. Holiday-makers could enjoy the beach, amusement arcades, amusing or scenic postcards, fish and chip shops, cafes, restaurants and pubs. But increasingly the call of the Mediterranean was heard by the working classes. In 1900 few if any working-class people would have dreamed of taking a vacation in a far-off sunny country in Southern Europe, because few if any could have afforded it. The 1950s and 1960s, however, witnessed the democratisation of voluntary foreign travel. Holidaying in Greece, Portugal and especially Spain became commonplace. By 1951, 1.5 million foreign holidays were enjoyed, mostly by the middle classes. By 1971 the figure had reached 4.2 million, and in 1999 it was in excess of 29 million. Aviation boomed. Laker Airways, for example, was launched in 1966. Other charter flight companies and commercial tour operators flew from the larger airports and also the smaller ones such as Luton. Since 1990, Luton Airport, in common with other smaller provincial airports, saw a second major wave of expansion on account of the budget airlines such as EasyJet and Ryan Air.

Television was intimately related to the postwar expansion in holidays, both reflecting and stimulating demand. In 1959 the BBC began *Whicker's World*, in which the roving journalist Alan Whicker travelled far and wide to report on holiday destinations. He was still doing it during the 1980s. In 1969 the BBC also launched *Holiday 69*, a series that ran every year thereafter, with the annual update flagged in its title. In 1976 Thames Television initiated *Wish You Were Here . . . ?*, hosted by Judith Chalmers and Chris Kelly. Both BBC and ITV also ran other travel shows, thereby helping to promote Australia and the USA as popular destinations for mass tourism.

As the proletarian holiday-makers arrived in their hundreds of thousands in foreign resorts, however, middle-class holiday-makers fastened upon different resorts and levels of accommodation to avoid them. Many of these were in 'remote' or 'unspoiled locations', code for 'there is no mass tourism here'. Much has been made of the environmental impact of budget airlines, but the continuing boom in flying beyond Europe during the postwar years was partly consequential upon the expanding horizons of the middle-class traveller, and business travellers too. In addition, the introduction of Eurostar services from London to France and Belgium during the 1990s reaffirmed France as a major holiday destination for the British and made the delights of Belgium accessible by rail, as well as air, sea and road.

In short, an island people continued to enjoy their islands but increasingly enjoyed getting away from it all to a growing number of foreign countries. Holiday-making reflected the expanding aspirations, expectations and horizons born of affluence, consumerism, the media and education during the twentieth century.

HOMOSEXUALITY Attitudes towards homosexuality and lesbianism were more tolerant by the end of the twentieth century than they had been a hundred years earlier. The imprisonment of Oscar Wilde in 1895 for 'a homosexual act not amounting to buggery' appears particularly punitive today, while the British government's treatment of Roger **Casement** during the Irish War of Independence amounted to a poisonous homophobic campaign. In all major spheres of public life, particularly in politics, law, the armed services and education, homosexuality was viewed as corrupting and dangerous throughout the first half of the twentieth century, although many psychologists increasingly came to view it as a 'condition' rather than a wicked pattern of behaviour born of innate debauchery.

The Victorian illegalisation of homosexuality was increasingly called into question during the postwar years. In 1957, the **Wolfenden Report** accelerated the revision of Victorian values by recommending that homosexual acts between consenting men over the age of twenty-one should be decriminalised. The blackmailing of homosexuals in senior or official positions was a problem that the report sought to address, a problem dramatised in the 1961 British film *Victim*, in which Dirk Bogarde played a lawyer taking on his blackmailer. The **Homosexual Law Reform Society** also lobbied professionally and politically for law reform. That came with the 1967 **Sexual Offences Act**, steered through parliament by the Labour MP Leo Abse. It decriminalised homosexuality, while also making it clear that the activity remained abnormal and not to be encouraged. The act of 1967 must be viewed within the context of the growing permissiveness

mentioned elsewhere in this book. Historically, the door to the closet had been opened and gay men increasingly came out into public life. The BBC television series *The Naked Civil Servant*, broadcast during the later 1970s, was based on the autobiography of the self-confessed old 'queen' Quentin Crisp, while famous gay television celebrities such as Larry Grayson and Russell Harty became household names. That term 'gay' appears to have come into use during the 1970s, an import from the United States of America, where the Stonewall riots of June 1969 encouraged the liberalisation of attitudes to homosexuals in that country.

With decriminalisation now a welcome fact, campaigns for equal civil rights for homosexual men began in earnest in 1969 with the formation of the **Committee for Homosexual Equality**, subsequently renamed the **Campaign for Homosexual Equality**. Gay Rights became increasingly militant. In 1989 the organisation Stonewall was set up to protest against the infamous Clause 28 of the Local Government Bill that prevented the dissemination of materials deemed to endorse or promote homosexuality. The group OutRage, formed by Peter Tatchell in 1990, was more militant still, seeking to 'out' from the closet those who appeared to be concealing their homosexuality. During the 1980s and 1990s, moreover, lesbian groups became involved with homosexual politics to fight for lesbian rights. Interestingly, lesbianism was never criminalised as was male same-sex activity, but many lesbians had been afraid publicly to declare their sexuality. Yet from 1985 most lesbians (and 'straight' men for that matter) were spared the apocalyptic spectre of AIDS that stalked many active gay men in Britain, as elsewhere. Tabloid newspaper articles continued to characterise homosexuals as innately promiscuous, and hence responsible for their own fates. The unwitting testimony of many such articles was that homophobia was never far from the surface of later twentieth-century Britain. Homosexual men, however, were a diverse group, often subjected to caricature, yet undoubtedly freer to live their lives more openly than just thirty years earlier. Oral historians and social historians have increasingly studied homosexuality in contemporary British history, with particular reference to the prejudices directed towards them both before and after 1967, the often vexed decision whether or not to 'come out', and the alternative masculinities and lifestyles pursued by gay men.

HORSE RACING Unlike most sports in Britain, horse racing has maintained its largely rural identity. Initially dominated by the aristocracy, the sport was increasingly penetrated by wealthy middle-class businessmen seeking to participate in 'the sport of kings' and to create or exploit elite networks connected with it. The very language of the two main forms of racing, 'flat' (or national hunt) racing and steeplechasing, are redolent of rusticity. The great flat race is the Epsom Derby, while the Grand National has been the world's most famous steeplechase since the 1920s, partly because of the height of its hedges and fences. Many of the sixty race courses in Britain are within large town or city boundaries – for example Aintree, the home of the Grand National – while the location of many smaller courses is decidedly rural in character – Chepstow in South Wales and Cartmel in the North-West of England are cases in point. Many small point-to-point races continue to be held at country courses, providing opportunities for horse-riding skills but also for betting. And that is the key to the popularity of horse racing, the second most regularly televised sport after football: not only does it remind millions of British people of a rural lifestyle and landscape, it

has long been established as a medium for betting and gambling.

During the twentieth century this symbiotic relationship between horses and punters was strengthened by the increasing application of technology to both racing and betting. At the race courses themselves, the 'Tote' or totalisator, introduced in 1929, was an alternative to the bookmaker, pooling the bets of punters and paying out to the winners, keeping the majority of stakes for its commercial operator. The governing authorities in horse racing, for example the National Hunt Committee and the Jockey Club, were in favour of the Tote, not only because it was a less corruptible form of betting than via bookmakers but also because it provided an opportunity to raise funds for the horses and the courses. However, the betting public was only lukewarm towards the Tote. In 1959, for example, it turned in just £28.5 million compared with an estimated £336.5 million accumulated by bookmakers. Hence those concerned with horse racing began to look increasingly towards a tax or levy on bookmakers. Away from the course, first the telegraph, then the telephone and later television, enabled racing results to be transmitted immediately to the bookmakers, the entrepreneurs at the heart of betting culture. The legalisation of off-course cash betting by the **Betting and Gaming Act**, 1960, was also a further stimulus to the popularity of the sport as a medium for betting, not least because the association of racing with unrespectable and illegal behaviour began to be lifted. It also coincided with the arrival of television as a mass medium, and live racing became a major feature of British life, even on the Reithian BBC. In addition, it led to the increased taxation of bookmakers, as once illegal bets were now recorded.

The excitement, glamour and betting opportunities of the largest horse races continued to appeal to all classes in society throughout the twentieth century. The sport retains an important place within the British national identity, from the race-going monarchy to sizeable sections of the working and middle classes. The most significant national events in the racing calendar were established before 1900 and have continued to the present day. In the year 2000 the Grand National, for example, provided a higher turnover for the betting company Ladbrokes than did football's Euro 2000. The world wide web hosts many betting and gambling sites dedicated to horse racing, and also the site of the bloodstock auctioneers Tattersalls and other institutions at the heart of the sport.

HOUSING AND HOME OWNERSHIP In an increasingly wealthy Britain, housing has remained one of the most profound indicators of both the material and the moral health of the country. Before the nineteenth century, progressive reformers had understood the need to clear away slums and build housing anew for the poorest sections of society. The **Housing and Town Planning Acts** promoted public sector housing, or council estates, across the length and breadth of the land, in town centres and suburbs, while the middle classes sprawled out into suburbia in even greater numbers.

Apart from the very poorest in rural and some inner-city areas, most homes were provided with electricity and gas between the wars as most people enjoyed improved housing. The older by-law terraced housing of the late Victorian and Edwardian years was extended and adapted to accommodate rising living standards and expectations, while huge swathes of semi-detached suburban housing provided Britain, and particularly England, with a distinctive heritage of Siamese-twinned houses. Increasingly since the 1920s the acquisition of the four- or five-bedroom detached home, labelled the 'executive' home from the 1960s by estate agents, became the goal of affluent middle-class householders, not all of whom had children. Many of these housing aspirations had begun during the Victorian years.

The 'house on the ground', with gardens, remained at the apex of the housing dream for most Britons. The tenement tradition was stronger in Scotland, however, but even in Scots cities known for high-density communal living the appearance of tower blocks proved controversial. The Red Road flats in Glasgow, among the highest blocks in Europe, were scheduled for demolition during the early twenty-first century. In common with other major cities, these towers were not popular with many of their tenants and developed many social problems. Among their abiding failures was the inability of large blocks of flats to look like 'home' in the traditional sense of that term, while the lack of defensible individual space and boundaries in the communal grass-lands and concretized walkways that surrounded them encouraged criminal activity. Hence by the 1990s the tower block was synonymous with the inner-city problem. However, some inner-city areas were increasingly gentrified and revived by the inward migration of middle-class households and wealthier ethnic minority households.

That housing and home ownership continued to reflect both improved living standards and inequalities in British society is emphasised by social and urban historians of housing. In 1914 just 10 per cent of householders in England and Wales were owner-occupiers, but by 1990 this had risen to over two-thirds of the population, or 67 per cent. Ethnic groupings manifested widely different levels of home ownership: by 1991, 82 per cent of Indians owned or were buying their accommodation, compared with 77 per cent of those of

Pakistani origin, 67 per cent of the white population, 48 per cent of black Caribbeans and 44 per cent of Bangladeshis. Clearly, the desire to own property was shared by the majority, but the means to that achievement were not always available.

I

IMMIGRATION Britain experienced successive waves of immigration after 1900, and rates of in-migration were higher during the first half of the century. In the decade 1900–09, for example, 2,287,000 people immigrated to the United Kingdom, and during the 1920s some 2,492,000 people moved here. During the 1950s and 1960s, the decades most commonly associated with mass immigration, fewer than 2,000,000 immigrants arrived. And, in each of these decades, emigration was in excess of immigration. Arithmetically, immigration did not 'put pressure' on accommodation, employment or public services, except in areas where these were already in short supply or contested by disadvantaged groups.

Britain remained mostly white throughout the twentieth and into the twenty-first century. Less than 7 per cent of the population was of colour by 1991. Yet by the year 2000 it was common to view Britain as a multicultural society. Britain was, however, never a monoculture – that is, a society characterised by a singular defining set of customs and values. Nor was it purely white by the beginning of the twentieth century. In London and other cities, small clusters of black communities and Jewish areas were to be found. Some had existed for centuries, but the numbers of Jews in Britain were augmented, especially

in London, by refugees escaping from anti-Semitism in Eastern and Central Europe. This immigration was partly curtailed by the **Aliens Act** of 1905.

At the turn of the century Jewish people were engaged in casual employment, in small trades such as jewellery making and furniture, in shop-keeping, and also in larger business and the professions. During the twentieth century, however, Jews progressively migrated away from their original areas of settlement such as the East End of London to more affluent suburbs, a consequence of increased wealth and occupational mobility and an indicator of decreasing segregation.

In London, and in the provincial cities of Bristol in the West of England, in Cardiff in South Wales, in Liverpool in North-West England, as well as in other waterside cities, lived communities of black people of African heritage. Comprised originally of escaped or manumitted slaves, and augmented by stowaways or immigrants from Africa, these black areas were relatively segregated from white society by 1900, hemmed in by social and economic discrimination that prevented advancement. A good example was the black community in Cardiff, near the docks. The First World War witnessed the minor expansion of numbers of blacks in these areas, as some black servicemen and war workers from the empire stayed on in Britain once the Armistice was declared.

Britain witnessed its first serious race riots after the war. In London and a number of other cities during 1919 blacks were blamed by whites for economic competition during a period of high unemployment. Jewish people had been subject to similar accusations, and both black and Jewish groups continued to suffer discrimination.

The Irish emigrated to Britain in large numbers during the industrial revolution, and by 1900 sizeable Irish communities existed in most large British cities and industrial towns. Ireland under British rule was economically a poor country, and 'the Mainland' offered work and opportunities denied to people living in the largely rural Irish social structure. The Irish too, most of whom were Catholics by religion, were sometimes mocked and discriminated against, and the **Irish War of Independence** led to hostility towards the 'Fenians'.

The Irish continued to migrate into Britain between the wars and after the Second World War, but other Europeans represented in postwar immigration were Italians, Poles, and Greek and Turkish Cypriots. Italians, for example, particularly those from the poor south of the country, emigrated to Britain to seek employment and housing. In the case of those from Poland and other Eastern and Central European countries, escape from totalitarian communism was a major push factor. It is pertinent to note that escape from Nazi Germany had led Poles, both Jewish and non-Jewish, to flee to Britain during the 1930s. In Cyprus, the political tensions between Greece and Turkey contributed to Greek-Cypriot emigration, both before and after the 1974 'invasion' of the island by Turkey.

The major phases of black and Asian immigration began in the wake of the British **Nationality Act** of 1948, which gave British citizenship to members of the British Commonwealth. The famous docking of the SS *Empire Windrush* in the same year, carrying immigrants from the Caribbean, is often viewed as the starting point for mass coloured immigration. In particular, Caribbean, Indian and Pakistani migrants moved to Britain to meet specific demands in the British labour market, mostly for manual labour but also for white-collar and professional employment. For much of the 1950s race relations appeared relatively stable, but in the autumn of 1958 race riots in Notting Hill,

London, and in Nottingham gave cause for concern. Further riots occurred during the 1980s and 1990s. In order to assuage fears, most infamously articulated by Enoch Powell in 1968, that Britain was being 'flooded' with migrants of colour, two **Commonwealth immigration acts** were passed during the 1960s, a further **Immigration Act** was passed in 1971, and a new **British Nationality Act** appeared on the statute books in 1981.

Restrictions on immigration accompanied progressive measures to encourage mutual respect and tolerance between different ethnic groups. The Labour governments of Harold Wilson during the second half of the 1960s introduced race relations legislation. Britain was an increasingly liberalised and tolerant country during the second half of the twentieth century. We should also not forget the fact that extreme right-wing parties performed very badly at most general and local elections. The British Union of Fascists during the 1930s and the Union Movement during the 1950s failed miserably in their attempts to exploit or foment racial tension. So too did the British National Party and the National Front, although there were a number of neo-fascist local councillors elected towards the end of the twentieth and during the early twenty-first century. This can be explained by racial prejudice, but also by a sense among poor whites that the political classes were more concerned with the social and economic fortunes of poorer ethnic minority groups. The East End of London remained an area where ethnic relations and tensions were studied by sociologists and social reformers who were worried about poverty, race and class. More generally, London throughout the twentieth century remained the most ethnically and religiously diverse city in Britain, and the capital developed large concentrations of different immigrant groups, giving rise to official fears about segregation, notably among poorer migrants of colour, and ethnic minorities whose identity owed much to religion. Increasingly, however, social historians are demonstrating greater understanding of the role of suburban dispersal in the unravelling of possibly dangerous levels of ethnic concentration.

INDIA AND PAKISTAN A suitable form of government for India, short of independence from the British Empire, had been experimented with by the British Raj in a number of **India Acts** in 1909, 1919 and 1935. This last act was passed during the decade when Gandhi's campaign for Indian secession was at its height. Dominion status was Britain's final and preferred option after the Second World War. Following growing violence between religious groupings in India, the **India Independence Act** created two new dominions, a predominantly Hindu India and a Muslim Pakistan. India also contained some sizeable Sikh and Buddhist minorities. Many Indians did not want dominion status, however, as it demanded allegiance to Britain and its monarchy, and in 1950, within a context of major internal difficulties, the Indian prime minister, Jawaharlal Nehru, established a republic. India thence became a member of the British Commonwealth. Pakistan, situated on India's north-western frontier, between the Arabian Sea and China, was led to independence by Muhammad Ali Jinnah. The country became a dominion of the British Commonwealth in 1956. Throughout these years, religious and nationalist tensions between India and Pakistan were never far from the surface of politics, and sometimes violently so. They continued to destabilise South Asia more generally, as did the growing disquiet between the two countries over the disputed territory of Kashmir. In 1972 Pakistan quit the Commonwealth in protest at the creation of the independent state of Bangladesh, where a minority of Bengali-Pakistanis lived.

Both predominantly poor rural countries, India and Pakistan became major source nations for the mass Asian immigration into Britain during the 1950s and 1960s that followed the passage of the Nationality Act of 1948. Many areas of British cities were transformed by this influx of South Asians, as were the eating habits of the British people. 'Going out for an Indian' became a common expression for eating in restaurants whose chefs and owners were as likely to come from Bangladesh or Pakistan as from India. Among the most famous culinary districts of the big cities were Sparkbrook, Birmingham, known by the early 1980s for its Balti cuisine, and Brick Lane in East London. More generally, in the inner suburbs as well as the inner cities, Asian restaurants flourished, as did shops with exotic foodstuffs to cater for both the immigrants and their children, and the adventurous tastes of the British people lapped this up. Thus did a post-colonial people, the British, enjoy the fruits of empire many years after the empire had become the Commonwealth.

INDUSTRIAL RELATIONS The term refers to the formal relations between management and workers, or employers' organisations and trade unions, and is not a term that was commonly used before the middle of the twentieth century. In general, benign industrial relations were the norm throughout the century, but, for some historians, conflicts in some of the most important industries came to signify 'what went wrong' with twentieth-century Britain. The most troubled decades were the years before the First World War, the 1920s, and the 1960s and 1970s, and the most troubled industries were the staple industries. Public transport was also prone to strike action.

The Conservative governments of the early years of the century facilitated the tamping down of industrial disputes via support for legal decisions that were later revoked by the Liberal governments before the First World War. The **Trades Disputes Act** of 1927 which followed the General Strike was overturned by the Labour government in 1946. The governments of the 1960s and 1970s also faced industrial action. During the 1980s the Conservative governments of Margaret Thatcher applied themselves to limiting the ability of trade unions to strike, with some success. In so doing, unfortunately, they also assisted employers to hire and fire with greater impunity.

Economic historians are by no means agreed on the effects of problems in industrial relations on the performance of the British economy. Some conservative historians argue, for example, that during the 1970s poor industrial relations were at the heart of Britain's economic crisis, but France also suffered from strikes and stoppages during that decade, while its economy grew faster than that of Britain. Other issues examined by historians are the solidarities involved in strike action; the causes of official strikes compared with 'wildcat' strikes – that is, those unsanctioned by the TUC; and the 'bread and butter' demands of strikers in comparison with the politicised nature of strike action.

INNER CITIES The term 'inner city' originated in urban social sciences in the United States, entering British popular usage via sociology during the early 1970s. 'Inner city' describes those urban areas characterised by social, economic and environmental problems. They are districts of cheap housing where many immigrants, often lacking in economic means, tended to settle. It is more accurate to conceive of inner cities socially rather than spatially, for the term 'inner city' includes the older areas of decaying housing that existed

between the town and city centres and the wealthier suburbs. Many older inner suburbs, those by-law terraced houses built during the later nineteenth century, for example, had become 'inner city' in terms of their dilapidated environment. Increasingly, some council estates, whether in the city centres or in outer suburbs, and built during the 1950s and 1960s, deteriorated rapidly, manifesting the social and environmental problems of poorer housing areas. And during the 1980s and 1990s many of the cottage estates of council housing built between the wars, and situated towards the edges of town in working-class suburbs, also developed inner-city characteristics, particularly in towns and regions associated with de-industrialisation. In terms of 'classic' inner cities, we can include Brixton in South London; Bethnal Green in East London; the Falls Road in Derry, Northern Ireland; the Gorbals district of Glasgow; Hulme and Moss Side in Manchester; and Toxteth in Liverpool. Hundreds of smaller marginal council estates in towns and cities across the length and breadth of Britain also developed inner-city characteristics. Some of these locations were associated with race riots during the 1980s.

IRELAND AND BRITAIN By 1900, the Irish question, to the English at any rate, seemed to have lost much of its force. The dynamism brought to Irish nationalism by James Stewart Parnell had dissipated and the campaign for 'home rule' had foundered. The combined forces of Ulster Protestant unionism, English Toryism and Chamberlainite imperialism had scuppered the opportunity which the largely peaceful home rule movement had generated. Moreover, under the leadership of John Redmond, the Irish Parliamentary Party regularly returned some eighty MPs to parliament, accompanied (if only physically) by an even more solidified group of

Irish Unionists, now sent there almost exclusively by the Protestants of north-eastern Ulster.

When the Liberals were returned to office in 1906, their lack of enthusiasm for reinvigorating the Liberal–Irish alliance was quite apparent. The party had split over Ireland and had been out of office for the best part of twenty years as a consequence. Indeed it was only the inconclusive outcomes of the two elections of 1910, held in the midst of the constitutional crisis over Lloyd George's 'People's Budget', which brought the Irish question back into the mainstream of British parliamentary life. Redmond's price for supporting the Liberals was a new Home Rule Bill, but as it made its way through parliament the Unionists of Ulster began arming to resist it, inspired as they were by Randolph Churchill's comment from the 1880s that 'Ulster will fight and Ulster will be right'. The gun, therefore, was reintroduced into Irish affairs not by the forces of nationalism but by the loyalists of Ulster, who, in no short order, had grouped themselves into a seemingly formidable private army, the Ulster Volunteer Force. In a story replete with ironies, one was that the loyalists of Ulster armed themselves with weapons from Germany, while another was that the Conservative Party supported them, 'to the brink of treason', in defence of the constitution. The prospects for a peaceful resolution to the home rule crisis seemed bleak, as the Bill passed into law in the summer of 1914.

Irish affairs were subsumed, however, in the greater crisis which overtook Europe in July and August of that year. With the outbreak of war, the Home Rule Act was suspended, and John Redmond now called on all Irishmen to enlist in the British Army in support of freedom for small nations. Redmond's call to the Southerners to enlist split the Volunteer movement. The majority joined up, while a minority, clinging to the name of Irish Volunteers, remained at home. But there was another strand to Irish nationalism, whose disciples had never been satisfied at the prospect of home rule within the empire and instead traced their roots via Fenianism, and the revolution of 1848, to the United Irishmen of 1798. Many nationalists had turned their backs on politics after the failure of Parnellism, and sought instead cultural and social outlets for their feelings of separateness from England. They formed themselves into such groups as the Gaelic League and the Gaelic Athletic Association, and strove to rediscover through sports a unique, separate Irishness which some saw as threatened, not expressed, by home rule. A political manifestation of many of these sentiments came in the formation of the **Sinn Féin** movement in 1905, which aimed at separation from Britain rather than a 'milk and water' home rule within the empire.

And within these groups were those inspired by the example of the threat of force, wielded by the armed Orangemen of Ulster. These were the men and women of the Irish Republican Brotherhood, who held that the English would only leave Ireland at the point of a gun, and that England's difficulty with Germany was Ireland's opportunity. It was this tiny group, led by P. H. Pearse, Tom Clarke, James **Connolly** and Sean MacDermott, who launched the Easter rising in Dublin in 1916, unilaterally declaring the freedom of 'The Irish Republic'. The week-long revolt was doomed to failure, as its leaders knew only too well. Connolly told one follower that they had 'no hope whatever' of success. They were 'all going out to be slaughtered'. Their aim instead, expressed regularly by Pearse in astonishingly powerful if atavistic prose, was to present to the Irish a 'blood sacrifice', to inspire the living by the selfless example of the dead. 'From the graves of dead patriots', said Pearse, 'spring living nations.'

At the general election of 1918, Sinn Féin, now associated in the public mind with the men of 1916, swept the board in nationalist Ireland. It is traditional to see the origins of this shift in the execution by the British of the leaders of the rebellion, and this was certainly a factor. More powerful, though, was the continued failure during the war to implement any measure of self-government for Ireland, even self-government at the cost of the exclusion from its provisions of an undefined part of Ulster. As the war dragged on relentlessly, Redmond, who died in March 1918, had secured nothing for Ireland, while the Ulster rebels of 1912 to 1914 were ensconced in the cabinet, in coalition with Lloyd George and their Tory supporters. Most disastrous of all perhaps was the decision, taken in the semi-panic conditions of the renewed German offensive of 1918, to try to impose conscription on Ireland. Sinn Féin policy became 'self-determination' (not home rule) by the end of the war.

So, when the war finally ended, the Sinn Féin MPs elected to the British parliament refused to attend it, and instead constituted themselves in Dublin as Dáil Éireann, refusing any longer to recognise the legitimacy of British rule in Ireland. In effect, they attempted to establish their own state, with their own revenue-raising mechanisms, courts system, and local and central government bodies. However, this was no programme of passive resistance, and instead a campaign of armed violence against the state was instituted by a body now styling itself the Irish Republican Army (IRA). As attacks were launched against policemen, soldiers and the physical infrastructure of the British state, the British responded with a series of draconian 'law and order' measures, using armed auxiliaries (the 'Black and Tans') to wage a campaign of counter-terrorism against the insurgents and their political supporters. Meanwhile a political 'solution' was imposed by the British government in the form of the Government of Ireland Act of 1920. This Act effectively partitioned Ireland and imposed two 'home rule' governments, one with jurisdiction over a new statelet, comprising the six north-eastern counties of the old province of Ulster, to be known as Northern Ireland, while a second (Southern Ireland) was to have jurisdiction over the remaining twenty-six counties. The Ulster Unionists, who had never wanted home rule, now accepted it, but for their 'own' bit of Ireland. The rest of Ireland, which had struggled for home rule for forty years, would no longer accept it.

The War of Independence, as it is now known, dragged on into 1921, with increasing violence on both sides. The IRA campaign, directed by Michael **Collins**, was brutally effective as an example of ruthless guerrilla warfare, but it seems unlikely that the organisation could have beaten the British Army had the latter been given a free rein against it. However, many in Britain were sick of war and sick of the atrocities being committed by their forces in Ireland, and there was increasing pressure on both sides for a truce and a compromise solution.

This came after months of wrangling and tortured negotiations in the form of the Anglo-Irish Treaty of December 1921. Great controversy still surrounds the signing of this agreement. Eamon de Valera, the public face of the Republican movement in Ireland, refused to attend the talks in person, instead sending Collins of the IRA. Collins, confronted by Lloyd George with the threat of terrible war, accepted a compromise which granted independence to Southern Ireland in all but name, in the form of a 'Free State' within the empire. Northern Ireland was to remain within the UK, but with its own devolved government in Belfast.

Ironically enough, given what was to come in the future, the partition of Ireland was scarcely discussed in the dáil when Collins returned to seek ratification of the London agreement. Instead, de Valera and his supporters argued that Collins had betrayed the Republic and refused to acknowledge that the British would never have conceded it. Much time was taken with a discussion of the obligation contained in the treaty, that members of the Free State parliament should take an oath of allegiance to the king of England. In fact, the British demand that Ireland remain within the empire merely disguised the extent of the concession to the Republicans of the reality of freedom.

De Valera's decision to walk out of the dáil and leave Collins to handle the British government probably made civil war inevitable in Ireland. This broke out in 1922 and lasted for a year. It is likely that more Irishmen died in this brutal struggle than had died in the fight against the British from 1916. Families were torn asunder in a conflict in which old friends, now on different sides, killed old friends. More Irishmen were executed by their fellow countrymen than had been executed by the British in the War of Independence.

The new state of Northern Ireland, meanwhile, was also born in violence. The IRA continued to wage an offensive against it, while atrocities were inflicted on the beleaguered nationalist minority in Belfast and elsewhere. The nationalists of Ulster, abandoned it seemed by their countrymen in the South, made little effort to make the new state workable, while it must be said that the Northern Ireland government made little or no effort to accommodate the very sizeable minority for which it was now responsible. Indeed, the minority safeguards under the 1920 Act, such as proportional representation at local and parliamentary elections, were swiftly abandoned by the new Unionist government,

while systematic gerrymandering of electoral boundaries ensured that, in areas where nationalists were in a majority, Unionist administrations were routinely returned. By the 1930s, any pretence at reconciling nationalists to the Northern Ireland state had been abandoned.

And, in the Free State, the fears of northern Unionists concerning 'Rome rule' appeared to have been justified, as the new state there enveloped itself in the cloak of a doubtless comforting Roman Catholicism. It might be pointed out that a more secular ethos might have been maintained (if only through necessity) had not a million Protestant Irishmen rejected self-government in a single Irish state. It should be recorded too that the Irish Free State – backward as it was in many respects – remained one of the few bastions of parliamentary democracy in interwar Europe. Born as it was in war and civil war, this was a remarkable achievement, its most remarkable aspect being the peaceful handing over of power to de Valera in 1932. De Valera had abandoned Sinn Féin's abstentionism and formed his Fianna Fáil party in 1926, entering the dáil the following year. He reluctantly took the oath of allegiance to the king, dismissing it as a 'form of words'. Many Irish lives could perhaps have been spared had he taken a similarly undogmatic view in 1921.

In power, de Valera sought to break the remaining links with Great Britain, to end partition, to promote Irish economic self-sufficiency and to restore the Irish language. He was successful at least at seeing off the IRA, but his attempts to promote Irish agriculture behind tariff walls produced only a damaging 'economic war' with Britain. The Irish language continued to decline, Ireland's young continued to emigrate and, if anything, partition was solidified under de Valera's rule. His new constitution of 1937 enshrined the 'special place' of the Roman

Catholic Church in Irish life, and renamed the state Éire. Relations with Britain were damaged, too, by de Valera's insistence on maintaining a studied neutrality during the Second World War.

For the British, the Irish question had been solved by Lloyd George in 1921. There was little fuss in Britain when Éire became an independent republic in 1949. And, while de Valera's wartime posturing may have irritated, few Britons thought much about Ireland until the 1960s. It came as a profound shock, therefore, when seemingly out of the blue violent political unrest broke out again in Northern Ireland in the autumn of 1968. The Troubles had begun.

ISLAM IN BRITAIN The historical account both of the Islamic religion and of Muslims in Britain often begins with Pakistani and Bangladeshi immigration during the 1960s and 1970s, mentions the radicalising affair of the *fatwa* issued against Salman Rushdie in 1989, and leads inexorably towards worries about inner cities and segregation, issues over the position of Islam in a secular multicultural society, and the terrorist atrocities in our present century. Yet Muslims lived in Britain before the 1950s, often in the port cities near their point of arrival. They were never a monolithic group, nor are they now. In his study *Negroes in Britain*, made during the 1940s and published in 1948, the sociologist Kenneth L. Little observed the small established Muslim community in Cardiff, South Wales. (Please note that in those days the common spelling was 'Moslem', not Muslim.) Writing of this community, Little observed that 'The bulk of its members are Arabs, mainly from Aden',

though there are also a fairly substantial number of Somalis from British Somaliland, Indians, Egyptians and Malays. Its total numbers

are difficult to estimate; but if the women and children are included – for most of the former and not a few of the latter have been 'Islamized' – it probably amounts to something not far short of two thousand. This segment is essentially religious and social rather than political in its interests, and is bound together by the strong ties of brotherhood inherent in the Islamic creed, despite some sectarianism in this respect. These religious ties and obligations are responsible to a considerable degree for the fact that the Arabs, at any rate, make social contacts almost exclusively amongst themselves, and particularly for the practice of a large amount of mutual assistance in respect of material possessions. For example, if a needy Moslem arrives in the district, one or two of the wealthier members of the group will see that he is properly set up with clothes, etc. This 'setting up' is not exactly an act of charity, as the recipient is expected to repay the obligation; and he usually does so when he returns to port from his next trip. The Moslems used to possess their own mosque, but this was destroyed by a bomb during the raids on Cardiff. A Moslem school and a temporary mosque have been established in a suitable building in Sophia Street, and are carried on under auspices of a resident sheikh and a small staff of assistants, and in the school instruction in the Koran is given to the Arab and other Moslem children of mixed blood.

(Kenneth Little, *Negroes in Britain: A Study of Racial Relations in English Society* (1948), pp. 110–11)

This quotation is enormously rich in content. The proximity of the community to the port and the docks revealed their immigrant origins and hinted at sources of labour and livelihood. The tradition of self-help, of relying upon other Muslims rather than wider society, is partly evident here, as is the obligation to pay back rather than remain indebted in financial terms. Little appears to be slightly worried at implications for segregation in this respect. It is also clear that Muslims in Cardiff had endured the privations of war, undertaken war work, and suffered from bomb damage, as did other groups. Little pointed out in a footnote that some Muslim men had been killed at sea by U Boat activities. In addition, this was a mixed profile of Muslims, from Arab and African countries, and many Muslims in late twentieth-century Britain were also from these source countries. Increasingly, however, most came from South Asia – Bangladesh and Pakistan – during the 1960s and 1970s. Some also came from Eastern Europe, notably the Balkan countries. By the year 2000 there were 1.6 million Muslims in Britain, almost 50 per cent of whom had been born in the United Kingdom.

J

JEWS IN BRITAIN Jews had lived in Britain for centuries, the largest Jewish population being in London. This was greatly added to by the immigration of Jews from Eastern and Central Europe as a consequence of the pogroms against them during the 1880s and 1890s. The East End of London became the early twentieth-century heartland of the Jewish population in Britain, although there were Jewish communities in other larger British cities. The number of Jews increased considerably during the 1930s as a result of anti-Semitism in Nazi Germany and Poland. By 1939 there were about 400,000 Jews in Britain, although that figure may not have accurately included all migrants during the immigration of the 1930s.

Historians have focused upon Jewish immigration and its consequences. Key themes include anti-Semitism and the complex negotiation of Jewish religious and cultural identities with British society. Most Jewish people desired to maintain various levels of religious and cultural identity while being integrated into British society. The spatial expression of this was Jewish suburbanisation. During the late 1960s the Jewish sociologist Ernest Krausz observed that most Jews had left the old 'ghetto' of the East End for home ownership in wealthier areas of North London, a north-by-north-west suburban dispersal that demonstrated just how prosperous many Jews had become, and also how far assimilation with English society and culture had occurred. By then hundreds of thousands of Jews had become increasingly assimilated into non-Jewish families through marriage to Christians and others.

Many Jews had been sympathetic to Labour and Liberal politics since the late nineteenth century, but from 1967, when conflict between Israel and the Palestinians and neighbouring Arab countries intensified, the political allegiances of British Jews began to change. However, the growing support for Palestinians on the British left alienated some Jews from socialism, and the endorsement in 1983 by the Labour Party of the Palestinian Liberation Organisation persuaded many Jews (a number of whom had been conservative business and professionals and who became more prominent during the 1970s and 1980s) to look to the Conservative Party. Several high-profile Jewish politicians became associated with Thatcherism – for example, Sir Leon Brittan, Sir Keith **Joseph** and Dame Shirley Porter. However, Jews were also influential in the rise of New Labour. Phillip Gould was in many ways the leading intellectual exponent of 'new' Labour politics, while Peter Mandelson, the grandson of Herbert Morrison, remained true to the New Labour cause.

Jews made a powerful contribution to Britain during the twentieth century. They were business leaders – both Marks and Spencer and Tesco were established by Jews – and contributed to a wide range of professions, including entertainments. By the 1990s some of the leading television personalities, for example Esther Rantzen and Sasha Baron Cohen, were hugely popular. Anti-Semitism had not disappeared, but nor was it as prevalent as it had been at mid-century.

JINGOISM A term for a heightened patriotism that became popular before the First World War. Deriving from a music hall song whose lyric included the sentiment 'we don't want to fight but by jingo if we do', jingoism encapsulated a sense of dogged Britishness, always triumphant yet not necessarily warlike unless pushed to it, whether the war in question was the Boer War or the war from 1914 to 1918. The word jingo increasingly became a part of the national vocabulary throughout the twentieth century, and could be heard in exclamation of shock or surprise ('oh, by jingo!').

K

KEYNESIANISM Derived from an interpretation of the theories of the economist John Maynard Keynes (1883–1946), Keynesianism was tantamount to heresy to many who believed in laissez-faire economic policies. In the post-Second World War period, Keynesians became hugely influential on government economic policies as the ideas of Keynes justified higher state spending on nationalisation. The first budgets of the postwar Labour governments have been much debated for their interventionist tendencies. Keynesians, who were present in all major political parties, attempted to achieve low levels of unemployment through managing the relative level of demand, using fiscal measures and interest rates. The ideas and economic tools associated with Keynes began to lose credibility during the 1970s, partly as a result of the increasing problem of inflation, and consequently monetarism became more influential as an economic creed, particularly on the right of the Conservative Party.

'KITCHEN SINK' ART AND DRAMA The 'Kitchen Sink School' was a term coined by the art critic David Sylvester in the mid-1950s to emphasise the social and provincial realism of key male artists of the time, notably John Bratby, Jack Smith and Edward Middleditch. The term was later applied to writers, notably the playwright Arnold Wesker, by no means a provincial writer, but who examined and evoked working-class Jewish life in the East End of London. His most famous work was *Chicken Soup with Barley* (1958), which related the disintegration of a Jewish family in the East End with the demise of communist and socialist optimism since the war. There was considerable overlap between kitchen sink drama and the Angry Young Men of the later 1950s, because both dealt with the atmospheres of urban Britain, the tang of the streets and personal issues in an urban (and suburban) context.

LABOUR PARTY AND THE LABOUR MOVE-MENT Begun in 1900 as the Labour Representation Committee (LRC), the Labour Party fused together the economic interests of the trade unions to pursue political representation for the working classes in Westminster and on local councils. At much the same time as New Liberalism emerged, so did more radical interventionist political parties to the left of politics. The LRC was a mosaic of Fabian Society gradualism, the socialism of the Independent Labour Party, trade union instrumentalism, and even New Liberalism. Revolutionary communism was never at home in the Labour Party, and Labour leaders were keen to put ideological distance between Labour and communism. Labour was always a reformist party.

The 1918 party conference saw Labour break away from its alliance with the Liberals and develop both its socialist platform and its party organisation. The Labour Party constitution, written mostly by Sidney Webb, committed the party to the nationalisation of the means of production, distribution and exchange and to the pursuit of redistributive social policies. Internal fractiousness and attacks from non-Labour Party socialist groups meant that its 'socialism' was always a flexible and contested ideology, and the two minority Labour governments pursued little that was socialist. However, the Attlee governments from 1945 to 1951 saw many of Labour's commitments since 1918 being put into practice.

Labour formed governments for little more than a quarter of the twentieth century. However, the party made a minor contribution to the wartime coalition of 1916–18, and during the Second World War leading Labour politicians played a significant role in the coalition government headed by Winston Churchill. This was one reason, but only one, why Labour won such a convincing general election victory towards the end of the war in 1945.

At Labour's lowest ebb during the 1980s, its reformist socialism was dogged both by accusations from communists that the party was betraying the industrial working class and by association with the Trotskyite Militant Tendency. More widely, however, the leftward shift in Labour's politics was at odds with the growing affluence of the working classes and lower middle classes. During the 1990s, following a fourth consecutive general election defeat by the Conservatives in the spring of 1992, the Labour Party remade itself as New Labour. In so doing, it completed its hundredth anniversary at its strongest in terms of its political appeal to a broad mass of voters. At the general elections of 1997 and 2001 the party of Tony Blair romped home.

Historians sympathetic to the Labour Party represent the left, right and centre of the Labour movement. Among key areas of study have been the first Labour minority governments, the Attlee years (1945–51), and the performance of the governments of Harold Wilson and of James Callaghan. After 1979, the tenor began to change as a growing revisionism among younger historians sought to widen the focus away from Labour's umbilical link with trade unions in order to understand the party's historical relationship both to social and cultural changes and to different sections of urban Britain.

LAISSEZ-FAIRE ECONOMICS The era of free trade, or laissez-faire economic policies that enshrined it, began with the abolition of the Corn Laws in 1846 and ended with the Ottawa Conference in 1932. From the early Victorian period to the 1920s, belief in free trade was economic orthodoxy for most politicians, although it was increasingly challenged by protectionism, in the form of the tariff reform movement, and imperial preference.

LEISURE Leisure may be defined as time spent in relaxation rather than in paid or unpaid work. Access to leisure, and ability to choose the growing number of leisure activities, was determined by income and purchasing power, by employment and unemployment, and by class and gender. Nonetheless, as a consequence of shorter working days over the last century, as well as growing entitlements to longer holidays, most people had more leisure time in 1999 than did their ancestors in 1899, although many might not have chosen to use 'free time' as leisure.

Social historians focus upon the relationship of leisure to popular culture, youth culture, affluence and consumerism, amateur and commercial impulses, and individual and collective identities (individual identities were – and still are – manifested in fashionable tastes and trends, while local and national solidarities were – and still are – expressed through sports). They also explore how leisure can be contested by different ideological positions. From the Victorian years, for example, betting and gambling formed a battleground between punters and puritan religious prohibitionists. Criticism of both betting and gaming as an offence to the self-help dynamic in the Protestant work ethic eroded only very slowly during the twentieth century. And Victorian campaigns against alcohol and the public house, or pub, continued long after 1900. Again, religious nonconformity was the major antagonist of the drinking classes, and in some areas of Britain, for example North Wales, where a nonconformist Protestant tradition or chapel culture was

a strong, access to alcohol was restricted relative to other areas.

As noted, the range of leisure activities grew and changed during the twentieth century. Some forms of leisure died out, for example music hall, while the consumption of food and alcohol and the taking of holidays reflected a widening of the tastes of the British people. Cinema and radio flourished in both the interwar and postwar years, but the growth of the television during the 1950s and the personal computer during the 1990s had massive impacts on people's recreational activities. It is interesting to note the findings of a MORI survey on leisure published in 1990. When a sample of people were asked 'Which of these things have you done in the past month?', the following were the most prominent:

Watched television or	
a video	89 per cent
Read a book	64 per cent
Ate with friends at home	51 per cent
Been to a restaurant	49 per cent
Been to pubs	46 per cent
General exercise	42 per cent
Gardening	40 per cent
DIY	39 per cent
Sunday afternoon drive	39 per cent
Away for the weekend	23 per cent
Been to sports club	20 per cent

(Eric Jacobs and Robert Worcester,
Britain under the Moriscope
(1990), p. 126)

This was just before the revolution in personal computers, but it indicated the strength of both individual pastimes and those shared with partners, families, friends and neighbours. These were important, reassuring continuities in the history of leisure during the twentieth century.

LIBERAL PARTY AND LIBERALISM During the Victorian period the Liberals, along with the Conservatives, dominated British politics. The twentieth century, however, witnessed less than ten years of Liberal government, although Liberals also served in coalition governments during the two world wars. Before 1900 'classical Liberalism' meant free trade and minimum but necessary social intervention. The Liberals were also identified with home rule. From 1906 to 1914, however, a more interventionist Liberalism known as New Liberalism profoundly influenced the agenda for domestic policy for many decades to come. The First World War, in alliance with internal splits, severely damaged the Liberal Party in Britain. Supplanted by the rise of Labour, it remained the third party for most of the twentieth century.

Hence, the history of the Liberal Party during the twentieth century was one of early high achievements followed by a miserable decline. The last three Liberal prime ministers were Sir Henry Campbell-Bannerman, Herbert Henry Asquith and David Lloyd George, in power from the years 1905 to 1922 inclusive. During the 1920s, as Liberalism lost its appeal to the electorate, Lloyd George and the party adopted Keynesianism in advance of the Labour Party, but it was all too late. The Liberals performed very badly at general elections during the 1930s, 1940s and 1950s, and it was not really until the 1960s that they began the slow crawl towards becoming a stronger third party. Some significant by-election results, and the rebuilding of party organisation under Jo **Grimond** and Jeremy **Thorpe**, gave them a new lease of life. Although this improvement continued under David Steel into the 1980s, the merger of the Liberals with the Social Democratic Party in 1988, to form the Liberal Democrats, turned out to be their biggest fillip. During the 1990s the 'Lib Dems' were clearly a much stronger third party than the Liberals had been.

It is difficult to avoid the conclusion that the rising sun of the Labour Party mostly eclipsed the working-class Liberal vote, notably in England, while the appeal of the Conservatives to a cross-class patriotism and hierarchical social order proved stronger than the less clearly defined Liberal vision of society. Liberalism from the 1920s was forced to adapt, becoming increasingly interventionist in social and economic policies while repudiating both socialism and conservatism, partly because Liberalism was neither socialist nor conservative, and partly because the party saw both as reflective of sectional class interests.

M

MASS OBSERVATION Formed in 1937 by the social anthropologist Tom **Harrisson** and the journalist Charles Madge, Mass Observation (MO) was dedicated to the social observation (as opposed to scientific social investigation) of the mass of British people. The documentary film maker Humphrey Jennings and the photographer Humphrey Spender were also at the heart of MO's work. Mass Observers lived in all areas of the country. A special interest in the industrial working classes, however, led to a great deal of activity in Bolton, Lancashire, which was generically titled Worktown. Harrisson, Madge and a team of volunteers assiduously wrote down their observations on everyday life at home, in the street, at the pub, at the cinema, in the football stadium, and in a variety of workplaces. Thanks to MO, social historians are fortunate to have access to a fascinating wealth of materials for Britain before and during the Second World War. MO made a number of studies on behalf of government during the war in addition to the everyday activities of observers. After the war it became a private company, making issue-based studies. Among its best-known publications are Humphrey Jennings and Charles Madge (eds), *May 12 1937: Mass Observation Day-Survey* (1937) and *Britain by Mass Observation* (1939), and Tom Harrisson, *Britain Revisited* (1961). Other titles give a tantalising flavour of MO's work, for example: *War Begins at Home* (1940), *Clothes Rationing Survey* (1941), *The Pub and the People* (1943), *People's Homes* (1943), *War Factory* (1943), *Peace and the Public* (1947) and *Living through the Blitz* (1976).

MEDIA A collective noun given to the **press** (namely newspapers and magazines), television and radio broadcasting, the cinema and, more recently, the internet. Literally these institutions – newspapers, magazines, cinema and television, the world wide web – mediate between people and the rest of the world. Historians of the media have focused on the newspapers, their ownership, readership, political biases and influences upon cultural and political developments in Britain; on the development of the BBC and its contribution to the cultural life of Britain; and on the cinema in British life and leisure.

MIDDLE CLASSES It is axiomatic for social historians to argue that the middle classes were rising in numbers, as well as in cultural, economic and political influence, throughout the twentieth century. Whereas the working classes rose and fell, service-sector expansion underpinned the growth of the middle classes and their increasing influence in cultural, economic and political spheres. Located between the landed aristocracy and gentry above them and the labouring proletariat below, the middle classes embraced a wide range of occupations, from lower-middle-class white-collar workers, or the much derided 'clerks', through the higher-paid professions and self-employed business people: in 1911 the combined categories of 'higher professions', 'lower professions', 'employers and proprietors', 'managers and administrators' and 'clerical workers' totalled 19 per cent of the working population. By 1991 this had risen to 54 per cent. These categories also reveal, of course, that the middle classes were not a homogeneous group. Furthermore, their lifestyles were diverse, varying by region, country, income and, increasingly, ethnicity and religion. After the 1960s, in particular, the Anglo-Indian middle classes expanded impressively.

Nonetheless, many broad shared characteristics defined the condition of being middle class. Education was a key factor. The middle classes were better qualified than the working classes, although by no means more intelligent. Private and home-centred, the majority of the middle classes preferred the suburbs to the inner cities, and were at the forefront of the suburbanisation of Britain, particularly England, after the Victorian years. This has been wittily termed 'the rise and sprawl of the middle classes'. The preferred housing was the single-family home, detached if possible, but a semi-detached home was also sought after. The expansion of Edwardian and interwar suburbs led to something akin to rings of middle-class suburbs surrounding the town and city centres; middle-class suburbanisation continued post-1945, although on a smaller scale than before the war, fuelled by the continuing aspiration for a suburban home and the increasing crossover of affluent working-class households into lower-middle-class suburban areas.

A postwar trend towards gentrification, however, a term coined by Ruth Glass, was evidence that a minority of middle-class people, often younger or in pursuit of an 'alternative' lifestyle, preferred to live in the inner city, or in the inner suburbs, the once declining poorer areas that were revitalised by bourgeois incomes and tastes. Yet tenure preferences remained dominated by the understanding that property ownership was essential to advancement, status and economic security: levels of home ownership among the middle classes remained above those of the working classes. From the 1980s, urban regeneration was in large part predicated on tempting the middle classes back to the poorer parts of town, because they would bring their economic and cultural capital with them.

Politically, the middle classes voted for all three major parties, but the Conservative Party remained the major beneficiary of middle-class voting. The majority of the membership of the Tory Party was also middle class. Labour was never purely a working-class movement, however. From the formation of the Fabian Society in the 1880s to the rise of New Labour in the 1990s, middle-class politicians and party activists were keen to identify themselves with socialism of varying shades of red. Many of Labour's leading politicians were middle class by birth.

By the final third of the twentieth century the middle classes formed the most contested political constituency at general elections. This was unsurprising because there were more of them than ever before. Any political party that ignored or repudiated the aspirations and values of the middle classes was doomed to failure.

MIDDLE ENGLAND Middle England does not refer to the geographical heart of the country, but to the middle classes and affluent working classes that live in the suburbs, or who enjoy home ownership in wealthier parts of the city and the country. This constituency, particularly the suburban middle classes and home-owning working classes, was targeted both by the Conservative Party during the 1980s and 1990s and by New Labour. The term was imported from the USA, where political parties had long since realised that middle America decided the fate of presidential elections.

MIXED ECONOMY The term given to the economy of Britain between the instigation of the Labour government's programme of nationalisation of key industries from 1946 to 1951 and the privatisation of the nationalised industries during the late 1980s and the 1990s. At no point was more than 20 per cent of the nation's industries controlled by government. The notion of a mixed economy enjoying both state investment and private enterprise was at the heart of the consensus politics of the 1950s and 1960s. It derived from John Maynard Keynes's view that governments needed to intervene strategically to support key industries in order to prevent a return to the crises of capitalism witnessed during the 1920s and 1930s. As the formulation of Conservative economic policies during the 1970s, and their enactment thereafter, was increasingly influenced by monetarism, the mixed economy was terminated. The governments of Margaret Thatcher and John Major viewed state subsidy as well meaning but wasteful, sustaining labour-intensive industries and leading to inertia rather than the much needed modernisation or even ruthless scaling-down of Britain's nationalised industries.

MONARCHY The apex of the British aristocracy and therefore of the class system, the monarchy remained hugely popular with the British public during the twentieth century. Difficult challenges were met and overcome. Criticisms of the unelected and subsidised excesses of the royal family surfaced time and again, and its legitimacy was often strongly attacked, but the many predictions about the death of the monarchy, or its diminution into a 'bicycle monarchy' akin to that of Denmark or the Netherlands, came to nothing.

The British monarchy was quintessentially British in image and manner, yet quite a multicultural familial network, with important connections to other crowned heads or deposed royal families in Europe. Queen Victoria, who reigned from 1837 to 1901, had famously been married to a German, and Queen Elizabeth II, on the throne since 1952, married a Greek, Prince Philip, in 1947.

Following the First World War, a number of crises threatened the public image of the royal family. The abdication crisis of December 1936, however, elicited probably more public sympathy for Edward VIII than hostility, and during the Second World War King George VI and Queen Elizabeth astutely avoided any semblance of a royal family cowering away in safety abroad. During the austerity years in early postwar Britain the glamour of the **royal wedding** in 1947 cheered up millions of people.

During the 1970s and 1980s the Labour MP Willie Hamilton was one of the more outspoken republican critics of the royal family. And Tom Nairn, in *The Enchanted Glass* (1983), viewed the monarchy as an essentially irrational continuation of a feudal institution, encouraging unhealthy attitudes and values in a democracy – for example deference, a tendency to accept or even revel in inequality and hierarchy.

Historians have taken up such themes, examining the role of the monarchy in an iconic sense, and questioning how far it was a conservative institution that was increasingly out of place in a progressive democracy. Even many socialist historians, however, have concluded that the monarchy was hardly any obstacle to progressive social change. Nor has the monarchy of Britain sustained a peculiarly conservative or even reactionary culture of politics.

The United States of America, for example – a republic – has long been characterised by a more conservative and anti-socialist mass politics than Britain. And fascist and reactionary movements in the French republic during the late twentieth century were more successful than in Britain. The monarchy played an important role in the ritualism and symbolism of British political life, and more widely contributed to a sense of national cohesion that was part of the complex issue of national identity.

MONETARISM Monetarism is opposed to Keynesianism. It aims to regulate inflation through control of the supply of money, and when allied to Thatcherism it was predisposed towards low taxation. In 1980, the medium-term financial strategy of the then chancellor of the exchequer, Geoffrey Howe, entailed the publishing of monetary targets. This approach was soon effectively abandoned, although the monetarist critique of high taxation and investment in nationalised industries was given expression in Tory economic policy until 1997.

MOTOR CAR MANUFACTURING From the 1920s to the 1980s a large-scale indigenous motor manufacturing industry existed in Britain: Austin, Morris, Rolls-Royce and Jaguar were among the best-known British companies, and the Morris Minor and the Mini were much-loved models. Vans and lorries were also manufactured in large quantities. However, foreign investment, particularly from the United States, also facilitated motor car manufacturing in Britain. Ford invested in a number of large plants between the wars: the factory at Dagenham and Becontree breathed life into the huge new council estate there. General Motors, later Vauxhall, also built plants in Britain. However, during the 1970s and subsequently, foreign competition rapidly undermined the viability of British vehicle manufacturing. The increasing numbers of European, Japanese and later South Korean cars on the roads was unwitting testimony to the failure of British motor companies to compete. Nationalisation and consolidation was one solution, although British Leyland was unable to become a fast-growing profitable enterprise. Instead, the governments of the 1980s turned to privatisation. By the end of the century, foreign interests owned most of the famous 'British' marques. The indigenous motor car industry, once a new industry between the wars and a symbol of national pride, was perhaps symbolised by the three-wheeled Robin Reliant. But motor vehicle production did not follow the road to near extinction endured by some of the staple industries. In 1938, 445,000 vehicles were built in Britain, and by the mid-1990s this had risen to over 1,600,000. The huge growth in motor car ownership and motorisation had been satisfied to a great degree by foreign imports, but also by foreign ownership in Britain. Large working-class communities had good reason to be grateful for inward investment from Europe, Asia and the United States of America.

MOTORISATION: CARS AND ROADS The internal combustion engine was invented in the nineteenth century but its impact was felt massively during the twentieth century. Before the 1920s, possession of a motor car was limited to the aristocracy and the wealthiest middle-class drivers: in 1914 fewer than one person in 230 owned a car, but this increased to one in fifteen by the eve of the Second World War. But the real growth came after the war: in 1951, 86 per cent of households had no car; by 1996, over 45 per cent of households owned one car, 21 per cent owned two, and 4 per cent had three cars – either on the drive, in the garage or parked on the road. In other words, by the 1990s over 70 per cent of households owned at least one car.

Consequences followed from this rise in motor car ownership. During the 1930s the motor vehicle was established as a killing machine. While the driving test was introduced in 1934, road deaths continued to rise into the postwar period until the 'road safety' campaigns for children, for example the Tufty Club, traffic-calming devices and speed limits began to reduce, but by no means remove, the tragedy of fatalities on the road. And roads had expanded massively. A major road-building programme began between the wars, and the Second World War itself saw the construction of many new metal roads for military traffic and other emergency needs. Major trunk roads were widened and lengthened during the postwar years, and the first road to be built to motorway standards was the Preston bypass in 1958, which later became part of the M6. The first section of the M1 motorway, from Watford to Rugby, was opened in November 1959. In 1909 there were just 175,470 miles of roads. By 2001, 246,987.57 miles (397,403 km) of roads crossed Great Britain, of which 48,713.49 miles (78,380 km) were trunk roads ('A' and 'B' roads) and 2,705.41 miles (4353 km) were motorways.

Today, environmentalism has made us aware of the impact of road building on the countryside and of fossil fuels (petrol and diesel) on the atmosphere. Social historians of motorisation, while cognisant of the physical consequences of the road system, emphasise the growing levels of mobility and choice afforded by the motor car, the democratisation of access to private transport, and the relationship of different brands of car to class and status. As with most areas of British life, private transport reflected inequalities. From the 1970s, notably, feminism condemned the greater access to cars for men compared with women. Wives and mothers at home often felt cut off from friends and family without a car, while working mothers needed one just as much as men did. This inequality diminished but was not removed with the rise of the two-car or even three-car household.

MULTICULTURALISM Multiculturalism refers to the respect and tolerance afforded to different cultures, ethnicities and religions. For many people, however, this scenario could lead to the dilution of a unifying national identity. In 2004, Trevor Phillips, the black chairman of the Commission for Racial Equality, called for the ending of the policy of multiculturalism. He was reacting to growing concerns about the relationship of multiculturalism to British national identity, and to a fear among many people that the common culture of Britishness was under attack from a relativism that privileged diversity rather than unity. The origins of multiculturalism may be dated to the views of Roy Jenkins, home secretary during the later 1960s, who argued that Britain should be a country mutually tolerant of cultural and ethnic differences. These sentiments accompanied the race relations legislation from 1965 and afterwards, and were also designed to negate the fears about immigration that became increasingly manifest during the 1960s. Although there was considerable evidence of fears about high rates of immigration, there was little to show that the majority of British people were in profound disagreement with Jenkins. The immigration acts of the 1970s and 1980s sought to allay these fears. The picture was nuanced, however. While wary of immigration, millions of people appeared to embrace the growing range of choices engendered by a fusion of different cultures and ethnicities. A poll for the BBC in August 2005, in the aftermath of the terrorist attacks in London the previous month, still found that over 60 per cent of British people thought multiculturalism made Britain a 'better place'. But 54 per cent of people also felt that parts of Britain were not very British any more because of immigration, and most considered that people who moved to Britain should adopt a British way of life and system of values. While this may superficially appear to throw into question a widespread faith in the relativism of multiculturalism, it also reveals a broad acceptance and tolerance of diversity. And it should be borne in mind that not everyone responding to the poll was British-born and white. Many immigrants wished to integrate into British culture, while negotiating this with the values and practices of their home countries. In the wake of a terrorist atrocity, most people in Britain appeared to agree with such aspirations.

MUSIC HALL During the Victorian era many pubs emerged as places to go to not only for a drink but also for a variety of entertainments. Some pubs were used as secret dens of street betting and illegal boxing, but they were additionally establishments where people could watch singers, dancers, singer-dancers, comedians and magicians. From this culture of pub-based entertainments grew the music hall. Many music halls remained small and informal affairs at the pub, while entrepreneurs in the larger towns and cities financed purpose-built variety palaces, some very grand in scale and decor. Before the rise of cinema between the wars, the music hall remained the big night out for many people.

The majority of the audience was working class, but the larger halls also catered for middle-class spectators. Most of the acts were also working class by birth, because music hall was an opportunity for upward social mobility for a talented few, as were sports and cinema. Among the most famous Victorian artistes who survived into the twentieth century were Marie **Lloyd**, a London singer, and Vesta Tilley, a female singer and drag act – that is, she used to play a man on stage. Of many male entertainers, to take one example, the singer Albert Chevalier used a market barrow as a prop, indicating the close connection of music hall acts to working-class life. Before the First World War, some music halls were converted to cinemas, a clear indication that the spectre of the screen in mass entertainment would eclipse the music hall stage. Much early cinema content owed something to music hall, however, and some early movie stars had trodden the boards of the most popular music halls before and, in some cases, after the war was over. It would be easy to write off the music hall as a mostly nineteenth-century entertainment that became obsolete during the twentieth century, but its influence was profound. Social historians emphasise the content of acts and the reactions of audiences as reported in contemporary newspaper and magazine articles to gain insights into the emotions and values of the Edwardian middle classes. These included escapism, a certain disdain as well as respect for authority, patriotism or jingoism, a love of sentimental and maudlin songs and stories, and an incorrigible affection for ribald jokes and innuendo. In Chevalier's song 'My Old Dutch', for example, a softly lilting ballad explained the enduring loyal affection of an elderly husband for his wife of many years, while one of Marie Lloyd's most famous songs, 'A little of what you fancy', was a song that cut against prevailing patriarchal notions of a woman's place as sexless and witless. Similar themes remained the stock-in-trade of working-class entertainments throughout the twentieth century. In such television soap operas as *Coronation Street* (begun 1960) and *East Enders* (begun 1985) bawdy and sentimental working-class culture is still thriving, and many of the characters resemble updated caricatures from the music hall of a hundred years ago.

N

NATIONAL HEALTH SERVICE (NHS) According to opinion polls in July 2008, the NHS on its sixtieth birthday was viewed by the majority of British people as far from perfect, but also as a national institution of which the country could be proud. Initiated by the **National Health Service Act** of 1946, and beginning life in 1948, the NHS was the creation of Aneurin Bevan, then minister for health and housing. Universal health care was engendered by Liberal as well as socialist policies, however. It consolidated the evolution of the contributory national insurance systems established during the New Liberal governments of 1906–14, developed in an *ad hoc* manner by interwar governments, and advocated by Beveridge and Keynes during the war. And in 1944 the Conservative Party's *A National Health Service* accepted an NHS for postwar Britain. Since its beginnings in an atmosphere of consensus, revisions to its scope and to its original pledge to be 'free' at the point of need were made many times: prescription charges are a case in point. It also became hugely expensive, not least because of an ageing and growing population and the advances in science and medicine which required expenditure on new brands of drugs. By 1980 the NHS accounted for almost 6 per cent of British gross domestic product. The Conservative government of Margaret Thatcher sought to rectify this, while claiming that the NHS was 'safe' in Tory hands. Entitlement to consultations with a general practitioner, however, and to hospital care that was free at the point of need, remained the *quid pro quo* of compulsory national insurance and income-tax deductions. Private health care, encouraged by governments in the 1980s in order to cut the costs of public health and to promote 'choice', ran alongside the NHS but did little to undermine its relationship to the health and medical care of most Britons. By 1997, the state of the NHS was an election issue: New Labour pledged to improve it while keeping broadly within Tory spending targets. In the following ten years, however, government spending on the health service greatly increased, and the developing synergies between public and private health facilities were continued by government. As the baby boomers of the 1940s and 1950s advance towards or reach retirement age, the conundrum of financing an expanding health service remains an urgent political and social issue.

NATIONAL IDENTITY Most people in Britain during the twentieth century felt 'British' to a greater or lesser degree. But some disliked being British, notably millions of Irish people before the Anglo-Irish Treaty of 1921. In addition, many Catholic Irish living in Northern Ireland following the treaty remained more Irish than British in religious sentiment and national identity. Others for various reasons, be it colour, culture, religion, politics or place of birth, felt less British than the majority of whites born in Britain. Many on the left were acutely ashamed of being British, and pointed to the existence of the legacy of the British Empire as the reason. Others questioned the very notion of 'Britain' as Scots and Welsh devolution gathered pace. The relationship between Scots and Welsh nationalism to an idea of Britain was different to that of English people and Britain. Most English people used the terms 'British' and 'English'

almost coterminously, but then England was the largest country, in terms of population as well as of cultural, economic and political influence. Both Plaid Cymru and the Scottish Nationalist Party, however, were by no means monolithic in their views: many individuals wished to remain within Britain via a devolved system; others wanted full-blown home government.

So what did 'Britishness' mean in relation to national identity? That question was probably easier to answer at the beginning of the twentieth century. With the exception of the Irish, millions of people were aware that they lived at the heart of empire, had faith in the system of parliamentary democracy based in London, saw the monarch as the legitimising figure of both government and the Anglican Church, and held that Britain was the most powerful and among the wealthiest countries on the planet. Popular patriotism and jingoism in Edwardian Britain were proof of such views. However, we should never lose sight of apathy and of the indifference of millions of British people to the 'British' Empire. For many, being British was simply taken for granted. Nonetheless 'Britishness' was qualified by many other forms of identity: in addition to Scots and Welsh nationalism, regionalism within England was another one. Class identity was also a powerful force for both collective and self-definition, and those who were more politically class conscious, for example Marxists and socialists, often felt that class was or should be a more important source of identification than country and empire. Between the wars, however, the appropriation of a sense of British nationhood by fascism led to hostile anti-patriotic statements on the left, while the majority continued to hold fast to less extreme visions of British identity than were assumed by ultra-right wing groups.

The Second World War heightened a

sense of British patriotism. Nazi Germany became a much hated common enemy, and historians used to view the war as having reduced class distinctions for a strengthened sense of Britishness, although that view has been increasingly contested since the 1980s. In the postwar period, however, the growth of immigration was seen by politicians, particularly in the Conservative Party, as threatening a British sense of national identity, and those fears began to grow as the language and ethos of multiculturalism became increasingly influential. Many on the left, particularly Marxist social and cultural historians, welcomed these challenges to British national identity and attempted to prove that the notion of Britishness itself was merely a series of outdated constructs – that is, myths and representations – that required interrogation. Hence the heritage industry was attacked for playing to a largely white notion of British cultural history. Cultural stereotypes, including 'pearly kings and queens', types of regional and national food such as the 'ploughman's lunch', and reassuring images of country villages, were all deconstructed as 'national fictions' that maintained an unquestioning belief system among the British, while contributing to a rather spurious assemblage of stereotypes that in combination constituted 'Britishness'.

At the end of the century, the notion that the very idea of Britishness might be inherently racist was mooted in the Parekh Report. Entitled *The Future of Multicultural Britain*, it argued that the majority of white British people should make accommodations to adjust to multiculturalism. This raised some difficult issues. Diversity was certainly a source of strength more than a sign of weakness, but many felt that a shared idea of 'Britishness' allied to citizenship could assist in fomenting a common identity across class, racial and religious divides. During the twenty-first century, these issues will continue to be debated, often passionately so.

NATIONAL INSURANCE A fundamental principle of social insurance, national insurance was pioneered in late nineteenth-century Germany. As concern grew in Britain about the need to address poverty and its consequences, the principle of compulsory contributions (deductions) from incomes in order to fund a state apparatus of unemployment insurance and old-age pensions was adopted by New Liberalism. Among its keenest proponents were Winston Churchill and David Lloyd George.

Whatever the iniquities of the system of universal national insurance, most politicians and welfare experts would now argue that it is a vastly superior scheme to the uneven and often crabbed system of Poor Law relief that predated unemployment benefits.

NATIONAL LOTTERY The first national lottery was abolished during the 1820s. In European countries regional and national government continued to promote and profit from lotteries, but the strength of nonconformity and the National Anti-Gambling League during the Victorian years and the early twentieth century meant that British punters – gamblers – were unlucky. Introduced in 1994 by the Conservative government of John Major, the National Lottery was the first nationwide state-sponsored gaming operation since the 1820s. It is now a leading activity in the culture of betting and gambling in Britain, held twice weekly, and televised, with different games and a paraphernalia of scratch-cards to induce the British people to have a flutter. Following the reform of the gaming laws during the 1960s, it was by no means inevitable that a national lottery would be introduced, but the drive of the Conservative governments of the 1980s and 1990s to reduce direct income tax meant that voluntary forms of taxation were increasingly acceptable. The National Lottery had generated over £12 billion for good causes by 2007. Among these, the most prominent beneficiaries were sportsmen and women: the achievements of British competitors in the Beijing Olympics of 2008 owed a great deal to the gambling habits of the nation. One of the lottery's negative consequences, however, was to reduce the turnover of the football pools, a weekly form of gaming introduced between the wars.

NATIONAL PARKS National parks were considered important for the reconstruction of postwar Britain, but the immediate needs of urban areas were addressed first: the **National Parks Act** was passed in 1949, some years after the major apparatus of town planning was introduced. Yet the appeal of the countryside for town dwellers was powerfully understood by the Labour government. For Lewis Silkin, the minister for town and country planning, the national parks were to protect Britain's areas of outstanding natural beauty from unwarranted development but also to become arenas for rational recreation. Silkin described his Bill as 'a people's charter for the open air, for the hikers and the ramblers, for everyone who likes to get out into the open air and enjoy the countryside'. The Act effectively nationalized private land and allowed the creation during the 1950s of the ten national parks in England and Wales: Dartmoor (1951); the Peak District (1951); the Lake District (1951); Snowdonia (1951); the North York Moors (1952); the Pembrokeshire Coast (1952); the Yorkshire Dales (1954); Exmoor (1954); Northumberland (1956); and the Brecon Beacons (1957). The Broads in Norfolk became a quasi-national park in 1988, and the New Forest was added in the early twenty-first century. In Scotland, two major national parks were finally created by an Act of 2000.

NATIONALISATION Nationalisation is the transfer of privately owned companies to the state. It is also referred to as 'public ownership'. At its conference in 1918, the Labour Party adopted a constitution committing it to the ownership by the state of the means of production, distribution and exchange. Coming towards the ending of the First World War, the timing of that conference was all important. The conflict had necessitated government control and coordination of industrial production, public transport and health services. For the duration of the war, therefore, key industries and public services had been effectively 'nationalised', and trade unions wished this to continue. In the staple industries, notably coal mining, trade unions felt that ownership and management by the state would be far fairer and more benign than in private hands. However, the Liberal–Conservative government of David Lloyd George returned industries to their owners. Significantly, the minority Labour governments of 1924 and of 1929–31 led by Ramsay MacDonald made no attempt to nationalise the mines.

The major catalyst for nationalisation, however, came with the Second World War. To a greater degree than in 1914–18, the state now coordinated the industries and services of the country. The Labour government from 1945 set about its plans to continue and extend state ownership of key industries, as outlined in **Landmarks**.

Road haulage and steel production were denationalised by the Tories during the early 1950s but most nationalised industries stayed in state ownership until 1979. During the 1970s, nationalisation was used as a tool to try to save ailing industries, but outcomes were often disappointing. The privatisation programme executed under Margaret Thatcher and

John Major between 1983 and 1997 effectively abolished the mixed economy and dealt a heavy blow to any lingering notions of consensus in economic policy. If anything, a new agenda emerged, shared by the Conservatives and New Labour: privatisation under government regulation was more effective than any Clause 4-inspired socialist reorganisation of the country's economy. The ditching of Clause 4 by Tony Blair during the mid-1990s, to the chagrin of the Labour left, was the sharpest illustration of Labour's change of heart. The onset of de-industrialisation, furthermore, also contributed to the death of nationalisation: by 2000 little more than a fifth of the economy was made up of manufacturing industry. What was once the percentage of state ownership and control in the entire economy was now the total sum of manufacturing. And to have nationalised service sector companies – for example, the banking and building societies, retail and tourism – was no longer on the political agenda. Interestingly, during the credit crunch crisis of 2008, nationalisation was viewed as a temporary safety net for ailing banks and building societies, but by no means as a permanent vision for the future. The postwar period had effectively witnessed the rise and fall of the socialist dream of a mixed economy.

NEW INDUSTRIES The term given to the manufacturing sectors that became established in interwar Britain in addition to the staple industries. The most significant new industries were motor car manufacturing and its allied trades. Morris in Oxford was the most successful interwar car manufacturing company, established by William **Morris** in 1914. Electrically powered goods and devices for the home, light engineering, pharmaceuticals and drugs were other leading new industries. These were mostly twentieth-century operations, whereas the staple industries were inherited from the previous century. London and the South-East and the Midlands of England enjoyed greater levels of growth from the unequal location of both domestic and overseas investment in these sectors. But then London has long held a competitive advantage over most other areas of Britain. Among the key foreign names associated with the new industries were Ford and Vauxhall (American; motor car manufacturing) and Hoover (American; domestic appliances).

NEW LABOUR Following the fourth consecutive general election defeat of the Labour Party in 1992, many of its younger members became frustrated at the slowness of the leadership to adapt to major changes and developments within the late twentieth century, and to grasp the complex values of the electorate, particularly those of middle England. Although John Smith's leadership promised to refresh the party, his untimely death in 1994 provided the opportunity for a fuller remaking of the image of Labour and its policies. This task, inspired in large part by the triumph of the New Democrats in the United States in 1992, following twelve years of Republican presidency, owed much to the thinking of the Labour strategist Philip Gould, but was effectively handled by Tony Blair, the leader of the Labour Party following the death of Smith. Young and charismatic, Blair set about dismantling older shibboleths held particularly on the left of the Labour Party. Nationalisation and higher rates of taxation for the wealthy were avoided by the new Blair agenda. He also argued that private sector finance was required to boost the effectiveness of public services. To a considerable degree, Blair and his supporters rebuilt the Labour Party on a Social Democratic model rather than a socialist one. Indeed, the 'Gang of Four' who had quit Labour to become the Social Democratic Party in 1981 would have felt mostly at home in the remodelled party of the mid-1990s. New Labour triumphed at the general election of 1997, and again in 2001, and Blair became the most successful Labour leader since the party had been formed at the beginning of the twentieth century. Other leading New Labour politicians were Gordon Brown and Peter Mandelson. Some socialist historians of postwar Labour politics, particularly on the left, are hostile to Blair, although others observe precedents in the thinking of Hugh Gaitskell during the 1950s. Even conservative historians have acknowledged Blair's undoubted political skills and accepted the wisdom of keeping to the centre ground of British politics.

NEW LIBERALISM New Liberalism was the interventionist reformist antidote to the laissez-faire model of Liberal politics associated with William Gladstone. Responding to unemployment and a worsening of social conditions in British cities, many intellectuals of the 1880s and 1890s began to question the social consequences of minimal government policies. The sociologist L. T. **Hobhouse** and the editor of the *Manchester Guardian* C. P. Scott were leading New Liberals. Prominent New Liberal politicians included Christopher Addison and David Lloyd George. The programme of social policy passed between 1906 and 1914 was essentially the enactment of New Liberalism, laying the foundations upon which an interventionist welfare state would later be constructed.

NEW TOWNS The new towns of Great Britain were initiated by the **New Towns Acts** of 1946 and 1965, both passed by Labour governments. The Act of 1946 was designed to relieve overcrowded and in some cases blitzed towns and cities of excess population and industrial concentration. In 1940, the **Barlow Report** had given explicit endorsement to this policy of decentralisation, and subsequent plans, such as the Greater London Plan and the Clyde Valley Regional Plan, both drawn up by Sir Patrick Abercrombie, became official policy. London, the largest city, gained eight new towns – namely Basildon, Bracknell, Crawley, Harlow, Hatfield, Hemel Hempstead, Stevenage and Welwyn Garden City. This last was a practical and symbolic link between the garden cities and the new towns that they influenced.

Arguably, the Act of 1965 was one of the few significantly consequential pieces of legislation to stem from the first Wilson government's much vaunted but ultimately disappointing commitment to a modernised economy and society based upon planning. For the new towns were not only intended to provide housing, they were also supposed to regenerate the economies of the regions in which they were designated. As the most populated country with the largest cities, England was granted the most new towns, over twenty in total, but a number were built in Northern Ireland, Scotland and Wales. Each town was seen into existence by a development corporation, which oversaw economic investment, construction and other issues for the first generation of its life. Like the garden cities, they were intended to provide self-contained cities in the country that conversely contained 'country' (parks and woodlands) in the city.

New towns privileged a low-density environment containing neighbourhoods set in parklands, houses with gardens, and some flats. This was accomplished with varying degrees of success, depending on the design of the neighbourhoods, the integrity of the town plan, and the money available from central government. New town development corporations, subsidised by governments, could offer favourable land prices to tempt companies to locate or relocate. Any worker who accepted employment in the new town was entitled to a new house, and that in itself was an attraction to many poorer or average-income households who wanted better economic and social opportunities than were offered in the poorer parts of older urban areas.

The new towns failed, however, to provide socially mixed and balanced communities by the 1960s. The reason was clear: the development corporations built most houses for rent. During the later 1940s, 1950s and 1960s, this was attractive to working-class families and couples seeking to escape the older cities, but it alienated the middle classes, who wanted to buy their own home and to make money from property. For this reason, the generation of new towns built since 1965, of which Milton Keynes has become the largest and best known, aimed for a mix of housing styles and tenures. Earlier new towns were also provided with more opportunities for home ownership.

By 1999 the twenty-eight new towns of Britain housed over 2 million people. Collectively they made up the largest programme of planned new communities in postwar Western Europe. Yet beyond the communities themselves, little national pride about the new towns was in evidence, for a variety of reasons. Conservatives often viewed them as socialist social engineering smuggled in by the development corporations. And many who criticised new towns for urbanising the countryside failed to understand that planned focused urban expansion was a containment strategy for unplanned suburbanisation. A failure to appreciate their achievements and to grasp the historical causes for their shortcomings was also symptomatic of misunderstandings about the role of town and country planning in modern Britain, and of a prejudice against modern urban environments, expressed in part in a general dislike of modern architecture. Yet the new towns had certainly raised the standards of living of most of their inhabitants.

NEWSPAPERS The predominant broadsheet or highbrow newspapers of the nineteenth and twentieth centuries were *The Times*, the *Daily Telegraph* and the *Manchester Guardian* (now *The Guardian*). During the later Victorian and the Edwardian periods, however, the so-called new journalism greatly increased the number of newspapers in Britain and changed the culture of daily and weekly newspapers. Characterised by more intrepid and investigative methods of enquiry and by writing in a manner that was more readily accessible to the increasingly literate public, the new journalism found its voice in a number of more radical local newspapers and in the new national newspapers of the Edwardian era, namely the *Daily Express*, the *Daily Mail* and the *Daily Mirror*.

Newspaper journalists are not always characterised by objectivity or fair-mindedness. The newspapers for which journalists work are usually identified with a political party – left, right or centre. This is often because of ownership and the politics and values of the newspaper's proprietor. To give some common examples, it did not take long for the *Daily Mail* and *Daily Mirror* to align themselves with the Conservative Party and the Liberal–Tory coalition of 1916 to 1922. The *Mail* remained Conservative but, due in part to a change of ownership, during the late 1930s the *Daily Mirror* adopted an Americanised tabloid style and increasingly moved towards a working-class readership. However, by the Second World War it was explicitly a 'Labour paper'. Another newspaper that explicitly supported the Labour Party, from its inception to its demise, was the *Daily Herald*. The *Mirror* has supported the Labour Party since the Second World War.

361

Further to the left, the *Daily Worker* was the longest-running communist newspaper: during the mid-1960s it became the *Morning Star*.

More mainstream daily newspapers supported the Conservative Party than Labour. During the 1970s and 1980s, for example, the *Daily Express*, the *Daily Mail*, the *Daily Telegraph* and *The Sun* were all Tory newspapers, although sometimes their support shifted: both the *Express* and *The Sun* moved in 1997 to advocate Tony Blair and New Labour, for example. The staunchest Conservative newspapers were the mid-market *Daily Express* and the *Daily Mail* and the broadsheet highbrow newspapers the *Daily Telegraph* and *The Times*. In common with the *Daily Mirror*, with which it was co-owned, the *Mail* lent support to Oswald Mosley during the years 1932–4.

Today, the other broadsheet newspaper of note is *The Independent*. This will only be useful for historians of the late twentieth century because it was established relatively late, in 1986, with a mission to remain 'independent' of the party politics of *The Times*, *Telegraph* or *Guardian*. Within ten years, however, *The Independent* was manifesting scepticism towards the Conservative governments of the later 1980s and 1990s.

Tabloid newspapers carried less weighty reporting or analysis than their more esteemed cousins, but are still useful for party-political views on major events and politicians, for historians of popular culture and populist journalism.

Local newspapers continued to thrive throughout the twentieth century, and all towns and cities had at least one. Counties also possessed newspapers. Both urban and county-based newspapers have tended to be understudied by media historians compared with the national press, although as contemporary sources they are hugely important. Many new local papers were established during the century, some becoming local institutions, others folding after just a few months or years. Political allegiances varied in the provincial press, but the latter's emphasis upon local and regional issues and events, both in themselves and in relation to the national-governmental context, meant that they often reflected views and a range of opinions that opposed government policies.

We should also recognise the significance of the sporting press, both newspapers and magazines. Essential for histories of sport and leisure, sporting papers were in addition vehicles for information useful for betting and gambling. The most enduring, such as the *Sporting Life*, along with the less successful or short-lived, are to be found at the **British Library Newspaper Library** in North London.

P

PACIFISM The history of pacifism in twentieth-century Britain began with the conscientious objectors to the First World War. As conscription was first introduced in 1916, many who felt the war was unnecessary and tragically wasteful of human life established the No-Conscription Fellowship. After 'the war to end all wars', popular and political fears began to grow at the destabilisation of Europe following the Paris Peace Conference in 1919. And in 1921 some of those involved in the No-Conscription Fellowship started the No More War Movement, headed by Fenner **Brockway**. The rise of fascism in Italy by 1922, and of Nazism in Germany, and the growing awareness of aerial bombardment as a consequence of innovations in military aircraft gave further succour to pacifism. The year the Nazis came to power in

Germany, 1933, also witnessed the publication of *Testament of Youth*, by Vera Brittain, and the pacifist victory at the **East Fulham by-election**. In the following year the Peace Pledge Union (PPU) was established. During the Second World War pacifists continued to argue that the war could be ended by negotiation, and some were arrested for exhortations to resist military service when fighting the evil of fascism and defending Britain were the major priorities. Members of the PPU were also publicly critical of the saturation bombing of German cities towards the end of the conflict. In the postwar period the pacifists found a home in the Campaign for Nuclear Disarmament and the left of the Labour Party. One of the most visible pacifist movements occurred in the mid-1980s at the Greenham Common Peace Camp, next to the little Berkshire town of Aldermaston. Women sang, skirled, ate, slept and climbed perimeter fences bearing placards against the bomb and the United States of America. Since then, some women involved at Greenham have remained as activists in pacifism.

PERMISSIVENESS AND THE 'PERMISSIVE SOCIETY' The 'permissive society' was the term used to capture the essence of the social and cultural changes that occurred in Britain during the 1960s. In the wake of the reforms of abortion, contraception, and divorce, Victorian values were under threat. The atmosphere of permissiveness was heightened by the liberal currents carried by rock and popular music, theatre, films and television programmes. Victorianism was also challenged by British youth culture, whose relationship with American popular culture and fashion was always close: Californian hippy-style libertarian values were the apogee of liberalisation and permissiveness – 'anything goes'.

This was not a one-dimensional lifting of the shackles, however. Mary White-house, for example, and her National Viewers' and Listeners' Association lambasted what she called 'BBC dirt', while millions of working-class and middle-class people, not all of them middle-aged or elderly, felt uncertain at the growing levels of what they viewed as increasingly promiscuous or disrespectful behaviour. Such sentiments may have influenced the general election result in 1970. They certainly surfaced during the 1980s, when Margaret Thatcher and her advisors launched an attack on permissiveness and called for a return to Victorian restraint and a spirit of self-help and deferred enjoyment rather than instant gratification.

POOR LAW The Old Poor Law was begun in the seventeenth century. Its replacement, the New Poor Law, initiated by the Poor Law (Amendment) Act of 1834, introduced a system of unemployment and poverty relief based upon indoor relief – the hated workhouse – and outdoor relief – payments to assist the family or individual in times of hardship. Payments were kept very low via the principle of 'less eligibility': they were to be lower than the lowest local incomes. Indoor relief was loathed because it separated parents from children and men from women, leading in many cases to the temporary break-up of the family. Moreover, the respectable poor down on their luck in these austere establishments often found themselves cheek by jowl with the 'unrespectable poor'. Increasingly the Poor Law was viewed, particularly by socialists, as demeaning to its recipients. Beatrice and Sidney Webb called for its abolition during the Edwardian years. New Liberal reforms, notably child welfare, national insurance and old-age pensions, weakened the Poor Law, as did reforms after 1918. It was mostly terminated in 1929–30 by the **Local Government Act**, and any lingering vestiges were ended after the Second World War.

POPULAR MUSIC In common with most other Western European countries, Britain enjoyed different forms of popular music throughout the twentieth century. To a greater degree than most Europeans, however, the British enjoyed a special relationship with the United States of America in popular music that encompassed the vaudeville-influenced music hall songs of the Edwardian years, the Tin Pan Alley gramophone records and dance-band music of the interwar period, through to the blues, jazz, soul, rock music, disco and trip hop of the postwar years. Some acts were distinctively British. The Beatles were an obvious case, as was Cliff **Richard**, with his clean-cut image. Some musical movements were more British than American, moreover. Skiffle during the 1950s, the Mersey beat of the 1960s, glam rock, northern soul and ska during the 1970s, the new romantics and grindcore metal in the 1980s, and trip hop during the 1990s – all owed something to American influences, but each had a decidedly British accent and flavour.

From the beginning of the charts in 1952 into the early twenty-first century, the ten best-selling singles acts in Britain were Cliff Richard, Elvis Presley, Madonna, Michael Jackson, the Beatles, **Queen**, Elton **John**, Rod Stewart, Kylie Minogue and David Bowie. Hence six were home-grown, three were American and one (Minogue) was Australian. In the USA, the Beatles, Elton John and the Rolling Stones were among the ten best-selling singles acts over the same period.

POPULATION In 1901 the population of Britain, including Ireland, amounted to 41.5 million people. By 1921 it was over 47 million, and by 1951 it had risen to 50 million. Over the course of the postwar years it continued to grow, to just under 60 million by 2001 (excluding Ireland). In the course of a century almost 20 million people were added to the landmasses of Britain and Ireland, and of course towns and services were forced to expand as a consequence. Population growth meant suburbanisation. Nine out of ten people in the twentieth century lived in urban areas.

Among the reasons for increases in population were the improvements in food, nutrition and health and welfare services – rising living standards that were a function of affluence and increased consumerism – and life expectancies improved across the developed world. Women lived longer than men, however. The introduction of antibiotics, vaccinations and other drugs, furthermore, decreased mortality rates as a consequence of illnesses. Immigration also increased the size of the population, but not by a great deal, because emigration counter-balanced a considerable degree of inward flow. Generally, the British population was never monolithic, but it became increasingly heterogeneous during the course of the twentieth century. In 1901 less than 0.5 per cent of people in Britain were of colour. By the 1990s Britain was still predominantly white: at the 2001 census the white population stood at 92.1 per cent, while 'Asian, Black, Chinese and others' amounted to 7.9 per cent of the total.

England was by far the largest country, numbering a little over 30 million in 1901 and 50 million in 2001. The population of Scotland rose from just 4.5 to 5.1 million over the course of the century, while the population of Wales never rose above 3 million. Out-migration from Ireland, Scotland and Wales certainly had a negative effect on population growth, particularly between the wars. Many emigrants from Scotland and Wales went abroad, but considerable numbers moved to England.

POVERTY During the 1880s, poverty was 'discovered' by social scientists, notably Charles Booth, as a large-scale problem in the big cities. Booth's great seventeen-volume *Life and Labour of the People in London* had found that almost a third of London's working-class population were living below his 'poverty line', an income per household below which subsistence became poverty. A little later, Benjamin Seebohm Rowntree, in *Poverty: A Study of Town Life* (1899), adopting a more sophisticated methodology than Booth, also found that a worrying percentage of the working-class population in York was in 'primary poverty', where income was insufficient to meet basic needs. Both Booth and Rowntree, as nonconformists, were keen to distinguish between primary poverty, which was caused by inadequate income and means, and secondary poverty, a degradation brought about not necessarily by insufficient income but by the wrong types of expenditure: spending money on alcohol and gambling were two causes of secondary poverty. Nonetheless, their major diagnosis was inadequate income. Between the wars, further social studies came to similar conclusions about causes of poverty, while accepting that the percentage of people in abject hardship was decreasing.

New Liberal social policies and piecemeal extensions to them between the wars drove down levels of poverty in Britain. The effect of high unemployment and underemployment during the 1930s, however, exacerbated the struggle for survival of hundreds of thousands of working-class households. Studies by the Pilgrim Trust and other charities, and the humane social observations of such writers as George Orwell, reminded the middle-class reading public that Britain was still a divided nation. And poverty was 'rediscovered' yet again during the Second World War as evacuation and abnormal wartime circumstances brought home to many middle-class people the low levels of health and dress of many working-class folk. The instigation of the welfare state between 1945 and 1950 failed to break down hard-core poverty. Brian Abel-Smith and Peter Townsend found that, even on the tightest definition of 'poverty' used to calculate **national assistance**, there were 2 million Britons in poverty in 1960. In *The Poor and the Poorest* (1965) they defined poverty as living on less than 140 per cent of the national assistance scale plus rent and other housing costs. Thus their figure of people living in poverty in 1960 was 7,438,000 (14.2 per cent of the population). Ken Coates and Richard Silburn, in *Poverty: the Forgotten Englishmen* (1967), reported on the appalling conditions of St Anns in Nottingham. Similar pockets of impoverishment could be found in almost every large town and city in Britain.

During the 1970s, the analysis of poverty was clouded by the introduction of the concept of 'relative deprivation' by the sociologist Peter Townsend and other social scientists. Whereas absolute deprivation was insufficient income and resources to be able to meet subsistence, relative deprivation was calibrated in relation to the rising standards of living in society and a subjective range of what was acceptable or even desirable. Hence definitions of poverty were partly, perhaps largely, cultural rather than simply economic. Certainly, many politicians argued that absolute poverty had been eradicated by national insurance, free health care, council housing and old-age pensions. At the end of the century, however, the University of Bristol's Centre for the Study of Poverty and Social Justice claimed that 9 million people were unable to access adequate housing, 5 million could not afford essential clothing for cold weather, and 12 million suffered from financial insecurity. There were elements of both absolute and relative deprivation in this analysis, but it was impossible to doubt the existence of poverty. The very rhetoric of

New Labour, and its continuing pledge to abolish child poverty, was further proof.

PRIVATISATION Privatisation is the process of turning state-owned industries into private companies by handing them to investors. Key staple industries and public transport were effectively nationalised during both the First and the Second World Wars, but returned to their private owners from 1918. Following 1945, however, the nationalisation of key sectors of the British economy meant that state ownership of the economy grew to over one-fifth. For socialists especially it remained a solution to many troubled sectors, for example the motor car industry. During the 1980s and 1990s, however, the Conservative governments of Margaret Thatcher and John Major privatised many manufacturing industries and also public transport: some thrived, some continued to struggle, others declined to almost nothing.

PROTECTIONISM The basic tenet of protectionism, a policy opposed to laissez-faire economics based upon tariff reform, was to insulate the British home market from foreign competition. Protectionism increasingly captured the imagination of the Conservative Party, but never a majority of it. Although the idea had nineteenth-century antecedents, the drive for tariff reform in the twentieth century began in 1903 with the decision of the Unionist colonial secretary Joseph Chamberlain to resign office in order to campaign for protectionism to encompass the British Empire. The conversion of Stanley Baldwin to protectionism probably cost the Conservatives the 1923 general election. However, following the Ottawa Conference of 1932, during the Great Depression, import controls were finally and formally adopted. Hence, under the Conservative-dominated National Government, the era of free trade was ended. Among other Conservatives, Winston Churchill was far from happy with the new economics. However, many on the left and also on the right, including Sir Oswald Mosley, a recent convert to fascism, were convinced of the need to protect British markets and jobs through a system of imperial preference.

PUB, THE Most of the alcohol consumed in Britain during the twentieth century was drunk at the local public house, or pub. This seemingly comfortable and traditional institution, however, was the site of significant social changes. When Mass Observation made their study of *The Pub and the People* (1943), it was mostly a male-dominated environment. A single woman entering a pub to buy a drink was regarded as morally dubious, so women were almost always accompanied by men, and men bought their drinks. With the rise of feminism during the 1970s, however, women became increasingly visible in pubs, usually in couples or groups. Children, by contrast, remained largely excluded from the interiors of most pubs, with the exception of the so-called children's room, increasingly often tagged onto the outside of the new public houses built in the expanding suburbs of the 1930s.

Until the 1960s, moreover, most of the ale drunk in pubs was in varying shades of brown, with the exception of stout. Bitter, mild and light ale were the favourites of both middle- and working-class men, but most commonly associated with the proletarian watering holes of the larger towns and cities. Lager was mostly served in little bottles, and was commonly regarded as a woman's drink, but the coldness of lager, especially during the summer months, led to its growing dominance in pub drinking. Marketing campaigns during the 1970s by American companies responsible for *Colt 45* and other so-called beers also enhanced the taste for lagers, but so too at that time did membership of the European Union. Danish and Dutch lagers were aggressively marketed, and British breweries turned to home-grown versions of this 'continental' drink. But the breweries also did a great deal to damage the reputation of bitter with the introduction of keg beers, fizzy and one-dimensional in taste. Hence the birth in 1971 of CAMRA, or the Campaign for the Revitalisation of Ale, later renamed the Campaign for Real Ale. Its largely but not exclusively middle-class membership pushed hard for the retention of the finest regional beers in Britain and for the preservation and promotion of the most attractive or comfortable pubs. This was consumerism in the context of alcohol.

Pubs and alcohol were not enjoyed by everyone, however. Since the Victorian period, nonconformist churches and tee-totallers had been campaigning for pro-hibition and for the closure of pubs, particularly in working-class districts. Drinkers were urged by ardent chapel-goers to sign the 'pledge' to reject alcohol. Inebriation was alleged to be a threat to industrial productivity, and expenditure on alcohol was castigated as improvident. To maintain levels of munitions produc-tion during the First World War, the Defence of the Realm Act in 1914 restricted access to alcohol by reducing pub opening hours. For David Lloyd George, secretary of state for war, beer was as much an enemy as the Germans. After the war, the Licensing Act of 1921 maintained the wartime restriction on pub opening, and only minor variations were entertained by local authorities. Until the late 1980s, pubs rarely opened before 11.00 a.m. and were closed again by 2.30 p.m. They opened again around 5.00 or 6.00 p.m. and were locked shut by 11.15 p.m.

These restrictions did nothing to erode the appeal of alcohol in working-class life. As George Orwell observed during the 1930s, a little drink was something to look forward to for the unemployed or the low paid, whose existence would have been unbearable without it. In his autobio-graphical work *The Classic Slum* (1971), Robert **Roberts** made much the same point: the pub was 'the shortest way out' of the Manchester slum. The coalition government of the wine-drinking Churchill was more relaxed about alcohol consump-tion during the Second World War, although beer strength was reduced.

Religious campaigns against drink fell away in the twentieth century. In some regions where a nonconformist tradition continued, access to pubs was correspond-ingly restricted, but concerns about drink could not successfully stop the tide of secu-larism or of alcohol flowing from the beer taps. The liberalisation of opening hours by the **Licensing Act** of 1988, allowing pubs to remain open all day if their owners wished, coincided with a growing fashion for wine bars, a context which was more comfortable for women than the back-street boozer. The appearance of wine bars also signalled a significant shift in the tastes of the alcohol-drinking public. For wines were becoming increasingly popular not only in bars but also in pubs and for drinking at home. Supermarket shelves began to sell wines from the 'New World' in addition to those from France, Germany (increasingly passé) and Italy, as well as Spanish reds. In order to cater for the wine-drinking and real-ale consuming customer, 'gastro-pubs' began to appear in larger cities, and in some country alehouses, from the beginning of the twenty-first century. This was also, in part, a reaction to the way in which breweries cashed in on the appetites generated by alcohol by serving cheap fast food. Hence both the appearance and the format of 'the pub' were in transition by the end of the twentieth century. Furthermore, in a development that might have pleased the teetotal campaigners of a hundred years ago, many pubs were forced to call 'last orders' permanently. Over 1,400 licensed premises closed down in 2007, for example. Among the causes of this were the afore-mentioned rise of wine bars and of home drinking; increased taxation levied on alcohol; competition from restaurant chains and pub conversions into restau-rants; immigration and the changing ethnic composition of inner-city areas where some cultures reject alcohol; the smoking ban from 2007; and the consolidation of the brewing industries, which made it harder for many smaller free houses – those pubs not owned by breweries – to compete. For CAMRA, this amounted to the loss of opportunities both for community activity and for drinking. Many social historians might agree.

PUBLIC EXPENDITURE; PUBLIC EXPENDI-TURE CUTS Public expenditure refers to the sums spent by governments to finance poli-cies, and public expenditure cuts to down-ward revisions of the sums to be spent. Throughout the twentieth century, public expenditure increased as the role of the state grew, although governments of different political persuasions were some-times forced to cut expenditure when the economy encountered problems and reve-nues from taxation declined. Government expenditure was also constrained by the overriding imperative to balance the budget. Significant examples of cuts in public expenditure came in 1921, when the Geddes axe fell, and during the Great Depression, following the recommenda-tions of the May committee. Chancellors of the exchequer during the Attlee govern-ments were hugely careful with public expenditure while committing to greater levels of state intervention than ever before – except during wartime. In the postwar years, a number of cuts to public expendi-ture resulted in disappointing delivery of

significant government policies, for example the National Plan during the mid-1960s and the cutbacks to public services of the late 1970s. The Thatcher govern-ments had promised to 'roll back the fron-tiers of the state', but by contrast the persistence of unemployment and poverty during the 1980s rendered this impossible.

R

RACE RELATIONS A positive facet of **Americanisation**, yet one often obscured by **anti-Americanism**, was the growth of race relations legislation in Britain. The very term 'race relations' was originally coined in the USA following the race riots in Chicago in 1919, and in the decades that followed American and British sociolo-gists, as well as progressive politicians, observed the evolution of race relations in their own society and across the Atlantic with interest. During the 1950s and 1960s this interest grew in consequence of an increasingly militant civil rights movement in the USA, and partly because of racial unrest in both countries. Hence progres-sive politicians and social scientists in Britain began to look to the United States for solutions to the growing hostility to immigration and minority groups of colour. This came in the form of the legis-lation of 1965, 1968 and 1976.

Good race relations were at the heart of the social policy of the Labour govern-ments of the 1960s, although many leading Conservatives and Liberals endorsed the principle. The demotion of J. Enoch Powell by Edward Heath in 1968, following the former's infamous warnings of 'rivers of blood', was partly proof of that. Nonetheless, unease at levels of immigra-tion, despite the fact that it was outstripped by emigration, led to the immigration acts of the 1960s, 1970s and since: they rested on the not unwise if morally skewed belief that good race relations are harmed by perceptions of the country being flooded by people of a different culture or colour. Race relations were also damaged by both race riots and rioting.

RACE RIOTS Race riots were an irregular blot on the social landscape of Britain's towns and cities during the twentieth century. Religion was also a factor. In 1905 and 1947–8, anti-Semitism was responsible for a number of ugly disturbances in London and some other major cities, and there were also anti-Jewish riots in South Wales in 1911. Rioting based on colour and ethnicity, however, is more accurately described as a race riot, and in 1919 Britain witnessed a number of disturbances, notably in Cardiff and London. Minor skirmishes also occurred in the early postwar period, as blacks were unfairly blamed by whites for disloyalty during the war and viewed as threats to employment during the years of mass demobilisation. Despite this, the governments of the 1950s continued to believe Britain was essentially a tolerant country, a belief that was compromised by the Notting Hill disturbances of 1958. A number of race riots occurred during the 1980s.

RADIO ('THE WIRELESS') The radio grew out of developments in military communications technology during the First World War, and boomed during the 1920s and 1930s. Over 80 per cent of British households had a broadcast licence by 1939. The British Broadcasting Company originally oversaw radio, but from 1926 it was replaced by the British Broadcasting Corporation, which maintained a monopoly over radio broadcasting. During the 1930s, however, Radio Luxembourg offered some choice, but not much. The

BBC offered three domestic channels from the end of the Second World War, namely the Home Service, the Light Programme and the Third Programme, until it increased its programming to four stations, **Radios 1**, **2**, **3 and 4**, in 1967. During the 1970s the introduction of commercial radio provided the BBC with further competition.

By the early twenty-first century, radio reflected the ethnic diversity of the British population and also the fast-growing range of tastes in music born of both multiculturalism and affluence. In addition talk radio, an American innovation, was increasingly influential, as **Radio 5 Live** and a host of commercial national and local radio stations proved. In short, listening to the radio remained a hugely popular leisure activity, and one reflective of the growing range of tastes enjoyed by the ever more diverse British population.

REARMAMENT Following a moderate regime of military expenditure between the end of the First World War and the mid-1930s, explained in part by economic problems, faith in the League of Nations, and a belief among politicians that the country was possessed of a growing pacifist sentiment, a rearmament programme was tentatively begun from 1935. The reasons were straightforward: the rise of fascism in Europe and fears of a possible if not inevitable war. Rearmament was therefore accompanied by the policy of appeasement. The British rearmament programme, begun under Stanley Baldwin and continued by Neville Chamberlain, has been viewed by economic historians as a programme of public works, an investment in the military resources of the country by the government that stimulated the staple industries of coal, iron and steel and benefited greatly the engineering industry. Each of these was essential to the production or modernisation of airplanes, ships and submarines. Yet the process of rearmament began and continued very slowly. In aircraft production, for example, an Air Ministry memorandum in February 1936 called for the provision of over 8,000 new aircraft over three years, yet by May 1938 only 4,500 had been delivered to the Royal Air Force, and not one Spitfire, the iconic fighter plane of the Battle of Britain, was battle-ready. It took the breakdown of relations between Britain and Germany in the wake of the Munich crisis to expedite production. Even then, when the crunch came in May 1940, the Luftwaffe was the larger force, but, thanks to the minister of aircraft production, Lord Beaverbrook, enough Hurricanes and Spitfires came through on time.

RECONSTRUCTION The period following major wars during which the country was both prepared for a return to normal life and improved by investments in public services and the built environment. The first **Ministry of Reconstruction** was established under the wartime coalition of David Lloyd George. As minister for reconstruction and also health, Christopher Addison steered through parliament a revolutionary Housing Act in 1919 which created local authority (council) housing subsidised from the centre.

The process of reconstruction following the Second World War was immeasurably more extensive and expensive than that of 1917–21, and had already begun to be planned for as early as 1940–41. Those were the darkest years of the war for Britain, but the *Picture Post* took the lead in promoting the appealing idea of a bright new reconstructed Britain. The founder of the *Picture Post*, Edward Hulton, was one of many significant social reformers, writers and politicians who formed the **1941 Committee** to press for greater and more effectively coordinated postwar planning powers which would rest upon common ownership

of industry, urban regeneration and welfare policies. The **Ministry of Town and Country Planning**, formed in 1943, gained considerable support from members of the 1941 Committee and drove forward the reconstruction of the built environment. All cities and towns that had been bombed, and many that had hardly been touched by aerial bombardment, were required by the government to draw up plans for the rebuilding of blitzed and blighted areas. Over 120 plans were produced between 1941 and 1952; some were almost fully realised, for example in Plymouth, while others were less successful.

The Town and Country Planning Act of 1947 provided much of the framework within which councils could plan and rebuild. On the outskirts of existing towns and cities, new council estates were allowed under strict circumstances. And in town and city centres, and some suburban overspill areas, high-rise housing was built, in line with recommendations by the **Dudley Report** of 1944. The experiment with high-rise housing had been pioneered by the London County Council from the 1940s. In addition, the New Towns Act of 1946 was a further key tool of reconstruction.

The 1960s saw the completion of reconstruction in Britain (although some bomb sites in London remained for decades afterwards). Interestingly, some of its less popular practices were to re-emerge later. The architectural fetish for high-rise and high-density apartment blocks, loathed by the 1970s, was rekindled during the 1990s by architects and town planners who now sought to use new designs for multi-storey living to tempt the middle classes back into the city centres, the inner cities and docklands. What had often failed for reconstruction was now at the heart of urban regeneration.

RELIGION Religion played an important but declining role in British life during the twentieth century. Secularisation was partly the reason, but so too was the growing range of leisure pursuits on offer, made available by growing affluence and consumerism. Anglicanism, or the Church of England, remained the religion of the majority, but Protestant nonconformist groups (Baptists, Methodists, Unitarians, etc.) and Roman Catholicism were central to the Christian culture of Britain, although these varied by country of origin and region. Many people who professed to be Christian did not attend church regularly during the twentieth century, and congregations declined. The church remained central to rites of passage in British life, however: most families opted to have their children baptised, to get married in church, and to bury their dead in a Christian funeral. The 2001 census found that 71.6 per cent of the population were Christian, 2.7 per cent were Muslim, 1 per cent were Hindu, 0.6 per cent were Sikh and 0.5 per cent were Jewish. A tiny minority were Rastafarians, and a tinier minority still described their religion as 'Jedi'. The census also found that people in Northern Ireland identified more strongly with a religion than did the English, Scots and Welsh. Over 10 per cent of the British population were atheists or agnostics by the end of the twentieth century.

RIOTS AND RIOTING Rioting was an infrequent but disturbing feature of British social and political life during the twentieth century, as it had been in previous centuries. Causes of rioting were varied. Frustration at the slowness of government to introduce enfranchisement for women at general elections led to suffragette riots during the Edwardian years. Racism also engendered rioting, as in the London and Cardiff race riots in 1919 and the anti-Semitic disturbances of 1947–8. The apparent peace in ethnic relations in postwar Britain was shattered in 1958 by the Notting Hill race riots, and subsequently in some other unpleasant manifestations of ethnic intolerance. The perceived racism of the police force and of white society among ethnic minorities of colour contributed to the outbreak of disturbances in **Southall** in 1979, and in St Pauls (Bristol), Brixton (London), Handsworth (Birmingham), Moss Side (Manchester) and Toxteth (Liverpool) during the first half of the 1980s. These were all areas with a large black population, some of them long-standing. Other riots were caused in 1919 by the threatened withdrawal of the out-of-work donation and in 1990 by the introduction of the poll tax. The Miners' strike of 1984–5 saw both civil and industrial unrest that led to violence. Hardly any riots lasted more than a few hours, although some continued, on and off, for days. The last set of disturbances of historic significance in Britain were the poll tax riots of 1990, when thousands of people demonstrated against the perceived iniquities of the new 'community charge' endorsed by Margaret Thatcher. The riots were one of the catalysts of her removal as prime minister.

ROCK MUSIC An American form of popular music born out of rhythm and blues, rock music arrived in Britain in 1955 with Bill Haley and the Comets, whose song *Rock Around the Clock* was featured in the film *The Blackboard Jungle* (1955). Rock has remained at the heart of youth culture in Britain ever since. Within a few years young British musicians, heavily influenced by American styles, were making their own rock music, and by the early 1960s a home-grown culture was displacing the American dominance in British popular music charts. It is difficult to imagine it now, but even Sir Cliff Richard posed as a smouldering, quasi-rebellious teenager during the later 1950s, as did a host of smaller acts. But the rise of the Beatles from 1962 was equally indicative of the oncoming British genius for making popular music. The swinging sixties were defined as much by music as by fashionable clothing and famous British actors and films, and the Beatles led a British invasion of the United States, as other bands followed them across the Atlantic.

The Rolling Stones and Led Zeppelin came to dominate the global rock culture of the later 1960s and the first half of the 1970s, while progressive rock and glam rock were also largely British music fashions at their most influential from about 1972 to 1977. Among leading exponents of progressive rock were Emerson, Lake and Palmer, Genesis and Yes, while the dominant glam rockers were Queen, led by the ebulliently gay Freddie Mercury. In reaction to both these music forms, however, punk rock surfaced in Britain in 1976.

Punk rock, which initially emanated from New York in the mid-1970s, signalled a decidedly different phase in British rock music. The originators of punk included the Ramones, Iggy and the Stooges, Patti Smith, and the New York Dolls. They inspired some British bands to adopt an angrier, harsher metallic guitar sound, thus rejecting the flamboyance and frippery of progressive and glam rock. Although many British cities produced some famous names, London became punk's British home.

The provenance of Anglo-American punk can be explained by a reaction to the perceived boredom and monotony of suburbs. Not a few punk banks, notably The Members and Siouxsie and the Banshees, sang about the tedium of suburban life for teenagers and women. Many punks were suburbanites who wished to live in the more dangerous and exotic inner cities. Outrageous dress, such as safety pins through noses and cheeks, ripped and filthy jeans, fishnet shirts, short skirts, tatty stockings and tights, loud footwear and vivid hair styling, characterised the more exhibitionist punks in their reaction to the greyness, as they saw it, of suburban life. This look became something of a cliché that continued to influence many copycat punks and punk bands. The fashion styles of Vivienne Westwood, who during the 1970s jointly ran the Sex boutique in London, a meeting place for the Sex Pistols and other punks, imaginatively promoted punk chic from the 1980s.

Following the punk revolt into style, the musical fashion turned to the contrived *poseurs* of the new romantic sound, while gritty rock music continued to be made by a handful of musicians. Grindcore, and the associated forms of heavy metal music – for example, thrash and speed metal – was another Anglo-American rock genre, deserving recognition for its ability to galvanise audiences and also for its ironic wit. Napalm Death was a leading grindcore outfit during the 1980s and 1990s. By then Britpop had emerged, and the now familiar bands of Oasis, Blur and Pulp became globally famous, a further assertion of the fact that young Brits were good at making rock music.

An aspect of British rock music that is often overlooked is its local resonance. It is of course impossible to conceive of the Beatles without Liverpool, but many lesser-known yet technically accomplished rock bands were associated with particular cities and regions. Manchester spawned lots of bands who took pride in their city, including the Smiths during the 1980s and Oasis in the 1990s. Some of the lyrics of British bands skilfully, even enigmatically, evoked their local roots. The song *Adventures in a Yorkshire landscape*, on the album *Axe Victim* (1974) by Be Bop Deluxe, conjures images of the rugged beauty of the county, beyond which lay declining mill towns and fatalistic council estates. More recently, both Catatonia and the Manic Street Preachers have been at the forefront of a new energy and pride in Welsh youth culture, particularly in South Wales.

RUGBY FOOTBALL Great divides, emanating from the nineteenth century, influenced the history of rugby in the twentieth. One was the split between soccer and rugby from 1865 and the rise of association football, in which players apart from goalkeepers were forbidden to use their hands. And within the sport of rugby itself the game is in two broad categories, namely rugby league and rugby union. Rugby league teams have thirteen players, while union teams have fifteen. The rules of the game also differ in significant respects. The North–South divide in Britain has long been manifested in the sport. In Northern England and South Wales, for example, and in some Midlands cities, rugby league was anchored in industrial towns and was both played and watched mostly by working-class people. Rugby union, by contrast, was redolent of a more genteel cohort of sportsmen and played more in the south of the country. A further and related bifurcation was that between amateurism and professionalism, but the latter eventually triumphed over the former. Although rugby matches had been regularly televised during the 'rugby season' on the BBC's *Grandstand*, the rise of satellite television and the internet greatly increased the sponsorship available to the sport. This led from the mid-1990s to increased commercialisation and internationalisation of club rugby league and the attraction of more players from overseas. It culminated in the Super League, which now draws a worldwide audience of millions.

In common with other major sports, rugby was a uniting force in the lives of millions of British people, whether in amateur union games, local league games or international matches. The annual Five Nations rugby union competitions between England, France, Ireland, Scotland and Wales (now Six Nations after the introduction of Italy) were occasions of sometimes intense national rivalry on the rugby pitch and in the stands. The standards of crowd behaviour have generally remained higher in rugby football than in soccer.

S

SECRET STATE To prevent communist infiltration by the activities of the KGB, the Russian spy organisation during Cold War, Britain relied upon MI5 and the wider security apparatus acting within a context that was mostly unknown to many politicians and to the public. The Attlee governments of 1945–51 were keen to keep extremists of both left and right out of positions of influence and power in Britain, as were subsequent governments. Fear of communist subversion can thus be viewed as an aspect of consensus. Vetting procedures were tightened during the 1950s in the light of the Burgess and Maclean affair, which in 1951 highlighted communist sympathies among some members of the secret services. Yet they could never be watertight: in 1963 Kim Philby of MI6 defected to the USSR, and the following year Anthony Blunt was discovered to be in league with the Russians. Hence counter-espionage activities had some successes. The early James Bond films and other movies and novels about secret agents during the Cold War did provide some insights, fictive or more realistic, into this official culture, but there was always a more mundane bureaucracy at work. Following the collapse of the communism in Eastern Europe historians have been able to access previously classified documents that throw light on the secret operations of the security services, the military and the Ministry of Defence at Whitehall.

The boundaries of legitimate secret action in protecting Britain from communism and other threats were never completely clear to the public and thus open to conspiracy theories. During the 1980s, for example, MI5 and the Conservative government deployed definitions of 'subversive' which civil rights lawyers have since enjoyed scrutinising. For example, in 1985 the government defined a 'subversive' as

> an individual [who] is a member of a subversive group . . . whose aims are to undermine or overthrow parliamentary democracy by political, industrial or violent means . . . is, or has recently been, sympathetic to or associated with members or sympathisers of such organisations or groups, in such a way as to raise reasonable doubts about his reliability.

An industrial subversive by this definition might have included Arthur Scargill, a known left-wing sympathiser and leader of industrial action, which during the Miners' Strike of 1984–5 sometimes involved violence. Yet he remained almost completely at liberty while no doubt being monitored to some degree by Whitehall. However, the actions of the British government occasionally ratcheted up the sense of secret conspiracy. In 1987 the attempts to ban *Spycatcher*, the book by an ex-MI5 agent Peter Wright, which claimed that there had been a secret service plot to bug and undermine the Wilson governments, had just that effect. The subsequent investigation found no evidence of an organised plot against the former Labour prime minister, despite expressions of outrage by

Tony **Benn**. The **Security Service Act** passed in December 1989, the year of communism's demise in Europe, placed MI5 on a statutory basis, allowing complaints to be investigated from politicians and members of the public. With the end of the Cold War came greater openness.

SECULARISM; SECULARISATION Secularism is defined as a condition of not being religious or spiritual. During the twentieth century Britain became a less religious, a less Christian society, and a more secular one. Overall, the number of church buildings fell, from 52,690 in 1900 to fewer than 48,550 by 2000. However, the secular trend was nuanced. Although not attending church regularly, many still claimed to believe in God. And the majority of Christians still observed the major rituals of baptisms, marriages, and funerals. The number of Church of England baptisms, however, fell from 564,000 in 1900 to 199,000 in 2000. This decline was mirrored to varying degrees in the smaller Protestant churches, but not among Roman Catholics. The number of Catholic baptisms rose from 55,000 in 1900 to 72,000 by the end of the century. This reflected partly the numbers of Irish in Britain, but also immigration from Catholic countries in Europe.

Historians have discussed the seemingly contradictory term 'secular Anglicanism' to attempt to characterise the belief system of the majority of British people. People of strong faith and fundamentalists, however, have been suspicious of secularisation in inverse proportion to the firmness of their belief. During the final years of the twentieth century and since, therefore, members of the National Secular Society looked on aghast as religious spokesmen (they were almost always men, with the exception of some Christian churches following the ordination of women) influenced ethical, moral and scientific debates. They privileged a belief in God, the Bible or the

Koran rather than humanistic and rational principles.

SEGREGATION The term entered British academic and policy approaches to housing from the United States as a consequence of the American civil rights campaigns during the 1960s. It refers to the inability of ethnic minority groups to access housing in white areas, and the consequent existence or growth of poor housing areas with distinct social, cultural and economic characteristics. The **Race Relations Acts** of 1968 and 1976 attempted to prevent segregation in housing. Furthermore, the voluntary dispersal of Jews, Asians and blacks from their original areas of settlement to the suburbs militated against the more profound levels of segregation to be found in the USA. Segregation is also underpinned by class: in the largest British cities, small and inward-looking communities of the poor, including the white working classes, still exist just a few streets or kilometres away from affluent housing districts.

SELF-HELP The 'bible' of self-help was the book of that name written by Samuel Smiles, the Victorian spokesman for thrift, abstinence and religious virtue. It refers to a condition of looking after oneself and one's family and household and avoiding, as far as is possible, any recourse to charity or to the state. The notion of self-help was always at the heart of the culture of the self-consciously 'respectable' working classes, who discerned a lack of it in the 'unrespectable' lower third beneath them. It remained too at the heart of the Protestant work ethic during the nineteenth and twentieth centuries. During the 1980s, the Conservative revival of Victorian values made much of the importance of self-help as an antidote to the so-called dependency culture of the welfare state and the public expenditure incurred by welfare benefits to 'scroungers'.

SITCOMS Situation comedies on television have remained hugely popular with the British viewing public since the 1950s. Many came from the United States of America, but Tony **Hancock**'s *Hancock's Half Hour* (BBC, 1956–60) was the first major home-grown sitcom. Its context was suburbia, a favoured subject for sitcoms to poke fun at. Sitcoms both launched the careers of relatively unknown actors and provided a new lease of life for those who were already major stars.

Little was sacred in situation comedy. In *All Gas and Gaiters* (BBC, 1967; 1969–71) the Church of England was the butt of jokes about the everyday world of organised religion, while in *Please, Sir!* (ITV, 1968–72) secondary schooling was satirised, the jokes being generated from the relationships between the old-fashioned or incompetent teachers and their working-class students. *It Ain't Half Hot Mum* (BBC, 1974–81) made jokes at the expense of the army in India during the British Empire. Some academic media analysts found the series mildly racist on account of the caricature of the Indians, although the British soldiers themselves were also stereotyped by accent and class. In *Man About the House* (ITV, 1973–6) the humorous potential was derived from the three young people who shared a flat in a house owned by the sexually repressed couple George and Mildred. It is interesting to note, however, that the relative permissiveness of the younger people, despite the title of the series, only partly undermined the gender roles of the women in the series, who were relentlessly daffy and obsessed with romantic love and with living in a nice clean apartment. In *Are You Being Served?* (BBC, 1973–83) among the first openly gay characters on TV since the decriminalisation of homosexuality was an explicitly effeminate man.

Older decrepit working-class areas of town during the 1960s provided the setting for the two most famous sitcoms that began in that decade, namely *Steptoe and Son* (BBC, 1962–5; 1970; 1972) and *Till Death Us Do Part* (BBC, 1966–8; 1972; 1974–5). The latter was based around the caricature of the white working-class racist Alf Garnett, whose family was relocated to a council flat. His foul language caused outrage among more conservative and religious-minded people: certainly Mary Whitehouse was unimpressed. The name 'Alf Garnett' later became synonymous in middle-class chatter with working-class prejudice and foul-mouthed behaviour. The ITV sitcom *Love thy Neighbour* (1972–6) also dealt with the theme of racism, but without the wittiness of *Till Death Us Do Part*.

Suburbia continued to provide a rich context for humour, however. Comfortable home-grown suburban sitcoms included *Terry and June* (BBC, 1979–87), which was developed from the preceding sitcom *Happy Ever After*. Both series starred Terry Scott and June Whitfield. In *The Likely Lads* (BBC, 1964–6) the lives of two young working-class men called Bob and Terry in the North-East of England reflected the growing presence of suburbia in sitcoms as the 1960s gave way to the 1970s. By 1973 and the second series, entitled *Whatever Happened to the Likely Lads?*, their lives had changed from a lad's culture of drinking and pursuing women in downtown pubs to the trials and tribulations of settling down. Bob had married Thelma and moved to a new home on an aspirational suburban housing estate. Bob himself travelled in life from an older housing area to a suburban home, and Terry was not amused. Perhaps that is why the opening visuals depicted an urban world also in transition during the late throes of reconstruction, as images of tower blocks and housing estates replaced the shabby terraced streets. In *The Fall and Rise of Reginald Perrin* (1976–9) the repetition of suburban life drove poor Reggie to distraction. Similar themes can also be identified in other much-loved sitcoms. *The Good Life* (BBC,1975–8) contrasted a couple of self-sufficient back-to-the-land suburbanites in Surbiton in South London who used their garden as a mini farm while their snobby neighbours looked on with varying degrees of condescension. (Surbiton is now where the Centre for Suburban Studies is based, at Kingston University.) In *Keeping Up Appearances* (BBC, 1990–95) the petty snobberies of a lower-middle-class woman were contrasted with the slob culture of a family on a suburban council estate. *One Foot in the Grave* (BBC, 1990–2000) evoked the surreal everyday life of an elderly couple in the twilight world of suburban retirement, while Ricky Gervais's *The Office*, a BBC sitcom of the early twenty-first century, was set in the quintessentially suburban and much-derided town of Slough on the outskirts of West London. David Brent, the character played by Gervais, even read some verses from John **Betjeman**'s poem *Slough* (1938) at the end of one episode.

Such sitcoms drew much of their comic power from reducing familiar people to cartoon-like characters in the caricatured context of the English suburbs. Above all, laughter was their main intention, not social realism. While sitcoms tended to reinforce negative or risible stereotypes, however, they also reflected social changes, even perhaps encouraging acceptance of those changes among the viewing public.

SLEAZE Sleaze in relation to British politics meant unseemly moral and sexual behaviour. Few governments in the postwar period were completely free of the nefarious sexual doings of some of their politicians, whether these became well known, as in the Profumo scandal of 1963, or remained mostly secretive, as in the life of Robert Boothby, a contemporary of

Profumo. A sleazy reputation could damage MPs and party leaders alike, as the fate of the Liberal leader Jeremy Thorpe painfully illustrated during the latter 1970s. However, sleaze became a particularly damaging issue for the Conservative government of John Major from 1992 to 1997, when, in the wake of a moralising 'back-to-basics' campaign emphasising family values, the tabloid press revelled in the exposure of the sexual peccadilloes and extra-marital affairs of Tory MPs. Such hypocrisy further weakened a government damaged by Black Wednesday in 1992 and by the increasingly fractious right wing of the party, led by John Redwood. It was later revealed that John Major himself was having an affair with the cabinet minister turned broadcaster and racy novelist Edwina Currie. Double standards were at the heart of the personal politics of many in the government of 1992–7.

SOAP OPERAS Many soap operas have been ephemeral, but the long-running *Coronation Street*, created by Tony Warren, retains a hugely important place in British television history. Begun by Granada for ITV in 1960, and set in an inner-city district between Manchester and Salford, the series depicts the lives of people in the 'traditional' urban working-class landscape of terraced houses, corner pubs and shops, and home interiors. The historical context of its beginnings is significant, because social realism was evident in the cinema films during the early 1960s. The series also portrayed the social divisions and hierarchies of the working-class areas: the snobbish pub landlady; the camaraderie of factory life; the familiar faces but spiteful gossip in the corner shop; and the hard-working woman, cleaning up after other people all day or making clothes in a workshop, coming home to a husband who demanded his 'tea' (not a cup of tea, but the working-class term for dinner, at 6 p.m.). By the latter 1980s, ironic or satirical representation of the inhabitants of the Street had replaced social realism.

Coronation Street also attempted to reflect social changes in the Victorian streets of Manchester. Divorce, homosexuality and immigration, this last personified by Asian shopkeepers, have been introduced. But ultimately the soap opera is there to entertain, not to provide an accurate picture of inner-city England since 1960. Similar points can be made about *EastEnders*, also set in a traditional working-class zone of terraced streets, in London. Devised by Julia Smith, the pub, shop, cafe and homes of Albert Square are the contexts for a parade of cockney characters or token representatives from minority groups to live out their dramas. Begun by the BBC in 1985, *EastEnders* has become one of the weekly staples of the viewing public, vying with *Coronation Street* for ratings and annual soap awards.

Significant exceptions to the urban grittiness of Albert Square and *Coronation Street* were *Emmerdale Farm* (later *Emmerdale*) and *Brookside*. *Emmerdale* began on ITV (now ITV 1) during the 1970s and is set in the Yorkshire Dales. *Brookside*, devised by Phil Redmond, and begun in 1982, was a flagship soap opera for the new Channel 4. Suburban life in a 1980s housing estate on the outskirts of Liverpool was the stuff of *Brookside*, which during its twenty-one-year run dealt with infidelity, incest, wife-beating, murder, petty crime, violent crime, more infidelity, and sometimes even love and romance, some of it heterosexual, some of it lesbian. *Brookside* was notable for its aspirational working-class and lower-middle-class characters, among whom was a black suburbanite, Mick, who may be seen as vaguely representative of the gathering trend of black suburbanisation by the 1980s. It is ironic that this suburban soap born of the late twentieth century was terminated in

2003, while the fictive Victorian hubs of Albert Square and *Coronation Street* are still going strong.

SOCIAL DARWINISM Following the popularising of the ideas of Charles Darwin by the philosopher Herbert Spencer, many came to believe that individuals, groups or sections of society, and even nations were involved in an evolutionary struggle for survival based upon the laws of natural selection that were evident in animal and plant species. This understanding was heightened by the 'discovery' of poor and degraded areas in British cities during the 1880s and 1890s, and by the inadequate physical conditions of many working-class recruits to the military during the Boer War. Several leading politicians and professionals began to argue that the poorest and least capable sections of society should be isolated from the mainstream lest they corrupt it. By the 1930s, a eugenicist argument had developed, calling for the sterilisation of lower orders of people and for selective breeding in order to maximise the highest inheritable qualities. Leading intellectuals on both left and right endorsed such views. The implications of this line of thinking became horribly clear in Nazi Germany. Furthermore, these bastardisations of Darwin's theories failed to account for the mitigating effects of culture, science and welfare policies in the 'struggle' for survival.

SOCIAL DEMOCRATIC PARTY (SDP) Formed in 1981 by the so-called Gang of Four, the Social Democratic Party was initially a breakaway faction of the Labour Party. Frustrated with the leadership selection process and the incumbency of Michael Foot as Labour leader, and disgusted with the party's leftward shift and declining electoral appeal, Roy Jenkins, David Owen, Bill Rodgers and Shirley Williams issued the **Limehouse**

Declaration in January 1981. Calling for a Council for Social Democracy, the declaration was the parting of the ways between Labour and these leading politicians. The SDP won a number of spectacular by-election victories during the 1980s but failed to break the mould of party politics at the general elections of 1983 and 1987. In 1988, following a tacit relationship with the Liberal Party and negotiations with the Liberal leadership, including David Steel, the SDP finally merged with its new ally, giving birth to the Liberal Democrats. The one member of the Gang of Four who refused to join was David Owen. He had been somewhat vilified by ITV's *Spitting Image* during the 1980s as the evil, calculating, dominant partner to the submissive, unctuous David Steel. The continuing SDP under Owen, however, was unsuccessful, and was terminated by the early 1990s.

SOCIAL POLICY Among the most important areas of social policy studied by historians are welfare, education, health and housing. Modern welfare policy began with the introduction of the Poor Law (Amendment Act) of 1834, which was subsequently adjusted to deal with large-scale local unemployment and the relief of the poor. It was mostly abolished in 1929 by Neville Chamberlain's Local Government Act. Increasingly, national insurance following the 1911 **National Insurance Act** aimed to insure the citizens of Britain from the worst depredations associated with ill health and unemployment.

The rise of New Liberalism during the late nineteenth and early twentieth centuries was given legislative form in the policies on education, national insurance, old-age pensions, health and child welfare passed before the First World War. The introduction of non-contributory pensions and of contributory national insurance for sickness and unemployment laid a foundation for welfare provision which was built upon to varying degrees by successive governments between the wars. As the Poor Law was terminated, new policies tackled unemployment, for example the Public Assistance Committees and the **Unemployment Assistance Board**.

The most significant chapter in the history of social policy, however, was the introduction from 1945 to 1951 of the welfare state, in the light of the Beveridge Report of 1942. The Keynesian commitment of the state to minimise unemployment and to provide social insurance for the citizens of Britain 'from the cradle to the grave' went largely unchallenged, even by the Conservative governments of the 1980s and 1990s. Public expenditure cuts, however, and changes in policy direction by incoming administrations changed the titles and sometimes the character of key policies, as was evident during those same Conservative governments. Family allowances, for example, were abolished and renamed 'child benefit' in the mid-1970s. Among the major themes emphasised by historians of social policy are the limitations in the reach of social legislation; the relationship of social policy to the functional maintenance of the family unit, despite its changing character; the relationship between social policy and citizenship; and the revisions to social policies in the wake of changing governments.

SOCIALISM Socialism is the political and economic ideology that calls for the ownership of the means of production, distribution and exchange to be placed in the hands of the people or the community and to be operated for need and redistributive equality, not profit. In modern Britain, the 1880s witnessed the formation of the Fabian Society (1884) and the Social Democratic Federation (1881) and the rise of new unions, organisations of unskilled workers, many of whose leaders were self-proclaimed socialists. In 1893 the establishment of the Independent Labour Party became another hugely important landmark in the evolution of socialism in Britain. Leading members of the trade unions, the Fabians and the ILP established the Labour Representation Committee in 1900. The socialist Labour Party was born.

Interpretations of socialism varied from the revolutionary left along a political spectrum to the most moderate of interventionist socialist politics that sought to modify rather than subvert or overthrow capitalism. As the major vehicle for socialism, the Labour Party, as partly defined in its manifesto of 1918 and in subsequent policies, was committed to nationalisation, an equalisation of wages, universal welfare provision and improved education for all workers 'by hand or by brain'. The legislative programme of Attlee's government came closest to achieving a framework for these high ideals to be realised, but by the end of the twentieth century socialism had palpably failed to remove poverty and inequality.

SPECIAL RELATIONSHIP In 2006 a US State Department official questioned whether there was any longer a special international bond between the British and American governments, claiming it to be a 'myth'. This proved to be embarrassing to Tony Blair, who had worked hard to retain Britain's special relationship with the American president George W. Bush, who was hardly popular in the United Kingdom. The War in Iraq from 2003 did much to generate a new phase of anti-Americanism in the UK. The maintenance of this connexion, however, had been at the heart of British defence and foreign policy since 1946, when Winston Churchill, still grateful for American assistance to the Allies during the Second World War, flagged the need for a special relationship in his speeches warning of the onset of the Cold War. The then foreign secretary, Ernest Bevin, welcomed **Marshall Aid** from 1947 and made an effort to keep Britain at the heart of a unique transatlantic nexus. Despite the damage done to the relationship by American criticisms of British incompetence during the Suez crisis of 1956, Harold Macmillan quickly rebuilt friendly terms with the USA. For reasons of mutual military expediency, American air bases remained on British soil, and were used in the attack on Libya in 1986, for example. Critics of the relationship, however, particularly in the Labour and Liberal parties, argued that the ending of the Cold War gave Britain a newer freedom to forsake dependence upon the arrogant USA and to become a larger power player in Europe. Similarly, others have seen the Westminster–Washington hook-up as placing London in an irresolute triangle between Brussels and North America. Yet the unique relationship between Britain and the USA arguably goes much wider and deeper than the dictates of foreign policy. Culturally, American cinema films, television programmes and popular music were more accessible to the British than to non-English speakers, and that led to a richly inventive Anglo-American vortex of cultural interaction alongside the political context. Many British TV series have been reworked in the USA (*The Office* is a significant recent example). British attitudes to the United States, therefore, have remained complex and often ambivalent into the early twenty-first century. Admiration for American glitz and glam rests alongside criticisms of its excess, while a continuing commitment to American foreign policy does not preclude uneasiness at American unilateralism.

SPORTS Sports played a huge role in the social and recreational life of twentieth-century Britain. The most popular sport was football, but cricket, rugby, tennis, and a variety of pub sports, notably darts, remain at the heart of the nation's leisure pursuits. And, as the performance by Team GB proved at the Beijing Olympics in 2008, many amateur sports are also practised and pursued in people's spare time.

Historians of sport focus on such key themes as class and status, notably the sociological class bases of certain sports and the role of sport as a vehicle for upward social mobility. Other key themes include the tensions between the amateur ethos and professionalisation. Professionals play sports for the money, of course, while amateurs are supposed to do so purely for the spirit of competition. Commercialisation was also viewed as a catalyst for financial inducements and potential corruption. The growing presence of women and ethnic minorities in sports that were once dominated by white men is a common focus in social histories. The role of sporting activities in the construction of gender identities – for example, 'masculinities' – sport as a spectacle, and the commercialisation of sports via television, their amplification and perhaps exaggeration in importance, are further growing areas of study. Whereas, for instance, football teams once drew their major reserves of support from within a town or city, it is commonplace now for the most successful teams to have a national and even an international following. Yet beyond the media glare historians still emphasise the role that small local teams play in forging local solidarities. Participation in sports, moreover, is also viewed as an important indicator not only of personal and team-based competitiveness but also of cooperation and of solidarities in such local contexts as clubs, schools and neighbourhoods. Another key theme in histories of sport is the role of animals.

STAPLE INDUSTRIES The staple industries of cotton and woollen textiles, steel manufacturing, shipbuilding and coal mining were at the heart of British economic growth and prosperity during the nineteenth century, and at the heart of British relative decline during the twentieth. Privatisation from 1979 was targeted in large part at the staples. Textile production and shipbuilding declined considerably between 1945 and 1990. By the year 2000, both of these once powerful heavy industries were more or less extinguished, although the reasons for their decline were complex, involving the rise of overseas competition, investment and management during the periods of both nationalisation and private ownership. The story of steel was more nuanced. In 1940 steel production was given a large boost by the needs of war, and 12 million tons were produced. This rose to a postwar peak of 28 million tons by 1970, but it declined thereafter. Nonetheless, by 1990 the industry produced nearly 17 million tons of steel for various other industries, more than during 1940. Coal mining was also a shadow of its former self: on the eve of the First World War over 284 million tons of coal was mined by hundreds of thousands of miners, many living in distinctive pit villages. By the end of the century the figure was less than 20 million tons, mined by a workforce of under 7,000 people.

By the 1990s, manufacturing industry in general accounted for a little over one-quarter of all employment in Britain. In 1979 considerably more than 7 million people were still employed in manufacturing, but this had shrunk by over 2.6 million to just over 4.5 million by 1992. The demise of the staple industries reflected the wider readjustments of de-industrialisation after the 1970s.

STERLING The pound sterling was and remains a symbol of national pride as well as a financial currency. Since decimalisation in 1971, in preparation for membership of the European Economic Community, sterling has been divided into pence and pounds, with 100 pence amounting to a pound. Before then, however, the imperial currency was divided into pounds (£), shillings (s.) and pence (d.), with a coinage system that many now look back on with some nostalgia. Twenty shillings equalled a pound, and a shilling was made up of 12 pennies. There were 'ten bob' notes (10s.), 'half a crown' (2/6), florins (2s.) and 1s. pieces, and also individual coins representing 6d., 3d., 1d., and a halfpenny.

The value of sterling was tied to the gold standard for much of the early twentieth century, while sterling policy in general was committed to retaining the value of the pound. However, devaluations occurred in 1949 and 1967 in order to render British goods more saleable abroad.

SUBURBANISATION AND SUBURBS England is the most suburban nation in Europe, a consequence of population growth, the expansion of public transport and roads, and the popular desire to live in a house with a garden somewhere between the town centre and the open countryside. A widespread suburban aspiration informed the lives of millions of English people after 1900. It is also a consequence of town and country planning. Those planners such as Frederic Osborn and others who were involved in the garden city and garden suburb movement may have disliked unplanned suburbanisation, but they certainly understood the appeal of suburban homes. A visit to Letchworth or Welwyn Garden City, products of the first half of the twentieth century, or to Milton Keynes, planned from 1967, proves this.

England remained geographically and demographically the 'dominant' country, and if anything that physical dominance increased as the population of England grew more than that of Scotland and Wales. The growing numbers of people were mostly housed in the expanding suburbs of existing British towns. In England more so than its neighbouring countries, suburbanisation was particularly significant, as people moved from town centres to the housing areas on the outskirts or towards the edges of towns. But almost all towns and cities in Britain expanded to varying extents: in Scotland, Wales and Northern Ireland residential suburbs also grew around towns and cities of any size.

Suburbanisation was dynamically related to social and economic change. Between the wars it grew rapidly: over 4 million homes were built, the majority in suburban areas, 2.5 million of them for home ownership among the middle classes. The classic semi-detached housing to be found in most English cities was at its apogee during the 1920s and 1930s. But the aspiration to live in the suburbs was also partly driven by the location of new council estates. Council houses were rented from the local authority (council), but many people in middle class occupations were able to afford new housing in the suburbs. Working-class suburbia, compared with middle-class suburbia, remains a neglected subject.

Today in England over 60 per cent of the population lives in suburbs. According to recent formulations used by the Independent Transport Commission, for example, based upon the work by Marcial Echenique and Rob Homewood, of the Centre for Architectural and Urban Studies at the University of Cambridge, England can be divided into the following categories:

    urban
    suburban/urban
    suburban
    suburban/rural
    rural.

The 'suburban' category currently amounts to 21 million people, or 44 per cent of the population, and covers about 17 per cent of the land in England. In addition about 7.9 million people, or 16 per cent of the population, live in 'suburban rural' areas. Thus 60 per cent of England is suburban or suburban rural. In addition, about 12 million live in the inner suburbs, the older terraced houses built during the Victorian and Edwardian periods. This means, quite starkly, that about 80 per cent of the English population resides neither in the urban centres nor in the countryside. It lives instead in a multi-tiered suburban gradient that stretches from the inner suburbs built before 1914, through the classic semi-detached housing estates built between the wars, in semi-detached and detached housing estates built since 1945, and also in suburbs on the edges of the countryside.

Suburbanisation was hugely significant for many reasons. It was the continuation of a nineteenth-century trend. As the outer suburbs expanded with middle class and affluent working-class households, the older inner suburbs and areas of town centre housing were places of settlement for incoming poorer groups, many of them immigrants. Hence the inner-city areas from the 1950s remained poorer than many suburbs and were targeted for urban regeneration during the 1980s and 1990s.

SUBURBIA Suburbia is composed of the culture, environment and lifestyles of the inhabitants of the suburbs. In Britain, suburbia is mostly identified as English. It is loved by many, hated by many others, and simultaneously both loved and hated by many more. It has been the subject of countless novels, some highbrow, many middlebrow, and lots lowbrow. Television sitcoms, from *Hancock's Half Hour* during the 1950s to *One Foot in the Grave* during the 1990s, were frequently located in a suburban street. A classic image of suburbia involves the 'Dunroamin' model of semi-detached houses of the interwar period, compulsively tended gardens and hedges, a car in the garage or on the drive, and families huddled around the television deriving vicarious enjoyment rather than the real pleasures of a truly urban lifestyle. Critics and admirers alike have made what they wanted of such a stereotype. The realities of suburban life, while fleetingly conjured up by such images, were always more complex than any risible representation, given that by the end of the twentieth century over two-thirds of the English population lived in a diverse range of suburban environments.

TENNIS Modern tennis began in Britain, as with so many other sports, during the Victorian years. The All England Croquet and Lawn Tennis Club, the governing body of the sport, had organised socially exclusive tennis events at Wimbledon since 1877 and, as the name of that organisation suggests, the sport had close links with the elite sport of croquet (in 1899 the name became the All England Lawn Tennis and Croquet Club). Both men's and women's singles and doubles matches had been established before the end of the nineteenth century. Whereas the cachet of croquet remained indubitably aristocratic and upper middle class, tennis became a mass spectator sport during the twentieth century, although in Britain, at least, the majority of both amateur county players and professionals emanated from the middle classes. The tennis club continued to play a not insignificant role in the informal networks in middle-class life.

The national home of tennis is Wimbledon, and the present site was opened by King George V in 1922. Any innate 'Britishness' associated with tennis, however, declined as a consequence of the growing international presence at Wimbledon. The American May Sutton won the ladies' singles title in 1905, while in 1907 the Australian Norman Brookes was the first overseas men's singles champion. Since then only two British men have won the coveted men's singles, namely Arthur Gore and Fred Perry. Perry dominated British and world tennis during the 1930s, as did Dorothy Round in the ladies' game. As with other sports, war interrupted Wimbledon, but the All England Club maintained the ground despite its uses for civil defence and military purposes. The war did nothing to stop American ascendancy in the sport, or that of France and other nations. Black tennis players also increasingly accustomed the British public to ethnic minority sportsmen and women during the postwar years: the American Althea Gibson, for example, rose from the Harlem ghetto to win the ladies' singles in 1957, while the Aboriginal Australian Evonne Goolagong triumphed in 1971. The African American Arthur Ashe became the first black winner of the men's singles in July 1975. The tennis courts of Wimbledon were also arenas for the Cold War, as the **Wimbledon boycott of 1973** demonstrated in absentia. A number of leading Eastern European tennis players defected to the West.

Internationalisation accompanied the growing commercialisation and professionalisation of tennis. While remaining more accessible to the wealthier sections in British society, it became a more open sport. Rather pathetically, however, the tennis-playing middle classes in Britain rarely rose to the highest levels of talent displayed by the nationals of other countries. The one and only Wimbledon victory in Britain's postwar singles tennis came with Virginia **Wade**'s ladies' title in 1977.

'Wimbledon fortnight' is as popular as ever. It is perhaps the world's leading tennis event, as the extensions to the ground and the addition to seating around Centre Court bear witness. Centre Court now accommodates 15,000 people and at the time of writing a retractable roof was being built.

TELEPHONE, THE Invented by Alexander Graham Bell in the USA in 1876, the telephone is an often overlooked but hugely significant device in any understanding of social change in twentieth-century Britain. In 1900, a million inland trunk calls (via a telephone exchange or automated router) were made in the UK; by 1990 this had risen to almost 4,000 million. The number of local calls in the latter year was in excess of 18,750 million.

The telephone enabled people to communicate over large distances, and thus contributed to the spatial widening of social networks. And, in tandem with the application of electricity to homes and businesses, it facilitated the outward and upward expansion of the city. If one was living in a far-flung suburb or on the twelfth floor of a block of flats, the phone was an enormously useful piece of household equipment. Only the privileged owned a telephone before the First World War, and the war itself demonstrated the military uses of this form of communications technology on the battlefield. The growing popularity of phone ownership between the wars was evident in fiction feature films, in which the telephone played an important role. At a couple of points in *The Thirty Nine Steps* (1939), for example, the actor on the telephone relays verbal information essential to the unfolding of the plot. Following the Second World War, the increasingly affluent British picked up the telephone. Its contribution

to changing family relationships and the rise of extended kinship and community networks was observed in East London by Michael Young and Peter Willmott. For those younger families who wished to leave the cramped and outdated accommodation in Bethnal Green in the East End of London, and the close-knit and even claustrophobic family life there, the telephone was essential. As one man who had moved to a new council estate testified:

There are two things that I think are essential when you live on an estate: one's a telephone, the other's a car. I don't like having to pay my telephone bill, but I think it's worth it. It means my brother can ring me up on the estate any time he wants to. And if you're in any trouble – if there's anything wrong with one of the boys say – I can ring up a doctor if I need one. You don't need a telephone in Bethnal Green, because the doctor's on the doorstep.

(Michael Young and Peter Willmott, *Family and Kinship in East London* (1979 edn), p. 158)

Given that during the 1930s hardly any working-class households had been able to afford a telephone, this quotation exemplifies the liberating and useful contribution that it made to poorer people's lives. Thus by the mid-1960s, for example, the planners of the forthcoming generation of new towns looked to the USA to understand both the increasing mobility of life facilitated by motorisation and the role played by communications technology that connected people up to formal and informal networks ranging far and wide. They understood that neighbourhood and locality were smaller influences on people's lives than when the first phase of new towns was planned during the 1940s. By 1970 almost every house or flat in Britain had a telephone. And, since 1990, further proof positive of the importance of community without propinquity in most people's lives was the rush to own or rent a mobile phone (cell phone), whether it was used for the purposes of work and business or to keep in touch with friends and family. The phrase 'flexible lifestyle' became something of an advertiser's cliché towards the end of the twentieth century, but life was indeed more mobile and varied than it was at the beginning of the century. The telephone was at the heart of this profound transition.

TELEVISION Beginning during the mid-1930s, and rudely interrupted by the Second World War, television broadcasting in Britain got off to a slow start. From its outset, the British Broadcasting Corporation (BBC) dominated television, but in 1955, when the number of televisions in Britain were expanding rapidly, Independent Television (ITV) was introduced to provide a commercially backed alternative to the BBC's monopoly. Between 1950 and 1965, the percentage of households owning or renting a television set rose from less than 1 to almost 90, and by 1970 almost every home had at least one set. During the 1970s, moreover, the black and white television was increasingly supplanted by the colour TV: in 1967, 88 per cent of homes had a black and white television licence; by 1977, 44.2 per cent had a black and white licence while 54.4 per cent were paying for a colour set.

Television was a window on Britain and the wider world through news, documentaries, dramas, soap operas and sitcoms. During the 1950s, moreover, the growing Americanisation of British life via the small screen led to considerable elite criticism of its alleged effects: the British public, however, remained almost addicted to the increasingly varied transatlantic menu of programmes offered by British

TV, and from the 1980s by the proliferation of channels. Key themes studied by media historians of television include representations of British life and different sections of British society; the ethos of BBC programming; the challenges of commercial TV; and the proliferation of the medium.

THATCHERISM The term refers to the values and policies associated with Margaret Thatcher, prime minister from 1979 to 1990. Thatcherism attacked nationalisation and pursued privatisation. It emphasised Victorian values rather than permissiveness, and was of course personified by Thatcher herself. Monetarism was at the heart of Thatcherite economic policies, and excessive state expenditure was frowned upon. Hatred of socialism and a certain contempt for trade unions were also key aspects of the ideology, as was a policy of de-industrialisation.

TOWN AND COUNTRY PLANNING The town and country planning movement began during the late nineteenth century in reaction to the environmental and social degradation that afflicted large areas of British towns and cities. It was powerfully influenced by the garden city and garden suburb movements. Overcrowded districts of the larger cities were to enjoy slum clearance and their populations were to be dispersed to garden cities built in the countryside. Two important exemplars of these principles were Letchworth Garden City, begun in 1903, and Welwyn Garden City, begun in 1920. These were working models of the self-sustaining and self-contained garden city, whose residents enjoyed quiet residential areas located away from industry and employment zones, a well-equipped city centre, and plenty of parks. The notion of the self-supporting garden city was based on the idea that employment would also locate there. People then only needed to walk or commute short distances to work. As a solution to the growing problem of commuting by public transport, this was only partly successful. Yet, from the vantage point of the twentieth-first century, it was an early if unconscious statement of environmentally conscious urban planning.

Both before, during and after the First World War, town planners were advocates of planned council estates. They also opposed suburban sprawl. The **Ribbon Development Act** of 1935 was an attempt to prevent the growth of what Clough Williams-Ellis termed 'the octopus' of urban sprawl caused by house building and the construction of industrial estates along the new arterial roads (octopus tentacles) that were spreading into the countryside as a consequence of motorisation. Increasingly influential on town and city councils, planners and architects were called upon by the government to begin planning for reconstruction during the Second World War. War empowered the profession of town planning. Formed in 1943, the Ministry of Town and Country Planning drove the **Town Planning (Blitz and Blight) Act** of 1944 and the Town and Country Planning Act of 1947, and subsequent acts thereafter. The New Towns Act of 1946 established the garden-city inspired programme of new towns in Britain. Both the redeveloped areas of existing towns and the new communities after 1946 reconstructed and renewed the built-environment of postwar Britain. Many people hated 'the planners', however. New town development corporations were loathed by a number of farmers and landowners for their powers of compulsory purchase of land upon which the new towns were to be built. Others hated the modern quality of the new towns or the rebuilt urban environments in comparison to 'traditional' townscapes. However, as a profession town planners were not uniform: many

working in local or county councils were relatively benign and well meaning, often operating with limited financial budgets, and frequently powerless to do little more than modify the overblown schemes of architects and local authorities that led to some of the 'great planning disasters' associated with the tower-block council estates of the 1950s and 1960s. During the 1970s and 1980s the reputation of town planning was particularly low, as social problems associated with inner-city estates, some less than twenty years old, were viewed as consequences of impoverished social planning. Conversely, however, the town and country planning legislation had also achieved a great deal. Although suburbanisation had continued to creep into the countryside, a great deal of countryside had been protected from sprawl by the green belt and other restrictions on development.

Historians of town planning have tended to be 'top down', focusing on professional networks, grand designs and influential individuals rather than on the social consequences of planning. Recently, however, the social effects of town planning have been increasingly studied.

TRADE UNIONS Collective organisations of workers within occupations and across sectional divides were at the heart of the Labour movement during the twentieth century. Before the 1880s trade unions had involved primarily skilled workers, but the rise of the 'new unions' in the late Victorian period witnessed growing levels of organisation among unskilled workers, continuing into the Edwardian years. Women also fought and won the right to belong to trade unions. If anything, for female workers who were traditionally paid less than men, and whose term of formal employment was expected to be shorter than that of men, the collective bargaining of the trade union was essential when negotiating with employers. Membership of trade unions grew dramatically before the First World War, and was closely related to the rise of the Labour Party. Attacks on industrial action and funding did nothing to prevent this growth in membership. Between 1914 and 1918 it intensified among both men and women, and during 1920 it reached almost a half of the workforce. Reasons include the rising expectations engendered by wartime and the consolidation of the Labour Party. Following the General Strike membership of unions declined, a trend exacerbated by the Great Depression, although the late 1930s witnessed heightened membership as trade improved. During the postwar years, the percentage of unionised workers increased slowly but steadily until the 1970s, when it soared upwards. By 1979, trade union density peaked at over 50 per cent. The proportion of women in unions in relation to their presence in the paid workforce overtook that of men. During the 1980s, however, for a number of reasons, not least Conservative legislation restricting union activities, heightened de-industrialisation, and privatisation, membership of trade unions declined among the manual working classes. This point indicates that trade union membership reflected structural changes in the economy. As the staple industries declined during the postwar years, particularly during the final quarter of the century, and as the service sector grew, the proportion of unionised middle-class white-collar workers increased. The expansion of white-collar work also partly explains the growing number of women in unions.

Historians of trade unions emphasise the close relationship of many – but not all – unions to the Labour Party and the funding of Labour through trade union levies. Their pivotal role in industrial relations has been explored by both economic and social historians, and Labour and communist historians have argued about the strength of communism among both the rank and file and the leadership. For many Conservative historians, the trade unions were bastions of restrictive practices, exhibiting a reluctance to embrace new technologies and a class-based selfishness. The ideology of trade unions and trade unionists is also a contested area. Some have emphasised the politicised nature of membership, while others stress the instrumentalism of the great majority of workers: they saw the unions as a means to the ends of higher wages and improved working conditions. The differing environments and memberships of public sector and private sector unions are also significant. The former tend to have more generalised cross-sectional unions, but the picture is a complex one. More widely still, reasons for the rise and fall of membership have embraced structural changes but also attempts to understand social and cultural changes.

TRANSSEXUALITY The most common term for transsexuality is 'sex change'. A tiny minority of people had been attempting to change their sex since ancient times. Genital mutilation was usually the commonest and excruciating means to this end. Transvestism – wearing the clothes of the opposite sex – is not the same as transsexuality, for transsexuals are psychologically and physically unhappy in their body and wish to belong to the opposite gender. Sex changes can work both ways, male to female (MTF) or female to male (FTM). The majority of sex changes are MTF but a growing number of sex-change operations have been carried out on women. Today termed 'gender reassignment', by 2007 over 400 operations were undertaken every year in Britain. Gender reassignment has its critics: from the viewpoint of some radical feminists, for example, MTF transsexuals imported highly conservative notions of femininity into the world of women. Many transsexuals, however, contest this perspective.

TROUBLES, THE The name given to the phase of Northern Irish history between 1968 and 1998 which saw a tragic deterioration in relations between the Irish Catholic minority in the Six Counties and the Protestant majority. The former wished to become part of a united Ireland, while the Northern Irish Protestants wanted to remain within the United Kingdom. The Troubles were initiated by the violence attending civil rights marches in 1968–9 and their aftermath, and the subsequent intervention of the British troops in 1971. From then on, many paramilitary groups on both sides waged terrorist campaigns of utter ruthlessness and cruelty.

In 1973, the British and Irish governments, working together with the mainstream Unionist and Nationalist parties, agreed on an innovative power-sharing arrangement for the governing of the province. This Sunningdale Agreement involved, for the first time, the active participation of representatives of the Nationalist community in running the state, and included a consultative 'Council of Ireland' involving input from the Republic. Many hopes were invested in this new dispensation, which began governing the province in early 1974. However, the odds were against it from the start. The IRA was profoundly hostile to this 'partitionist' arrangement, which fell far short of a united Ireland. The Republican movement was determined therefore to 'blow it out of the water'. Meanwhile, while many Unionists were probably prepared to swallow the inclusion of Nationalists in government in return for an end to violence, even a consultative role for the Republic was too much for most of them. Harder-line Unionists, in cahoots with the sinister figures of the paramilitary Ulster Defence Association, organized a general strike in the spring of 1974, which brought the new executive to its knees. Nationalists complained of the weakness of the incoming Labour government in supporting the executive against the strikers, and it is undeniable that intimidation by paramilitaries was widespread. Nevertheless it is undeniable also that the majority of the Unionist community did not give their support to the institutions of the power-sharing administration, and at least acquiesced in its overthrow by what amounted to a coup d'état. The cynic might suggest that neither community had suffered enough at this stage to make the necessary compromises.

And suffering was to come on all sides. As the IRA continued its campaign of assassination and bombing, both in Northern Ireland and in Great Britain, and the loyalists continued butchering Catholics in Belfast and elsewhere, the British government abandoned hope of a political 'solution' and played down any institutional links with the Irish Republic. The IRA had by now given up on the assumption that 'victory' was imminent, and instead adopted a strategy of a 'long war'. The same tactics – bombing, assassination, intimidation, robbery, and disruption of ordinary life and political processes – were to be continued indefinitely until 'victory' could be secured when the British finally lost patience and went 'home'.

Meanwhile, the British had decided that Northern Irish politicians were hopeless and that there was nothing to be gained from negotiating with terrorists. The way forward therefore was to pretend that violence in Northern Ireland was not political, but criminal and sectarian. Northern Ireland was a 'normal' part of the UK, but one blighted by abnormal levels of gangsterism. The correct body to deal with terrorists therefore was the police, not the army, and, once captured, terrorists were to be treated not as prisoners of war but as ordinary criminals. Moreover, internment was an inappropriate mechanism to deal with a crime wave, and 'criminals' would no longer by locked up as an administrative measure. Instead they would be dealt with by the courts, albeit courts which would sit without a jury. These were the policies of 'normalization, criminalization, Ulsterization'.

In the short term, these policies paid off. The ability of terrorist groups to strike was significantly impaired by the late 1970s by the greatly increased power of the state to infiltrate them, arrest them, interrogate them (often with considerable brutality), get confessions out of them, and 'process' them through the courts. By 1980 it is likely that there were more IRA men in prison than outside it, and it is at this stage that their 'struggle' took on a new and highly significant character. 'Special category status' for terrorist prisoners had been abolished in 1976, and thereafter those convicted of terrorist offences were to be treated as 'ordinary' prisoners. They were to be housed in cells, in the specially created 'H Blocks' of the Maze prison, rather than in compounds, as had hitherto been the case. They would wear prison uniform and do prison work. For IRA prisoners, this was anathema. They regarded themselves as members of an army who had been taken prisoner on 'active service', and to accept 'criminalization' meant to deny the legitimacy of their 'armed struggle', to accept that it was a 'crime'. Since 1976, hundreds of IRA prisoners had been 'on the blanket', refusing to wear uniforms, and choosing to sit naked in their empty cells. This had escalated into the 'dirty' protests, with prisoners squatting for twenty-four hours a day in their own excrement. These tactics had failed to excite other than local sympathy, but a renewed strike in 1981 ended only after the deaths of ten hunger strikers. These strikes

are also significant, however, because they marked the beginning of a shift in IRA strategy away from an exclusively armed aspect. Hitherto the IRA had eschewed all things political. They were an army, the armed wing of the legitimate government of Ireland. Their job was to strike with utter ruthlessness against the enemies of Ireland. Now, though, they found themselves in the unusual position of portraying themselves as victims of a cruelly unjust system. They were suffering, not inflicting suffering. Moreover, the unexpected arrival of a parliamentary by-election in the constituency of Fermanagh-South Tyrone afforded them the opportunity to maximize publicity by standing one of their number, Bobby Sands, as a candidate. This was a high-risk strategy, as many in their ranks realized. A humiliating turnout for Sands would allow their enemies to portray the IRA as simply a bunch of criminal fanatics. But Sands polled 30,000 votes, handing a huge propaganda coup to the Republican movement. Equally astonishing was the fact that two other prisoners were elected as members of parliament in the general election in the Irish Republic. The experience of standing for, and actually winning, elections was a new one for the IRA, and had profound implications for their thinking. In the short term it was the direct cause of a new strategy, summed up in the slogan 'the armalite and the ballot box', whereby the IRA would pursue its aims through a joint programme of violence combined with politics. As will be shown shortly, this was unsustainable.

The hunger strikes had other implications, and the rise in electoral support for Sinn Féin, the political wing of the IRA, was deeply unsettling, not least for the government of the Republic. With the exception of a number of horrendous UVF bomb attacks in the early 1970s, the Republic had somehow managed to escape the chaos, destruction and loss of life which had beset the North. Now, however, supporters of the prisoners were bringing demonstrations and violence to the streets of Dublin, and IRA men were being elected to the dáil. The moderate nationalist SDLP, to which governments of the Republic had traditionally been close, was being undermined by Sinn Féin.

The British too were alarmed at developments in the early 1980s, not least by the IRA's success in almost assassinating the entire cabinet at Brighton in October 1984. Mrs Thatcher is unlikely to have been moved to compromise by this attack, but it is clear that she allowed herself to be persuaded by some colleagues and officials that improved relations with the Republic were necessary if support for Sinn Féin was to be constrained. The interest of improvement in security cooperation was another factor. The result was the Anglo-Irish Agreement of 1985.

The 1985 agreement is significant not so much for what it achieved as for what it represented, namely the reinternationalisation of the Irish question. As has been shown, the search for a 'solution' had effectively been abandoned in 1975, and relations with the Republic had often been frosty during the hunger strike crisis. By 1985 it was clear that no entirely internal solution was possible, and, much to the indignation of the Unionists, the Republic was given a consultative role in the governing of Northern Ireland. A permanent Anglo-Irish secretariat was established at Maryfield, which, along with the Inter-Governmental Conference, 'reinstitutionalized' Anglo-Irish relations. In the long run these arrangements helped produce a new bipartisan approach to Northern Ireland which would bring violence to an end.

The Troubles, however, were far from over. Recognition should be given to the efforts of John Hume, of the moderate nationalist SDLP. Hume worked tirelessly, and at much cost to his own reputation (and indeed his personal security), to convince the IRA, in the person of Gerry Adams, that the British were now effectively neutral, and that the IRA campaign was prolonging divisions in Ireland rather than helping end them. Much behind-the-scenes work remained to be done, but as early as 1989 Adams was talking of a 'non-armed political movement, to seek self-determination for Ireland'. Following the departure of the staunchly unionist Mrs Thatcher in 1990, a succession of secretaries of state, clearly influenced by Hume, began using language more accommodating to nationalism. Nevertheless, the early 1990s were marked with horrendous violence from both sides.

Another door was opened, however, with the Anglo-Irish Downing Street Declaration of December 1993. This cleverly ambiguous document, in which the voice of John Hume can clearly be heard, declared formally that Britain had 'no selfish strategic or economic interest in Ireland'; Britain committed herself to promoting 'peace, stability and reconciliation . . . by agreement among all people who inhabit the island'. Her role was to 'encourage, facilitate and enable' agreement. It was for 'the people of the island of Ireland alone, by agreement between the two parts respectively, to exercise the right of self-determination'. Albert Reynolds for the Republic agreed that 'self-determination' could only be achieved with and subject to the consent of the majority in the existing state of Northern Ireland. Both governments pledged to organise inclusive talks for all those committed to entirely peaceful means of achieving their aims. The Downing Street declaration thus acknowledged the Nationalist demand for 'self-determination' while preserving the Unionist right to consent or withhold their consent. This text elicited the IRA ceasefire in August 1994.

The initial optimism which accompanied this ceasefire did not last, as the vexed issue of the 'decommissioning' of the IRA's arsenal reared its head. John Major's fragile government depended upon the continued support of the Ulster Unionists at Westminster, and they in turn were deeply suspicious about the reality of the IRA's intentions. Major first of all demanded proof that the ceasefire was permanent, then fudged this with a 'working assumption' that it was. The British government demanded that the IRA begin decommissioning before Sinn Féin could enter talks. As the stalemate dragged on, the IRA returned to violence in January 1996 with a huge bomb in Canary Wharf in London. This attack was greeted with almost universal dismay. Meanwhile, tension in Northern Ireland was being heightened by repeated stand-offs at a rerouted Orange Order parade at Drumcree, while the loyalist paramilitaries continued their campaign of sectarian murder.

The landslide election victory of Tony Blair's Labour Party in the UK general election of May 1997 provided the key to progress. His massive majority freed him from dependence on the Unionists, and his new secretary of state, Marjorie **Mowlam**, immediately renewed contacts with Sinn Féin. The leadership of the Republican movement now came under intense pressure to renew their ceasefire, which they duly did in July 1997, having signed up to the so-called Mitchell principles that committed them to entirely non-violent methods. David Trimble, leader of the Ulster Unionists, and hitherto regarded as a hard-liner, agree to participate in inclusive talks. This was the first occasion on which a Unionist leader had sat down with an IRA leader since James Craig had met Michael Collins in January 1922. Ian Paisley's Democratic Unionist Party was the only significant group to boycott these talks.

After tortuous and prolonged negotiations, led by Blair and taoiseach Bertie Ahern, the parties came to the Good Friday Agreement in April 1998. The main feature of the agreement was a complex three-strand set of constitutional structures, described by one authority as a combination of consociational and confederal elements. Strand 1 consisted of a local assembly and executive for Northern Ireland with complex checks and balances to ensure full power-sharing; strand 2 was a North–South ministerial council 'to develop consultation, co-operation and action within the island of Ireland . . . on matters of mutual interest'; and strand 3 was a British–Irish council and a so-called British–Irish intergovernmental conference. Other key items included the commitment by the Republic to give up its claim to the territory of Northern Ireland; the stipulation that Irish 'self-determination' would be recognised and expressed through joint referenda North and South; recognition by all parties that constitutional change could come about only by 'consent'; the commitment that all paramilitary prisoners would be released within two years; that all parties would use their influence to secure complete decommissioning of paramilitary arsenals; that 'parity of esteem' would be accorded to the cultural identities of both communities; that the 'equality' and 'human rights' agenda were to be respected and institutionalised; and that there would be major reforms of policing and the administration of criminal justice.

U

UNEMPLOYMENT Unemployment was an almost permanent feature in Britain during

the twentieth century, although its incidence fluctuated greatly. It rose before the
First World War, as the staple industries
were challenged by foreign competition.
The war itself witnessed a return to almost
full employment as the conscription of
young servicemen created a labour
shortage on the home front that was in
part remedied by female workers. The
problem surged temporarily in 1918 as the
demobilisation of soldiers flooded the
workforce, and protests against the out-of-
work donation reflected the disappointment felt by many soldiers who had
expected to return to regular work.
Between the wars, however, joblessness
returned to haunt Britain, or those who
were jobless and those who cared about
them, and protests against unemployment
continued. Hunger marches brought the
plight of the staple industries to the attention of the nation. Britain was a divided
country, and the more prosperous South
and Midlands were less harshly affected by
the slump than the depressed areas in the
North and in Scotland and Wales. There
were in fact only seven hunger marches,
the first in 1922 and the seventh in 1936.
The largest numbered 2,000 workers, by
no means an impressive total, yet large
enough to have imprinted the marches
onto the historical record of unemployment and its effects between the wars. Six
of the marches were organised by the
National Unemployed Workers' Movement
(NUWM). Unemployed workers, both
men and women, walked from the
depressed areas of South Wales, Scotland,
the North-East and North-West of
England to London, where rallies were
held in Trafalgar Square. *En route* they
were fed by well-wishers and communists,
and slept rough outdoors or in makeshift
accommodation. Theirs was a poignant
gesture, mostly peaceful but occasionally
marked by disturbances. The most famous
march of all, that of the brave 300 from the

shipbuilding town of Jarrow in 1936, was
organised not by the NUWM but by the
Labour MP Ellen Wilkinson and other
officials from the town. The marches were
effective at gaining the attention of the
media, both newsreel and newspapers, and
at reminding the nation of the plight of
those in the depressed areas. The National
Government, however, did not really
respond with policies formulated in the
flurry of news generated by the processions
of the poor to London. Poor Law, public
assistance and unemployment assistance
payments remained low, and the most
significant legislation, the Special Areas
Act of 1934, was limited.

Unemployment was effectively reduced
by the upturn in trade from the mid-1930s
and almost eradicated by the onset of war
from 1939. After 1945, the economy was
able to absorb most demobilised men, not
least because so many women returned to
unpaid domestic labour from war work,
and during the 1950s and 1960s, although
unemployment rates fluctuated, they were
relatively low compared with the 1920s and
1930s before them and the 1970s and 1980s
afterwards. Unemployment reached a peak
of 3 million by the mid-1980s, a level not
seen in Britain since the Great Depression.

URBAN REGENERATION Urban regeneration refers to the concerted attempt since
the mid-1980s, by government, local councils, private developers and a variety of
professional agencies and urban development corporations, to revitalise old and
obsolete housing and buildings through
the injection of much needed capital and
through major environmental improvements. One important sociological principle of urban regeneration is to 'get the
middle classes in', because politicians and
planners expected the middle classes to
revive areas through their spending power
and to create new cultural and leisure facilities. The vogue for American-style loft-

living, for example, coincided with the regeneration of the docks in Cardiff, Glasgow, Liverpool and London. In the larger cities, unelected urban development corporations, comprised of architects, town planners, civil engineers and other professionals, coordinated and planned the regeneration of often vast areas of dereliction, notably the docklands and industrial zones. This was another sphere of Americanisation: the regeneration of watersides in Britain during the 1980s and 1990s owed much to the models pioneered in Baltimore and Boston, although increasingly European solutions and a more mixed-use pattern in streets and squares was evident in some schemes. Considerable obstacles to successful urban regeneration were inadequate funding from central government, misuse of some funding and other resources, and the problems in coordinating a multi-agency 'delivery' of regeneration projects. There have certainly been a number of failures and underwhelming schemes, but also a number of impressive revitalisations of inner cities and decaying industrial hinterlands.

URBANISATION Excluding Ireland, there were 37 million people in Britain in 1900. By the time of the 1991 census the population of England, Northern Ireland, Scotland and Wales was 58 million, and was growing rapidly. This expanding population required housing and amenities.

During the course of the nineteenth century Britain became an urban nation, and throughout the twentieth century it remained so. In 1900, 77 per cent of people in England and Wales, for example, lived in a town or city. By the 1990s, the figure was 90 per cent. Towns varied in size from smallish settlements of perhaps 10,000 up to the largest of up to 200,000 inhabitants, and there were huge concentrations of people in the great conurbations. The Greater London region, for example,

housed over 8 million by the mid-twentieth century. But the Birmingham to Coventry axis, Manchester and its satellites, and Liverpool and its neighbouring towns comprised millions of people within sprawling urban regions.

Mostly, urbanisation meant suburbanisation. However, the new towns from 1946 were planned alternatives to suburbanisation. In 1947 the Town and Country Planning Act put restrictions on suburban growth and created a green belt around larger towns and cities which limited construction of industry and residential development in the nearby countryside. Nonetheless, (sub)urbanisation continued to grow as a consequence of population pressures and strategic relaxations of the town and country planning laws. The Conservative governments of the 1950s more effectively dealt with the housing shortage than their Labour predecessor by promoting expanded towns via the 1952 **Town Development Act**, by continuing funding for the new towns, and by relaxing restrictions on private development. The reorganisation of **local government** during the early 1970s created large metropolitan councils in order to streamline and improve services to these great urban populations. Those councils have been one of the many organisations involved in the urban regeneration of the declining inner cities and de-industrialised zones of urban areas.

VICTORIAN VALUES The Conservative governments of the 1980s rejected the permissiveness of the 1960s as socially corrosive and threatening of traditional values such as thrift, hard work, self-help and moderation in leisure habits, and resurrected the values which they claimed had made Britain great during the previous century. This strategy was undermined by the sleaze attaching to prominent politicians.

W

WELFARE STATE Introduced between 1946 and 1951, the welfare state remains the greatest achievement of the Labour Party, the party that has continued until the present day to claim credit for it. Offering the citizens of Britain support 'from the cradle to the grave', its major institutions were the National Health Service, from 1948, and universal systems of **national assistance** and national insurance. Old-age pensions were similarly underpinned by national insurance contributions. The principle of free universal entitlement to health care was subsequently modified through public expenditure cuts and via the introduction of prescription charges and payments for dental care, but health care has remained mostly free at the point of need. The Liberal Party also greatly influenced Labour's creation, however. The policies associated with New Liberalism before 1914 had established national insurance and old-age pensions, and between the wars it was the Liberals who first adopted Keynesianism, the economic system that legitimised the taxation-funded welfare system post 1945. During the Second World War, moreover, the publication of the Beveridge Report stimulated public interest in the notion of a greatly improved welfare system, and its principles were adopted in 1945 by the Labour Party in its general election manifesto, written by Michael Young. By 1951 the Conservative Party, for the purposes of electoral expedi-

ency, had accepted both the welfare legislation passed by Labour and the Keynesian economic policies to support it. This was the basis of consensus politics, mostly but not completely unchallenged until the emergence of Thatcherism. For Labour and Liberal historians, and many Conservatives of the 'one-nation' school, the aggregate impact of postwar welfare was both benign and positive, but from the 1980s Thatcherism led to a revisionist school which highlighted the negative effects of welfare policy. High taxation was criticised for funding a culture of dependency among the working classes. However, attempts to roll back the frontiers of the welfare state after 1979 were mostly unsuccessful. The new policy directions and adjustments outlined in **Landmarks** failed significantly to reduce welfare expenditure.

WOMEN The social, economic and political opportunities for women at the beginning of the twenty-first century were considerably greater than they had been a hundred years previously. The causes of this qualified improvement in their status were many and varied, and owed much to the actions and efforts of women themselves during the course of the twentieth century.

Family limitation via the use of contraception was hugely important and empowering for women. By 'empowering' in this context we do not mean the acquisition of influence and control over others. Instead, it refers to the manner in which women were freed from obligations and pressures in order to use their time more meaningfully to pursue their own interests. The middle classes pioneered family limitation during the later nineteenth and into the twentieth century, as the number of children per married couple fell. This enabled many women to engage in public life, particularly in the voluntary fields of charity and philanthropy.

In politics, women could vote in local elections by 1914. They had been eligible to vote in and stand for school boards until the ending of the latter in 1904 closed off an avenue of advancement for public-spirited women. Nonetheless, education was an increasingly important profession for female preferment, as was law. National politics was opened up to women from the ending of the First World War with the passage of the Representation of the People Act of 1918 and the **Sex Disqualification Removal Act** of 1919. In 1928, women's voting rights became the same as those of men.

Many key pieces of legislation within the penumbra of social policy particularly affected the lives of women. The **Family Allowances Act** of 1945 paid child allowances directly to mothers. And later developments in welfare payments, such as family income supplement and supplementary benefit, although they affected all members of a household, were of particular importance to poorer women, for example in single-parent households.

The relaxation of the divorce laws encouraged the liberation of women from unhappy marriages. For many women, divorce was true emancipation, but discriminatory income practices often meant that women earned less than men and had to struggle harder to raise families or to look after themselves and their children. Nonetheless, the figures for divorce are striking, particularly following the 1969 Divorce Act, and illustrate that women lower down the social scale took advantage of their new ability to initiate divorce proceedings.

The history of abortion law reform and the complex issue of a woman's right to choose is most often focused on the Abortion Act of 1967. Abortion was and remained a terribly difficult choice for women, and before 1968, for poorer women, the choice had been even more difficult, and sometimes tragic in its consequences.

Both abortion and divorce reform were at the heart the 'permissive moment' in social legislation. Also significant was the rise of second-wave feminism and of concerted political attempts by the liberal left to produce pay and employment rights for women on an equal basis with men. The **Employment Act** of 1971 was the first of a number of pieces of legislation intended to promote equality of income.

As noted at the beginning of this section, girls and women by the year 2000 were in a measurably superior social, economic and political situation than they had been one hundred years previously. Their educational performances and qualifications were surpassing those of boys and men in some subjects and professions. In politics, too, more women were sitting in both parliamentary houses than ever before. And in entertainments and popular culture, women were almost as prominent as men.

In occupational terms there were also significant advances. Before the First World War women formed 30 per cent of the waged labour force, but this had risen to almost 54 per cent by the end of the 1990s. However, both class and ethnic dimensions qualified these achievements: like most successful men, most successful women remained resolutely middle class in origin. Furthermore, much of the increase of women in the labour force occurred in part-time employment.

WOMEN'S SUFFRAGE The major Victorian parliamentary reforms of 1867 and 1884–5 had enfranchised the working classes, but both middle-class and working-class women were excluded from voting in general elections. The campaign for women's suffrage – the right to vote in those elections – was given considerable momentum by the formation in 1897 of the

National Union of Women's Suffrage Societies and a more militant edge from 1903 by the **Women's Social and Political Union**. The great strides in the United States of America, where women had the right to vote in some states before 1914, also led to cooperation between British and American suffrage campaigners, ensuring that the cause was associated with mostly progressive politicians in both countries. The First World War witnessed the partial enfranchisement of women in Britain, in the Representation of the People Act of 1918. In the USA, all women achieved the vote on equal terms with men by 1919. But in Britain it was not until 1928 that all women aged twenty-one and over gained enfranchisement on equal terms with men, and, even then, this was in the teeth of criticism from Conservative daily newspapers of the 'flapper vote folly'.

WORKING CLASSES When assessing the history of the British working classes during the twentieth century, historians emphasise structural change, the differences between the organised working classes and those who were not in trade unions, and the related contexts of community and culture. Surprisingly, furthermore, a key theme in the social history of the working classes is their rise from about the 1880s until the 1950s, and then their decline in an era of increasing affluence, consumerism and unprecedented welfare state provision. This view of cultural and spiritual decline was influenced in part by perspectives on working-class history in the nineteenth century, proposed by the Hammonds and the Webbs, and in part by the Institute of Community Studies and some pessimistic sociological studies of working-class life during the 1950s and 1960s.

The rise apparently occurred during the first half of the twentieth century. From the late Victorian years to the 1930s the manual working classes numbered over 70 per cent of the working population. The aspirations of millions of them were reflected in trade unions, expressing the hopes and interests of organised labour that gave birth to the Labour Party. The latter's programme of welfare legislation and nationalisation of key industries protected the industrial working class from the worst consequences of unregulated capitalism: low wages and unemployment. The trade unions, the institutional expression of working-class collectivism, were at the peak of their influence and membership during the 1920s. And trade union membership rose between 1945 and 1979, particularly during the 1970s. Not all were blue-collar union members, but the majority certainly were.

The 'decline' argument is usually presented as follows: before about the mid-1950s the working class lived in 'traditional' working-class urban areas. These were mostly tightly knit and homogeneous communities, thousands of which were anchored to the coal mines, the iron and steel factories, the textile mills and the docks that gave them a livelihood. Think of Coronation Street a hundred years ago, set in a landscape of smoking factory chimneys, textile mills and warehouses, street corner pubs, fish and chip and corner shops of the type to be found in such sitcoms as *Open All Hours*, with a nearby football ground and a tram rattling along the main road. Add in to this landscape hundreds of men in cloth caps, children in clean but cheap school uniforms, and weary but hard-working women trying their best to raise their families in a poor but decent household, and you get the idea of the 'traditional' working class. Of course, such communities varied by location: in South Wales, for example, little villages and small towns of regimented terraced housing owed their livelihood less to textile mills and more to coal mining and iron making. Such communities were still to be commonly found by the 1950s, and even during the 1970s, but after Margaret Thatcher came to power what was left of them were forced to adapt or die. From the 1970s, however, de-industrialisation and economic restructuring denuded and demoralised many poorer traditional working-class areas. Furthermore, a more middle-class range of service-based occupations increased the size of the middle classes at the expense of the working classes. Concomitantly, working-class membership of trade unions declined after 1980. Unions in the staple industries were particularly affected.

Education also contributed to the numeric demise of the working classes, enhancing the lives and prospects of thousands of working-class students and enabling upward social mobility into the middle classes. The grammar school system provided scholarships for the brightest of those working-class products from primary schools, and the postwar introduction of comprehensive education and the expansion of university places from the 1960s also contributed to the upward social mobility of working-class youths. Furthermore, unprecedented levels of affluence from the 1950s enabled working-class households to afford more expensive items and luxury goods. Here, it seems, the working-class people wanted what the middle classes had already got, and many sociologists during the 1950s and 1960s were convinced that a process of cultural assimilation was occurring as the working class apparently became more consumerist and materialistic. The impressive-sounding term *embourgeoisement* was used to describe the sharing of lifestyles between the lower middle classes and the working classes as the latter became more suburbanised. The most famous reading of this change was Michael Young and Peter Willmott's *Family and Kinship in East London* (1957) and *Family and Class in a London Suburb* (1960).

However, increasing affluence, home ownership, upward mobility and economic restructuring did not lead to the total erosion of the working classes. Over 30 per cent of all workers were in skilled, semi-skilled or unskilled manual employment by 1991. Whether all of those unskilled workers resemble the loud-mouthed slobs of television comedy or cling desperately, in the words of Corelli Barnett, to the 'nipple' of the welfare state is a highly debateable point. Not all are the residual poor. And it is interesting, if depressing, to note that, whereas the Edwardians used the term 'residuum', the equivalent word today is 'underclass'. The tragedies of Baby P and of Shannon Matthews in 2008 were certainly awful reminders of the amoral and desperate circumstances of many marginal working-class households who were unable to cope with the demands and pressures of modern life. In the early twenty-first century, as in the early twentieth, the poorest working-class children of Britain were its most vulnerable citizens, cruelly treated by their inadequate parents, and let down by inadequate social services.

YOUTH CULTURE It is commonly assumed that youth culture in Britain began with the teenager during the later 1950s and mushroomed during the 1960s: the baby boomers, those born between the end of the Second World War and 1960, began making popular music, experimenting with drugs and wearing seemingly outrageous fashions. Exciting though this picture is, a little qualification is required. Social historians have pointed to earlier cultures of young people, for example the 'monkey parades' of the Edwardian years, and between the wars youthful fashions and trends emerged, particularly among those with money to spare. The 'flapper' woman of the 1920s was young, stylish and seemingly prepared to flout convention, while the leisure of working-class boys and young men often involved public houses, snooker halls and cheap suits. American cinema stars and music styles were particularly copied and enjoyed by young people. Jazz was adopted by university students and self-consciously intellectual young people, and such trends re-emerged once the war was over, albeit muted by the austerity from 1945 to 1954. Perceptions of juvenile delinquency during the 1940s and 1950s led in part to the provision of youth clubs on council estates and in other residential areas. These clubs coincided with the appearance from 1955 of the teenager, leading to further fears of juvenile misbehaviour in age-specific clubs. All this coincided with the Americanisation and commercialisation of youth culture. The permissiveness of the 1960s and the 1970s would have been unthinkable without the new youth culture that burgeoned during the 1950s.

The prominence of youth culture in the media since the 1960s has meant that 'age' became increasingly studied by social historians and other academics and youth became categorised as an agency for sociocultural and even political change. Many Marxist writers in the fields of cultural history, cultural studies and literary studies wrote excitedly of the potential of youthful subcultures to change society, perhaps even along radical lines. The French students' revolt of 1968 was viewed as an example *par excellence* of how young people could ally themselves with the workers to form a collective force for change. Many youth 'subcultures', however, reflected other social values. The Teddy boy rockers of the 1950s and early 1960s, dressed to mock the dress sense of the Edwardian man of leisure (hence their name), were often conservative working-class young men in low-paid employment. In the case of the Notting Hill race riots some Teds were guilty of racist behaviour and language. And during the later 1970s punk rock was viewed by sociologists as subversive, as if it possessed a counter-cultural potential to mount a challenge to the New Right. In 1979, however, when Margaret Thatcher was elected, no doubt more than a few punks voted for her. During the 1990s some pop bands, such as Blur, Oasis and Simply Red, did become anti-Conservative in their language, but the landslide victory of New Labour in 1997 owed little that was quantifiable to these twenty-something and thirty-something musicians. Youth cultures continue to thrive today, but they are more a reflection of commercialism and youthful hedonism than any subversive menace.

BIBLIOGRAPHY AND INTERNET SOURCES

Books

Addison, Paul, and Jones, Harriet (eds), *A Companion to Contemporary Britain: 1939–2001* (2007)

Black, Jeremy, *Modern British History since 1900* (2000)

Black, Jeremy, and MacRaild, Donald, *Studying History* (2000)

Black, Lawrence, and Pemberton, Hugh (eds), *An Affluent Society? Britain's Postwar Golden Age Revisited* (2004)

Butler, L. J., and Gorst, Anthony (eds), *Modern British History* (1997)

Butler, Lawrence, and Jones, Harriet, *Britain in the Twentieth Century: A Documentary Reader*, Vol. 1: *1900–1939* (1994)

—— *Britain in the Twentieth Century: A Documentary Reader*, Vol. 2: *1939–1970* (1994)

Caunce, Stephen, *Oral History and the Local Historian* (1994)

Cherry, Gordon, *Town Planning in Britain since 1900* (1996)

Clapson, Mark, *Invincible Green Suburbs, Brave New Towns: Social Change and Urban Dispersal in Postwar England* (1998)

Clarke, Peter, *Hope and Glory: Britain, 1900–1990* (1995)

Constantine, Stephen, *Social Conditions in Britain, 1918–1939* (1983)

—— *Unemployment in Britain between the Wars* (1980)

Cook, Chris, *Routledge Guide to British Political Archives: Sources Since 1945* (2006)

Cook, Chris, and Stevenson, John, *Britain since 1945* (1996)

—— *Modern British History, 1714–2001* (2001)

Evans, Richard J., *In Defence of History* (1997)

Garnett, Mark, and Weight, Richard, *Modern British History: The Essential A–Z Guide* (2004)

George, Stephen, *Britain and European Integration since 1945* (1991)

George-Warren, Holly, and Romanowski, Patricia, *The Rolling Stone Encyclopaedia of Rock and Roll* (2005)

Gourvish, Terry, and O'Day, Alan (eds), *Britain since 1945* (1991)

Graves, Robert and Hodge, Alan, *The Long Weekend: A Social History of Britain, 1918–1939* (1941)

Halsey, A. H., *Change in British Society: From 1900 to the Present Day* (1995)

Halsey, A. H., with Webb, Josephine (eds), *Twentieth-Century British Social Trends* (2000)

Harris, José, *Private Lives, Public Spirit: Britain 1870–1914* (1994)

Hennessey, Peter, *Having it So Good: Britain in the Fifties* (2006)

Hennessey, Peter, and Seldon, Anthony (eds), *Ruling Performance: British Government from Attlee to Thatcher* (1989)

Hollowell, Jonathan, *Britain since 1945* (2003)
Hutchinson Encyclopedia of Modern Political Biography (1999)
Jacobs, Eric, and Worcester, Robert, *Britain under the Moriscope* (1990)
James, Lawrence, *The Rise and Fall of the British Empire* (1994)
—— *The Middle Class: A History* (2006)
Jenkins, Keith, *Rethinking History* (1992)
Johnson, Paul (ed.), *Twentieth-Century Britain: Social, Cultural and Economic Change* (1994)
Kynaston, David, *Austerity Britain: 1945–1951* (2007)
Lowe, Norman, *Mastering Modern British History* (1998)
Marwick, Arthur, *British Society since 1945* (2001)
—— *Culture in Britain since 1945* (1991)
—— *The New Nature of History* (2001)
McAleer, Dave, *Hit Singles: Top 20 Charts from 1954 to the Present Day* (2007)
Mowat, C. L., *Britain between the Wars, 1918–1940* (1979)
May, Alex, *Britain and Europe since 1945* (1999)
Ovendale, Ritchie, *British Defence Policy since 1945* (1994)
Palmer, Alan, *The Penguin Dictionary of Twentieth-Century History* (1999)
Pugh, Martin, *Britain: A Concise History, 1789–1998* (1999)
—— *We Danced All Night: A Social History of Britain Between the Wars* (2008)
Rubinstein, W. D., *Twentieth-Century Britain: A Political History* (2003)
Sandbrook, Dominic, *White Heat: A History of Britain in the Swinging Sixties* (2006)
Seldon, Anthony (ed.), *Contemporary History: Practice and Method* (1988)
Sked, Alan, and Cook, Chris, *Postwar Britain: A Political History* (1990)
Stevenson, John, *British Society, 1914–45* (1994)
Thompson, Paul, *The Edwardians: The Remaking of British Society* (1984)
Tiratsoo, Nick (ed.), *From Blitz to Blair: A New History of Britain, 1939–1997* (1997)
Tosh, John, *The Pursuit of History: Aims, Methods and New Directions in the Study of Modern History* (1998)
Vahimagi, Tise, *British Television* (1996)
Vincent, David, *Poor Citizens: The State and the Poor in Twentieth-Century Britain* (1991)
Ward, Steven V., *Planning and Urban Change* (2006)
Weigall, David, and Murphy, Michael, *A Level British History* (1996)
Wilson, A. N., *After the Victorians: The World our Parents Knew* (2005)
Wrigley, Chris, *A Companion to Early Twentieth-Century Britain* (2002)

World Wide Web

http://hansard.millbanksystems.com
http://parlipapers.chadwyck.co.uk
www.bbc.co.uk
www.bbchistorymagazine.com
www.bl.uk
www.bl.uk/collections/sound-archive
www.british-history.ac.uk
www.guardian.co.uk

BIBLIOGRAPHY

www.historytoday.org
www.iamhist.org
www.ihr.ac.uk
www.independent.co.uk
www.margaretthatcher.org
www.movietone.com
www.nationalarchives.gov.uk
www.nfo.ac.uk
www.ohs.org.uk
www.opsi.gov.uk
www.oxforddnb.com
www.parliament.uk/publications/index.cfm
www.terramedia.co.uk
www.30yearrulereview.org.uk
www.timesonline.co.uk/archive
www.statistics.gov.uk
www.spartacus.schoolnet.co.uk

INDEX